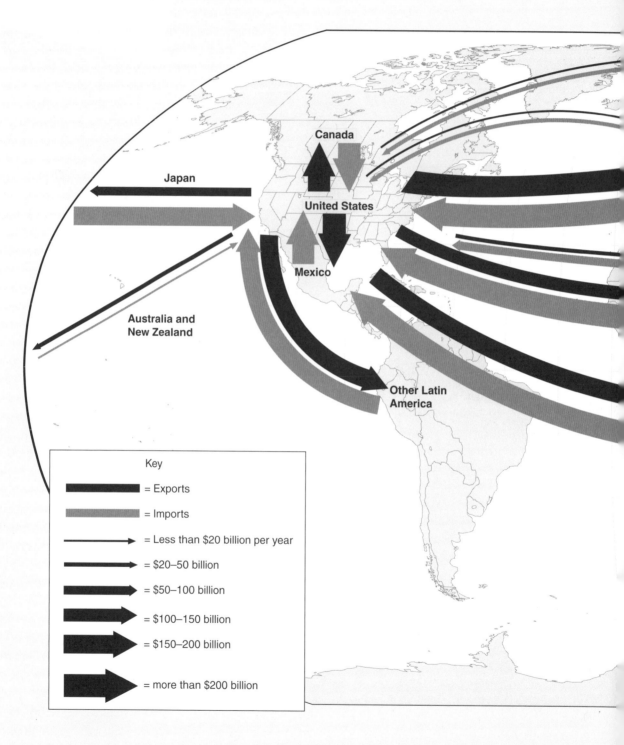

Canada

Japan

United States

Mexico

Australia and
New Zealand

Other Latin
America

Key

= Exports

= Imports

→ = Less than $20 billion per year

→ = $20–50 billion

→ = $50–100 billion

→ = $100–150 billion

→ = $150–200 billion

→ = more than $200 billion

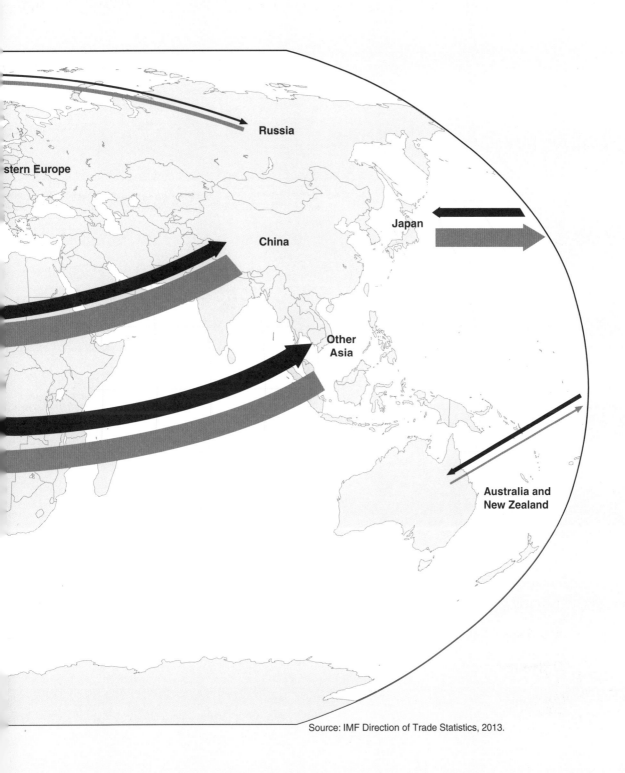

Russia

stern Europe

China

Japan

Other
Asia

Australia and
New Zealand

Source: IMF Direction of Trade Statistics, 2013.

THE PEARSON SERIES IN ECONOMICS

Abel/Bernanke/Croushore
*Macroeconomics**

Bade/Parkin
*Foundations of Economics**

Berck/Helfand
The Economics of the Environment

Bierman/Fernandez
Game Theory with Economic Applications

Blanchard
*Macroeconomics**

Blau/Ferber/Winkler
The Economics of Women, Men, and Work

Boardman/Greenberg/Vining/Weimer
Cost-Benefit Analysis

Boyer
Principles of Transportation Economics

Branson
Macroeconomic Theory and Policy

Bruce
Public Finance and the American Economy

Carlton/Perloff
Modern Industrial Organization

Case/Fair/Oster
*Principles of Economics**

Chapman
Environmental Economics: Theory, Application, and Policy

Cooter/Ulen
Law & Economics

Daniels/VanHoose
International Monetary & Financial Economics

Downs
An Economic Theory of Democracy

Ehrenberg/Smith
Modern Labor Economics

Farnham
Economics for Managers

Folland/Goodman/Stano
The Economics of Health and Health Care

Fort
Sports Economics

Froyen
Macroeconomics

Fusfeld
The Age of the Economist

Gerber
*International Economics**

González-Rivera
Forecasting for Economics and Business

Gordon
*Macroeconomics**

Greene
Econometric Analysis

Gregory
Essentials of Economics

Gregory/Stuart
Russian and Soviet Economic Performance and Structure

Hartwick/Olewiler
The Economics of Natural Resource Use

Heilbroner/Milberg
The Making of the Economic Society

Heyne/Boettke/Prychitko
The Economic Way of Thinking

Holt
Markets, Games, and Strategic Behavior

Hubbard/O'Brien
*Economics**

*Money, Banking, and the Financial System**

Hubbard/O'Brien/Rafferty
*Macroeconomics**

Hughes/Cain
American Economic History

Husted/Melvin
International Economics

Jehle/Reny
Advanced Microeconomic Theory

Johnson-Lans
A Health Economics Primer

Keat/Young/Erfle
Managerial Economics

Klein
Mathematical Methods for Economics

Krugman/Obstfeld/Melitz
*International Economics: Theory & Policy**

Laidler
The Demand for Money

Leeds/von Allmen
The Economics of Sports

Leeds/von Allmen/Schiming
*Economics**

Lynn
Economic Development: Theory and Practice for a Divided World

Miller
*Economics Today**

Understanding Modern Economics

Miller/Benjamin
The Economics of Macro Issues

Miller/Benjamin/North
The Economics of Public Issues

Mills/Hamilton
Urban Economics

Mishkin
*The Economics of Money, Banking, and Financial Markets**

*The Economics of Money, Banking, and Financial Markets, Business School Edition**

*Macroeconomics: Policy and Practice**

Murray
Econometrics: A Modern Introduction

O'Sullivan/Sheffrin/Perez
*Economics: Principles, Applications and Tools**

Parkin
*Economics**

Perloff
*Microeconomics**

*Microeconomics: Theory and Applications with Calculus**

Perloff/Brander
*Managerial Economics and Strategy**

Phelps
Health Economics

Pindyck/Rubinfeld
*Microeconomics**

Riddell/Shackelford/Stamos/Schneider
Economics: A Tool for Critically Understanding Society

Roberts
The Choice: A Fable of Free Trade and Protection

Rohlf
Introduction to Economic Reasoning

Roland
Development Economics

Scherer
Industry Structure, Strategy, and Public Policy

Schiller
The Economics of Poverty and Discrimination

Sherman
Market Regulation

Stock/Watson
Introduction to Econometrics

Studenmund
Using Econometrics: A Practical Guide

Tietenberg/Lewis
Environmental and Natural Resource Economics

Environmental Economics and Policy

Todaro/Smith
Economic Development

Waldman/Jensen
Industrial Organization: Theory and Practice

Walters/Walters/Appel/Callahan/Centanni/Maex/O'Neill
Econversations: Today's Students Discuss Today's Issues

Weil
Economic Growth

Williamson
Macroeconomics

*denotes MyEconLab Visit www.myeconlab.com to learn more.

MyEconLab® Provides the Power of Practice

Optimize your study time with **MyEconLab**, the online assessment and tutorial system. When you take a sample test online, **MyEconLab** gives you targeted feedback and a personalized Study Plan to identify the topics you need to review.

Study Plan

The Study Plan shows you the sections you should study next, gives easy access to practice problems, and provides you with an automatically generated quiz to prove mastery of the course material.

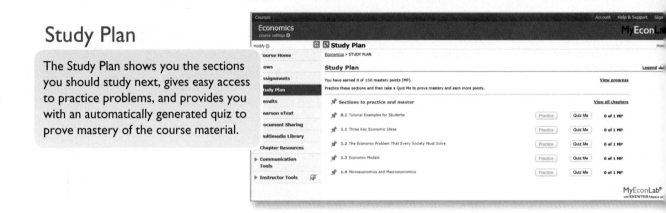

Unlimited Practice

As you work each exercise, instant feedback helps you understand and apply the concepts. Many Study Plan exercises contain algorithmically generated values to ensure that you get as much practice as you need.

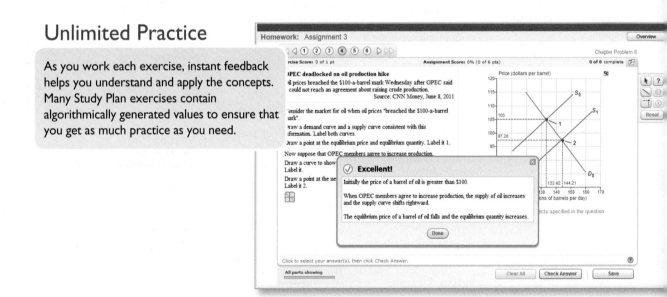

Learning Resources

Study Plan problems link to learning resources that further reinforce concepts you need to master.

- **Help Me Solve This** learning aids help you break down a problem much the same way as an instructor would do during office hours. Help Me Solve This is available for select problems.

- **eText links** are specific to the problem at hand so that related concepts are easy to review just when they are needed.

- A **graphing tool** enables you to build and manipulate graphs to better understand how concepts, numbers, and graphs connect.

MyEconLab

Find out more at www.myeconlab.com

Real-Time Data Analysis Exercises

Up-to-date macro data is a great way to engage in and understand the usefulness of macro variables and their impact on the economy. Real-Time Data Analysis exercises communicate directly with the Federal Reserve Bank of St. Louis's FRED® site, so every time FRED posts new data, students see new data.

End-of-chapter exercises accompanied by the Real-Time Data Analysis icon 🌐 include Real-Time Data versions in **MyEconLab**.

Select in-text figures labeled **MyEconLab** Real-Time Data update in the electronic version of the text using FRED data.

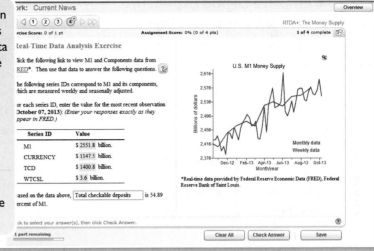

Current News Exercises

Posted weekly, we find the latest microeconomic and macroeconomic news stories, post them, and write auto-graded multi-part exercises that illustrate the economic way of thinking about the news.

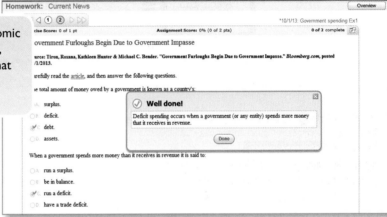

Interactive Homework Exercises

Participate in a fun and engaging activity that helps promote active learning and mastery of important economic concepts.

Pearson's experiments program is flexible and easy for instructors and students to use. For a complete list of available experiments, visit *www.myeconlab.com*.

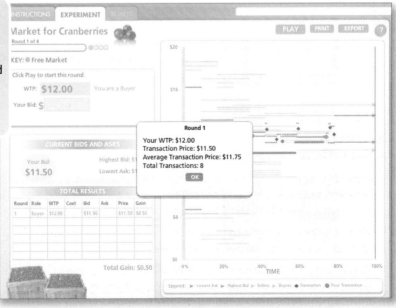

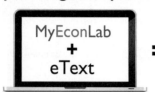

Digital

Complete **Digital Experience**

MyEconLab + eText =

Allow your students to save by purchasing a stand-alone MyEconLab directly from Pearson at **www.myeconlab.com**. Pearson's industry-leading learning solution features a **full Pearson eText** and course management functionality. Most importantly, MyEconLab helps you hold students accountable for class preparation and supports more active learning styles. Visit **www.myeconlab.com** to find out more.

Students can purchase a three-hole-punched, full-color version of the text via myeconlab.com at a **significant discount delivered right to their door**. →

Instant eText Access

 =

The **CourseSmart eBookstore** provides instant, online access to the textbook and course materials students need at a lower price. CourseSmart's eTextbooks are fully searchable and offer the same paging and appearance as the printed texts. You can preview eTextbooks online anytime at **www.coursesmart.com**.

Homework and Tutorial Only

MyEconLab =

Same great assessment technology without the **Pearson eText**.

Students can purchase a three-hole-punched, full-color version of the text via myeconlab.com at a **significant discount delivered right to their door**. →

Digital + Print

Great Content + Great Value

 =

Package our premium bound textbook with a MyEconLab access code for the most enduring student experience. Find out more at **www.myeconlab.com**.

Great Content + Great Price

 =

Save your students money and promote an active learning environment by offering a Student Value Edition—a three-hole-punched, full-color version of the premium textbook that's available at a 35% discount—packaged with a MyEconLab access code at your bookstore.

Custom

Customized Solutions

 =

Customize your textbook to match your syllabus. Trim your text to include just the chapters you need or add chapters from multiple books. With no unused material or unnecessary expense, Pearson Learning Solutions provides the right content you need for a course that's entirely your own. **www.pearsonlearningsolutions.com**

Contact your Pearson representative for more information on Pearson Choices

International Finance

THEORY AND POLICY

TENTH EDITION

Paul R. Krugman
Princeton University

Maurice Obstfeld
University of California, Berkeley

Marc J. Melitz
Harvard University

PEARSON

Boston   Columbus   Indianapolis   New York   San Francisco   Upper Saddle River
Amsterdam   Cape Town   Dubai   London   Madrid   Milan   Munich   Paris   Montréal   Toronto
Delhi   Mexico City   São Paulo   Sydney   Hong Kong   Seoul   Singapore   Taipei   Tokyo

For Robin—P.K.
For my family—M.O.
For Clair, Benjamin, and Max—M.M.

Editor in Chief: Donna Battista
Acquisitions Editor: Christina Masturzo
Program Manager: Carolyn Philips
Editorial Assistants: Patrick Henning and Christine Mallon
Executive Marketing Manager: Lori DeShazo
Managing Editor: Jeff Holcomb
Production Project Manager: Carla Thompson
Procurement Specialist: Carol Melville
Senior Art Director: Jonathan Boylan
Cover Design: Jonathan Boylan
Interior Design: Integra-Chicago
Image Manager: Rachel Youdelman
Photo Research: Aptara, Inc.

Text Permissions Associate Project Manager: Samantha Graham
Text Permissions Research: Electronic Publishing Services, Inc.
Director of Media: Susan Schoenberg
Content Leads, MyEconLab: Courtney Kamauf and Noel Lotz
Senior Media Producer: Melissa Honig
Full-Service Project Management and Composition: Integra-Chicago
Printer/Binder: Courier/Kendallville
Cover Printer: Lehigh-Phoenix Color/Hagerstown
Text Font: 10/12 Times New Roman

Acknowledgments of material borrowed from other sources and reproduced, with permission, in this textbook appear on appropriate page within text. Credits appear on page 431, which constitutes a continuation of the copyright page.

FRED ® is a registered trademark and the FRED ® Logo and ST. LOUIS FED are trademarks of the Federal Reserve Bank of St. Louis. http://research.stlouisfed.org/fred2/

Microsoft and/or its respective suppliers make no representations about the suitability of the information contained in the documents and related graphics published as part of the services for any purpose. All such documents and related graphics are provided "as is" without warranty of any kind. Microsoft and/or its respective suppliers hereby disclaim all warranties and conditions with regard to this information, including all warranties and conditions of merchantability, whether express, implied or statutory, fitness for a particular purpose, title and non-infringement. In no event shall Microsoft and/or its respective suppliers be liable for any special, indirect or consequential damages or any damages whatsoever resulting from loss of use, data or profits, whether in an action of contract, negligence or other tortious action, arising out of or in connection with the use or performance of information available from the services.

The documents and related graphics contained herein could include technical inaccuracies or typographical errors. Changes are periodically added to the information herein. Microsoft and/or its respective suppliers may make improvements and/or changes in the product(s) and/or the program(s) described herein at any time. Partial screen shots may be viewed in full within the software version specified.

Microsoft®, Excel®, PowerPoint®, Windows®, and Word® are registered trademarks of the Microsoft Corporation in the U.S.A. and other countries. This book is not sponsored or endorsed by or affiliated with the Microsoft Corporation.

Library of Congress Cataloging-in-Publication Data
Krugman, Paul R.
    International Finance: theory and policy/Paul R. Krugman, Princeton University, Maurice Obstfeld,
    University of California, Berkeley, Marc J. Melitz, Harvard University.—10th edition.
      pages cm
    Includes bibliographical references and index.
    ISBN 978-0-13-342364-8—ISBN 978-0-13-342363-1 (finance split) —ISBN 978-0-13-342367-9 (trade split)
      1. International economic relations. 2. International finance.
I. Obstfeld, Maurice. II. Melitz, Marc J. III. Title.
    HF1359.K78 2015
    337—dc23
                                      2013046411

10 9 8 7 6 5 4 3 2

ISBN 10:   0-13-342363-8
ISBN 13: 978-0-13-342363-1

Brief Contents

Contents

Preface

Years after the global financial crisis that broke out in 2007–2008, the industrial world's economies are still growing too slowly to restore full employment. Emerging markets, despite impressive income gains in many cases, remain vulnerable to the ebb and flow of global capital. And finally, an acute economic crisis in the euro area has lasted since 2009, bringing the future of Europe's common currency into question. This tenth edition therefore comes out at a time when we are more aware than ever before of how events in the global economy influence each country's economic fortunes, policies, and political debates. The world that emerged from World War II was one in which trade, financial, and even communication links between countries were limited. More than a decade into the 21st century, however, the picture is very different. Globalization has arrived, big time. International trade in goods and services has expanded steadily over the past six decades thanks to declines in shipping and communication costs, globally negotiated reductions in government trade barriers, the widespread outsourcing of production activities, and a greater awareness of foreign cultures and products. New and better communications technologies, notably the Internet, have revolutionized the way people in all countries obtain and exchange information. International trade in financial assets such as currencies, stocks, and bonds has expanded at a much faster pace even than international product trade. This process brings benefits for owners of wealth but also creates risks of contagious financial instability. Those risks were realized during the recent global financial crisis, which spread quickly across national borders and has played out at huge cost to the world economy. Of all the changes on the international scene in recent decades, however, perhaps the biggest one remains the emergence of China—a development that is already redefining the international balance of economic and political power in the coming century.

Imagine the astonishment of the generation that lived through the depressed 1930s as adults, had its members been able to foresee the shape of today's world economy! Nonetheless, the economic concerns that continue to cause international debate have not changed that much from those that dominated the 1930s, nor indeed since they were first analyzed by economists more than two centuries ago. What are the merits of free trade among nations compared with protectionism? What causes countries to run trade surpluses or deficits with their trading partners, and how are such imbalances resolved over time? What causes banking and currency crises in open economies, what causes financial contagion between economies, and how should governments handle international financial instability? How can governments avoid unemployment and inflation, what role do exchange rates play in their efforts, and how can countries best cooperate to achieve their economic goals? As always in international economics, the interplay of events and ideas has led to new modes of analysis. In turn, these analytical advances, however abstruse they may seem at first, ultimately do end up playing a major role in governmental policies, in international negotiations, and in people's everyday lives. Globalization has made citizens of all countries much more aware than ever before of the worldwide economic forces that influence their fortunes, and globalization is here to stay.

New to the Tenth Edition

For this edition, we are offering an Economics volume as well as Trade and Finance splits. The goal with these distinct volumes is to allow professors to use the book that best suits their needs based on the topics they cover in their International Economics course. In the Economics volume for a two-semester course, we follow the standard practice of dividing the book into two halves, devoted to trade and to monetary questions. Although the trade and monetary portions of international economics are often treated as unrelated subjects, even within one textbook, similar themes and methods recur in both subfields. We have made it a point to illuminate connections between the trade and monetary areas when they arise. At the same time, we have made sure that the book's two halves are completely self-contained. Thus, a one-semester course on trade theory can be based on Chapters 2 through 12, and a one-semester course on international monetary economics can be based on Chapters 13 through 22. For professors' and students' convenience, however, they can now opt to use either the Trade or the Finance volume, depending on the length and scope of their course.

We have thoroughly updated the content and extensively revised several chapters. These revisions respond both to users' suggestions and to some important developments on the theoretical and practical sides of international economics. The most far-reaching changes in the Finance volume are the following:

- **Chapter 6, Output and the Exchange Rate in the Short Run** In response to the global economic crisis of 2007–2009, countries throughout the world adopted countercyclical fiscal responses. Renewed academic research on the size of the fiscal multiplier soon followed, although most of it was set in the closed economy and so ignored the exchange rate effects stressed in this chapter's model. For this edition, we have added a new Case Study on the size of the fiscal multiplier in the open economy. In line with recent academic literature, which focuses on fiscal policy at the zero lower interest-rate bound, we integrate the discussion with our model of the liquidity trap.
- **Chapter 7, Fixed Exchange Rates and Foreign Exchange Intervention** The chapter now includes additional discussion of "inflow attacks" on exchange rates being held at appreciated levels through foreign exchange intervention and other measures, a phenomenon seen in China and other countries. A new Case Study focuses on the Swiss National Bank's policy of capping the Swiss franc's level against the euro.
- **Chapter 8, International Monetary Systems: An Historical Overview** A detailed derivation of an open economy's multi-period intertemporal budget constraint now complements the discussion of external balance. (Instructors who do not want to cover this relatively more technical material can skip it without loss of continuity.) The intertemporal analysis is applied to analyze the sustainability of New Zealand's persistent foreign borrowing. In addition, the chapter's discussion of recent events in the global economy has been updated.
- **Chapter 9, Financial Globalization: Opportunity and Crisis** For this new edition, we have switched the earlier order of Chapters 9 and 10 so that the book now covers the international capital market before covering optimum currency areas and the euro crisis. Our reasoning is that the euro crisis is in large part a crisis of the banks, which students cannot understand without a good prior grasp of international banking and its problems. Consistent with this approach, the new Chapter 9 covers bank balance sheets and bank fragility in detail, with emphasis on bank capital and capital regulation. Ever since this book's first edition, we have stressed the global context of banking regulation. In this edition, we explain the "financial trilemma," which forces national policymakers to choose at most two from among the potential objectives of financial openness, financial stability, and national control over financial policy.

- **Chapter 10, Optimum Currency Areas and the Euro** The crisis in the euro area escalated dramatically after the last edition of this book went to press. For this new edition, we have brought our coverage of the euro crisis up to date with new material on initiatives for closer policy coordination in the euro countries, such as banking union. Our theoretical discussion of optimum currency areas also reflects lessons of the euro crisis.
- **Chapter 11, Developing Countries: Growth, Crisis, and Reform** Our coverage of capital flows to developing countries now includes recent research on the small size of those flows, as well as their paradoxical tendency to favor low-growth over high-growth developing economies. We point out the close link between theories of capital allocation to developing countries and theories of the cross-country distribution of income.

In addition to these structural changes, we have updated the book in other ways to maintain current relevance. Thus, in the Finance volume, we examine the causes of the large measured global current account surplus (Chapter 2); we describe the outbreak and resolution of Zimbabwe's hyperinflation (Chapter 4); and we describe the evolving infrastructure of international bank regulation, including Basel III and the Financial Stability Board (Chapter 9).

About the Book

The idea of writing this book came out of our experience in teaching international economics to undergraduates and business students since the late 1970s. We perceived two main challenges in teaching. The first was to communicate to students the exciting intellectual advances in this dynamic field. The second was to show how the development of international economic theory has traditionally been shaped by the need to understand the changing world economy and analyze actual problems in international economic policy.

We found that published textbooks did not adequately meet these challenges. Too often, international economics textbooks confront students with a bewildering array of special models and assumptions from which basic lessons are difficult to extract. Because many of these special models are outmoded, students are left puzzled about the real-world relevance of the analysis. As a result, many textbooks often leave a gap between the somewhat antiquated material to be covered in class and the exciting issues that dominate current research and policy debates. That gap has widened dramatically as the importance of international economic problems—and enrollments in international economics courses—have grown.

This book is our attempt to provide an up-to-date and understandable analytical framework for illuminating current events and bringing the excitement of international economics into the classroom. In analyzing both the real and monetary sides of the subject, our approach has been to build up, step by step, a simple, unified framework for communicating the grand traditional insights as well as the newest findings and approaches. To help the student grasp and retain the underlying logic of international economics, we motivate the theoretical development at each stage by pertinent data and policy questions.

The Place of This Book in the Economics Curriculum

Students assimilate international economics most readily when it is presented as a method of analysis vitally linked to events in the world economy, rather than as a body of abstract theorems about abstract models. Our goal has therefore been to stress concepts and their application rather than theoretical formalism. Accordingly, the book does not presuppose an extensive background in economics. Students who have had a course in economic principles will find the book accessible, but students who have taken further courses in microeconomics or macroeconomics will find an abundant supply of new material. Specialized appendices and mathematical postscripts have been included to challenge the most advanced students.

Some Distinctive Features

This book covers the most important recent developments in international economics without shortchanging the enduring theoretical and historical insights that have traditionally formed the core of the subject. We have achieved this comprehensiveness by stressing how recent theories have evolved from earlier findings in response to an evolving world economy. The text is divided into a core of chapters focused on theory, followed by chapters applying the theory to major policy questions, past and current.

In Chapter 1, we describe in some detail how this book addresses the major themes of international economics. Here we emphasize several of the topics that previous authors failed to treat in a systematic way.

Asset Market Approach to Exchange Rate Determination

The modern foreign exchange market and the determination of exchange rates by national interest rates and expectations are at the center of our account of open-economy macroeconomics. The main ingredient of the macroeconomic model we develop is the interest parity relation, augmented later by risk premiums (Chapter 3). Among the topics we address using the model are exchange rate "overshooting"; inflation targeting; behavior of real exchange rates; balance-of-payments crises under fixed exchange rates; and the causes and effects of central bank intervention in the foreign exchange market (Chapters 4 through 7).

International Macroeconomic Policy Coordination

Our discussion of international monetary experience (Chapters 8 through 11) stresses the theme that different exchange rate systems have led to different policy coordination problems for their members. Just as the competitive gold scramble of the interwar years showed how beggar-thy-neighbor policies can be self-defeating, the current float challenges national policymakers to recognize their interdependence and formulate policies cooperatively.

The World Capital Market and Developing Countries

A broad discussion of the world capital market is given in Chapter 9 which takes up the welfare implications of international portfolio diversification as well as problems of prudential supervision of internationally active banks and other financial institutions. Chapter 11 is devoted to the long-term growth prospects and to the specific macroeconomic stabilization and liberalization problems of industrializing and newly industrialized countries. The chapter reviews emerging market crises and places in historical perspective the interactions among developing country borrowers, developed country lenders, and official financial institutions such as the International Monetary Fund. Chapter 11 also reviews China's exchange-rate policies and recent research on the persistence of poverty in the developing world.

Learning Features

This book incorporates a number of special learning features that will maintain students' interest in the presentation and help them master its lessons.

Case Studies

Case studies that perform the threefold role of reinforcing material covered earlier, illustrating its applicability in the real world, and providing important historical information often accompany theoretical discussions.

Special Boxes

Less central topics that nonetheless offer particularly vivid illustrations of points made in the text are treated in boxes. Among these markets for nondeliverable forward exchange (Chapter 3); and the rapid accumulation of foreign exchange reserves by developing countries (Chapter 11).

Captioned Diagrams

More than 200 diagrams are accompanied by descriptive captions that reinforce the discussion in the text and help the student in reviewing the material.

Learning Goals

A list of essential concepts sets the stage for each chapter in the book. These learning goals help students assess their mastery of the material.

Summary and Key Terms

Each chapter closes with a summary recapitulating the major points. Key terms and phrases appear in boldface type when they are introduced in the chapter and are listed at the end of each chapter. To further aid student review of the material, key terms are italicized when they appear in the chapter summary.

Problems

Each chapter is followed by problems intended to test and solidify students' comprehension. The problems range from routine computational drills to "big picture" questions suitable for classroom discussion. In many problems we ask students to apply what they have learned to real-world data or policy questions.

Further Readings

For instructors who prefer to supplement the textbook with outside readings, and for students who wish to probe more deeply on their own, each chapter has an annotated bibliography that includes established classics as well as up-to-date examinations of recent issues.

MyEconLab

MyEconLab

MyEconLab is the premier online assessment and tutorial system, pairing rich online content with innovative learning tools. MyEconLab includes comprehensive homework, quiz, test, and tutorial options, allowing instructors to manage all assessment needs in one program. Key innovations in the MyEconLab course for the tenth edition of *International Economics: Theory & Policy* include the following:

- *Real-Time Data Analysis Exercises,* marked with , allow students and instructors to use the latest data from FRED, the online macroeconomic data bank from the Federal Reserve Bank of St. Louis. By completing the exercises, students become familiar with a key data source, learn how to locate data, and develop skills to interpret data.
- In the *enhanced eText* available in MyEconLab, figures labeled MyEconLab Real-Time Data allow students to display a pop-up graph updated with real-time data from FRED.
- *Current News Exercises,* new to this edition of the MyEconLab course, provide a turn-key way to assign gradable news-based exercises in MyEconLab. Every week, Pearson scours the news, finds a current article appropriate for an economics course, creates an exercise around the news article, and then automatically adds it to MyEconLab. Assigning and grading current news-based exercises that deal with the latest economic events has never been more convenient.

Students and MyEconLab

This online homework and tutorial system puts students in control of their own learning through a suite of study and practice tools correlated with the online, interactive version of the textbook and learning aids such as animated figures. Within MyEconLab's structured environment, students practice what they learn, test their understanding, and then pursue a study plan that MyEconLab generates for them based on their performance.

Instructors and MyEconLab

MyEconLab provides flexible tools that allow instructors easily and effectively to customize online course materials to suit their needs. Instructors can create and assign tests, quizzes, or homework assignments. MyEconLab saves time by automatically grading all questions and tracking results in an online gradebook. MyEconLab can even grade assignments that require students to draw a graph.

After registering for MyEconLab instructors have access to downloadable supplements such as an instructor's manual, PowerPoint lecture notes, and a test bank. The test bank can also be used within MyEconLab, giving instructors ample material from which they can create assignments—or the Custom Exercise Builder makes it easy for instructors to create their own questions.

Weekly news articles, video, and RSS feeds help keep students updated on current events and make it easy for instructors to incorporate relevant news in lectures and homework.

For more information about MyEconLab or to request an instructor access code, visit www.myeconlab.com.

Additional Supplementary Resources

A full range of additional supplementary materials to support teaching and learning accompanies this book.

- The Online Instructor's Manual—updated by Hisham Foad of San Diego State University—includes chapter overviews and answers to the end-of-chapter problems.

- The Online Test Bank offers a rich array of multiple-choice and essay questions, including some mathematical and graphing problems, for each textbook chapter. It is available in Word, PDF, and TestGen formats. This Test Bank was carefully revised and updated by Robert F. Brooker of Gannon University.
- The Computerized Test Bank reproduces the Test Bank material in the TestGen software that is available for Windows and Macintosh. With TestGen, instructors can easily edit existing questions, add questions, generate tests, and print the tests in variety of formats.
- The Online PowerPoint Presentation with Tables, Figures, & Lecture Notes was revised by Amy Glass of Texas A&M University. This resource contains all text figures and tables and can be used for in-class presentations.
- The Companion Web Site at www.pearsonhighered.com/krugman contains additional appendices. (See page xvi of the Contents for a detailed list of the Online Appendices.)

Instructors can download supplements from our secure Instructor's Resource Center. Please visit www.pearsonhighered.com/irc.

Acknowledgments

Our primary debt is to Christina Masturzo, the Acquisitions Editor in charge of the project. We also are grateful to the Program Manager, Carolyn Philips, and the Project Manager, Carla Thompson. Heather Johnson's efforts as Project Manager with Integra-Chicago were essential and efficient. We would also like to thank the media team at Pearson—Denise Clinton, Noel Lotz, Courtney Kamauf, and Melissa Honig—for all their hard work on the MyEconLab course for the tenth edition. Last, we thank the other editors who helped make the first nine editions of this book as good as they were.

We also wish to acknowledge the sterling research assistance of Tatjana Kleineberg and Sandile Hlatshwayo. Camille Fernandez provided superb logistical support, as usual. For helpful suggestions and moral support, we thank Jennifer Cobb, Gita Gopinath, Vladimir Hlasny, and Phillip Swagel.

We thank the following reviewers, past and present, for their recommendations and insights:

Jaleel Ahmad, *Concordia University*

Lian An, *University of North Florida*

Anthony Paul Andrews, *Governors State University*

Myrvin Anthony, *University of Strathclyde, U.K.*

Michael Arghyrou, *Cardiff University*

Richard Ault, *Auburn University*

Amitrajeet Batabyal, *Rochester Institute of Technology*

Tibor Besedes, *Georgia Tech*

George H. Borts, *Brown University*

Robert F. Brooker, *Gannon University*

Francisco Carrada-Bravo, *W.P. Carey School of Business, ASU*

Debajyoti Chakrabarty, *University of Sydney*

Adhip Chaudhuri, *Georgetown University*

Jay Pil Choi, *Michigan State University*

Jaiho Chung, *National University of Singapore*

Jonathan Conning, *Hunter College and The Graduate Center, The City University of New York*

Brian Copeland, *University of British Columbia*

Kevin Cotter, *Wayne State University*

Barbara Craig, *Oberlin College*

Susan Dadres, *University of North Texas*

Ronald B. Davies, *University College Dublin*

Ann Davis, *Marist College*

Gopal C. Dorai, *William Paterson University*

Robert Driskill, *Vanderbilt University*

Gerald Epstein, *University of Massachusetts at Amherst*

JoAnne Feeney, *State University of New York*

at Albany
Robert Foster, *American Graduate School of International Management*
Patrice Franko, *Colby College*
Diana Fuguitt, *Eckerd College*
Byron Gangnes, *University of Hawaii at Manoa*
Ranjeeta Ghiara, *California State University, San Marcos*
Neil Gilfedder, *Stanford University*
Amy Glass, *Texas A&M University*
Patrick Gormely, *Kansas State University*
Thomas Grennes, *North Carolina State* University
Bodil Olai Hansen, *Copenhagen Business School*
Michael Hoffman, *U.S. Government Accountability Office*
Henk Jager, *University of Amsterdam*
Arvind Jaggi, *Franklin & Marshall College*
Mark Jelavich, *Northwest Missouri State University*
Philip R. Jones, *University of Bath and University of Bristol, U.K.*
Tsvetanka Karagyozova, *Lawrence University*
Hugh Kelley, *Indiana University*
Michael Kevane, *Santa Clara University*
Maureen Kilkenny, *University of Nevada*
Hyeongwoo Kim, *Auburn University*
Stephen A. King, *San Diego State University, Imperial Valley*
Faik Koray, *Louisiana State University*
Corinne Krupp, *Duke University*
Bun Song Lee, *University of Nebraska, Omaha*
Daniel Lee, *Shippensburg University*
Francis A. Lees, *St. Johns University*
Jamus Jerome Lim, *World Bank Group*
Rodney Ludema, *Georgetown University*
Stephen V. Marks, *Pomona College*
Michael L. McPherson, *University of North Texas*
Marcel Mérette, *University of Ottawa*
Shannon Mitchell, *Virginia Commonwealth University*
Kaz Miyagiwa, *Emory University*
Shannon Mudd, *Ursinus College*

Marc-Andreas Muendler, *University of California, San Diego*
Ton M. Mulder, *Erasmus University, Rotterdam*
Robert G. Murphy, *Boston College*
E. Wayne Nafziger, *Kansas State University*
Steen Nielsen, *University of Aarhus*
Dmitri Nizovtsev, *Washburn University*
Terutomo Ozawa, *Colorado State University*
Arvind Panagariya, *Columbia University*
Nina Pavcnik, *Dartmouth College*
Iordanis Petsas, *University of Scranton*
Thitima Puttitanun, *San Diego State University*
Peter Rangazas, *Indiana University-Purdue University Indianapolis*
James E. Rauch, *University of California, San Diego*
Michael Ryan, *Western Michigan University*
Donald Schilling, *University of Missouri, Columbia*
Patricia Higino Schneider, *Mount Holyoke College*
Ronald M. Schramm, *Columbia University*
Craig Schulman, *Texas A&M University*
Yochanan Shachmurove, *University of Pennsylvania*
Margaret Simpson, *The College of William and Mary*
Enrico Spolaore, *Tufts University*
Robert Staiger, *University of Wisconsin-Madison*
Jeffrey Steagall, *University of North Florida*
Robert M. Stern, *University of Michigan*
Abdulhamid Sukar, *Cameron University*
Rebecca Taylor, *University of Portsmouth, U.K.*
Scott Taylor, *University of British Columbia*
Aileen Thompson, *Carleton University*
Sarah Tinkler, *Portland State University*
Arja H. Turunen-Red, *University of New Orleans*
Dick vander Wal, *Free University of Amsterdam*
Gerald Willmann, *University of Kiel*
Rossitza Wooster, *California State University, Sacramento*
Bruce Wydick, *University of San Francisco*
Jiawen Yang, *The George Washington University*
Kevin H. Zhang, *Illinois State University*

Although we have not been able to make each and every suggested change, we found reviewers' observations invaluable in revising the book. Obviously, we bear sole responsibility for its remaining shortcomings.

Paul R. Krugman
Maurice Obstfeld
Marc J. Melitz
October 2013

CHAPTER 1

INTRODUCTION

You could say that the study of international trade and finance is where the discipline of economics as we know it began. Historians of economic thought often describe the essay "Of the Balance of Trade" by the Scottish philosopher David Hume as the first real exposition of an economic model. Hume published his essay in 1758, almost 20 years before his friend Adam Smith published *The Wealth of Nations*. And the debates over British trade policy in the early 19th century did much to convert economics from a discursive, informal field to the model-oriented subject it has been ever since.

Yet the study of international economics has never been as important as it is now. In the early 21st century, nations are more closely linked than ever before through trade in goods and services, flows of money, and investment in each other's economies. And the global economy created by these linkages is a turbulent place: Both policy makers and business leaders in every country, including the United States, must now pay attention to what are sometimes rapidly changing economic fortunes halfway around the world.

A look at some basic trade statistics gives us a sense of the unprecedented importance of international economic relations. Figure 1-1 shows the levels of U.S. exports and imports as shares of gross domestic product from 1960 to 2012. The most obvious feature of the figure is the long-term upward trend in both shares: International trade has roughly tripled in importance compared with the economy as a whole.

Almost as obvious is that, while both imports and exports have increased, imports have grown more, leading to a large excess of imports over exports. How is the United States able to pay for all those imported goods? The answer is that the money is supplied by large inflows of capital—money invested by foreigners willing to take a stake in the U.S. economy. Inflows of capital on that scale would once have been inconceivable; now they are taken for granted. And so the gap between imports and exports is an indicator of another aspect of growing international linkages—in this case the growing linkages between national capital markets.

Finally, notice that both imports and exports took a plunge in 2009. This decline reflected the global economic crisis that began in 2008 and is a reminder of the close links between world trade and the overall state of the world economy.

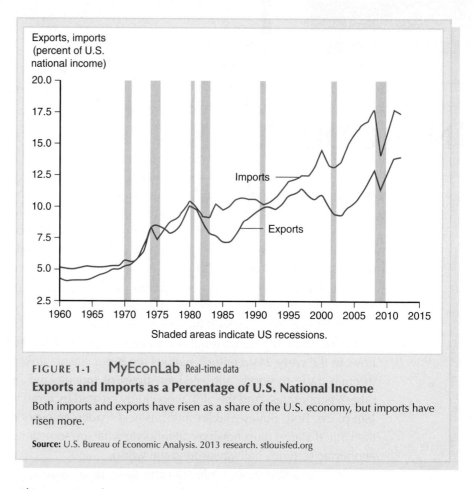

FIGURE 1-1 MyEconLab Real-time data

Exports and Imports as a Percentage of U.S. National Income

Both imports and exports have risen as a share of the U.S. economy, but imports have risen more.

Source: U.S. Bureau of Economic Analysis. 2013 research. stlouisfed.org

If international economic relations have become crucial to the United States, they are even more crucial to other nations. Figure 1-2 shows the average of imports and exports as a share of GDP for a sample of countries. The United States, by virtue of its size and the diversity of its resources, relies less on international trade than almost any other country.

International Economics—now available alternatively in two volumes, *International Trade* and *International Finance*—introduces the main concepts and methods of international economics and illustrates them with applications drawn from the real world. Much of the text is devoted to old ideas that are still as valid as ever: The 19th-century trade theory of David Ricardo and even the 18th-century monetary analysis of David Hume remain highly relevant to the 21st-century world economy. At the same time, we have made a special effort to bring the analysis up to date. In particular, the economic crisis that began in 2007 threw up major new challenges for the global economy. Economists were able to apply existing analyses to some of these challenges, but they were also forced to rethink some important concepts. Furthermore, new approaches have emerged to old questions, such as the impacts of changes in monetary and fiscal policy. We have attempted to convey the key ideas that have emerged in recent research while stressing the continuing usefulness of old ideas.

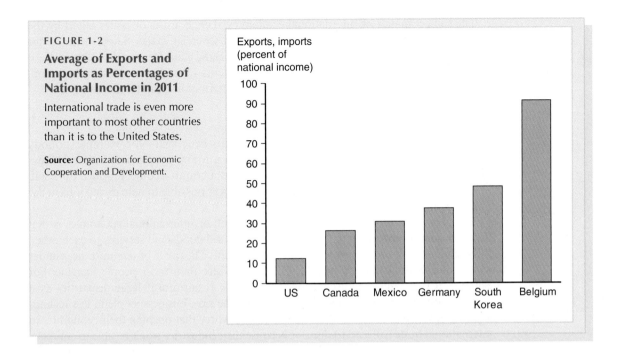

FIGURE 1-2

Average of Exports and Imports as Percentages of National Income in 2011

International trade is even more important to most other countries than it is to the United States.

Source: Organization for Economic Cooperation and Development.

Exports, imports (percent of national income)

LEARNING GOALS

After reading this chapter, you will be able to:

■ Distinguish between international and domestic economic issues.
■ Explain why seven themes recur in international economics, and discuss their significance.
■ Distinguish between the trade and monetary aspects of international economics.

What Is International Economics About?

International economics uses the same fundamental methods of analysis as other branches of economics because the motives and behavior of individuals are the same in international trade as they are in domestic transactions. Gourmet food shops in Florida sell coffee beans from both Mexico and Hawaii; the sequence of events that brought those beans to the shop is not very different, and the imported beans traveled a much shorter distance than the beans shipped within the United States! Yet international economics involves new and different concerns because international trade and investment occur between independent nations. The United States and Mexico are sovereign states; Florida and Hawaii are not. Mexico's coffee shipments to Florida could be disrupted if the U.S. government imposed a quota that limits imports; Mexican coffee could suddenly become cheaper to U.S. buyers if the peso were to fall in value against the dollar. By contrast, neither of those events can happen in commerce within the United States because the Constitution forbids restraints on interstate trade and all U.S. states use the same currency.

The subject matter of international economics, then, consists of issues raised by the special problems of economic interaction between sovereign states. Seven themes recur throughout the study of international economics: (1) the gains from trade, (2) the pattern of trade, (3) protectionism, (4) the balance of payments, (5) exchange rate determination, (6) international policy coordination, and (7) the international capital market.

The Gains from Trade

Everybody knows that some international trade is beneficial—for example, nobody thinks that Norway should grow its own oranges. Many people are skeptical, however, about the benefits of trading for goods that a country could produce for itself. Shouldn't Americans buy American goods whenever possible to help create jobs in the United States?

Probably the most important single insight in all of international economics is that there are *gains from trade*—that is, when countries sell goods and services to each other, this exchange is almost always to their mutual benefit. The range of circumstances under which international trade is beneficial is much wider than most people imagine. For example, it is a common misconception that trade is harmful if large disparities exist between countries in productivity or wages. On one side, businesspeople in less technologically advanced countries, such as India, often worry that opening their economies to international trade will lead to disaster because their industries won't be able to compete. On the other side, people in technologically advanced nations where workers earn high wages often fear that trading with less advanced, lower-wage countries will drag their standard of living down—one presidential candidate memorably warned of a "giant sucking sound" if the United States were to conclude a free trade agreement with Mexico.

Yet two countries can trade to their mutual benefit even when one of them is more efficient than the other at producing everything and when producers in the less efficient country can compete only by paying lower wages. Trade provides benefits by allowing countries to export goods whose production makes relatively heavy use of resources that are locally abundant while importing goods whose production makes heavy use of resources that are locally scarce. International trade also allows countries to specialize in producing narrower ranges of goods, giving them greater efficiencies of large-scale production.

Nor are the benefits of international trade limited to trade in tangible goods. International migration and international borrowing and lending are also forms of mutually beneficial trade—the first a trade of labor for goods and services, the second a trade of current goods for the promise of future goods. Finally, international exchanges of risky assets such as stocks and bonds can benefit all countries by allowing each country to diversify its wealth and reduce the variability of its income. These invisible forms of trade yield gains as real as the trade that puts fresh fruit from Latin America in Toronto markets in February.

Although nations generally gain from international trade, it is quite possible that international trade may hurt particular groups *within* nations—in other words, that international trade will have strong effects on the distribution of income. The effects of trade on income distribution have long been a concern of international trade theorists who have pointed out that:

International trade can adversely affect the owners of resources that are "specific" to industries that compete with imports, that is, cannot find alternative employment in other industries. Examples would include specialized machinery, such as power looms made less valuable by textile imports, and workers with specialized skills, like fishermen who find the value of their catch reduced by imported seafood.

Trade can also alter the distribution of income between broad groups, such as workers and the owners of capital.

These concerns have moved from the classroom into the center of real-world policy debate as it has become increasingly clear that the real wages of less-skilled workers in the United States have been declining—even though the country as a whole is continuing to grow richer. Many commentators attribute this development to growing international trade, especially the rapidly growing exports of manufactured goods from low-wage countries. Assessing this claim has become an important task for international economists.

The Pattern of Trade

Economists cannot discuss the effects of international trade or recommend changes in government policies toward trade with any confidence unless they know their theory is good enough to explain the international trade that is actually observed. As a result, attempts to explain the pattern of international trade—who sells what to whom—have been a major preoccupation of international economists.

Some aspects of the pattern of trade are easy to understand. Climate and resources clearly explain why Brazil exports coffee and Saudi Arabia exports oil. Much of the pattern of trade is more subtle, however. Why does Japan export automobiles, while the United States exports aircraft? In the early 19th century, English economist David Ricardo offered an explanation of trade in terms of international differences in labor productivity, an explanation that remains a powerful insight. In the 20th century, however, alternative explanations also were proposed. One of the most influential explanations links trade patterns to an interaction between the relative supplies of national resources such as capital, labor, and land on one side and the relative use of these factors in the production of different goods on the other. This basic model must be extended in order to generate accurate empirical predictions for the volume and pattern of trade. Also, some international economists have proposed theories that suggest a substantial random component, along with economies of scale, in the pattern of international trade.

How Much Trade?

If the idea of gains from trade is the most important theoretical concept in international economics, the seemingly eternal debate over how much trade to allow is its most important policy theme. Since the emergence of modern nation-states in the 16th century, governments have worried about the effect of international competition on the prosperity of domestic industries and have tried either to shield industries from foreign competition by placing limits on imports or to help them in world competition by subsidizing exports. The single most consistent mission of international economics has been to analyze the effects of these so-called protectionist policies—and usually, though not always, to criticize protectionism and show the advantages of freer international trade.

The debate over how much trade to allow took a new direction in the 1990s. After World War II the advanced democracies, led by the United States, pursued a broad policy of removing barriers to international trade; this policy reflected the view that free trade was a force not only for prosperity but also for promoting world peace.

In the first half of the 1990s, several major free trade agreements were negotiated. The most notable were the North American Free Trade Agreement (NAFTA) between the United States, Canada, and Mexico, approved in 1993, and the so-called Uruguay Round agreement, which established the World Trade Organization in 1994.

Since that time, however, an international political movement opposing "globalization" has gained many adherents. The movement achieved notoriety in 1999, when demonstrators representing a mix of traditional protectionists and new ideologies disrupted a major international trade meeting in Seattle. If nothing else, the anti-globalization movement has forced advocates of free trade to seek new ways to explain their views.

Over the years, international economists have developed a simple yet powerful analytical framework for determining the effects of government policies that affect international trade. This framework helps predict the effects of trade policies, while also allowing for cost-benefit analysis and defining criteria for determining when government intervention is good for the economy.

In the real world, however, governments do not necessarily do what the cost-benefit analysis of economists tells them they should. This does not mean that analysis is useless. Economic analysis can help make sense of the politics of international trade policy by showing who benefits and who loses from such government actions as quotas on imports and subsidies to exports. The key insight of this analysis is that conflicts of interest *within* nations are usually more important in determining trade policy than conflicts of interest *between* nations. Trade usually has very strong effects on income distribution within countries, while the relative power of different interest groups within countries, rather than some measure of overall national interest, is often the main determining factor in government policies toward international trade.

Balance of Payments

In 1998, both China and South Korea ran large trade surpluses of about $40 billion each. In China's case, the trade surplus was not out of the ordinary—the country had been running large surpluses for several years, prompting complaints from other countries, including the United States, that China was not playing by the rules. So is it good to run a trade surplus and bad to run a trade deficit? Not according to the South Koreans: Their trade surplus was forced on them by an economic and financial crisis, and they bitterly resented the necessity of running that surplus.

This comparison highlights the fact that a country's *balance of payments* must be placed in the context of an economic analysis to understand what it means. It emerges in a variety of specific contexts: in discussing foreign direct investment by multinational corporations, in relating international transactions to national income accounting, and in discussing virtually every aspect of international monetary policy, the subject of this volume. Like the problem of protectionism, the balance of payments has become a central issue for the United States because the nation has run huge trade deficits every year since 1982.

Exchange Rate Determination

In September 2010, Brazil's finance minister, Guido Mantegna, made headlines by declaring that the world was "in the midst of an international currency war." The occasion for his remarks was a sharp rise in the value of Brazil's currency, the *real*, which was worth less than 45 cents at the beginning of 2009 but had risen to almost 60 cents when he spoke (and would rise to 65 cents over the next few months). Mantegna accused wealthy countries—the United States in particular—of engineering this rise, which was devastating to Brazilian exporters. However, the surge in the *real* proved short-lived; the currency began dropping in mid-2011, and by the summer of 2013 it was back down to only 45 cents.

A key difference between international economics and other areas of economics is that countries usually have their own currencies—the euro, which is shared by a number of European countries, being the exception that proves the rule. And as the example of the *real* illustrates, the relative values of currencies can change over time, sometimes drastically.

For historical reasons, the study of exchange rate determination is a relatively new part of international economics. For much of modern economic history, exchange rates were fixed by government action rather than determined in the marketplace. Before World War I, the values of the world's major currencies were fixed in terms of gold; for a generation after World War II, the values of most currencies were fixed in terms of the U.S. dollar. The analysis of international monetary systems that fix exchange rates remains an important subject. Chapter 7 is devoted to the working of fixed-rate systems, Chapter 8 to the historical performance of alternative exchange-rate systems, and Chapter 10 to the economics of currency areas such as the European monetary union. For the time being, however, some of the world's most important exchange rates fluctuate minute by minute and the role of changing exchange rates remains at the center of the international economics story. Chapters 3 through 6 focus on the modern theory of floating exchange rates.

International Policy Coordination

The international economy comprises sovereign nations, each free to choose its own economic policies. Unfortunately, in an integrated world economy, one country's economic policies usually affect other countries as well. For example, when Germany's Bundesbank raised interest rates in 1990—a step it took to control the possible inflationary impact of the reunification of West and East Germany—it helped precipitate a recession in the rest of Western Europe. Differences in goals among countries often lead to conflicts of interest. Even when countries have similar goals, they may suffer losses if they fail to coordinate their policies. A fundamental problem in international economics is determining how to produce an acceptable degree of harmony among the international trade and monetary policies of different countries in the absence of a world government that tells countries what to do.

For almost 70 years, international trade policies have been governed by an international agreement known as the General Agreement on Tariffs and Trade (GATT). Since 1994, trade rules have been enforced by an international organization, the World Trade Organization, that can tell countries, including the United States, that their policies violate prior agreements.

While cooperation on international trade policies is a well-established tradition, coordination of international macroeconomic policies is a newer and more uncertain topic. Attempts to formulate principles for international macroeconomic coordination date to the 1980s and 1990s and remain controversial to this day. Nonetheless, attempts at international macroeconomic coordination are occurring with growing frequency in the real world. Both the theory of international macroeconomic coordination and the developing experience are reviewed in Chapter 8.

The International Capital Market

In 2007, investors who had bought U.S. mortgage-backed securities—claims on the income from large pools of home mortgages—received a rude shock: as home prices began to fall, mortgage defaults soared, and investments they had been assured were safe turned out to be highly risky. Since many of these claims were owned by financial institutions, the housing bust soon turned into a banking crisis. And here's the thing: it wasn't just a U.S. banking crisis, because banks in other countries, especially in Europe, had also bought many of these securities.

The story didn't end there: Europe soon had its own housing bust. And while the bust mainly took place in southern Europe, it soon became apparent that many northern European banks—such as German banks that had lent money to their Spanish counterparts—were also very exposed to the financial consequences.

In any sophisticated economy, there is an extensive capital market: a set of arrangements by which individuals and firms exchange money now for promises to pay in the future. The growing importance of international trade since the 1960s has been accompanied by a growth in the *international* capital market, which links the capital markets of individual countries. Thus in the 1970s, oil-rich Middle Eastern nations placed their oil revenues in banks in London or New York, and these banks in turn lent money to governments and corporations in Asia and Latin America. During the 1980s, Japan converted much of the money it earned from its booming exports into investments in the United States, including the establishment of a growing number of U.S. subsidiaries of Japanese corporations. Nowadays, China is funneling its own export earnings into a range of foreign assets, including dollars that its government holds as international reserves.

International capital markets differ in important ways from domestic capital markets. They must cope with special regulations that many countries impose on foreign investment; they also sometimes offer opportunities to evade regulations placed on domestic markets. Since the 1960s, huge international capital markets have arisen, most notably the remarkable London Eurodollar market, in which billions of dollars are exchanged each day without ever touching the United States.

Some special risks are associated with international capital markets. One risk is currency fluctuations: If the euro falls against the dollar, U.S. investors who bought euro bonds suffer a capital loss. Another risk is national default: A nation may simply refuse to pay its debts (perhaps because it cannot), and there may be no effective way for its creditors to bring it to court. Fears of default by highly indebted European nations have been a major concern in recent years.

The growing importance of international capital markets and their new problems demand greater attention than ever before. This text devotes two chapters to issues arising from international capital markets: one on the functioning of global asset markets (Chapter 9) and one on foreign borrowing by developing countries (Chapter 11).

International Economics: Trade and Money

The economics of the international economy can be divided into two broad subfields: the study of *international trade* and the study of *international money*. International trade analysis focuses primarily on the *real* transactions in the international economy, that is, transactions involving a physical movement of goods or a tangible commitment of economic resources. International monetary analysis focuses on the *monetary* side of the international economy, that is, on financial transactions such as foreign purchases of U.S. dollars. An example of an international trade issue is the conflict between the United States and Europe over Europe's subsidized exports of agricultural products; an example of an international monetary issue is the dispute over whether the foreign exchange value of the dollar should be allowed to float freely or be stabilized by government action.

In the real world, there is no simple dividing line between trade and monetary issues. Most international trade involves monetary transactions, while, as the examples in this chapter already suggest, many monetary events have important consequences for trade. Nonetheless, the distinction between international trade and international money is useful. *International Trade* covers international trade issues, developing the analytical theory of international trade and applying trade theory to the analysis of government policies toward trade. *International Finance* is devoted to international monetary issues, developing international monetary theory and applying this analysis to international monetary policy.

MyEconLab Can Help You Get a Better Grade

MyEconLab   If your exam were tomorrow, would you be ready? For each chapter, MyEconLab Practice Tests and Study Plans pinpoint sections you have mastered and those you need to study. That way, you are more efficient with your study time, and you are better prepared for your exams.

Here's how it works:

1. Make sure you have a Course ID from your instructor. Register and log in at www.myeconlab.com
2. Click on "Study Plan" and select the "Practice" button for the first section in this chapter.
3. Work the Practice questions. MyEconLab will grade your work automatically.
4. The Study Plan will serve up additional Practice Problems and tutorials to help you master the specific areas where you need to focus. By practicing online, you can track your progress in the Study Plan.
5. If you do well on the practice questions, the "Quiz Me" button will become highlighted. Work the Quiz questions.
6. Once you have mastered a section via the "Quiz Me" test, you will receive a Mastery Point and be directed to work on the next section.

CHAPTER 2

NATIONAL INCOME ACCOUNTING AND THE BALANCE OF PAYMENTS

Between 2004 and 2007, the world economy boomed, its total real product growing at an annual average rate of about 5 percent per year. The growth rate of world production slowed to around 3 percent per year in 2008, before dropping to *minus* 0.6 percent in 2009—a reduction in world output unprecedented in the period since World War II. In many countries, including the United States, unemployment soared. While the world's developing and emerging countries quickly returned to an annual growth rate close to 6 per cent per year, advanced economies struggled to grow quickly enough to return to full employment, and the European countries that use the euro again grew at a negative rate in 2012. Can economic analysis help us to understand the behavior of the global economy and the reasons why individual countries' fortunes often differ?

The theory of international *trade* is concerned primarily with the problem of making the best use of the world's scarce productive resources at a single point in time. The branch of economics called **microeconomics** studies this problem from the perspective of individual firms and consumers. Microeconomics works "from the bottom up" to show how individual economic actors, by pursuing their own interests, collectively determine how resources are used. In the study of international microeconomics, we learn how individual production and consumption decisions produce patterns of international trade and specialization. International trade theory demonstrates that while free trade usually encourages efficient resource use, government intervention or market failures can cause waste even when all factors of production are fully employed.

In this book, we shift the focus and ask: How can economic policy ensure that factors of production *are* fully employed? And what determines how an economy's capacity to produce goods and services changes over time? To answer these questions, we must understand **macroeconomics**, the branch of economics that studies how economies' overall levels of employment, production, and growth are determined. Like microeconomics, macroeconomics is concerned with the effective use of scarce resources. But while microeconomics focuses on

11

the economic decisions of individuals, macroeconomics analyzes the behavior of an economy as a whole. In our study of international macroeconomics, we will learn how the interactions of national economies influence the worldwide pattern of macroeconomic activity.

Macroeconomic analysis emphasizes four aspects of economic life that are usually kept in the background to simplify discussions of the microeconomic theory of international trade:

1. *Unemployment.* We know that in the real world, workers may be unemployed and factories may be idle. Macroeconomics studies the factors that cause unemployment and the steps governments can take to prevent it. A main concern of international macroeconomics is the problem of ensuring full employment in economies open to international trade.

2. *Saving.* The theory of international trade usually assumes that every country consumes an amount exactly equal to its income—no more and no less. In reality, though, households can put aside part of their income to provide for the future, or they can borrow temporarily to spend more than they earn. A country's saving or borrowing behavior affects domestic employment and future levels of national wealth. From the standpoint of the international economy as a whole, the world saving rate determines how quickly the world stock of productive capital can grow.

3. *Trade imbalances.* The value of a country's imports equals the value of its exports when spending equals income. This state of balanced trade is seldom attained by actual economies, however. In the following chapters, trade imbalances play a large role because they redistribute wealth among countries and are a main channel through which one country's macroeconomic policies affect its trading partners. It should be no surprise, therefore, that trade imbalances, particularly when they are large and persistent, quickly can become a source of international discord.

4. *Money and the price level.* The microeconomic theory of international trade is a barter theory, one in which goods are exchanged directly for other goods on the basis of their relative prices. In practice, it is more convenient to use money— a widely acceptable medium of exchange—in transactions, and to quote prices in terms of money. Because money changes hands in virtually every transaction that takes place in a modern economy, fluctuations in the supply of money or in the demand for it can affect both output and employment. International macroeconomics takes into account that every country uses a currency and that a monetary change (for example, a change in money supply) in one country can have effects that spill across its borders to other countries. Stability in money price levels is an important goal of international macroeconomic policy.

This chapter takes the first step in our study of international macroeconomics by explaining the accounting concepts economists use to describe a country's level of production and its international transactions. To get a complete picture of the macroeconomic linkages among economies that engage in international trade, we have to master two related and essential tools. The first of these tools, **national income accounting**, records all the expenditures that contribute to a country's income and output. The second tool, **balance of payments accounting**, helps us keep track of both changes in a country's indebtedness to foreigners and the fortunes of its export and import-competing industries. The balance of payments accounts also show the connection between foreign transactions and national money supplies.

After reading this chapter, you will be able to:

- Discuss the concept of the current account balance.
- Use the current account balance to extend national income accounting to open economies.
- Apply national income accounting to the interaction of saving, investment, and net exports.
- Describe the balance of payments accounts and explain their relationship to the current account balance.
- Relate the current account to changes in a country's net foreign wealth.

The National Income Accounts

Of central concern to macroeconomic analysis is a country's **gross national product (GNP)**, the value of all final goods and services produced by the country's factors of production and sold on the market in a given time period. GNP, which is the basic measure of a country's output studied by macroeconomists, is calculated by adding up the market value of all expenditures on final output. GNP therefore includes the value of goods like bread sold in a supermarket and textbooks sold in a bookstore as well as the value of services provided by stock brokers and plumbers. Because output cannot be produced without the aid of factor inputs, the expenditures that make up GNP are closely linked to the employment of labor, capital, and other factors of production.

To distinguish among the different types of expenditure that make up a country's GNP, government economists and statisticians who compile national income accounts divide GNP among the four possible uses for which a country's final output is purchased: *consumption* (the amount consumed by private domestic residents), *investment* (the amount put aside by private firms to build new plant and equipment for future production), *government purchases* (the amount used by the government), and the *current account balance* (the amount of net exports of goods and services to foreigners). The term *national income accounts*, rather than *national output accounts*, is used to describe this fourfold classification because a country's income in fact equals its output. Thus, the national income accounts can be thought of as classifying each transaction that contributes to national income according to the type of expenditure that gives rise to it. Figure 2-1 shows how U.S. GNP was divided among its four components in the first quarter of 2013.[1]

---

[1] In Figure 2-1 quarterly GNP and its components are measured at an annual rate (that is, they are multiplied by four). Our definition of the current account is not strictly accurate when a country is a net donor or recipient of foreign gifts. This possibility, along with some others, also complicates our identification of GNP with national income. We describe later in this chapter how the definitions of national income and the current account must be changed in such cases.

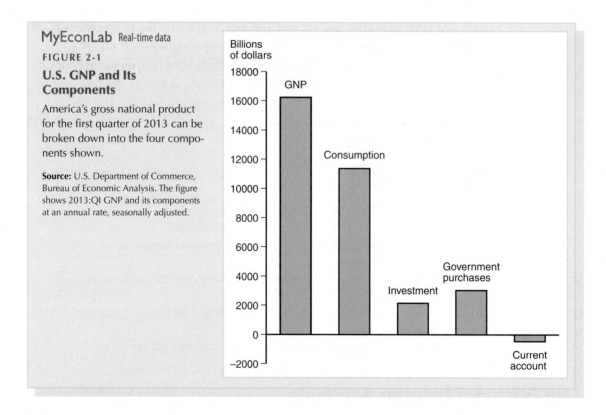

MyEconLab Real-time data

FIGURE 2-1

U.S. GNP and Its Components

America's gross national product for the first quarter of 2013 can be broken down into the four components shown.

Source: U.S. Department of Commerce, Bureau of Economic Analysis. The figure shows 2013:QI GNP and its components at an annual rate, seasonally adjusted.

Why is it useful to divide GNP into consumption, investment, government purchases, and the current account? One major reason is that we cannot hope to understand the cause of a particular recession or boom without knowing how the main categories of spending have changed. And without such an understanding, we cannot recommend a sound policy response. In addition, the national income accounts provide information essential for studying why some countries are rich—that is, have a high level of GNP relative to population size—while some are poor.

National Product and National Income

Our first task in understanding how economists analyze GNP is to explain in greater detail why the GNP a country generates over some time period must equal its **national income**, the income earned in that period by its factors of production.

The reason for this equality is that every dollar used to purchase goods or services automatically ends up in somebody's pocket. A visit to the doctor provides a simple example of how an increase in national output raises national income by the same amount. The $75 you pay the doctor represents the market value of the services he or she provides for you, so your visit raises GNP by $75. But the $75 you pay the doctor also raises his or her income. So national income rises by $75.

The principle that output and income are the same also applies to goods, even goods produced with the help of many factors of production. Consider the example of an economics textbook. When you purchase a new book from the publisher, the value of your purchase enters GNP. But your payment enters the income of the productive factors that cooperated in producing the book because the publisher must pay for their services with the proceeds of sales. First, there are the authors, editors, artists, and compositors who provide the labor inputs necessary for the book's production. Second, there are the publishing company's shareholders, who receive dividends for having financed acquisition of the capital used in production. Finally, there are the suppliers of paper and ink, who provide the intermediate materials used in producing the book.

The paper and ink purchased by the publishing house to produce the book are *not* counted separately in GNP because their contribution to the value of national output is already included in the book's price. It is to avoid such double counting that we allow only the sale of *final* goods and services to enter into the definition of GNP. Sales of intermediate goods, such as paper and ink purchased by a publisher, are not counted. Notice also that the sale of a used textbook does not enter GNP. Our definition counts only final goods and services that are *produced*, and a used textbook does not qualify: It was counted in GNP at the time it was first sold. Equivalently, the sale of a used textbook does not generate income for any factor of production.

Capital Depreciation and International Transfers

Because we have defined GNP and national income so that they are necessarily equal, their equality is really an identity. Two adjustments to the definition of GNP must be made, however, before the identification of GNP and national income is entirely correct in practice.

1. GNP does not take into account the economic loss due to the tendency of machinery and structures to wear out as they are used. This loss, called *depreciation*, reduces the income of capital owners. To calculate national income over a given period, we must therefore subtract from GNP the depreciation of capital over the period. GNP less depreciation is called *net national product* (NNP).
2. A country's income may include gifts from residents of foreign countries, called *unilateral transfers*. Examples of unilateral transfers of income are pension payments to retired citizens living abroad, reparation payments, and foreign aid such as relief funds donated to drought-stricken nations. For the United States in 2012, the balance of such payments amounted to around –$129.7 billion, representing a 0.8 percent of GNP net transfer to foreigners. Net unilateral transfers are part of a country's income but are not part of its product, and they must be added to NNP in calculations of national income.

National income equals GNP *less* depreciation *plus* net unilateral transfers. The difference between GNP and national income is by no means an insignificant amount, but macroeconomics has little to say about it, and it is of little importance for macroeconomic analysis. Therefore, for the purposes of this text, we usually use the terms *GNP* and *national income* interchangeably, emphasizing the distinction between the two only when it is essential.[2]

Gross Domestic Product

Most countries other than the United States have long reported **gross domestic product (GDP)** rather than GNP as their primary measure of national economic activity. In 1991, the United States began to follow this practice as well. GDP is supposed to

---

[2]Strictly speaking, government statisticians refer to what we have called "national income" as *national disposable income*. Their official concept of national income omits foreign net unilateral transfers. Once again, however, the difference between national income and national disposable income is usually unimportant for macroeconomic analysis. Unilateral transfers are alternatively referred to as *secondary income payments* to distinguish them from *primary income payments* consisting of cross-border wage and investment income. We will see this terminology later when we study balance of payments accounting.

measure the volume of production within a country's borders, whereas GNP equals GDP *plus* net receipts of factor income from the rest of the world. For the United States, these net receipts are primarily the income domestic residents earn on wealth they hold in other countries less the payments domestic residents make to foreign owners of wealth that is located in the domestic country.

GDP does not correct, as GNP does, for the portion of countries' production carried out using services provided by foreign-owned capital and labor. Consider an example: The profits of a Spanish factory with British owners are counted in Spain's GDP but are part of Britain's GNP. The services British capital provides in Spain are a service export from Britain, therefore they are added to British GDP in calculating British GNP. At the same time, to figure Spain's GNP, we must subtract from its GDP the corresponding service import from Britain.

As a practical matter, movements in GDP and GNP usually do not differ greatly. We will focus on GNP in this text, however, because GNP tracks national income more closely than GDP does, and national welfare depends more directly on national income than on domestic product.

National Income Accounting for an Open Economy

In this section, we extend to the case of an open economy, the closed-economy national income accounting framework you may have seen in earlier economics courses. We begin with a discussion of the national income accounts because they highlight the key role of international trade in open-economy macroeconomic theory. Since a closed economy's residents cannot purchase foreign output or sell their own to foreigners, all of national income must be allocated to domestic consumption, investment, or government purchases. In an economy open to international trade, however, the closed-economy version of national income accounting must be modified because some domestic output is exported to foreigners while some domestic income is spent on imported foreign products.

The main lesson of this section is the relationship among national saving, investment, and trade imbalances. We will see that in open economies, saving and investment are not necessarily equal, as they are in a closed economy. This occurs because countries can save in the form of foreign wealth by exporting more than they import, and they can *dissave*—that is, reduce their foreign wealth—by exporting less than they import.

Consumption

The portion of GNP purchased by private households to fulfill current wants is called **consumption**. Purchases of movie tickets, food, dental work, and washing machines all fall into this category. Consumption expenditure is the largest component of GNP in most economies. In the United States, for example, the fraction of GNP devoted to consumption has fluctuated in a range from about 62 to 70 percent over the past 60 years.

Investment

The part of output used by private firms to produce future output is called **investment**. Investment spending may be viewed as the portion of GNP used to increase the nation's stock of capital. Steel and bricks used to build a factory are part of investment spending, as are services provided by a technician who helps build business computers. Firms' purchases of inventories are also counted in investment spending because carrying inventories is just another way for firms to transfer output from current use to future use.

Investment is usually more variable than consumption. In the United States, (gross) investment has fluctuated between 11 and 22 percent of GNP in recent years. We often use the word *investment* to describe individual households' purchases of stocks, bonds, or real estate, but you should be careful not to confuse this everyday meaning of the word with the economic definition of investment as a part of GNP. When you buy a share of Microsoft stock, you are buying neither a good nor a service, so your purchase does not show up in GNP.

Government Purchases

Any goods and services purchased by federal, state, or local governments are classified as **government purchases** in the national income accounts. Included in government purchases are federal military spending, government support of cancer research, and government funds spent on highway repair and education. Government purchases include investment as well as consumption purchases. Government transfer payments such as social security and unemployment benefits do not require the recipient to give the government any goods or services in return. Thus, transfer payments are not included in government purchases.

Government purchases currently take up about 20 percent of U.S. GNP, and this share has not changed much since the late 1950s. (The corresponding figure for 1959, for example, was around 20 percent.) In 1929, however, government purchases accounted for only 8.5 percent of U.S. GNP.

The National Income Identity for an Open Economy

In a closed economy, any final good or service not purchased by households or the government must be used by firms to produce new plant, equipment, and inventories. If consumption goods are not sold immediately to consumers or the government, firms (perhaps reluctantly) add them to existing inventories, thereby increasing their investment.

This information leads to a fundamental identity for closed economies. Let Y stand for GNP, C for consumption, I for investment, and G for government purchases. Since all of a closed economy's output must be consumed, invested, or bought by the government, we can write

$$Y = C + I + G.$$

We derived the national income identity for a closed economy by assuming all output is consumed or invested by the country's citizens or purchased by its government. When foreign trade is possible, however, some output is purchased by foreigners while some domestic spending goes to purchase goods and services produced abroad. The GNP identity for open economies shows how the national income a country earns by selling its goods and services is divided between sales to domestic residents and sales to foreign residents.

Since residents of an open economy may spend some of their income on imports, that is, goods and services purchased from abroad, only the portion of their spending not devoted to imports is part of domestic GNP. The value of imports, denoted by IM, must be subtracted from total domestic spending, $C + I + G$, to find the portion of domestic spending that generates domestic national income. Imports from abroad add to foreign countries' GNPs but do not add directly to domestic GNP.

Similarly, the goods and services sold to foreigners make up a country's exports. Exports, denoted by *EX*, are the amount foreign residents' purchases add to the national income of the domestic economy.

The national income of an open economy is therefore the sum of domestic and foreign expenditures on the goods and services produced by domestic factors of production. Thus, the national income identity for an open economy is

$$Y = C + I + G + EX - IM. \tag{2-1}$$

An Imaginary Open Economy

To make identity (2-1) concrete, let's consider an imaginary closed economy, Agraria, whose only output is wheat. Each citizen of Agraria is a consumer of wheat, but each is also a farmer and therefore can be viewed as a firm. Farmers invest by putting aside a portion of each year's crop as seed for the next year's planting. There is also a government that appropriates part of the crop to feed the Agrarian army. Agraria's total annual crop is 100 bushels of wheat. Agraria can import milk from the rest of the world in exchange for exports of wheat. We cannot draw up the Agrarian national income accounts without knowing the price of milk in terms of wheat because all the components in the GNP identity (2-1) must be measured in the same units. If we assume the price of milk is 0.5 bushel of wheat per gallon, and that at this price, Agrarians want to consume 40 gallons of milk, then Agraria's imports are equal in value to 20 bushels of wheat.

In Table 2-1 we see that Agraria's total output is 100 bushels of wheat. Consumption is divided between wheat and milk, with 55 bushels of wheat and 40 gallons of milk (equal in value to 20 bushels of wheat) consumed over the year. The value of consumption in terms of wheat is $55 + (0.5 \times 40) = 55 + 20 = 75$.

The 100 bushels of wheat produced by Agraria are used as follows: 55 are consumed by domestic residents, 25 are invested, 10 are purchased by the government, and 10 are exported abroad. National income ($Y = 100$) equals domestic spending ($C + I + G = 110$) plus exports ($EX = 10$) less imports ($IM = 20$).

The Current Account and Foreign Indebtedness

In reality, a country's foreign trade is exactly balanced only rarely. The difference between exports of goods and services and imports of goods and services is known as the **current account balance** (or current account). If we denote the current account by *CA*, we can express this definition in symbols as

$$CA = EX - IM.$$

TABLE 2-1	National Income Accounts for Agraria, an Open Economy (bushels of wheat)				
GNP (total output)	= Consumption	+ Investment	+ Government purchases	+ Exports	− Imports
100	= 75[a]	+ 25	+ 10	+ 10	− 20[b]

[a] 55 bushels of wheat + (0.5 bushel per gallon) × (40 gallons of milk).
[b] 0.5 bushel per gallon × 40 gallons of milk.

When a country's imports exceed its exports, we say the country has a *current account deficit*. A country has a *current account surplus* when its exports exceed its imports.[3]

The GNP identity, equation (2-1), shows one reason why the current account is important in international macroeconomics. Since the right-hand side of (2-1) gives total expenditures on domestic output, changes in the current account can be associated with changes in output and, thus, employment.

The current account is also important because it measures the size and direction of international borrowing. When a country imports more than it exports, it is buying more from foreigners than it sells to them and must somehow finance this current account deficit. How does it pay for additional imports once it has spent its export earnings? Since the country as a whole can import more than it exports only if it can borrow the difference from foreigners, a country with a current account deficit must be increasing its net foreign debts by the amount of the deficit. This is currently the position of the United States, which has a significant current account deficit (and borrowed a sum equal to roughly 3 percent of its GNP in 2012).[4]

Similarly, a country with a current account surplus is earning more from its exports than it spends on imports. This country finances the current account deficit of its trading partners by lending to them. The foreign wealth of a surplus country rises because foreigners pay for any imports not covered by their exports by issuing IOUs that they will eventually have to redeem. The preceding reasoning shows that *a country's current account balance equals the change in its net foreign wealth.*[5]

We have defined the current account as the difference between exports and imports. Equation (2-1) says that the current account is also equal to the difference between national income and domestic residents' total spending $C + I + G$:

$$Y - (C + I + G) = CA.$$

It is only by borrowing abroad that a country can have a current account deficit and use more output than it is currently producing. If it uses less than its output, it has a current account surplus and is lending the surplus to foreigners.[6] International borrowing and lending can be thought of as *intertemporal trade* (trades of present and future consumption). A country with a current account deficit is importing present consumption and exporting future consumption. A country with a current account surplus is exporting present consumption and importing future consumption.

---

[3]In addition to net exports of goods and services, the current account balance includes net unilateral transfers of income, which we discussed briefly above. Following our earlier assumption, we continue to ignore such transfers for now to simplify the discussion. Later in this chapter, when we analyze the U.S. balance of payments in detail, we will see how transfers of current income enter the current account.

[4]Alternatively, a country could finance a current account deficit by using previously accumulated foreign wealth to pay for imports. This country would be running down its net foreign wealth, which has the same effect on overall wealth as running up its net foreign debts.

Our discussion here is ignoring the possibility that a country receives *gifts* of foreign assets (or gives such gifts), such as when one country agrees to forgive another's debts. As we will discuss below, such asset transfers (unlike transfers of current income) are not part of the current account, but they nonetheless do affect net foreign wealth. They are recorded in the *capital account* of the balance of payments.

[5]Alas, this statement is also not exactly correct, because there are factors that influence net foreign wealth that are not captured in the national income and product accounts. We will abstract from this fact until this chapter's concluding Case Study.

[6]The sum $A = C + I + G$ is often called domestic *absorption* in the literature on international macroeconomics. Using this terminology, we can describe the current account surplus as the difference between income and absorption, $Y - A$.

As an example, consider again the imaginary economy of Agraria described in Table 2-1. The total value of its consumption, investment, and government purchases, at 110 bushels of wheat, is greater than its output of 100 bushels. This inequality would be impossible in a closed economy; it is possible in this open economy because Agraria now imports 40 gallons of milk, worth 20 bushels of wheat, but exports only 10 bushels of wheat. The current account deficit of 10 bushels is the value of Agraria's borrowing from foreigners, which the country will have to repay in the future.

Figure 2-2 gives a vivid illustration of how a string of current account deficits can add up to a large foreign debt. The figure plots the U.S. current account balance since the late 1970s along with a measure of the nation's stock of net foreign wealth, its **net international investment position** (or *IIP*), the difference between its claims on foreigners and its liabilities to them. As you can see, the United States had accumulated substantial foreign wealth by the early 1980s, when a sustained current account deficit of proportions unprecedented in the 20th century opened up. In 1987, the country became

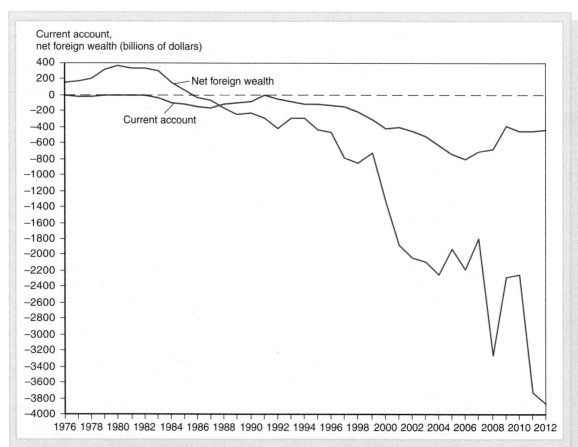

FIGURE 2-2   MyEconLab Real-time data

The U.S. Current Account and Net International Investment Position, 1976–2012

A string of current account deficits starting in the early 1980s reduced America's net foreign wealth until, by the early 21st century, the country had accumulated a substantial net foreign debt.

Source: U.S. Department of Commerce, Bureau of Economic Analysis.

a net debtor to foreigners for the first time since World War I. That foreign debt has continued to grow, and at the start of 2013, it stood at about 25 percent of GNP.

Saving and the Current Account

Simple as it is, the GNP identity has many illuminating implications. To explain the most important of these implications, we define the concept of **national saving**, that is, the portion of output, Y, that is not devoted to household consumption, C, or government purchases, G.[7] *In a closed economy, national saving always equals investment.* This tells us that the closed economy as a whole can increase its wealth only by accumulating new capital.

Let S stand for national saving. Our definition of S tells us that

$$S = Y - C - G.$$

Since the closed-economy GNP identity, $Y = C + I + G$, may also be written as $I = Y - C - G$, then

$$S = I,$$

and national saving must equal investment in a closed economy.

Whereas in a closed economy, saving and investment must always be equal, in an open economy they can differ. Remembering that national saving, S, equals $Y - C - G$ and that $CA = EX - IM$, we can rewrite the GNP identity (2-1) as

$$S = I + CA.$$

The equation highlights an important difference between open and closed economies: An open economy can save either by building up its capital stock or by acquiring foreign wealth, but a closed economy can save only by building up its capital stock.

Unlike a closed economy, an open economy with profitable investment opportunities does not have to increase its saving in order to exploit them. The preceding expression shows that it is possible simultaneously to raise investment and foreign borrowing without changing saving. For example, if New Zealand decides to build a new hydroelectric plant, it can import the materials it needs from the United States and borrow American funds to pay for them. This transaction raises New Zealand's domestic investment because the imported materials contribute to expanding the country's capital stock. The transaction also raises New Zealand's current account deficit by an amount equal to the increase in investment. New Zealand's saving does not have to change, even though investment rises. For this to be possible, however, U.S. residents must be willing to save more so that the resources needed to build the plant are freed for New Zealand's use. The result is another example of intertemporal trade, in which New Zealand imports present output (when it borrows from the United States) and exports future output (when it pays off the loan).

Because one country's savings can be borrowed by a second country in order to increase the second country's stock of capital, a country's current account surplus

---

[7]The U.S. national income accounts assume that government purchases are not used to enlarge the nation's capital stock. We follow this convention here by subtracting *all* government purchases from output to calculate national saving. Most other countries' national accounts distinguish between government consumption and government investment (for example, investment by publicly owned enterprises) and include the latter as part of national saving. Often, however, government investment figures include purchases of military equipment.

is often referred to as its *net foreign investment*. Of course, when one country lends to another to finance investment, part of the income generated by the investment in future years must be used to pay back the lender. Domestic investment and foreign investment are two different ways in which a country can use current savings to increase its future income.

Private and Government Saving

So far our discussion of saving has not stressed the distinction between saving decisions made by the private sector and saving decisions made by the government. Unlike private saving decisions, however, government saving decisions are often made with an eye toward their effect on output and employment. The national income identity can help us to analyze the channels through which government saving decisions influence domestic macroeconomic conditions. To use the national income identity in this way, we first have to divide national saving into its private and government components.

Private saving is defined as the part of disposable income that is saved rather than consumed. Disposable income is national income, Y, less the net taxes collected from households and firms by the government, T.[8] Private saving, denoted S^p, can therefore be expressed as

$$S^p = Y - T - C.$$

Government saving is defined similarly to private saving. The government's "income" is its net tax revenue, T, while its "consumption" is government purchases, G. If we let S^g stand for government saving, then

$$S^g = T - G.$$

The two types of saving we have defined, private and government, add up to national saving. To see why, recall the definition of national saving, S, as $Y - C - G$. Then

$$S = Y - C - G = (Y - T - C) + (T - G) = S^p + S^g.$$

We can use the definitions of private and government saving to rewrite the national income identity in a form that is useful for analyzing the effects of government saving decisions on open economies. Because $S = S^p + S^g = I + CA$,

$$S^p = I + CA - S^g = I + CA - (T - G) = I + CA + (G - T). \qquad \text{(2-2)}$$

Equation (2-2) relates private saving to domestic investment, the current account surplus, and government saving. To interpret equation (2-2), we define the **government budget deficit** as $G - T$, that is, as government saving preceded by a minus sign. The government budget deficit measures the extent to which the government is borrowing to finance its expenditures. Equation (2-2) then states that a country's private saving can take three forms: investment in domestic capital (I), purchases of wealth from foreigners (CA), and purchases of the domestic government's newly issued debt $(G - T)$.[9]

---

[8]Net taxes are taxes less government transfer payments. The term *government* refers to the federal, state, and local governments considered as a single unit.
[9]In a closed economy, the current account is always zero, so equation (2-2) is simply $S^p = I + (G - T)$.

THE MYSTERY OF THE MISSING DEFICIT

Because each country's exports are other countries' imports, the world's current account balances must add up to zero. But they don't. The accompanying figure shows the pattern in the data. Between 1980 and 2003, the sum of global current accounts was negative, implying either that surpluses were understated or that deficits were overstated. But in 2004, the "mystery of the missing surplus" became a "mystery of the missing deficit." Since that year, the measured global current account has been positive.

Given the inevitable errors in collecting detailed international payments data from many national agencies with differing accuracy and coverage, some discrepancy is unavoidable. What is puzzling is that the global discrepancy should be *persistently* positive or negative. That pattern suggests that something systematic is going on.

When the global current account balance was negative, it was thought that a big contributing factor was incomplete reporting of international investment income. For example, banks report these to their home governments, but the recipients, some of whom wish to avoid taxes, may not report them at the receiving end.

Not only have tax authorities become better at enforcing compliance, however, the general level of interest rates is now lower than it was in the 1980s and 1990s. Better measurement of international investment income could be responsible for a shrinking negative world current account. But what could have made it turn positive?

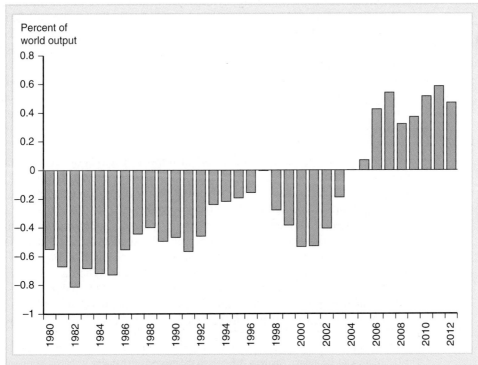

The Global Current Account Discrepancy since 1980

Once big and negative, implying missing current account credits, the global current account balance has become big and positive, implying missing current account debits.

Source: International Monetary Fund, *World Economic Outlook* database, April 2013.

(*Continued*)

One possible culprit is growing international trade in services. For example, a big law firm is likely to report its service exports fairly accurately, but the purchases by many of its smaller customers may escape detection. In a recent detailed review of the question, however, the *Economist* magazine pointed out that errors in measuring merchandise trade have also risen dramatically, and it is less clear that these would create a systematic bias toward an apparent global surplus.* The mystery remains a mystery. In 2012, it was worth $336 billion, or nearly half a percent of world output.

*See "Economics Focus: Exports to Mars," *Economist*, November 12, 2011, at http://www.economist.com/node/21538100.

The Balance of Payments Accounts

In addition to national income accounts, government economists and statisticians also keep balance of payments accounts, a detailed record of the composition of the current account balance and of the many transactions that finance it.[10] Balance of payments figures are of great interest to the general public, as indicated by the attention that various news media pay to them. But press reports sometimes confuse different measures of international payments flows. Should we be alarmed or cheered by a *Wall Street Journal* headline proclaiming, "U.S. Chalks Up Record Balance of Payments Deficit"? A thorough understanding of balance of payments accounting will help us evaluate the implications of a country's international transactions.

A country's balance of payments accounts keep track of both its payments to and its receipts from foreigners. Any transaction resulting in a receipt from foreigners is entered in the balance of payments accounts as a *credit*. Any transaction resulting in a payment to foreigners is entered as a *debit*. Three types of international transaction are recorded in the balance of payments:

1. Transactions that arise from the export or import of goods or services and therefore enter directly into the current account. When a French consumer imports American blue jeans, for example, the transaction enters the U.S. balance of payments accounts as a credit on the current account.
2. Transactions that arise from the purchase or sale of financial assets. An **asset** is any one of the forms in which wealth can be held, such as money, stocks, factories, or government debt. The **financial account** of the balance of payments records all international purchases or sales of financial assets. When an American company buys a French factory, the transaction enters the U.S. balance of payments as a debit in the financial account. It enters as a debit because the transaction requires a payment from the United States to foreigners. Correspondingly, a U.S.

[10]The U.S. Bureau of Economic Analysis (BEA) is in the process of changing its balance of payments presentation to conform to prevailing international standards, so our discussion in this chapter differs in some respects from that in editions one through eight of this book. We follow the new methodology described by Kristy L. Howell and Robert E. Yuskavage, "Modernizing and Enhancing BEA's International Economic Accounts: Recent Progress and Future Directions," *Survey of Current Business* (May 2010), pp. 6–20. For an update, see Kristy L. Howell and Kyle L. Westmoreland, "Modernizing and Enhancing BEA's International Economic Accounts: A Progress Report and Plans for Implementation," *Survey of Current Business* (May 2013), pp. 44–60. As of this writing, the BEA has not completed a full transition to the new system, but it hopes to do so in June 2014.

sale of assets to foreigners enters the U.S. financial account as a credit. The difference between a country's purchases and sales of foreign assets is called its *financial account balance*, or its *net financial flows.*

3. Certain other activities resulting in transfers of wealth between countries are recorded in the **capital account**. These international asset movements—which are generally very small for the United States—differ from those recorded in the financial account. For the most part they result from nonmarket activities or represent the acquisition or disposal of nonproduced, nonfinancial, and possibly intangible assets (such as copyrights and trademarks). For example, if the U.S. government forgives $1 billion in debt owed to it by the government of Pakistan, U.S. wealth declines by $1 billion and a $1 billion debit is recorded in the U.S. capital account.

You will find the complexities of the balance of payments accounts less confusing if you keep in mind the following simple rule of double-entry bookkeeping: *Every international transaction automatically enters the balance of payments twice, once as a credit and once as a debit.* This principle of balance of payments accounting holds true because every transaction has two sides: If you buy something from a foreigner, you must pay him in some way, and the foreigner must then somehow spend or store your payment.

Examples of Paired Transactions

Some examples will show how the principle of double-entry bookkeeping operates in practice.

1. Imagine you buy an ink-jet fax machine from the Italian company Olivetti and pay for your purchase with a $1,000 check. Your payment to buy a good (the fax machine) from a foreign resident enters the U.S. current account as a debit. But where is the offsetting balance of payments credit? Olivetti's U.S. salesperson must do something with your check—let's say he deposits it in Olivetti's account at Citibank in New York. In this case, Olivetti has purchased, and Citibank has sold, a U.S. asset—a bank deposit worth $1,000—and the transaction shows up as a $1,000 credit in the U.S. financial account. The transaction creates the following two offsetting bookkeeping entries in the U.S. balance of payments:

	Credit	Debit
Fax machine purchase (Current account, U.S. good import)		$1,000
Sale of bank deposit by Citibank (Financial account, U.S. asset sale)	$1,000	

2. As another example, suppose that during your travels in France, you pay $200 for a fine dinner at the Restaurant de l'Escargot d'Or. Lacking cash, you place the charge on your Visa credit card. Your payment, which is a tourist expenditure, will be counted as a service import for the United States, and therefore as a current account debit. Where is the offsetting credit? Your signature on the Visa slip entitles the restaurant to receive $200 (actually, its local currency equivalent) from First Card, the company that issued your Visa card. It is therefore an asset, a claim on a future payment from First Card. So when you pay for your meal abroad with your credit card, you are selling an asset to France and generating

a $200 credit in the U.S. financial account. The pattern of offsetting debits and credits in this case is:

	Credit	Debit
Meal purchase (Current account, U.S. service import)		$200
Sale of claim on First Card		
(Financial account, U.S. asset sale)	$200	

3. Imagine next that your Uncle Sid from Los Angeles buys a newly issued share of stock in the U.K. oil giant British Petroleum (BP). He places his order with his U.S. stockbroker, Go-for-Broke, Inc., paying $95 with funds from his Go-for-Broke money market account. BP, in turn, deposits the $95 Sid has paid into its own U.S. bank account at Second Bank of Chicago. Uncle Sid's acquisition of the stock creates a $95 debit in the U.S. financial account (he has purchased an asset from a foreign resident, BP), while BP's $95 deposit at its Chicago bank is the offsetting financial account credit (BP has expanded its U.S. asset holdings). The mirror-image effects on the U.S. balance of payments therefore both appear in the financial account:

	Credit	Debit
Uncle Sid's purchase of a share of BP		$95
(Financial account, U.S. asset purchase)		
BP's deposit of Uncle Sid's payment at Second Bank of Chicago		
(Financial account, U.S. asset sale)	$95	

4. Finally, let's consider how the U.S. balance of payments accounts are affected when U.S. banks forgive (that is, announce that they will simply forget about) $5,000 in debt owed to them by the government of the imaginary country of Bygonia. In this case, the United States makes a $5,000 capital transfer to Bygonia, which appears as a $5,000 debit entry in the capital account. The associated credit is in the financial account, in the form of a $5,000 reduction in U.S. assets held abroad (a negative "acquisition" of foreign assets, and therefore a balance of payments credit):

	Credit	Debit
U.S. banks' debt forgiveness		$5,000
(Capital account, U.S. transfer payment)		
Reduction in banks' claims on Bygonia		
(Financial account, U.S. asset sale)	$5,000	

These examples show that many circumstances can affect the way a transaction generates its offsetting balance of payments entry. We can never predict with certainty where the flip side of a particular transaction will show up, but we can be sure that it will show up somewhere.

The Fundamental Balance of Payments Identity

Because any international transaction automatically gives rise to offsetting credit and debit entries in the balance of payments, the sum of the current account balance and the capital account balance automatically equals the financial account balance:

$$\text{Current account } + \text{ capital account } = \text{ Financial account.} \qquad (2\text{-}3)$$

In examples 1, 2, and 4 previously, current or capital account entries have offsetting counterparts in the financial account, while in example 3, two financial account entries offset each other.

You can understand this identity another way. Recall the relationship linking the current account to international lending and borrowing. Because the sum of the current and capital accounts is the total change in a country's net foreign assets (including, through the capital account, nonmarket asset transfers), that sum necessarily equals the difference between a country's purchases of assets from foreigners and its sales of assets to them—that is, the financial account balance (also called net financial flows).

We now turn to a more detailed description of the balance of payments accounts, using as an example the U.S. accounts for 2012.

The Current Account, Once Again

As you have learned, the current account balance measures a country's net exports of goods and services. Table 2-2 shows that U.S. exports (on the credit side) were $2,986.9 billion in 2012, while U.S. imports (on the debit side) were $3,297.7 billion.

The balance of payments accounts divide exports and imports into three finer categories. The first is *goods* trade, that is, exports or imports of merchandise. The second category, *services*, includes items such as payments for legal assistance, tourists' expenditures, and shipping fees. The final category, *income*, is made up mostly of international interest and dividend payments and the earnings of domestically owned firms operating abroad. If you own a share of a German firm's stock and receive a dividend payment of $5, that payment shows up in the accounts as a U.S. investment income receipt of $5. Wages that workers earn abroad can also enter the income account.

We include income on foreign investments in the current account because that income really is compensation for the *services* provided by foreign investments. This idea, as we saw earlier, is behind the distinction between GNP and GDP. When a U.S. corporation builds a plant in Canada, for instance, the productive services the plant generates are viewed as a service export from the United States to Canada equal in value to the profits the plant yields for its American owner. To be consistent, we must be sure to include these profits in American GNP and not in Canadian GNP. Remember, the definition of GNP refers to goods and services generated by a country's factors of production, but it does *not* specify that those factors must work within the borders of the country that owns them.

Before calculating the current account, we must include one additional type of international transaction that we have largely ignored until now. In discussing the relationship between GNP and national income, we defined unilateral transfers between countries as international gifts, that is, payments that do not correspond to the purchase of any good, service, or asset. Net unilateral transfers are considered part of the current account as well as a part of national income, and the identity $Y = C + I + G + CA$ holds exactly if Y is interpreted as GNP *plus* net transfers. In 2012, the U.S. balance of unilateral transfers was −$129.7 billion.

MyEconLab Real-time data

TABLE 2-2	U.S. Balance of Payments Accounts for 2012 (billions of dollars)
Current Account	
(1) Exports	**2,986.9**
Of which:	
Goods	1,561.2
Services	649.3
Income receipts (primary income)	776.3
(2) Imports	**3,297.7**
Of which:	
Goods	2,302.7
Services	442.5
Income payments (primary income)	552.4
(3) Net unilateral transfers (secondary income)	−129.7
Balance on current account	**−440.4**
[(1) − (2) + (3)]	
Capital Account	
(4)	**7.0**
Financial Account	
(5) Net U.S. acquisition of financial assets, excluding financial derivatives	**97.5**
Of which:	
Official reserve assets	4.5
Other assets	93.0
(6) Net U.S. incurrence of liabilities, excluding financial derivatives	**543.9**
Of which:	
Official reserve assets	393.9
Other assets	150.0
(7) Financial derivatives, net	**7.1**
Net financial flows	**−439.4**
[(5) − (6) + (7)]	
Net errors and omissions	−6.0
[Net financial flows less sum of current and capital accounts]	

Source: U.S. Department of Commerce, Bureau of Economic Analysis, June 14, 2013, release. Totals may differ from sums because of rounding.

The table shows a 2012 current account balance of $2,986.9 billion − $3,297.7 − $129.7 billion = −$440.4 billion, a deficit.

The negative sign means that current payments to foreigners exceeded current receipts and that U.S. residents used more output than they produced. Since these current account transactions were paid for in some way, we know that this $440.4 billion net debit entry must be offset by a net $440.4 billion credit elsewhere in the balance of payments.

The Capital Account

The capital account entry in Table 2-2 shows that in 2012, the United States received net capital asset transfers of roughly $7.0 billion. These payments to the United States are a net balance of payments credit. After we add them to the payments deficit implied by the current account, we find that the United States' need to cover its excess payments to foreigners is reduced very slightly, from $440.4 billion to $433.4 billion. Because an excess of national spending over income must be covered by net borrowing from foreigners, this negative current plus capital account balance must be matched by an equal negative balance of net financial flows, representing the net liabilities the United States incurred to foreigners in 2012 in order to fund its deficit.

The Financial Account

While the current account is the difference between sales of goods and services to foreigners and purchases of goods and services from them, the financial account measures the difference between acquisitions of assets from foreigners and the buildup of liabilities to them. When the United States borrows $1 from foreigners, it is selling them an asset—a promise that they will be repaid $1, with interest, in the future. Likewise, when the United States lends abroad, it acquires an asset: the right to claim future repayment from foreigners.

To cover its 2012 current plus capital account deficit of $433.4 billion, the United States needed to borrow from foreigners (or otherwise sell assets to them) in the net amount of $433.4 billion. We can look again at Table 2-2 to see exactly how this net sale of assets to foreigners came about.

The table records separately U.S. acquisitions of foreign financial assets (which are balance of payments debits, because the United States must pay foreigners for those assets) and increases in foreign claims on residents of the United States (which are balance of payments credits, because the United States receives payments when it sells assets overseas).

These data on increases in U.S. asset holdings abroad and foreign holdings of U.S. assets do not include holdings of *financial derivatives*, which are a class of assets that are more complicated than ordinary stocks and bonds, but have values that can depend on stock and bond values. (We will describe some specific derivative securities in the next chapter.) Starting in 2006, the U.S. Department of Commerce was able to assemble data on *net* cross-border derivative flows for the United States (U.S. net purchases of foreign-issued derivatives less foreign net purchases of U.S.-issued derivatives). Derivatives transactions enter the balance of payments accounts in the same way as do other international asset transactions.

According to Table 2-2, U.S.-owned assets abroad (other than derivatives) increased (on a net basis) by $97.5 billion in 2012. The figure is "on a net basis" because some U.S. residents bought foreign assets while others sold foreign assets they already owned, the difference between U.S. gross purchases and sales of foreign assets being $97.5 billion. In the same year (again on a net basis), the United States incurred new liabilities to foreigners equal to $543.9 billion. Some U.S. residents undoubtedly repaid foreign debts, but new borrowing from foreigners exceeded these repayments by $543.9 billion. The balance of U.S. purchases and sales of financial derivatives was $7.1 billion: The United States acquired derivative claims on foreigners greater in value than the derivative claims on the U.S. that foreigners acquired. We calculate the balance on financial account (net financial flows) as $97.5 billion − $543.9 billion + $7.1 billion = −$439.4 billion. The negative value for net financial flows means that in 2012, the United States increased its net liability to foreigners (liabilities minus assets) by $439.4 billion.

Net Errors and Omissions

We come out with net financial flows of −$439.4 billion rather than the −$433.4 billion that we'd expected after adding up the current and capital account balances. According to our data on trade and financial flows, the United States incurred $6.0 billion more in foreign debt than it actually needed to fund its current plus capital account deficit. If every balance of payments credit automatically generates an equal counterpart debit and vice versa, how is this difference possible? The reason is that information about the offsetting debit and credit items associated with a given transaction may be collected from different sources. For example, the import debit that a shipment of DVD players from Japan generates may come from a U.S. customs inspector's report and the corresponding financial account credit from a report by the U.S. bank in which the check paying for the DVD players is deposited. Because data from different sources may differ in coverage, accuracy, and timing, the balance of payments accounts seldom balance in practice as they must in theory. Account keepers force the two sides to balance by adding to the accounts a *net errors and omissions* item. For 2012, unrecorded (or misrecorded) international transactions generated a balancing accounting debit of −$6.0 billion—the difference between the recorded net financial flows and the sum of the recorded current and capital accounts.

We have no way of knowing exactly how to allocate this discrepancy among the current, capital, and financial accounts. (If we did, it wouldn't be a discrepancy!) The financial account is the most likely culprit, since it is notoriously difficult to keep track of the complicated financial trades between residents of different countries. But we cannot conclude that net financial flows were $6 billion higher than recorded because the current account is also highly suspect. Balance of payments accountants consider merchandise trade data relatively reliable, but data on services are not. Service transactions such as sales of financial advice and computer programming assistance may escape detection. Accurate measurement of international interest and dividend receipts is particularly difficult.

Official Reserve Transactions

Although there are many types of financial account transactions, one type is important enough to merit separate discussion. This type of transaction is the purchase or sale of official reserve assets by central banks.

An economy's **central bank** is the institution responsible for managing the supply of money. In the United States, the central bank is the Federal Reserve System. **Official international reserves** are foreign assets held by central banks as a cushion against national economic misfortune. At one time, official reserves consisted largely of gold, but today, central banks' reserves include substantial foreign financial assets, particularly U.S. dollar assets such as Treasury bills. The Federal Reserve itself holds only a small level of official reserve assets other than gold; its own holdings of U.S. dollar assets are not considered international reserves.

Central banks often buy or sell international reserves in private asset markets to affect macroeconomic conditions in their economies. Official transactions of this type are called **official foreign exchange intervention**. One reason why foreign exchange intervention can alter macroeconomic conditions is that it is a way for the central bank to inject money into the economy or withdraw it from circulation. We will have much more to say later about the causes and consequences of foreign exchange intervention.

Government agencies other than central banks may hold foreign reserves and intervene officially in exchange markets. The U.S. Treasury, for example, operates an Exchange Stabilization Fund that at times has played an active role in market trading.

Because the operations of such agencies usually have no noticeable impact on the money supply, however, we will simplify our discussion by speaking (when it is not too misleading) as if the central bank alone holds foreign reserves and intervenes.

When a central bank purchases or sells a foreign asset, the transaction appears in its country's financial account just as if the same transaction had been carried out by a private citizen. A transaction in which the central bank of Japan (the Bank of Japan) acquires dollar assets might occur as follows: A U.S. auto dealer imports a Nissan sedan from Japan and pays the auto company with a check for $20,000. Nissan does not want to invest the money in dollar assets, but it so happens that the Bank of Japan is willing to give Nissan Japanese money in exchange for the $20,000 check. The Bank of Japan's international reserves rise by $20,000 as a result of the deal. Because the Bank of Japan's dollar reserves are part of total Japanese assets held in the United States, the latter rise by $20,000. This transaction therefore results in a $20,000 credit in the U.S. financial account, the other side of the $20,000 debit in the U.S. current account due to the import of the car.[11]

Table 2-2 shows the size and direction of official reserve transactions involving the United States in 2012. U.S. official reserve assets rose by $4.5 billion. Foreign central banks purchased $393.9 billion to add to their reserves. The net increase in U.S. official reserves *less* the increase in foreign official reserve claims on the United States is the level of net central bank financial flows, which stood at $4.5 billion − $393.9 = −$389.4 billion in 2012.

You can think of this −$389.4 billion net central bank financial flow as measuring the degree to which monetary authorities in the United States and abroad joined with other lenders to cover the U.S. current account deficit. In the example above, the Bank of Japan, by acquiring a $20,000 U.S. bank deposit, indirectly finances an American import of a $20,000 Japanese car. The level of net central bank financial flows is called the **official settlements balance** or (in less formal usage) the **balance of payments**. This balance is the sum of the current account and capital account balances, less the nonreserve portion of the financial account balance, and it indicates the payments gap that official reserve transactions need to cover. Thus, the U.S. balance of payments in 2012 was −$389.4 billion.

The balance of payments played an important historical role as a measure of disequilibrium in international payments, and for many countries it still plays this role. A negative balance of payments (a deficit) may signal a crisis, for it means that a country is running down its international reserve assets or incurring debts to foreign monetary authorities. If a country faces the risk of being suddenly cut off from foreign loans, it will want to maintain a "war chest" of international reserves as a precaution. Developing countries, in particular, are in this position (see Chapter 11).

Like any summary measure, however, the balance of payments must be interpreted with caution. To return to our running example, the Bank of Japan's decision to expand its U.S. bank deposit holdings by $20,000 swells the measured U.S. balance of payments deficit by the same amount. Suppose the Bank of Japan instead places its $20,000 with Barclays Bank in London, which in turn deposits the money with Citibank in New York. The United States incurs an extra $20,000 in liabilities to *private* foreigners in this case, and the U.S. balance of payments deficit does not rise. But this "improvement" in the balance of payments is of little economic importance: It makes no real difference to the United States whether it borrows the Bank of Japan's money directly or through a London bank.

---

[11]To test your understanding, see if you can explain why the same sequence of actions causes a $20,000 improvement in Japan's current account and a $20,000 increase in its net financial flows.

CASE STUDY   The Assets and Liabilities of the World's Biggest Debtor

We saw earlier that the current account balance measures the flow of new net claims on foreign wealth that a country acquires by exporting more goods and services than it imports. This flow is not, however, the only important factor that causes a country's net foreign wealth to change. In addition, changes in the market price of wealth previously acquired can alter a country's net foreign wealth. When Japan's stock market lost three-quarters of its value over the 1990s, for example, American and European owners of Japanese shares saw the value of their claims on Japan plummet, and Japan's net *foreign* wealth increased as a result. Exchange rate changes have a similar effect. When the dollar depreciates against foreign currencies, for example, foreigners who hold dollar assets see their wealth fall when measured in their home currencies.

The Bureau of Economic Analysis (BEA) of the U.S. Department of Commerce, which oversees the vast job of data collection behind the U.S. national income and balance of payments statistics, reports annual estimates of the net international investment position of the United States—the country's foreign assets less its foreign liabilities. Because asset price and exchange rate changes alter the dollar values of foreign assets and liabilities alike, the BEA must adjust the values of existing claims to reflect such capital gains and losses in order to estimate U.S. net foreign wealth. These estimates show that at the end of 2012, the United States had a *negative* net foreign wealth position far greater than that of any other country.

Until 1991, foreign direct investments such as foreign factories owned by U.S. corporations were valued at their historical, that is, original, purchase prices. Now the BEA uses two different methods to place current values on foreign direct investments: the *current cost* method, which values direct investments at the cost of buying them today, and the *market value* method, which is meant to measure the price at which the investments could be sold. These methods can lead to different valuations because the cost of replacing a particular direct investment and the price it would command if sold on the market may be hard to measure. (The net foreign wealth data graphed in Figure 2-2 are current cost estimates, which are believed to be more accurate.)

Table 2-3 reproduces the BEA's account of how it made its valuation adjustments to find the U.S. net IIP at the end of 2012. This "headline" estimate values direct investments at current cost. Starting with its estimate of 2011 net foreign wealth (−$3,730.6 billion), the BEA (column a) added the amount of the 2012 U.S. net financial flow of −$439.4 billion—recall the figure reported in Table 2-2. Then the BEA adjusted the values of previously held assets and liabilities for various changes in their dollar prices (columns b, c, and d). As a result of these valuation changes, U.S. net foreign wealth fell by an amount smaller than the $439.4 billion in new net borrowing from foreigners—in fact, U.S. net foreign wealth only declined by $133.3 billion. The BEA's 2012 estimate of U.S. net foreign wealth, therefore, was −$3,863.9 billion.

TABLE 2-3 — International Investment Position of the United States at Year End, 2011 and 2012 (millions of dollars)

Line	Type of investment	Position, 2011[r]	Financial flows (a)	Price changes (b)	Exchange-rate changes[1] (c)	Other changes[2] (d)	Total (a+b+c+d)	Position, 2012[r]
1	Net international investment position of the United States (lines 2+3)	−3,730,590	−439,351	489,566	5,100	−188,618	−133,302	−3,863,892
2	Financial derivatives, net (line 5 less line 25)[3]	86,039	7,064	(4)	(4)	[4]−35,327	−28,263	57,776
3	Net international investment position, excluding financial derivatives (line 6 less line 26)	−3,816,629	−446,415	489,566	5,100	−153,291	−105,039	−3,921,668
4	U.S.-owned assets abroad (lines 5+6)	21,636,152	(3)	(3)	(3)	(3)	1,466	21,637,618
5	Financial derivatives (gross positive fair value)	4,716,578	(3)	(3)	(3)	(3)	−1,096,817	3,619,761
6	U.S.-owned assets abroad, excluding financial derivatives (lines 7+12+17)	16,919,574	97,469	990,880	5,909	4,024	1,098,283	18,017,857
7	U.S. official reserve assets	537,037	4,460	33,079	−2,208	0	35,331	572,368
8	Gold	400,355	0	[5]33,079	.....	[6]0	33,079	433,434
9	Special drawing rights	54,956	37	.....	57	0	94	55,050
10	Reserve position in the International Monetary Fund	30,080	4,032	.....	49	0	4,081	34,161
11	Foreign currencies	51,646	391	.....	−2,314	0	−1,923	49,723
12	U.S. government assets, other than official reserve assets	178,901	−85,331	.....	(*)	0	−85,331	93,570
13	U.S. credits and other long-term assets[7]	78,373	5,656	.....	(*)	0	5,656	84,029
14	Repayable in dollars	78,100	5,656	.....	.....	0	5,656	83,756
15	Other[8]	273	0	.....	(*)	.....	0	273
16	U.S. foreign currency holdings and U.S. short-term assets[9]	100,528	−90,987	.....	(*)	.....	−90,987	9,541
17	U.S. private assets	16,203,636	178,341	957,801	8,117	4,024	1,148,283	17,351,919
18	Direct investment at current cost	4,663,142	388,293	25,339	16,234	−15,258	414,608	5,077,750
19	Foreign securities	6,441,350	144,823	932,462	−7,412	20,000	1,089,873	7,531,223
20	Bonds	1,939,912	62,243	139,503	−973	0	200,773	2,140,685
21	Corporate stocks	4,501,438	82,580	792,959	−6,439	20,000	889,100	5,390,538
22	U.S. claims on unaffiliated foreigners reported by U.S. nonbanking concerns	792,953	25,723	.....	3,194	22,882	51,799	844,752
23	U.S. claims reported by U.S. banks and securities brokers, not included elsewhere	4,306,191	−380,498	.....	−3,899	−23,600	−407,997	3,898,194
24	Foreign-owned assets in the United States (lines 25+26)	25,366,742	(3)	(3)	(3)	(3)	134,768	25,501,510
25	Financial derivatives (gross negative fair value)	4,630,539	(3)	(3)	(3)	(3)	−1,068,554	3,561,985
26	Foreign-owned assets in the United States, excluding financial derivatives (lines 27+34)	20,736,203	543,884	501,314	809	157,315	1,203,322	21,939,525
27	Foreign official assets in the United States	5,256,358	393,922	42,110	58	0	436,090	5,692,448
28	U.S. government securities	4,235,886	314,660	−23,650	.....	0	291,010	4,526,896
29	U.S. Treasury securities	3,620,580	433,155	−21,531	.....	0	411,624	4,032,204
30	Other	615,306	−118,495	−2,119	.....	0	−120,614	494,692
31	Other U.S. government liabilities[10]	119,980	8,241	.....	58	0	8,299	128,279
32	U.S. liabilities reported by U.S. banks and securities brokers, not included elsewhere	205,973	−1,572	.....	.....	0	−1,572	204,401
33	Other foreign official assets	694,519	72,593	65,760	.....	0	138,353	832,872
34	Other foreign assets	15,479,845	149,962	459,204	751	157,315	767,232	16,247,077
35	Direct investment at current cost	2,879,531	166,411	20,385	606	−9,607	177,795	3,057,326
36	U.S. Treasury securities	1,386,274	156,385	−1,090	0	0	155,295	1,541,569
37	U.S. securities other than U.S. Treasury securities	6,151,552	196,908	439,909	−897	116,578	752,498	6,904,050
38	Corporate and other bonds	2,894,604	23,584	125,774	−897	18,898	167,359	3,061,963
39	Corporate stocks	3,256,948	173,324	314,135	.....	97,680	585,139	3,842,087
40	U.S. currency	397,086	57,141	.....	.....	0	57,141	454,227
41	U.S. liabilities to unaffiliated foreigners reported by U.S. nonbanking concerns	630,925	−39,505	.....	3,158	61,944	25,597	656,522
42	U.S. liabilities reported by U.S. banks and securities brokers, not included elsewhere	4,034,477	−387,378	.....	−2,116	−11,600	−401,094	3,633,383
	Memoranda:							
43	Direct investment abroad at market value	4,513,863	388,293	301,652	48,194	−2,463	735,676	5,249,539
44	Direct investment in the United States at market value	3,510,395	166,411	260,399	.....	−13,236	413,574	3,923,969

r Revised
* Less than $500,000 (+/−)
..... Not applicable

1. Represents gains or losses on foreign-currency-denominated assets and liabilities due to their revaluation at current exchange rates.
2. Includes changes due to year-to-year shifts in the composition of reporting panels, primarily for bank and nonbank estimates , and to the incorporation of more comprehensive survey results. Also includes capital gains and losses of direct investment affiliates and changes in positions that cannot be allocated to financial flows, price changes, or exchange-rate changes.
3. Financial flows and valuation adjustments for financial derivatives are available only on a net basis, which is shown on line 2; they are not separately available for gross positive fair values and gross negative fair values of financial derivatives. Consequently, columns (a) through (d) on lines 4, 5, 24, and 25 are not available.
4. Data are not separately available for the three types of valuation adjustments; therefore, the sum of all three types is shown in column (d).
5. Reflects changes in the value of the official gold stock due to fluctuations in the market price of gold.
6. Reflects changes in gold stock from U.S. Treasury sales of gold medallions and commemorative and bullion coins; also reflects replenishment through open market purchases. These demonetizations/monetizations are not included in international transactions financial flows.
7. Also includes paid-in capital subscriptions to international financial institutions and outstanding amounts of miscellaneous claims that have been settled through international agreements to be payable to the U.S. government over periods in excess of 1 year. Excludes World War I debts that are not being serviced.
8. Includes indebtedness that the borrower may contractually, or at its option, repay with its currency, or by delivery of materials or transfer of services.
9. Includes foreign-currency-denominated assets obtained through temporary reciprocal currency arrangements between the Federal Reserve System and foreign central banks. These assets are included in the investment position at the dollar value established at the time they were received, reflecting the valuation of these assets in the Federal Reserve System's balance sheet. Changes in exchange rates are not included in the investment position at the dollar value established at the time they were received, reflecting the valuation of these assets in the Federal Reserve System's balance sheet. Changes in exchange rates
10. Includes U.S. government liabilities associated with military sales contracts and U.S. government reserve-related liabilities from allocations of special drawing rights (SDRs).

Source: U.S. Department of Commerce, Bureau of Economic Analysis, June 2013.

This debt is larger than the total foreign debt owed by all the Central and Eastern European countries, which was about $1,240 billion in 2012. To put these figures in perspective, however, it is important to realize that the U.S. net foreign debt amounted to about 25 percent of its GDP, while the foreign liability of Hungary, Poland, Romania, and the other Central and Eastern European debtors was about 67 percent of their collective GDP! Thus, the U.S. external debt represents a much lower domestic income drain.

Changes in exchange rates and securities prices have the potential to change the U.S. net foreign debt sharply, however, because the *gross* foreign assets and liabilities of the United States have become so large in recent years. Figure 2-3 illustrates this dramatic trend. In 1976, U.S. foreign assets stood at only 25 percent of U.S. GDP and liabilities at 16 percent (making the United States a net foreign creditor in the amount of roughly 9 percent of its GDP). In 2012, however, the country's foreign assets amounted to roughly 138 percent of GDP and its liabilities to roughly 163 percent. The tremendous growth in these stocks of wealth reflects the rapid globalization of financial markets in the late 20th century, a phenomenon we will discuss further in Chapter 9.

Think about how wealth positions of this magnitude amplify the effects of exchange rate changes, however. Suppose 70 percent of U.S. foreign assets are denominated in foreign currencies, but all U.S. liabilities to foreigners are denominated in dollars (these are approximately the correct numbers). Because the 2012 U.S. GDP was around $15.7 trillion, a 10 percent depreciation of the dollar would leave U.S. liabilities unchanged but would increase U.S. assets (measured in dollars)

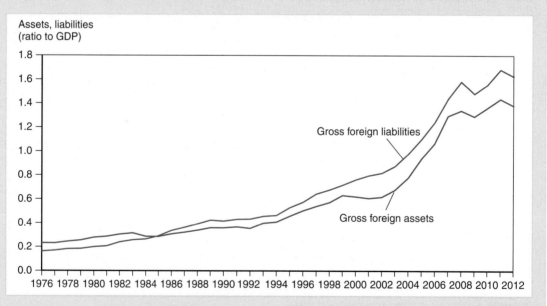

FIGURE 2-3   MyEconLab Real-time data

U.S. Gross Foreign Assets and Liabilities, 1976–2012

Since 1976, both the foreign assets and the liabilities of the United States have increased sharply. But liabilities have risen more quickly, leaving the United States with a substantial net foreign debt.

Source: U.S. Department of Commerce, Bureau of Economic Analysis, June 2013.

by $0.1 \times 0.7 \times 1.38 = 9.7$ percent of GDP, or about \$1.5 trillion. This number is approximately 3.4 times the U.S. current account deficit of 2012! Indeed, due to sharp movements in exchange rates and stock prices, the U.S. economy lost about \$800 billion in this way between 2007 and 2008 and gained a comparable amount between 2008 and 2009 (see Figure 2-2). The corresponding redistribution of wealth between foreigners and the United States would have been much smaller back in 1976.

Does this possibility mean that policy makers should ignore their countries' current accounts and instead try to manipulate currency values to prevent large buildups of net foreign debt? That would be a perilous strategy because, as we will see in the next chapter, expectations of future exchange rates are central to market participants' behavior. Systematic government attempts to reduce foreign investors' wealth through exchange rate changes would sharply reduce foreigners' demand for domestic currency assets, thus decreasing or eliminating any wealth benefit from depreciating the home currency.

SUMMARY

1. International *macroeconomics* is concerned with the full employment of scarce economic resources and price level stability throughout the world economy. Because they reflect national expenditure patterns and their international repercussions, the *national income accounts* and the *balance of payments accounts* are essential tools for studying the macroeconomics of open, interdependent economies.

2. A country's *gross national product* (GNP) is equal to the income received by its factors of production. The national income accounts divide national income according to the types of spending that generate it: *consumption, investment, government purchases,* and the *current account balance. Gross domestic product* (GDP), equal to GNP less net receipts of factor income from abroad, measures the output produced within a country's territorial borders.

3. In an economy closed to international trade, GNP must be consumed, invested, or purchased by the government. By using current output to build plant, equipment, and inventories, investment transforms present output into future output. For a closed economy, investment is the only way to save in the aggregate, so the sum of the saving carried out by the private and public sectors, *national saving,* must equal investment.

4. In an open economy, GNP equals the sum of consumption, investment, government purchases, and net exports of goods and services. Trade does not have to be balanced if the economy can borrow from and lend to the rest of the world. The difference between the economy's exports and imports, the current account balance, equals the difference between the economy's output and its total use of goods and services.

5. The current account also equals the country's net lending to foreigners. Unlike a closed economy, an open economy can save through domestic *and* foreign investments. National saving therefore equals domestic investment plus the current account balance. The current account is closely related to the change in the *net international investment position,* though usually not equal to that change because of fluctuations in asset values not recorded in the national income and product accounts.

6. Balance of payments accounts provide a detailed picture of the composition and financing of the current account. All transactions between a country and the rest of the world are recorded in the country's balance of payments accounts. The accounts are based on the convention that any transaction resulting in a payment to foreigners is entered as a debit while any transaction resulting in a receipt from foreigners is entered as a credit.

7. Transactions involving goods and services appear in the current account of the balance of payments, while international sales or purchases of *assets* appear in the *financial account.* The *capital account* records mainly nonmarket asset transfers and tends to be small for the United States. The sum of the current and capital account balances must equal the financial account balance (net financial flows). This feature of the accounts reflects the fact that discrepancies between export earnings and import expenditures must be matched by a promise to repay the difference, usually with interest, in the future.

8. International asset transactions carried out by *central banks* are included in the financial account. Any central bank transaction in private markets for foreign currency assets is called *official foreign exchange intervention.* One reason intervention is important is that central banks use it as a way to change the amount of money in circulation. A country has a deficit in its *balance of payments* when it is running down its *official international reserves* or borrowing from foreign central banks; it has a surplus in the opposite case.

KEY TERMS

asset, p. 24
balance of payments accounting, p. 13
capital account, p. 25
central bank, p. 30
consumption, p. 16
current account balance, p. 18
financial account, p. 24
government budget deficit,p. 22
government purchases, p. 17

gross domestic product (GDP), p. 15
gross national product (GNP), p. 13
investment, p. 16
macroeconomics, p. 11
microeconomics, p. 11
national income, p. 14
national income accounting, p. 13

national saving, p. 21
net international investment position, p. 20
official foreign exchange intervention, p. 30
official international reserves, p. 30
official settlements balance (or balance of payments), p. 31
private saving, p. 22

PROBLEMS   MyEconLab

1. We stated in this chapter that GNP accounts avoid double counting by including only the value of *final* goods and services sold on the market. Should the measure of imports used in the GNP accounts therefore be defined to include only imports of final goods and services from abroad? What about exports?

2. Equation (2-2) tells us that to reduce a current account deficit, a country must increase its private saving, reduce domestic investment, or cut its government budget deficit. Nowadays, some people recommend restrictions on imports from China (and other countries) to reduce the American current account deficit. How would higher U.S. barriers to imports affect its private saving, domestic investment, and government deficit? Do you agree that import restrictions would necessarily reduce a U.S. current account deficit?

3. Explain how each of the following transactions generates two entries—a credit and a debit—in the American balance of payments accounts, and describe how each entry would be classified:

   a. An American buys a share of German stock, paying by writing a check on an account with a Swiss bank.

   b. An American buys a share of German stock, paying the seller with a check on an American bank.

   c. The Korean government carries out an official foreign exchange intervention in which it uses dollars held in an American bank to buy Korean currency from its citizens.

   d. A tourist from Detroit buys a meal at an expensive restaurant in Lyons, France, paying with a traveler's check.

   e. A California winemaker contributes a case of cabernet sauvignon for a London wine tasting.

   f. A U.S.-owned factory in Britain uses local earnings to buy additional machinery.

4. A New Yorker travels to New Jersey to buy a $100 telephone answering machine. The New Jersey company that sells the machine then deposits the $100 check in its account at a New York bank. How would these transactions show up in the balance of payments accounts of New York and New Jersey? What if the New Yorker pays cash for the machine?

5. The nation of Pecunia had a current account deficit of $1 billion and a nonreserve financial account surplus of $500 million in 2014.

   a. What was the balance of payments of Pecunia in that year? What happened to the country's net foreign assets?

   b. Assume that foreign central banks neither buy nor sell Pecunian assets. How did the Pecunian central bank's foreign reserves change in 2014? How would this official intervention show up in the balance of payments accounts of Pecunia?

   c. How would your answer to (b) change if you learned that foreign central banks had purchased $600 million of Pecunian assets in 2014? How would these official purchases enter foreign balance of payments accounts?

   d. Draw up the Pecunian balance of payments accounts for 20014 under the assumption that the event described in (c) occurred in that year.

6. Can you think of reasons why a government might be concerned about a large current account deficit or surplus? Why might a government be concerned about its official settlements balance (that is, its balance of payments)?

7. Do data on the U.S. official settlements balance give an accurate picture of the extent to which foreign central banks buy and sell dollars in currency markets?

8. Is it possible for a country to have a current account deficit at the same time it has a surplus in its balance of payments? Explain your answer, using hypothetical figures for the current and nonreserve financial accounts. Be sure to discuss the possible implications for official international reserve flows.

9. Suppose the U.S. net foreign debt is 25 percent of U.S. GDP and foreign assets and liabilities pay an interest rate of 5 percent per year. What would be the drain on U.S. GDP (as a percentage) from paying interest on the net foreign debt? Do you think this is a large number? What if the net foreign debt were 100 percent of GDP? At what point do you think a country's government should become worried about the size of its foreign debt?

10. If you go to the BEA website (http://www.bea.gov) and look at the *Survey of Current Business* for July 2013, the table on "U.S. International Transactions," you will find that in 2012, U.S. income receipts on its foreign assets were $770.1 billion

(line 13), while the country's payments on liabilities to foreigners were $537.8 billion (line 30). Yet we saw in this chapter that the United States is a substantial net debtor to foreigners. How, then, is it possible that the United States received more foreign asset income than it paid out?

11. Return to the example in this chapter's final Case Study of how a 10 percent dollar depreciation affects U.S. net foreign wealth (pages 32–35). Show the size of the effect on *foreigners'* net foreign claims on the U.S. measured in dollars (as a percent of U.S. GDP).

12. We mentioned in the chapter that capital gains and losses on a country's net foreign assets are not included in the national income measure of the current account. How would economic statisticians have to modify the national income identity (2-1) if they wish to include such gains and losses as part of the definition of the current account? In your opinion, would this make sense? Why do you think this is not done in practice?

13. Go to the BEA website at http://www.bea.gov/newsreleases/international/intinv/intinvnewsrelease.htm and download annual data starting in 1976 on the United States' end-of-year international investment position. For the same time period, download annual data on U.S. nominal GDP from http://www.bea.gov/national/index.htm#gdp. Then compute the annual ratio of the IIP to nominal GDP starting in 1976, and graph the data. The United States has run current account deficits in almost every year since the mid-1980s. Do the data you have graphed therefore surprise you? (Hint: To answer this question, you will need to compare the current account deficit, as a percent of nominal GDP, with the growth rate of nominal GDP, so you will also need to examine the annual current account data from the BEA website. You may wish to return to this problem after reading Chapter 8.)

FURTHER READINGS

European Commission, International Monetary Fund, Organisation for Economic Co-operation and Development, United Nations, and World Bank. *System of National Accounts 2008.* New York: United Nations, 2009. Definitive guidelines for constructing national income and product accounts.

Christopher A. Gohrband and Kristy L. Howell. "U.S. International Financial Flows and the U.S. Net Investment Position: New Perspectives Arising from New International Standards," in Charles Hulten and Marshall Reinsdorff, eds., *Wealth, Financial Intermediation, and the Real Economy.* Chicago: University of Chicago Press, 2014. Detailed discussion of the IIP statistics for the United States.

William Griever, Gary Lee, and Francis Warnock. "The U.S. System for Measuring Cross-Border Investment in Securities: A Primer with a Discussion of Recent Developments." *Federal Reserve Bulletin* 87 (October 2001), pp. 633–650. Critical description of U.S. procedures for measuring foreign assets and liabilities.

International Monetary Fund. *Balance of Payments and International Investment Position Manual*, 6th edition. Washington, D.C.: International Monetary Fund, 2009. Authoritative treatment of balance of payments accounting.

Philip R. Lane and Gian Maria Milesi-Ferretti. "The External Wealth of Nations Mark II: Revised and Extended Estimates of Foreign Assets and Liabilities, 1970–2004." *Journal of International Economics* 73 (November 2007), pp. 223–250. Applies a common methodology to construct international position data for a large sample of countries.

Catherine L. Mann. "Perspectives on the U.S. Current Account Deficit and Sustainability." *Journal of Economic Perspectives* 16 (Summer 2002), pp. 131–152. Examines the causes and consequences of recent U.S. current account deficits.

James E. Meade. *The Balance of Payments*, Chapters 1–3. London: Oxford University Press, 1952. A classic analytical discussion of balance of payments concepts.

Maurice Obstfeld. "Does the Current Account Still Matter?" *American Economic Review* 102 (May 2012): 1–23. Discusses the significance of the current account in a world of large two-way international asset flows.

Cédric Tille. "The Impact of Exchange Rate Movements on U.S. Foreign Debt." *Current Issues in Economics and Finance* (Federal Reserve Bank of New York) 9 (January 2003), pp. 1–7. Discusses the implications of asset price changes for U.S. foreign assets and liabilities.

MyEconLab Can Help You Get a Better Grade

MyEconLab   If your exam were tomorrow, would you be ready? For each chapter, MyEconLab Practice Tests and Study Plans pinpoint sections you have mastered and those you need to study. That way, you are more efficient with your study time, and you are better prepared for your exams.

To see how it works, turn to page 9 and then go to

www.myeconlab.com

CHAPTER 3

EXCHANGE RATES AND THE FOREIGN EXCHANGE MARKET: AN ASSET APPROACH

Around Christmas 2012, Shinzo Abe became prime minister of Japan, immediately pledging to revive its sluggish economy through forceful economic measures including "bold monetary policy." Over the next six months, the prices of Japanese goods measured in the domestic currency, the yen, fell sharply compared to the prices of foreign goods when also measured in yen. One immediate effect was on tourism: A record number of foreign visitors came during Japan's sping 2013 cherry blossom season; at the same time, the number of Japanese travelers to South Korea, a popular tourist destination, dropped sharply. What economic forces made the relative prices of Japanese goods fall so suddenly? One major factor was a 15 percent fall in the dollar price of the yen in the six months after Abe's government came to power.

The price of one currency in terms of another is called an **exchange rate**. At 4 P.M. London time on June 7, 2013, you would have needed 1.3221 dollars to buy one unit of the European currency, the euro, so the dollar's exchange rate against the euro was $1.3221 per euro. Because of their strong influence on the current account and other macroeconomic variables, exchange rates are among the most important prices in an open economy.

Because an exchange rate, the price of one country's money in terms of another's, is also an asset price, the principles governing the behavior of other asset prices also govern the behavior of exchange rates. As you will recall from Chapter 2, the defining characteristic of an asset is that it is a form of wealth, a way of transferring purchasing power from the present into the future. The price an asset commands today is therefore directly related to the purchasing power over goods and services that buyers expect it to yield in the future. Similarly, *today's* dollar/euro exchange rate is closely tied to people's expectations about the *future* level of that rate. Just as the price of Google stock rises immediately upon favorable news about Google's future prospects, so do exchange rates respond immediately to any news concerning future currency values.

Our general goals in this chapter are to understand the role of exchange rates in international trade and to understand how exchange rates are determined. To begin, we first learn how exchange rates allow us to compare the prices of different countries' goods and services. Next, we describe the international asset market in which currencies are traded and show how equilibrium exchange rates are determined in that market. A final section underlines our asset market approach by showing how today's exchange rate responds to changes in the expected future values of exchange rates.

LEARNING GOALS

After reading this chapter, you will be able to:

- Relate exchange rate changes to changes in the relative prices of countries' exports.
- Describe the structure and functions of the foreign exchange market.
- Use exchange rates to calculate and compare returns on assets denominated in different currencies.
- Apply the interest parity condition to find equilibrium exchange rates.
- Find the effects of interest rates and expectation shifts on exchange rates.

Exchange Rates and International Transactions

Exchange rates play a central role in international trade because they allow us to compare the prices of goods and services produced in different countries. A consumer deciding which of two American cars to buy must compare their dollar prices, for example, $44,000 (for a Lincoln Continental) or $27,000 (for a Ford Taurus). But how is the same consumer to compare either of these prices with the 2,500,000 Japanese yen it costs to buy a Nissan Maxima from Japan? To make this comparison, he or she must know the relative price of dollars and yen.

The relative prices of currencies can be viewed in real time on the Internet. Exchange rates are also reported daily in newspapers' financial sections. Table 3-1 shows the dollar exchange rates for currencies traded in London at 4 P.M. on June 7, 2013, as reported in the *Financial Times*. An exchange rate can be quoted in two ways: as the price of the foreign currency in terms of dollars (for example, $0.0102685 per yen) or as its inverse, the price of dollars in terms of the foreign currency (for example, ¥97.3850 per dollar). The first of these exchange rate quotations (dollars per foreign currency unit) is said to be in *direct* (or "American") terms; the second (foreign currency units per dollar) is in *indirect* (or "European") terms.[1]

Households and firms use exchange rates to translate foreign prices into domestic currency terms. Once the money prices of domestic goods and imports have been expressed in terms of the same currency, households and firms can compute the *relative* prices that affect international trade flows.

---

[1] The "mid" rates shown are the average of "bid" and "ask" prices for the U.S. dollar. Generally, a buyer of dollars will pay more (the ask price) than a seller will receive (the bid price) due to costs of intermediating the trade (for example by a bank or broker). The difference—the bid-ask spread—is a measure of transaction costs. In Chapter 8, we will refer to "effective" exchange rate indexes, which are averages of exchange rates against individual trading partner currencies.

TABLE 3-1 Exchange Rate Quotations

CURRENCIES www.ft.com/currencies

FX - EFFECTIVE INDICES

	Jun 7	Jun 6	Mth ago		Jun 7	Jun 6	Mth ago
Australia	105.2	106.0	113.0	Sweden	87.1	87.3	88.6
Canada	111.6	110.5	113.6	Switzerland	143.4	143.7	143.7
Denmark	107.3	107.3	106.9	UK	81.1	81.2	80.9
Japan	145.7	144.3	143.4	USA	85.6	86.1	85.9
New Zealand	114.6	115.9	121.8	Euro	95.03	95.04	94.43
Norway	107.5	107.6	106.8				

Source: Bank of England. New Sterling ERI base Jan 2005 = 100. Other indices base average 1990 = 100. Index rebased 1/2/95. for further information about ERIs see www.bankofengland.co.uk

Bank of England Indices

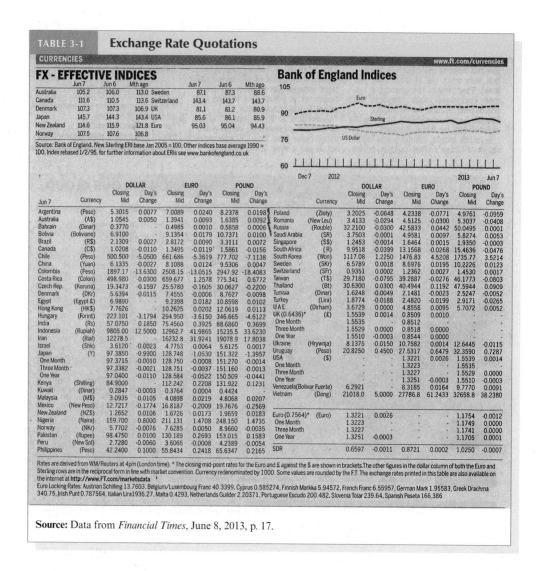

Jun 7	Currency	DOLLAR Closing Mid	Day's Change	EURO Closing Mid	Day's Change	POUND Closing Mid	Day's Change
Argentina	(Peso)	5.3015	0.0077	7.0089	0.0240	8.2378	0.0198
Australia	(A$)	1.0545	0.0050	1.3941	0.0093	1.6385	0.0092
Bahrain	(Dinar)	0.3770	-	0.4985	0.0010	0.5858	0.0006
Bolivia	(Boliviano)	6.9100	-	9.1354	0.0179	10.7371	0.0100
Brazil	(R$)	2.1309	0.0027	2.8172	0.0090	3.3111	0.0072
Canada	(C$)	1.0208	-0.0110	1.3495	-0.0119	1.5861	-0.0156
Chile	(Peso)	500.500	-5.0500	661.686	-5.3619	777.702	-7.1138
China	(Yuan)	6.1335	-0.0027	8.1088	0.0124	9.5306	0.0047
Colombia	(Peso)	1897.17	-13.6300	2508.15	-13.0515	2947.92	-18.4083
Costa Rica	(Colon)	498.980	-0.0300	659.677	1.2578	775.341	0.6772
Czech Rep.	(Koruna)	19.3473	-0.1597	25.5780	-0.1605	30.0627	-0.2200
Denmark	(DKr)	5.6394	-0.0115	7.4555	-0.0006	8.7627	-0.0098
Egypt	(Egypt £)	6.9890	-	9.2398	0.0182	10.8598	0.0102
Hong Kong	(HK$)	7.7626	-	10.2625	0.0202	12.0619	0.0113
Hungary	(Forint)	223.101	-3.1794	294.950	-3.6150	346.665	-4.6122
India	(Rs)	57.0750	0.1850	75.4560	0.3925	88.6860	0.3699
Indonesia	(Rupiah)	9805.00	12.5000	12962.7	41.9865	15235.5	33.6230
Iran	(Rial)	12278.5	-	16232.8	31.9241	19078.9	17.8038
Israel	(Shk)	3.6120	-0.0023	4.7753	0.0064	5.6125	0.0017
Japan	(Y)	97.3850	-0.9900	128.748	-1.0530	151.322	-1.3957
One Month		97.3715	-0.0010	128.750	-0.0008	151.270	-0.0014
Three Month		97.3382	-0.0021	128.751	-0.0037	151.160	-0.0013
One Year		97.0400	-0.0110	128.584	-0.0522	150.509	-0.0441
Kenya	(Shilling)	84.9000	-	112.242	0.2208	131.922	0.1231
Kuwait	(Dinar)	0.2847	-0.0003	0.3764	0.0004	0.4424	
Malaysia	(M$)	3.0935	0.0105	4.0898	0.0219	4.8068	0.0207
Mexico	(New Peso)	12.7217	-0.1774	16.8187	-0.2009	19.7676	-0.2569
New Zealand	(NZ$)	1.2652	0.0106	1.6726	0.0173	1.9659	0.0183
Nigeria	(Naira)	159.700	0.8000	211.131	1.4708	248.150	1.4735
Norway	(NKr)	5.7702	-0.0076	7.6285	0.0050	8.9660	-0.0035
Pakistan	(Rupee)	98.4750	0.0100	130.189	0.2693	153.015	0.1583
Peru	(New Sol)	2.7280	-0.0060	3.6066	-0.0008	4.2389	-0.0054
Philippines	(Peso)	42.2400	0.1000	55.8434	0.2418	65.6347	0.2165

Jun 7	Currency	DOLLAR Closing Mid	Day's Change	EURO Closing Mid	Day's Change	POUND Closing Mid	Day's Change
Poland	(Zloty)	3.2025	-0.0648	4.2338	-0.0771	4.9761	-0.0959
Romania	(New Leu)	3.4133	-0.0294	4.5125	-0.0300	5.3037	-0.0408
Russia	(Rouble)	32.2100	-0.0300	42.5833	0.0442	50.0495	0.0001
Saudi Arabia	(SR)	3.7503	-0.0001	4.9581	0.0097	5.8274	0.0053
Singapore	(S$)	1.2453	-0.0014	1.6464	0.0015	1.9350	-0.0003
South Africa	(R)	9.9518	-0.0399	13.1568	-0.0268	15.4636	-0.0476
South Korea	(Won)	1117.08	1.2250	1476.83	4.5208	1735.77	3.5214
Sweden	(SKr)	6.5789	0.0018	8.6976	0.0195	10.2226	0.0123
Switzerland	(SFr)	0.9351	0.0002	1.2362	0.0027	1.4530	0.0017
Taiwan	(T$)	29.7180	-0.0795	39.2887	-0.0276	46.1773	-0.0803
Thailand	(Bt)	30.6300	0.0300	40.4944	0.1192	47.5944	0.0909
Tunisia	(Dinar)	1.6248	-0.0049	2.1481	-0.0023	2.5247	-0.0052
Turkey	(Lira)	1.8774	-0.0188	2.4820	-0.0199	2.9171	-0.0265
UAE	(Dirham)	3.6729	0.0000	4.8558	0.0095	5.7072	0.0052
UK (0.6436)*	(£)	1.5539	0.0014	0.8509	0.0010	-	-
One Month		1.5535		0.8512			
Three Month		1.5529	0.0000	0.8518	0.0000		
One Year		1.5510	-0.0003	0.8544	0.0000		
Ukraine	(Hrywnja)	8.1375	-0.0150	10.7582	0.0014	12.6445	-0.0115
Uruguay	(Peso)	20.8250	0.4500	27.5317	0.6479	32.3590	0.7287
USA	($)	-		1.3221	0.0026	1.5539	0.0014
One Month				1.3223		1.5535	
Three Month				1.3227		1.5529	0.0000
One Year				1.3251		1.5510	-0.0003
Venezuela	(Bolivar Fuerte)	6.2921	-	8.3185	0.0164	9.7770	0.0091
Vietnam	(Dong)	21018.0	5.0000	27786.8	61.2433	32658.8	38.2380
Euro (0.7564)*	(Euro)	1.3221	0.0026	-		1.1754	-0.0012
One Month		1.3223		-		1.1749	0.0000
Three Month		1.3227		-		1.1741	0.0000
One Year		1.3251	-0.0003	-		1.1705	0.0001
SDR		0.6597	-0.0011	0.8721	0.0002	1.0250	-0.0007

Rates are derived from WM/Reuters at 4pm (London time). * The closing mid-point rates for the Euro and £ against the $ are shown in brackets. The other figures in the dollar column of both the Euro and Sterling rows are in the reciprocal form in line with market convention. Currency redenominated by 1000. Some values are rounded by the F.T. The exchange rates printed in this table are also available on the internet at http://www.FT.com/marketsdata
Euro Locking Rates: Austrian Schilling 13.7603, Belgium/Luxembourg Franc 40.3399, Cyprus 0.585274, Finnish Markka 5.94572, French Franc 6.55957, German Mark 1.95583, Greek Drachma 340.75, Irish Punt 0.787564, Italian Lira1936.27, Malta 0.4293, Netherlands Guilder 2.20371, Portuguese Escudo 200.482, Slovenia Tolar 239.64, Spanish Peseta 166.386

Source: Data from *Financial Times*, June 8, 2013, p. 17.

Domestic and Foreign Prices

If we know the exchange rate between two countries' currencies, we can compute the price of one country's exports in terms of the other country's money. For example, how many dollars would it cost to buy an Edinburgh Woolen Mill sweater costing 50 British pounds (£50)? The answer is found by multiplying the price of the sweater in pounds, 50, by the price of a pound in terms of dollars—the dollar's exchange rate against the pound. At an exchange rate of $1.50 per pound (expressed in American terms), the dollar price of the sweater is

$$(1.50\$/\pounds) \times (\pounds 50) = \$75.$$

A change in the dollar/pound exchange rate would alter the sweater's dollar price. At an exchange rate of 1.25 per pound, the sweater would cost only

$$(1.25\$/\pounds) \times (\pounds 50) = \$62.50,$$

assuming its price in terms of pounds remained the same. At an exchange rate of $1.75 per pound, the sweater's dollar price would be higher, equal to

$$(1.75\$/£) \times (£50) = \$87.50.$$

Changes in exchange rates are described as depreciations or appreciations. A **depreciation** of the pound against the dollar is a fall in the dollar price of pounds, for example, a change in the exchange rate from $1.50 per pound to $1.25 per pound. The preceding example shows that *all else equal, a depreciation of a country's currency makes its goods cheaper for foreigners*. A rise in the pound's price in terms of dollars— for example, from $1.50 per pound to $1.75 per pound—is an **appreciation** of the pound against the dollar. *All else equal, an appreciation of a country's currency makes its goods more expensive for foreigners*.

The exchange rate changes discussed in the example simultaneously alter the prices Britons pay for American goods. At an exchange rate of $1.50 per pound, the pound price of a pair of American designer jeans costing $45 is $(\$45)/(1.50\$/£) = £30$. A change in the exchange rate from $1.50 per pound to $1.25 per pound, while a depreciation of the pound against the dollar, is also a rise in the pound price of dollars, an *appreciation* of the dollar against the pound. This appreciation of the dollar makes the American jeans more expensive for Britons by raising their pound price from £30 to

$$(\$45)/(1.25\$/£) = £36.$$

The change in the exchange rate from $1.50 per pound to $1.75 per pound—an appreciation of the pound against the dollar but a depreciation of the dollar against the pound—lowers the pound price of the jeans from £30 to

$$(\$45)/(1.75\$/£) = £25.71.$$

As you can see, descriptions of exchange rate changes as depreciations or appreciations can be bewildering because when one currency depreciates against another, the second currency must simultaneously appreciate against the first. To avoid confusion in discussing exchange rates, we must always keep track of which of the two currencies we are examining has depreciated or appreciated against the other.

If we remember that a depreciation of the dollar against the pound is at the same time an appreciation of the pound against the dollar, we reach the following conclusion: *When a country's currency depreciates, foreigners find that its exports are cheaper and domestic residents find that imports from abroad are more expensive. An appreciation has opposite effects: Foreigners pay more for the country's products and domestic consumers pay less for foreign products.*

Exchange Rates and Relative Prices

Import and export demands, like the demands for all goods and services, are influenced by *relative* prices, such as the price of sweaters in terms of designer jeans. We have just seen how exchange rates allow individuals to compare domestic and foreign money prices by expressing them in a common currency unit. Carrying this analysis one step further, we can see that exchange rates also allow individuals to compute the relative prices of goods and services whose money prices are quoted in different currencies.

An American trying to decide how much to spend on American jeans and how much to spend on British sweaters must translate their prices into a common currency to compute the price of sweaters in terms of jeans. As we have seen, an exchange rate of $1.50 per pound means that an American pays $75 for a sweater priced at £50 in

TABLE 3-2	\$/£ Exchange Rates and the Relative Price of American Designer Jeans and British Sweaters		
Exchange rate (\$/£)	1.25	1.50	1.75
Relative price (pairs of jeans/sweater)	1.39	1.67	1.94

Note: The above calculations assume unchanged money prices of \$45 per pair of jeans and £50 per sweater.

Britain. Because the price of a pair of American jeans is \$45, the price of a sweater in terms of a pair of jeans is (\$75 per sweater)/(\$45 per pair of jeans) = 1.67 pairs of jeans per sweater. Naturally, a Briton faces the same relative price of (£50 per sweater)/(£30 per pair of jeans) = 1.67 pairs of jeans per sweater.

Table 3-2 shows the relative prices implied by exchange rates of \$1.25 per pound, \$1.50 per pound, and \$1.75 per pound, on the assumption that the dollar price of jeans and the pound price of sweaters are unaffected by the exchange rate changes. To test your understanding, try to calculate these relative prices for yourself and confirm that the outcome of the calculation is the same for a Briton and for an American.

The table shows that if the goods' money prices do not change, an appreciation of the dollar against the pound makes sweaters cheaper in terms of jeans (each pair of jeans buys more sweaters) while a depreciation of the dollar against the pound makes sweaters more expensive in terms of jeans (each pair of jeans buys fewer sweaters). The computations illustrate a general principle: *All else equal, an appreciation of a country's currency raises the relative price of its exports and lowers the relative price of its imports. Conversely, a depreciation lowers the relative price of a country's exports and raises the relative price of its imports.*

The Foreign Exchange Market

Just as other prices in the economy are determined by the interaction of buyers and sellers, exchange rates are determined by the interaction of the households, firms, and financial institutions that buy and sell foreign currencies to make international payments. The market in which international currency trades take place is called the **foreign exchange market**.

The Actors

The major participants in the foreign exchange market are commercial banks, corporations that engage in international trade, nonbank financial institutions such as asset-management firms and insurance companies, and central banks. Individuals may also participate in the foreign exchange market—for example, the tourist who buys foreign currency at a hotel's front desk—but such cash transactions are an insignificant fraction of total foreign exchange trading.

We now describe the major actors in the market and their roles.

1. *Commercial banks.* Commercial banks are at the center of the foreign exchange market because almost every sizable international transaction involves the debiting and crediting of accounts at commercial banks in various financial centers. Thus, the vast majority of foreign exchange transactions involve the exchange of bank deposits denominated in different currencies.

Let's look at an example. Suppose ExxonMobil Corporation wishes to pay €160,000 to a German supplier. First, ExxonMobil gets an exchange rate quotation

EXCHANGE RATES, AUTO PRICES, AND CURRENCY WARS

Automobiles make up a significant share of international trade, and many advanced economies are significant exporters as well as importers of cars. Competition is fierce—the United States exports Fords, Sweden exports Volvos, Germany exports BMWs, Japan exports Hondas, and Britain exports Land Rovers, to name just a few—and increased auto imports from abroad are likely to mean fewer sales for the domestic producer.

Exchange rates are therefore of critical importance to auto makers. For example, when Korea's currency, the won, appreciates in the foreign exchange market, this hurts Korean producers in two distinct ways. First, the prices of competing imported cars go down because foreign prices look lower when measured in terms of won. Thus, imports flood in and create a more competitive home pricing environment for Korean producers like Hyundai and Kia. Second, foreigners (whose currencies have depreciated against the won) find that the home-currency prices of Korean cars have risen, and they switch their purchases to cheaper suppliers. Korean auto exports suffer as a result. Later in the book (Chapter 5) we will discuss the pricing strategies that producers of specialized products like autos may adopt when trying to defend market shares in the face of exchange rate changes.

These effects of exchange rates on manufacturing producers explain why export industries complain when foreign countries adopt policies that weaken their currencies. In September 2010, as many industrial countries' currencies depreciated because of slow economic growth, Brazil's finance minister accused the richer countries of waging "currency wars" against the poorer emerging market economies. After reading Chapter 6, you will understand why sluggish economic growth and currency depreciation might go together. Chapter 7 discusses how a similar phenomenon of "competitive depreciation" occurred during the Great Depression of the 1930s.

Talk of currency wars emerged once again when Japan's yen depreciated sharply early in 2013 (as described in this chapter's first paragraph). Of course, Japanese auto firms were major beneficiaries, at the expense of their many foreign competitors. According to an Associated Press (AP) report in May 2013, Nissan was able to cut the dollar prices of seven of the 18 models it sells in the United States: at the new dollar exchange rate of the yen, even somewhat lower *dollar* prices produced enough *yen* revenue to cover Japanese production costs as well as higher yen profits. Nissan cut the price of its Altima by $580 and that of its Armada SUV by $4,400. As the AP reported, "Although Nissan denies it, industry analysts say the company can afford to cut prices because of efforts in Japan to weaken the yen against the dollar. That makes cars and parts made in Japan cheaper than goods made in the U.S."*

*"Nissan Cuts Prices on 7 of Its U.S. Models," *USA Today,* May 1, 2013, available at: http://www.usatoday.com/story/money/cars/2013/05/01/nissan-cuts-prices-juke/2127721/

from its own commercial bank, the Third National Bank. Then it instructs Third National to debit ExxonMobil's dollar account and pay €160,000 into the supplier's account at a German bank. If the exchange rate quoted to ExxonMobil by Third National is $1.2 per euro, $192,000 ($= $1.2 per euro × €160,000$) is debited from ExxonMobil's account. The final result of the transaction is the exchange of a $192,000 deposit at Third National Bank (now owned by the German bank that supplied the euros) for the €160,000 deposit used by Third National to pay Exxon-Mobil's German supplier.

As the example shows, banks routinely enter the foreign exchange market to meet the needs of their customers—primarily corporations. In addition, a bank will also quote to other banks exchange rates at which it is willing to buy currencies from them and sell currencies to them. Foreign currency trading among banks—called **interbank trading**—accounts for much of the activity in the foreign exchange market. In fact, the exchange rates listed in Table 3-1 are interbank rates, the rates banks charge each other. No amount less than $1 million is traded at those rates. The rates available to corporate customers, called "retail" rates, are usually less favorable than the "wholesale" interbank rates. The difference between the retail and the wholesale rates is the bank's compensation for doing the business.

Because their international operations are so extensive, large commercial banks are well suited to bring buyers and sellers of currencies together. A multinational corporation wishing to convert $100,000 into Swedish kronor might find it difficult and costly to locate other corporations wishing to sell the right amount of kronor. By serving many customers simultaneously through a single large purchase of kronor, a bank can economize on these search costs.

2. *Corporations.* Corporations with operations in several countries frequently make or receive payments in currencies other than that of the country in which they are headquartered. To pay workers at a plant in Mexico, for example, IBM may need Mexican pesos. If IBM has only dollars earned by selling computers in the United States, it can acquire the pesos it needs by buying them with its dollars in the foreign exchange market.

3. *Nonbank financial institutions.* Over the years, deregulation of financial markets in the United States, Japan, and other countries has encouraged nonbank financial institutions such as mutual funds to offer their customers a broader range of services, many of them indistinguishable from those offered by banks. Among these have been services involving foreign exchange transactions. Institutional investors such as pension funds often trade foreign currencies. So do insurance companies. Hedge funds, which cater to very wealthy individuals and are not bound by the government regulations that limit mutual funds' trading strategies, trade actively in the foreign exchange market.

4. *Central banks.* In the last chapter, we learned that central banks sometimes intervene in foreign exchange markets. While the volume of central bank transactions is typically not large, the impact of these transactions may be great. The reason for this impact is that participants in the foreign exchange market watch central bank actions closely for clues about future macroeconomic policies that may affect exchange rates. Government agencies other than central banks may also trade in the foreign exchange market, but central banks are the most regular official participants.

Characteristics of the Market

Foreign exchange trading takes place in many financial centers, with the largest volumes of trade occurring in such major cities as London (the largest market), New York, Tokyo, Frankfurt, and Singapore. The worldwide volume of foreign exchange trading is enormous, and it has ballooned in recent years. In April 1989, the average total value of global foreign exchange trading was close to $600 billion *per day*. A total of $184 billion was traded daily in London, $115 billion in the United States, and $111 billion in Tokyo. Twenty-one years later, in April 2010, the daily global value of foreign exchange trading had jumped to around $4.0 trillion. A total of $1.85 trillion was traded daily in Britain, $904 billion in the United States, and $312 billion in Japan.[2]

---

[2]April 1989 figures come from surveys carried out simultaneously by the Federal Reserve Bank of New York, the Bank of England, the Bank of Japan, the Bank of Canada, and monetary authorities from France, Italy, the Netherlands, Singapore, Hong Kong, and Australia. The April 2010 survey was carried out by 53 central banks. Revised figures are reported in "Triennial Central Bank Survey of Foreign Exchange and Derivatives Market Activity in April 2010: Preliminary Global Results," Bank for International Settlements, Basel, Switzerland, September 2010. Daily U.S. foreign currency trading in 1980 averaged only around $18 billion.

Telephone, fax, and Internet links among the major foreign exchange trading centers make each a part of a single world market on which the sun never sets. Economic news released at any time of the day is immediately transmitted around the world and may set off a flurry of activity by market participants. Even after trading in New York has finished, New York–based banks and corporations with affiliates in other time zones can remain active in the market. Foreign exchange traders may deal from their homes when a late-night communication alerts them to important developments in a financial center on another continent.

The integration of financial centers implies that there can be no significant difference between the dollar/euro exchange rate quoted in New York at 9 A.M. and the dollar/euro exchange rate quoted in London at the same time (which corresponds to 2 P.M. London time). If the euro were selling for $1.1 in New York and $1.2 in London, profits could be made through **arbitrage**, the process of buying a currency cheap and selling it dear. At the prices listed above, a trader could, for instance, purchase €1 million in New York for $1.1 million and immediately sell the euros in London for $1.2 million, making a pure profit of $100,000. If all traders tried to cash in on the opportunity, however, their demand for euros in New York would drive up the dollar price of euros there, and their supply of euros in London would drive down the dollar price of euros there. Very quickly, the difference between the New York and London exchange rates would disappear. Since foreign exchange traders carefully watch their computer screens for arbitrage opportunities, the few that arise are small and very short-lived.

While a foreign exchange transaction can match any two currencies, most transactions (roughly 85 percent in April 2010) are exchanges of foreign currencies for U.S. dollars. This is true even when a bank's goal is to sell one nondollar currency and buy another! A bank wishing to sell Swiss francs and buy Israeli shekels, for example, will usually sell its francs for dollars and then use the dollars to buy shekels. While this procedure may appear roundabout, it is actually cheaper for the bank than the alternative of trying to find a holder of shekels who wishes to buy Swiss francs. The advantage of trading through the dollar is a result of the United States' importance in the world economy. Because the volume of international transactions involving dollars is so great, it is not hard to find parties willing to trade dollars against Swiss francs or shekels. In contrast, relatively few transactions require direct exchanges of Swiss francs for shekels.[3]

Because of its pivotal role in so many foreign exchange deals, the U.S. dollar is sometimes called a **vehicle currency**. A vehicle currency is one that is widely used to denominate international contracts made by parties who do not reside in the country that issues the vehicle currency. It has been suggested that the euro, which was introduced at the start of 1999, will evolve into a vehicle currency on a par with the dollar. By April 2010, about 39 percent of foreign exchange trades were against euros—less than half the share of the dollar, albeit above the figure of 37 percent clocked three years earlier. Japan's yen is the third most important currency, with a market share of 19 percent (out of 200). The pound sterling, once second only to the dollar as a key international currency, has declined greatly in importance.[4]

---

[3]The Swiss franc/shekel exchange rate can be calculated from the dollar/franc and dollar/shekel exchange rates as the dollar/shekel rate divided by the dollar/franc rate. If the dollar/franc rate is $0.80 per franc and the dollar/shekel rate is $0.20 per shekel, then the Swiss franc/shekel rate is (0.20 $/shekel)/(0.80 $/franc) = 0.25 Swiss francs/shekel. Exchange rates between nondollar currencies are called "cross rates" by foreign exchange traders.

[4]For a more detailed discussion of vehicle currencies, see Richard Portes and Hélène Rey, "The Emergence of the Euro as an International Currency," *Economic Policy* 26 (April 1998), pp. 307–343. Data on currency shares come from Bank for International Settlements, *op. cit.*, table 3. For an assessment of the future roles of the dollar and the euro, see the essays in Jean Pisani-Ferry and Adam S. Posen, eds., *The Euro at Ten: The Next Global Currency?* (Washington, D.C.: Peterson Institute for International Economics, 2009). These essays were written before the euro area crisis, to be discussed in Chapter 10.

Spot Rates and Forward Rates

The foreign exchange transactions we have been discussing take place on the spot: Two parties agree to an exchange of bank deposits and execute the deal immediately. Exchange rates governing such "on-the-spot" trading are called **spot exchange rates** and the deal is called a spot transaction.

Foreign exchange deals sometimes specify a *future* transaction date—one that may be 30 days, 90 days, 180 days, or even several years away. The exchange rates quoted in such transactions are called **forward exchange rates**. In a 30-day forward transaction, for example, two parties may commit themselves on April 1 to a spot exchange of £100,000 for $155,000 on May 1. The 30-day forward exchange rate is therefore $1.55 per pound, and it is generally different from the spot rate and from the forward rates applied to different future dates. When you agree to sell pounds for dollars on a future date at a forward rate agreed on today, you have "sold pounds forward" and "bought dollars forward." The future date on which the currencies are actually exchanged is called the *value date*.[5] Table 3-1 shows forward exchange rates for some major currencies.

Forward and spot exchange rates, while not necessarily equal, do move closely together, as illustrated for monthly data on dollar/pound rates in Figure 3-1. The appendix to this chapter, which discusses how forward exchange rates are determined, explains this close relationship between movements in spot and forward rates.

An example shows why parties may wish to engage in forward exchange transactions. Suppose Radio Shack knows that in 30 days it must pay yen to a Japanese supplier for a shipment of radios arriving then. Radio Shack can sell each radio for $100 and must pay its supplier ¥9,000 per radio; its profit depends on the dollar/yen

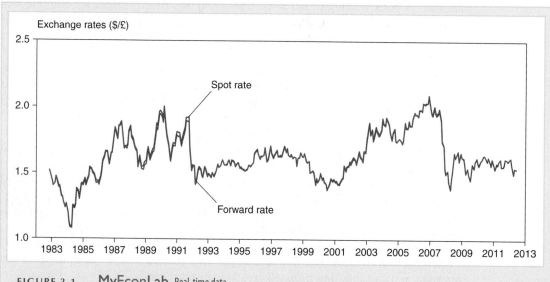

FIGURE 3-1   MyEconLab Real-time data

Dollar/Pound Spot and Forward Exchange Rates, 1983–2013

Spot and forward exchange rates tend to move in a highly correlated fashion.

Source: *Datastream.* Rates shown are 90-day forward exchange rates and spot exchange rates, at end of month.

---

[5]In days past, it would take up to two days to settle even spot foreign exchange transactions. In other words, the value date for a spot transaction was actually two days after the deal was struck. Nowadays, most spot trades of major currencies settle on the same day.

exchange rate. At the current spot exchange rate of $0.0105 per yen, Radio Shack would pay ($0.0105 per yen) × (¥9,000 per radio) = $94.50 per radio and would therefore make $5.50 on each radio imported. But Radio Shack will not have the funds to pay the supplier until the radios arrive and are sold. If over the next 30 days the dollar unexpectedly depreciates to $0.0115 per yen, Radio Shack will have to pay ($0.0115 per yen) × (¥9,000 per radio) = $103.50 per radio and so will take a $3.50 *loss* on each.

To avoid this risk, Radio Shack can make a 30-day forward exchange deal with Bank of America. If Bank of America agrees to sell yen to Radio Shack in 30 days at a rate of $0.0107, Radio Shack is assured of paying exactly ($0.0107 per yen) × (¥9,000 per radio) = $96.30 per radio to the supplier. By buying yen and selling dollars forward, Radio Shack is guaranteed a profit of $3.70 per radio and is insured against the possibility that a sudden exchange rate change will turn a profitable importing deal into a loss. In the jargon of the foreign exchange market, we would say that Radio Shack has *hedged* its foreign currency risk.

From now on, when we mention an exchange rate but don't specify whether it is a spot rate or a forward rate, we will always be referring to the spot rate.

Foreign Exchange Swaps

A foreign exchange *swap* is a spot sale of a currency combined with a forward repurchase of that currency. For example, suppose the Toyota auto company has just received $1 million from American sales and knows it will have to pay those dollars to a California supplier in three months. Toyota's asset-management department would meanwhile like to invest the $1 million in euro bonds. A three-month swap of dollars into euros may result in lower brokers' fees than the two separate transactions of selling dollars for spot euros and selling the euros for dollars on the forward market. Swaps make up a significant proportion of all foreign exchange trading.

Futures and Options

Several other financial instruments traded in the foreign exchange market, like forward contracts, involve future exchanges of currencies. The timing and terms of the exchanges can differ, however, from those specified in forward contracts, giving traders additional flexibility in avoiding foreign exchange risk.

When you buy a *futures contract*, you buy a promise that a specified amount of foreign currency will be delivered on a specified date in the future. A forward contract between you and some other private party is an alternative way to ensure that you receive the same amount of foreign currency on the date in question. But while you have no choice about fulfilling your end of a forward deal, you can sell your futures contract on an organized futures exchange, realizing a profit or loss right away. Such a sale might appear advantageous, for example, if your views about the future spot exchange rate were to change.

A *foreign exchange option* gives its owner the right to buy or sell a specified amount of foreign currency at a specified price at any time up to a specified expiration date. The other party to the deal, the option's seller, is required to sell or buy the foreign currency at the discretion of the option's owner, who is under no obligation to exercise his right.

Imagine you are uncertain about when in the next month a foreign currency payment will arrive. To avoid the risk of a loss, you may wish to buy a *put option* giving you the right to sell the foreign currency at a known exchange rate at any time during the month. If instead you expect to make a payment abroad sometime in the month, a *call option*, which gives you the right to buy foreign currency to make the payment at a known price, might be attractive. Options can be written on many underlying assets (including foreign exchange futures), and, like futures, they are freely bought and sold. Forwards, swaps, futures, and options are all examples of *financial derivatives*, which we encountered in Chapter 2.

The Demand for Foreign Currency Assets

We have now seen how banks, corporations, and other institutions trade foreign currency bank deposits in a worldwide foreign exchange market that operates 24 hours a day. To understand how exchange rates are determined by the foreign exchange market, we first must ask how the major actors' demands for different types of foreign currency deposits are determined.

The demand for a foreign currency bank deposit is influenced by the same considerations that influence the demand for any other asset. Chief among these considerations is our view of what the deposit will be worth in the future. A foreign currency deposit's future value depends in turn on two factors: the interest rate it offers and the expected change in the currency's exchange rate against other currencies.

Assets and Asset Returns

As you will recall, people can hold wealth in many forms—stocks, bonds, cash, real estate, rare wines, diamonds, and so on. The object of acquiring wealth—of saving—is to transfer purchasing power into the future. We may do this to provide for our retirement years, for our heirs, or simply because we earn more than we need to spend in a particular year and prefer to save the balance for a rainy day.

Defining Asset Returns Because the object of saving is to provide for future consumption, we judge the desirability of an asset largely on the basis of its **rate of return**, that is, the percentage increase in value it offers over some time period. For example, suppose that at the beginning of 2015 you pay $100 for a share of stock issued by Financial Soothsayers, Inc. If the stock pays you a dividend of $1 at the beginning of 2016, and if the stock's price rises from $100 to $109 per share over the year, then you have earned a rate of return of 10 percent on the stock over 2015—that is, your initial $100 investment has grown in value to $110, the sum of the $1 dividend and the $109 you could get by selling your share. Had Financial Soothsayers stock still paid out its $1 dividend but dropped in price to $89 per share, your $100 investment would be worth only $90 by year's end, giving a rate of return of *negative* 10 percent.

You often cannot know with certainty the return that an asset will actually pay after you buy it. Both the dividend paid by a share of stock and the share's resale price, for example, may be hard to predict. Your decision therefore must be based on an *expected* rate of return. To calculate an expected rate of return over some time period, you make your best forecast of the asset's total value at the period's end. The percentage difference between that expected future value and the price you pay for the asset today equals the asset's expected rate of return over the time period.

When we measure an asset's rate of return, we compare how an investment in the asset changes in total value between two dates. In the previous example, we compared how the value of an investment in Financial Soothsayers stock changed between 2015 ($100) and 2016 ($110) to conclude that the rate of return on the stock was 10 percent per year.

We call this a *dollar* rate of return because the two values we compare are expressed in terms of dollars. It is also possible, however, to compute different rates of return by expressing the two values in terms of a foreign currency or a commodity such as gold.

The Real Rate of Return The expected rate of return that savers consider in deciding which assets to hold is the expected **real rate of return**, that is, the rate of return computed by measuring asset values in terms of some broad representative basket

NONDELIVERABLE FORWARD EXCHANGE TRADING IN ASIA

In a standard forward exchange contract, two parties agree to exchange two different currencies at an agreed rate on a future date. The currencies of many developing countries are, however, not fully *convertible*, meaning that they cannot be freely traded on international foreign exchange markets. An important example of an inconvertible currency is China's renminbi, which can be traded within China's borders (by residents) but not freely outside of them (because China's government does not allow nonresidents unrestricted ownership of renminbi deposits in China). Thus, for currencies such as the renminbi, the customary way of trading forward exchange is not possible.

Developing countries with inconvertible currencies such as China's have entered the ranks of the world's largest participants in international trade and investment. Usually, traders use the forward exchange market to hedge their currency risks, but in cases such as China's, as we have seen, a standard forward market cannot exist. Is there no way for foreigners to hedge the currency risk they may take on when they trade with inconvertible-currency countries?

Since the early 1990s, markets in *nondeliverable forward exchange* have sprung up in centers such as Hong Kong and Singapore to facilitate hedging in inconvertible Asian currencies. Among the currencies traded in offshore nondeliverable forward markets are the Chinese renminbi, the Taiwan dollar, and the Indian rupee. By using nondeliverable forward contracts, traders can hedge currency risks without ever actually having to trade inconvertible currencies.

Let's look at a hypothetical example to see how this hedging can be accomplished. General Motors has just sold some car components to China. Its contract with the Chinese importer states that in three months, GM will receive the dollar equivalent of 10 million yuan in payment for its shipment. (The yuan is the unit in which amounts of renminbi are measured, just as British sterling is measured in pounds.) The People's Bank of China (PBC), the central bank, tightly controls its currency's exchange rate by trading dollars that it holds for renminbi with domestic residents.*

Today, the PBC will buy or sell a U.S. dollar for 6.8 yuan. But assume the PBC has been gradually allowing its currency to appreciate against the dollar, and the rate it will quote in three months is uncertain: It could be anywhere between, say, 6.7 and 6.5 yuan per dollar. GM would like to lock in a forward exchange rate of 6.6 yuan per dollar, which the company's chief financial officer might typically do simply by selling the expected 10 million yuan receipts forward for dollars at that rate. Unfortunately, the renminbi's inconvertibility means that GM will actually receive, not renminbi that it can sell forward, but the dollar equivalent of 10 million yuan, dollars that the importer can buy through China's banking system.

Nondeliverable forwards result in a "virtual" forward market, however. They do this by allowing non-Chinese traders to make bets on the renminbi's value that are *payable in dollars*. To lock in a nondeliverable forward exchange rate of 6.6 yuan per dollar, GM can sign a contract requiring it to pay the difference between the number of dollars it actually receives in three months and the amount it would receive if the exchange rate were exactly 6.6 yuan per dollar, equivalent to $1/6.6$ dollars per yuan = \$0.1515 per yuan (after rounding). Thus, if the exchange rate turns out to be 6.5 yuan per dollar (which otherwise would be

(Continued)

*China's currency regime is an example of a fixed exchange rate system, which we will study in greater detail in Chapter 7.

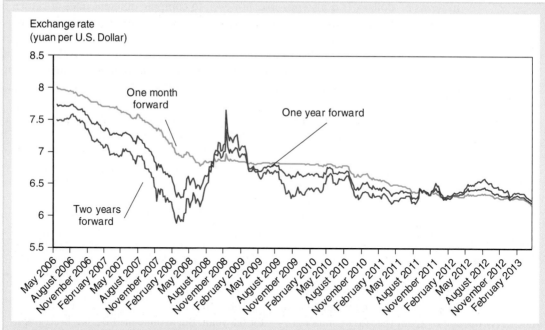

Nondeliverable Forward Exchange Rates, China Yuan per Dollar

Source: *Datastream*.

good luck for GM), GM will have to pay out on its contract $(1/6.5 - 1/6.6 \text{ dollars per yuan}) \times (10,000,000 \text{ yuan}) = (\$0.1538 - \$0.1515 \text{ per yuan}) \times (10,000,000 \text{ yuan}) = \$23,310$.

On the other hand, by giving up the possibility of good luck, GM also avoids the risk of bad luck. If the exchange rate turns out instead to be 6.7 yuan per dollar (which otherwise would be unfavorable for GM), GM will pay the negative amount $(\$0.1493 - \$0.1515 \text{ per yuan}) \times (10,000,000 \text{ yuan}) = -\$22,614$, that is, it will receive \$22,614 from the other contracting party. The nondeliverable forward contract allows GM to immunize itself from exchange risk, even though the parties to the contract need never actually exchange Chinese currency.

The chart above shows daily data on nondeliverable forward rates of yuan for dollars with value dates one month, one year, and two years away. (Far longer maturities are also quoted.) Changes in these rates are more variable at the longer maturities because the rates reflect expectations about China's future exchange rate policy and the far future is relatively more uncertain than the near future.

How have China's exchange rate policies evolved? From July 2005 until July 2008, China followed a widely understood policy of gradually allowing its currency to appreciate against the U.S. dollar. Because of expectations during this period that the yuan/dollar rate would fall over time, the forward rates at which people were willing to trade to cover transactions two years away are below the one-year-ahead forward rates, which in turn are below the one-month-ahead forward rates.

China changed its policy in the summer of 2008, pegging the yuan rigidly to the dollar without any announced end date for that policy. That action altered the relationship among the three forward rates, as you can see in the chart. Two years later, in June 2010, China announced its return to a supposedly more flexible exchange rate for the yuan. Since then, the yuan has continued to appreciate against the dollar—but at a gradual pace.

China's exchange rate system and policies have been a focus of international controversy in recent years, and we will say more about them in later chapters.

of products that savers regularly purchase. It is the expected real return that matters because the ultimate goal of saving is future consumption, and only the *real* return measures the goods and services a saver can buy in the future in return for giving up some consumption (that is, saving) today.

To continue our example, suppose the dollar value of an investment in Financial Soothsayers stock increases by 10 percent between 2015 and 2016 but the dollar prices of all goods and services *also* increase by 10 percent. Then in terms of output—that is, in *real terms*—the investment would be worth no more in 2015 than in 2016. With a real rate of return of zero, Financial Soothsayers stock would not be a very desirable asset.

Although savers care about expected real rates of return, rates of return expressed in terms of a currency can still be used to *compare* real returns on *different* assets. Even if all dollar prices rise by 10 percent between 2015 and 2016, a rare bottle of wine whose dollar price rises by 25 percent is still a better investment than a bond whose dollar value rises by 20 percent. The real rate of return offered by the wine is 15 percent (= 25 percent − 10 percent) while that offered by the bond is only 10 percent (= 20 percent − 10 percent). Notice that the difference between the dollar returns of the two assets (25 percent − 20 percent) must equal the difference between their real returns (15 percent − 10 percent). The reason for this equality is that given the two assets' dollar returns, a change in the rate at which the dollar prices of goods are rising changes both assets' real returns by the same amount.

The distinction between real rates of return and dollar rates of return illustrates an important concept in studying how savers evaluate different assets: The returns on two assets cannot be compared unless they are measured in the *same* units. For example, it makes no sense to compare directly the real return on the bottle of wine (15 percent in our example) with the dollar return on the bond (20 percent) or to compare the dollar return on old paintings with the euro return on gold. Only after the returns are expressed in terms of a common unit of measure—for example, all in terms of dollars—can we tell which asset offers the highest expected real rate of return.

Risk and Liquidity

All else equal, individuals prefer to hold those assets offering the highest expected real rate of return. Our later discussions of particular assets will show, however, that "all else" often is not equal. Some assets may be valued by savers for attributes other than the expected real rate of return they offer. Savers care about two main characteristics of an asset other than its return: its **risk**, the variability it contributes to savers' wealth, and its **liquidity**, the ease with which the asset can be sold or exchanged for goods.

   1. *Risk*. An asset's real return is usually unpredictable and may turn out to be quite different from what savers expected when they purchased the asset. In our last example, savers found the expected real rate of return on an investment in bonds (10 percent) by subtracting from the expected rate of increase in the investment's dollar value (20 percent) the expected rate of increase in dollar prices (10 percent). But if expectations are wrong and the bonds' dollar value stays constant instead of rising by 20 percent, the saver ends up with a real return of negative 10 percent (= 0 percent − 10 percent). Savers dislike uncertainty and are reluctant to

hold assets that make their wealth highly variable. An asset with a high expected rate of return may thus appear undesirable to savers if its realized rate of return fluctuates widely.

2. *Liquidity.* Assets also differ according to the cost and speed at which savers can dispose of them. A house, for example, is not very liquid because its sale usually requires time and the services of brokers and inspectors. To sell a house quickly, one might have to sell at a relatively low price. In contrast, cash is the most liquid of all assets: It is always acceptable at face value as payment for goods or other assets. Savers prefer to hold some liquid assets as a precaution against unexpected pressing expenses that might force them to sell less liquid assets at a loss. They will therefore consider an asset's liquidity as well as its expected return and risk in deciding how much of it to hold.

Interest Rates

As in other asset markets, participants in the foreign exchange market base their demands for deposits of different currencies on a comparison of these assets' expected rates of return. To compare returns on different deposits, market participants need two pieces of information. First, they need to know how the money values of the deposits will change. Second, they need to know how exchange rates will change so that they can translate rates of return measured in different currencies into comparable terms.

The first piece of information needed to compute the rate of return on a deposit of a particular currency is the currency's **interest rate**, the amount of that currency an individual can earn by lending a unit of the currency for a year. At a dollar interest rate of 0.10 (quoted as 10 percent per year), the lender of $1 receives $1.10 at the end of the year, $1 of which is principal and 10 cents of which is interest. Looked at from the other side of the transaction, the interest rate on dollars is also the amount that must be paid to borrow $1 for a year. When you buy a U.S. Treasury bill, you earn the interest rate on dollars because you are lending dollars to the U.S. government.

Interest rates play an important role in the foreign exchange market because the large deposits traded there pay interest, each at a rate reflecting its currency of denomination. For example, when the interest rate on dollars is 10 percent per year, a $100,000 deposit is worth $100,000 after a year; when the interest rate on euros is 5 percent per year, a €100,000 deposit is worth €105,000 after a year. Deposits pay interest because they are really loans from the depositor to the bank. When a corporation or a financial institution deposits a currency in a bank, it is lending that currency to the bank rather than using it for some current expenditure. In other words, the depositor is acquiring an asset denominated in the currency it deposits.

The dollar interest rate is simply the dollar rate of return on dollar deposits. You "buy" the deposit by lending a bank $100,000, and when you are paid back with 10 percent interest at the end of the year, your asset is worth $110,000. This gives a rate of return of $(110,000 - 100,000)/100,000 = 0.10$, or 10 percent per year. Similarly, a foreign currency's interest rate measures the foreign currency return on deposits of that currency. Figure 3-2 shows the monthly behavior of interest rates on the dollar and the Japanese yen from 1978 to 2013. These interest rates are not measured in comparable terms, so there is no reason for them to be close to each other or to move in similar ways over time.

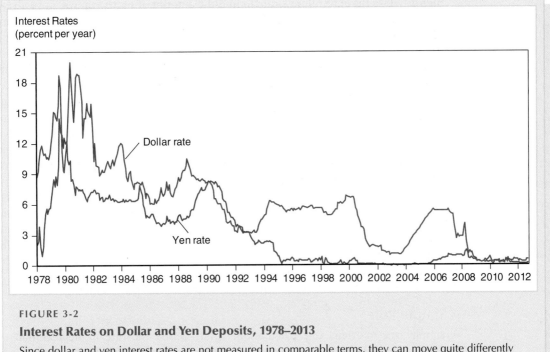

FIGURE 3-2

Interest Rates on Dollar and Yen Deposits, 1978–2013

Since dollar and yen interest rates are not measured in comparable terms, they can move quite differently over time.

Source: *Datastream*. Three-month interest rates are shown.

Exchange Rates and Asset Returns

The interest rates offered by a dollar and a euro deposit tell us how their dollar and euro values will change over a year. The other piece of information we need in order to compare the rates of return offered by dollar and euro deposits is the expected change in the dollar/euro exchange rate over the year. To see which deposit, euro or dollar, offers a higher expected rate of return, you must ask the question: If I use dollars to buy a euro deposit, how many dollars will I get back after a year? When you answer this question, you are calculating the *dollar* rate of return on a euro deposit because you are comparing its *dollar* price today with its *dollar* value a year from today.

To see how to approach this type of calculation, let's look at the following situation: Suppose that today's exchange rate (quoted in American terms) is $1.10 per euro, but that you expect the rate to be $1.165 per euro in a year (perhaps because you expect unfavorable developments in the U.S. economy). Suppose also that the dollar interest rate is 10 percent per year while the euro interest rate is 5 percent per year. This means a deposit of $1.00 pays $1.10 after a year while a deposit of €1 pays €1.05 after a year. Which of these deposits offers the higher return?

The answer can be found in five steps.

Step 1.   Use today's dollar/euro exchange rate to figure out the dollar price of a euro deposit of, say, €1. If the exchange rate today is $1.10 per euro, the dollar price of a €1 deposit is just $1.10.

Step 2.   Use the euro interest rate to find the amount of euros you will have a year from now if you purchase a €1 deposit today. You know that the interest rate on euro deposits is 5 percent per year. So at the end of a year, your €1 deposit will be worth €1.05.

Step 3.   Use the exchange rate you expect to prevail a year from today to calculate the expected dollar value of the euro amount determined in Step 2. Since you expect the dollar to depreciate against the euro over the coming year so that the exchange rate 12 months from today is $1.165 per euro, you expect the dollar value of your euro deposit after a year to be $1.165 per euro × €1.05 = $1.223.

Step 4.   Now that you know the dollar price of a €1 deposit today ($1.10) and can forecast its value in a year ($1.223), you can calculate the expected *dollar* rate of return on a euro deposit as $(1.223 - 1.10)/1.10 = 0.11$, or 11 percent per year.

Step 5.   Since the dollar rate of return on dollar deposits (the dollar interest rate) is only 10 percent per year, you expect to do better by holding your wealth in the form of euro deposits. Despite the fact that the dollar interest rate exceeds the euro interest rate by 5 percent per year, the euro's expected appreciation against the dollar gives euro holders a prospective capital gain that is large enough to make euro deposits the higher-yield asset.

A Simple Rule

A simple rule shortens this calculation. First, define the **rate of depreciation** of the dollar against the euro as the percentage increase in the dollar/euro exchange rate over a year. In the last example, the dollar's expected depreciation rate is $(1.165 - 1.10)/1.10 = 0.059$, or roughly 6 percent per year. Once you have calculated the rate of depreciation of the dollar against the euro, our rule is this: *The dollar rate of return on euro deposits is approximately the euro interest rate plus the rate of depreciation of the dollar against the euro*. In other words, to translate the euro return on euro deposits into dollar terms, you need to add the rate at which the euro's dollar price rises over a year to the euro interest rate.

In our example, the sum of the euro interest rate (5 percent) and the expected depreciation rate of the dollar (roughly 6 percent) is about 11 percent, which is what we found to be the expected dollar return on euro deposits in our first calculation.

We summarize our discussion by introducing some notation:

$R_€$ = today's interest rate on one-year euro deposits,

$E_{\$/€}$ = today's dollar/euro exchange rate (number of dollars per euro),

$E^e_{\$/€}$ = dollar/euro exchange rate (number of dollars per euro) expected to prevail a year from today.

(The superscript ^{e} attached to this last exchange rate indicates that it is a forecast of the future exchange rate based on what people know today.)

Using these symbols, we write the expected rate of return on a euro deposit, measured in terms of dollars, as the sum of (1) the euro interest rate and (2) the expected rate of dollar depreciation against the euro:

$$R_€ + (E^e_{\$/€} - E_{\$/€})/E_{\$/€}.$$

This expected return is what must be compared with the interest rate on one-year dollar deposits, $R_\$$, in deciding whether dollar or euro deposits offer the higher expected rate of return.[6] The expected rate of return difference between dollar and euro deposits is therefore equal to $R_\$$ less the previous expression,

$$R_\$ - [R_€ + (E^e_{\$/€} - E_{\$/€})/E_{\$/€}] = R_\$ - R_€ - (E^e_{\$/€} - E_{\$/€})/E_{\$/€}. \quad (3\text{-}1)$$

When the difference above is positive, dollar deposits yield the higher expected rate of return; when it is negative, euro deposits yield the higher expected rate of return.

Table 3-3 carries out some illustrative comparisons. In case 1, the interest difference in favor of dollar deposits is 4 percent per year ($R_\$ - R_€ = 0.10 - 0.06 = 0.04$), and no change in the exchange rate is expected [$(E^e_{\$/€} - E_{\$/€})/E_{\$/€} = 0.00$]. This means that the expected annual real rate of return on dollar deposits is 4 percent higher than that on euro deposits, so that, other things equal, you would prefer to hold your wealth as dollar rather than euro deposits.

In case 2, the interest difference is the same (4 percent), but it is just offset by an expected depreciation rate of the dollar of 4 percent. The two assets therefore have the same expected rate of return.

Case 3 is similar to the one discussed earlier: A 4 percent interest difference in favor of dollar deposits is more than offset by an 8 percent expected depreciation of the dollar, so euro deposits are preferred by market participants.

In case 4, there is a 2 percent interest difference in favor of euro deposits, but the dollar is expected to *appreciate* against the euro by 4 percent over the year. The expected rate of return on dollar deposits is therefore 2 percent per year higher than that on euro deposits.

So far, we have been translating all returns into dollar terms. But the rate of return differentials we calculated would have been the same had we chosen to express

TABLE 3-3	Comparing Dollar Rates of Return on Dollar and Euro Deposits			
Case	**Dollar Interest Rate** $R_\$$	**Euro Interest Rate** $R_€$	**Expected Rate of Dollar Depreciation against Euro** $\dfrac{E^e_{\$/€} - E_{\$/€}}{E_{\$/€}}$	**Rate of Return Difference between Dollar and Euro Deposits** $R_\$ - R_€ - \dfrac{(E^e_{\$/€} - E_{\$/€})}{E_{\$/€}}$
1	0.10	0.06	0.00	0.04
2	0.10	0.06	0.04	0.00
3	0.10	0.06	0.08	−0.04
4	0.10	0.12	−0.04	0.02

---

[6] If you compute the expected dollar return on euro deposits using the exact five-step method we described before introducing the simple rule, you'll find that it actually equals

$$(1 + R_€) (E^e_{\$/€}/ E_{\$/€}) - 1.$$

This exact formula can be rewritten, however, as

$$R_€ + (E^e_{\$/€} - E_{\$/€})/E_{\$/€} + R_€ \times (E^e_{\$/€} - E_{\$/€})/E_{\$/€}.$$

The expression above is very close to the formula derived from the simple rule when, as is usually the case, the product $R_€ \times (E^e_{\$/€} - E_{\$/€})/E_{\$/€}$ is a small number.

returns in terms of euros or in terms of some third currency. Suppose, for example, we wanted to measure the return on dollar deposits in terms of euros. Following our simple rule, we would add to the dollar interest rate $R_\$$ the expected rate of depreciation of the euro against the dollar. But the expected rate of depreciation of the euro against the dollar is approximately the expected **rate of appreciation** of the dollar against the euro, that is, the expected rate of depreciation of the dollar against the euro with a minus sign in front of it. This means that in terms of euros, the return on a dollar deposit is

$$R_\$ - (E^e_{\$/\euro} - E_{\$/\euro})/E_{\$/\euro}.$$

The difference between the expression above and $R_\euro$ is identical to expression (3-1). Thus, it makes no difference to our comparison whether we measure returns in terms of dollars or euros, as long as we measure them both in terms of the same currency.

Return, Risk, and Liquidity in the Foreign Exchange Market

We observed earlier that a saver deciding which assets to hold may care about the assets' riskiness and liquidity in addition to their expected real rates of return. Similarly, the demand for foreign currency assets depends not only on returns but also on risk and liquidity. Even if the expected dollar return on euro deposits is higher than that on dollar deposits, for example, people may be reluctant to hold euro deposits if the payoff to holding them varies erratically.

There is no consensus among economists about the importance of risk in the foreign exchange market. Even the definition of "foreign exchange risk" is a topic of debate. For now, we will avoid these complex questions by assuming that the real returns on all deposits have equal riskiness, regardless of the currency of denomination. In other words, we are assuming that risk differences do not influence the demand for foreign currency assets. We discuss the role of foreign exchange risk in greater detail, however, in Chapter 7.[7]

Some market participants may be influenced by liquidity factors in deciding which currencies to hold. Most of these participants are firms and individuals conducting international trade. An American importer of French fashion products or wines, for example, may find it convenient to hold euros for routine payments even if the expected rate of return on euros is lower than that on dollars. Because payments connected with international trade make up a very small fraction of total foreign exchange transactions, we ignore the liquidity motive for holding foreign currencies.

We are therefore assuming for now that participants in the foreign exchange market base their demands for foreign currency assets exclusively on a comparison of those assets' expected rates of return. The main reason for making this assumption is that it simplifies our analysis of how exchange rates are determined in the foreign exchange market. In addition, the risk and liquidity motives for holding foreign currencies

---

[7]In discussing spot and forward foreign exchange transactions, some textbooks make a distinction between foreign exchange "speculators"—market participants who allegedly care only about expected returns—and "hedgers"—market participants whose concern is to avoid risk. We depart from this textbook tradition because it can mislead the unwary: While the speculative and hedging motives are both potentially important in exchange rate determination, the same person can be both a speculator and a hedger if she cares about both return and risk. Our tentative assumption that risk is unimportant in determining the demand for foreign currency assets means, in terms of the traditional language, that the speculative motive for holding foreign currencies is far more important than the hedging motive.

appear to be of secondary importance for many of the international macroeconomic issues discussed in the next few chapters.

Equilibrium in the Foreign Exchange Market

We now use what we have learned about the demand for foreign currency assets to describe how exchange rates are determined. We will show that the exchange rate at which the market settles is the one that makes market participants content to hold existing supplies of deposits of all currencies. When market participants willingly hold the existing supplies of deposits of all currencies, we say that the foreign exchange market is in equilibrium.

The description of exchange rate determination given in this section is only a first step: A full explanation of the exchange rate's current level can be given only after we examine how participants in the foreign exchange market form their expectations about the exchange rates they expect to prevail in the future. The next two chapters look at the factors that influence expectations of future exchange rates. For now, however, we will take expected future exchange rates as given.

Interest Parity: The Basic Equilibrium Condition

The foreign exchange market is in equilibrium when deposits of all currencies offer the same expected rate of return. The condition that the expected returns on deposits of any two currencies are equal when measured in the same currency is called the **interest parity condition**. It implies that potential holders of foreign currency deposits view them all as equally desirable assets, provided their expected rates of return are the same.

Let's see why the foreign exchange market is in equilibrium only when the interest parity condition holds. Suppose the dollar interest rate is 10 percent and the euro interest rate is 6 percent, but that the dollar is expected to depreciate against the euro at an 8 percent rate over a year. (This is case 3 in Table 3-3.) In the circumstances described, the expected rate of return on euro deposits would be 4 percent per year higher than that on dollar deposits. We assumed at the end of the last section that individuals always prefer to hold deposits of currencies offering the highest expected return. This implies that if the expected return on euro deposits is 4 percent greater than that on dollar deposits, no one will be willing to continue holding dollar deposits, and holders of dollar deposits will be trying to sell them for euro deposits. There will therefore be an excess supply of dollar deposits and an excess demand for euro deposits in the foreign exchange market.

As a contrasting example, suppose dollar deposits again offer a 10 percent interest rate but euro deposits offer a 12 percent rate and the dollar is expected to *appreciate* against the euro by 4 percent over the coming year. (This is case 4 in Table 3-3.) Now the return on dollar deposits is 2 percent higher. In this case, no one would demand euro deposits, so they would be in excess supply and dollar deposits would be in excess demand.

When, however, the dollar interest rate is 10 percent, the euro interest rate is 6 percent, and the dollar's expected depreciation rate against the euro is 4 percent, dollar and euro deposits offer the same rate of return and participants in the foreign exchange market are equally willing to hold either. (This is case 2 in Table 3-3.)

Only when all expected rates of return are equal—that is, when the interest parity condition holds—is there no excess supply of some type of deposit and no excess demand for another. The foreign exchange market is in equilibrium when no type of deposit is in excess demand or excess supply. We can therefore say that the foreign exchange market is in equilibrium when, and only when, the interest parity condition holds.

To represent interest parity between dollar and euro deposits symbolically, we use expression (3-1), which shows the difference between the two assets' expected rates of return measured in dollars. The expected rates of return are equal when

$$R_\$ = R_€ + (E^e_{\$/€} - E_{\$/€})/E_{\$/€}. \qquad (3\text{-}2)$$

You probably suspect that when dollar deposits offer a higher return than euro deposits, the dollar will appreciate against the euro as investors all try to shift their funds into dollars. Conversely, the dollar should depreciate against the euro when it is euro deposits that initially offer the higher return. This intuition is exactly correct. To understand the mechanism at work, however, we must take a careful look at how exchange rate changes like these help to maintain equilibrium in the foreign exchange market.

How Changes in the Current Exchange Rate Affect Expected Returns

As a first step in understanding how the foreign exchange market finds its equilibrium, we examine how changes in today's exchange rate affect the expected return on a foreign currency deposit when interest rates and expectations about the future exchange rate do not change. Our analysis will show that, other things equal, depreciation of a country's currency today *lowers* the expected domestic currency return on foreign currency deposits. Conversely, appreciation of the domestic currency today, all else equal, *raises* the domestic currency return expected of foreign currency deposits.

It is easiest to see why these relationships hold by looking at an example: How does a change in today's dollar/euro exchange rate, all else held constant, change the expected return, measured in terms of dollars, on euro deposits? Suppose today's dollar/euro rate is $1.00 per euro and the exchange rate you expect for this day next year is $1.05 per euro. Then the expected rate of dollar depreciation against the euro is $(1.05 - 1.00)/1.00 = 0.05$, or 5 percent per year. This means that when you buy a euro deposit, you not only earn the interest $R_€$ but also get a 5 percent "bonus" in terms of dollars. Now suppose today's exchange rate suddenly jumps up to $1.03 per euro (a depreciation of the dollar and an appreciation of the euro), but the expected future rate is *still* $1.05 per euro. What happens to the "bonus" you expected to get from the euro's increase in value in terms of dollars? The expected rate of dollar depreciation is now only $(1.05 - 1.03)/1.03 = 0.019$, or 1.9 percent instead of 5 percent. Since $R_€$ has not changed, the dollar return on euro deposits, which is the sum of $R_€$ and the expected rate of dollar depreciation, has *fallen* by 3.1 percentage points per year (5 percent − 1.9 percent).

In Table 3-4, we work out the dollar return on euro deposits for various levels of today's dollar/euro exchange rate $E_{\$/€}$, always assuming that the expected *future* exchange rate remains fixed at $1.05 per euro and the euro interest rate is 5 percent per year. As you can see, a rise in today's dollar/euro exchange rate (a depreciation of the dollar against the euro) always *lowers* the expected dollar return on euro deposits (as in our example), while a fall in today's dollar/euro exchange rate (an appreciation of the dollar against the euro) always *raises* this return.

It may run counter to your intuition that a depreciation of the dollar against the euro makes euro deposits less attractive relative to dollar deposits (by lowering the expected dollar return on euro deposits) while an appreciation of the dollar makes euro deposits more attractive. This result will seem less surprising if you remember we have assumed that the expected future dollar/euro rate and interest rates do

TABLE 3-4	Today's Dollar/Euro Exchange Rate and the Expected Dollar Return on Euro Deposits When $E^e_{\$/\euro}$ = \$1.05 per Euro			
Today's Dollar / Euro Exchange Rate	Interest Rate on Euro Deposits	Expected Dollar Depreciation Rate against Euro		Expected Dollar Return on Euro Deposits
$E_{\$/\euro}$	$R_\euro$	$\dfrac{1.05 - E_{\$/\euro}}{E_{\$/\euro}}$		$R_\euro + \dfrac{1.05 - E_{\$/\euro}}{E_{\$/\euro}}$
1.07	0.05	− 0.019		0.031
1.05	0.05	0.00		0.05
1.03	0.05	0.019		0.069
1.02	0.05	0.029		0.079
1.00	0.05	0.05		0.10

not change. A dollar depreciation today, for example, means the dollar now needs to depreciate by a *smaller* amount to reach any given expected future level. If the expected future dollar/euro exchange rate does not change when the dollar depreciates today, the dollar's expected future depreciation against the euro therefore falls, or, alternatively, the dollar's expected future appreciation rises. Since interest rates also are unchanged, today's dollar depreciation thus makes euro deposits less attractive compared with dollar deposits.

Put another way, a current dollar depreciation that affects neither exchange rate expectations nor interest rates leaves the expected future dollar payoff of a euro deposit the same but raises the deposit's current dollar cost. This change naturally makes euro deposits less attractive relative to dollar deposits.

It may also run counter to your intuition that *today's* exchange rate can change while the exchange rate expected for the *future* does not. We will indeed study cases later in this book when both of these rates do change at once. We nonetheless hold the expected future exchange rate constant in the present discussion because that is the clearest way to illustrate the effect of today's exchange rate on expected returns. If it helps, you can imagine we are looking at the impact of a *temporary* change so brief that it has no effect on the exchange rate expected for next year.

Figure 3-3 shows the calculations in Table 3-4 in a graphic form that will be helpful in our analysis of exchange rate determination. The vertical axis in the figure measures today's dollar/euro exchange rate and the horizontal axis measures the expected dollar return on euro deposits. For *fixed* values of the expected future dollar/euro exchange rate and the euro interest rate, the relation between today's dollar/euro exchange rate and the expected dollar return on euro deposits defines a downward-sloping schedule.

The Equilibrium Exchange Rate

Now that we understand why the interest parity condition must hold for the foreign exchange market to be in equilibrium and how today's exchange rate affects the expected return on foreign currency deposits, we can see how equilibrium exchange rates are determined. Our main conclusion will be that exchange rates always adjust to maintain interest parity. We continue to assume the dollar interest rate $R_\$$, the euro interest rate $R_\euro$, and the expected future dollar/euro exchange rate $E^e_{\$/\euro}$ are all *given*.

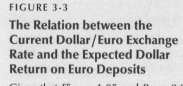

FIGURE 3-3

The Relation between the Current Dollar/Euro Exchange Rate and the Expected Dollar Return on Euro Deposits

Given that $E^e_{\$/€} = 1.05$ and $R_€ = 0.05$, an appreciation of the dollar against the euro raises the expected return on euro deposits, measured in terms of dollars.

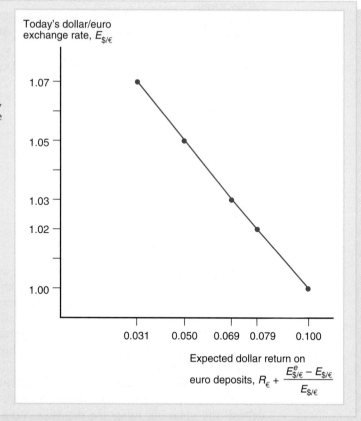

Today's dollar/euro exchange rate, $E_{\$/€}$

Expected dollar return on

euro deposits, $R_€ + \dfrac{E^e_{\$/€} - E_{\$/€}}{E_{\$/€}}$

Figure 3-4 illustrates how the equilibrium dollar/euro exchange rate is determined under these assumptions. The vertical schedule in the graph indicates the given level of $R_\$$, the return on dollar deposits measured in terms of dollars. The downward-sloping schedule shows how the expected return on euro deposits, measured in terms of dollars, depends on the current dollar/euro exchange rate. This second schedule is derived in the same way as the one shown in Figure 3-3.

The equilibrium dollar/euro rate is the one indicated by the intersection of the two schedules at point 1, $E^1_{\$/€}$. At this exchange rate, the returns on dollar and euro deposits are equal, so that the interest parity condition (3-2),

$$R_\$ = R_€ + (E^e_{\$/€} - E^1_{\$/€})/E^1_{\$/€},$$

is satisfied.

Let's see why the exchange rate will tend to settle at point 1 in Figure 3-4 if it is initially at a point such as 2 or 3. Suppose first that we are at point 2, with the exchange rate equal to $E^2_{\$/€}$. The downward-sloping schedule measuring the expected dollar return on euro deposits tells us that at the exchange rate $E^2_{\$/€}$, the rate of return on euro deposits is less than the rate of return on dollar deposits, $R_\$$. In this situation, anyone holding euro deposits wishes to sell them for the more lucrative dollar deposits: The foreign exchange market is out of equilibrium because participants such as banks and multinational corporations are *unwilling* to hold euro deposits.

How does the exchange rate adjust? The unhappy owners of euro deposits attempt to sell them for dollar deposits, but because the return on dollar deposits is higher

FIGURE 3-4

Determination of the Equilibrium Dollar/Euro Exchange Rate

Equilibrium in the foreign exchange market is at point 1, where the expected dollar returns on dollar and euro deposits are equal.

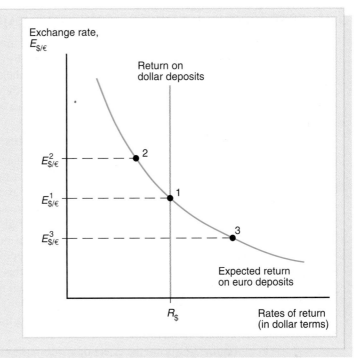

than that on euro deposits at the exchange rate $E^2_{\$/€}$, no holder of a dollar deposit is willing to sell it for a euro deposit at that rate. As euro holders try to entice dollar holders to trade by offering them a better price for dollars, the dollar/euro exchange rate falls toward $E^1_{\$/€}$; that is, euros become cheaper in terms of dollars. Once the exchange rate reaches $E^1_{\$/€}$, euro and dollar deposits offer equal returns, and holders of euro deposits no longer have an incentive to try to sell them for dollars. The foreign exchange market is therefore in equilibrium. In falling from $E^2_{\$/€}$ to $E^1_{\$/€}$, the exchange rate equalizes the expected returns on the two types of deposit by increasing the rate at which the dollar is expected to depreciate in the future, thereby making euro deposits more attractive.

The same process works in reverse if we are initially at point 3 with an exchange rate of $E^3_{\$/€}$, At point 3, the return on euro deposits exceeds that on dollar deposits, so there is now an excess supply of the latter. As unwilling holders of dollar deposits bid for the more attractive euro deposits, the price of euros in terms of dollars tends to rise; that is, the dollar tends to depreciate against the euro. When the exchange rate has moved to $E^1_{\$/€}$, rates of return are equalized across currencies and the market is in equilibrium. The depreciation of the dollar from $E^3_{\$/€}$ to $E^1_{\$/€}$ makes euro deposits less attractive relative to dollar deposits by reducing the rate at which the dollar is expected to depreciate in the future.[8]

---

[8] We could have developed our diagram from the perspective of Europe, with the euro/dollar exchange rate $E_{€/\$}\,(=1/E_{\$/€})$ on the vertical axis, a schedule vertical at $R_€$ to indicate the euro return on euro deposits, and a downward-sloping schedule showing how the euro return on dollar deposits varies with $E_{€/\$}$. An exercise at the end of the chapter asks you to show that this alternative way of looking at equilibrium in the foreign exchange market gives the same answers as the method used here in the text.

Interest Rates, Expectations, and Equilibrium

Having seen how exchange rates are determined by interest parity, we now take a look at how current exchange rates are affected by changes in interest rates and in expectations about the future, the two factors we held constant in our previous discussions. We will see that the exchange rate (which is the relative price of two assets) responds to factors that alter the expected rates of return on those two assets.

The Effect of Changing Interest Rates on the Current Exchange Rate

We often read in the newspaper that the dollar is strong because U.S. interest rates are high or that it is falling because U.S. interest rates are falling. Can these statements be explained using our analysis of the foreign exchange market?

To answer this question, we again turn to a diagram. Figure 3-5 shows a rise in the interest rate on dollars, from $R_\$^1$ to $R_\$^2$ as a rightward shift of the vertical dollar deposits return schedule. At the initial exchange rate $E_{\$/\text{€}}^1$, the expected return on dollar deposits is now higher than that on euro deposits by an amount equal to the distance between points 1 and 1′. As we have seen, this difference causes the dollar to appreciate to $E_{\$/\text{€}}^2$ (point 2). Because there has been no change in the euro interest rate or in the expected future exchange rate, the dollar's appreciation today raises the expected dollar return on euro deposits by increasing the rate at which the dollar is expected to depreciate in the future.

Figure 3-6 shows the effect of a rise in the euro interest rate $R_\text{€}$. This change causes the downward-sloping schedule (which measures the expected dollar return on euro deposits) to shift rightward. (To see why, ask yourself how a rise in the euro interest rate alters the dollar return on euro deposits, given the current exchange rate and the expected future rate.)

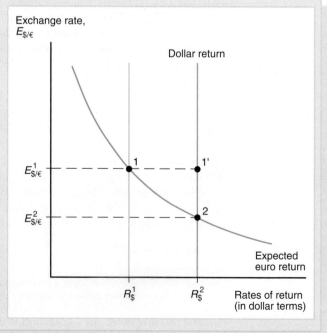

FIGURE 3-5

Effect of a Rise in the Dollar Interest Rate

A rise in the interest rate offered by dollar deposits from R_s^1 to R_s^2 causes the dollar to appreciate from $E_{\$/\text{€}}^1$ (point 1) to $E_{\$/\text{€}}^2$ (point 2).

FIGURE 3-6

Effect of a Rise in the Euro Interest Rate

A rise in the interest rate paid by euro deposits causes the dollar to depreciate from $E^1_{\$/\euro}$ (point 1) to $E^2_{\$/\euro}$ (point 2). (This figure also describes the effect of a rise in the expected future $/€ exchange rate.)

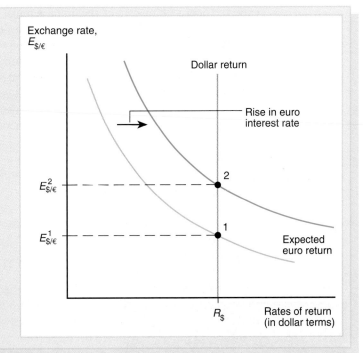

At the initial exchange rate $E^1_{\$/\euro}$, the expected depreciation rate of the dollar is the same as before the rise in $R_\euro$, so the expected return on euro deposits now exceeds that on dollar deposits. The dollar/euro exchange rate rises (from $E^1_{\$/\euro}$ to $E^2_{\$/\euro}$ to eliminate the excess supply of dollar assets at point 1. As before, the dollar's depreciation against the euro eliminates the excess supply of dollar assets by lowering the expected dollar rate of return on euro deposits. A rise in European interest rates therefore leads to a depreciation of the dollar against the euro or, looked at from the European perspective, an appreciation of the euro against the dollar.

Our discussion shows that, all else equal, *an increase in the interest paid on deposits of a currency causes that currency to appreciate against foreign currencies.*

Before we conclude that the newspaper account of the effect of interest rates on exchange rates is correct, we must remember that our assumption of a *constant* expected future exchange rate often is unrealistic. In many cases, a change in interest rates will be accompanied by a change in the expected future exchange rate. This change in the expected future exchange rate will depend, in turn, on the economic causes of the interest rate change. We compare different possible relationships between interest rates and expected future exchange rates in Chapter 5. Keep in mind for now that in the real world, we cannot predict how a given interest rate change will alter exchange rates unless we know *why* the interest rate is changing.

The Effect of Changing Expectations on the Current Exchange Rate

Figure 3-6 may also be used to study the effect on today's exchange rate of a rise in the expected future dollar/euro exchange rate, $E^e_{\$/\euro}$.

Given today's exchange rate, a rise in the expected future price of euros in terms of dollars raises the dollar's expected depreciation rate. For example, if today's exchange rate is $1.00 per euro and the rate expected to prevail in a year is $1.05 per euro, the expected depreciation rate of the dollar against the euro is $(1.05 - 1.00)/1.00 = 0.05$; if the expected future exchange rate now rises to \$1.06 per euro, the expected depreciation rate also rises, to $(1.06 - 1.00)/1.00 = 0.06$.

Because a rise in the expected depreciation rate of the dollar raises the expected dollar return on euro deposits, the downward-sloping schedule shifts to the right, as in Figure 3-6. At the initial exchange rate $E_{\$/€}^1$, there is now an excess supply of dollar deposits: Euro deposits offer a higher expected rate of return (measured in dollar terms) than do dollar deposits. The dollar therefore depreciates against the euro until equilibrium is reached at point 2.

 We conclude that, all else equal, *a rise in the expected future exchange rate causes a rise in the current exchange rate. Similarly, a fall in the expected future exchange rate causes a fall in the current exchange rate.*

CASE STUDY   What Explains the Carry Trade?

Over much of the 2000s, Japanese yen interest rates were close to zero (as Figure 3-2 shows) while Australia's interest rates were comfortably positive, climbing to over 7 percent per year by the spring of 2008. While it might therefore have appeared attractive to borrow yen and invest the proceeds in Australian dollar bonds, the interest parity condition implies that such a strategy should not be *systematically* profitable: On average, shouldn't the interest advantage of Australian dollars be wiped out by relative appreciation of the yen?

Nonetheless, market actors ranging from Japanese housewives to sophisticated hedge funds did in fact pursue this strategy, investing billions in Australian dollars and driving that currency's value up, rather than down, against the yen. More generally, international investors frequently borrow low-interest currencies (called "funding" currencies) and buy high-interest currencies (called "investment" currencies), with results that can be profitable over long periods. This activity is called the *carry trade*, and while it is generally impossible to document the extent of carry trade positions accurately, they can become very large when sizable international interest differentials open up. Is the prevalence of the carry trade evidence that interest parity is wrong?

The honest answer is that while interest parity does not hold exactly in practice—in part because of the risk and liquidity factors mentioned above—economists are still working hard to understand if the carry trade requires additional explanation. Their work is likely to throw further light on the functioning of foreign exchange markets in particular and financial markets in general.

One important hazard of the carry trade is that investment currencies (the high-interest currencies that carry traders target) may experience abrupt crashes. Figure 3-7 illustrates this feature of foreign exchange markets, comparing the cumulative return to investing ¥100 in yen bonds and in Australian dollar bonds over different investment horizons, with the initial investment being made in the final quarter of 2002. As you can see, the yen investment yields next to nothing, whereas Australian dollars pay off handsomely, not only because of a high interest rate but because the yen tended to fall against the Australian dollar through the summer of 2008. But in 2008, the Australian dollar crashed against the yen, falling in price from ¥104 to only ¥61 between July and December. As Figure 3-7 shows, this crash did not wipe out the gains to the carry trade strategy entirely—*if* the strategy had been initiated early enough! Of course, anyone who got into the business late, for example, in 2007, did very poorly indeed. Conversely, anyone savvy enough to unwind the strategy in June 2008 would have doubled his or her money in five and a half years. The carry trade is obviously a very risky business.

We can gain some insight into this pattern by imagining that investors expect a gradual 1 percent annual appreciation of the Australian dollar to occur with high probability (say, 90 percent) and a big 40 percent depreciation to occur with a 10 percent probability. Then the expected appreciation rate of the Australian dollar is:

$$\text{Expected appreciation} = (0.9) \times 1 - (0.1) \times 40 = -3.1 \text{ percent per year.}$$

The negative expected appreciation rate means that the yen is actually expected to appreciate *on average* against the Australian dollar. Moreover, the probability of a crash occurring in the first six years of the investment is only $1 - (0.9)^6 = 1 - 0.53 = 47$ percent, less than fifty-fifty.[9] The resulting pattern of cumulative returns could easily look much like the one shown in Figure 3-7. Calculations like these are suggestive,

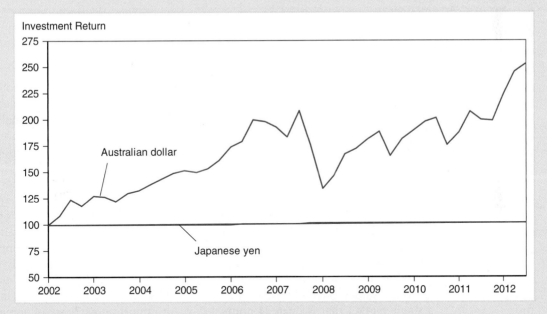

FIGURE 3-7

Cumulative Total Investment Return in Australian Dollar Compared to Japanese Yen, 2003–2013

The Australian dollar-yen carry trade has been profitable on average but is subject to sudden large reversals, as in 2008.

Source: Exchange rates and three-month treasury yields from Global Financial Data.

---

[9]If crashes are independent events over time, the probability that a crash does *not* occur over six years is $(0.9)^6$. Therefore, the probability that a crash does occur in the six-year period is $1 - (0.9)^6$.

and although they are unlikely to explain the full magnitude of carry trade returns, researchers have found that investment currencies are particularly subject to abrupt crashes, and funding currencies to abrupt appreciations.[10]

Complementary explanations based on risk and liquidity considerations have also been advanced. Often, abrupt currency movements occur during financial crises, which are situations in which other wealth is being lost and liquid cash is particularly valuable. In such circumstances, large losses on carry trade positions are extra painful and may force traders to sell other assets they own at a loss.[11] We will say much more about crises in later chapters, but we note for now that the Australian dollar collapse of late 2008 occurred in the midst of a severe global financial crisis.

When big carry trade positions emerge, the government officials responsible for international economic policies often lose sleep. In their early phase, carry trade dynamics will drive investment currencies higher as investors pile in and build up ever-larger exposures to a sudden depreciation of the investment currency. This makes the crash bigger when it occurs, as wrong-footed investors all scramble to repay their funding loans. The result is greater exchange rate volatility in general, as well as the possibility of big trader losses with negative repercussions in stock markets, bond markets, and markets for interbank loans.

SUMMARY

1. An *exchange rate* is the price of one country's currency in terms of another country's currency. Exchange rates play a role in spending decisions because they enable us to translate different countries' prices into comparable terms. All else equal, a *depreciation* of a country's currency against foreign currencies (a rise in the home currency prices of foreign currencies) makes its exports cheaper and its imports more expensive. An *appreciation* of its currency (a fall in the home currency prices of foreign currencies) makes its exports more expensive and its imports cheaper.

2. Exchange rates are determined in the *foreign exchange market*. The major participants in that market are commercial banks, international corporations, nonbank financial institutions, and national central banks. Commercial banks play a pivotal role in the market because they facilitate the exchange of interest-bearing bank deposits, which make up the bulk of foreign exchange trading. Even though foreign exchange trading takes place in many financial centers around the world, modern communication technology links those centers together into a single market that is open 24 hours a day. An important category of foreign

---

[10]See Markus K. Brunnermeier, Stefan Nagel, and Lasse H. Pedersen, "Carry Trades and Currency Crashes," *NBER Macroeconomics Annual* 23 (2008), pp. 313–347. These findings are consistent with the apparently greater empirical success of the interest parity condition over relatively long periods, as documented by Menzie Chinn, "The (Partial) Rehabilitation of Interest Rate Parity in the Floating Rate Era: Longer Horizons, Alternative Expectations, and Emerging Markets," *Journal of International Money and Finance* 25 (February 2006), pp. 7–21.

[11]See Brunnermeier et al., *ibid.*, as well as Craig Burnside, "Carry Trades and Risk," in Jessica James, Ian Marsh, and Lucio Sarno, eds., *Handbook of Exchange Rates* (Hoboken, NJ: John Wiley & Sons, 2012), pp. 283–312.

exchange trading is *forward* trading, in which parties agree to exchange currencies on some future date at a prenegotiated exchange rate. In contrast, *spot* trades are settled immediately.

3. Because the exchange rate is the relative price of two assets, it is most appropriately thought of as being an asset price itself. The basic principle of asset pricing is that an asset's current value depends on its expected future purchasing power. In evaluating an asset, savers look at the expected *rate of return* it offers, that is, the rate at which the value of an investment in the asset is expected to rise over time. It is possible to measure an asset's expected rate of return in different ways, each depending on the units in which the asset's value is measured. Savers care about an asset's expected *real rate of return*, the rate at which its value expressed in terms of a representative output basket is expected to rise.

4. When relative asset returns are relevant, as in the foreign exchange market, it is appropriate to compare expected changes in assets' currency values, provided those values are expressed in the same currency. If *risk* and *liquidity* factors do not strongly influence the demands for foreign currency assets, participants in the foreign exchange market always prefer to hold those assets yielding the highest expected rate of return.

5. The returns on deposits traded in the foreign exchange market depend on *interest rates* and expected exchange rate changes. To compare the expected rates of return offered by dollar and euro deposits, for example, the return on euro deposits must be expressed in dollar terms by adding to the euro interest rate the expected *rate of depreciation* of the dollar against the euro (or *rate of appreciation* of the euro against the dollar) over the deposit's holding period.

6. Equilibrium in the foreign exchange market requires *interest parity*; that is, deposits of all currencies must offer the same expected rate of return when returns are measured in comparable terms.

7. For given interest rates and a given expectation of the future exchange rate, the interest parity condition tells us the current equilibrium exchange rate. When the expected dollar return on euro deposits exceeds that on dollar deposits, for example, the dollar immediately depreciates against the euro. Other things equal, a dollar depreciation today reduces the expected dollar return on euro deposits by reducing the depreciation rate of the dollar against the euro expected for the future. Similarly, when the expected return on euro deposits is below that on dollar deposits, the dollar must immediately appreciate against the euro. Other things equal, a current appreciation of the dollar makes euro deposits more attractive by increasing the dollar's expected future depreciation against the European currency.

8. All else equal, a rise in dollar interest rates causes the dollar to appreciate against the euro while a rise in euro interest rates causes the dollar to depreciate against the euro. Today's exchange rate is also altered by changes in its expected future level. If there is a rise in the expected future level of the dollar/euro rate, for example, then at unchanged interest rates, today's dollar/euro exchange rate will also rise.

KEY TERMS

appreciation, p. 43	interbank trading, p. 46	rate of depreciation, p. 56
arbitrage, p. 47	interest parity condition, p. 59	rate of return, p. 50
depreciation, p. 43		real rate of return, p. 51
exchange rate, p. 40	interest rate, p. 54	risk, p. 53
foreign exchange market, p. 44	liquidity, p. 53	spot exchange rate, p. 48
forward exchange rate, p. 48	rate of appreciation, p. 58	vehicle currency, p. 47

PROBLEMS

1. In Munich, a bratwurst costs 5 euros; a hot dog costs $4 at Boston's Fenway Park. At an exchange rate of $1.05/per euro, what is the price of a bratwurst in terms of a hot dog? All else equal, how does this relative price change if the dollar depreciates to $1.25 per euro? Compared with the initial situation, has a hot dog become more or less expensive relative to a bratwurst?

2. As defined in footnote 3, cross exchange rates are exchange rates quoted against currencies other than the U.S. dollar. If you return to Table 3-1, you will notice that it lists not only exchange rates against the dollar, but also cross rates against the euro and the pound sterling. The fact that we can derive the Swiss franc/Israeli shekel exchange rate, say, from the dollar/franc rate and the dollar/shekel rate follows from ruling out a potentially profitable arbitrage strategy known as *triangular arbitrage*. As an example, suppose the Swiss franc price of a shekel were below the Swiss franc price of a dollar times the dollar price of a shekel. Explain why, rather than buying shekels with dollars, it would be cheaper to buy Swiss francs with dollars and use the francs to buy the shekels. Thus, the hypothesized situation offers a riskless profit opportunity and therefore is not consistent with profit maximization.

3. Table 3-1 reports exchange rates not only against the US dollar, but also against the euro and the pound sterling. (Each row gives the price of the dollar, euro, and pound, respectively, in terms of a different currency.) At the same time, the table gives the spot dollar prices of the euro ($1.3221 per euro) and the pound sterling ($1.5539 per pound). Pick any five currencies from the table and show that the three quoted spot exchange rates (in terms of dollars, euros, and pounds) approximately rule out triangular arbitrage. Why do we need to add the word "approximately"?

4. Petroleum is sold in a world market and tends to be priced in U.S. dollars. The Nippon Steel Chemical Group of Japan must import petroleum to use in manufacturing plastics and other products. How are its profits affected when the yen depreciates against the dollar?

5. Calculate the dollar rates of return on the following assets:
   a. A painting whose price rises from $200,000 to $250,000 in a year.
   b. A bottle of a rare Burgundy, Domaine de la Romanée-Conti 2011, whose price rises from $255 to $275 between 2013 and 2014.
   c. A £10,000 deposit in a London bank in a year when the interest rate on pounds is 10 percent and the $/£ exchange rate moves from $1.50 per pound to $1.38 per pound.

6. What would be the real rates of return on the assets in the preceding question if the price changes described were accompanied by a simultaneous 10 percent increase in all dollar prices?

7. Suppose the dollar interest rate and the pound sterling interest rate are the same, 5 percent per year. What is the relation between the current equilibrium $/£ exchange rate and its expected future level? Suppose the expected future $/£ exchange rate, $1.52 per pound, remains constant as Britain's interest rate rises to 10 percent per year. If the U.S. interest rate also remains constant, what is the new equilibrium $/£ exchange rate?

8. Traders in asset markets suddenly learn that the interest rate on dollars will decline in the near future. Use the diagrammatic analysis of this chapter to determine the effect on the *current* dollar/euro exchange rate, assuming current interest rates on dollar and euro deposits do not change.

9. We noted that we could have developed our diagrammatic analysis of foreign exchange market equilibrium from the perspective of Europe, with the euro/dollar exchange rate $E_{€/\$}(= 1/E_{\$/€})$ on the vertical axis, a schedule vertical at $R_€$ to indicate the euro return on euro deposits, and a downward-sloping schedule showing how the euro return on dollar deposits varies with $E_{€/\$}$. Derive this alternative picture of equilibrium and use it to examine the effect of changes in interest rates and the expected future exchange rate. Do your answers agree with those we found earlier?

10. The following report appeared in the *New York Times* on August 7, 1989 ("Dollar's Strength a Surprise," p. D1):

    But now the sentiment is that the economy is heading for a "soft landing," with the economy slowing significantly and inflation subsiding, but without a recession.

    This outlook is good for the dollar for two reasons. A soft landing is not as disruptive as a recession, so the foreign investments that support the dollar are more likely to continue.

    Also, a soft landing would not force the Federal Reserve to push interest rates sharply lower to stimulate growth. Falling interest rates can put downward pressure on the dollar because they make investments in dollar-denominated securities less attractive to foreigners, prompting the selling of dollars. In addition, the optimism sparked by the expectation of a soft landing can even offset some of the pressure on the dollar from lower interest rates.

    a. Show how you would interpret the third paragraph of this report using this chapter's model of exchange rate determination.

    b. What additional factors in exchange rate determination might help you explain the second paragraph?

11. Suppose the dollar exchange rates of the euro and the yen are equally variable. The euro, however, tends to depreciate unexpectedly against the dollar when the return on the rest of your wealth is unexpectedly high, while the yen tends to appreciate unexpectedly in the same circumstances. As a U.S. resident, which currency, the euro or the yen, would you consider riskier?

12. Does any of the discussion in this chapter lead you to believe that dollar deposits may have liquidity characteristics different from those of other currency deposits? If so, how would the differences affect the interest differential between, say, dollar and Mexican peso deposits? Do you have any guesses about how the liquidity of euro deposits may be changing over time?

13. In October 1979, the U.S. central bank (the Federal Reserve System) announced it would play a less active role in limiting fluctuations in dollar interest rates. After this new policy was put into effect, the dollar's exchange rates against foreign currencies became more volatile. Does our analysis of the foreign exchange market suggest any connection between these two events?

14. Imagine everyone in the world pays a tax of τ percent on interest earnings and on any capital gains due to exchange rate changes. How would such a tax alter the analysis of the interest parity condition? How does your answer change if the tax applies to interest earnings but *not* to capital gains, which are untaxed?

15. Suppose the one-year forward $\$/€$ exchange rate is $1.26 per euro and the spot exchange rate is $1.2 per euro. What is the forward premium on euros (the forward discount on dollars)? What is the difference between the interest rate on one-year dollar deposits and that on one-year euro deposits (assuming no repayment risk)?

16. Europe's single currency, the euro, was introduced in January 1999, replacing the currencies of 11 European Union members, including France, Germany, Italy,

and Spain (but not Britain; see Chapter 10). Do you think that, immediately after the euro's introduction, the value of foreign exchange trading in euros was greater or less than the euro value of the pre-1999 trade in the 11 original national currencies? Explain your answer.

17. Multinationals generally have production plants in a number of countries. Consequently, they can move production from expensive locations to cheaper ones in response to various economic developments—a phenomenon called *outsourcing* when a domestically based firm moves part of its production abroad. If the dollar depreciates, what would you expect to happen to outsourcing by American companies? Explain and provide an example.

18. The interest rate on U.S. three-month Treasury bills dropped to very low levels at the end of 2008 and remained there for several years. Starting in January 2009 and ending in December 2013, find data on the three-month Treasury bill rate from Federal Reserve Economic Data (FRED) at the Federal Reserve Bank of St. Louis; find data on the exchange rate of the U.S. dollar against the Korean won from the Bank of Korea Economic Statistics System at http://ecos.bok.or.kr/flex/EasySearch_e.jsp; and from the same source, find data on the Korean 91-day Monetary Stabilization Bond interest rate. Imagine that you borrow dollars at the Treasury bill rate to invest in Korean stabilization bonds, thus doing a carry trade that exposes you to the risk of won/dollar exchange rate fluctuations. As in the case study in the text, calculate the total return on your carry trade for every month starting in February 2009 and ending in December 2013.

19. The chapter explained why exporters cheer when their home currency depreciates. At the same time, domestic consumers find that they pay higher prices, so they should be disappointed when the currency becomes weaker. Why do the exporters usually win out, so that governments often seem to welcome depreciations while trying to avoid appreciations? (Hint: Think about the analogy with protective tariffs.)

FURTHER READINGS

Sam Y. Cross. *All about the Foreign Exchange Market in the United States*. New York: Books for Business, 2002. Primer on the United States portion of the market.

Federal Reserve Bank of New York. *The Basics of Foreign Trade and Exchange*, at http://www.ny.frb.org/education/fx/index.html. Broad-ranging but highly accessible account of exchange markets and their role. Also supplies many useful Web links.

Philipp Hartmann. *Currency Competition and Foreign Exchange Markets: The Dollar, the Yen and the Euro*. Cambridge: Cambridge University Press, 1999. Theoretical and empirical micro-oriented study of the role of international currencies in world trade and asset markets.

John Maynard Keynes. *A Tract on Monetary Reform*, Chapter 3. London: MacMillan, 1923. Classic analysis of the forward exchange market and covered interest parity.

Michael R. King, Carol Osler, and Dagfinn Rime. "Foreign Exchange Market Structure, Players, and Evolution," in Jessica James, Ian Marsh, and Lucio Sarno, eds., *Handbook of Exchange Rates*. Hoboken, NJ: John Wiley & Sons, 2012, pp. 3–44. Up-to-date overview of foreign exchange market structure.

Paul R. Krugman. "The International Role of the Dollar: Theory and Prospect," in John F. O. Bilson and Richard C. Marston, eds. *Exchange Rate Theory and Practice*. Chicago: University of Chicago Press, 1984, pp. 261–278. Theoretical and empirical analysis of the dollar's position as an "international money."

Richard M. Levich. *International Financial Markets: Prices and Policies*, 2nd edition. Boston: Irwin McGraw-Hill, 2001. Chapters 3–8 of this comprehensive text focus on the foreign exchange market.

Michael Mussa. "Empirical Regularities in the Behavior of Exchange Rates and Theories of the Foreign Exchange Market," in Karl Brunner and Allan H. Meltzer, eds., *Policies for Employment, Prices and Exchange Rates*, Carnegie-Rochester Conference Series on Public Policy 11. Amsterdam: North-Holland, 1979, pp. 9–57. A classic paper that examines the empirical basis of the asset price approach to exchange rate determination.

David Sawyer. "Continuous Linked Settlement (CLS) and Foreign Exchange Settlement Risk." *Financial Stability Review* 17 (December 2004), pp. 86–92. Describes the functioning of and rationale for the Continuous Linked Settlement system for rapid settlement of foreign exchange transactions.

Julian Walmsley. *The Foreign Exchange and Money Markets Guide*, 2nd edition. New York: John Wiley and Sons, 2000. A basic text on the terminology and institutions of the foreign exchange market.

Tim Weithers. *Foreign Exchange: A Practical Guide to the FX Markets.* Hoboken, NJ: John Wiley & Sons, 2006. A clear introduction to foreign exchange instruments and markets.

MyEconLab Can Help You Get a Better Grade

MyEconLab   If your exam were tomorrow, would you be ready? For each chapter, MyEconLab Practice Tests and Study Plans pinpoint sections you have mastered and those you need to study. That way, you are more efficient with your study time, and you are better prepared for your exams.

To see how it works, turn to page 9 and then go to

www.myeconlab.com

3

Forward Exchange Rates and Covered Interest Parity

This appendix explains how forward exchange rates are determined. Under the assumption that the interest parity condition always holds, a forward exchange rate equals the spot exchange rate expected to prevail on the forward contract's value date.

As the first step in the discussion, we point out the close connection among the forward exchange rate between two currencies, their spot exchange rate, and the interest rates on deposits denominated in those currencies. The connection is described by the *covered interest parity* condition, which is similar to the (noncovered) interest parity condition defining foreign exchange market equilibrium but involves the forward exchange rate rather than the expected future spot exchange rate.

To be concrete, we again consider dollar and euro deposits. Suppose you want to buy a euro deposit with dollars but would like to be *certain* about the number of dollars it will be worth at the end of a year. You can avoid exchange rate risk by buying a euro deposit and, at the same time, selling the proceeds of your investment forward. When you buy a euro deposit with dollars and at the same time sell the principal and interest forward for dollars, we say you have "covered" yourself, that is, avoided the possibility of an unexpected depreciation of the euro.

The covered interest parity condition states that the rates of return on dollar deposits and "covered" foreign deposits must be the same. An example will clarify the meaning of the condition and illustrate why it must always hold. Let $F_{\$/€}$ stand for the one-year forward price of euros in terms of dollars, and suppose $F_{\$/€} = \$1.113$ per euro. Assume that at the same time, the spot exchange rate $E_{\$/€} = 1.05$ per euro, $R_\$ = 0.10$, and $R_€ = 0.04$. The (dollar) rate of return on a dollar deposit is clearly 0.10, or 10 percent, per year. What is the rate of return on a covered euro deposit?

We answer this question as we did in the chapter. A €1 deposit costs €1.05 today, and it is worth €1.04 after a year. If you sell €1.04 forward today at the forward exchange rate of $1.113 per euro, the dollar value of your investment at the end of a year is ($1.113 per euro) $\times$ (€1.04) = $1.158. The rate of return on a covered purchase of a euro deposit is therefore $(1.158 - 1.05)/1.05 = 0.103$. This 10.3 percent per year rate of return exceeds the 10 percent offered by dollar deposits, so covered interest parity does not hold. In this situation, no one would be willing to hold dollar deposits; everyone would prefer covered euro deposits.

More formally, we can express the covered return on euro deposits as

$$\frac{F_{\$/€}(1 + R_€) - E_{\$/€}}{E_{\$/€}},$$

which is approximately equal to

$$R_€ + \frac{F_{\$/€} - E_{\$/€}}{E_{\$/€}}$$

when the product $R_€ \times (F_{\$/€} - E_{\$/€})/E_{\$/€}$ is a small number. The covered interest parity condition can therefore be written

$$R_\$ = R_€ + (F_{\$/€} - E_{\$/€})/E_{\$/€}.$$

The quantity

$$(F_{\$/\euro} - E_{\$/\euro})/E_{\$/\euro}$$

is called the *forward premium* on euros against dollars. (It is also called the *forward discount* on dollars against euros.) Using this terminology, we can state the covered interest parity condition as follows: *The interest rate on dollar deposits equals the interest rate on euro deposits plus the forward premium on euros against dollars (the forward discount on dollars against euros).*

There is strong empirical evidence that the covered interest parity condition holds for different foreign currency deposits issued within a single financial center. Indeed, currency traders often set the forward exchange rates they quote by looking at current interest rates and spot exchange rates and using the covered interest parity formula.[12] Deviations from covered interest parity can occur, however, if the deposits being compared are located in different countries. These deviations occur when asset holders fear that governments may impose regulations that will prevent the free movement of foreign funds across national borders. Our derivation of the covered interest parity condition implicitly assumed there was no political risk of this kind. Deviations can occur also because of fears that banks will fail, making them unable to pay off large deposits.[13]

By comparing the (noncovered) interest parity condition,

$$R_\$ = R_\euro + (E^e_{\$/\euro} - E_{\$/\euro})/E_{\$/\euro},$$

with the *covered* interest parity condition, you will find that both conditions can be true at the same time only if the one-year forward rate quoted today equals the spot exchange rate people expect to materialize a year from today:

$$F_{\$/\euro} = E^e_{\$/\euro}.$$

This makes intuitive sense. When two parties agree to trade foreign exchange on a date in the future, the exchange rate they agree on is the spot rate they expect to prevail on that date. The important difference between covered and noncovered transactions should be kept in mind, however. Covered transactions do not involve exchange rate risk, whereas noncovered transactions do.

The theory of covered interest parity helps explain the close correlation between the movements in spot and forward exchange rates shown in Table 3-1, a correlation typical of all major currencies. The unexpected economic events that affect expected asset returns often have a relatively small effect on international interest rate differences between deposits with short maturities (for example, three months). To maintain covered

---

[12]Empirical evidence supporting the covered interest parity condition is provided by Frank McCormick in "Covered Interest Arbitrage: Unexploited Profits? Comment," *Journal of Political Economy* 87 (April 1979), pp. 411–417, and by Kevin Clinton in "Transactions Costs and Covered Interest Arbitrage: Theory and Evidence," *Journal of Political Economy* 96 (April 1988), pp. 358–370.

[13]For a more detailed discussion of the role of political risk in the forward exchange market, see Robert Z. Aliber, "The Interest Parity Theorem: A Reinterpretation," *Journal of Political Economy* 81 (November/December 1973), pp. 1451–1459. Of course, actual government restrictions on cross-border money movements can also cause covered interest parity deviations. On the fear of bank failure as a cause for deviations from covered interest parity, see Naohiko Baba and Frank Packer, "Interpreting Deviations from Covered Interest Parity During the Financial Market Turmoil of 2007–2008," Working Paper No. 267, Bank for International Settlements, December 2008. The events underlying this last paper are discussed in Chapter 9.

interest parity, therefore, spot and forward rates for the corresponding maturities must change roughly in proportion to each other.

We conclude this appendix with one further application of the covered interest parity condition. To illustrate the role of forward exchange rates, the chapter used the example of an American importer of Japanese radios anxious about the $/¥ exchange rate it would face in 30 days when the time came to pay the supplier. In the example, Radio Shack solved the problem by selling forward for yen enough dollars to cover the cost of the radios. But Radio Shack could have solved the problem in a different, more complicated way. It could have (1) borrowed dollars from a bank; (2) sold those dollars immediately for yen at the spot exchange rate and placed the yen in a 30-day yen bank deposit; (3) then, after 30 days, used the proceeds of the maturing yen deposit to pay the Japanese supplier; and (4) used the realized proceeds of the U.S. radio sales, less profits, to repay the original dollar loan.

Which course of action—the forward purchase of yen or the sequence of four transactions described in the preceding paragraph—is more profitable for the importer? We leave it to you, as an exercise, to show that the two strategies yield the same profit when the covered interest parity condition holds.

4

MONEY, INTEREST RATES, AND EXCHANGE RATES

Chapter 3 showed how the exchange rate between currencies depends on two factors—the interest that can be earned on deposits of those currencies and the expected future exchange rate. To understand fully the determination of exchange rates, however, we have to learn how interest rates themselves are determined and how expectations of future exchange rates are formed. In this and the next two chapters, we examine these topics by building an economic model that links exchange rates, interest rates, and other important macroeconomic variables such as the inflation rate and output.

The first step in building the model is to explain the effects of a country's money supply and of the demand for its money on its interest rate and exchange rate. Because exchange rates are the relative prices of national monies, factors that affect a country's money supply or demand are among the most powerful determinants of its currency's exchange rate against foreign currencies. It is therefore natural to begin a deeper study of exchange rate determination with a discussion of money supply and money demand.

Monetary developments influence the exchange rate by changing *both* interest rates *and* people's expectations about future exchange rates. Expectations about future exchange rates are closely connected with expectations about the future money prices of countries' products; these price movements, in turn, depend on changes in money supply and demand. In examining monetary influences on the exchange rate, we therefore look at how monetary factors influence output prices along with interest rates. Expectations of future exchange rates depend on many factors other than money, however, and these nonmonetary factors are taken up in the next chapter.

Once the theories and determinants of money supply and demand are laid out, we use them to examine how equilibrium interest rates are determined by the equality of money supply and money demand. Then we combine our model of interest rate determination with the interest parity condition to study the effects of monetary shifts on the exchange rate, given the prices of goods and services, the level of output, and market expectations about the future. Finally, we take a first look at the long-term effects of monetary changes on output prices and expected future exchange rates.

After reading this chapter, you will be able to:

- Describe and discuss the national money markets in which interest rates are determined.
- Show how monetary policy and interest rates feed into the foreign exchange market.
- Distinguish between the economy's long-run position and the short run, in which money prices and wages are sticky.
- Explain how price levels and exchange rates respond to monetary factors in the long run.
- Outline the relationship between the short-run and the long-run effects of monetary policy, and explain the concept of short-run exchange rate overshooting.

Money Defined: A Brief Review

We are so accustomed to using money that we seldom notice the roles it plays in almost all of our everyday transactions. As with many other modern conveniences, we take money for granted until something goes wrong with it! In fact, the easiest way to appreciate the importance of money is to imagine what economic life would be like without it.

In this section, we do just that. Our purpose in carrying out this "thought experiment" is to distinguish money from other assets and to describe the characteristics of money that lead people to hold it. These characteristics are central to an analysis of the demand for money.

Money as a Medium of Exchange

The most important function of money is to serve as a *medium of exchange*, a generally accepted means of payment. To see why a medium of exchange is necessary, imagine how time-consuming it would be for people to purchase goods and services in a world where the only type of trade possible is barter trade—the direct trade of goods or services for other goods or services. To have her car repaired, for example, your professor would have to find a mechanic in need of economics lessons!

Money eliminates the enormous search costs connected with a barter system because money is universally acceptable. It eliminates these search costs by enabling an individual to sell the goods and services she produces to people other than the producers of the goods and services she wishes to consume. A complex modern economy would cease functioning without some standardized and convenient means of payment.

Money as a Unit of Account

Money's second important role is as a *unit of account*, that is, as a widely recognized measure of value. It is in this role that we encountered money in Chapter 3: Prices of goods, services, and assets are typically expressed in terms of money. Exchange rates allow us to translate different countries' money prices into comparable terms.

The convention of quoting prices in money terms simplifies economic calculations by making it easy to compare the prices of different commodities. The international price comparisons in Chapter 3, which used exchange rates to compare the prices of different countries' outputs, are similar to the calculations you would have to do many times each day if different commodities' prices were not expressed in terms of a standardized unit of account. If the calculations in Chapter 3 gave you a headache, imagine what it would be like to have to calculate the relative prices of each good and service you consume in terms of several other goods and services—for example, the price of a slice of pizza in terms of bananas. This thought experiment should give you a keener appreciation of using money as a unit of account.

Money as a Store of Value

Because money can be used to transfer purchasing power from the present into the future, it is also an asset, or a *store of value*. This attribute is essential for any medium of exchange because no one would be willing to accept it in payment if its value in terms of goods and services evaporated immediately.

Money's usefulness as a medium of exchange, however, automatically makes it the most *liquid* of all assets. As you will recall from the last chapter, an asset is said to be liquid when it can be transformed into goods and services rapidly and without high transaction costs, such as brokers' fees. Since money is readily acceptable as a means of payment, money sets the standard against which the liquidity of other assets is judged.

What Is Money?

Currency and bank deposits on which checks may be written certainly qualify as money. These are widely accepted means of payment that can be transferred between owners at low cost. Households and firms hold currency and checking deposits as a convenient way of financing routine transactions as they arise. Assets such as real estate do not qualify as money because, unlike currency and checking deposits, they lack the essential property of liquidity.

When we speak in this book of the **money supply**, we are referring to the monetary aggregate the Federal Reserve calls M1, that is, the total amount of currency and checking deposits held by households and firms. In the United States at the end of 2012, the total money supply amounted to $2.5 trillion, equal to roughly 16 percent of that year's GNP.[1]

The large deposits traded by participants in the foreign exchange market are not considered part of the money supply. These deposits are less liquid than money and are not used to finance routine transactions.

How the Money Supply Is Determined

An economy's money supply is controlled by its central bank. The central bank directly regulates the amount of currency in existence and also has indirect control over the amount of checking deposits issued by private banks. The procedures through which the central bank controls the money supply are complex, and we assume for now that the central bank simply sets the size of the money supply at the level it desires. We go into the money supply process in more detail, however, in Chapter 7.

---

[1]A broader Federal Reserve measure of money supply, M2, includes time deposits, but these are less liquid than the assets included in M1 because the funds in them typically cannot be withdrawn early without penalty. An even broader measure, known as M3, is also tracked by the Fed. A decision on where to draw the line between money and near-money must be somewhat arbitrary and therefore controversial. For further discussion of this question, see Chapter 3 of Frederic S. Mishkin, *The Economics of Money, Banking and Financial Markets*, 10th edition (Upper Saddle River, NJ: Prentice Hall, 2013).

The Demand for Money by Individuals

Having discussed the functions of money and the definition of the money supply, we now examine the factors that determine the amount of money an individual desires to hold. The determinants of individual money demand can be derived from the theory of asset demand discussed in the last chapter.

We saw in the last chapter that individuals base their demand for an asset on three characteristics:

1. The expected return the asset offers compared with the returns offered by other assets.
2. The riskiness of the asset's expected return.
3. The asset's liquidity.

While liquidity plays no important role in determining the relative demands for assets traded in the foreign exchange market, households and firms hold money *only* because of its liquidity. To understand how the economy's households and firms decide the amount of money they wish to hold, we must look more closely at how the three considerations listed above influence money demand.

Expected Return

Currency pays no interest. Checking deposits often do pay some interest, but they offer a rate of return that usually fails to keep pace with the higher returns offered by less liquid forms of wealth. When you hold money, you therefore sacrifice the higher interest rate you could earn by holding your wealth in a government bond, a large time deposit, or some other relatively illiquid asset. It is this last rate of interest we have in mind when we refer to "the" interest rate. Since the interest paid on currency is zero while that paid on "checkable" deposits tends to be relatively constant, the difference between the rate of return of money in general and that of less liquid alternative assets is reflected by the market interest rate: The higher the interest rate, the more you sacrifice by holding wealth in the form of money.[2]

Suppose, for example, the interest rate you could earn from a U.S. Treasury bill is 10 percent per year. If you use $10,000 of your wealth to buy a Treasury bill, you will be paid $11,000 by Uncle Sam at the end of a year, but if you choose instead to keep the $10,000 as cash in a safe-deposit box, you give up the $1,000 interest you could have earned by buying the Treasury bill. You thus sacrifice a 10 percent rate of return by holding your $10,000 as money.

The theory of asset demand developed in the last chapter shows how changes in the rate of interest affect the demand for money. The theory states that, other things equal, people prefer assets offering higher expected returns. Because an increase in the interest rate is a rise in the rate of return on less liquid assets relative to the rate of return on money, individuals will want to hold more of their wealth in nonmoney assets that pay the market interest rate and less of their wealth in the form of money

---

[2]Many of the illiquid assets that individuals can choose from do not pay their returns in the form of interest. Stocks, for example, pay returns in the forms of dividends and capital gains. The family summer house on Cape Cod pays a return in the forms of capital gains and the pleasure of vacations at the beach. The assumption behind our analysis of money demand is that once allowance is made for risk, all assets other than money offer an expected rate of return (measured in terms of money) equal to the interest rate. This assumption allows us to use the interest rate to summarize the return an individual forgoes by holding money rather than an illiquid asset.

if the interest rate rises. We conclude that, *all else equal, a rise in the interest rate causes the demand for money to fall.*

We can also describe the influence of the interest rate on money demand in terms of the economic concept of *opportunity cost*—the amount you sacrifice by taking one course of action rather than another. The interest rate measures the opportunity cost of holding money rather than interest-bearing bonds. A rise in the interest rate therefore raises the cost of holding money and causes money demand to fall.

Risk

Risk is not an important factor in money demand. It is risky to hold money because an unexpected increase in the prices of goods and services could reduce the value of your money in terms of the commodities you consume. Since interest-paying assets such as government bonds have face values fixed in terms of money, however, the same unexpected increase in prices would reduce the real value of those assets by the same percentage. Because any change in the riskiness of money causes an equal change in the riskiness of bonds, changes in the risk of holding money need not cause individuals to reduce their demand for money and increase their demand for interest-paying assets.

Liquidity

The main benefit of holding money comes from its liquidity. Households and firms hold money because it is the easiest way of financing their everyday purchases. Some large purchases can be financed through the sale of a substantial illiquid asset. An art collector, for example, could sell one of her Picassos to buy a house. To finance a continuing stream of smaller expenditures at various times and for various amounts, however, households and firms have to hold some money.

An individual's need for liquidity rises when the average daily value of his transactions rises. A student who takes the bus every day, for example, does not need to hold as much cash as a business executive who takes taxis during rush hour. We conclude that *a rise in the average value of transactions carried out by a household or firm causes its demand for money to rise.*

Aggregate Money Demand

Our discussion of how individual households and firms determine their demands for money can now be applied to derive the determinants of **aggregate money demand**, the total demand for money by all households and firms in the economy. Aggregate money demand is just the sum of all the economy's individual money demands.

Three main factors determine aggregate money demand:

1. *The interest rate.* A rise in the interest rate causes each individual in the economy to reduce her demand for money. All else equal, aggregate money demand therefore falls when the interest rate rises.

2. *The price level.* The economy's **price level** is the price of a broad reference basket of goods and services in terms of currency. Generally, the reference basket includes standard, everyday consumption items such as food, clothing, and housing and less routine purchases such as medical care and legal fees. If the price level rises, individual households and firms must spend more money than before to purchase their usual weekly baskets of goods and services. To maintain the same level of liquidity as before the price level increase, they will therefore have to hold more money.

3. *Real national income.* When real national income (GNP) rises, more goods and services are sold in the economy. This increase in the real value of transactions raises the demand for money, given the price level.

If P is the price level, R is the interest rate, and Y is real GNP, the aggregate demand for money, M^d, can be expressed as

$$M^d = P \times L(R, Y), \tag{4-1}$$

where the value of $L(R, Y)$ falls when R rises, and rises when Y rises.[3] To see why we have specified that aggregate money demand is *proportional* to the price level, imagine that all prices doubled but the interest rate and everyone's *real* incomes remained unchanged. The money value of each individual's average daily transactions would then simply double, as would the amount of money each wished to hold.

We usually write the aggregate money demand relation (4-1) in the equivalent form

$$M^d/P = L(R, Y), \tag{4-2}$$

and call $L(R, Y)$ aggregate *real* money demand. This way of expressing money demand shows that the aggregate demand for liquidity, $L(R, Y)$, is not a demand for a certain number of currency units but is instead a demand to hold a certain amount of real purchasing power in liquid form. The ratio M^d/P—that is, desired money holdings measured in terms of a typical reference basket of commodities—equals the amount of real purchasing power people would like to hold in liquid form. For example, if people wished to hold $1,000 in cash at a price level of $100 per commodity basket, their real money holdings would be equivalent to $1,000/($100 per basket) = 10 baskets. If the price level doubled (to $200 per basket), the purchasing power of their $1,000 in cash would be halved, since it would now be worth only 5 baskets.

Figure 4-1 shows how aggregate real money demand is affected by the interest rate for a fixed level of real income, Y. The aggregate real money demand schedule $L(R, Y)$

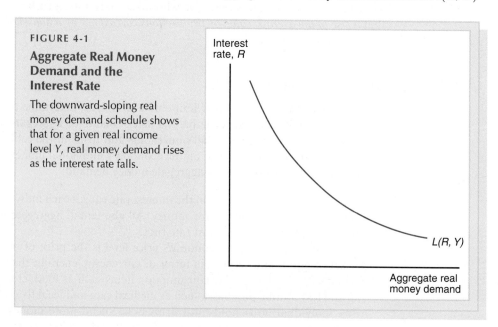

FIGURE 4-1

Aggregate Real Money Demand and the Interest Rate

The downward-sloping real money demand schedule shows that for a given real income level Y, real money demand rises as the interest rate falls.

Interest rate, R

$L(R, Y)$

Aggregate real money demand

---

[3]Naturally, $L(R, Y)$ rises when R falls, and falls when Y falls.

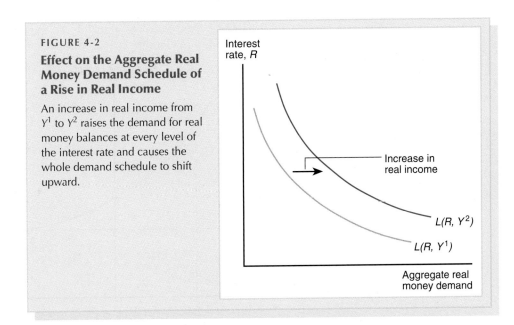

FIGURE 4-2

Effect on the Aggregate Real Money Demand Schedule of a Rise in Real Income

An increase in real income from Y^1 to Y^2 raises the demand for real money balances at every level of the interest rate and causes the whole demand schedule to shift upward.

slopes downward because a fall in the interest rate raises the desired real money holdings of each household and firm in the economy.

For a given level of real GNP, changes in the interest rate cause movements *along* the $L(R, Y)$ schedule. Changes in real GNP, however, cause the schedule itself to shift. Figure 4-2 shows how a rise in real GNP from Y^1 to Y^2 affects the position of the aggregate real money demand schedule. Because a rise in real GNP raises aggregate real money demand for a given interest rate, the schedule $L(R, Y^2)$ lies to the right of $L(R, Y^1)$ when Y^2 is greater than Y^1.

The Equilibrium Interest Rate: The Interaction of Money Supply and Demand

As you might expect from other economics courses you've taken, the money market is in equilibrium when the money supply set by the central bank equals aggregate money demand. In this section, we see how the interest rate is determined by money market equilibrium, given the price level and output, both of which are temporarily assumed to be unaffected by monetary changes.

Equilibrium in the Money Market

If M^s is the money supply, the condition for equilibrium in the money market is

$$M^s = M^d. \tag{4-3}$$

After dividing both sides of this equality by the price level, we can express the money market equilibrium condition in terms of aggregate real money demand as

$$M^s/P = L(R, Y). \tag{4-4}$$

Given the price level, P, and the level of output, Y, the equilibrium interest rate is the one at which aggregate real money demand equals the real money supply.

FIGURE 4-3

Determination of the Equilibrium Interest Rate

With P and Y given and a real money supply of M^s/P, money market equilibrium is at point 1. At this point, aggregate real money demand and the real money supply are equal and the equilibrium interest rate is R^1.

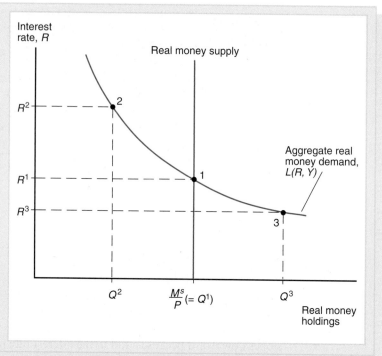

In Figure 4-3, the aggregate real money demand schedule intersects the real money supply schedule at point 1 to give an equilibrium interest rate of R^1. The money supply schedule is vertical at M^s/P because M^s is set by the central bank while P is taken as given.

Let's see why the interest rate tends to settle at its equilibrium level by considering what happens if the market is initially at point 2, with an interest rate, R^2, that is above R^1.

At point 2, the demand for real money holdings falls short of the supply by $Q^1 - Q^2$, so there is an excess supply of money. If individuals are holding more money than they desire given the interest rate of R^2, they will attempt to reduce their liquidity by using some money to purchase interest-bearing assets. In other words, individuals will attempt to get rid of their excess money by lending it to others. Since there is an aggregate excess supply of money at R^2, however, not everyone can succeed in doing this: There are more people who would like to lend money to reduce their liquidity than there are people who would like to borrow money to increase theirs. Those who cannot unload their extra money try to tempt potential borrowers by lowering the interest rate they charge for loans below R^2. The downward pressure on the interest rate continues until the rate reaches R^1. At this interest rate, anyone wishing to lend money can do so because the aggregate excess supply of money has disappeared; that is, supply once again equals demand. Once the market reaches point 1, there is therefore no further tendency for the interest rate to drop.[4]

---

[4]Another way to view this process is as follows: We saw in the last chapter that an asset's rate of return falls when its current price rises relative to its future value. When there is an excess supply of money, the current money prices of illiquid assets that pay interest will be bid up as individuals attempt to reduce their money holdings. This rise in current asset prices lowers the rate of return on nonmoney assets, and since this rate of return is equal to the interest rate (after adjustment for risk), the interest rate also must fall.

Similarly, if the interest rate is initially at a level R^3 below R^1, it will tend to rise. As Figure 4-3 shows, there is excess demand for money equal to $Q^3 - Q^1$ at point 3. Individuals therefore attempt to sell interest-bearing assets such as bonds to increase their money holdings (that is, they sell bonds for cash). At point 3, however, not everyone can succeed in selling enough interest-bearing assets to satisfy his or her demand for money. Thus, people bid for money by offering to borrow at progressively higher interest rates and push the interest rate upward toward R^1. Only when the market has reached point 1 and the excess demand for money has been eliminated does the interest rate stop rising.

We can summarize our findings as follows: *The market always moves toward an interest rate at which the real money supply equals aggregate real money demand. If there is initially an excess supply of money, the interest rate falls, and if there is initially an excess demand, it rises.*

Interest Rates and the Money Supply

The effect of increasing the money supply at a given price level is illustrated in Figure 4-4. Initially, the money market is in equilibrium at point 1, with a money supply M^1 and an interest rate R^1. Since we are holding P constant, a rise in the money supply to M^2 increases the real money supply from M^1/P to M^2/P. With a real money supply of M^2/P, point 2 is the new equilibrium and R^2 is the new, lower interest rate that induces people to hold the increased available real money supply.

The process through which the interest rate falls is by now familiar. After M^s is increased by the central bank, there is initially an excess real supply of money at the old equilibrium interest rate, R^1, which previously balanced the market. Since people are holding more money than they desire, they use their surplus funds to bid for assets that pay interest. The economy as a whole cannot reduce its money holdings,

FIGURE 4-4

Effect of an Increase in the Money Supply on the Interest Rate

For a given price level, P, and real income level, Y, an increase in the money supply from M^1 to M^2 reduces the interest rate from R^1 (point 1) to R^2 (point 2).

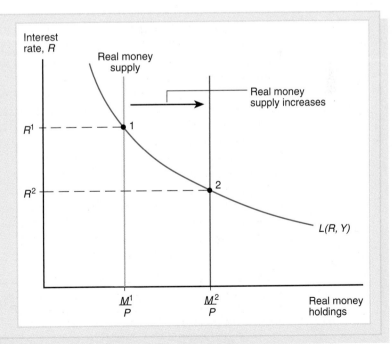

so interest rates are driven down as unwilling money holders compete to lend their excess cash balances. At point 2 in Figure 4-4, the interest rate has fallen sufficiently to induce an increase in real money demand equal to the increase in the real money supply.

By running the above policy experiment in reverse, we can see how a reduction of the money supply forces interest rates upward. A fall in M^s causes an excess demand for money at the interest rate that previously balanced supply and demand. People attempt to sell interest-bearing assets—that is, to borrow—to rebuild their depleted real money holdings. Since they cannot all be successful when there is excess money demand, the interest rate is pushed upward until everyone is content to hold the smaller real money stock.

We conclude that *an increase in the money supply lowers the interest rate, while a fall in the money supply raises the interest rate, given the price level and output.*

Output and the Interest Rate

Figure 4-5 shows the effect on the interest rate of a rise in the level of output from Y^1 to Y^2, given the money supply and the price level. As we saw earlier, an increase in output causes the entire aggregate real money demand schedule to shift to the right, moving the equilibrium away from point 1. At the old equilibrium interest rate, R^1, there is an excess demand for money equal to $Q^2 - Q^1$ (point 1′). Since the real money supply is given, the interest rate is bid up until it reaches the higher, new equilibrium level R^2 (point 2). A fall in output has opposite effects, causing the aggregate real money demand schedule to shift to the left and therefore causing the equilibrium interest rate to fall.

We conclude that *an increase in real output raises the interest rate, while a fall in real output lowers the interest rate, given the price level and the money supply.*

FIGURE 4-5

Effect on the Interest Rate of a Rise in Real Income

Given the real money supply, M^S/P ($= Q^1$), a rise in real income from Y^1 to Y^2 raises the interest rate from R^1 (point 1) to R^2 (point 2).

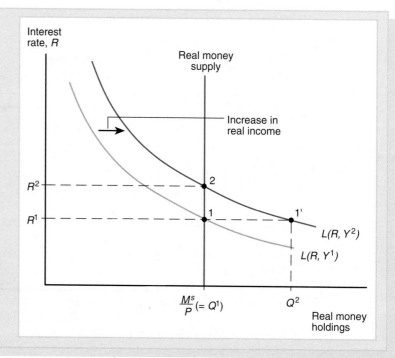

The Money Supply and the Exchange Rate in the Short Run

In Chapter 3, we learned about the interest parity condition, which predicts how interest rate movements influence the exchange rate, given expectations about the exchange rate's future level. Now that we know how shifts in a country's money supply affect the interest rate on nonmoney assets denominated in its currency, we can see how monetary changes affect the exchange rate. We will discover that *an increase in a country's money supply causes its currency to depreciate in the foreign exchange market, while a reduction in the money supply causes its currency to appreciate.*

In this section, we continue to take the price level (along with real output) as given, and for that reason we label the analysis of this section **short run**. The **long-run** analysis of an economic event allows for the complete adjustment of the price level (which may take a long time) and for full employment of all factors of production. Later in this chapter, we examine the long-run effects of money supply changes on the price level, the exchange rate, and other macroeconomic variables. Our long-run analysis will show how the money supply influences exchange rate expectations, which we also continue to take as given for now.

Linking Money, the Interest Rate, and the Exchange Rate

To analyze the relationship between money and the exchange rate in the short run in Figure 4-6, we combine two diagrams we have already studied separately. Let's assume once again we are looking at the dollar/euro exchange rate, that is, the price of euros in terms of dollars.

The first diagram (introduced as Figure 3-4) shows equilibrium in the foreign exchange market and how it is determined given interest rates and expectations about future exchange rates. This diagram appears as the top part of Figure 4-6. The dollar interest rate, $R_\$^1$, which is determined in the money market, defines the vertical schedule.

As you will remember from Chapter 3, the downward-sloping expected euro return schedule shows the expected return on euro deposits, measured in dollars. The schedule slopes downward because of the effect of current exchange rate changes on expectations of future depreciation: A strengthening of the dollar today (a fall in $E_{\$/€}$) relative to its *given* expected future level makes euro deposits more attractive by leading people to anticipate a sharper dollar depreciation in the future.

At the intersection of the two schedules (point 1′), the expected rates of return on dollar and euro deposits are equal, and therefore interest parity holds. $E_{\$/€}^1$ is the equilibrium exchange rate.

In the second diagram we need to examine the relationship between money and the exchange rate was introduced as Figure 4-3. This figure shows how a country's equilibrium interest rate is determined in its money market, and it appears as the bottom part of Figure 4-6. For convenience, however, the figure has been rotated clockwise by 90 degrees so that dollar interest rates are measured from 0 on the horizontal axis and the U.S. real money supply is measured from 0 on the descending vertical axis. Money market equilibrium is shown at point 1, where the dollar interest rate $R_\$^1$ induces people to demand real balances equal to the U.S. real money supply, M_{US}^s/P_{US}.

Figure 4-6 emphasizes the link between the U.S. money market (bottom) and the foreign exchange market (top)—the U.S. money market determines the dollar interest rate, which in turn affects the exchange rate that maintains interest parity. (Of course,

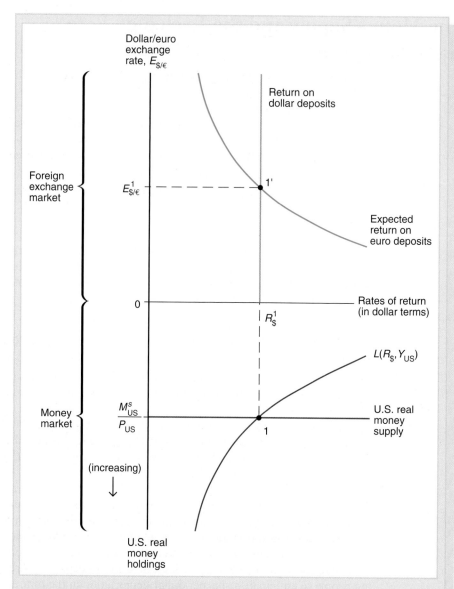

FIGURE 4-6

Simultaneous Equilibrium in the U.S. Money Market and the Foreign Exchange Market

Both asset markets are in equilibrium at the interest rate $R_\$^1$ and exchange rate $E_{\$/€}^1$; at these values, money supply equals money demand (point 1) and the interest parity condition holds (point 1').

there is a similar link between the European money market and the foreign exchange market that operates through changes in the euro interest rate.)

Figure 4-7 illustrates these linkages. The U.S. and European central banks, the Federal Reserve System and the European Central Bank (ECB), respectively, determine the U.S. and European money supplies, M_{US}^s and M_E^s. Given the price levels and national incomes of the two countries, equilibrium in national money markets leads to

FIGURE 4-7

Money Market/Exchange Rate Linkages

Monetary policy actions by the Fed affect the U.S. interest rate, changing the dollar/euro exchange rate that clears the foreign exchange market. The ECB can affect the exchange rate by changing the European money supply and interest rate.

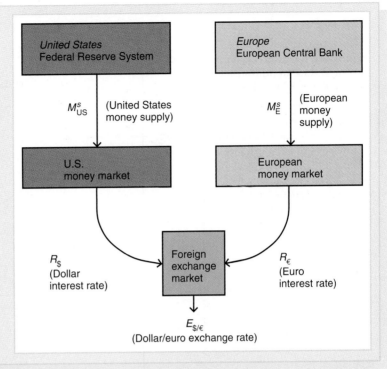

the dollar and euro interest rates $R_\$$ and $R_€$. These interest rates feed into the foreign exchange market, where, given expectations about the future dollar/euro exchange rate, the current rate $E_{\$/€}$ is determined by the interest parity condition.

U.S. Money Supply and the Dollar/Euro Exchange Rate

We now use our model of asset market linkages (the links between the money and foreign exchange markets) to ask how the dollar/euro exchange rate changes when the Federal Reserve changes the U.S. money supply M_{US}^s. The effects of this change are summarized in Figure 4-8.

At the initial money supply M_{US}^1, the money market is in equilibrium at point 1 with an interest rate $R_\$^1$. Given the euro interest rate and the expected future exchange rate, a dollar interest rate of $R_\$^1$ implies that foreign exchange market equilibrium occurs at point 1′, with an exchange rate equal to $E_{\$/€}^1$.

What happens when the Federal Reserve, perhaps fearing the onset of a recession, raises the U.S. money supply to M_{US}^2? This increase sets in motion the following sequence of events: (1) At the initial interest rate $R_\$^1$, there is an excess supply of money in the U.S. money market, so the dollar interest rate falls to $R_\$^2$ as the money market reaches its new equilibrium position (point 2). (2) Given the initial exchange rate $E_{\$/€}^1$ and the new, lower interest rate on dollars, $R_\$^2$, the expected return on euro deposits is greater than that on dollar deposits. Holders of dollar deposits therefore try to sell them for euro deposits, which are momentarily more attractive. (3) The dollar depreciates to $E_{\$/€}^2$ as holders of dollar deposits bid for euro deposits. The foreign exchange market is once again in equilibrium at point 2′ because the exchange rate's move to $E_{\$/€}^2$ causes a fall in the dollar's expected future depreciation rate sufficient to offset the fall in the dollar interest rate.

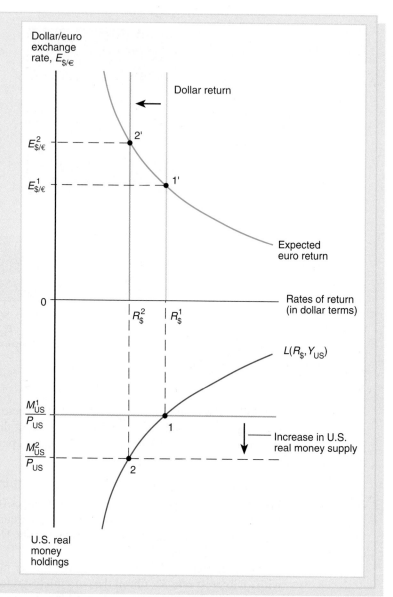

FIGURE 4-8

Effect on the Dollar/Euro Exchange Rate and Dollar Interest Rate of an Increase in the U.S. Money Supply

Given P_{US} and Y_{US} when the money supply rises from M^1_{US} to M^2_{US} the dollar interest rate declines (as money market equilibrium is reestablished at point 2) and the dollar depreciates against the euro (as foreign exchange market equilibrium is reestablished at point 2′).

~We conclude that *an increase in a country's money supply causes its currency to depreciate in the foreign exchange market. By running Figure 4-8 in reverse, you can see that a reduction in a country's money supply causes its currency to appreciate in the foreign exchange market.*

Europe's Money Supply and the Dollar/Euro Exchange Rate

The conclusions we have reached also apply when the ECB changes Europe's money supply. Suppose the ECB fears a recession in Europe and hopes to head it off through a looser monetary policy. An increase in M^s_E causes a depreciation of the euro (that is, an appreciation of the dollar, or a fall in $E_{\$/\euro}$), while a reduction in M^s_E causes an appreciation of the euro (that is, a depreciation of the dollar, or a rise in $E_{\$/\euro}$).

The mechanism at work, which runs from the European interest rate to the exchange rate, is the same as the one we just analyzed. It is good exercise to verify

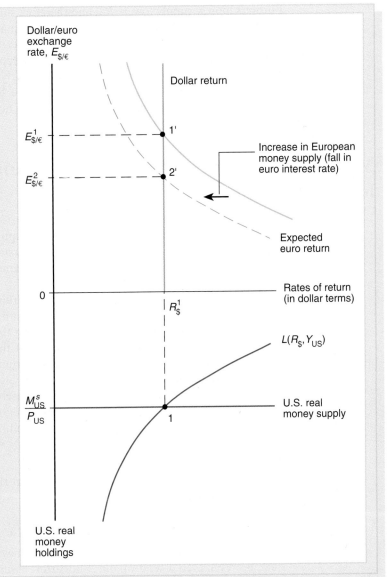

FIGURE 4-9

Effect of an Increase in the European Money Supply on the Dollar/Euro Exchange Rate

By lowering the dollar return on euro deposits (shown as a leftward shift in the expected euro return curve), an increase in Europe's money supply causes the dollar to appreciate against the euro. Equilibrium in the foreign exchange market shifts from point 1′ to point 2′ but equilibrium in the U.S. money market remains at point 1.

these assertions by drawing figures similar to Figures 4-6 and 4-8 that illustrate the linkage between the European money market and the foreign exchange market.

Here we use a different approach to show how changes in Europe's money supply affect the dollar/euro exchange rate. In Chapter 3, we learned that a fall in the euro interest rate, $R_{\euro}$, shifts the downward-sloping schedule in the upper part of Figure 4-6 to the left. The reason is that for any level of the exchange rate, a fall in $R_{\euro}$ lowers the expected rate of return on euro deposits. Since a rise in the European money supply M_E^s lowers $R_{\euro}$, we can see the effect on the exchange rate by shifting the expected euro return schedule in the top part of Figure 4-6 to the left.

The result of an increase in the European money supply is shown in Figure 4-9. Initially, the U.S. money market is in equilibrium at point 1 and the foreign exchange market is in equilibrium at point 1′, with an exchange rate $E_{\$/\euro}^1$. An increase in

Europe's money supply lowers R_{ϵ}, and therefore shifts to the left the schedule linking the expected return on euro deposits to the exchange rate. Foreign exchange market equilibrium is restored at point 2′, with an exchange rate $E^2_{\$/\epsilon}$. We see that the increase in European money causes the euro to depreciate against the dollar (that is, causes a fall in the dollar price of euros). Similarly, a fall in Europe's money supply would cause the euro to appreciate against the dollar (that is, $E_{\$/\epsilon}$ would rise). The change in the European money supply does not disturb the U.S. money market equilibrium, which remains at point 1.[5]

Money, the Price Level, and the Exchange Rate in the Long Run

Our short-run analysis of the link between countries' money markets and the foreign exchange market rested on the simplifying assumption that price levels and exchange rate expectations were given. To extend our understanding of how money supply and money demand affect exchange rates, we must examine how monetary factors affect a country's price level in the long run.

An economy's **long-run equilibrium** is the position it would eventually reach if no new economic shocks occurred during the adjustment to full employment. You can think of long-run equilibrium as the equilibrium that would be maintained after all wages and prices had had enough time to adjust to their market-clearing levels. An equivalent way of thinking of it is as the equilibrium that would occur if prices were perfectly flexible and always adjusted immediately to preserve full employment.

In studying how monetary changes work themselves out over the long run, we will examine how such changes shift the economy's long-run equilibrium. Our main tool is once again the theory of aggregate money demand.

Money and Money Prices

If the price level and output are fixed in the short run, the condition (4-4) of money market equilibrium,

$$M^s/P = L(R, Y),$$

determines the domestic interest rate, R. The money market always moves to equilibrium, however, even if we drop our "short-run" assumption and think of periods over which P and Y, as well as R, can vary. The above equilibrium condition can therefore be rearranged to give

$$P = M^s/L(R, Y), \tag{4-5}$$

which shows how the price level depends on the interest rate, real output, and the domestic money supply.

The *long-run equilibrium price level* is just the value of P that satisfies condition (4-5) when the interest rate and output are at their long-run levels, that is, at levels consistent with full employment. When the money market is in equilibrium and all factors of production are fully employed, the price level will remain steady if the money

---

[5]The U.S. money market equilibrium remains at point 1 because the price adjustments that equilibrate the European money market and the foreign exchange market after the increase in Europe's money supply do not change either the money supply or money demand in the United States, given Y_{US} and P_{US}.

supply, the aggregate money demand function, and the long-run values of R and Y remain steady.

One of the most important predictions of the previous equation for P concerns the relationship between a country's price level and its money supply, M^s: *All else equal, an increase in a country's money supply causes a proportional increase in its price level.* If, for example, the money supply doubles (to $2M^s$) but output and the interest rate do not change, the price level must also double (to $2P$) to maintain equilibrium in the money market.

The economic reasoning behind this very precise prediction follows from our observation above that the demand for money is a demand for *real* money holdings: Real money demand is not altered by an increase in M^s that leaves R and Y (and thus aggregate real money demand $L(R, Y)$) unchanged. If aggregate real money demand does not change, however, the money market will remain in equilibrium only if the real money supply also stays the same. To keep the real money supply M^s/P constant, P must rise in proportion to M^s.

The Long-Run Effects of Money Supply Changes

Our theory of how the money supply affects the price level *given* the interest rate and output is not yet a theory of how money supply changes affect the price level in the long run. To develop such a theory, we still have to determine the long-run effects of a money supply change on the interest rate and output. This is easier than you might think. As we now argue, *a change in the supply of money has no effect on the long-run values of the interest rate or real output.*[6]

The best way to understand the long-run effects of money supply on the interest rate and output is to think first about a *currency reform*, in which a country's government redefines the national currency unit. For example, the government of Turkey reformed its currency on January 1, 2005, simply by issuing "new" Turkish lira, each equal to 1 million "old" Turkish lira. The effect of this reform was to lower the number of currency units in circulation, and all lira prices, to $\frac{1}{1,000,000}$ of their old lira values. But the redefinition of the monetary unit had no effect on real output, the interest rate, or the relative prices of goods: All that occurred was a one-time change in all values measured in lira. A decision to measure distance in half-miles rather than miles would have as little effect on real economic variables as the Turkish government's decision to chop six zeros off the end of every magnitude measured in terms of money.

An increase in the supply of a country's currency has the same effect in the long run as a currency reform. A doubling of the money supply, for example, has the same long-run effect as a currency reform in which each unit of currency is replaced by two units of "new" currency. If the economy is initially fully employed, every money price in the economy eventually doubles, but real GNP, the interest rate, and all relative prices return to their long-run or full-employment levels.

Why is a money supply change just like a currency reform in its effects on the economy's long-run equilibrium? The full-employment output level is determined by the

---

[6]The preceding statement refers only to changes in the *level* of the nominal money supply and not, for example, to changes in the *rate* at which the money supply is growing over time. The proposition that a one-time change in the level of the money supply has no effects on the long-run values of real economic variables is often called the *long-run neutrality of money*. In contrast, changes in the money supply growth rate need not be neutral in the long run. At the very least, a sustained change in the monetary growth rate will eventually affect equilibrium real money balances by raising the money interest rate (as discussed in the next chapter).

economy's endowments of labor and capital, so in the long run, real output does not depend on the money supply. Similarly, the interest rate is independent of the money supply in the long run. If the money supply and all prices double permanently, there is no reason why people previously willing to exchange $1 today for $1.10 a year from now should not be willing afterward to exchange $2 today for $2.20 a year from now, so the interest rate will remain at 10 percent per annum. Relative prices also remain the same if all money prices double, since relative prices are just ratios of money prices. Thus, money supply changes do not change the long-run allocation of resources. Only the absolute level of money prices changes.[7]

When studying the effect of an increase in the money supply over long time periods, we are therefore justified in assuming that the long-run values of R and Y will not be changed by a change in the supply of money. Thus, we can draw the following conclusion from equation (4-5): *A permanent increase in the money supply causes a proportional increase in the price level's long-run value. In particular, if the economy is initially at full employment, a permanent increase in the money supply eventually will be followed by a proportional increase in the price level.*

Empirical Evidence on Money Supplies and Price Levels

In looking at actual data on money and prices, we should not expect to see an exactly proportional relationship over long periods, partly because output, the interest rate, and the aggregate real money demand function can shift for reasons that have nothing to do with the supply of money. Output changes as a result of capital accumulation and technological advance (for example, more powerful computers), and money demand behavior may change as a result of demographic trends or financial innovations such as electronic cash-transfer facilities. In addition, actual economies are rarely in positions of long-run equilibrium. Nonetheless, we should expect the data to show a clear-cut positive association between money supplies and price levels. If real-world data did not provide strong evidence that money supplies and price levels move together in the long run, the usefulness of the theory of money demand we have developed would be in severe doubt.

The wide swings in Latin American rates of price level increase in recent decades make the region an ideal case study of the relationship between money supplies and price levels. Price level inflation had been high and variable in Latin America for more than a decade, when efforts at macroeconomic reform began to bring inflation lower by the mid-1990s.

On the basis of our theories, we would expect to find such sharp swings in inflation rates accompanied by swings in growth rates of money supplies. This expectation is confirmed by Figure 4-10, which plots annual average growth rates of the money supply against annual inflation rates over the two decades 1987–2007. On average, years with higher money growth also tend to be years with higher inflation. In addition, the data points cluster around the 45-degree line, along which money supplies and price levels increase in proportion.

---

[7]To understand more fully why a one-time change in the money supply does not change the long-run level of the interest rate, it may be useful to think of interest rates measured in terms of money as defining relative prices of currency units available on different dates. If the dollar interest rate is R percent per annum, giving up $1 today buys you $(1 + R)$ next year. Thus, $1/(1 + R)$ is the relative price of future dollars in terms of current dollars, and this relative price would not change if the real value of the monetary units were scaled up or down by the same factor on all dates.

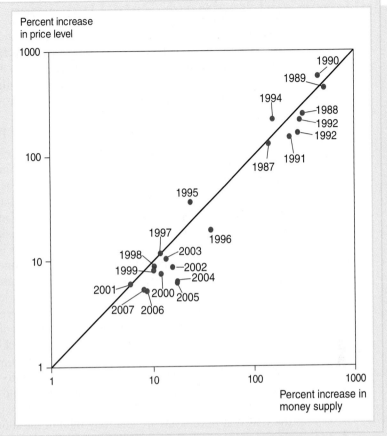

Source: IMF, *World Economic Outlook*, various issues. Regional aggregates are weighted by shares of dollar GDP in total regional dollar GDP.

FIGURE 4-10

Average Money Growth and Inflation in Western Hemisphere Developing Countries, by Year, 1987–2007

Even year by year, there is a strong positive relation between average Latin American money supply growth and inflation. (Both axes have logarithmic scales.)

The main lesson to be drawn from Figure 4-10 is that the data confirm the strong long-run link between national money supplies and national price levels predicted by economic theory.

Money and the Exchange Rate in the Long Run

The domestic currency price of foreign currency is one of the many prices in the economy that rise in the long run after a permanent increase in the money supply. If you think again about the effects of a currency reform, you will see how the exchange rate moves in the long run. Suppose the U.S. government replaced every pair of "old" dollars with one "new" dollar. Then, if the dollar/euro exchange rate had been 1.20 *old* dollars per euro before the reform, it would change to 0.60 *new* dollars per euro immediately after the reform. In much the same way, a halving of the U.S. money supply would eventually lead the dollar to appreciate from an exchange rate of 1.20 dollars/euro to one of 0.60 dollars/euro. Since the dollar prices of all U.S. goods and services would also decrease by half, this 50 percent appreciation of the dollar leaves the *relative* prices of all U.S. and foreign goods and services unchanged.

We conclude that, all else equal, *a permanent increase in a country's money supply causes a proportional long-run depreciation of its currency against foreign currencies. Similarly, a permanent decrease in a country's money supply causes a proportional long-run appreciation of its currency against foreign currencies.*

Inflation and Exchange Rate Dynamics

In this section, we tie together our short- and long-run findings about the effects of monetary changes by examining the process through which the price level adjusts to its long-run position. An economy experiences **inflation** when its price level is rising and **deflation** when its price level is falling. Our examination of inflation will give us a deeper understanding of how the exchange rate adjusts to monetary disturbances in the economy.

Short-Run Price Rigidity versus Long-Run Price Flexibility

Our analysis of the short-run effects of monetary changes assumed that a country's price level, unlike its exchange rate, does not jump immediately. This assumption cannot be exactly correct because many commodities, such as agricultural products, are traded in markets where prices adjust sharply every day as supply or demand conditions shift. In addition, exchange rate changes themselves may affect the prices of some tradable goods and services that enter into the commodity basket defining the price level.

Many prices in the economy, however, are written into long-term contracts and cannot be changed immediately when changes in the money supply occur. The most important prices of this type are workers' wages, which are negotiated only periodically in many industries. Wages do not enter indices of the price level directly, but they make up a large fraction of the cost of producing goods and services. Since output prices depend heavily on production costs, the behavior of the overall price level is influenced by the sluggishness of wage movements. The short-run "stickiness" of price levels is illustrated by Figure 4-11, which compares data on month-to-month percentage changes in the dollar/yen exchange rate, $E_{\$/\yen}$, with data on month-to-month percentage changes in the ratio of money price levels in the United States and Japan, P_{US}/P_J. As you can see, the exchange rate is much more variable than relative price levels, a fact consistent with the view that price levels are relatively rigid in the short run. The pattern shown in the figure applies to all of the main industrial countries in recent decades. In light of this and other evidence, we will therefore continue to assume the price level is given in the short run and does not make significant jumps in response to policy changes.

This assumption would not be reasonable, however, for all countries at all times. In extremely inflationary conditions, such as those seen in the 1980s in some Latin American countries, long-term contracts specifying domestic money payments may go out of use. Automatic price level indexation of wage payments may also be widespread under highly inflationary conditions. Such developments make the price level much less rigid than it would be under moderate inflation, and large price level jumps become possible. Some price rigidity can remain, however, even in the face of inflation rates that would be high by everyday industrial-country standards. For example, Turkey's 30 percent inflation rate for 2002 seems high until it is compared with the 114 percent depreciation of the Turkish lira against the U.S. dollar over the same year.

Our analysis assuming short-run price rigidity is nonetheless most applicable to countries with histories of comparative price level stability, such as the United States. Even in the cases of low-inflation countries, there is a lively academic debate over the possibility that seemingly sticky wages and prices are in reality quite flexible.[8]

---

[8]For a discussion of this debate and empirical evidence that U.S. aggregate prices and wages show significant rigidity, see the book by Hall and Papell listed in Further Readings. Other summaries of U.S. evidence are given by Mark A. Wynne, "Sticky Prices: What Is the Evidence?" *Federal Reserve Bank of Dallas Economic Review* (First Quarter 1995), pp. 1–12; and by Peter J. Klenow and Benjamin A. Malin, "Microeconomic Evidence on Price Setting,"in Benjamin M. Friedman and Michael Woodford, eds., *Handbook of Monetary Economics*, Vol. 3 (Amsterdam: Elsevier, 2010).

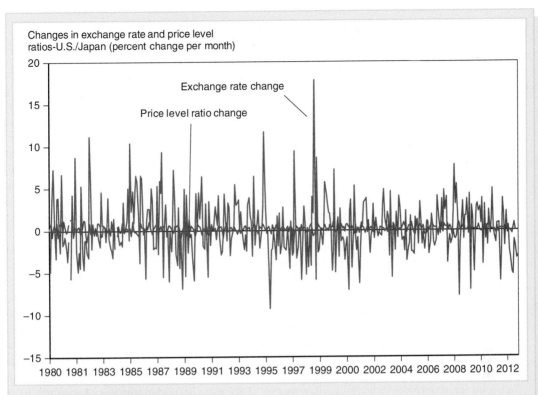

Changes in exchange rate and price level
ratios-U.S./Japan (percent change per month)

FIGURE 4-11   MyEconLab Real-time data

Month-to-Month Variability of the Dollar/Yen Exchange Rate and of the U.S./Japan Price Level Ratio, 1980–2013

The much greater month-to-month variability of the exchange rate suggests that price levels are relatively sticky in the short run.

Source: Price levels from International Monetary Fund, *International Financial Statistics*. Exchange rate from Global Financial Data.

Although the price level appears to display short-run stickiness in many countries, a change in the money supply creates immediate demand and cost pressures that eventually lead to *future* increases in the price level. These pressures come from three main sources:

1. *Excess demand for output and labor.* An increase in the money supply has an expansionary effect on the economy, raising the total demand for goods and services. To meet this demand, producers of goods and services must employ workers overtime and make new hires. Even if wages are given in the short run, the additional demand for labor allows workers to ask for higher wages in the next round of wage negotiations. Producers are willing to pay these higher wages, for they know that in a booming economy, it will not be hard to pass higher wage costs on to consumers through higher product prices.

2. *Inflationary expectations.* If everyone expects the price level to rise in the future, their expectation will increase the pace of inflation today. Workers bargaining over wage contracts will insist on higher money wages to counteract the effect on their real wages of the anticipated general increase in prices. Producers, once

MONEY SUPPLY GROWTH AND HYPERINFLATION IN ZIMBABWE

Since the French Revolution, there have been thirty recorded episodes of *hyperinflation*: an explosive and seemingly uncontrollable inflation in which money loses value rapidly and may even go out of use. All hyperinflations have been driven by massive money-supply growth, starting with the French revolutionary government's issuance of a paper currency, called *assignats*, to pay for its spending needs.

The lone episode of hyperinflation in the 21st century, but one of the most extreme ever, occurred in the African nation of Zimbabwe between 2007 and 2009. During hyperinflations, the magnitudes of monetary changes are so enormous that the "long-run" effects of money on the price level can occur very quickly. These episodes therefore provide laboratory conditions well suited for testing long-run theories about the effects of money supplies on prices.*

Like other hyperinflations, Zimbabwe's was fueled by the government's need to cover its expenses by printing money. These expenses included a four-year war in the Congo that began in 1998 and large-scale support of agriculture, all at a time when foreigners were withdrawing loans, investment, and aid because of domestic political turbulence. Inflation was the result, and the currency's exchange rate, while officially controlled by the government, depreciated rapidly in a parallel black market where market forces prevailed. On April 1, 2006, the government carried out a currency reform, creating a new Zimbabwean dollar (Z$) equivalent to 1,000 old ones.

In 2007, high inflation crossed the line into hyperinflation, as illustrated in the accompanying figure. The monthly inflation rate surpassed 50 percent in March 2007 and generally rose from there. On July 1, 2008, the government issued a Z$100 billion note—at the time, roughly equal to the price of three eggs—and the following month carried out a further currency reform with each *new* new Z$ equivalent to 10 billion *old* new dollars. But the situation only worsened. According to the official CPI statistics of the Reserve Bank of Zimbabwe (RBZ), the central bank, the price level rose by a factor of 36,661,304.13 between January 2007 and July 2008 (when the bank stopped reporting price data). The RBZ's numbers may be underestimates. According to one report, the rate of inflation for the month of October 2008 alone exceeded 33,000,000 percent![†] Yet another currency reform, on February 3, 2009, created the fourth Z$, equivalent to 1 trillion of the former currency units.

By early 2009, however, the hyperinflation was coming to an end on its own because people

---

*In a classic paper, the late Columbia University economist Phillip Cagan drew the line between inflation and hyperinflation at an inflation rate of 50 percent per month (which, through the power of compounding, comes out to 12,875 percent per year). See "The Monetary Dynamics of Hyperinflation," in Milton Friedman, ed., *Studies in the Quantity Theory of Money* (Chicago: University of Chicago Press, 1956), pp. 25–117. Such eighteenth-century data as are available indicate that the French Revolution episode (1789–1796) reached a peak monthly inflation rate of more than 143 percent.
[†]See Tara McIndoe-Calder, "Hyperinflation in Zimbabwe," unpublished manuscript, Central Bank of Ireland, March 2011.

---

again, will give in to these wage demands if they expect product prices to rise and cover the additional wage costs.

3. *Raw materials prices.* Many raw materials used in the production of final goods, for example, petroleum products and metals, are sold in markets where prices adjust sharply even in the short run. By causing the prices of such materials to jump upward, a money supply increase raises production costs in materials-using industries. Eventually, producers in those industries will raise product prices to cover their higher costs.

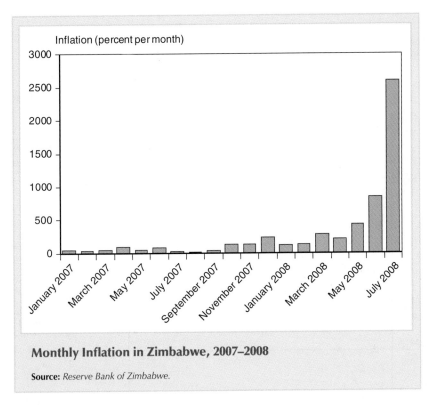

Monthly Inflation in Zimbabwe, 2007–2008

Source: *Reserve Bank of Zimbabwe.*

were avoiding the unstable Z$ and instead relying on foreign currencies such as the U.S. dollar, the South African rand, and the pula of Botswana. A new coalition government legalized foreign currency use, suspended the legal tender status of the Z$, and announced that it would conduct all of its own transactions in U.S. dollars. Importantly, the government (which could no longer print money) adopted a "cash budgeting" rule, allowing itself to spend only the money it brings in through taxes. Because the Z$ quickly went out of use, the RBZ gave up reporting its exchange

rate after November 6, 2009. Inflation (now measured in U.S. dollar terms) dropped dramatically in 2009. Although several currencies continue to circulate side by side, the U.S. dollar is by far dominant. In effect, the U.S. Federal Reserve now determines monetary conditions in Zimbabwe.

Zimbabwe still suffers from numerous economic problems, many of them stemming from its years of extreme macroeconomic instability, but inflation is not one of them. Recent inflation has remained low, under 5 percent per year since 2010.**

**For more detailed accounts, see Janet Koech, "Hyperinflation in Zimbabwe," in *Globalization and Monetary Policy Institute 2011 Annual Report,* Federal Reserve Bank of Dallas, pp. 2–12; and Joseph Noko, "Dollarization: The Case of Zimbabwe," *Cato Journal* 31 (Spring/Summer 2011), pp. 339–365.

Permanent Money Supply Changes and the Exchange Rate

We now apply our analysis of inflation to study the adjustment of the dollar/euro exchange rate following a *permanent* increase in the U.S. money supply. Figure 4-12 shows both the short-run (Figure 4-12a) and the long-run (Figure 4-12b) effects of this disturbance. We suppose the economy starts with all variables at their long-run

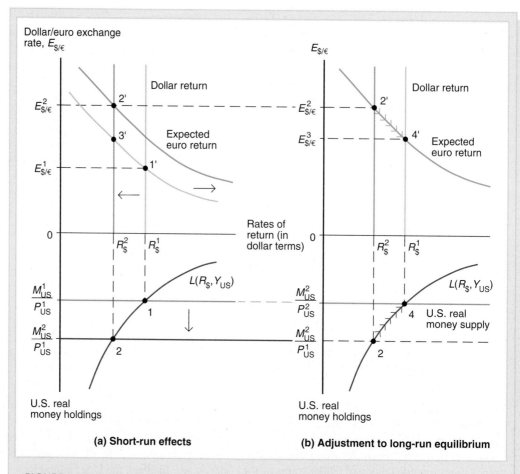

FIGURE 4-12

Short-Run and Long-Run Effects of an Increase in the U.S. Money Supply (Given Real Output, Y)

(a) Short-run adjustment of the asset markets. (b) How the interest rate, price level, and exchange rate move over time as the economy approaches its long-run equilibrium.

levels and that output remains constant as the economy adjusts to the money supply change.

Figure 4-12a assumes the U.S. price level is initially given at P_{US}^1. An increase in the nominal money supply from M_{US}^1 to M_{US}^2 therefore raises the real money supply from M_{US}^1/P_{US}^1 to M_{US}^2/P_{US}^1 in the short run, lowering the interest rate from $R_\$^1$ (point 1) to $R_\$^2$ (point 2). So far, our analysis proceeds exactly as it did earlier in this chapter.

The first change in our analysis comes when we ask how the American money supply change (shown in the bottom part of panel (a)) affects the foreign exchange market (shown in the top part of panel (a)). As before, the fall in the U.S. interest rate is shown as a leftward shift in the vertical schedule giving the dollar return on dollar deposits. This is no longer the whole story, however, for the money supply increase now affects *exchange rate expectations*. Because the U.S. money supply change is permanent, people expect a long-run increase in all dollar prices, including the exchange rate, which is the dollar price of euros. As you know will recall from Chapter 3, a rise in the expected future dollar/euro exchange rate (a future dollar depreciation) raises the expected dollar return on euro deposits; it thus shifts the downward-sloping schedule in the top part of Figure 4-12a to the right. The dollar depreciates against the euro, moving from an exchange rate of $E^1_{\$/€}$ (point 1′) to $E^2_{\$/€}$ (point 2′). Notice that the dollar depreciation is *greater* than it would be if the expected future dollar/euro exchange rate stayed fixed (as it might if the money supply increase were temporary rather than permanent). If the expectation $E^e_{\$/€}$ did not change, the new short-run equilibrium would be at point 3′ rather than at point 3′.

Figure 4-12b shows how the interest rate and exchange rate behave as the price level rises during the economy's adjustment to its long-run equilibrium. The price level begins to rise from the initially given level P^1_{US}, eventually reaching P^2_{US}. Because the long-run increase in the price level must be proportional to the increase in the money supply, the final *real* money supply, M^1_{US}/P^2_{US}, is shown equal to the initial real money supply, M^1_{US}/P^1_{US}. Since output is given and the real money supply has returned to its original level, the equilibrium interest rate must again equal $R^1_\$$ in the long run (point 4). The interest rate therefore rises from $R^2_\$$ (point 2) to $R^1_\$$ (point 4) as the price level rises from P^1_{US} to P^2_{US}.

The rising U.S. interest rate has exchange rate effects that can also be seen in Figure 4-12b: The dollar *appreciates* against the euro in the process of adjustment. If exchange rate expectations do not change further during the adjustment process, the foreign exchange market moves to its long-run position along the downward-sloping schedule defining the dollar return on euro deposits. The market's path is just the path traced out by the vertical dollar interest rate schedule as it moves rightward because of the price level's gradual rise. In the long run (point 4′), the equilibrium exchange rate, $E^3_{\$/€}$, is higher than at the original equilibrium, point 1′. Like the price level, the dollar/euro exchange rate has risen in proportion to the increase in the money supply.

Figure 4-13 shows time paths like the ones just described for the U.S. money supply, the dollar interest rate, the U.S. price level, and the dollar/euro exchange rate. The figure is drawn so that the long-run increases in the price level (Figure 4-13c) and exchange rate (Figure 4-13d) are proportional to the increase in the money supply (Figure 4-13a).

Exchange Rate Overshooting

In its initial depreciation after a money supply rise, the exchange rate jumps from $E^1_{\$/€}$ up to $E^2_{\$/€}$, a depreciation greater than its *long-run* depreciation from $E^1_{\$/€}$ to $E^3_{\$/€}$ (see Figure 4-13d). The exchange rate is said to overshoot when its immediate response to a disturbance is greater than its long-run response. **Exchange rate overshooting** is an important phenomenon because it helps explain why exchange rates move so sharply from day to day.

The economic explanation of overshooting comes from the interest parity condition. The explanation is easiest to grasp if we assume that before the money supply increase first occurs, no change in the dollar/euro exchange rate is expected, so that $R^1_\$$ equals $R_€$, the given interest rate on euro deposits. A permanent increase in the U.S.

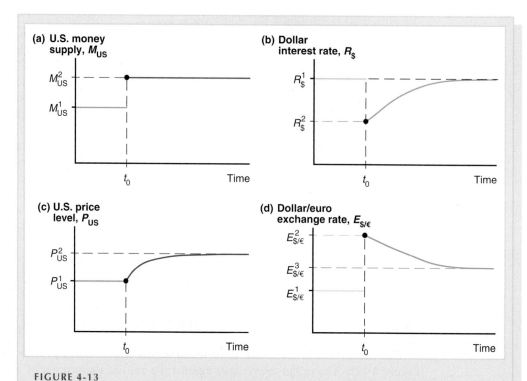

FIGURE 4-13

Time Paths of U.S. Economic Variables after a Permanent Increase in the U.S. Money Supply

After the money supply increases at t_0 in panel (a), the interest rate (in panel (b)), price level (in panel (c)), and exchange rate (in panel (d)) move as shown toward their long-run levels. As indicated in panel (d) by the initial jump from $E^1_{\$/€}$ to $E^2_{\$/€}$, the exchange rate overshoots in the short run before settling down to its long-run level, $E^3_{\$/€}$.

money supply doesn't affect $R_€$, so it causes $R^1_\$$ to fall below $R_€$ and remain below that interest rate (Figure 4-13b) until the U.S. price level has completed the long-run adjustment to P^2_{US} shown in Figure 4-13c. For the foreign exchange market to be in equilibrium during this adjustment process, however, the interest difference in favor of euro deposits must be offset by an expected *appreciation* of the dollar against the euro, that is, by an expected fall in $E_{\$/€}$. Only if the dollar/euro exchange rate overshoots $E^3_{\$/€}$ initially will market participants expect a subsequent appreciation of the dollar against the euro.

Overshooting is a direct consequence of the short-run rigidity of the price level. In a hypothetical world where the price level could adjust immediately to its new, long-run level after a money supply increase, the dollar interest rate would not fall because prices *would* adjust immediately and prevent the real money supply from rising. Thus, there would be no need for overshooting to maintain equilibrium in the foreign exchange market. The exchange rate would maintain equilibrium simply by jumping to its new, long-run level right away.

CASE STUDY   Can Higher Inflation Lead to Currency *Appreciation*? The Implications of Inflation Targeting

In the overshooting model we have just examined, an increase in the money supply leads to higher inflation and currency depreciation, as shown in Figure 4–13. It may seem puzzling, then, that readers of the financial press often see headlines such as the following one from the *Financial Times* of May 24, 2007: "Inflation Drives Canadian Dollar Higher." In light of the seemingly reasonable model set out in this chapter, can such statements possibly make sense?

A clue comes from reading further in the *Financial Times* news story on Canadian inflation. According to the *FT*:

> [A]nalysts said that the main driver of the recent bout of Canadian dollar appreciation was higher-than-expected April inflation data, which saw the bond market fully price in a 25 basis point rise in Canadian interest rates by the end of the year.

If central banks act to raise interest rates when inflation rises, then because higher interest rates cause currency appreciation, it might be possible to resolve the apparent contradiction to our model. To do so fully, however, we must consider two aspects of the way in which modern central banks actually formulate and implement monetary policy.

    1. *The interest rate, not the money supply, is the prime instrument of monetary policy.* Nowadays, most central banks do not actually target the money supply in order to control inflation. They instead target a benchmark short-term rate of interest (such as the overnight "federal funds" rate in the United States). How does our discussion of money market equilibrium help us to understand this process? Consider Figure 4-3, and assume that the central bank wishes to set an interest rate of R^1. It can do so simply by agreeing to provide or take up all of the cash that the market wishes to trade at that rate of interest. If the money supply is initially Q^2, for example, there will be an excess demand for money at the interest rate R^1, so people will sell bonds to the central bank for money (in effect, borrowing) until the money supply has expanded to Q^1 and the excess demand is gone. Central banks tend to set an interest rate, rather than the money supply, because the money demand schedule $L(R, Y)$ shifts around unpredictably in practice. If the central bank were to fix the money supply, the result would be high and possibly damaging interest rate volatility; it is thus more practical to fix the interest rate and let the money supply adjust automatically when necessary.[9]

---

[9]For a nontechnical account of modern central bank policy implementation, see Michael Woodford, "Monetary Policy in a World without Money," *International Finance* 3 (July 2000), pp. 229–260. Woodford's provocative title points to another advantage of the interest rate instrument for central banks: It is possible to conduct monetary policy even if checking deposits pay interest at competitive rates. For many purposes, however, it is reasonable to ignore the variability of the $L(R, Y)$ schedule and simply assume that the central bank directly sets the money supply. In the rest of the book we shall, for the most part, make that simplifying assumption. The major exception will be when we introduce fixed exchange rates in Chapter 7. For a simple reformulation of the theory of monetary policy in terms of an interest rate rather than money supply instrument, see the paper by David Romer in this chapter's Further Readings.

Our preceding discussion of the positive relationship between the money supply and price level will tip you off, however, to one potential problem of an interest rate instrument. If the money supply is free to grow or shrink as markets collectively desire, how can the price level and inflation be kept under control? For example, if market actors doubt the central bank's resolve to control inflation, and suddenly push the price level up because they expect higher prices in the future, they could simply borrow more money from the central bank, thereby bringing about the money supply increase needed to sustain higher prices in the long run. This worrisome possibility brings us to the second pillar of modern monetary policy.

2. *Most central banks adjust their policy interest rates expressly so as to keep inflation in check.* A central bank can keep inflation from getting too high or too low by raising the interest rate when it learns that inflation is running higher than expected, and lowering it when inflation is running lower. As we will see more fully in Chapter 6, a rise in the interest rate, which causes the currency to appreciate, dampens the demand for a country's products by making them more expensive compared to foreign goods. This fall in demand, in turn, promotes lower domestic prices. A fall in the interest rate, symmetrically, supports domestic prices. Indeed, many central banks now follow formal strategies of *inflation targeting*, under which they announce a target (or target range) for the inflation rate and adjust the interest rate to keep inflation on target. Some central banks target so-called *core* inflation, which is inflation in the price level excluding volatile components such as energy prices, rather than *headline* inflation, which is inflation in the total consumer price index. The formal practice of inflation targeting was initiated by New Zealand's central bank in 1990, and the central banks of many other developed and developing areas, including Canada, Chile, Mexico, South Africa, Sweden, Thailand, the United Kingdom, and the euro zone, have followed suit.[10]

We can now understand the "paradox" of higher-than-expected inflation causing currency appreciation rather than depreciation. Suppose market participants unexpectedly push up prices and borrow to enlarge the money supply. Thus, when the Canadian government releases new price data, the data show a price level higher than what market participants had previously predicted. If the Bank of Canada is expected to raise interest rates quickly so as to push the price level and money supply back on course, there is no reason for the future expected exchange rate to change. But with higher Canadian interest rates, interest parity requires an expected future *depreciation* of the Canadian dollar, which is consistent with an unchanged future exchange rate only if the Canadian dollar *appreciates* immediately. The picture of the economy's adjustment after the unexpected increase in money and prices

---

[10]On inflation-targeting practices and the theory behind them, see the books by Bernanke et al., and by Truman in Further Readings. For a critique of the idea of targeting core rather than headline inflation, see Stephen Cecchetti, "Core Inflation Is an Unreliable Guide," *Financial Times*, September 12, 2006.

would look like Figure 4–13 in reverse (that is, constructed to reflect a monetary contraction rather than an expansion)—with the added assumption that the Bank of Canada gradually moves interest rates back to their initial level as the price level returns to its targeted path.[11]

Economists Richard Clarida of Columbia University and Daniel Waldman of Barclays Capital offer striking statistical evidence consistent with this explanation.[12] These writers measure unexpected inflation as the inflation rate estimate initially announced by a government, prior to any data revisions, less the median of inflation forecasts for that period previously published by a set of banking industry analysts. For a sample of ten countries—Australia, Britain, Canada, the euro area, Japan, New Zealand, Norway, Sweden, Switzerland, and the United States—Clarida and Waldman examine the exchange rate changes that occur in the period lasting from five minutes prior to an inflation announcement to five minutes afterward. Their key findings are these:

1. On average for the ten currencies that they study, news that inflation is unexpectedly high does indeed lead a currency to appreciate, not depreciate.
2. The effect is stronger for core than for headline inflation.
3. The effect is much stronger for the inflation-targeting countries than for the United States and Japan, the two countries that did not announce inflation targets. In the case of Canada, for example, the announcement of an annual core inflation rate that is 1 percent per year above the market expectation leads the Canadian dollar to appreciate immediately by about 3 percent against the U.S. dollar. The corresponding effect for the U.S. dollar/euro exchange rate, while in the same direction, is only about one-quarter as big.
4. For countries where sufficiently long data series are available, the strengthening effect of unexpected inflation on the currency is present after the introduction of inflation targeting, but not before.

Scientific theories can be conclusively disproved, of course, but never conclusively proved. So far, however, the theory that strict inflation targeting makes bad news on inflation good news for the currency looks quite persuasive.

---

[11]Strictly speaking, the narrative in the text describes a setting with price level rather than inflation rate targeting. (Can you see the difference?) The reasoning in the case of inflation targeting is nearly identical, however, provided that the central bank's interest rate response to unexpectedly high inflation is sufficiently strong.

[12]See Clarida and Waldman, "Is Bad News About Inflation Good News for the Exchange Rate? And If So, Can That Tell Us Anything about the Conduct of Monetary Policy?" in John Y. Campbell, ed., *Asset Prices and Monetary Policy* (Chicago: University of Chicago Press, 2008). Michael W. Klein of Tufts University and Linda S. Goldberg of the Federal Reserve Bank of New York used a related approach to investigate changing market perceptions of the European Central Bank's inflation aversion after its launch in 1999. See "Evolving Perceptions of Central Bank Credibility: The European Central Bank Experience," *NBER International Seminar on Macroeconomics* 33 (2010), pp. 153–182.

SUMMARY

1. Money is held because of its liquidity. When considered in real terms, *aggregate money demand* is not a demand for a certain number of currency units but is instead a demand for a certain amount of purchasing power. Aggregate real money demand depends negatively on the opportunity cost of holding money (measured by the domestic interest rate) and positively on the volume of transactions in the economy (measured by real GNP).

2. The money market is in equilibrium when the real *money supply* equals aggregate real money demand. With the *price level* and real output given, a rise in the money supply lowers the interest rate and a fall in the money supply raises the interest rate. A rise in real output raises the interest rate, given the price level, while a fall in real output has the opposite effect.

3. By lowering the domestic interest rate, an increase in the money supply causes the domestic currency to depreciate in the foreign exchange market (even when expectations of future exchange rates do not change). Similarly, a fall in the domestic money supply causes the domestic currency to appreciate against foreign currencies.

4. The assumption that the price level is given in the *short run* is a good approximation to reality in countries with moderate *inflation*, but it is a misleading assumption over the *long run*. Permanent changes in the money supply push the *long-run equilibrium* price level proportionally in the same direction but do not influence the long-run values of output, the interest rate, or any relative prices. One important money price whose long-run equilibrium level rises in proportion to a permanent money supply increase is the exchange rate, the domestic currency price of foreign currency.

5. An increase in the money supply can cause the exchange rate to overshoot its long-run level in the short run. If output is given, a permanent money supply increase, for example, causes a more-than-proportional short-run depreciation of the currency, followed by an appreciation of the currency to its long-run exchange rate. *Exchange rate overshooting*, which heightens the volatility of exchange rates, is a direct result of sluggish short-run price level adjustment and the interest parity condition.

KEY TERMS

aggregate money demand, p. 81
deflation, p. 96
exchange rate overshooting,
    p. 101

inflation, p. 96
long run, p. 87
long-run equilibrium,
    p. 92

money supply, p. 79
price level, p. 81
short run, p. 87

PROBLEMS

MyEconLab

1. Suppose there is a reduction in aggregate real money demand, that is, a negative shift in the aggregate real money demand function. Trace the short- and long-run effects on the exchange rate, interest rate, and price level.

2. How would you expect a fall in a country's population to alter its aggregate money demand function? Would it matter if the fall in population were due to a fall in the number of households or to a fall in the size of the average household?

3. The velocity of money, V, is defined as the ratio of real GNP to real money holdings, $V = Y/(M/P)$ in this chapter's notation. Use equation (4-4) to derive an

expression for velocity and explain how velocity varies with changes in R and in Y. (Hint: The effect of output changes on V depends on the elasticity of aggregate money demand with respect to real output, which economists believe to be less than unity.) What is the relationship between velocity and the exchange rate?

4. What is the short-run effect on the exchange rate of an increase in domestic real GNP, given expectations about future exchange rates?

5. Does our discussion of money's usefulness as a medium of exchange and unit of account suggest reasons why some currencies become vehicle currencies for foreign exchange transactions? (The concept of a vehicle currency was discussed in Chapter 3.)

6. If a currency reform has no effects on the economy's real variables, why do governments typically institute currency reforms in connection with broader programs aimed at halting runaway inflation? (There are many instances in addition to the Turkish case mentioned in the text. Other examples include Israel's switch from the pound to the shekel, Argentina's switches from the peso to the austral and back to the peso, and Brazil's switches from the cruzeiro to the cruzado, from the cruzado to the cruzeiro, from the cruzeiro to the cruzeiro real, and from the cruzeiro real to the real, the current currency, which was introduced in 1994.)

7. In 1984 and 1985, the small Latin American country of Bolivia experienced hyperinflation. Below are some key macroeconomic data from those years:

Macroeconomic Data for Bolivia, April 1984–October 1985

Month	Money Supply (Billions of Pesos)	Price Level (Relative to 1982 Average = 1	Exchange Rate (Pesos per Dollar)
1984			
April	270	21.1	3,576
May	330	31.1	3,512
June	440	32.3	3,342
July	599	34.0	3,570
August	718	39.1	7,038
September	889	53.7	13,685
October	1,194	85.5	15,205
November	1,495	112.4	18,469
December	3,296	180.9	24,515
1985			
January	4,630	305.3	73,016
February	6,455	863.3	141,101
March	9,089	1,078.6	128,137
April	12,885	1,205.7	167,428
May	21,309	1,635.7	272,375
June	27,778	2,919.1	481,756
July	47,341	4,854.6	885,476
August	74,306	8,081.0	1,182,300
September	103,272	12,647.6	1,087,440
October	132,550	12,411.8	1,120,210

Source: Juan-Antonio Morales, "Inflation Stabilization in Bolivia," in Michael Bruno et al., eds., *Inflation Stabilization: The Experience of Argentina, Brazil, Bolivia, and Mexico*. Cambridge, MA: MIT Press, 1988, table 7A-1. Money supply is M1.

a. Do the money supply, price level, and exchange rate against the U.S. dollar move broadly as you would expect? Explain.

b. Calculate the percent changes in the general price level and price of the dollar between April 1984 and July 1985. How do these compare to each other and to the percent increase in the money supply? Can you explain the results? (Hint: Refer back to the discussion of the *velocity* of money in question 3.)

c. The Bolivian government introduced a dramatic stabilization plan near the end of August 1985. Looking at the price levels and exchange rates for the following two months, do you think it was successful? In light of your answer, explain why the money supply increased by a large amount between September and October 1985.

8. Below is a table of some inflation targeting countries and the years in which they adopted the practice:

Country	Year of adoption
New Zealand	1990
Chile	1991
Canada	1991
Israel	1991
Sweden	1993
Finland	1993
Australia	1994
Brazil	1999
Mexico	1999
South Africa	2000
Indonesia	2005

Go to the International Monetary Fund's most recent *World Economic Outlook* database (accessible directly or through www.imf.org) and collect the annual inflation rate series PCPIEPCH for these countries, starting in 1980. Then graph the data for each country using Excel or some other data analysis package. Just looking at the data, does inflation appear to behave differently after the adoption of inflation targeting?

9. In our discussion of short-run exchange rate overshooting, we assumed real output was given. Assume instead that an increase in the money supply raises real output in the short run (an assumption that will be justified in Chapter 6). How does this affect the extent to which the exchange rate overshoots when the money supply first increases? Is it likely that the exchange rate undershoots? (Hint: In Figure 4-12a, allow the aggregate real money demand schedule to shift in response to the increase in output.)

10. Figure 14-2 shows that Japan's short-term interest rates have had periods during which they are near or equal to zero. Is the fact that the yen interest rates shown never drop below zero a coincidence, or can you think of some reason why interest rates might be bounded below by zero?

11. How might a zero interest rate complicate the task of monetary policy? (Hint: At a zero rate of interest, there is no advantage in switching from money to bonds.)

12. As we observed in this chapter, central banks, rather than purposefully setting the level of the money supply, usually set a target level for a short-term interest rate by standing ready to lend or borrow whatever money people wish to trade at that interest rate. (When people need more money for a reason other than a change in the interest rate, the money supply therefore expands, and it contracts when they wish to hold less.)

   a. Describe the problems that might arise if a central bank sets monetary policy by holding the market interest rate constant. (First, consider the flexible-price case, and ask yourself if you can find a unique equilibrium price level when the central bank simply gives people all the money they wish to hold at the pegged interest rate. Then consider the sticky-price case.)

   b. Does the situation change if the central bank raises the interest rate when prices are high, according to a formula such as $R - R_0 = a(P - P_0)$, where a is a positive constant and P_0 a target price level?

   c. Suppose the central bank's policy rule is $R - R_0 = a(P - P_0) + u$, where u is a random movement in the policy interest rate. In the overshooting model shown in Figure 4-13, describe how the economy would adjust to a permanent one-time unexpected fall in the random factor u, and say why. You can interpret the fall in u as an interest rate cut by the central bank, and therefore as an expansionary monetary action. Compare your story with the one depicted in Figure 4-13.

13. Since 1942, the small country of Panama has had no paper currency other than the United States dollar, which circulates freely internally. What would you expect to be true about the inflation rate in Panama compared to that in the United States, and why? Go to the International Monetary Fund's most recent *World Economic Outlook* database (accessible directly or through www.imf.org) and examine comparable consumer-price inflation rates for Panama and the United States? Do the inflation rates you see there conform to your earlier prediction? (After you have read Chapters 5 and 7, you should return to this question as you will then have a deeper understanding of the factors that determine the price level in a country like Panama.)

FURTHER READINGS

Ben S. Bernanke, Thomas Laubach, Frederic S. Mishkin, and Adam S. Posen. *Inflation Targeting: Lessons from the International Experience.* Princeton, NJ: Princeton University Press, 1999. Discusses recent monetary policy experience and the consequences for inflation and other macroeconomic variables.

Rudiger Dornbusch. "Expectations and Exchange Rate Dynamics." *Journal of Political Economy* 84 (December 1976), pp. 1161–1176. A theoretical analysis of exchange rate overshooting.

Jacob A. Frenkel and Michael L. Mussa. "The Efficiency of Foreign Exchange Markets and Measures of Turbulence." *American Economic Review* 70 (May 1980), pp. 374–381. Contrasts the behavior of national price levels with that of exchange rates and other asset prices.

Robert E. Hall and David H. Papell. *Macroeconomics: Economic Growth, Fluctuations, and Policy*, 6th edition. New York: W. W. Norton & Company, 2005. Chapter 15 discusses some theories of nominal price rigidity.

David Romer. "Keynesian Macroeconomics without the *LM* Curve." *Journal of Economic Perspectives* 14 (Spring 2000), pp. 149–169. A macroeconomic model in which the central bank implements monetary policy through the interest rate rather than the money supply.

Edwin M. Truman. *Inflation Targeting in the World Economy*. Washington, D.C.: Institute for International Economics, 2003. Overview of the international aspects of monetary policy frameworks that target low inflation.

MyEconLab Can Help You Get a Better Grade

MyEconLab   If your exam were tomorrow, would you be ready? For each chapter, MyEconLab Practice Tests and Study Plans pinpoint sections you have mastered and those you need to study. That way, you are more efficient with your study time, and you are better prepared for your exams.

To see how it works, turn to page 9 and then go to

www.myeconlab.com

PRICE LEVELS AND THE EXCHANGE RATE IN THE LONG RUN

At the end of 1970, you could have bought 358 Japanese yen with a single American dollar; by Christmas 1980, a dollar was worth only 203 yen. Despite a temporary comeback during the 1980s, the dollar's price in yen slumped to 100 by the summer of 2013. Many investors found these price changes difficult to predict, and as a result fortunes were lost—and made—in the foreign exchange market. What economic forces lie behind such dramatic long-term movements in exchange rates?

We have seen that exchange rates are determined by interest rates and expectations about the future, which are, in turn, influenced by conditions in national money markets. To understand fully long-term exchange rate movements, however, we have to extend our model in two directions. First, we must complete our account of the linkages among monetary policies, inflation, interest rates, and exchange rates. Second, we must examine factors other than money supplies and demands—for example, demand shifts in markets for goods and services—that also can have sustained effects on exchange rates.

The model of long-run exchange rate behavior that we develop in this chapter provides the framework that actors in asset markets use to forecast future exchange rates. Because the expectations of these agents influence exchange rates immediately, however, predictions about *long-run* movements in exchange rates are important *even in the short run*. We therefore will draw heavily on this chapter's conclusions when we begin our study in Chapter 6 of *short-run* interactions between exchange rates and output.

In the long run, national price levels play a key role in determining both interest rates and the relative prices at which countries' products are traded. A theory of how national price levels interact with exchange rates is thus central to understanding why exchange rates can change dramatically over periods of several years. We begin our analysis by discussing the theory of **purchasing power parity (PPP)**, which explains movements in the exchange rate between two countries' currencies by changes in the countries' price levels. Next, we examine reasons why PPP may fail to give accurate long-run predictions and show how the theory must sometimes be modified to account for supply or demand shifts in countries' output markets. Finally, we look at what our extended PPP theory predicts about how changes in money and output markets affect exchange and interest rates.

LEARNING GOALS

After reading this chapter, you will be able to:

- Explain the purchasing power parity theory of exchange rates and the theory's relationship to international goods-market integration.
- Describe how monetary factors such as ongoing price level inflation affect exchange rates in the long run.
- Discuss the concept of the real exchange rate.
- Understand factors that affect real exchange rates and relative currency prices in the long run.
- Explain the relationship between international real interest rate differences and expected changes in real exchange rates.

The Law of One Price

To understand the market forces that might give rise to the results predicted by the purchasing power parity theory, we discuss first a related but distinct proposition known as the **law of one price**. The law of one price states that in competitive markets free of transportation costs and official barriers to trade (such as tariffs), identical goods sold in different countries must sell for the same price when their prices are expressed in terms of the same currency. For example, if the dollar/pound exchange rate is $1.50 per pound, a sweater that sells for $45 in New York must sell for £30 in London. The dollar price of the sweater when sold in London is then ($1.50 per pound) × (£30 per sweater) = $45 per sweater, the same as its price in New York.

Let's continue with this example to see why the law of one price must hold when trade is free and there are no transport costs or other trade barriers. If the dollar/pound exchange rate were $1.45 per pound, you could buy a sweater in London by converting $43.50 (= $1.45 per pound × £30) into £30 in the foreign exchange market. Thus, the dollar price of a sweater in London would be only $43.50. If the same sweater were selling for $45 in New York, U.S. importers and British exporters would have an incentive to buy sweaters in London and ship them to New York, pushing the London price up and the New York price down until prices were equal in the two locations. Similarly, at an exchange rate of $1.55 per pound, the dollar price of sweaters in London would be $46.50 (= $1.55 per pound × £30), $1.50 more than in New York. Sweaters would be shipped from west to east until a single price prevailed in the two markets.

The law of one price is a restatement, in terms of currencies, of a principle that was important in the trade theory portion of this book: When trade is open and costless, identical goods must trade at the same relative prices regardless of where they are sold. We remind you of that principle here because it provides one link between the domestic prices of goods and exchange rates. We can state the law of one price formally as follows: Let P_{US}^i be the dollar price of good i when sold in the United States, P_E^i the corresponding euro price in Europe. Then the law of one price implies that the dollar price of good i is the same wherever it is sold.

$$P_{US}^i = (E_{\$/\euro}) \times (P_E^i).$$

Equivalently, the dollar/euro exchange rate is the ratio of good i's U.S. and European money prices,

$$E_{\$/€} = P_{US}^i / P_E^i.$$

Purchasing Power Parity

The theory of purchasing power parity states that the exchange rate between two countries' currencies equals the ratio of the countries' price levels. Recall from Chapter 4 that the domestic purchasing power of a country's currency is reflected in the country's price level, the money price of a reference basket of goods and services. The PPP theory therefore predicts that a fall in a currency's domestic purchasing power (as indicated by an increase in the domestic price level) will be associated with a proportional currency depreciation in the foreign exchange market. Symmetrically, PPP predicts that an increase in the currency's domestic purchasing power will be associated with a proportional currency appreciation.

The basic idea of PPP was put forth in the writings of 19th-century British economists, among them David Ricardo (the originator of the theory of comparative advantage). Gustav Cassel, a Swedish economist writing in the early 20th century, popularized PPP by making it the centerpiece of a theory of exchange rates. While there has been much controversy about the general validity of PPP, the theory does highlight important factors behind exchange rate movements.

To express the PPP theory in symbols, let P_{US} be the dollar price of a reference commodity basket sold in the United States and P_E the euro price of the same basket in Europe. (Assume for now that a single basket accurately measures money's purchasing power in both countries.) Then PPP predicts a dollar/euro exchange rate of

$$E_{\$/€} = P_{US}/P_E. \tag{5-1}$$

If, for example, the reference commodity basket costs $200 in the United States and €160 in Europe, PPP predicts a dollar/euro exchange rate of $1.25 per euro ($200 per basket/€160 per basket). If the U.S. price level were to triple (to $600 per basket), so would the dollar price of a euro: PPP would imply an exchange rate of $3.75 per euro (= $600 per basket/€160 per basket).

By rearranging equation (5-1) to read

$$P_{US} = (E_{\$/€}) \times (P_E),$$

we get an alternative interpretation of PPP. The left side of this equation is the dollar price of the reference commodity basket in the United States; the right side is the dollar price of the reference basket when purchased in Europe (that is, its euro price multiplied by the dollar price of a euro). These two prices are the same if PPP holds. PPP thus asserts that all countries' price levels are equal when measured in terms of the same currency.

Equivalently, the right side of the last equation measures the purchasing power of a dollar when exchanged for euros and spent in Europe. PPP therefore holds when, at going exchange rates, every currency's domestic purchasing power is always the same as its foreign purchasing power.

The Relationship between PPP and the Law of One Price

Superficially, the statement of PPP given by equation (5-1) looks like the law of one price, which says that $E_{\$/€} = P_{US}^i / P_E^i$ for any commodity i. There is a difference between PPP and the law of one price, however: The law of one price applies to individual commodities (such as commodity i), while PPP applies to the general price level, which is a composite of the prices of all the commodities that enter into the reference basket.

If the law of one price holds true for every commodity, of course, PPP must hold automatically as long as the reference baskets used to reckon different countries' price levels are the same. Proponents of the PPP theory argue, however, that its validity (in particular, its validity as a long-run theory) does not require the law of one price to hold exactly.

Even when the law of one price fails to hold for each individual commodity, the argument goes, prices and exchange rates should not stray too far from the relation predicted by PPP. When goods and services become temporarily more expensive in one country than in others, the demands for its currency and its products fall, pushing the exchange rate and domestic prices back in line with PPP. The opposite situation of relatively cheap domestic products leads, analogously, to currency appreciation and price level inflation. PPP thus asserts that even when the law of one price is not literally true, the economic forces behind it will help eventually to equalize a currency's purchasing power in all countries.

Absolute PPP and Relative PPP

The statement that exchange rates equal relative price levels (equation (5-1)) is sometimes referred to as **absolute PPP**. Absolute PPP implies a proposition known as **relative PPP**, which states that the percentage change in the exchange rate between two currencies over any period equals the difference between the percentage changes in national price levels. Relative PPP thus translates absolute PPP from a statement about price and exchange rate *levels* into one about price and exchange rate *changes*. It asserts that prices and exchange rates change in a way that preserves the ratio of each currency's domestic and foreign purchasing powers.

If the U.S. price level rises by 10 percent over a year while Europe's rises by only 5 percent, for example, relative PPP predicts a 5 percent depreciation of the dollar against the euro. The dollar's 5 percent depreciation against the euro just cancels the 5 percent by which U.S. inflation exceeds European inflation, leaving the relative domestic and foreign purchasing powers of both currencies unchanged.

More formally, relative PPP between the United States and Europe would be written as

$$(E_{\$/€,\,t} - E_{\$/€,\,t-1})/E_{\$/€,\,t-1} = \pi_{US,\,t} - \pi_{E,\,t} \tag{5-2}$$

where π_t denotes an inflation rate (that is, $\pi_t = (P_t - P_{t-1})/P_{t-1}$, the percentage change in a price level between dates t and $t - 1$).[1] Unlike absolute PPP, relative PPP can be defined only with respect to the time interval over which price levels and the exchange rate change.

In practice, national governments do not take pains to compute the price level indexes they publish using an internationally standardized basket of commodities.

---

[1]To be precise, equation (5-1) implies a good approximation to equation (5-2) when rates of change are not too large. The *exact* relationship is

$$E_{\$/€,\,t}/E_{\$/€,\,t-1} = (P_{US,\,t}/P_{US,\,t-1})/(P_{E,\,t}/P_{E,\,t-1}).$$

After subtracting 1 from both sides, we write the preceding exact equation as

$$
\begin{aligned}
(E_{\$/€,\,t} - E_{\$/€,\,t-1})/E_{\$/€,\,t-1} &= (\pi_{US,\,t} + 1)(P_{E,\,t-1}/P_{E,\,t}) - (P_{E,\,t}/P_{E,\,t}) \\
&= (\pi_{US,\,t} - \pi_{E,\,t})/(1 + \pi_{E,\,t}) \\
&= (\pi_{US,\,t} - \pi_{E,\,t}) - \pi_{E,\,t}(\pi_{US,\,t} - \pi_{E,\,t})/(1 + \pi_{E,\,t}).
\end{aligned}
$$

But if $\pi_{US,\,t}$ and $\pi_{E,\,t}$ are small, the term $-\pi_{E,\,t}(\pi_{US,\,t} - \pi_{E,\,t})/(1 + \pi_{E,\,t})$ in the last equality is negligibly small, implying a very good approximation to (5-2).

Absolute PPP makes no sense, however, unless the two baskets whose prices are compared in equation (5-1) are the same. (There is no reason to expect *different* commodity baskets to sell for the same price!) The notion of relative PPP therefore comes in handy when we have to rely on government price level statistics to evaluate PPP. It makes logical sense to compare percentage exchange rate changes to inflation differences, as above, even when countries base their price *level* estimates on product baskets that differ in coverage and composition.

Relative PPP is important also because it may be valid even when absolute PPP is not. Provided the factors causing deviations from absolute PPP are more or less stable over time, percentage *changes* in relative price levels can still approximate percentage *changes* in exchange rates.

A Long-Run Exchange Rate Model Based on PPP

When combined with the framework of money demand and supply that we developed in Chapter 4, the assumption of PPP leads to a useful theory of how exchange rates and monetary factors interact in the long run. Because factors that do not influence money supply or money demand play no explicit role in this theory, it is known as the **monetary approach to the exchange rate**. The monetary approach is this chapter's first step in developing a general long-run theory of exchange rates.

We think of the monetary approach as a *long-run* and not a short-run theory because it does not allow for the price rigidities that seem important in explaining short-run macroeconomic developments, in particular departures from full employment. Instead, the monetary approach proceeds as if prices can adjust right away to maintain full employment as well as PPP. Here, as in the previous chapter, when we refer to a variable's "long-run" value, we mean the variable's equilibrium value in a hypothetical world of perfectly flexible output and factor market prices.

There is actually considerable controversy among macroeconomists about the sources of apparent price level stickiness, with some maintaining that prices and wages only appear rigid and in reality adjust immediately to clear markets. To an economist of the aforementioned school, this chapter's models would describe the short-run behavior of an economy in which the speed of price level adjustment is so great that no significant unemployment ever occurs.

The Fundamental Equation of the Monetary Approach

To develop the monetary approach's predictions for the dollar/euro exchange rate, we will assume that in the long run, the foreign exchange market sets the rate so that PPP holds (see equation (5-1)):

$$E_{\$/€} = P_{US}/P_E.$$

In other words, we assume the above equation would hold in a world where there are no market rigidities to prevent the exchange rate and other prices from adjusting immediately to levels consistent with full employment.

In the previous chapter, equation (4-5) showed how we can explain domestic price levels in terms of domestic money demands and supplies. In the United States,

$$P_{US} = M_{US}^s/L(R_\$, Y_{US}), \tag{5-3}$$

while in Europe,

$$P_E = M_E^s/L(R_€, Y_E). \tag{5-4}$$

As before, we have used the symbol M^s to stand for a country's money supply and $L(R, Y)$ to stand for its aggregate real money demand, which decreases when the interest rate rises and increases when real output rises.[2]

Equations (5-3) and (5-4) show how the monetary approach to the exchange rate comes by its name. According to the statement of PPP in equation (5-1), the dollar price of a euro is simply the dollar price of U.S. output divided by the euro price of European output. These two price levels, in turn, are determined completely by the supply and demand for each currency area's money: The United States' price level is the U.S. money supply divided by U.S. real money demand, as shown in (5-3), and Europe's price level similarly is the European money supply divided by European real money demand, as shown in (5-4). The monetary approach therefore makes the general prediction that *the exchange rate, which is the relative price of American and European money, is fully determined in the long run by the relative supplies of those monies and the relative real demands for them.* Shifts in interest rates and output levels affect the exchange rate only through their influences on money demand.

In addition, the monetary approach makes a number of specific predictions about the long-run effects on the exchange rate of changes in money supplies, interest rates, and output levels:

1. *Money supplies.* Other things equal, a permanent rise in the U.S. money supply M^s_{US} causes a proportional increase in the long-run U.S. price level P_{US}, as equation (5-3) shows. Because under PPP $E_{\$/\euro} = P_{US}/P_E$, however, $E_{\$/\euro}$ also rises in the long run in proportion to the increase in the U.S. money supply. (For example, if M^s_{US} rises by 10 percent, P_{US} and $E_{\$/\euro}$ both eventually rise by 10 percent as well.) Thus, an increase in the U.S. money supply causes a proportional long-run *depreciation* of the dollar against the euro. Conversely, equation (5-4) shows that a permanent increase in the European money supply causes a proportional increase in the long-run European price level. Under PPP, this price level rise implies a proportional long-run *appreciation* of the dollar against the euro (which is the same as a proportional depreciation of the euro against the dollar).

2. *Interest rates.* A rise in the interest rate $R_\$$ on dollar-denominated assets lowers real U.S. money demand $L(R_\$, Y_{US})$. By (5-3), the long-run U.S. price level rises, and under PPP the dollar must depreciate against the euro in proportion to this U.S. price level increase. A rise in the interest rate $R_\euro$ on euro-denominated assets has the reverse long-run exchange rate effect. Because real European money demand $L(R_\euro, Y_E)$ falls, Europe's price level rises, by (5-4). Under PPP, the dollar must appreciate against the euro in proportion to Europe's price level increase.

3. *Output levels.* A rise in U.S. output raises real U.S. money demand $L(R_\$, Y_{US})$, leading by (5-3) to a fall in the long-run U.S. price level. According to PPP, there is an appreciation of the dollar against the euro. Symmetrically, a rise in European output raises $L(R_\euro, Y_E)$ and, by (5-4), causes a fall in Europe's long-run price level. PPP predicts that this development will make the dollar depreciate against the euro.

To understand these predictions, remember that the monetary approach, like any long-run theory, essentially assumes price levels adjust as quickly as exchange rates do—that is, right away. For example, a rise in real U.S. output raises the transactions demand for real U.S. money balances. According to the monetary approach, the U.S.

---

[2]To simplify the notation, we assume identical money demand functions for the United States and Europe.

price level drops *immediately* to bring about a market-clearing increase in the supply of real money balances. PPP implies that this instantaneous American price deflation is accompanied by an instantaneous dollar appreciation on the foreign exchanges.

The monetary approach leads to a result familiar from Chapter 4, that the long-run foreign exchange value of a country's currency moves in proportion to its money supply (prediction 1). The theory also raises what seems to be a paradox (prediction 2). In our previous examples, we always found that a currency *appreciates* when the interest rate it offers rises relative to foreign interest rates. How is it that we have now arrived at precisely the opposite conclusion—that a rise in a country's interest rate *depreciates* its currency by lowering the real demand for its money?

At the end of Chapter 3, we warned that no account of how a change in interest rates affects the exchange rate is complete until we specify *exactly why interest rates have changed*. This point explains the apparent contradiction in our findings about interest and exchange rates. To resolve the puzzle, however, we must first examine more closely how monetary policies and interest rates are connected in the long run.

Ongoing Inflation, Interest Parity, and PPP

In the last chapter, we saw that a permanent increase in the level of a country's money supply ultimately results in a proportional rise in its price level but has no effect on the long-run values of the interest rate or real output. While the conceptual experiment of a one-time, stepwise money supply change is useful for thinking about the long-run effects of money, it is not very realistic as a description of actual monetary policies. More plausibly, the monetary authorities choose a growth rate for the money supply, say, 5, 10, or 50 percent per year and then allow money to grow gradually, through incremental but frequent increases. What are the long-run effects of a policy that allows the money supply to grow smoothly forever at a positive rate?

The reasoning in Chapter 4 suggests that continuing money supply growth will require a continuing rise in the price level—a situation of *ongoing* inflation. As firms and workers catch on to the fact that the money supply is growing steadily at, say, a 10 percent annual rate, they will adjust by raising prices and wages by the same 10 percent every year, thus keeping their real incomes constant. Full-employment output depends on supplies of productive factors, but it is safe to assume that factor supplies, and thus output, are unaffected over the long run by different choices of a constant growth rate for the money supply. *Other things equal, money supply growth at a constant rate eventually results in ongoing price level inflation at the same rate, but changes in this long-run inflation rate do not affect the full-employment output level or the long-run relative prices of goods and services.*

The interest rate, however, is definitely not independent of the money supply growth rate in the long run. While the long-run interest rate does not depend on the absolute *level* of the money supply, continuing *growth* in the money supply eventually will affect the interest rate. The easiest way to see how a permanent increase in inflation affects the long-run interest rate is by combining PPP with the interest rate parity condition on which our previous analysis of exchange rate determination was built.

As in the preceding two chapters, the condition of interest parity between dollar and euro assets is

$$R_\$ = R_€ + (E^e_{\$/€} - E_{\$/€})/E_{\$/€}$$

(recall equation (3-2), page 60). Now let's ask how this parity condition, which must hold in the long run as well as in the short run, fits with the other parity condition we are assuming in our long-run model, purchasing power parity. According to relative PPP, the percentage change in the dollar/euro exchange rate over the next year, say, will equal the difference between the inflation rates of the United States and Europe over that year (see equation (5-2)). Since people understand this relationship, however, it must also be true that they *expect* the percentage exchange rate change to equal the U.S.–Europe inflation difference. The interest parity condition written on the previous page now tells us the following: *If people expect relative PPP to hold, the difference between the interest rates offered by dollar and euro deposits will equal the difference between the inflation rates expected, over the relevant horizon, in the United States and in Europe.*

Some additional notation is helpful in deriving this result more formally. If P^e is the price level expected in a country for a year from today, the expected inflation rate in that country, π^e, is the expected percentage increase in the price level over the coming year:

$$\pi^e = (P^e - P)/P.$$

If relative PPP holds, however, market participants will also *expect* relative PPP to hold, which means that we can replace the actual depreciation and inflation rates in equation (5-2) with the values the market expects to materialize:

$$(E^e_{\$/€} - E_{\$/€})/E_{\$/€} = \pi^e_{US} - \pi^e_{E}.$$

By combining this "expected" version of relative PPP with the interest parity condition

$$R_\$ = R_€ + (E^e_{\$/€} - E_{\$/€})/E_{\$/€}$$

and rearranging, we arrive at a formula that expresses the international interest rate difference as the difference between expected national inflation rates:

$$R_\$ - R_€ = \pi^e_{US} - \pi^e_{E}. \tag{5-5}$$

If, as PPP predicts, currency depreciation is expected to offset the international inflation difference (so that the expected dollar depreciation rate is $\pi^e_{US} - \pi^e_{E}$), the interest rate difference must equal the expected inflation difference.

The Fisher Effect

Equation (5-5) gives us the long-run relationship between ongoing inflation and interest rates that we need to explain the monetary approach's predictions about how interest rates affect exchange rates. The equation tells us that *all else equal, a rise in a country's expected inflation rate will eventually cause an equal rise in the interest rate that deposits of its currency offer. Similarly, a fall in the expected inflation rate will eventually cause a fall in the interest rate.*

This long-run relationship between inflation and interest rates is called the **Fisher effect**. The Fisher effect implies, for example, that if U.S. inflation were to rise permanently from a constant level of 5 percent per year to a constant level of 10 percent per year, dollar interest rates would eventually catch up with the higher inflation, rising by 5 percentage points per year from their initial level. These changes would leave the *real rate of return* on dollar assets, measured in terms of U.S. goods and services, unchanged. The Fisher effect is therefore another example of the general idea that in the long run, purely monetary developments should have no effect on an economy's relative prices.[3]

[3]The effect is named after Irving Fisher of Yale University, one of the great American economists of the early 20th century. The effect is discussed at length in his book *The Theory of Interest* (New York: Macmillan, 1930). Fisher, incidentally, gave an early account of the interest parity condition on which our theory of foreign exchange market equilibrium is based.

The Fisher effect is behind the seemingly paradoxical monetary approach prediction that a currency depreciates in the foreign exchange market when its interest rate rises relative to foreign currency interest rates. In the long-run equilibrium assumed by the monetary approach, a rise in the difference between home and foreign interest rates occurs only when expected home inflation rises relative to expected foreign inflation. This is certainly not the case in the short run, when the domestic price level is sticky. In the short run, as we saw in Chapter 4, the interest rate can rise when the domestic money supply *falls* because the sticky domestic price level leads to an excess demand for real money balances at the initial interest rate. Under the flexible-price monetary approach, however, the price level would fall right away, leaving the *real* money supply unchanged and thus making the interest rate change unnecessary.

We can better understand how interest rates and exchange rates interact under the monetary approach by thinking through an example. Our example illustrates why the monetary approach associates sustained interest rate hikes with current as well as future currency depreciation, and sustained interest rate declines with appreciation.

Imagine that at time t_0, the Federal Reserve unexpectedly increases the growth rate of the U.S. money supply from π to the higher level $\pi + \Delta\pi$. Figure 5-1 illustrates how this change affects the dollar/euro exchange rate, $E_{\$/€}$, as well as other U.S. variables, under the assumptions of the monetary approach. To simplify the graphs, we assume that in Europe, the inflation rate remains constant at zero.

Figure 5-1a shows the sudden acceleration of U.S. money supply growth at time t_0. (We have scaled the vertical axes of the graphs so that constant slopes represent constant proportional growth rates of variables.) The policy change generates expectations of more rapid currency depreciation in the future: Under PPP the dollar will now depreciate at the rate $\pi + \Delta\pi$ rather than at the lower rate π. Interest parity therefore requires the dollar interest rate to rise, as shown in Figure 5-1b, from its initial level $R_\$^1$ to a new level that reflects the extra expected dollar depreciation, $R_\$^2 = R_\$^1 + \Delta\pi$ (see equation (5-5)). Notice that this adjustment leaves the euro interest rate unchanged; but since Europe's money supply and output haven't changed, the original euro interest rate will still maintain equilibrium in Europe's money market.

You can see from Figure 5-1a that the *level* of the money supply does not actually jump upward at t_0—only the *future growth rate* changes. Since there is no immediate increase in the money supply—but there is an interest rate rise that reduces money demand—there would be an excess supply of real U.S. money balances at the price level prevailing just prior to t_0. In the face of this potential excess supply, the U.S. price level jumps upward at t_0 (see Figure 5-1c), reducing the real money supply so that it again equals real money demand (see equation (5-3)). Consistently with the upward jump in P_{US} at t_0, Figure 5-1d shows the simultaneous proportional upward jump in $E_{\$/€}$ implied by PPP.

How can we visualize the reaction of the foreign exchange market at time t_0? The dollar interest rate rises not because of a change in current levels of money supply or demand, but solely because people expect more rapid future money supply growth and dollar depreciation. As investors respond by moving into foreign deposits, which momentarily offer higher expected returns, the dollar depreciates sharply in the foreign exchange market, moving to a new trend line along which depreciation is more rapid than it was up to time t_0.[4]

Notice how different assumptions about the speed of price level adjustment lead to contrasting predictions about how exchange and interest rates interact. In the example of a fall in the level of the money supply under sticky prices, an interest rate

---

[4]In the general case in which Europe's inflation rate π_E is not zero, the dollar, rather than depreciating against the euro at rate π before t_0 and at rate $\pi + \Delta\pi$ afterward, depreciates at rate $\pi - \pi_E$ until t_0 and at rate $\pi + \Delta\pi - \pi_E$ thereafter.

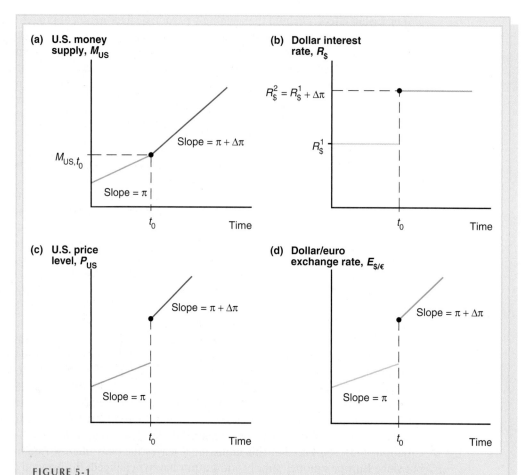

FIGURE 5-1

Long-Run Time Paths of U.S. Economic Variables after a Permanent Increase in the Growth Rate of the U.S. Money Supply

After the money supply growth rate increases at time t_0 in panel (a), the interest rate (in panel (b)), price level (in panel (c)), and exchange rate (in panel (d)) move to new long-run equilibrium paths. (The money supply, price level, and exchange rate are all measured on a *natural logarithmic* scale, which makes variables that change at constant proportional rates appear as straight lines when they are graphed against time. The slope of the line equals the variable's proportional growth rate.)

rise is needed to preserve money market equilibrium, given that the price level cannot do so by dropping immediately in response to the money supply reduction. In that sticky-price case, an interest rate rise is associated with lower expected inflation and a long-run currency appreciation, so the currency appreciates immediately. In our monetary approach example of a rise in money supply growth, however, an interest rate increase is associated with higher expected inflation and a currency that will be weaker on all future dates. An immediate currency *depreciation* is the result.[5]

---

[5]National money supplies typically trend upward over time, as in Figure 5-1a. Such trends lead to corresponding upward trends in price levels; if two countries' price level trends differ, PPP implies a trend in their exchange rate as well. From now on, when we refer to a change in the money supply, price level, or exchange rate, we will mean by this a change in the level of the variable relative to its previously expected trend path—that is, a parallel shift in the trend path. When instead we want to consider changes in the slopes of trend paths themselves, we will say so explicitly.

These contrasting results of interest rate changes underlie our earlier warning that an explanation of exchange rates based on interest rates must carefully account for the factors that cause interest rates to move. These factors can simultaneously affect expected future exchange rates and can therefore have a decisive impact on the foreign exchange market's response to the interest rate change. The appendix to this chapter shows in detail how expectations change in the case we analyzed.

Empirical Evidence on PPP and the Law of One Price

How well does the PPP theory explain actual data on exchange rates and national price levels? A brief answer is that *all versions of the PPP theory do badly* in explaining the facts. In particular, changes in national price levels often tell us relatively little about exchange rate movements.

Do not conclude from this evidence, however, that the effort you've put into learning about PPP has been wasted. As we'll see later in this chapter, PPP is a key building block of exchange rate models that are more realistic than the monetary approach. Indeed, the empirical failures of PPP give us important clues about how more realistic models should be set up.

To test *absolute* PPP, economic researchers compare the international prices of a broad reference basket of commodities, making careful adjustments for intercountry quality differences among supposedly identical goods. These comparisons typically conclude that absolute PPP is way off the mark: The prices of identical commodity baskets, when converted to a single currency, differ substantially across countries. Even the law of one price has not fared well in some recent studies of price data broken down by commodity type. Manufactured goods that seem to be very similar to each other have sold at widely different prices in various markets since the early 1970s. Because the argument leading to absolute PPP builds on the law of one price, it is not surprising that PPP does not stand up well to the data.[6]

Relative PPP is sometimes a reasonable approximation to the data, but it, too, usually performs poorly. Figure 5-2 illustrates relative PPP's weakness by plotting both the yen/dollar exchange rate, $E_{¥/\$}$, and the ratio of the Japanese and U.S. price levels, P_J/P_{US}, through 2012. Price levels are measured by indexes reported by the Japanese and U.S. governments.[7]

Relative PPP predicts that $E_{¥/\$}$ and P_J/P_{US} will move in proportion, but clearly they do not. In the early 1980s, there was a steep appreciation of the dollar against the yen even though, with Japan's price level consistently falling relative to that in the

---

[6]Some of the negative evidence on absolute PPP is discussed in the Case Study to follow. Regarding the law of one price, see, for example, Peter Isard, "How Far Can We Push the Law of One Price?" *American Economic Review* 67 (December 1977), pp. 942–948; Gita Gopinath, Pierre-Olivier Gourinchas, Chang-Tai Hsieh, and Nicholas Li, "International Prices, Costs, and Markup Differences," *American Economic Review* 101 (October 2011), pp. 2450–2486; Mario J. Crucini and Anthony Landry, "Accounting for Real Exchange Rates Using Micro-Data," Working Paper 17812, National Bureau of Economic Research, February 2012; and the paper by Goldberg and Knetter in Further Readings.

[7]The price level measures in Figure 5-2 are index numbers, not dollar amounts. For example, the U.S. consumer price index (CPI) was 100 in the base year 2000 and only about 50 in 1980, so the dollar price of a reference commodity basket of typical U.S. consumption purchases doubled between 1980 and 2000. For Figure 5-2, base years for the U.S. and Japanese price indexes were chosen so that their 1980 ratio would equal the 1980 exchange rate, but this imposed equality does not mean that absolute PPP held in 1980. Although Figure 5-2 uses CPIs, other price indexes lead to similar pictures.

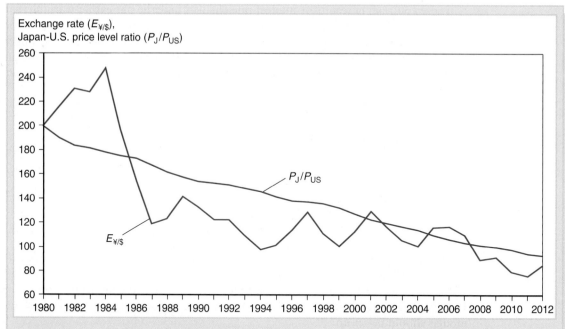

Exchange rate ($E_{¥/\$}$),
Japan-U.S. price level ratio (P_J/P_{US})

FIGURE 5-2   MyEconLab Real-time data

The Yen/Dollar Exchange Rate and Relative Japan–U.S. Price Levels, 1980–2012

The graph shows that relative PPP does not track the yen/dollar exchange rate during 1980–2012.

Source: IMF, *International Financial Statistics*. Exchange rates and price levels are end-of-year data.

United States, relative PPP suggests that the dollar should have *de*preciated instead. The same inflation trends continued after the mid-1980s, but the yen then appreciated by far more than the amount that PPP would have predicted. Only over fairly long periods is relative PPP approximately satisfied. In view of the lengthy departures from PPP in between, however, that theory appears to be of limited use even as a long-run explanation.

Studies of other currencies largely confirm the results in Figure 5-2. Relative PPP has not held up well.[8] As you will learn later in this book, between the end of World War II in 1945 and the early 1970s, exchange rates were fixed within narrow, internationally agreed-upon margins through the intervention of central banks in the foreign exchange market. During that period of fixed exchange rates, PPP did not do too badly. However, during the first half of the 1920s, when many exchange rates were market-determined as in the 1970s and after, important deviations from relative PPP occurred, just as in recent decades.[9]

---

[8]See, for example, the paper by Taylor and Taylor in this chapter's Further Readings.

[9]See Paul R. Krugman, "Purchasing Power Parity and Exchange Rates: Another Look at the Evidence," *Journal of International Economics* 8 (August 1978), pp. 397–407; Paul De Grauwe, Marc Janssens, and Hilde Leliaert, *Real-Exchange-Rate Variability from 1920 to 1926 and 1973 to 1982*, Princeton Studies in International Finance 56 (International Finance Section, Department of Economics, Princeton University, September 1985); and Hans Genberg, "Purchasing Power Parity under Fixed and Flexible Exchange Rates," *Journal of International Economics* 8 (May 1978), pp. 247–276.

Explaining the Problems with PPP

What explains the negative empirical results described in the previous section? There are several immediate problems with our rationale for the PPP theory of exchange rates, which was based on the law of one price:

1. Contrary to the assumption of the law of one price, transport costs and restrictions on trade certainly do exist. These trade barriers may be high enough to prevent some goods and services from being traded between countries.

2. Monopolistic or oligopolistic practices in goods markets may interact with transport costs and other trade barriers to weaken further the link between the prices of similar goods sold in different countries.

3. Because the inflation data reported in different countries are based on different commodity baskets, there is no reason for exchange rate changes to offset official measures of inflation differences, even when there are no barriers to trade and all products are tradable.

Trade Barriers and Nontradables

Transport costs and governmental trade restrictions make it expensive to move goods between markets located in different countries and therefore weaken the law of one price mechanism underlying PPP. Suppose once again that the same sweater sells for $45 in New York and for £30 in London, but that it costs $2 to ship a sweater between the two cities. At an exchange rate of $1.45 per pound, the dollar price of a London sweater is ($1.45 per pound) × (£30) = $43.50 but an American importer would have to pay $43.50 + $2 = $45.50 to purchase the sweater in London and get it to New York. At an exchange rate of $1.45 per pound, it therefore would not pay to ship sweaters from London to New York even though their dollar price would be higher in the latter location. Similarly, at an exchange rate of $1.55 per pound, an American exporter would lose money by shipping sweaters from New York to London even though the New York price of $45 would then be below the dollar price of the sweater in London, $46.50.

The lesson of this example is that transport costs sever the close link between exchange rates and goods prices implied by the law of one price. The greater the transport costs, the greater the range over which the exchange rate can move, given goods prices in different countries. Official trade restrictions such as tariffs have a similar effect, because a fee paid to the customs inspector affects the importer's profit in the same way as an equivalent shipping fee. Either type of trade impediment weakens the basis of PPP by allowing the purchasing power of a given currency to differ more widely from country to country. For example, in the presence of trade impediments, a dollar need not go as far in London as in Chicago—and it doesn't, as anyone who has ever been to London has found out.

As you will recall from the theory of international trade, transport costs may be so large relative to the cost of producing some goods and services that those items can never be traded internationally at a profit. Such goods and services are called *nontradables*. The time-honored classroom example of a nontradable is the haircut. A Frenchman desiring an American haircut would have to transport himself to the United States or transport an American barber to France; in either case, the cost of transport is so large relative to the price of the service being purchased that (tourists excepted) French haircuts are consumed only by residents of France while American haircuts are consumed only by residents of the United States.

The existence in all countries of nontraded goods and services, whose prices are not linked internationally, allows systematic deviations even from relative PPP. Because the price of a nontradable is determined entirely by its *domestic* supply and demand curves, shifts in those curves may cause the domestic price of a broad commodity basket to change relative to the foreign price of the same basket. Other things equal, a rise in the price of a country's nontradables will raise its price level relative to foreign price levels (measuring all countries' price levels in terms of a single currency). Looked at another way, the purchasing power of any given currency will fall in countries where the prices of nontradables rise.

Each country's price level includes a wide variety of nontradables, including (along with haircuts) routine medical treatment, dance instruction, and housing, among others. Broadly speaking, we can identify traded goods with manufactured products, raw materials, and agricultural products. Nontradables are primarily services and the outputs of the construction industry. There are, naturally, exceptions to this rule. For example, financial services provided by banks and brokerage houses often can be traded internationally. (The rise of the Internet, in particular, has expanded the range of tradable services.) In addition, trade restrictions, if sufficiently severe, can cause goods that would normally be traded to become nontraded. Thus, in most countries, some manufactures are nontraded.

We can get a rough idea of the importance of nontradables in the American economy by looking at the contribution of the service industries to U.S. GNP. In recent years, services have accounted for around 75 percent of the value of U.S. output. While services tend to have smaller shares in poorer economies, nontradables make up an important component of GNP everywhere. Nontradables help explain the wide departures from relative PPP illustrated by Figure 5-2.

Departures from Free Competition

When trade barriers and imperfectly competitive market structures occur together, linkages between national price levels are weakened further. An extreme case occurs when a single firm sells a commodity for different prices in different markets.

When a firm sells the same product for different prices in different markets, we say that it is practicing **pricing to market**. Pricing to market may reflect different demand conditions in different countries. For example, countries where demand is more price-inelastic will tend to be charged higher markups over a monopolistic seller's production cost. Empirical studies of firm-level export data have yielded strong evidence of pervasive pricing to market in manufacturing trade.[10]

In 2011, for example, a Volkswagen Passat cost $4,000 more in Austria than in Ireland despite those countries' shared currency (the euro) and despite the European Union's efforts over many years to remove intra-European trade barriers (see Chapter 10). Such price differentials would be difficult to enforce if it were not costly for consumers to buy autos in Ireland and drive or ship them to Austria or if consumers viewed cheaper cars available in Austria as good substitutes for the Passat. The combination of product differentiation and segmented markets, however, leads to large violations

---

[10]For a detailed review of the evidence, see the paper by Goldberg and Knetter in this chapter's Further Readings. Theoretical contributions on pricing to market include Rudiger Dornbusch, "Exchange Rates and Prices," *American Economic Review* 77 (March 1987), pp. 93–106; Paul R. Krugman, "Pricing to Market When the Exchange Rate Changes," in Sven W. Arndt and J. David Richardson, eds., *Real-Financial Linkages among Open Economies* (Cambridge, MA: MIT Press, 1987); and Andrew Atkeson and Ariel Burstein, "Pricing-to-Market, Trade Costs, and International Relative Prices," *American Economic Review* 98 (December 2008), pp. 1998–2031.

of the law of one price and absolute PPP. Shifts in market structure and demand over time can invalidate relative PPP.

Differences in Consumption Patterns and Price Level Measurement

Government measures of the price level differ from country to country. One reason for these differences is that people living in different countries spend their incomes in different ways. In general, people consume relatively higher proportions of their own country's products—including its tradable products—than of foreign-made products. The average Norwegian consumes more reindeer meat than her American counterpart, the average Japanese more sushi, and the average Indian more chutney. In constructing a reference commodity basket to measure purchasing power, it is therefore likely that the Norwegian government will put a relatively high weight on reindeer, the Japanese government a high weight on sushi, and the Indian government a high weight on chutney.

SOME MEATY EVIDENCE ON THE LAW OF ONE PRICE

In the summer of 1986, the *Economist* magazine conducted an extensive survey on the prices of Big Mac hamburgers at McDonald's restaurants throughout the world. This apparently whimsical undertaking was not the result of an outbreak of editorial giddiness. Rather, the magazine wanted to poke fun at economists who confidently declare exchange rates to be "overvalued" or "undervalued" on the basis of PPP comparisons. Since Big Macs are "sold in 41 countries, with only the most trivial changes of recipe," the magazine argued, a comparison of hamburger prices should serve as a "medium-rare guide to whether currencies are trading at the right exchange rates."* Since 1986, the *Economist* has periodically updated its calculations.

One way of interpreting the *Economist* survey is as a test of the law of one price. Viewed in this way, the results of the initial test were quite startling. The dollar prices of Big Macs turned out to be wildly different in different countries. For example, the price of a Big Mac in New York was 50 percent higher than in Australia and 64 percent higher than in Hong Kong. In contrast, a Parisian Big Mac cost 54 percent more than its New York counterpart, and a Tokyo Big Mac cost 50 percent more. Only in Britain and Ireland were the dollar prices of the burgers close to New York levels.

How can this dramatic violation of the law of one price be explained? As the *Economist* noted, transport costs and government regulations are part of the explanation. Product differentiation is probably an important additional factor. Because relatively few close substitutes for Big Macs are available in some countries, product differentiation may give McDonald's some power to tailor prices to the local market. Finally, remember that the price of a Big Mac must cover not only the cost of ground meat and buns, but also the wages of serving people, rent, electricity, and so on. The prices of these nonfood inputs can differ sharply in different countries. Indeed, the *Economist* has now

---

*"On the Hamburger Standard," *Economist*, September 6–12, 1986.

(*Continued*)

introduced a refined version of their index that corrects for the fact that labor costs tend to be lower in poorer countries.**

We have reproduced the results of the *Economist*'s January 2013 survey report. The table shows various countries' prices of Big Macs,

The hamburger standard					
	Big Mac prices		Implied PPP* of the dollar	Actual exchange rate: January 30th	Under (−)/over(+) Valuation against the dollar, %
	in local currency	in dollars			
United States	$4.37	4.37	1.00	1.00	0.0
Argentina	Peso 19.00	3.82	4.35	4.98	−12.6
Australia	A$4.70	4.90	1.08	0.96	12.2
Brazil	Real 11.25	5.64	2.58	1.99	29.2
Britain	£2.69	4.25	0.62	0.63	−2.7
Canada	C$5.41	5.39	1.24	1.00	23.5
Chile	Peso 2,050.00	4.35	469.39	471.75	−0.5
China	Yuan 16.00	2.57	3.66	6.22	−41.1
Czech Republic	Koruna 70.33	3.72	16.10	18.89	−14.8
Denmark	DK 28.50	5.18	6.53	5.50	18.7
Egypt	Pound 16.00	2.39	3.66	6.69	−45.2
Euro area	€3.59	4.88	0.82	0.74	11.7
Hong Kong	HK$ 17.00	2.19	3.89	7.76	−49.8
Hungary	Forint 830.00	3.82	190.04	217.47	−12.6
Indonesia	Rupiah 27,939.00	2.86	6,397.18	9,767.50	−34.5
Israel	Shekel 14.90	4.00	3.41	3.72	−8.4
Japan	¥320.00	3.51	73.27	91.07	−19.5
Malaysia	Ringgit 7.95	2.58	1.82	3.08	−41.0
Mexico	Peso 37.00	2.90	8.47	12.74	−33.5
New Zealand	NZ$5.20	4.32	1.19	1.20	−1.0
Norway	Kroner 43.00	7.84	9.84	5.48	79.6
Peru	Sol 10.00	3.91	2.29	2.56	−10.5
Philippines	Peso 118.00	2.91	27.02	40.60	−33.5
Poland	Zloty 9.10	2.94	2.08	3.09	−32.6
Russia	Ruble 72.88	2.43	16.69	30.05	−44.5
Saudi Arabia	Riyal 11.00	2.93	2.52	3.75	−32.8
Singapore	S$4.50	3.64	1.03	1.23	−16.6
South Africa	Rand 18.33	2.03	4.20	9.05	−53.6
South Korea	Won 3,700.00	3.41	847.19	1,085.48	−22.0
Sweden	SKR 48.40	7.62	11.08	6.35	74.5
Switzerland	CHF 6.50	7.12	1.49	0.91	63.1
Taiwan	NT$75.00	2.54	17.17	29.50	−41.8
Thailand	Baht 87.00	2.92	19.92	29.76	−33.1
Turkey	Lire 8.45	4.78	1.93	1.77	9.4

*Purchasing power parity: local price divided by price in United States.

Sources: McDonald's; the *Economist*, January 2013 survey. Exchange rates are local currency per dollar.

**See the Big Mac index website at http://www.economist.com/content/big-mac-index, from which the data below are drawn.

measured in U.S. dollar terms. These range from a high of $7.84 in Norway (79.4 percent above the U.S. price) to only $2.19 in Hong Kong (half the U.S. price).

For each country, we can figure out a "Big Mac PPP," which is the hypothetical level of the exchange rate that would equate the dollar price of a locally sold Big Mac to its $4.37 U.S. price. For example, in January 2013 an American dollar cost only 5.48 kroner in the foreign exchange market, making the dollar price of a Norwegian Big Mac $7.84, quite bit higher than in the U.S. The exchange rate that would have equalized U.S. and Norwegian burger prices, however, was (43 kroner per burger)/(4.37 dollars per burger) = 9.84 kroner per dollar, an exchange rate making the kroner much cheaper in terms of dollars (and therefore making Norwegian burgers cheaper as well).

It is often said that a currency is overvalued when its exchange rate makes domestic goods expensive relative to similar goods sold abroad and undervalued in the opposite case. For the Norwegian krone, for example, the degree of overvaluation on the Big Mac scale is the percentage by which the hypothetical Big Mac PPP kroner price of the dollar exceeds the market rate, or

$$100 \times (9.84 - 5.48)/5.48 = 79.6 \text{ percent.}$$

Of course, apart from rounding error, this is the percentage by which the dollar price of a Norwegian burger exceeds that of a U.S. burger, and therefore the percentage by which the actual dollar price of a kroner exceeds the hypothetical Big Mac price.

Likewise, in January 2013 the dollar price of the Chinese yuan was 41.1 percent *below* the level needed to bring about burger price parity:

That country's currency was *under*valued by 41.1 percent, according to the Big Mac measure. China's currency would have had to appreciate substantially against the dollar to bring the Chinese and U.S. prices of Big Macs into line. Norway's currency, in contrast, would have had to depreciate substantially.

In general, a "PPP exchange rate" is defined as one that equates the international prices of some broad basket of goods and services, not just hamburgers. As we shall see, there are several reasons why we might expect PPP not to hold exactly, even over long periods. Thus, despite the widespread use of terms like *overvaluation*, policy makers have to be very cautious in judging whether any particular level of the exchange rate may signal the need for economic policy changes.

Policy makers would be wise, however, to take into account extremes of over- or undervaluation. Consider the case of Iceland. In January 2006, Iceland had a dollar Big Mac price of $7.44 and a whopping 131 percent currency overvaluation on the Big Mac scale. Then the tiny country was swept up in a global financial crisis that we will discuss in detail in Chapters 8 and 9. From around 68 kronur per dollar in 2006, the currency depreciated all the way to around 120 per dollar by 2010. Unlike many other countries, Iceland imports the burgers' ingredients, the kronur prices of which rose sharply because of the depreciation. The sudden cost increase made the franchise unprofitable without a big rise in prices to customers. But Iceland's economy had suffered severely in the crisis. Rather than boosting prices, the franchise owner closed all three of Iceland's McDonald's restaurants. As a result, the country no longer appears in the *Economist*'s survey.[†]

[†]See Omar R. Valdimarsson, "McDonald's Closes in Iceland after Krona Collapse," Bloomberg News, October 26, 2009. Available at http://www.bloomberg.com/apps/ news?pid=newsarchive&sid=amu4.WTVaqjI

Because relative PPP makes predictions about price *changes* rather than price *levels*, it is a sensible concept regardless of the baskets used to define price levels in the countries being compared. If all U.S. prices increase by 10 percent and the dollar depreciates against foreign currencies by 10 percent, relative PPP will be satisfied (assuming there are no changes abroad) for any domestic and foreign choices of price level indexes.

Change in the relative prices of basket components, however, can cause relative PPP to fail tests that are based on official price indexes. For example, a rise in the relative price of fish would raise the dollar price of a Japanese government reference commodity basket relative to that of a U.S. government basket, simply because fish takes up a larger share of the Japanese basket. Relative price changes could lead to PPP violations like those shown in Figure 5-2 even if trade were free and costless.

PPP in the Short Run and in the Long Run

The factors we have examined so far in explaining the PPP theory's poor empirical performance can cause national price levels to diverge even in the long run, after all prices have had time to adjust to their market-clearing levels. As we discussed in Chapter 4, however, many prices in the economy are sticky and take time to adjust fully. Departures from PPP may therefore be even greater in the short run than in the long run.

An abrupt depreciation of the dollar against foreign currencies, for example, makes farm equipment in the United States cheaper relative to similar equipment produced abroad. As farmers throughout the world shift their demand for tractors and reapers to U.S. producers, the price of American farm equipment tends to rise to reduce the divergence from the law of one price caused by the dollar's depreciation. It takes time for this process of price increase to be complete, however, and prices for U.S. and foreign farm equipment may differ considerably while markets adjust to the exchange rate change.

You might suspect that short-run price stickiness and exchange rate volatility help explain a phenomenon we noted in discussing Figure 5-2—that violations of relative PPP have been much more flagrant over periods when exchange rates have floated. Empirical research supports this interpretation of the data. Figure 4-11, which we used to illustrate the stickiness of goods prices compared with exchange rates, is quite typical of floating-rate episodes. In a careful study covering many countries and historical episodes, economist Michael Mussa compared the extent of short-run deviations from PPP under fixed and floating exchange rates. He found that floating exchange rates systematically lead to much larger and more frequent short-run deviations from relative PPP.[11] The box on pages 133–134 provides an especially vivid illustration of how price stickiness can generate violations of the law of one price even for absolutely identical goods.

Recent research suggests that short-run deviations from PPP such as those due to volatile exchange rates die away over time, with only half the effect of a temporary departure from PPP remaining after four years.[12] Even when these temporary PPP deviations are removed from the data, however, it still appears that the cumulative effect of certain long-run trends causes predictable departures from PPP for many countries. The Case Study entitled "Why Price Levels Are Lower in Poorer Countries" discusses one of the major mechanisms behind such trends.

---

[11]See Mussa, "Nominal Exchange Rate Regimes and the Behavior of Real Exchange Rates: Evidence and Implications," in Karl Brunner and Allan H. Meltzer, eds., *Real Business Cycles, Real Exchange Rates and Actual Policies*, Carnegie-Rochester Conference Series on Public Policy 25 (Amsterdam: North-Holland, 1986), pp. 117–214. Charles Engel of the University of Wisconsin has found that under a floating exchange rate, international price differences for the same good can be more variable than the relative price of different goods within a single country. See Engel, "Real Exchange Rates and Relative Prices: An Empirical Investigation," *Journal of Monetary Economics* 32 (August 1993), pp. 35–50. Also see Gopinath, Gourinchas, Hsieh, and Li, *op. cit.* (footnote 6).

[12]See, for example, Jeffrey A. Frankel and Andrew K. Rose, "A Panel Project on Purchasing Power Parity: Mean Reversion within and between Countries," *Journal of International Economics* 40 (February 1996), pp. 209–224. The statistical validity of these results is challenged by Paul G. J. O'Connell in "The Overvaluation of Purchasing Power Parity," *Journal of International Economics* 44 (February 1998), pp. 1–19.

CASE STUDY

Why Price Levels Are Lower in Poorer Countries

Research on international price level differences has uncovered a striking empirical regularity: When expressed in terms of a single currency, countries' price levels are positively related to the level of real income per capita. In other words, a dollar, when converted to local currency at the market exchange rate, generally goes much further in a poor country than in a rich one. Figure 5-3 illustrates the relation between price levels and income, with each dot representing a different country.

The previous section's discussion of the role of nontraded goods in the determination of national price levels suggests that international variations in the prices of nontradables may contribute to price level discrepancies between rich and poor nations. The available data indeed show that nontradables tend to be more expensive (relative to tradables) in richer countries.

One reason for the lower relative price of nontradables in poor countries was suggested by Bela Balassa and Paul Samuelson.[13] The Balassa-Samuelson theory

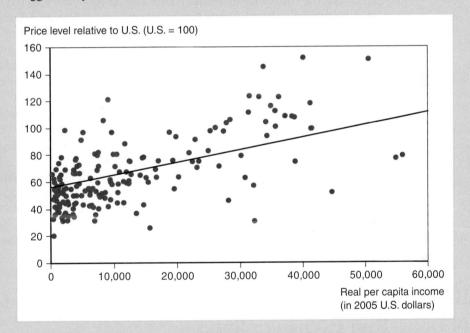

FIGURE 5-3

Price Levels and Real Incomes, 2010

Countries' price levels tend to rise as their real incomes rise. Each dot represents a country. The straight line indicates a statistician's best prediction of a country's price level relative to that of the United States based on knowing its real per capita income.

Source: Penn World Table, version 7.1.

---

[13]See Balassa, "The Purchasing Power Parity Doctrine: A Reappraisal," *Journal of Political Economy* 72 (December 1964), pp. 584–596; and Samuelson, "Theoretical Notes on Trade Problems," *Review of Economics and Statistics* 46 (May 1964), pp. 145–154. The Balassa-Samuelson theory was foreshadowed by some observations of Ricardo. See Jacob Viner, *Studies in the Theory of International Trade* (New York: Harper & Brothers, 1937), p. 315.

assumes the labor forces of poor countries are less productive than those of rich countries in the tradables sector but international productivity differences in nontradables are negligible. If the prices of traded goods are roughly equal in all countries, however, lower labor productivity in the tradables industries of poor countries implies lower wages than abroad, lower production costs in nontradables, and therefore a lower price of nontradables. Rich countries with higher labor productivity in the tradables sector will tend to have higher nontradables prices and higher price levels. Productivity statistics give some empirical support to the Balassa-Samuelson differential productivity postulate. And it is plausible that international productivity differences are sharper in traded than in nontraded goods. Whether a country is rich or poor, a barber can give only so many haircuts in a week, but there may be a significant scope for productivity differences across countries in the manufacture of traded goods like personal computers.

An alternative theory that attempts to explain the lower price levels of poor countries was put forth by Jagdish Bhagwati of Columbia University, and by Irving Kravis of the University of Pennsylvania and Robert Lipsey of the City University of New York.[14] The Bhagwati-Kravis-Lipsey view relies on differences in endowments of capital and labor rather than productivity differences, but it also predicts that the relative price of nontradables increases as real per capita income increases. Rich countries have high capital-labor ratios, while poor countries have more labor relative to capital. Because rich countries have higher capital-labor ratios, the marginal productivity of labor is greater in rich countries than in poor countries, and the former will therefore have a higher wage level than the latter.[15] Nontradables, which consist largely of services, are naturally labor-intensive relative to tradables. Because labor is cheaper in poor countries and is used intensively in producing nontradables, nontradables also will be cheaper there than in the rich, high-wage countries. Once again, this international difference in the relative price of nontradables suggests that overall price levels, when measured in a single currency, should be higher in rich countries than in poor countries.

Beyond Purchasing Power Parity: A General Model of Long-Run Exchange Rates

Why devote so much discussion to the purchasing power parity theory when it is fraught with exceptions and apparently contradicted by the data? We examined the implications of PPP so closely because its basic idea of relating long-run exchange rates to long-run national price levels is a very useful starting point. The monetary approach presented previously, which assumed PPP, is too simple to give accurate

[14]See Kravis and Lipsey, *Toward an Explanation of National Price Levels*, Princeton Studies in International Finance 52 (International Finance Section, Department of Economics, Princeton University, November 1983); and Bhagwati, "Why Are Services Cheaper in the Poor Countries?" *Economic Journal* 94 (June 1984), pp. 279–286.
[15]This argument assumes that factor endowment differences between rich and poor countries are sufficiently great that factor-price equalization cannot hold.

predictions about the real world, but we can generalize it by taking account of some of the reasons why PPP predicts badly in practice. In this section, we do just that.

The long-run analysis below continues to ignore short-run complications caused by sticky prices. An understanding of how exchange rates behave in the long run is, as mentioned earlier, a prerequisite for the more complicated short-run analysis that we undertake in the next chapter.

The Real Exchange Rate

As the first step in extending the PPP theory, we define the concept of a **real exchange rate**. The real exchange rate between two countries' currencies is a broad summary measure of the prices of one country's goods and services relative to the other country's. It is natural to introduce the real exchange rate concept at this point because the major prediction of PPP is that real exchange rates never change, at least not permanently. To extend our model so that it describes the world more accurately, we need to examine systematically the forces that can cause dramatic and permanent changes in real exchange rates.

As we will see, real exchange rates are important not only for quantifying deviations from PPP but also for analyzing macroeconomic demand and supply conditions in open economies. When we wish to differentiate a real exchange rate—which is the relative price of two output baskets—from a relative price of two currencies, we will refer to the latter as a **nominal exchange rate**. But when there is no risk of confusion, we will continue to use the shorter term, *exchange rate*, to refer to nominal exchange rates.

Real exchange rates are defined in terms of nominal exchange rates and price levels. Before we can give a more precise definition of real exchange rates, however, we need to clarify the price level measure we will be using. Let P_{US}, as usual, be the price level in the United States, and P_E the price level in Europe. Since we will not be assuming absolute PPP (as we did in our discussion of the monetary approach), we no longer assume the price level can be measured by the same basket of commodities in the United States as in Europe. Because we will soon want to link our analysis to monetary factors, we require instead that each country's price index give a good representation of the purchases that motivate its residents to demand its money supply.

No measure of the price level does this perfectly, but we must settle on some definition before we can formally define the real exchange rate. To be concrete, you can think of P_{US} as the dollar price of an unchanging basket containing the typical weekly purchases of U.S. households and firms; P_E, similarly, is based on an unchanging basket reflecting the typical weekly purchases of European households and firms. The point to remember is that *the U.S. price level will place a relatively heavy weight on commodities produced and consumed in America, and the European price level a relatively heavy weight on commodities produced and consumed in Europe.*[16]

Having described the reference commodity baskets used to measure price levels, we now formally define the *real dollar/euro exchange rate*, denoted $q_{\$/€}$, as the dollar price of the European basket relative to that of the American basket. We can express the real exchange rate as the dollar value of Europe's price level divided by the U.S. price level or, in symbols, as

$$q_{\$/€} = (E_{\$/€} \times P_E)/P_{US}. \tag{5-6}$$

---

[16]Nontradables are one important factor behind the relative preference for home products.

A numerical example will clarify the concept of the real exchange rate. Imagine the European reference commodity basket costs €100 (so that $P_E = €100$ per European basket), the U.S. basket costs $120 (so that $P_{US} = 120 per U.S. basket), and the nominal exchange rate is $E_{\$/€} = 1.20 per euro. The real dollar/euro exchange rate would then be

$$q_{\$/€} = \frac{(\$1.20 \text{ per euro}) \times (€100 \text{ per European basket})}{(\$120 \text{ per U.S. basket})}$$
$$= (\$120 \text{ per European basket})/(\$120 \text{ per U.S. basket})$$
$$= 1 \text{ U.S. basket per European basket.}$$

A rise in the real dollar/euro exchange rate $q_{\$/€}$, (which we call a **real depreciation** of the dollar against the euro) can be thought of in several equivalent ways. Most obviously, (5-6) shows this change to be a fall in the purchasing power of a dollar within Europe's borders relative to its purchasing power within the United States. This change in relative purchasing power occurs because the dollar prices of European goods ($E_{\$/€} \times P_E$) rise relative to those of U.S. goods (P_{US}).

In terms of our numerical example, a 10 percent nominal dollar depreciation, to $E_{\$/€} = 1.32 per euro, causes $q_{\$/€}$ to rise to 1.1 U.S. baskets per European basket, a *real* dollar depreciation of 10 percent against the euro. (The same change in $q_{\$/€}$ could result from a 10 percent rise in P_E or a 10 percent fall in P_{US}.) The real depreciation means the dollar's purchasing power over European goods and services falls by 10 percent relative to its purchasing power over U.S. goods and services.

Alternatively, even though many of the items entering national price levels are nontraded, it is useful to think of the real exchange rate $q_{\$/€}$ as the relative price of European products in general in terms of American products, that is, the price at which hypothetical trades of American for European commodity baskets would occur if trades at domestic prices were possible. The dollar is considered to *depreciate* in real terms against the euro when $q_{\$/€}$ rises because the hypothetical purchasing power of America's products in general over Europe's declines. America's goods and services thus become cheaper relative to Europe's.

A **real appreciation** of the dollar against the euro is a fall in $q_{\$/€}$. This fall indicates a decrease in the relative price of products purchased in Europe, or a rise in the dollar's European purchasing power compared with that in the United States.[17]

Our convention for describing real depreciations and appreciations of the dollar against the euro is the same one we use for nominal exchange rates (that is, $E_{\$/€}$ up is a dollar depreciation, $E_{\$/€}$ down is an appreciation). Equation (5-6) shows that at *unchanged* output prices, nominal depreciation (appreciation) implies real depreciation (appreciation). Our discussion of real exchange rate changes thus includes, as a special case, an observation we made in Chapter 3: With the domestic money prices of goods held constant, a nominal dollar depreciation makes U.S. goods cheaper compared with foreign goods, while a nominal dollar appreciation makes them more expensive.

Equation (5-6) makes it easy to see why the real exchange rate can never change when relative PPP holds. Under relative PPP, a 10 percent rise in $E_{\$/€}$, for instance, would always be exactly offset by a 10 percent fall in the price level ratio P_E/P_{US}, leaving $q_{\$/€}$ unchanged.

---

[17]This is true because $E_{\$/€} = 1/E_{€/\$}$, implying that a real depreciation of the dollar against the euro is the same as a real appreciation of the euro against the dollar (that is, a rise in the purchasing power of the euro within the United States relative to its purchasing power within Europe, or a fall in the relative price of American products in terms of European products).

Demand, Supply, and the Long-Run Real Exchange Rate

It should come as no surprise that in a world where PPP does not hold, the long-run values of real exchange rates—just like other relative prices that clear markets—depend on demand and supply conditions. Since a real exchange rate tracks changes in the relative price of two countries' expenditure baskets, however, conditions in *both* countries matter. Changes in countries' output markets can be complex, and we do not want to digress into an exhaustive (and exhausting) catalogue of the possibilities. We focus instead on two specific cases that are both easy to grasp and important in practice for explaining why the long-run values of real exchange rates can change.

1. *A change in world relative demand for American products.* Imagine total world spending on American goods and services rises relative to total world spending on European goods and services. Such a change could arise from several sources—for example, a shift in private U.S. demand away from European goods and toward American goods; a similar shift in private foreign demand toward American goods; or an increase in U.S. government demand falling primarily on U.S. output. Any increase in relative world demand for U.S. products causes an excess demand for them at the previous real exchange rate. To restore equilibrium, the relative price of American output in terms of European output will therefore have to rise: The relative prices of U.S. nontradables will rise, and the prices of tradables produced in the United States, and consumed intensively there, will rise relative to the prices of tradables made in Europe. These changes all work to reduce $q_{\$/€}$, the relative price of Europe's reference expenditure basket in terms of the United States'.

STICKY PRICES AND THE LAW OF ONE PRICE: EVIDENCE FROM SCANDINAVIAN DUTY-FREE SHOPS

Sticky nominal prices and wages are central to macroeconomic theories, but just why might it be difficult for money prices to change from day to day as market conditions change? One reason is based on the idea of "menu costs." Menu costs could arise from several factors, such as the actual costs of printing new price lists and catalogs. In addition, firms may perceive a different type of menu cost due to their customers' imperfect information about competitors' prices. When a firm raises its price, some customers will shop around elsewhere and find it convenient to remain with a competing seller even if all sellers have raised their prices. In the presence of these various types of menu costs, sellers will often hold prices constant after a change in market conditions until they are certain the change is permanent enough to make incurring the costs of price changes worthwhile.*

If there were truly no barriers between two markets with goods priced in different currencies, sticky prices would be unable to survive in the face of an exchange rate change. All buyers would simply flock to the market where a good had become cheapest. But when some trade impediments exist, deviations from the law of one price do not induce unlimited arbitrage, so it is feasible for sellers to hold prices constant despite exchange rate changes. In the real world, trade barriers appear to be significant, widespread, and often subtle in nature.

Apparently, arbitrage between two markets may be limited even when the physical distance between them is zero, as a surprising study of pricing behavior in Scandinavian duty-free outlets shows. Swedish economists Marcus Asplund and Richard Friberg studied pricing behavior in the duty-free stores of two Scandinavian ferry

---

*It is when economic conditions are very volatile that prices seem to become most flexible. For example, restaurant menus will typically price their catch of the day at "market" so that the price charged (and the fish offered) can reflect the high variability in fishing outcomes.

(*Continued*)

lines whose catalogs quote the prices of each good in several currencies for the convenience of customers from different countries.[†] Since it is costly to print the catalogs, they are reissued with revised prices only from time to time. In the interim, however, fluctuations in exchange rates induce multiple, changing prices for the *same* good. For example, on the Birka Line of ferries between Sweden and Finland, prices were listed in both Finnish markka and Swedish kronor between 1975 and 1998, implying that a relative depreciation of the markka would make it cheaper to buy cigarettes or vodka by paying markka rather than kronor.

Despite such price discrepancies, Birka Line was always able to do business in both currencies—passengers did not rush to buy at the lowest price. Swedish passengers, who held relatively large quantities of their own national currency, tended to buy at the kronor prices, whereas Finnish customers tended to buy at the markka prices.

Often, Birka Line would take advantage of publishing a new catalog to reduce deviations from the law of one price. The average deviation from the law of one price in the month just before such a price adjustment was 7.21 percent, but only 2.22 percent in the month of the price adjustment. One big impediment to taking advantage of the arbitrage opportunities was the cost of changing currencies at the onboard foreign exchange booth—roughly 7.5 percent. That transaction cost, given different passengers' currency preferences at the time of embarkation, acted as an effective trade barrier.[‡]

Surprisingly, Birka Line did not completely eliminate law of one price deviations when it changed catalog prices. Instead, Birka Line practiced a kind of pricing to market on its ferries. Usually, exporters who price to market discriminate among different consumers based on their different locations, but Birka was able to discriminate based on different nationality and currency preferences, even with all potential consumers located on the same ferry boat.

[†]"The Law of One Price in Scandinavian Duty-Free Stores," *American Economic Review* 91 (September 2001), pp. 1072–1083.

[‡]Customers could pay in the currency of their choice not only with cash, but also with credit cards, which involve lower foreign exchange conversion fees but convert at an exchange rate prevailing a few days after the purchase of the goods. Asplund and Friberg suggest that for such small purchases, uncertainty and the costs of calculating relative prices (in addition to the credit-card exchange fees) might have been a sufficient deterrent to transacting in a relatively unfamiliar currency.

We conclude that *an increase in world relative demand for U.S. output causes a long-run real appreciation of the dollar against the euro (a fall in $q_{\$/€}$). Similarly, a decrease in world relative demand for U.S. output causes a long-run real depreciation of the dollar against the euro (a rise in $q_{\$/€}$).*

2. *A change in relative output supply.* Suppose the productive efficiency of U.S. labor and capital rises. Since Americans spend part of their increased income on foreign goods, the supplies of all types of U.S. goods and services increase relative to the demand for them, the result being an excess relative supply of American output at the previous real exchange rate. A fall in the relative price of American products—both nontradables and tradables—shifts demand toward them and eliminates the excess supply. This price change is a real depreciation of the dollar against the euro, that is, an increase in $q_{\$/€}$. *A relative expansion of U.S. output causes a long-run real depreciation of the dollar against the euro ($q_{\$/€}$ rises). A relative expansion of European output causes a long-run real appreciation of the dollar against the euro ($q_{\$/€}$ falls).*[18]

---

[18]Our discussion of the Balassa-Samuelson effect in the Case Study on pages 129–130 would lead you to expect that a productivity increase concentrated in the U.S. tradables sector might cause the dollar to appreciate, rather than depreciate, in real terms against the euro. In the last paragraph, however, we have in mind a balanced productivity increase that benefits the traded and nontraded sectors in equal proportion, thus resulting in a real dollar depreciation by causing a drop in the prices of nontraded goods and in those of traded goods that are more important in America's consumer price index than in Europe's.

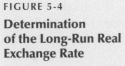

FIGURE 5-4

Determination of the Long-Run Real Exchange Rate

The long-run equilibrium real exchange rate equates world relative demand to the full-employment level of relative supply.

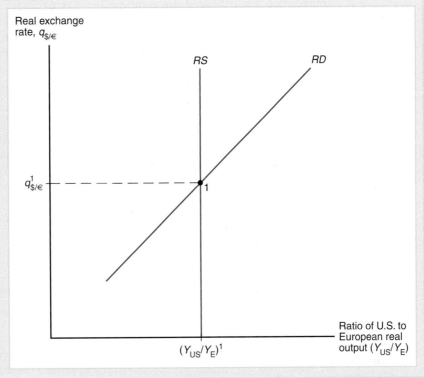

Real exchange rate, $q_{\$/€}$

RS

RD

$q^1_{\$/€}$

1

$(Y_{US}/Y_E)^1$

Ratio of U.S. to European real output (Y_{US}/Y_E)

A useful diagram summarizes our discussion of demand, supply, and the long-run real exchange rate. In Figure 5-4, the supply of U.S. output relative to European output, Y_{US}/Y_E, is plotted along the horizontal axis while the real dollar/euro exchange rate, $q_{\$/€}$, is plotted along the vertical axis.

The equilibrium real exchange rate is determined by the intersection of two schedules. The upward-sloping schedule *RD* shows that the relative demand for U.S. products in general, relative to the demand for European products, rises as $q_{\$/€}$ rises, that is, as American products become relatively cheaper. This "demand" curve for U.S. relative to European goods has a positive slope because we are measuring a *fall* in the relative price of U.S. goods by a move *upward* along the vertical axis. What about relative supply? In the long run, relative national output levels are determined by factor supplies and productivity, with little, if any, effect on the real exchange rate. The relative supply curve, *RS*, therefore is vertical at the long-run (that is, full-employment) relative output ratio, $(Y_{US}/Y_E)^1$. The equilibrium long-run real exchange rate is the one that sets relative demand equal to long-run relative supply (point 1).[19]

The diagram easily illustrates how changes in world markets affect the real exchange rate. Suppose world gasoline prices fall, making American sport-utility vehicles more desirable for people everywhere. This change would be a rise in world relative demand for American goods and would shift *RD* to the right, causing $q_{\$/€}$ to fall (a real dollar

---

[19]Notice that these *RD* and *RS* schedules differ from the ones used in Chapter 6 of our companion textbook, *International Trade: Theory and Policy*. Those schedules referred to relative world demand for and supply of two products that could be produced in either of two countries. In contrast, the *RD* and *RS* curves in this chapter refer to the relative world demand for and supply of one country's overall output (its GDP) relative to another's.

appreciation against the euro). Suppose the United States improves its health-care system, reducing illness throughout the American workforce. If workers are able to produce more goods and services in an hour as a result, the rise in U.S. productivity shifts RS to the right, causing $q_{\$/€}$ to rise (a real dollar depreciation against the euro).

Nominal and Real Exchange Rates in Long-Run Equilibrium

We now pull together what we have learned in this chapter and the last one to show how long-run nominal exchange rates are determined. One central conclusion is that changes in national money supplies and demands give rise to the proportional long-run movements in nominal exchange rates and international price level ratios predicted by the relative purchasing power parity theory. Demand and supply shifts in national output markets, however, cause nominal exchange rate movements that do not conform to PPP.

Recall our definition of the real dollar/euro exchange rate as

$$q_{\$/€} = (E_{\$/€} \times P_E)/P_{US}.$$

(See equation (5-6).) If we now solve this equation for the nominal exchange rate, we get an equation that gives us the nominal dollar/euro exchange rate as the real dollar/euro exchange rate times the U.S.–Europe price level ratio:

$$E_{\$/€} = q_{\$/€} \times (P_{US}/P_E). \tag{5-7}$$

Formally speaking, the only difference between (5-7) and equation (5-1), on which we based our exposition of the monetary approach to the exchange rate, is that (5-7) accounts for possible deviations from PPP by adding the *real* exchange rate as an additional determinant of the nominal exchange rate. *The equation implies that for a given real dollar/euro exchange rate, changes in money demand or supply in Europe or the United States affect the long-run nominal dollar/euro exchange rate as in the monetary approach. Changes in the long-run real exchange rate, however, also affect the long-run nominal exchange rate.* The long-run theory of exchange rate determination implied by equation (5-7) thus includes the valid elements of the monetary approach, but in addition it corrects the monetary approach by allowing for nonmonetary factors that can cause sustained deviations from purchasing power parity.

Assuming all variables start out at their long-run levels, we can now understand the most important determinants of long-run swings in nominal exchange rates:

1. *A shift in relative money supply levels.* Suppose the Fed wishes to stimulate the economy and therefore carries out an increase in the level of the U.S. money supply. As you will remember from Chapter 4, a permanent, one-time increase in a country's money supply has no effect on the long-run levels of output, the interest rate, or any relative price (including the real exchange rate). Thus, (5-3) implies once again that P_{US} rises in proportion to M_{US}, while (5-7) shows that the U.S. price level is the sole variable changing in the long run along with the nominal exchange rate $E_{\$/€}$. Because the real exchange rate $q_{\$/€}$ does not change, the nominal exchange rate change is consistent with relative PPP: The only long-run effect of the U.S. money supply increase is to raise all dollar prices, including the dollar price of the euro, in proportion to the increase in the money supply. It should be no surprise that this result is the same as the one we found using the monetary approach, since that approach is designed to account for the long-run effects of monetary changes.

2. *A shift in relative money supply growth rates.* Suppose the Fed concludes, to its dismay, that over the next few years the U.S. price level will fall. (A consistently falling price level is called *deflation.*) A permanent increase in the *growth rate* of the U.S. money supply raises the long-run U.S. inflation rate and, through the Fisher effect, raises the dollar interest rate relative to the euro interest rate. Because relative U.S. real money demand therefore declines, equation (5-3) implies that P_{US} rises (as shown in Figure 5-1). Because the change bringing this outcome about is purely monetary, however, it is neutral in its long-run effects; specifically, it does not alter the long-run *real* dollar/euro exchange rate. According to (5-7), then, $E_{\$/€}$ rises in proportion to the increase in P_{US} (a depreciation of the dollar against the euro). Once again, a purely monetary change brings about a long-run nominal exchange rate shift in line with relative PPP, just as the monetary approach predicted.

3. *A change in relative output demand.* This type of change is *not* covered by the monetary approach, so now the more general perspective we've developed, in which the real exchange rate can change, is essential. Since a change in relative output demand does not affect long-run national price levels—these depend solely on the factors appearing in equations (5-3) and (5-4)—the long-run nominal exchange rate in (5-7) will change only insofar as the real exchange rate changes. Consider an increase in world relative demand for U.S. products. Earlier in this section, we saw that a rise in demand for U.S. products causes a long-run real appreciation of the dollar against the euro (a fall in $q_{\$/€}$); this change is simply a rise in the relative price of U.S. output. Given that long-run national price levels are unchanged, however, (5-7) tells us that a long-run *nominal* appreciation of the dollar against the euro (a fall in $E_{\$/€}$) must also occur. This prediction highlights the important fact that even though exchange rates are nominal prices, they respond to nonmonetary as well as monetary events, even over long horizons.

4. *A change in relative output supply.* As we saw earlier in this section, an increase in relative U.S. output supply causes the dollar to depreciate in real terms against the euro, lowering the relative price of U.S. output. This rise in $q_{\$/€}$ is not, however, the only change in equation (5-7) implied by a relative rise in U.S. output. In addition, the U.S. output increase raises the transaction demand for real U.S. money balances, raising aggregate U.S. real money demand and, by (5-3), pushing the long-run U.S. price level down. Referring back to equation (5-7), you will see that since $q_{\$/€}$ rises while P_{US} falls, the output and money market effects of a change in output supply work in opposite directions, thus making the net effect on $E_{\$/€}$ is *ambiguous.* Our analysis of an output-supply change illustrates that even when a disturbance originates in a single market (in this case, the output market), its influence on exchange rates may depend on repercussion effects that are channeled through other markets.

We conclude that when all disturbances are monetary in nature, exchange rates obey relative PPP in the long run. In the long run, a monetary disturbance affects only the general purchasing power of a currency, and this change in purchasing power changes equally the currency's value in terms of domestic and foreign goods. When disturbances occur in output markets, the exchange rate is unlikely to obey relative PPP, even in the long run. Table 5-1 summarizes these conclusions regarding the effects of monetary and output market changes on long-run nominal exchange rates.

In the chapters that follow, we will appeal to this section's general long-run exchange rate model even when we are discussing *short-run* macroeconomic events. Long-run

TABLE 5-1	Effects of Money Market and Output Market Changes on the Long-Run Nominal Dollar/Euro Exchange Rate, $E_{\$/€}$	
Change	**Effect on the Long-Run Nominal Dollar/Euro Exchange Rate, $E_{\$/€}$**
Money market	
1. Increase in U.S. money supply level	Proportional increase (nominal depreciation of $)
2. Increase in European money supply level	Proportional decrease (nominal depreciation of euro)
3. Increase in U.S. money supply growth rate	Increase (nominal depreciation of $)
4. Increase in European money supply growth rate	Decrease (nominal depreciation of euro)
Output market	
1. Increase in demand for U.S. output	Decrease (nominal appreciation of $)
2. Increase in demand for European output	Increase (nominal appreciation of euro)
3. Output supply increase in the United States	Ambiguous
4. Output supply increase in Europe	Ambiguous

factors are important in the short run because of the central role that expectations about the future play in the day-to-day determination of exchange rates. That is why news about the current account, for example, can have a big impact on the exchange rate. The long-run exchange rate model of this section will provide the anchor for market expectations, that is, the framework market participants use to forecast future exchange rates on the basis of information at hand today.

International Interest Rate Differences and the Real Exchange Rate

Earlier in this chapter, we saw that relative PPP, when combined with interest parity, implies that international interest rate differences equal differences in countries' expected inflation rates. Because relative PPP does not hold true in general, however, the relation between international interest rate differences and national inflation rates is likely to be more complex in practice than that simple formula suggests. Despite this complexity, economic policy makers who hope to influence exchange rates, as well as private individuals who wish to forecast them, cannot succeed without understanding the factors that cause countries' interest rates to differ.

In this section, we therefore extend our earlier discussion of the Fisher effect to include real exchange rate movements. We do this by showing that in general, interest rate differences between countries depend not only on differences in expected inflation, as the monetary approach asserts, but also on expected changes in the real exchange rate.

We begin by recalling that the change in $q_{\$/€}$, the real dollar/euro exchange rate, is the *deviation* from relative PPP; that is, the change in $q_{\$/€}$ is the percentage change in the nominal dollar/euro exchange rate less the international difference in inflation rates between the United States and Europe. We thus arrive at the corresponding relationship among the *expected* change in the real exchange rate, the *expected* change in the nominal rate, and *expected* inflation:

$$(q^e_{\$/\euro} - q_{\$/\euro})/q_{\$/\euro} = [(E^e_{\$/\euro} - E_{\$/\euro})/E_{\$/\euro}] - (\pi^e_{US} - \pi^e_E), \qquad (5\text{-}8)$$

where $q^e_{\$/\euro}$ (as per our usual notation) is the real exchange rate expected for a year from today.

Now we return to the interest parity condition between dollar and euro deposits,

$$R_\$ - R_\euro = (E^e_{\$/\euro} - E_{\$/\euro})/E_{\$/\euro}.$$

An easy rearrangement of (5-8) shows the expected rate of change in the *nominal* dollar/euro exchange rate is just the expected rate of change in the *real* dollar/euro exchange rate *plus* the U.S.–Europe expected inflation difference. Combining (5-8) with the above interest parity condition, we thus are led to the following breakdown of the international interest rate gap:

$$R_\$ - R_\euro = [(q^e_{\$/\euro} - q_{\$/\euro})/q_{\$/\euro}] + (\pi^e_{US} - \pi^e_E). \qquad (5\text{-}9)$$

Notice that when the market expects relative PPP to prevail, $q^e_{\$/\euro} = q_{\$/\euro}$ and the first term on the right side of this equation drops out. In this special case, (5-9) reduces to the simpler (5-5), which we derived by assuming relative PPP.

In general, however, the dollar/euro interest difference is the sum of *two* components: (1) the expected rate of real dollar depreciation against the euro and (2) the expected inflation difference between the United States and Europe. For example, if U.S. inflation will be 5 percent per year forever and European inflation will be zero forever, the long-run interest difference between dollar and euro deposits need not be the 5 percent that PPP (when combined with interest parity) would suggest. If, in addition, everyone knows that output demand and supply trends will make the dollar depreciate against the euro in real terms at a rate of 1 percent per year, the international interest spread will actually be 6 percent.

Real Interest Parity

Economics makes an important distinction between **nominal interest rates**, which are rates of return measured in monetary terms, and **real interest rates**, which are rates of return measured in *real* terms, that is, in terms of a country's output. Because real rates of return often are uncertain, we usually will refer to *expected* real interest rates. The interest rates we discussed in connection with the interest parity condition and the determinants of money demand were nominal rates, for example, the dollar return on dollar deposits. But for many other purposes, economists need to analyze behavior in terms of real rates of return. No one who is thinking of investing money, for example, could make a decision knowing only that the nominal interest rate is 15 percent. The investment would be quite attractive at zero inflation, but disastrously unattractive if inflation were bounding along at 100 percent per year![20]

We conclude this chapter by showing that when the nominal interest parity condition equates nominal interest rate differences between currencies to expected changes in *nominal* exchange rates, a *real* interest parity condition equates expected real interest

---

[20]We could get away with examining nominal return differences in the foreign exchange market because (as Chapter 3 showed) nominal return differences equal real return differences for any given investor. In the context of the demand for money, the nominal interest rate is the real rate of return you sacrifice by holding interest-barren currency.

rate differences to expected changes in *real* exchange rates. Only when relative PPP is expected to hold (meaning no real exchange rate change is anticipated) are expected real interest rates in all countries identical.

The expected real interest rate, denoted r^e, is defined as the nominal interest rate, R, less the expected inflation rate, π^e:

$$r^e = R - \pi^e.$$

In other words, the expected real interest rate in a country is just the real rate of return a domestic resident expects to earn on a loan of his or her currency. The definition of the expected real interest rate clarifies the generality of the forces behind the Fisher effect: Any increase in the expected inflation rate that does not alter the expected real interest rate must be reflected, one for one, in the nominal interest rate.

A useful consequence of the preceding definition is a formula for the difference in expected real interest rates between two currency areas such as the United States and Europe:

$$r^e_{US} - r^e_E = (R_\$ - \pi^e_{US}) - (R_€ - \pi^e_E).$$

If we rearrange equation (5-9) and combine it with the equation above, we get the desired *real interest parity condition*:

$$r^e_{US} - r^e_E = (q^e_{\$/€} - q_{\$/€})/q_{\$/€}. \tag{5-10}$$

Equation (5-10) looks much like the nominal interest parity condition from which it is derived, but it explains differences in expected *real* interest rates between the United States and Europe by expected movements in the dollar/euro *real* exchange rate.

Expected real interest rates are the same in different countries when relative PPP is expected to hold (in which case (5-10) implies that $r^e_{US} = r^e_E$). More generally, however, expected real interest rates in different countries need not be equal, even in the long run, if continuing change in output markets is expected.[21] Suppose, for example, that productivity in the South Korean tradables sector is expected to rise during the next two decades, while productivity stagnates in South Korean nontradables and in all U.S. industries. If the Balassa-Samuelson hypothesis is valid, people should expect the U.S. dollar to depreciate in real terms against South Korea's currency, the won, as the prices of South Korea's nontradables trend upward. Equation (5-10) thus implies that the expected real interest rate should be higher in the United States than in South Korea.

Do such real interest differences imply unnoticed profit opportunities for international investors? Not necessarily. A cross-border real interest difference does imply that residents of two countries perceive different real rates of return on wealth. Nominal interest parity tells us, however, that any *given* investor expects the same real return on domestic and foreign currency assets. Two investors residing in different countries need not calculate this single real rate of return in the same way if relative PPP does not link the prices of their consumption baskets, but there is no way either can profit from their disagreement by shifting funds between currencies.

---

[21]In the two-period analysis of international borrowing and lending in Chapter 6 of our companion textbook, *International Trade: Theory and Policy*, all countries face a single worldwide real interest rate. Relative PPP must hold in that analysis, however, because there is only one consumption good in each period.

SUMMARY

1. The *purchasing power parity* theory, in its absolute form, asserts that the exchange rate between countries' currencies equals the ratio of their price levels, as measured by the money prices of a reference commodity basket. An equivalent statement of PPP is that the purchasing power of any currency is the same in any country. *Absolute PPP* implies a second version of the PPP theory, *relative PPP*, which predicts that percentage changes in exchange rates equal differences in national inflation rates.

2. A building block of the PPP theory is the *law of one price*, which states that under free competition and in the absence of trade impediments, a good must sell for a single price regardless of where in the world it is sold. Proponents of the PPP theory often argue, however, that its validity does not require the law of one price to hold for every commodity.

3. The *monetary approach to the exchange rate* uses PPP to explain long-term exchange rate behavior exclusively in terms of money supply and demand. In that theory, long-run international interest differentials result from different national rates of ongoing inflation, as the *Fisher effect* predicts. Sustained international differences in monetary growth rates are, in turn, behind different long-term rates of continuing inflation. The monetary approach thus finds that a rise in a country's interest rate will be associated with a depreciation of its currency. Relative PPP implies that international interest differences, which equal the expected percentage change in the exchange rate, also equal the international expected inflation gap.

4. The empirical support for PPP and the law of one price is weak in recent data. The failure of these propositions in the real world is related to trade barriers and departures from free competition, factors that can result in *pricing to market* by exporters. In addition, different definitions of price levels in different countries bedevil attempts to test PPP using the price indices governments publish. For some products, including many services, international transport costs are so steep that these products become nontradable.

5. Deviations from relative PPP can be viewed as changes in a country's *real exchange rate*, the price of a typical foreign expenditure basket in terms of the typical domestic expenditure basket. All else equal, a country's currency undergoes a long-run *real appreciation* against foreign currencies when the world relative demand for its output rises. In this case, the country's real exchange rate, as just defined, falls. The home currency undergoes a long-run *real depreciation* against foreign currencies when home output expands relative to foreign output. In this case, the real exchange rate rises.

6. The long-run determination of *nominal exchange rates* can be analyzed by combining two theories: the theory of the long-run *real* exchange rate and the theory of how domestic monetary factors determine long-run price levels. A stepwise increase in a country's money stock ultimately leads to a proportional increase in its price level and a proportional fall in its currency's foreign exchange value, just as relative PPP predicts. Changes in monetary growth rates also have long-run effects consistent with PPP. Supply or demand changes in output markets, however, result in exchange rate movements that do not conform to PPP.

7. The interest parity condition equates international differences in *nominal interest rates* to the expected percentage change in the nominal exchange rate. If interest parity holds in this sense, a real interest parity condition equates international differences in expected *real interest rates* to the expected

change in the real exchange rate. Real interest parity also implies that international differences in nominal interest rates equal the difference in expected inflation *plus* the expected percentage change in the real exchange rate.

KEY TERMS

absolute PPP, p. 118
Fisher effect, p. 118
law of one price, p. 112
monetary approach to
   the exchange rate, p. 115

nominal exchange rate, p. 131
nominal interest rate, p. 139
pricing to market, p. 124
purchasing power parity
   (PPP), p. 111

real appreciation, p. 132
real depreciation, p. 132
real exchange rate, p. 131
real interest rate, p. 139
relative PPP, p. 114

PROBLEMS

MyEconLab

1. Suppose Russia's inflation rate is 100 percent over one year but the inflation rate in Switzerland is only 5 percent. According to relative PPP, what should happen over the year to the Swiss franc's exchange rate against the Russian ruble?

2. Discuss why it is often asserted that exporters suffer when their home currencies appreciate in real terms against foreign currencies and prosper when their home currencies depreciate in real terms.

3. Other things equal, how would you expect the following shifts to affect a currency's real exchange rate against foreign currencies?
   a. The overall level of spending doesn't change, but domestic residents decide to spend more of their income on nontraded products and less on tradables.
   b. Foreign residents shift their demand away from their own goods and toward the home country's exports.

4. Large-scale wars typically bring a suspension of international trading and financial activities. Exchange rates lose much of their relevance under these conditions, but once the war is over, governments wishing to fix exchange rates face the problem of deciding what the new rates should be. The PPP theory has often been applied to this problem of postwar exchange rate realignment. Imagine that you are a British Chancellor of the Exchequer and that World War I has just ended. Explain how you would figure out the dollar/pound exchange rate implied by PPP. When might it be a bad idea to use the PPP theory in this way?

5. In the late 1970s, Britain seemed to have struck it rich. Having developed its North Sea oil-producing fields in earlier years, Britain suddenly found its real income higher as a result of a dramatic increase in world oil prices in 1979–1980. In the early 1980s, however, oil prices receded as the world economy slid into a deep recession and world oil demand faltered.

   In the following chart, we show index numbers for the average real exchange rate of the pound against several foreign currencies. (Such average index numbers are called real *effective* exchange rates.) A rise in one of these numbers indicates a real *appreciation* of the pound, that is, an increase in Britain's price level relative to the average price level abroad measured in pounds. A fall is a real depreciation.

Real Effective Exchange Rate of the Pound Sterling, 1976–1984 (1980 = 100)

1976	1977	1978	1979	1980	1981	1982	1983	1984
68.3	66.5	72.2	81.4	100.0	102.8	100.0	92.5	89.8

Source: International Monetary Fund, *International Financial Statistics*. The real exchange rate measures are based on indices of net output prices called value-added deflators.

Use the clues we have given about the British economy to explain the rise and fall of the pound's real effective exchange rate between 1978 and 1984. Pay particular attention to the role of nontradables.

6. Explain how permanent shifts in national real money demand functions affect real and nominal exchange rates in the long run.

7. At the end of World War I, the Treaty of Versailles imposed an indemnity on Germany, a large annual payment from it to the victorious Allies. (Many historians believe this indemnity played a role in destabilizing financial markets in the interwar period and even in bringing on World War II.) In the 1920s, economists John Maynard Keynes and Bertil Ohlin had a spirited debate in the *Economic Journal* over the possibility that the transfer payment would impose a "secondary burden" on Germany by worsening its terms of trade. Use the theory developed in this chapter to discuss the mechanisms through which a permanent transfer from Poland to the Czech Republic would affect the real zloty/koruna exchange rate in the long run.

8. Continuing with the preceding problem, discuss how the transfer would affect the long-run *nominal* exchange rate between the two currencies.

9. A country imposes a tariff on imports from abroad. How does this action change the long-run real exchange rate between the home and foreign currencies? How is the long-run nominal exchange rate affected?

10. Imagine two identical countries have restricted imports to identical levels, but one has done so using tariffs while the other has done so using quotas. After these policies are in place, both countries experience identical, balanced expansions of domestic spending. Where should the demand expansion cause a greater real currency appreciation, in the tariff-using country or in the quota-using country?

11. Explain how the nominal dollar/euro exchange rate would be affected (all else equal) by permanent changes in the expected rate of real depreciation of the dollar against the euro.

12. Can you suggest an event that would cause a country's nominal interest rate to rise and its currency to appreciate simultaneously, in a world of perfectly flexible prices?

13. Suppose the expected real interest rate in the United States is 9 percent per year while that in Europe is 3 percent per year. What do you expect to happen to the real dollar/euro exchange rate over the next year?

14. In the short run of a model with sticky prices, a reduction in the money supply raises the nominal interest rate and appreciates the currency (see Chapter 4). What happens to the expected real interest rate? Explain why the subsequent path of the real exchange rate satisfies the real interest parity condition.

15. Discuss the following statement: "When a change in a country's nominal interest rate is caused by a rise in the expected real interest rate, the domestic currency appreciates. When the change is caused by a rise in expected inflation, the currency depreciates." (It may help to refer back to Chapter 4.)

16. Nominal interest rates are quoted at a variety of maturities, corresponding to different lengths of loans. For example, in late 2004 the U.S. government could take out ten-year loans at an annual interest rate of slightly over 4 percent, whereas the annual rate it paid on loans of only three months' duration was slightly under 2 percent. (An annualized interest rate of 2 percent on a three-month loan means that if you borrow a dollar, you repay $1.005 = \$1 + (3/12) \times \$0.02$ at the end of three months.) Typically, though not always, long-term interest rates are above short-term rates, as in the preceding example from 2004. In terms of the Fisher effect, what would that pattern say about expected inflation and/or the expected future real interest rate?

17. Continuing with the preceding problem, we can define short- and long-term *real* rates of interest. In all cases, the relevant real interest rate (annualized, that is, expressed in percent per year) is the annualized nominal interest rate at the maturity in question, less the annualized expected inflation rate over the period of the loan. Recall the evidence that relative PPP seems to hold better over long horizons than short ones. In that case, will international real interest differentials be larger at short than at long maturities? Explain your reasoning.

18. Why might it be true that relative PPP holds better in the long run than the short run? (Think about how international trading firms might react to large and persistent cross-border differences in the prices of a tradable good.)

19. Suppose residents of the U.S. consume relatively more of U.S. export goods than residents of foreign countries. In other words, U.S. export goods have a higher weight in the U.S. CPI than they do in other countries. Conversely, foreign exports have a lower weight in the U.S. CPI than they do abroad. What would be the effect on the dollar's real exchange rate of a rise in the U.S. terms of trade (the relative price of U.S. exports in terms of U.S. imports)?

20. The *Economist* magazine has observed that the price of Big Macs is systematically positively related to a country's income level, just as is the general price level (recall the box on pages 125–127). If you go to the *Economist*'s Big Mac standard website, at http://www.economist.com/content/big-mac-index, you will find an Excel spreadsheet containing the data on under/overvaluation for January 2013 (as well as for previous years' surveys). Go to the World Bank's World Development Indicators website, http://data.worldbank.org/indicator/, and find the most recent data on GNI (Gross National Income) per capita, PPP, for all countries. Use these data, together with the *Economist* data on Big Mac dollar prices, to make a graph of income per capita (horizontal axis) versus dollar Big Mac price (vertical axis). What do you find?

FURTHER READINGS

James E. Anderson and Eric van Wincoop. "Trade Costs." *Journal of Economic Literature* 42 (September 2004), pp. 691–751. Comprehensive survey of the nature and effects of costs of international trade.

Gustav Cassel. *Post-War Monetary Stabilization*. New York: Columbia University Press, 1928. Applies the purchasing power parity theory of exchange rates in analyzing the monetary problems that followed World War I.

Robert E. Cumby. "Forecasting Exchange Rates and Relative Prices with the Hamburger Standard: Is What You Want What You Get with McParity?" Working Paper 5675. National Bureau of Economic Research, July 1996. Studies the statistical forecasting power of Big Mac measures of over- and under-valuation.

Angus Deaton and Alan Heston. "Understanding PPPs and PPP-Based National Accounts." *American Economic Journal: Macroeconomics* 2 (October 2010): 1–35. Critical overview of the many obstacles to constructing accurate international price comparisons.

Michael B. Devereux. "Real Exchange Rates and Macroeconomics: Evidence and Theory." *Canadian Journal of Economics* 30 (November 1997), pp. 773–808. Reviews theories of the determinants and effects of real exchange rates.

Rudiger Dornbusch. "The Theory of Flexible Exchange Rate Regimes and Macroeconomic Policy," in Jan Herin, Assar Lindbeck, and Johan Myhrman, eds. *Flexible Exchange Rates and Stabilization Policy*. Boulder, CO: Westview Press, 1977, pp. 123–143. Develops a long-run model of exchange rates incorporating traded and nontraded goods and services.

Pinelopi Koujianou Goldberg and Michael M. Knetter. "Goods Prices and Exchange Rates: What Have We Learned?" *Journal of Economic Literature* 35 (September 1997), pp. 1243–1272. Excellent survey of micro-level evidence on the law of one price, exchange rate pass-through, and pricing to market.

David Hummels. "Transportation Costs and International Trade in the Second Era of Globalization." *Journal of Economic Perspectives* 21 (Summer 2007), pp. 131–154. Surveys the economics of transportation costs in modern international trade.

Jaewoo Lee, Gian Maria Milesi-Ferretti, Jonathan Ostry, Alessandro Prati, and Luca Antonio Ricci. *Exchange Rate Assessments: CGER Methodologies.* Occasional Paper 261, International Monetary Fund, 2008. Describes International Monetary Fund models for evaluating real exchange rates.

Lloyd A. Metzler. "Exchange Rates and the International Monetary Fund," in *International Monetary Policies.* Postwar Economic Studies 7. Washington, D.C.: Board of Governors of the Federal Reserve System, 1947, pp. 1–45. The author applies purchasing power parity with skill and skepticism to evaluate the fixed exchange rates established by the International Monetary Fund after World War II.

Frederic S. Mishkin. *The Economics of Money, Banking and Financial Markets*, 10th edition. Upper Saddle River, NJ: Prentice Hall, 2013. Chapter 5 discusses inflation and the Fisher effect.

Kenneth Rogoff. "The Purchasing Power Parity Puzzle." *Journal of Economic Literature* 34 (June 1996), pp. 647–668. Critical survey of theory and empirical work.

Alan C. Stockman. "The Equilibrium Approach to Exchange Rates." *Federal Reserve Bank of Richmond Economic Review* 73 (March/April 1987), pp. 12–30. Theory and evidence on an equilibrium exchange rate model similar to the long-run model of this chapter.

Alan M. Taylor and Mark P. Taylor. "The Purchasing Power Parity Debate." *Journal of Economic Perspectives* 18 (Fall 2004), pp. 135–158. Surveys recent research on PPP.

MyEconLab Can Help You Get a Better Grade

MyEconLab   If your exam were tomorrow, would you be ready? For each chapter, MyEconLab Practice Tests and Study Plans pinpoint sections you have mastered and those you need to study. That way, you are more efficient with your study time, and you are better prepared for your exams.

To see how it works, turn to page 9 and then go to

www.myeconlab.com

The Fisher Effect, the Interest Rate, and the Exchange Rate under the Flexible-Price Monetary Approach

The monetary approach to exchange rates—which assumes the prices of goods are perfectly flexible—implies that a country's currency depreciates when its nominal interest rates rise because of higher expected future inflation. This appendix supplies a detailed analysis of that important result.

Consider again the dollar/euro exchange rate, and imagine the Federal Reserve raises the future rate of U.S. money supply growth by the amount $\Delta\pi$. Figure 5A-1 provides a diagram that will help us keep track of how various markets respond to that change.

The lower right quadrant in the figure is our usual depiction of equilibrium in the U.S. money market. It shows that before the increase in U.S. money supply growth, the nominal interest rate on dollars equals $R_\$^1$ (point 1). The Fisher effect tells us that a rise $\Delta\pi$ in the future rate of U.S. money supply growth, all else equal, will raise the nominal interest rate on dollars to $R_\$^2 = R_\$^1 + \Delta\pi$ (point 2).

As the diagram shows, the rise in the nominal dollar interest rate reduces money demand and therefore requires an equilibrating fall in the real money supply. But the nominal money stock is unchanged in the short run because it is only the *future* rate of U.S. money supply growth that has risen. What happens? Given the unchanged nominal money supply M_{US}^1, an upward jump in the U.S. price level from P_{US}^1 to P_{US}^2 brings about the needed reduction in American real money holdings. The assumed flexibility of prices allows this jump to occur even in the short run.

To see the exchange rate response, we turn to the lower-left quadrant. The monetary approach assumes purchasing power parity, implying that as P_{US} rises (while the European price level remains constant, which we assume), the dollar/euro exchange rate $E_{\$/€}$ must rise (a depreciation of the dollar). The lower-left quadrant of Figure 5A-1 graphs the implied relationship between U.S. real money holdings, M_{US}/P_{US}, and the nominal exchange rate, $E_{\$/€}$, given an unchanged *nominal* money supply in the United States and an unchanged European price level. Using PPP, we can write the equation graphed there (which is a downward-sloping *hyperbola*) as:

$$E_{\$/€} = P_{US}/P_E = \frac{M_{US}/P_E}{M_{US}/P_{US}}.$$

This equation shows that the fall in the U.S. real money supply, from M_{US}^1/P_{US}^1 to M_{US}^1/P_{US}^2, is associated with a dollar depreciation in which the dollar/euro nominal exchange rate rises from $E_{\$/€}^1$ to $E_{\$/€}^2$ (shown as a movement to the left along the horizontal axis).

The 45-degree line in the upper-left quadrant of Figure 5A-1 allows you to translate the exchange rate change given in the lower-left quadrant to the vertical axis of the upper-right quadrant's diagram. The upper-right quadrant contains our usual portrayal of equilibrium in the foreign exchange market.

There you can see the dollar's depreciation against the euro is associated with a move in the foreign exchange market's equilibrium from point 1′ to point 2′. The picture shows why the dollar depreciates, despite the rise in $R_\$$. The reason is an outward

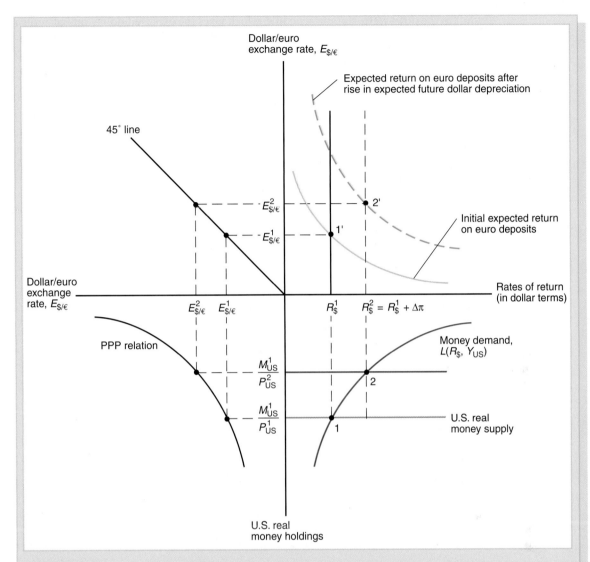

FIGURE 5A-1

How a Rise in U.S. Monetary Growth Affects Dollar Interest Rates and the Dollar/Euro Exchange Rate When Goods Prices Are Flexible

When goods prices are perfectly flexible, the money market equilibrium diagram (southeast quadrant) shows two effects of an increase, $\Delta\pi$, in the future rate of U.S. money supply growth. The change (i) raises the dollar interest rate from $R_\$^1$ to $R_\$^2 = R_\$^2 + \Delta\pi$, in line with the Fisher effect, and (ii) causes the U.S. price level to jump upward, from P_{US}^1 to P_{US}^2. Money market equilibrium therefore moves from point 1 to point 2. (Because M_{US}^1 doesn't change immediately, the real U.S. money supply falls to M_{US}^1/P_{US}^2, bringing the real money supply into line with reduced money demand.) The PPP relationship in the southwest quadrant shows that the price level jump from P_{US}^1 to P_{US}^2 requires a depreciation of the dollar against the euro (the dollar/euro exchange rate moves up, from $E_{\$/€}^1$ to $E_{\$/€}^2$). In the foreign exchange market diagram (northeast quadrant), this dollar depreciation is shown as the move from point 1' to point 2'. The dollar depreciates despite a rise in $R_\$$ because heightened expectations of future dollar depreciation against the euro cause an outward shift of the locus measuring the expected dollar return on euro deposits.

shift in the downward-sloping schedule, which gives the expected dollar rate of return on euro deposits. Why does that schedule shift outward? Higher expected future monetary growth implies faster expected future depreciation of the dollar against the euro and therefore a rise in the attractiveness of euro deposits. It is this change in expectations that leads simultaneously to a rise in the nominal interest rate on dollars and to a depreciation of the dollar in the foreign exchange market.

To summarize, we cannot predict how a rise in the dollar interest rate will affect the dollar's exchange rate without knowing *why* the nominal interest rate has risen. In a flexible-price model in which the home nominal interest rate rises because of higher expected future money supply growth, the home currency will depreciate—not appreciate—thanks to expectations of more rapid future depreciation.

6

OUTPUT AND THE EXCHANGE RATE IN THE SHORT RUN

The U.S. and Canadian economies registered similar negative rates of output growth during 2009, a year of deep global recession. But while the U.S. dollar depreciated against foreign currencies by about 8 percent over the year, the Canadian dollar *appreciated* by roughly 16 percent. What explains these contrasting experiences? By completing the macroeconomic model built in the last three chapters, this chapter will sort out the complicated factors that cause output, exchange rates, and inflation to change. Chapters 4 and 5 presented the connections among exchange rates, interest rates, and price levels but always assumed that output levels were determined outside of the model. Those chapters gave us only a partial picture of how macroeconomic changes affect an open economy because events that change exchange rates, interest rates, and price levels may also affect output. Now we complete the picture by examining how output and the exchange rate are determined in the short run.

Our discussion combines what we have learned about asset markets and the long-run behavior of exchange rates with a new element, a theory of how the output market adjusts to demand changes when product prices in the economy are themselves slow to adjust. As we learned in Chapter 4, institutional factors like long-term nominal contracts can give rise to "sticky" or slowly adjusting output market prices. By combining a short-run model of the output market with our models of the foreign exchange and money markets (the asset markets), we build a model that explains the short-run behavior of all the important macroeconomic variables in an open economy. The long-run exchange rate model of the preceding chapter provides the framework that participants in the asset markets use to form their expectations about future exchange rates.

Because output changes may push the economy away from full employment, the links among output and other macroeconomic variables, such as the trade balance and the current account, are of great concern to economic policy makers. In the last part of this chapter, we use our short-run model to examine how macroeconomic policy tools affect output and the current account and how those tools can be used to maintain full employment.

After reading this chapter, you will be able to:

- Explain the role of the real exchange rate in determining the aggregate demand for a country's output.
- See how an open economy's short-run equilibrium can be analyzed as the intersection of an asset market equilibrium schedule (*AA*) and an output market equilibrium schedule (*DD*).
- Understand how monetary and fiscal policies affect the exchange rate and national output in the short run.
- Describe and interpret the long-run effects of permanent macroeconomic policy changes.
- Explain the relationship among macroeconomic policies, the current account balance, and the exchange rate.

Determinants of Aggregate Demand in an Open Economy

To analyze how output is determined in the short run when product prices are sticky, we introduce the concept of **aggregate demand** for a country's output. Aggregate demand is the amount of a country's goods and services demanded by households, firms, and governments throughout the world. Just as the output of an individual good or service depends in part on the demand for it, a country's overall short-run output level depends on the aggregate demand for its products. The economy is at full employment in the long run (by definition) because wages and the price level eventually adjust to ensure full employment. In the long run, domestic output therefore depends only on the available domestic supplies of factors of production such as labor and capital. As we will see, however, these productive factors can be over- or underemployed in the short run as a result of shifts in aggregate demand that have not yet had their full long-run effects on prices.

In Chapter 2, we learned an economy's output is the sum of four types of expenditure that generate national income: consumption, investment, government purchases, and the current account. Correspondingly, aggregate demand for an open economy's output is the sum of consumption demand (C), investment demand (I), government demand (G), and net export demand, that is, the current account (CA). Each of these components of aggregate demand depends on various factors. In this section we examine the factors that determine consumption demand and the current account. We discuss government demand later in this chapter when we examine the effects of fiscal policy; for now, we assume that G is given. To avoid complicating our model, we also assume investment demand is given. The determinants of investment demand are incorporated into the model in the Online Appendix to this chapter.

Determinants of Consumption Demand

In this chapter, we view the amount a country's residents wish to consume as depending on disposable income, Y^d (that is, national income less taxes, $Y - T$).[1] (C, Y, and T are all measured in terms of domestic output units.) With this assumption,

---

[1]A more complete model would allow other factors, such as real wealth, expected future income, and the real interest rate, to affect consumption plans. This chapter's Appendix 1 links the formulation here to the microeconomic theory of the consumer.

a country's desired consumption level can be written as a function of disposable income:

$$C = C(Y^d).$$

Because each consumer naturally demands more goods and services as his or her real income rises, we expect consumption to increase as disposable income increases at the aggregate level, too. Thus, consumption demand and disposable income are positively related. However, when disposable income rises, consumption demand generally rises by *less* because part of the income increase is saved.

Determinants of the Current Account

The current account balance, viewed as the demand for a country's exports less that country's own demand for imports, is determined by two main factors: the domestic currency's real exchange rate against foreign currency (that is, the price of a typical foreign expenditure basket in terms of domestic expenditure baskets) and domestic disposable income. (In reality, a country's current account depends on many other factors, such as the level of foreign expenditure, but for now we regard these other factors as being held constant.)[2]

We express a country's current account balance as a function of its currency's real exchange rate, $q = EP^*/P$, and of domestic disposable income, Y^d:

$$CA = CA(EP^*/P, Y^d).$$

As a reminder of the last chapter's discussion, note that the domestic currency prices of representative foreign and domestic expenditure baskets are, respectively, EP^* and P, where E (the nominal exchange rate) is the price of foreign currency in terms of domestic currency, P^* is the foreign price level, and P is the home price level. The *real* exchange rate q, defined as the price of the foreign basket in terms of the domestic one, is therefore EP^*/P. If, for example, the representative basket of European goods and services costs €40 (P^*), the representative U.S. basket costs $50 ($P$), and the dollar/euro exchange rate is $1.10 per euro ($E$), then the price of the European basket in terms of U.S. baskets is

$$EP^*/P = \frac{(1.10\,\$/€) \times (40\,€/\text{European basket})}{(50\,\$/\text{U.S. basket})}$$

$$= 0.88\,\text{U.S. baskets/European basket}.$$

Real exchange rate changes affect the current account because they reflect changes in the prices of domestic goods and services relative to foreign goods and services. Disposable income affects the current account through its effect on total spending by domestic consumers. To understand how these real exchange rate and disposable income effects work, it is helpful to look separately at the demand for a country's exports, EX, and the demand for imports by the country's residents, IM. As we saw in Chapter 2, the current account is related to exports and imports by the identity

$$CA = EX - IM,$$

when CA, EX, and IM all are measured in terms of domestic output.

---

[2]As the previous footnote observed, we are ignoring a number of factors (such as wealth and interest rates) that affect consumption along with disposable income. Since some part of any consumption change goes into imports, these omitted determinants of consumption also help to determine the current account. Following the convention of Chapter 2, we are also ignoring unilateral transfers in analyzing the current account balance.

How Real Exchange Rate Changes Affect the Current Account

You will recall that a representative domestic expenditure basket includes some imported products but places a relatively heavier weight on goods and services produced domestically. At the same time, the representative foreign basket is skewed toward goods and services produced in the foreign country. Thus, a rise in the price of the foreign basket in terms of domestic baskets, say, will be associated with a rise in the relative price of foreign output in general relative to domestic output.[3]

To determine how such a change in the relative price of national outputs affects the current account, other things equal, we must ask how it affects both EX and IM. When EP^*/P rises, for example, foreign products have become more expensive relative to domestic products: Each unit of domestic output now purchases fewer units of foreign output. Foreign consumers will respond to this price shift (a real domestic currency depreciation) by demanding more of our exports. This response by foreigners will therefore raise EX and improve the domestic country's current account.

The effect of the same real exchange rate increase on IM is more complicated. Domestic consumers respond to the price shift by purchasing fewer units of the more expensive foreign products. Their response does not imply, however, that IM must fall, because IM denotes the *value* of imports measured in terms of domestic output, not the *volume* of foreign products imported. Since a rise in EP^*/P (a real depreciation of the domestic currency) tends to raise the value of each unit of imports in terms of domestic output units, imports measured in domestic output units may rise as a result of a rise in EP^*/P even if imports decline when measured in foreign output units. IM can therefore rise or fall when EP^*/P rises, so the effect of a real exchange rate change on the current account CA is ambiguous.

Whether the current account improves or worsens depends on which effect of a real exchange rate change is dominant—the *volume effect* of consumer spending shifts on export and import quantities, or the *value effect*, which changes the domestic output equivalent of a *given* volume of foreign imports. We assume for now that the volume effect of a real exchange rate change always outweighs the value effect, so that, other things equal, a real depreciation of the currency improves the current account and a real appreciation of the currency worsens the current account.[4]

While we have couched our discussion of real exchange rates and the current account in terms of consumers' responses, producers' responses are just as important and work in much the same way. When a country's currency depreciates in real terms, foreign firms will find that the country can supply intermediate production inputs more cheaply. These effects have become stronger as a result of the increasing tendency for multinational firms to locate different stages of their production processes in a variety of countries. For example, the German auto manufacturer BMW can shift production from Germany to its Spartanburg, South Carolina, plant if a dollar depreciation lowers the relative cost of producing in the United States. The production shift represents an increase in world demand for U.S. labor and output.

---

[3]The real exchange rate is being used here essentially as a convenient summary measure of the relative prices of domestic against foreign products. A more exact (but much more complicated) analysis would work explicitly with separate demand and supply functions for each country's nontradables and tradables but would lead to conclusions very much like those we reach below.

[4]This assumption requires that import and export demands be relatively *elastic* with respect to the real exchange rate. Appendix 2 to this chapter describes a precise mathematical condition, called the Marshall-Lerner condition, under which the assumption in the text is valid. The appendix also examines empirical evidence on the time horizon over which the Marshall-Lerner condition holds.

TABLE 6-1	Factors Determining the Current Account
Change	**Effect on Current Account, *CA***
Real exchange rate, $EP^*/P\uparrow$	$CA\uparrow$
Real exchange rate, $EP^*/P\downarrow$	$CA\downarrow$
Disposable income, $Y^d\uparrow$	$CA\downarrow$
Disposable income, $Y^d\downarrow$	$CA\uparrow$

How Disposable Income Changes Affect the Current Account

The second factor influencing the current account is domestic disposable income. Since a rise in Y^d causes domestic consumers to increase their spending on *all* goods, including imports from abroad, an increase in disposable income worsens the current account, other things equal. (An increase in Y^d has no effect on export demand because we are holding foreign income constant and not allowing Y^d to affect it.)

Table 6-1 summarizes our discussion of how real exchange rate and disposable income changes influence the domestic current account.

The Equation of Aggregate Demand

We now combine the four components of aggregate demand to get an expression for total aggregate demand, denoted D:

$$D = C(Y - T) + I + G + CA(EP^*/P, Y - T),$$

where we have written disposable income Y^d as output, Y, less taxes, T. This equation shows that aggregate demand for home output can be written as a function of the real exchange rate, disposable income, investment demand, and government spending:

$$D = D(EP^*/P, Y - T, I, G).$$

We now want to see how aggregate demand depends on the real exchange rate and domestic GNP given the level of taxes, T, investment demand, I, and government purchases, G.[5]

The Real Exchange Rate and Aggregate Demand

A rise in EP^*/P makes domestic goods and services cheaper relative to foreign goods and services and shifts both domestic and foreign spending from foreign goods to domestic goods. As a result, CA rises (as assumed in the previous section) and aggregate demand, D, therefore goes up. *A real depreciation of the home currency*

---

[5]As noted above, investment I is taken as given, though we may imagine that it shifts for reasons that are outside the model (in other words, we assume it is an exogenous rather than an endogenous variable). We make the same assumption about G. It would not be hard to make I endogenous, however, as is done in the Online Appendix, where investment is a declining function of the domestic real rate of interest. (That is the assumption made in the standard *IS-LM* model of intermediate macroeconomics courses.) For a given expected future exchange rate and a given full-employment output level, the model of the Online Appendix implies that investment demand can be expressed as $I(E,Y)$, where a rise in E (depreciation of domestic currency) raises investment demand, as does an increase in domestic output Y. Modeling investment in this way within the setup of this chapter would not change our predictions in any important way.

raises aggregate demand for home output, other things equal; a real appreciation lowers aggregate demand for home output.

Real Income and Aggregate Demand

The effect of domestic real income on aggregate demand is slightly more complicated. If taxes are fixed at a given level, a rise in Y represents an equal rise in disposable income Y^d. While this rise in Y^d raises consumption, it worsens the current account by raising home spending on foreign imports. The first of these effects raises aggregate demand, but the second lowers it. Since the increase in consumption is divided between higher spending on home products and higher spending on foreign imports, however, the first effect (the effect of disposable income on total consumption) is greater than the second (the effect of disposable income on import spending alone). Therefore, *a rise in domestic real income raises aggregate demand for home output, other things equal, and a fall in domestic real income lowers aggregate demand for home output.*

Figure 6-1 shows the relation between aggregate demand and real income Y for fixed values of the real exchange rate, taxes, investment demand, and government spending. As Y rises, consumption rises by a fraction of the increase in income. Part of this increase in consumption, moreover, goes into import spending. The effect of an increase in Y on the aggregate demand for home output is therefore smaller than the accompanying rise in consumption demand, which is smaller, in turn, than the increase in Y. We show this in Figure 6-1 by drawing the aggregate demand schedule with a slope less than 1. (The schedule intersects the vertical axis above the origin because investment, government, and foreign demand would make aggregate demand greater than zero, even in the hypothetical case of zero domestic output.)

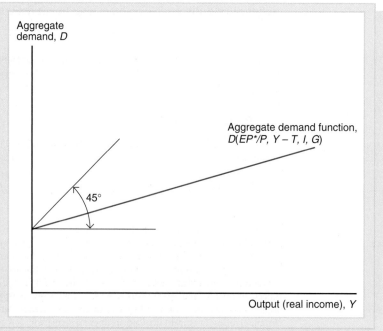

FIGURE 6-1

Aggregate Demand as a Function of Output

Aggregate demand is a function of the real exchange rate (EP^*/P), disposable income $(Y - T)$, investment demand (I), and government spending (G). If all other factors remain unchanged, a rise in output (real income), Y, increases aggregate demand. Because the increase in aggregate demand is less than the increase in output, the slope of the aggregate demand function is less than 1 (as indicated by its position within the 45-degree angle).

Aggregate demand, D

Aggregate demand function, $D(EP^*/P, Y - T, I, G)$

$45°$

Output (real income), Y

How Output Is Determined in the Short Run

Having discussed the factors that influence the demand for an open economy's output, we now study how output is determined in the short run. We show that the output market is in equilibrium when real domestic output, Y, equals the aggregate demand for domestic output:

$$Y = D(EP^*/P, Y - T, I, G). \qquad (6\text{-}1)$$

The equality of aggregate supply and demand therefore determines the short-run equilibrium output level.[6]

Our analysis of real output determination applies to the short run because we assume that the money prices of goods and services are *temporarily fixed*. As we will see later in the chapter, the short-run real output changes that occur when prices are temporarily fixed eventually cause price level changes that move the economy to its long-run equilibrium. In long-run equilibrium, factors of production are fully employed, the level of real output is completely determined by factor supplies, and the real exchange rate has adjusted to equate long-run real output to aggregate demand.[7]

The determination of national output in the short run is illustrated in Figure 6-2, where we again graph aggregate demand as a function of output for fixed levels of the

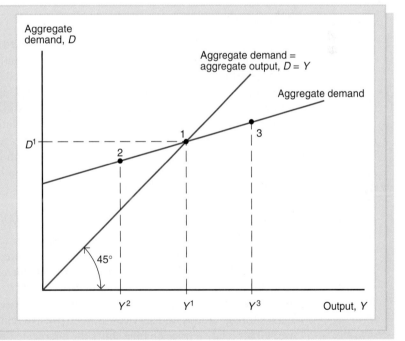

FIGURE 6-2

The Determination of Output in the Short Run

In the short run, output settles at Y^1 (point 1), where aggregate demand, D^1, equals aggregate output, Y^1.

---

[6]Superficially, equation (6-1), which may be written as $Y = C(Y^d) + I + G + CA(EP^*/P, Y^d)$, looks like the GNP identity we discussed in Chapter 2, $Y = C + I + G + CA$. How do the two equations differ? They differ in that (6-1) is an equilibrium condition, not an identity. As you will recall from Chapter 2, the investment quantity I appearing in the GNP identity includes *undesired* or involuntary inventory accumulation by firms, so the GNP identity always holds as a matter of definition. The investment demand appearing in equation (6-1), however, is *desired* or planned investment. Thus, the GNP identity always holds, but equation (6-1) holds only if firms are not unwillingly building up or drawing down inventories of goods.

[7]Thus, equation (6-1) also holds in long-run equilibrium, but the equation determines the long-run real exchange rate when Y is at its long-run value, as in Chapter 5. (We are holding foreign conditions constant.)

real exchange rate, taxes, investment demand, and government spending. The intersection (at point 1) of the aggregate demand schedule and a 45-degree line drawn from the origin (the equation $D = Y$) gives us the unique output level Y^1 at which aggregate demand equals domestic output.

Let's use Figure 6-2 to see why output tends to settle at Y^1 in the short run. At an output level of Y^2, aggregate demand (point 2) is higher than output. Firms therefore increase their production to meet this excess demand. (If they did not, they would have to meet the excess demand out of inventories, reducing investment below the desired level, I.) Thus, output expands until national income reaches Y^1.

At point 3, there is an excess supply of domestic output, and firms find themselves involuntarily accumulating inventories (and involuntarily raising their investment spending above its desired level). As inventories start to build up, firms cut back on production; only when output has fallen to Y^1 will firms be content with their level of production. Once again, output settles at point 1, the point at which output exactly equals aggregate demand. In this short-run equilibrium, consumers, firms, the government, and foreign buyers of domestic products are all able to realize their desired expenditures with no output left over.

Output Market Equilibrium in the Short Run: The *DD* Schedule

Now that we understand how output is determined for a given real exchange rate EP^*/P, let's look at how the exchange rate and output are simultaneously determined in the short run. To understand this process, we need two elements. The first element, developed in this section, is the relationship between output and the exchange rate (the *DD* schedule) that must hold when the output market is in equilibrium. The second element, developed in the next section, is the relationship between output and the exchange rate that must hold when the home money market and the foreign exchange market (the asset markets) are in equilibrium. Both elements are necessary because the economy as a whole is in equilibrium only when both the output market and the asset markets are in equilibrium.

Output, the Exchange Rate, and Output Market Equilibrium

Figure 6-3 illustrates the relationship between the exchange rate and output implied by output market equilibrium. Specifically, the figure illustrates the effect of a depreciation of the domestic currency against foreign currency (that is, a rise in E from E^1 to E^2) for fixed values of the domestic price level, P, and the foreign price level, P^*. With fixed price levels at home and abroad, the rise in the nominal exchange rate makes foreign goods and services more expensive relative to domestic goods and services. This relative price change shifts the aggregate demand schedule upward.

The fall in the relative price of domestic output shifts the aggregate demand schedule upward because at each level of domestic output, the demand for domestic products is higher. For example, foreign and American consumers of autos alike shift their demands toward American models when the dollar depreciates. Output expands from Y^1 to Y^2 as firms find themselves faced with excess demand at initial production levels.

Although we have considered the effect of a change in E with P and P^* held fixed, it is straightforward to analyze the effects of changes in P or P^* on output. *Any rise in the real exchange rate EP^*/P (whether due to a rise in E, a rise in P^*, or a fall in P) will cause an upward shift in the aggregate demand function and an expansion of output, all else equal.* (A rise in P^*, for example, has effects qualitatively identical to those of

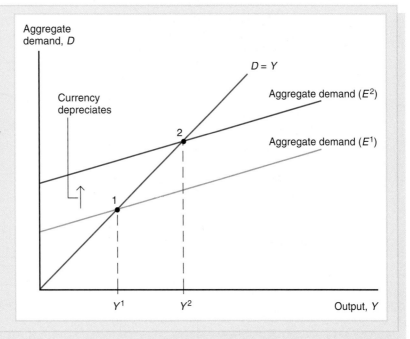

FIGURE 6-3

Output Effect of a Currency Depreciation with Fixed Output Prices

A rise in the exchange rate from E^1 to E^2 (a currency depreciation) raises aggregate demand to *Aggregate demand* (E^2) and output to Y^2, all else equal.

a rise in E.) *Similarly, any fall in $EP*/P$, regardless of its cause (a fall in E, a fall in P*, or a rise in P), will cause output to contract, all else equal.* (A rise in P, with E and $P*$ held fixed, for example, makes domestic products more expensive relative to foreign products, reduces aggregate demand for domestic output, and causes output to fall.)

Deriving the *DD* Schedule

If we assume P and $P*$ are fixed in the short run, a depreciation of the domestic currency (a rise in E) is associated with a rise in domestic output, Y, while an appreciation (a fall in E) is associated with a fall in Y. This association provides us with one of the two relationships between E and Y needed to describe the short-run macroeconomic behavior of an open economy. We summarize this relationship by the **DD schedule**, which shows all combinations of output and the exchange rate for which the output market is in short-run equilibrium (aggregate demand = aggregate output).

Figure 6-4 shows how to derive the *DD* schedule, which relates E and Y when P and $P*$ are fixed. The upper part of the figure reproduces the result of Figure 6-3 (a depreciation of the domestic currency shifts the aggregate demand function upward, causing output to rise). The *DD* schedule in the lower part graphs the resulting relationship between the exchange rate and output (given that P and $P*$ are held constant). Point 1 on the *DD* schedule gives the output level, Y^1, at which aggregate demand equals aggregate supply when the exchange rate is E^1. A depreciation of the currency to E^2 leads to the higher output level Y^2 according to the figure's upper part, and this information allows us to locate point 2 on *DD*.

Factors that Shift the *DD* Schedule

A number of factors affect the position of the *DD* schedule: the levels of government demand, taxes, and investment; the domestic and foreign price levels; variations in domestic consumption behavior; and the foreign demand for home output. To understand the effects of shifts in each of these factors, we must study how the *DD* schedule shifts when it changes. In the following discussions, we assume all other factors remain fixed.

FIGURE 6-4

Deriving the *DD* Schedule

The *DD* schedule (shown in the lower panel) slopes upward because a rise in the exchange rate from E^1 to E^2, all else equal, causes output to rise from Y^1 to Y^2.

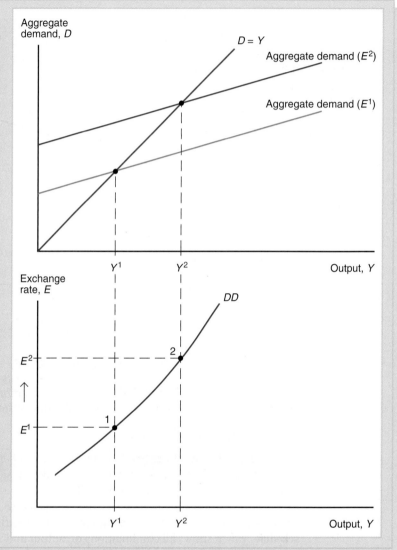

1. *A change in G.* Figure 6-5 shows the effect on *DD* of a rise in government purchases from G^1 to G^2, given a constant exchange rate of E^0. An example would be the increase in U.S. military and security expenditures following the September 11, 2001, attacks. As shown in the upper part of the figure, the exchange rate E^0 leads to an equilibrium output level Y^1 at the initial level of government demand; so point 1 is one point on DD^1.

   An increase in G causes the aggregate demand schedule in the upper part of the figure to shift upward. Everything else remaining unchanged, output increases from Y^1 to Y^2. Point 2 in the bottom part shows the higher level of output at which aggregate demand and supply are now equal, *given an unchanged exchange rate of E^0.* Point 2 is on a new *DD* curve, DD^2.

   For any given exchange rate, the level of output equating aggregate demand and supply is higher after the increase in G. This implies that *an increase in G causes*

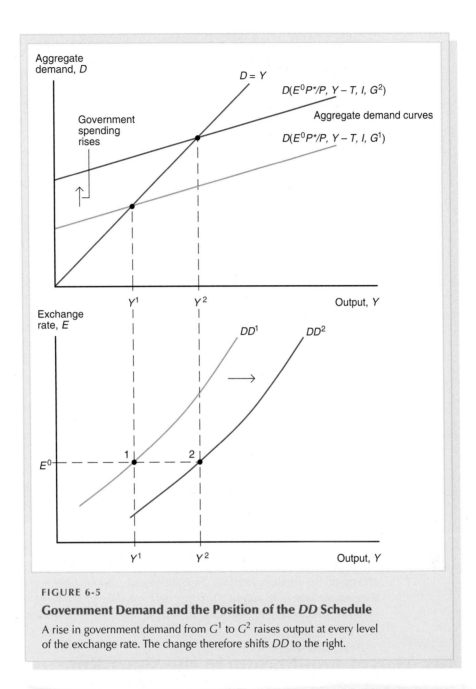

FIGURE 6-5

Government Demand and the Position of the *DD* Schedule

A rise in government demand from G^1 to G^2 raises output at every level of the exchange rate. The change therefore shifts *DD* to the right.

DD to shift to the right, as shown in Figure 6-5. Similarly, a decrease in G causes DD to shift to the left.

The method and reasoning we have just used to study how an increase in *G* shifts the *DD* curve can be applied to all the cases that follow. Here, we summarize the results. To test your understanding, use diagrams similar to Figure 6-5 to illustrate how the economic factors listed below change the curves.

2. *A change in T.* Taxes, *T*, affect aggregate demand by changing disposable income, and thus consumption, for any level of *Y*. It follows that an increase in taxes causes the aggregate demand function of Figure 6-1 to shift *downward* given

the exchange rate E. Since this effect is the opposite of that of an increase in G, an increase in T must cause the DD schedule to shift leftward. Similarly, a fall in T, such as the tax cut enacted after 2001 by U.S. President George W. Bush, causes a rightward shift of DD.

3. *A change in I.* An increase in investment demand has the same effect as an increase in G: The aggregate demand schedule shifts upward and DD shifts to the right. A fall in investment demand shifts DD to the left.

4. *A change in P.* Given E and P^*, an increase in P makes domestic output more expensive relative to foreign output and lowers net export demand. The DD schedule shifts to the left as aggregate demand falls. A fall in P makes domestic goods cheaper and causes a rightward shift of DD.

5. *A change in P*.* Given E and P, a rise in P^* makes foreign goods and services relatively more expensive. Aggregate demand for domestic output therefore rises and DD shifts to the right. Similarly, a fall in P^* causes DD to shift to the left.

6. *A change in the consumption function.* Suppose residents of the home economy suddenly decide they want to consume more and save less at each level of disposable income. This could occur, for example, if home prices increase and homeowners borrow against their additional wealth. If the increase in consumption spending is not devoted entirely to imports from abroad, aggregate demand for domestic output rises and the aggregate demand schedule shifts upward for any given exchange rate E. This implies a shift to the right of the DD schedule. An autonomous fall in consumption (if it is not entirely due to a fall in import demand) shifts DD to the left.

7. *A demand shift between foreign and domestic goods.* Suppose there is no change in the domestic consumption function but domestic and foreign residents suddenly decide to devote more of their spending to goods and services produced in the home country. (For example, fears of mad cow disease abroad raise the demand for U.S. beef products.) If home disposable income and the real exchange rate remain the same, this shift in demand *improves* the current account by raising exports and lowering imports. The aggregate demand schedule shifts upward and DD therefore shifts to the right. The same reasoning shows that a shift in world demand away from domestic products and toward foreign products causes DD to shift to the left.

You may have noticed that a simple rule allows you to predict the effect on DD of any of the disturbances we have discussed: *Any disturbance that raises aggregate demand for domestic output shifts the DD schedule to the right; any disturbance that lowers aggregate demand for domestic output shifts the DD schedule to the left.*

Asset Market Equilibrium in the Short Run: The *AA* Schedule

We have now derived the first element in our account of short-run exchange rate and income determination, the relation between the exchange rate and output that is consistent with the equality of aggregate demand and supply. That relation is summarized by the DD schedule, which shows all exchange rate and output levels at which the output market is in short-run equilibrium. As we noted at the beginning of the preceding section, however, equilibrium in the economy as a whole requires equilibrium in the asset markets as well as in the output market, and there is no reason in general why points on the DD schedule should lead to asset market equilibrium.

To complete the story of short-run equilibrium, we therefore introduce a second element to ensure that the exchange rate and output level consistent with output market equilibrium are also consistent with asset market equilibrium. The schedule of exchange rate and output combinations that are consistent with equilibrium in the domestic money market and the foreign exchange market is called the *AA* **schedule**.

Output, the Exchange Rate, and Asset Market Equilibrium

In Chapter 3, we studied the interest parity condition, which states that the foreign exchange market is in equilibrium only when the expected rates of return on domestic and foreign currency deposits are equal. In Chapter 4, we learned how the interest rates that enter the interest parity relationship are determined by the equality of real money supply and real money demand in national money markets. Now we combine these asset market equilibrium conditions to see how the exchange rate and output must be related when all asset markets simultaneously clear. Because the focus for now is on the domestic economy, the foreign interest rate is taken as given.

For a given expected future exchange rate, E^e, the interest parity condition describing foreign exchange market equilibrium is equation (3-2),

$$R = R^* + (E^e - E)/E,$$

where R is the interest rate on domestic currency deposits and R^* is the interest rate on foreign currency deposits. In Chapter 4, we saw that the domestic interest rate satisfying the interest parity condition must also equate the real domestic money supply, M^s/P, to aggregate real money demand (see equation (4-4)):

$$M^s/P = L(R, Y).$$

You will recall that aggregate real money demand, $L(R, Y)$, rises when the interest rate falls because a fall in R makes interest-bearing nonmoney assets less attractive to hold. (Conversely, a rise in the interest rate lowers real money demand.) A rise in real output, Y, increases real money demand by raising the volume of monetary transactions people must carry out (and a fall in real output reduces real money demand by reducing people's transactions needs).

We now use the diagrammatic tools developed in Chapter 4 to study the changes in the exchange rate that must accompany output changes so that asset markets remain in equilibrium. Figure 6-6 shows the equilibrium domestic interest rate and exchange rate associated with the output level Y^1 for a given nominal money supply, M^s; a given domestic price level, P; a given foreign interest rate, R^*; and a given value of the expected future exchange rate, E^e. In the lower part of the figure, we see that with real output at Y^1 and the real money supply at M^s/P, the interest rate R^1 clears the home money market (point 1), while the exchange rate E^1 clears the foreign exchange market (point 1'). The exchange rate E^1 clears the foreign exchange market because it equates the expected rate of return on foreign deposits, measured in terms of domestic currency, to R^1.

A rise in output from Y^1 to Y^2 raises aggregate real money demand from $L(R, Y^1)$ to $L(R, Y^2)$, shifting out the entire money demand schedule in the lower part of Figure 6-6. This shift, in turn, raises the equilibrium domestic interest rate to R^2 (point 2). With E^e and R^* fixed, the domestic currency must appreciate from E^1 to E^2 to bring the foreign exchange market back into equilibrium at point 2'. The domestic currency appreciates by just enough that the increase in the rate at which it is expected to *depreciate* in the future offsets the increased interest rate advantage of

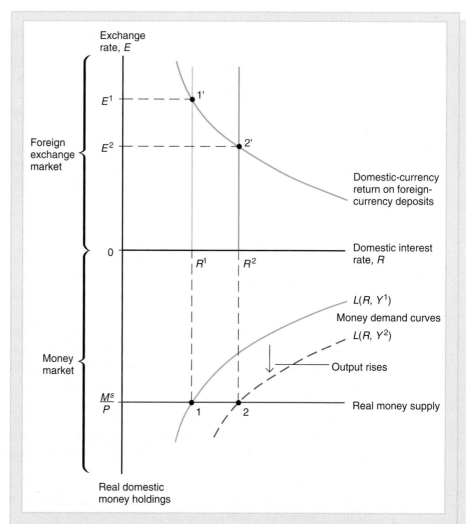

FIGURE 6-6

Output and the Exchange Rate in Asset Market Equilibrium

For the asset (foreign exchange and money) markets to remain in equilibrium, a rise
in output must be accompanied by an appreciation of the currency, all else equal.

home currency deposits. *For asset markets to remain in equilibrium, a rise in domestic
output must be accompanied by an appreciation of the domestic currency, all else equal,
and a fall in domestic output must be accompanied by a depreciation.*

Deriving the *AA* Schedule

While the *DD* schedule plots exchange rates and output levels at which the output
market is in equilibrium, the *AA* schedule relates exchange rates and output levels
that keep the money and foreign exchange markets in equilibrium. Figure 6-7 shows
the *AA* schedule. From Figure 6-6, we see that for any output level Y, there is a unique
exchange rate E satisfying the interest parity condition (given the real money supply, the foreign interest rate, and the expected future exchange rate). Our previous

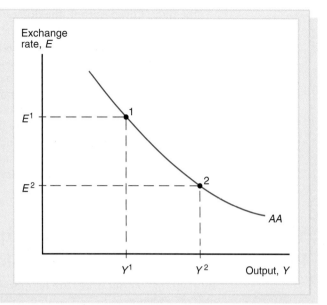

FIGURE 6-7

The *AA* Schedule

The asset market equilibrium schedule (*AA*) slopes downward because a rise in output from Y^1 to Y^2, all else equal, causes a rise in the home interest rate and a domestic currency appreciation from E^1 to E^2.

reasoning tells us that other things equal, a rise in Y^1 to Y^2 will produce an appreciation of the domestic currency, that is, a fall in the exchange rate from E^1 to E^2. The *AA* schedule therefore has a negative slope, as shown in Figure 6-7.

Factors that Shift the *AA* Schedule

Five factors cause the *AA* schedule to shift: changes in the domestic money supply, M^s; changes in the domestic price level, P; changes in the expected future exchange rate, E^e; changes in the foreign interest rate, R^*; and shifts in the aggregate real money demand schedule.

1. *A change in M^s.* For a fixed level of output, an increase in M^s causes the domestic currency to depreciate in the foreign exchange market, all else equal (that is, E rises). Since for each level of output the exchange rate, E, is higher after the rise in M^s, the rise in M^s causes *AA* to shift *upward*. Similarly, a fall in M^s causes *AA* to shift *downward*.

2. *A change in P.* An increase in P reduces the real money supply and drives the interest rate upward. Other things (including Y) equal, this rise in the interest rate causes E to fall. The effect of a rise in P is therefore a downward shift of *AA*. A fall in P results in an upward shift of *AA*.

3. *A change in E^e.* Suppose participants in the foreign exchange market suddenly revise their expectations about the exchange rate's future value so that E^e rises. Such a change shifts the curve in the top part of Figure 6-6 (which measures the expected domestic currency return on foreign currency deposits) to the right. The rise in E^e therefore causes the domestic currency to depreciate, other things equal. Because the exchange rate producing equilibrium in the foreign exchange market is higher after a rise in E^e, given output, *AA* shifts upward when a rise in the expected future exchange rate occurs. It shifts downward when the expected future exchange rate falls.

4. *A change in R^*.* A rise in R^* raises the expected return on foreign currency deposits and therefore shifts the downward-sloping schedule at the top of Figure 6-6 to

the right. Given output, the domestic currency must depreciate to restore interest parity. A rise in R^* therefore has the same effect on AA as a rise in E^e: It causes an upward shift. A fall in R^* results in a downward shift of AA.

5. *A change in real money demand.* Suppose domestic residents decide they would prefer to hold lower real money balances at each output level and interest rate. (Such a change in asset-holding preferences is a *reduction in money demand.*) A reduction in money demand implies an inward shift of the aggregate real money demand function $L\ (R, Y)$ for any fixed level of Y, and it thus results in a lower interest rate and a rise in E. A reduction in money demand therefore has the same effect as an increase in the money supply, in that it shifts AA upward. The opposite disturbance of an increase in money demand would shift AA downward.

Short-Run Equilibrium for an Open Economy: Putting the *DD* and *AA* Schedules Together

By assuming output prices are temporarily fixed, we have derived two separate schedules of exchange rate and output levels: the *DD* schedule, along which the output market is in equilibrium, and the *AA* schedule, along which the asset markets are in equilibrium. A short-run equilibrium for the economy as a whole must lie on *both* schedules because such a point must bring about equilibrium simultaneously in the output and asset markets. We can therefore find the economy's short-run equilibrium by finding the intersection of the *DD* and *AA* schedules. Once again, it is the assumption that domestic output prices are temporarily fixed that makes this intersection a *short-run* equilibrium. The analysis in this section continues to assume the foreign interest rate R^*, the foreign price level P^*, and the expected future exchange rate E^e also are fixed.

Figure 6-8 combines the *DD* and *AA* schedules to locate short-run equilibrium. The intersection of *DD* and *AA* at point 1 is the only combination of exchange rate

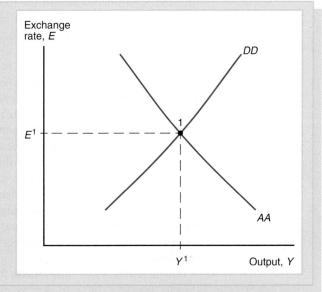

FIGURE 6-8

Short-Run Equilibrium: The Intersection of *DD* and *AA*

The short-run equilibrium of the economy occurs at point 1, where the output market (whose equilibrium points are summarized by the *DD* curve) and the asset market (whose equilibrium points are summarized by the *AA* curve) simultaneously clear.

FIGURE 6-9

How the Economy Reaches Its Short-Run Equilibrium

Because asset markets adjust very quickly, the exchange rate jumps immediately from point 2 to point 3 on AA. The economy then moves to point 1 along AA as output rises to meet aggregate demand.

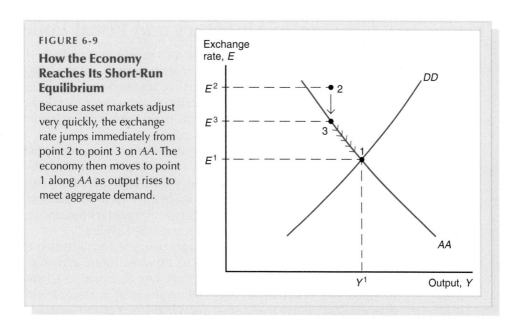

and output consistent with both the equality of aggregate demand and aggregate supply *and* asset market equilibrium. The short-run equilibrium levels of the exchange rate and output are therefore E^1 and Y^1.

To convince yourself that the economy will indeed settle at point 1, imagine the economy is instead at a position like point 2 in Figure 6-9. At point 2, which lies above AA and DD, both the output and asset markets are out of equilibrium. Because E is so high relative to AA, the rate at which E is expected to fall in the future is also high relative to the rate that would maintain interest parity. The high expected future appreciation rate of the domestic currency implies that the expected domestic currency return on foreign deposits is below that on domestic deposits, so there is an excess demand for the domestic currency in the foreign exchange market. The high level of E at point 2 also makes domestic goods cheap for foreign buyers (given the goods' domestic currency prices), causing an excess demand for output at that point.

The excess demand for domestic currency leads to an immediate fall in the exchange rate from E^2 to E^3. This appreciation equalizes the expected returns on domestic and foreign deposits and places the economy at point 3 on the asset market equilibrium curve AA. But since point 3 is above the DD schedule, there is still excess demand for domestic output. As firms raise production to avoid depleting their inventories, the economy travels along AA to point 1, where aggregate demand and supply are equal. Because asset prices can jump immediately while changes in production plans take some time, the asset markets remain in continual equilibrium even while output is changing.

The exchange rate falls as the economy approaches point 1 along AA because rising national output causes money demand to rise, pushing the interest rate steadily upward. (The currency must appreciate steadily to lower the expected rate of future domestic currency appreciation and maintain interest parity.) Once the economy has reached point 1 on DD, aggregate demand equals output and producers no longer face involuntary inventory depletion. The economy therefore settles at point 1, the only point at which the output *and* asset markets clear.

Temporary Changes in Monetary and Fiscal Policy

Now that we have seen how the economy's short-run equilibrium is determined, we can study how shifts in government macroeconomic policies affect output and the exchange rate. Our interest in the effects of macroeconomic policies stems from their usefulness in counteracting economic disturbances that cause fluctuations in output, employment, and inflation. In this section, we learn how government policies can be used to maintain full employment in open economies.

We concentrate on two types of government policy, **monetary policy**, which works through changes in the money supply, and **fiscal policy**, which works through changes in government spending or taxes.[8] To avoid the complications that would be introduced by ongoing inflation, however, we do not look at situations in which the money supply grows over time. Thus, the only type of monetary policies we will study explicitly are one-shot increases or decreases in money supplies.[9]

In this section, we examine *temporary* policy shifts, shifts that the public expects to be reversed in the near future. The expected future exchange rate, E^e, is now assumed to equal the long-run exchange rate discussed in Chapter 5, that is, the exchange rate that prevails once full employment is reached and domestic prices have adjusted fully to past disturbances in the output and asset markets. In line with this interpretation, a temporary policy change does *not* affect the long-run expected exchange rate, E^e.

We assume throughout that events in the economy we are studying do not influence the foreign interest rate, R^*, or price level, P^*, and that the domestic price level, P, is fixed in the short run.

Monetary Policy

The short-run effect of a temporary increase in the domestic money supply is shown in Figure 6-10. An increased money supply shifts AA^1 upward to AA^2 but does not affect the position of DD. The upward shift of the asset market equilibrium schedule moves the economy from point 1, with exchange rate E^1 and output Y^1, to point 2, with exchange rate E^2 and output Y^2. An increase in the money supply causes a depreciation of the domestic currency, an expansion of output, and therefore an increase in employment.

We can understand the economic forces causing these results by recalling our earlier discussions of asset market equilibrium and output determination. At the initial output level Y^1 and given the fixed price level, an increase in money supply must push down the home interest rate, R. We have been assuming that the monetary change is temporary and does not affect the expected future exchange rate, E^e, so to preserve interest parity in the face of a decline in R (given that the foreign interest rate, R^*, does not change), the exchange rate must depreciate immediately to create the expectation that the home currency will appreciate in the future at a faster rate than was expected before R fell. The immediate depreciation of the domestic currency, however, makes home products cheaper relative to foreign products. There is therefore an increase in aggregate demand, which must be matched by an increase in output.

---

[8]An example of the latter (as noted earlier) would be the tax cut enacted during the 2001–2005 administration of President George W. Bush. Other policies, such as commercial policies (tariffs, quotas, and so on), have macroeconomic side effects. Such policies, however, are not used routinely for purposes of macroeconomic stabilization, so we do not discuss them in this chapter. (A problem at the end of this chapter does ask you to think about the macroeconomic effects of a tariff.)

[9]You can extend the results below to a setting with ongoing inflation by thinking of the exchange rate and price level changes we describe as departures from time paths along which E and P trend upward at constant rates.

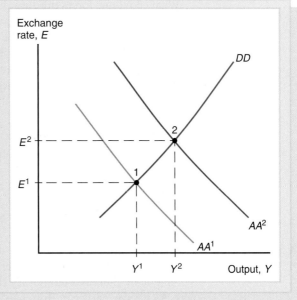

FIGURE 6-10

Effects of a Temporary Increase in the Money Supply

By shifting AA^1 upward, a temporary increase in the money supply causes a currency depreciation and a rise in output.

Fiscal Policy

As we saw earlier, expansionary fiscal policy can take the form of an increase in government spending, a cut in taxes, or some combination of the two that raises aggregate demand. A temporary fiscal expansion (which does not affect the expected future exchange rate) therefore shifts the DD schedule to the right but does not move AA.

Figure 6-11 shows how expansionary fiscal policy affects the economy in the short run. Initially the economy is at point 1, with an exchange rate E^1 and output Y^1. Suppose the government decides to spend \$30 billion to develop a new space shuttle. This one-time increase in government purchases moves the economy to point 2, causing the currency to appreciate to E^2 and output to expand to Y^2. The economy would respond in a similar way to a temporary cut in taxes.

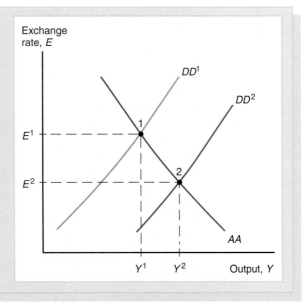

FIGURE 6-11

Effects of a Temporary Fiscal Expansion

By shifting DD^1 to the right, a temporary fiscal expansion causes a currency appreciation and a rise in output.

What economic forces produce the movement from point 1 to point 2? The increase in output caused by the increase in government spending raises the transactions demand for real money holdings. Given the fixed price level, this increase in money demand pushes the interest rate, R, upward. Because the expected future exchange rate, E^e, and the foreign interest rate, R^*, have not changed, the domestic currency must appreciate to create the expectation of a subsequent depreciation just large enough to offset the higher international interest rate difference in favor of domestic currency deposits.

Policies to Maintain Full Employment

The analysis of this section can be applied to the problem of maintaining full employment in open economies. Because temporary monetary expansion and temporary fiscal expansion both raise output and employment, they can be used to counteract the effects of temporary disturbances that lead to recession. Similarly, disturbances that lead to overemployment can be offset through contractionary macroeconomic policies.

Figure 6-12 illustrates this use of macroeconomic policy. Suppose the economy's initial equilibrium is at point 1, where output equals its full-employment level, denoted Y^f. Suddenly there is a temporary shift in consumer tastes away from domestic products. As we saw earlier in this chapter, such a shift is a decrease in aggregate demand for domestic goods, and it causes the curve DD^1 to shift leftward, to DD^2. At point 2, the new short-run equilibrium, the currency has depreciated to E^2 and output, at Y^2, is below its full-employment level: The economy is in a recession. Because the shift in preferences is assumed to be temporary, it does not affect E^e, so there is no change in the position of AA^1.

To restore full employment, the government may use monetary or fiscal policy, or both. A temporary fiscal expansion shifts DD^2 back to its original position, restoring full employment and returning the exchange rate to E^1. A temporary money supply increase shifts the asset market equilibrium curve to AA^2 and places the economy

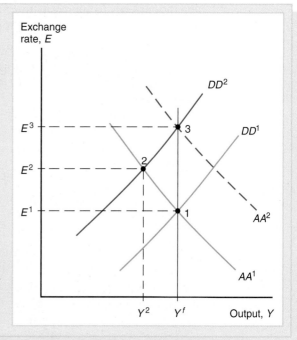

FIGURE 6-12

Maintaining Full Employment after a Temporary Fall in World Demand for Domestic Products

A temporary fall in world demand shifts DD^1 to DD^2, reducing output from Y^f to Y^2 and causing the currency to depreciate from E^1 to E^2 (point 2). Temporary fiscal expansion can restore full employment (point 1) by shifting the DD schedule back to its original position. Temporary monetary expansion can restore full employment (point 3) by shifting AA^1 to AA^2. The two policies differ in their exchange rate effects: The fiscal policy restores the currency to its previous value (E^1), whereas the monetary policy causes the currency to depreciate further, to E^3.

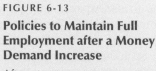

FIGURE 6-13

Policies to Maintain Full Employment after a Money Demand Increase

After a temporary money demand increase (shown by the shift from AA^1 to AA^2), either an increase in the money supply or temporary fiscal expansion can be used to maintain full employment. The two policies have different exchange rate effects: The monetary policy restores the exchange rate back to E^1, whereas the fiscal policy leads to greater appreciation (E^3).

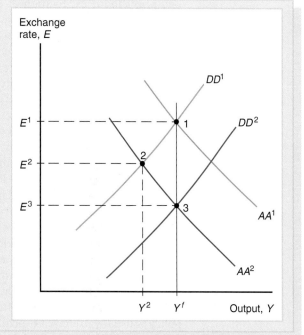

at point 3, a move that restores full employment but causes the home currency to depreciate even further.

Another possible cause of recession is a temporary increase in the demand for money, illustrated in Figure 6-13. An increase in money demand pushes up the domestic interest rate and appreciates the currency, thereby making domestic goods more expensive and causing output to contract. Figure 6-13 shows this asset market disturbance as the downward shift of AA^1 to AA^2, which moves the economy from its initial, full-employment equilibrium at point 1 to point 2.

Expansionary macroeconomic policies can again restore full employment. A temporary money supply increase shifts the AA curve back to AA^1 and returns the economy to its initial position at point 1. This temporary increase in money supply completely offsets the increase in money demand by giving domestic residents the additional money they desire to hold. Temporary fiscal expansion shifts DD^1 to DD^2 and restores full employment at point 3. But the move to point 3 involves an even greater appreciation of the currency.

Inflation Bias and Other Problems of Policy Formulation

The apparent ease with which full employment is maintained in our model is misleading, and you should not come away from our discussion of policy with the idea that it is easy to keep the macroeconomy on a steady course. Here are just a few of the many problems that can arise:

    1. Sticky nominal prices not only give a government the power to raise output when it is abnormally low, but also may tempt it to create a politically useful economic boom, say, just before a close election. This temptation causes problems when workers and firms anticipate it in advance, for they will raise wage demands and prices in the expectation of expansionary policies. The government will then find itself in the position of having to use expansionary policy tools merely to prevent the recession that higher domestic prices otherwise would cause! As a result, macroeconomic policy can display an **inflation bias**, leading to high inflation but no average gain in output. Such an increase in inflation occurred in the United States, as well as in many other countries, during the 1970s. The inflation bias problem has led to a search for institutions—for example, central banks that operate independently of the government in power—that might convince market actors that government policies will not be used in a shortsighted way, at the expense of long-term price stability. As we noted in Chapter 4, many central banks throughout the world now seek to reach announced target levels of (low) inflation. Chapters 10 and 11 will discuss some of these efforts in greater detail.[10]

2. In practice, it is sometimes hard to be sure whether a disturbance to the economy originates in the output or the asset markets. Yet a government concerned about the exchange rate effect of its policy response needs to know the source of the disturbance before it can choose between monetary and fiscal policy.

3. Real-world policy choices are frequently determined by bureaucratic necessities rather than by detailed consideration of whether shocks to the economy are real (that is, they originate in the output market) or monetary. Shifts in fiscal policy often can be made only after lengthy legislative deliberation, while monetary policy is usually exercised expeditiously by the central bank. To avoid procedural delays, governments are likely to respond to disturbances by changing monetary policy even when a shift in fiscal policy would be more appropriate.

4. Another problem with fiscal policy is its impact on the government budget. A tax cut or spending increase may lead to a larger government budget deficit, which must sooner or later be closed by a fiscal reversal, as happened following the multibillion-dollar fiscal stimulus package sponsored by the Obama administration in the United States in 2009. Unfortunately, there is no guarantee the government will have the political will to synchronize these actions with the state of the business cycle. The state of the electoral cycle may be more important, as we have seen.

5. Policies that appear to act swiftly in our simple model operate in reality with lags of varying lengths. At the same time, the difficulty of evaluating the size and persistence of a given shock makes it hard to know precisely how much monetary or fiscal medicine to administer. These uncertainties force policy makers to base their actions on forecasts and hunches that may turn out to be quite wide of the mark.

Permanent Shifts in Monetary and Fiscal Policy

A permanent policy shift affects not only the current value of the government's policy instrument (the money supply, government spending, or taxes) but also the *long-run* exchange rate. This in turn affects expectations about future exchange rates. Because these changes in expectations have a major influence on the exchange rate prevailing

---

[10]For a clear and detailed discussion of the inflation bias problem, see Chapter 14 in Andrew B. Abel, Ben S. Bernanke, and Dean Croushore, *Macroeconomics*, 8th ed. (Upper Saddle River, NJ: Prentice Hall, 2014). The inflation bias problem can arise even when the government's policies are not politically motivated, as Abel, Bernanke, and Croushore explain. The basic idea is that when factors like minimum wage laws keep output inefficiently low by lowering employment, monetary expansion that raises employment may move the economy toward a more efficient use of its total resources. The government might wish to reach a better resource allocation purely on the grounds that such a change potentially benefits everyone in the economy. But the private sector's expectation of such policies still will generate inflation.

in the short run, the effects of permanent policy shifts differ from those of temporary shifts. In this section, we look at the effects of permanent changes in monetary and fiscal policy, in both the short and long runs.[11]

To make it easier to grasp the long-run effects of policies, we assume the economy is initially at a long-run equilibrium position and that the policy changes we examine are the only economic changes that occur (our usual "other things equal" clause). These assumptions mean that the economy starts out at full employment with the exchange rate at its long-run level and with no change in the exchange rate expected. In particular, we know that the domestic interest rate must initially equal the foreign rate, R^*.

A Permanent Increase in the Money Supply

Figure 6-14 shows the short-run effects of a permanent increase in the money supply on an economy initially at its full-employment output level Y^f (point 1). As we saw earlier, even a temporary increase in M^s causes the asset market equilibrium schedule to shift upward from AA^1 to AA^2. Because the increase in M^s is now permanent, however, it also affects the exchange rate expected for the future, E^e. Chapter 4 showed how a permanent increase in the money supply affects the long-run exchange rate: A permanent increase in M^s must ultimately lead to a proportional rise in E. Therefore, the permanent rise in M^s causes E^e, the expected future exchange rate, to rise proportionally.

Because a rise in E^e accompanies a *permanent* increase in the money supply, the upward shift of AA^1 to AA^2 is *greater* than that caused by an equal, but transitory,

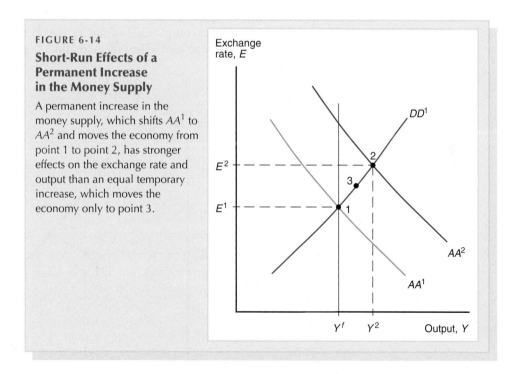

FIGURE 6-14

Short-Run Effects of a Permanent Increase in the Money Supply

A permanent increase in the money supply, which shifts AA^1 to AA^2 and moves the economy from point 1 to point 2, has stronger effects on the exchange rate and output than an equal temporary increase, which moves the economy only to point 3.

---

[11]You may be wondering whether a permanent change in fiscal policy is always possible. For example, if a government starts with a balanced budget, doesn't a fiscal expansion lead to a deficit, and thus require an eventual fiscal contraction? Problem 3 at the end of this chapter suggests an answer.

increase. At point 2, the economy's new short-run equilibrium, Y and E are both higher than they would be were the change in the money supply temporary. (Point 3 shows the equilibrium that might result from a temporary increase in M^s.)

Adjustment to a Permanent Increase in the Money Supply

The increase in the money supply shown in Figure 6-14 is not reversed by the central bank, so it is natural to ask how the economy is affected *over time*. At the short-run equilibrium, shown as point 2 in Figure 6-14, output is above its full-employment level and labor and machines are working overtime. Upward pressure on the price level develops as workers demand higher wages and producers raise prices to cover their increasing production costs. Chapter 4 showed that while an increase in the money supply must eventually cause all money prices to rise in proportion, it has no lasting effect on output, relative prices, or interest rates. Over time, the inflationary pressure that follows a permanent money supply expansion pushes the price level to its new long-run value and returns the economy to full employment.

Figure 6-15 will help you visualize the adjustment back to full employment. Whenever output is greater than its full-employment level, Y^f, and productive factors are working overtime, the price level P is rising to keep up with rising production costs. Although the DD and AA schedules are drawn for a constant price level P, we have seen how increases in P cause the schedules to shift. A rise in P makes domestic goods more expensive relative to foreign goods, discouraging exports and encouraging imports. A rising domestic price level therefore causes DD^1 to shift to the left over time. Because a rising price level steadily reduces the real money supply over time, AA^2 also travels to the left as prices rise.

The DD and AA schedules stop shifting only when they intersect at the full-employment output level Y^f; as long as output differs from Y^f, the price level will change and the two schedules will continue to shift. The schedules' final positions are shown

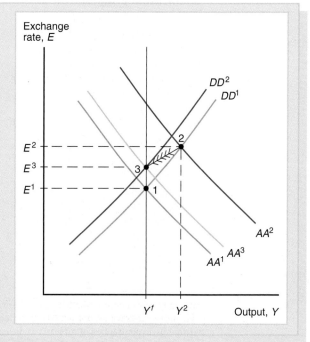

FIGURE 6-15

Long-Run Adjustment to a Permanent Increase in the Money Supply

After a permanent money supply increase, a steadily increasing price level shifts the DD and AA schedules to the left until a new long-run equilibrium (point 3) is reached.

in Figure 6-15 as DD^2 and AA^3. At point 3, their intersection, the exchange rate, E, and the price level, P, have risen in proportion to the increase in the money supply, as required by the long-run neutrality of money. (AA^2 does not shift all the way back to its original position because E^e is permanently higher after a permanent increase in the money supply: It too has risen by the same percentage as M^s.)

Notice that along the adjustment path between the initial short-run equilibrium (point 2) and the long-run equilibrium (point 3), the domestic currency actually appreciates (from E^2 to E^3) following its initial sharp depreciation (from E^1 to E^2). This exchange rate behavior is an example of the *overshooting* phenomenon discussed in Chapter 4, in which the exchange rate's initial response to some change is greater than its long-run response.[12]

We can draw on our conclusions to describe the proper policy response to a permanent monetary disturbance. A permanent increase in money demand, for example, can be offset with a permanent increase of equal magnitude in the money supply. Such a policy maintains full employment, but because the price level would fall in the absence of the policy, the policy will not have inflationary consequences. Instead, monetary expansion can move the economy straight to its long-run, full-employment position. Keep in mind, however, that it is hard in practice to diagnose the origin or persistence of a particular shock to the economy.

A Permanent Fiscal Expansion

A permanent fiscal expansion not only has an immediate impact in the output market but also affects the asset markets through its impact on long-run exchange rate expectations. Figure 6-16 shows the short-run effects of a government decision to spend an

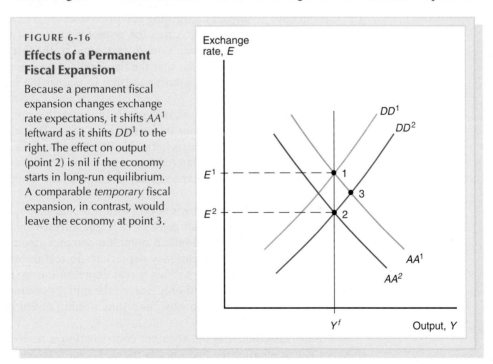

FIGURE 6-16

Effects of a Permanent Fiscal Expansion

Because a permanent fiscal expansion changes exchange rate expectations, it shifts AA^1 leftward as it shifts DD^1 to the right. The effect on output (point 2) is nil if the economy starts in long-run equilibrium. A comparable *temporary* fiscal expansion, in contrast, would leave the economy at point 3.

---

[12]While the exchange rate initially overshoots in the case shown in Figure 6-15, overshooting does not have to occur in all circumstances. Can you explain why, and does the "undershooting" case seem reasonable?

extra $10 billion a year on its space travel program *forever*. As before, the direct effect of this rise in G on aggregate demand causes DD^1 to shift right to DD^2. But because the increase in government demand for domestic goods and services is permanent in this case, it causes a long-run appreciation of the currency, as we saw in Chapter 5. The resulting fall in E^e pushes the asset market equilibrium schedule AA^1 downward to AA^2. Point 2, where the new schedules DD^2 and AA^2 intersect, is the economy's short-run equilibrium, and at that point the currency has appreciated to E^2 from its initial level while output is unchanged at Y^f.

The important result illustrated in Figure 6-16 is that when a fiscal expansion is permanent, the additional currency appreciation caused by the shift in exchange rate expectations reduces the policy's expansionary effect on output. Without this additional expectations effect due to the permanence of the fiscal change, equilibrium would initially be at point 3, with higher output and a smaller appreciation. The greater the downward shift of the asset market equilibrium schedule, the greater the appreciation of the currency. This appreciation "crowds out" aggregate demand for domestic products by making them more expensive relative to foreign products.

Figure 6-16 is drawn to show a case in which fiscal expansion, contrary to what you might have guessed, has *no* net effect on output. This case is not, however, a special one; in fact, it is inevitable under the assumptions we have made. The argument that establishes this point requires five steps; by taking the time to understand them, you will solidify your understanding of the ground we have covered so far:

1. As a first step, convince yourself (perhaps by reviewing Chapter 4) that because the fiscal expansion does not affect the money supply, M^s; the long-run values of the domestic interest rate (which equals the foreign interest rate); or output (Y^f), it can have no impact on the long-run price level.

2. Next, recall our assumption that the economy starts out in long-run equilibrium with the domestic interest rate, R, just equal to the foreign rate, R^*, and output equal to Y^f. Observe also that the fiscal expansion leaves the real money supply, M^s/P, unchanged in the short run (that is, neither the numerator nor the denominator changes).

3. Now imagine, contrary to what Figure 6-16 shows, that output did rise above Y^f. Because M^s/P doesn't change in the short run (Step 2), the domestic interest rate, R, would have to rise above its initial level of R^* to keep the money market in equilibrium. Since the foreign interest rate remains at R^*, however, a rise in Y to any level above Y^f implies an expected depreciation of the domestic currency (by interest parity).

4. Notice next that something is wrong with this conclusion. We already know (from Step 1) that the long-run price level is not affected by the fiscal expansion, so people can expect a nominal domestic currency depreciation just after the policy change only if the currency depreciates in real terms as the economy returns to long-run equilibrium. Such a real depreciation, by making domestic products relatively cheap, would only worsen the initial situation of overemployment that we have imagined to exist, and thus would prevent output from ever actually returning to Y^f.

5. Finally, conclude that the apparent contradiction is resolved only if output does not rise at all after the fiscal policy move. The only logical possibility is that the currency appreciates right away to its new long-run value. This appreciation crowds out just enough net export demand to leave output at the full-employment level despite the higher level of G.

Notice that this exchange rate change, which allows the output market to clear at full employment, leaves the asset markets in equilibrium as well. Since the exchange rate has jumped to its new long-run value, R remains at R^*. With output also at Y^f, however, the long-run money market equilibrium condition $M^s/P = L(R^*, Y^f)$ still holds, as it did before the fiscal action. So our story hangs together: The currency appreciation that a permanent fiscal expansion provokes immediately brings the asset markets as well as the output market to positions of long-run equilibrium.

We conclude that if the economy starts at long-run equilibrium, a permanent change in fiscal policy has no net effect on output. Instead, it causes an immediate and permanent exchange rate jump that offsets exactly the fiscal policy's direct effect on aggregate demand. A fall in net export demand counteracts the rise in government demand.

Macroeconomic Policies and the Current Account

Policy makers are often concerned about the level of the current account. As we will discuss more fully in Chapter 8, an excessive imbalance in the current account—either a surplus or a deficit—may have undesirable long-run effects on national welfare. Large external imbalances may also generate political pressures for governments to impose restrictions on trade. It is therefore important to know how monetary and fiscal policies aimed at domestic objectives affect the current account.

Figure 6-17 shows how the *DD-AA* model can be extended to illustrate the effects of macroeconomic policies on the current account. In addition to the *DD* and *AA* curves, the figure contains a new curve, labeled *XX*, which shows combinations of the exchange rate and output at which the current account balance would be equal to some desired level, say $CA(EP^*/P, Y - T) = X$. The curve slopes upward because, other things equal, a rise in output encourages spending on imports and thus worsens the current account if it is not accompanied by a currency depreciation. Since the

FIGURE 6-17

How Macroeconomic Policies Affect the Current Account

Along the curve *XX*, the current account is constant at the level $CA = X$. Monetary expansion moves the economy to point 2 and thus raises the current account balance. Temporary fiscal expansion moves the economy to point 3 while permanent fiscal expansion moves it to point 4; in either case, the current account balance falls.

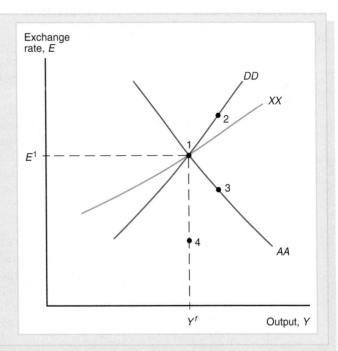

actual level of CA can differ from X, the economy's short-run equilibrium does *not* have to be on the XX curve.

The central feature of Figure 6-17 is that XX is *flatter* than DD. The reason is seen by asking how the current account changes as we move up along the DD curve from point 1, where all three curves intersect (so that, initially, $CA = X$). As we increase Y in moving up along DD, the *domestic* demand for domestic output rises by less than the rise in output itself (since some income is saved and some spending falls on imports). Along DD, however, *total aggregate demand has to equal supply.* To prevent an excess supply of home output, E therefore must rise sharply enough along DD to make export demand rise faster than import demand. In other words, net foreign demand—the current account—must rise sufficiently along DD as output rises to take up the slack left by domestic saving. Thus, to the right of point 1, DD is above the XX curve, where $CA > X$; similar reasoning shows that to the left of point 1, DD lies below the XX curve (where $CA < X$).

The current account effects of macroeconomic policies can now be examined. As shown earlier, an increase in the money supply, for example, shifts the economy to a position like point 2, expanding output and depreciating the currency. Since point 2 lies above XX, the current account has improved as a result of the policy action. *Monetary expansion causes the current account balance to increase in the short run.*

Consider next a temporary fiscal expansion. This action shifts DD to the right and moves the economy to point 3 in the figure. Because the currency appreciates and income rises, there is a deterioration in the current account. A permanent fiscal expansion has the additional effect of shifting AA leftward, producing an equilibrium at point 4. Like point 3, point 4 is below XX, so once again the current account worsens, and by more than in the temporary case. *Expansionary fiscal policy reduces the current account balance.*

Gradual Trade Flow Adjustment and Current Account Dynamics

An important assumption underlying the DD-AA model is that, other things equal, a real depreciation of the home currency immediately improves the current account while a real appreciation causes the current account immediately to worsen. In reality, however, the behavior underlying trade flows may be far more complex than we have so far suggested, involving dynamic elements—on the supply as well as the demand side—that lead the current account to adjust only gradually to exchange rate changes. In this section, we discuss some dynamic factors that seem important in explaining actual patterns of current account adjustment and indicate how their presence might modify the predictions of our model.

The J-Curve

It is sometimes observed that a country's current account *worsens* immediately after a real currency depreciation and begins to improve only some months later, contrary to the assumption we made in deriving the DD curve. If the current account initially worsens after a depreciation, its time path, shown in Figure 6-18, has an initial segment reminiscent of a J and therefore is called the **J-curve**.

The current account, measured in domestic output, can deteriorate sharply right after a real currency depreciation (the move from point 1 to point 2 in the figure) because most import and export orders are placed several months in advance. In the

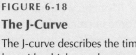

FIGURE 6-18

The J-Curve

The J-curve describes the time lag with which a real currency depreciation improves the current account.

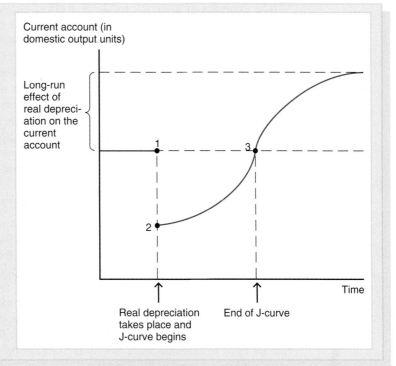

first few months after the depreciation, export and import volumes therefore may reflect buying decisions that were made on the basis of the old real exchange rate: The primary effect of the depreciation is to raise the value of the pre-contracted level of imports in terms of domestic products. Because exports measured in domestic output do not change, while imports measured in domestic output rise, there is an initial fall in the current account, as shown.

Even after the old export and import contracts have been fulfilled, it still takes time for new shipments to adjust fully to the relative price change. On the production side, producers of exports may have to install additional plant and equipment and hire new workers. To the extent that imports consist of intermediate materials used in domestic manufacturing, import adjustment will also occur gradually as importers switch to new production techniques that economize on intermediate inputs. There are lags on the consumption side as well. To expand significantly foreign consumption of domestic exports, for example, it may be necessary to build new retailing outlets abroad, a time-consuming process.

The result of these lags in adjustment is the gradually improving current account shown in Figure 6-18 as the move from point 2 to point 3 and beyond. Eventually, the increase in the current account tapers off as the adjustment to the real depreciation is completed.

Empirical evidence indicates for most industrial countries a J-curve lasting more than six months but less than a year. Thus, point 3 in the figure is typically reached within a year of the real depreciation, and the current account continues to improve afterward.[13]

---

[13]See the discussion of Table 6A2-1 in Appendix 2 of this chapter.

The existence of a significant J-curve effect forces us to modify some of our earlier conclusions, at least for the short run of a year or less. Monetary expansion, for example, can depress output initially by depreciating the home currency. In this case, it may take some time before an increase in the money supply results in an improved current account and therefore in higher aggregate demand.

If expansionary monetary policy actually depresses output in the short run, the domestic interest rate will need to fall further than it normally would to clear the home money market. Correspondingly, the exchange rate will overshoot more sharply to create the larger expected domestic currency appreciation required for foreign exchange market equilibrium. By introducing an additional source of overshooting, J-curve effects amplify the volatility of exchange rates.

Exchange Rate Pass-Through and Inflation

Our discussion of how the current account is determined in the *DD-AA* model has assumed that nominal exchange rate changes cause proportional changes in real exchange rates in the short run. Because the *DD-AA* model assumes that the nominal output prices P and P^* cannot suddenly jump, movements in the real exchange rate, $q = EP^*/P$, correspond perfectly in the short run to movements in the nominal rate, E. In reality, however, even the short-run correspondence between nominal and real exchange rate movements, while quite close, is less than perfect. To understand fully how *nominal* exchange rate movements affect the current account in the short run, we need to examine more closely the linkage between the nominal exchange rate and the prices of exports and imports.

The domestic currency price of foreign output is the product of the exchange rate and the foreign currency price, or EP^*. We have assumed until now that when E rises, for example, P^* remains fixed so that the domestic currency price of goods imported from abroad rises in proportion. The percentage by which import prices rise when the home currency depreciates by 1 percent is known as the degree of **pass-through** from the exchange rate to import prices. In the version of the *DD-AA* model we studied above, the degree of pass-through is 1; any exchange rate change is passed through completely to import prices.

Contrary to this assumption, however, exchange rate pass-through can be incomplete. One possible reason for incomplete pass-through is international market segmentation, which allows imperfectly competitive firms to price to market by charging different prices for the same product in different countries (recall Chapter 5). For example, a large foreign firm supplying automobiles to the United States may be so worried about losing market share that it does not immediately raise its U.S. prices by 10 percent when the dollar depreciates by 10 percent, despite the fact that its revenue from American sales, measured in its own currency, will decline. Similarly, the firm may hesitate to lower its U.S. prices by 10 percent after a dollar appreciation of that size because it can thereby earn higher profits without investing resources immediately in expanding its shipments to the United States. In either case, the firm may wait to find out if the currency movement reflects a definite trend before making price and production commitments that are costly to undo. In practice, many U.S. import prices tend to rise by only around half of a typical dollar depreciation over the following year.

We thus see that while a permanent nominal exchange rate change may be fully reflected in import prices in the long run, the degree of pass-through may be far less than 1 in the short run. Incomplete pass-through will have complicated effects, however, on the timing of current account adjustment. On the one hand, the short-run J-curve effect of a nominal currency change will be dampened by a low responsiveness of import prices to the exchange rate. On the other hand, incomplete pass-through implies that currency movements have less-than-proportional effects on the relative prices determining trade volumes. The failure of relative prices to adjust quickly will in turn be accompanied by a slow adjustment of trade volumes. Notice also how the link between nominal and real exchange rates may be further weakened by *domestic* price responses. In highly inflationary economies, for example, it is difficult to alter the real exchange rate, EP^*/P, simply by changing the nominal rate E, because the resulting increase in aggregate demand quickly sparks domestic inflation, which in turn raises P. To the extent that a country's export prices rise when its currency depreciates, any favorable effect on its competitive position in world markets will be dissipated. Such price increases, however, like partial pass-through, may weaken the J-curve.

The Current Account, Wealth, and Exchange Rate Dynamics

Our theoretical model showed that a permanent fiscal expansion would cause both an appreciation of the currency and a current account deficit. Although our discussion earlier in this chapter focused on the role of price level movements in bringing the economy from its immediate position after a permanent policy change to its long-run position, the definition of the current account should alert you to another underlying dynamic: The net foreign wealth of an economy with a deficit is falling over time.

Although we have not explicitly incorporated wealth effects into our model, we would expect people's consumption to fall as their wealth falls. Because a country with a current account deficit is transferring wealth to foreigners, domestic consumption is falling over time and foreign consumption is rising. What are the exchange rate effects of this international redistribution of consumption demand in favor of foreigners? Foreigners have a relative preference for consuming the goods that they produce, and as a result, the relative world demand for home goods will fall and the home currency will tend to depreciate in real terms.

This longer-run perspective leads to a more complicated picture of the real exchange rate's evolution following a permanent change such as a fiscal expansion. Initially, the home currency will appreciate as the current account balance falls sharply. But then, over time, the currency will begin to depreciate as market participants' expectations focus increasingly on the current account's effect on relative international wealth levels.[14]

The Liquidity Trap

During the lengthy Great Depression of the 1930s, the nominal interest rate hit zero in the United States, and the country found itself caught in what economists call a **liquidity trap**.

Recall from Chapter 4 that money is the most *liquid* of assets, unique in the ease with which it can be exchanged for goods. A liquidity trap is a trap because once an economy's nominal interest rate falls to zero, the central bank cannot reduce it further by increasing the money supply (that is, by increasing the economy's liquidity). Why? At negative nominal interest rates, people would find money strictly preferable to bonds, and bonds therefore would be in excess supply. While a zero interest rate

---

[14]An influential model of exchange rates and the current account is presented by Rudiger Dornbusch and Stanley Fischer, "Exchange Rates and the Current Account," *American Economic Review* 70 (December 1980), pp. 960–971.

may please borrowers who can borrow for free it worries makers of macroeconomic policy, who are trapped in a situation where they may no longer be able to steer the economy through conventional monetary expansion.

Economists thought liquidity traps were a thing of the past until Japan fell into one in the late 1990s. Despite a dramatic lowering of interest rates by the country's central bank, the Bank of Japan (BOJ), the country's economy has stagnated and suffered *de*flation (a falling price level) since at least the mid-1990s. By 1999, the country's short-term interest rates had effectively reached zero. In September 2004, for example, the Bank of Japan reported that the overnight interest rate (the one most immediately affected by monetary policy) was only 0.001 percent per year.

Seeing signs of economic recovery, the BOJ raised interest rates slightly starting in 2006, but retreated back toward zero as a global financial crisis gathered force late in 2008 (see Chapter 8). That crisis also hit the United States hard, and as Figure 3-2 (page 55) suggests, interest rates then plummeted toward zero in the United States as well as in Japan. Simultaneously, other central banks throughout the world slashed their own rates dramatically. The liquidity trap had gone global.

The dilemma a central bank faces when the economy is in a liquidity trap slowdown can be seen by considering the interest parity condition when the domestic interest rate $R = 0$,

$$R = 0 = R^* + (E^e - E)/E.$$

Assume for the moment that the expected future exchange rate, E^e, is fixed. Suppose the central bank raises the domestic money supply so as to depreciate the currency temporarily (that is, to raise E today but return the exchange rate to the level E^e later). The interest parity condition shows that E cannot rise once $R = 0$ because the interest rate would have to become *negative*. Instead, despite the increase in the money supply, the exchange rate remains steady at the level

$$E = E^e/(1 - R^*).$$

The currency cannot depreciate further.

How is this possible? Our usual argument that a temporary increase in the money supply reduces the interest rate (and depreciates the currency) rests on the assumption that people will add money to their portfolios only if bonds become less attractive to hold. At an interest rate of $R = 0$, however, people are indifferent about trades between bonds and money—both yield a nominal rate of return rate equal to zero. An open-market purchase of bonds for money, say, will not disturb the markets: People will be happy to accept the additional money in exchange for their bonds with no change in the interest rate from zero and, thus, no change in the exchange rate. In contrast to the case we examined earlier in this chapter, an increase in the money supply will have no effect on the economy! A central bank that progressively *reduces* the money supply by selling bonds will eventually succeed in pushing the interest rate up—the economy cannot function without some money—but that possibility is not helpful when the economy is in a slump and a *fall* in interest rates is the medicine that it needs.

Figure 6-19 shows how the *DD-AA* diagram can be modified to depict the region of potential equilibrium positions involving a liquidity trap. The *DD* schedule is the same, but the *AA* schedule now has a flat segment at levels of output so low that the money market finds its equilibrium at an interest rate R equal to zero. The flat segment of *AA* shows the currency cannot depreciate beyond the level $E^e/(1 - R^*)$. At the equilibrium point 1 in the diagram, output is trapped at a level Y^1 that is below the full-employment level Y^f.

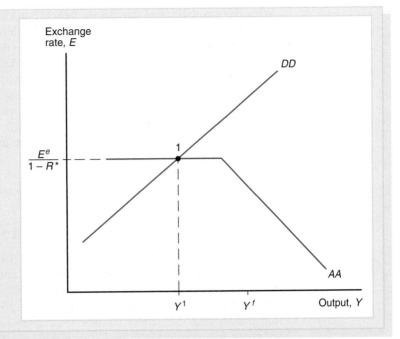

FIGURE 6-19

A Low-Output Liquidity Trap

At point 1, output is below its full employment level. Because exchange rate expectations E^e are fixed, however, a monetary expansion will merely shift AA to the right, leaving the initial equilibrium point the same. The horizontal stretch of AA gives rise to the liquidity trap.

Let's consider next how an open-market expansion of the money supply works in this strange, zero-interest world. Although we do not show it in Figure 6-19, that action would shift *AA to the right*: At an unchanged exchange rate, higher output Y raises money demand, leaving people content to hold the additional money at the unchanged interest rate $R = 0$. The horizontal stretch of AA becomes longer as a result. With more money in circulation, real output and money demand can rise further than before without driving the nominal interest rate to a positive level. (Eventually, as Y rises even further, increased money demand results in progressively higher interest rates R and therefore in progressive currency appreciation along the downward-sloping segment of AA.) The surprising result is that the equilibrium simply remains at point 1. Monetary expansion thus has no effect on output or the exchange rate. This is the sense in which the economy is "trapped."

Our earlier assumption that the expected future exchange rate is fixed is a key ingredient in this liquidity trap story. Suppose the central bank can credibly promise to raise the money supply *permanently*, so that E^e rises at the same time as the current money supply. In that case, the AA schedule will shift up as well as to the right, output will therefore expand, and the currency will depreciate. Observers of Japan's experience have argued, however, that BOJ officials were so fearful of depreciation and inflation (as were many central bankers during the early 1930s) that markets did not believe the officials would be willing to depreciate the currency permanently. Instead, markets suspected an intention to restore an appreciated exchange rate later on, and treated any monetary expansion as temporary. Only in the first half of 2013 did the Japanese government finally announce a credible intention to expand the money supply enough, and keep interest rates at zero long enough, to attain a 2 percent rate of annual inflation. At that point the yen depreciated sharply, as described at the start of Chapter 3.[15]

---

[15]A similar policy was advocated by Paul R. Krugman, "It's Baaack: Japan's Slump and the Return of the Liquidity Trap," *Brookings Papers on Economic Activity* 2 (1998), pp. 137–205

With the United States and Japan maintaining zero interest rates through 2013, some economists feared the Fed would be powerless to stop an American deflation similar to Japan's. The Fed and other central banks responded by adopting what came to be called *unconventional monetary policies*, in which the central bank buys specific categories of assets with newly issued money, greatly increasing the money supply in the process. One such policy involves purchasing long-term government bonds so as to reduce long-term interest rates. Those rates play a big role in determining the interest charged for home loans, and when they fall, housing demand therefore rises. Another possible unconventional policy, which we will discuss in the next chapter, is the purchase of foreign exchange.

CASE STUDY

How Big Is the Government Spending Multiplier?

Many students first encounter the **government spending multiplier** during their initial exposure to macroeconomics. The multiplier measures the size of the increase in output caused by an increase in government spending, or in symbols, $\Delta Y / \Delta G$.

While at first glance it may seem that the multiplier is big, students quickly learn about factors that can reduce its size. If an increase in government spending also leads to an increase in the interest rate, and this, in turn, discourages spending on consumption and investment, then the multiplier is smaller: A part of the potential expansionary impact of the fiscal policy is "crowded out" by the rise in the interest rate.

In the open economy, the multiplier is smaller still. Some private spending leaks out of the economy through imports, and if the exchange rate appreciates, then as we have seen in this chapter, the resulting reduction in net exports is an additional channel for crowding out.

Finally, under conditions of price flexibility and full employment, the multiplier is essentially zero: if the government wishes to consume more, and resources are already fully employed in production, then the private sector must part with the output that the government wants. There is no way to get much more out of the existing, fully employed stocks of productive factors, and so $\Delta Y / \Delta G \approx 0$.

Uncertainty about the multiplier's size raised concerns outside of academia once the world slipped into recession in 2008 as a result of the global financial crisis that we will discuss in later chapters (starting with Chapter 8). The United States, China, and other countries mounted big programs of fiscal expansion, including increased government spending, to prop up their stricken economies. Were these resources wasted, or were they helpful in reducing the severity of the slump? Would it be easy or painful later on to reduce government spending in order to roll back the government deficits the recession caused? The answers depended on the size of the government spending multiplier.

Economists have been studying the question of the multiplier's size for years, but the severity of the 2008–2009 recession inspired a new crop of theoretical and empirical studies. We saw earlier that in the open economy, permanent government spending has no impact on output—the multiplier is zero—but temporary government spending can raise output (recall Figure 6-16). Countercyclical fiscal expansion is most likely to be temporary (because the recession is temporary), and so this is also the case focused upon by recent research.

In an exhaustive survey, Robert E. Hall of Stanford University suggests that most studies find a multiplier between 0.5 and 1.0 (see his paper in Further Readings). That is, when the government raises its consumption by $1, the resulting increase in output will be at most $1—smaller than the big multipliers of the simplest closed-economy models, but still an effect likely to have a substantial positive impact on employment.

We saw earlier, however, that in 2009, many industrial economies lowered their interest rates dramatically, sometimes entering liquidity traps with zero rates of interest. Hall explained that this situation is exceptional because the usual "crowding out" does not occur, and he thought that for economies in liquidity traps the multiplier might be as high as 1.7. Lawrence Christiano, Martin Eichenbaum, and Sergio Rebelo of Northwestern University have suggested a much higher number based on their theoretical modeling: While below 1 normally, their multiplier can be as high as 3.7 in a liquidity trap! Alan Auerbach and Yuriy Gorodnichenko of the University of California, Berkeley, analyze data from the (mostly wealthy) member countries of the Organization for Economic Cooperation and Development and find that for economies in recession (though not necessarily in a liquidity trap), the multiplier is about 2.[16]

Our model of the liquidity trap allow us to see easily that the multiplier is larger when the interest rate is held at zero, and it also yields an interesting additional prediction for the open-economy case. Not only is there no crowding out through the interest rate, there is also no crowding out through the exchange rate.

Figure 6-16 shows the output effect of a temporary increase in G under normal (positive interest rate) conditions. Compare this with the effect on Y of a similar spending increase in Figure 6-19 (assuming R remains at zero). Because (by assumption) the expected future exchange rate E^e does not change when the rise in G is temporary, DD simply slides to the right along the horizontal portion of AA, which itself does not shift. Neither the interest rate nor the expected future exchange rate changes in Figure 6-19, so interest parity implies that the current exchange rate cannot change either. In Figure 6-16, in contrast, the increase in output raises money demand, pushing up R and appreciating the currency. Because the currency appreciation reduces net exports, thereby limiting the net positive effect on output, the multiplier is smaller in Figure 6-16 than in Figure 6-19. In Figure 6-19, in fact, the multiplier is the same as under a *fixed exchange rate*, a case that we will examine in the next chapter.

One region where the multiplier's size became a topic of contentious debate was Europe, where countries simultaneously cut government spending sharply after 2009 in order to reduce public deficits and debts. Our discussion of the multiplier might lead you to believe that the effects were highly contractionary. This is exactly what happened, as we shall see in Chapter 10.

SUMMARY

1. The *aggregate demand* for an open economy's output consists of four components corresponding to the four components of GNP: consumption demand, investment demand, government demand, and the current account (net export demand). An important determinant of the current account is the real exchange rate, the ratio of the foreign price level (measured in domestic currency) to the domestic price level.

---

[16]See Christiano, Eichenbaum, and Rebelo, "When Is the Government Spending Multiplier Large?" *Journal of Political Economy* 119 (February 2011), pp. 78–121; and Auerbach and Gorodnichenko, "Fiscal Multipliers in Recession and Expansion," in Alberto Alesina and Francesco Giavazzi, eds., *Fiscal Policy after the Financial Crisis* (Chicago: University of Chicago Press, 2013), pp. 63–102.

2. Output is determined in the short run by the equality of aggregate demand and aggregate supply. When aggregate demand is greater than output, firms increase production to avoid unintended inventory depletion. When aggregate demand is less than output, firms cut back production to avoid unintended accumulation of inventories.

3. The economy's short-run equilibrium occurs at the exchange rate and output level where—given the price level, the expected future exchange rate, and foreign economic conditions—aggregate demand equals aggregate supply and the asset markets are in equilibrium. In a diagram with the exchange rate and real output on its axes, the short-run equilibrium can be visualized as the intersection of an upward-sloping *DD schedule,* along which the output market clears, and a downward-sloping *AA schedule,* along which the asset markets clear.

4. A temporary increase in the money supply, which does not alter the long-run expected nominal exchange rate, causes a depreciation of the currency and a rise in output. Temporary fiscal expansion also results in a rise in output, but it causes the currency to appreciate. *Monetary policy* and *fiscal policy* can be used by the government to offset the effects of disturbances to output and employment. Temporary monetary expansion is powerless to raise output or move the exchange rate, however, when the economy is in a zero-interest *liquidity trap.*

5. Permanent shifts in the money supply, which do alter the long-run expected nominal exchange rate, cause sharper exchange rate movements and therefore have stronger short-run effects on output than transitory shifts. If the economy is at full employment, a permanent increase in the money supply leads to a rising price level, which ultimately reverses the effect on the real exchange rate of the nominal exchange rate's initial depreciation. In the long run, output returns to its initial level and all money prices rise in proportion to the increase in the money supply.

6. Because permanent fiscal expansion changes the long-run expected exchange rate, it causes a sharper currency appreciation than an equal temporary expansion. If the economy starts out in long-run equilibrium, the additional appreciation makes domestic goods and services so expensive that the resulting "crowding out" of net export demand nullifies the policy's effect on output and employment. In this case, a permanent fiscal expansion has no expansionary effect at all. The *government spending multiplier* is zero for permanent fiscal expansion, unlike for temporary fiscal expansion.

7. A major practical problem is ensuring that the government's ability to stimulate the economy does not tempt it to gear policy to short-term political goals, thus creating an *inflation bias.* Other problems include the difficulty of identifying the sources or durations of economic changes and time lags in implementing policies.

8. If exports and imports adjust gradually to real exchange rate changes, the current account may follow a *J-curve* pattern after a real currency depreciation, first worsening and then improving. If such a J-curve exists, currency depreciation may have an initial contractionary effect on output, and exchange rate overshooting will be amplified. Limited exchange rate *pass-through*, along with domestic price increases, may reduce the effect of a nominal exchange rate change on the real exchange rate.

KEY TERMS

PROBLEMS

1. How does the *DD* schedule shift if there is a decline in investment demand?

2. Suppose the government imposes a tariff on all imports. Use the *DD-AA* model to analyze the effects this measure would have on the economy. Analyze both temporary and permanent tariffs.

3. Imagine Congress passes a constitutional amendment requiring the U.S. government to maintain a balanced budget at all times. Thus, if the government wishes to change government spending, it must always change taxes by the same amount, that is, $\Delta G = \Delta T$. Does the constitutional amendment imply that the government can no longer use fiscal policy to affect employment and output? (Hint: Analyze a "balanced-budget" increase in government spending, one that is accompanied by an equal tax hike.)

4. Suppose there is a permanent fall in private aggregate demand for a country's output (a downward shift of the entire aggregate demand schedule). What is the effect on output? What government policy response would you recommend?

5. Why does a temporary increase in government spending cause the current account to fall by a smaller amount than does a permanent increase in government spending?

6. If a government initially has a balanced budget but then cuts taxes, it is running a deficit that it must somehow finance. Suppose people think the government will finance its deficit by printing the extra money it now needs to cover its expenditures. Would you still expect the tax cut to cause a currency appreciation?

7. You observe that a country's currency depreciates while its current account worsens. What data might you look at to decide if you are witnessing a J-curve effect? What other macroeconomic change might bring about a currency depreciation coupled with a deterioration of the current account, even if there is no J-curve?

8. A new government is elected and announces that once it is inaugurated, it will increase the money supply. Use the *DD-AA* model to study the economy's response to this announcement.

9. How would you draw the *DD-AA* diagram when the current account's response to exchange rate changes follows a J-curve? Use this modified diagram to examine the effects of temporary and permanent changes in monetary and fiscal policy.

10. What does the Marshall-Lerner condition look like if the country whose real exchange rate changes does *not* start out with a current account of zero? (The Marshall-Lerner condition is derived in Appendix 2 under the "standard" assumption of an initially balanced current account.)

11. Our model takes the price level *P* as given in the short run, but in reality the currency appreciation caused by a permanent fiscal expansion might cause *P* to fall a bit by lowering some import prices. If *P* can fall slightly as a result of a permanent fiscal expansion, is it still true that there are no output effects? (As above, assume an initial long-run equilibrium.)

12. Suppose interest parity does not hold exactly, but the true relationship is $R = R^* + (E^e - E)/E + \rho$, where ρ is a term measuring the differential riskiness of domestic versus foreign deposits. Suppose a permanent rise in domestic government spending, by creating the prospect of future government deficits, also raises ρ, that is, makes domestic currency deposits more risky. Evaluate the policy's output effects in this situation.

13. If an economy does *not* start out at full employment, is it still true that a permanent change in fiscal policy has no current effect on output?

14. Consider the following linear version of the *AA-DD* model in the text: Consumption is given by $C = (1 - s)Y$ and the current account balance is given by $CA = aE - mY$. (In macroeconomics textbooks, s is sometimes referred to as the *marginal propensity to save* and m is called the *marginal propensity to import*.) Then the condition of equilibrium in the goods market is $Y = C + I + G + CA = (1 - s)Y + I + G + aE - mY$. We will write the condition of money-market equilibrium as $M^s/P = bY - dR$. On the assumption that the central bank can hold both the interest rate R and the exchange rate E constant, and assuming that investment I also is constant, what is the effect of an increase in government spending G on output Y? (This number is often called the *open-economy government spending multiplier*, but as you can see it is relevant only under strict conditions.) Explain your result intuitively.

15. See if you can retrace the steps in the five-step argument on page 174 to show that a permanent fiscal expansion cannot cause output to *fall*.

16. The chapter's discussion of "Inflation Bias and Other Problems of Policy Formulation" suggests (page 170, paragraph 4) that there may not really be any such thing as a *permanent* fiscal expansion. What do you think? How would these considerations affect the exchange rate and output effects of fiscal policy? Do you see any parallels with this chapter's discussion of the longer-run impact of current account imbalances?

17. If you compare low-inflation economies with economies in which inflation is high and very volatile, how might you expect the degree of exchange rate pass-through to differ, and why?

18. During the passage of the U.S. fiscal stimulus bill of February 2009, many members of Congress demanded "buy American" clauses, which would have prevented the government from spending money on imported goods. According to the analysis of this chapter, would U.S. government spending constrained by "buy American" restrictions have had a bigger effect on U.S. output than unconstrained U.S. government spending? Why or why not?

19. Return to problem 14 above and notice that, to complete the model described there, we must add the interest parity conditions. Observe also that if Y^f is the full-employment output level, then the long-run expected exchange rate, E^e, satisfies the equation: $Y^f = (aE^e + I + G)/(s + m)$. (We are again taking investment I as given.) Using these equations, demonstrate algebraically that if the economy starts at full employment with $R = R^*$, an increase in G has no effect on output. What is the effect on the exchange rate? How does the exchange rate change depend on a, and why?

20. We can express a linear approximation to the interest parity condition (accurate for small exchange rate changes) as: $R = R^* + (E^e - E)/E^e$. Adding this to the model of problems 14 and 19, solve for Y as a function of G. What is the government spending multiplier for temporary changes in G (those that do not alter E^e)? How does your answer depend on the parameters a, b, and d, and why?

FURTHER READINGS

Victor Argy and Michael G. Porter. "The Forward Exchange Market and the Effects of Domestic and External Disturbances under Alternative Exchange Rate Systems." *International Monetary Fund Staff Papers* 19 (November 1972), pp. 503–532. Advanced analysis of a macroeconomic model similar to the one in this chapter.

Victor Argy and Joanne K. Salop. "Price and Output Effects of Monetary and Fiscal Policies under Flexible Exchange Rates." *International Monetary Fund Staff Papers* 26 (June 1979), pp. 224–256. Discusses the effects of macroeconomic policies under alternative institutional assumptions about wage indexation and the wage-price adjustment process in general.

Rudiger Dornbusch. "Exchange Rate Expectations and Monetary Policy." *Journal of International Economics* 6 (August 1976), pp. 231–244. A formal examination of monetary policy and the exchange rate in a model with a J-curve.

Rudiger Dornbusch and Paul Krugman. "Flexible Exchange Rates in the Short Run." *Brookings Papers on Economic Activity* 3 (1976), pp. 537–575. Theory and evidence on short-run macroeconomic adjustment under floating exchange rates.

Joseph E. Gagnon. "Productive Capacity, Product Varieties, and the Elasticities Approach to the Trade Balance." *Review of International Economics* 15 (September 2007), pp. 639–659. Looks at the role of new products in determining long-run trade elasticities.

Robert E. Hall. "By How Much Does GDP Rise if the Government Buys More Output?" *Brookings Papers on Economic Activity* 2 (2009), pp. 183–231. Thorough (but advanced) discussion of the government spending multiplier in contemporary macroeconomic models and in practice.

Jaime Marquez. *Estimating Trade Elasticities.* Boston: Kluwer Academic Publishers, 2002. Comprehensive survey on the estimation of trade elasticities.

Subramanian Rangan and Robert Z. Lawrence. *A Prism on Globalization.* Washington, D.C.: Brookings Institution, 1999. An examination of multinational firms' responses to exchange rate movements.

Lars E. O. Svensson. "Escaping from a Liquidity Trap and Deflation: The Foolproof Way and Others." *Journal of Economic Perspectives* 17 (Fall 2003), pp. 145–166. Clear discussion of policy options for economies facing deflation, including unconventional monetary policies.

MyEconLab Can Help You Get a Better Grade

MyEconLab   If your exam were tomorrow, would you be ready? For each chapter, MyEconLab Practice Tests and Study Plans pinpoint sections you have mastered and those you need to study. That way, you are more efficient with your study time, and you are better prepared for your exams.

To see how it works, turn to page 9 and then go to

www.myeconlab.com

Intertemporal Trade and Consumption Demand

We assume in the chapter that private consumption demand is a function of disposable income, $C = C(Y^d)$, with the property that when Y^d rises, consumption rises by less (so that saving, $Y^d - C(Y^d)$, goes up too). This appendix interprets this assumption in the context of the intertemporal model of consumption behavior discussed in the appendix to Chapter 6 of our companion textbook, *International Trade: Theory and Policy*.

The intertemporal model assumes that consumers' welfare depends on present consumption demand D_P and future consumption demand D_F. If present income is Q_P and future income is Q_F, consumers can use borrowing or saving to allocate their consumption over time in any way consistent with the *intertemporal budget constraint*

$$D_P + D_F/(1 + r) = Q_P + Q_F/(1 + r),$$

where r is the real rate of interest.

Figure 6A1-1 illustrates how consumption and saving are determined in the intertemporal consumer model. If present and future output are initially described by the point labeled 1 in the figure, a consumer's wish to pick the highest utility indifference curve consistent with his or her budget constraints leads to consumption at point 1 as well.

We have assumed zero saving at point 1 to show most clearly the effect of a rise in current output, which we turn to next. Suppose present output rises while future output doesn't, moving the income endowment to point 2', which lies horizontally to

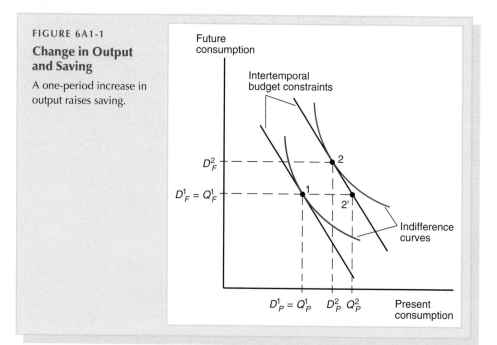

FIGURE 6A1-1

Change in Output and Saving

A one-period increase in output raises saving.

the right of point 1. You can see that the consumer will wish to spread the increase in consumption this allows her over her *entire* lifetime. She can do this by saving some of the present income rise, $Q_P^2 - Q_P^1$, and moving up to the left along her budget line from her endowment point 2′ to point 2.

If we now reinterpret the notation so that present output, Q_P, corresponds to disposable income, Y^d, and present consumption demand corresponds to $C(Y^d)$, we see that while consumption certainly depends on factors other than current disposable income—notably, future income and the real interest rate—its behavior implies a rise in lifetime income that is concentrated in the present will indeed lead to a rise in current consumption less than the rise in current income. Since the output changes we have been considering in this chapter are all temporary changes that result from the short-run stickiness of domestic money prices, the consumption behavior we simply assumed in the chapter does capture the feature of intertemporal consumption behavior essential for the *DD-AA* model to work.

We could also use 6A1-1 to look at the consumption effects of the real interest rate, which we mentioned in footnote 1. If the economy is initially at point 1, a fall in the real interest rate *r* causes the budget line to rotate counterclockwise about point 1, causing a rise in present consumption. If initially the economy had been saving a positive amount, however, as at point 2, this effect would be ambiguous, a reflection of the contrary pulls of the income and substitution effects we introduced in the first part of this book on international trade theory. In this second case, the endowment point is point 2′, so a fall in the real interest rate causes a counterclockwise rotation of the budget line about point 2′. Empirical evidence indicates that the positive effect of a lower real interest rate on consumption probably is weak.

Use of the preceding framework to analyze the intertemporal aspects of fiscal policy would lead us too far afield, although this is one of the most fascinating topics in macroeconomics. We refer readers instead to any good intermediate macroeconomics text.[17]

---

[17]For example, see Abel, Bernanke, and Croushore, *op. cit.*, Chapter 15.

The Marshall-Lerner Condition and Empirical Estimates of Trade Elasticities

The chapter assumed a real depreciation of a country's currency improves its current account. As we noted, however, the validity of this assumption depends on the response of export and import volumes to real exchange rate changes. In this appendix, we derive a condition on those responses for the assumption in the text to be valid. The condition, called the *Marshall-Lerner condition*, states that, all else equal, a real depreciation improves the current account if export and import volumes are sufficiently elastic with respect to the real exchange rate. (The condition is named after two of the economists who discovered it, Alfred Marshall and Abba Lerner.) After deriving the Marshall-Lerner condition, we look at empirical estimates of trade elasticities and analyze their implications for actual current account responses to real exchange rate changes.

To start, write the current account, measured in domestic output units, as the difference between exports and imports of goods and services similarly measured:

$$CA(EP^*/P, Y^d) = EX(EP^*/P) - IM(EP^*/P, Y^d).$$

Above, export demand is written as a function of EP^*/P alone because foreign income is being held constant.

Let q denote the real exchange rate EP^*/P and let EX^* denote domestic imports measured in terms of *foreign*, rather than domestic, output. The notation EX^* is used because domestic imports from abroad, measured in foreign output, equal the volume of foreign exports to the home country. If we identify q with the price of foreign products in terms of domestic products, then IM and EX^* are related by

$$IM = q \times EX^*,$$

that is, imports measured in domestic output = (domestic output units/foreign output unit) × (imports measured in foreign output units).[18]

The current account can therefore be expressed as

$$CA(q, Y^d) = EX(q) - q \times EX^*(q, Y^d).$$

Now let EX_q stand for the effect of a rise in q (a real depreciation) on export demand, and let EX_q^* stand for the effect of a rise in q on import volume. Thus,

$$EX_q = \Delta EX/\Delta q, EX_q^* = \Delta EX^*/\Delta q.$$

---

[18]As we warned earlier in the chapter, the identification of the real exchange rate with relative output prices is not quite exact since, as we defined it, the real exchange rate is the relative price of expenditure baskets. For most practical purposes, however, the discrepancy is not qualitatively important. A more serious problem with our analysis is that national outputs consist in part of nontradables, and the real exchange rate covers their prices as well as those of tradables. To avoid the additional complexity that would result from a more detailed treatment of the composition of national outputs, we assume in deriving the Marshall-Lerner condition that the real exchange rate can be approximately identified with the relative price of imports in terms of exports.

As we saw in the chapter, EX_q is positive (a real depreciation makes home products relatively cheaper and stimulates exports) while EX_q^* is negative (a relative cheapening of home products reduces domestic import demand). Using these definitions, we can now ask how a rise in q affects the current account, all else equal.

If superscript 1 indicates the initial value of a variable while superscript 2 indicates its value after q has changed by $\Delta q = q^2 - q^1$, then the change in the current account caused by a real exchange rate change Δq is

$$\Delta CA = CA^2 - CA^1 = (EX^2 - q^2 \times EX^{*2}) - (EX^1 - q^1 \times EX^{*1})$$
$$= \Delta EX - (q^2 \times \Delta EX^*) - (\Delta q \times EX^{*1}).$$

Dividing through by Δq gives the current account's response to a change in q,

$$\Delta CA/\Delta q = EX_q - (q^2 \times EX_q^*) - EX^{*1}.$$

This equation summarizes the two current account effects of a real depreciation discussed in the text, the *volume* effect and the *value* effect. The terms involving EX_q and EX_q^* represent the volume effect, the effect of the change in q on the number of output units exported and imported. These terms are always positive because $EX_q > 0$ and $EX_q^* < 0$. The last term above, EX^{*1}, represents the value effect, and it is preceded by a minus sign. This last term tells us that a rise in q worsens the current account to the extent that it raises the domestic output value of the initial volume of imports.

We are interested in knowing when the right-hand side of the equation above is positive, so that a real depreciation causes the current account balance to increase. To answer this question, we first define the *elasticity of export demand* with respect to q,

$$\eta = (q^1/EX^1)EX_q,$$

and the elasticity of import demand with respect to q,

$$\eta^* = -(q^1/EX^{*1})EX_q^*.$$

(The definition of η^* involves a minus sign because $EX_q^* < 0$, and we are defining trade elasticities as positive numbers.) Returning to our equation for $\Delta CA/\Delta q$, we multiply its right-hand side by (q^1/EX^1) to express it in terms of trade elasticities. Then, if the current account is initially zero (that is, $EX^1 = q^1 \times EX^{*1}$), this last step shows that $\Delta CA/\Delta q$ is positive when

$$\eta + (q^2/q^1)\eta^* - 1 > 0.$$

If the change in q is assumed to be small, so that $q^2 \approx q^1$, the condition for an increase in q to improve the current account is

$$\eta + \eta^* > 1.$$

This is the Marshall-Lerner condition, which states that if the current account is initially zero, a real currency depreciation causes a current account surplus if the sum of the relative price elasticities of export and import demand exceeds 1. (If the current account is not zero initially, the condition becomes more complex.) In applying the Marshall-Lerner condition, remember that its derivation assumes that disposable income is held constant when q changes.

TABLE 6A2-1	Estimated Price Elasticities for International Trade in Manufactured Goods					
	η			η^*		
Country	Impact	Short-run	Long-run	Impact	Short-run	Long-run
Austria	0.39	0.71	1.37	0.03	0.36	0.80
Belgium	0.18	0.59	1.55	—	—	0.70
Britain	—	—	0.31	0.60	0.75	0.75
Canada	0.08	0.40	0.71	0.72	0.72	0.72
Denmark	0.82	1.13	1.13	0.55	0.93	1.14
France	0.20	0.48	1.25	—	0.49	0.60
Germany	—	—	1.41	0.57	0.77	0.77
Italy	—	0.56	0.64	0.94	0.94	0.94
Japan	0.59	1.01	1.61	0.16	0.72	0.97
Netherlands	0.24	0.49	0.89	0.71	1.22	1.22
Norway	0.40	0.74	1.49	—	0.01	0.71
Sweden	0.27	0.73	1.59	—	—	0.94
Switzerland	0.28	0.42	0.73	0.25	0.25	0.25
United States	0.18	0.48	1.67	—	1.06	1.06

Source: Estimates are taken from Jacques R. Artus and Malcolm D. Knight, *Issues in the Assessment of the Exchange Rates of Industrial Countries*. Occasional Paper 29. Washington, D.C.: International Monetary Fund, July 1984, table 4. Unavailable estimates are indicated by dashes.

Now that we have the Marshall-Lerner condition, we can ask whether empirical estimates of trade equations imply price elasticities consistent with this chapter's assumption that a real exchange rate depreciation improves the current account. Table 6A2-1 presents International Monetary Fund elasticity estimates for trade in manufactured goods. The table reports export and import price elasticities measured over three successively longer time horizons and thus allows for the possibility that export and import demands adjust gradually to relative price changes, as in our discussion of the J-curve effect. Impact elasticities measure the response of trade flows to relative price changes in the first six months after the change, short-run elasticities apply to a one-year adjustment period, and long-run elasticities measure the response of trade flows to the price changes over a hypothetical infinite adjustment period.

For most countries, the impact elasticities are so small that the sum of the impact export and import elasticities is less than 1. Since the impact elasticities usually fail to satisfy the Marshall-Lerner condition, the estimates support the existence of an initial J-curve effect that causes the current account to deteriorate immediately following a real depreciation.

It is also true, however, that most countries represented in the table satisfy the Marshall-Lerner condition in the short run and that virtually all do so in the long run. The evidence is therefore consistent with the assumption made in the chapter: Except over short time periods, a real depreciation is likely to improve the current account, while a real appreciation is likely to worsen it.

CHAPTER 7

FIXED EXCHANGE RATES AND FOREIGN EXCHANGE INTERVENTION

In the past several chapters, we developed a model that helps us understand how a country's exchange rate and national income are determined by the interaction of asset and output markets. Using that model, we saw how monetary and fiscal policies can be used to maintain full employment and a stable price level.

To keep our discussion simple, we assumed exchange rates are *completely* flexible, that is, that national monetary authorities themselves do not trade in the foreign exchange market to influence exchange rates. In reality, however, the assumption of complete exchange rate flexibility is not always accurate. As we mentioned earlier, the world economy operated under a system of *fixed* dollar exchange rates between the end of World War II and 1973, with central banks routinely trading foreign exchange to hold their exchange rates at internationally agreed levels. Industrialized countries now operate under a hybrid system of **managed floating exchange rates**—a system in which governments may attempt to moderate exchange rate movements without keeping exchange rates rigidly fixed. A number of developing countries have retained some form of government exchange rate fixing, for reasons that we discuss in Chapter 11.

In this chapter, we study how central banks intervene in the foreign exchange market to fix exchange rates and how macroeconomic policies work when exchange rates are fixed. The chapter will help us understand the role of central bank foreign exchange intervention in the determination of exchange rates under a system of managed floating.

After reading this chapter, you will be able to:

- Understand how a central bank must manage monetary policy so as to fix its currency's value in the foreign exchange market.

- Describe and analyze the relationship among the central bank's foreign exchange reserves, its purchases and sales in the foreign exchange market, and the money supply.

- Explain how monetary, fiscal, and sterilized intervention policies affect the economy under a fixed exchange rate.

- Discuss causes and effects of balance of payments crises.

- Describe how alternative multilateral systems for pegging exchange rates work.

Why Study Fixed Exchange Rates?

A discussion of fixed exchange rates may seem outdated in an era when newspaper headlines regularly highlight sharp changes in the exchange rates of the major industrial-country currencies. There are four reasons why we must understand fixed exchange rates, however, before analyzing contemporary macroeconomic policy problems:

1. *Managed floating.* As previously noted, central banks may intervene in currency markets to influence exchange rates. So while the dollar exchange rates of the industrial countries' currencies are not currently fixed by governments, they are not always left to fluctuate freely, either. The system of floating dollar exchange rates is sometimes referred to as a dirty float, to distinguish it from a clean float in which governments make no direct attempts to influence foreign currency values. (The model of the exchange rate developed in earlier chapters assumed a cleanly floating, or completely flexible, exchange rate.)[1] Because the present monetary system is a hybrid of the "pure" fixed and floating rate systems, an understanding of fixed exchange rates gives us insight into the effects of foreign exchange intervention when it occurs under floating rates.

2. *Regional currency arrangements.* Some countries belong to *exchange rate unions*, organizations whose members agree to fix their mutual exchange rates while allowing their currencies to fluctuate in value against the currencies of nonmember countries. Currently, for example, Denmark pegs its currency's value against the euro within the European Union's *Exchange Rate Mechanism.*

3. *Developing countries.* While industrial countries generally allow their currencies to float against the dollar, these economies account for less than a sixth of the world's countries. Many developing countries try to peg or manage the values of their currencies, often in terms of the dollar, but sometimes in terms of a nondollar currency or some "basket" of currencies chosen by the authorities. Morocco pegs its currency to a basket, for example, while Barbados pegs to the U.S. dollar and Senegal pegs to the euro. No examination of the problems of developing

---

[1]It is questionable whether a truly clean float has ever existed in reality. Most government policies affect the exchange rate, and governments rarely undertake policies without considering the policies' exchange rate implications.

countries would get very far without taking into account the implications of fixed exchange rates.[2]

4. *Lessons of the past for the future.* Fixed exchange rates were the norm in many periods, such as the decades before World War I, between the mid-1920s and 1931, and again between 1945 and 1973. Today, economists and policy makers dissatisfied with floating exchange rates sometimes propose new international agreements that would resurrect a form of fixed-rate system. Would such plans benefit the world economy? Who would gain or lose? To compare the merits of fixed and floating exchange rates, we must understand the functioning of fixed rates.

Central Bank Intervention and the Money Supply

In Chapter 4, we defined an economy's money supply as the total amount of currency and checking deposits held by its households and firms and assumed that the central bank determined the amount of money in circulation. To understand the effects of central bank intervention in the foreign exchange market, we need to look first at how central bank financial transactions affect the money supply.[3]

The Central Bank Balance Sheet and the Money Supply

The main tool we use in studying central bank transactions in asset markets is the **central bank balance sheet**, which records the assets held by the central bank and its liabilities. Like any other balance sheet, the central bank balance sheet is organized according to the principles of double-entry bookkeeping. Any acquisition of an asset by the central bank results in a positive change on the assets side of the balance sheet, while any increase in the bank's liabilities results in a positive change on the balance sheet's liabilities side.

---

[2]The International Monetary Fund (IMF), an international agency that we will discuss in the next chapter, publishes a useful classification of its member countries' exchange rate arrangements. Arrangements as of end-April 2012 can be found on page 4 of its publication, *Annual Report on Exchange Arrangements and Exchange Restrictions 2012*, available at http://www.imf.org/external/pubs/cat/longres.aspx?sk=26012.0. (The IMF calls these "de facto"exchange rate arrangements because they are based on what countries actually do, not what they *say* they do.) As of April 2012, 66 countries, including most major industrial countries and the 17 countries that then used the euro, had "floating" or "freely floating" currencies. (The euro itself floats independently against the dollar and other major currencies, as we discuss in Chapter 10.) Thirteen countries did not have their own currencies (including Ecuador, Panama, and Zimbabwe). Forty-three had "conventional pegs" of the type we will study in this chapter, while 12 more had "currency boards" (a special type of fixed exchange rate scheme to which the analysis of this chapter largely applies). Among the conventional pegs were many mostly poorer countries but also oil-rich Saudi Arabia and European Union member Denmark. Sixteen more countries, including Cambodia, Iraq, Macedonia, and Vietnam, had "stabilized arrangements" in which the authorities fix exchange rates, but without any formal commitment to do so. One country (Tonga) allowed its exchange rate to move within horizontal bands; fifteen others had "crawling pegs," in which the exchange rate is forced to follow a predetermined path, or "crawl-like arrangements." (The latter group includes China.) Finally, 24 countries (including Bangladesh, Nigeria, Russia, and Singapore) had "other managed arrangements." As you can see, there is a bewildering array of different exchange rate systems, and the case of fixed exchange rates remains quite important.

[3]As we pointed out in Chapter 2, government agencies other than central banks may intervene in the foreign exchange market, but their intervention operations, unlike those of central banks, have no significant effect on national money supplies. (In the terminology introduced in the coming pages, interventions by agencies other than central banks are automatically sterilized.) To simplify our discussion, we continue to assume, when the assumption is not misleading, that central banks alone carry out foreign exchange intervention.

A balance sheet for the central bank of the imaginary country of Pecunia is shown below.

Central Bank Balance Sheet

Assets		Liabilities	
Foreign assets	$1,000	Deposits held by private banks	$500
Domestic assets	$1,500	Currency in circulation	$2,000

The assets side of the Bank of Pecunia's balance sheet lists two types of assets, *foreign assets* and *domestic assets*. Foreign assets consist mainly of foreign currency bonds owned by the central bank. These foreign assets make up the central bank's official international reserves, and their level changes when the central bank intervenes in the foreign exchange market by buying or selling foreign exchange. For historical reasons discussed later in this chapter, a central bank's international reserves also include any gold that it owns. The defining characteristic of international reserves is that they be either claims on foreigners or a universally acceptable means of making international payments (for example, gold). In the present example, the central bank holds $1,000 in foreign assets.

Domestic assets are central bank holdings of claims to future payments by its own citizens and domestic institutions. These claims usually take the form of domestic government bonds and loans to domestic private banks. The Bank of Pecunia owns $1,500 in domestic assets. Its total assets therefore equal $2,500, the sum of foreign and domestic asset holdings.

The liabilities side of the balance sheet lists as liabilities the deposits of private banks and currency in circulation, both notes and coin. (Nonbank firms and households generally cannot deposit money at the central bank, while banks are generally required by law to hold central bank deposits as partial backing for their own liabilities.) Private bank deposits are liabilities of the central bank because the money may be withdrawn whenever private banks need it. Currency in circulation is considered a central bank liability mainly for historical reasons: At one time, central banks were obliged to give a certain amount of gold or silver to anyone wishing to exchange domestic currency for one of those precious metals. The balance sheet above shows that Pecunia's private banks have deposited $500 at the central bank. Currency in circulation equals $2,000, so the central bank's total liabilities amount to $2,500.

The central bank's total assets equal its total liabilities plus its net worth, which we have assumed in the present example to be zero. Because changes in central bank net worth are not important to our analysis, we will ignore them.[4]

The additional assumption that net worth is constant means that the changes in central bank assets we will consider *automatically* cause equal changes in central bank liabilities. When the central bank purchases an asset, for example, it can pay for it in one of two ways. A cash payment raises the supply of currency in circulation by the amount of the bank's asset purchase. A payment by check promises the check's owner a central bank deposit equal in value to the asset's price. When the recipient of the check deposits it in her account at a private bank, the private bank's claims on the central bank (and thus the central bank's liabilities to private banks) rise by the same

---

[4]There are several ways in which a central bank's net worth (also called the central bank's *capital*) could change. For example, the government might allow its central bank to keep a fraction of the interest earnings on its assets, and this interest flow would raise the bank's net worth if reinvested. Such changes in net worth tend to be small enough empirically that they can usually be ignored for purposes of macroeconomic analysis. However, see end-of-chapter problem 19.

amount. In either case, the central bank's purchase of assets automatically causes an equal increase in its liabilities. Similarly, asset sales by the central bank involve either the withdrawal of currency from circulation or the reduction of private banks' claims on the central bank, and thus a fall in central bank liabilities to the private sector.

An understanding of the central bank balance sheet is important because changes in the central bank's assets cause changes in the domestic money supply. The preceding paragraph's discussion of the equality between changes in central bank assets and liabilities illustrates the mechanism at work.

When the central bank buys an asset from the public, for example, its payment— whether cash or check—directly enters the money supply. The increase in central bank liabilities associated with the asset purchase thus causes the money supply to expand. The money supply shrinks when the central bank sells an asset to the public because the cash or check the central bank receives in payment goes out of circulation, reducing the central bank's liabilities to the public. Changes in the level of central bank asset holdings cause the money supply to change in the same direction because they require equal changes in the central bank's liabilities.

The process we have described may be familiar to you from studying central bank open-market operations in earlier courses. By definition, open-market operations involve the purchase or sale of domestic assets, but official transactions in foreign assets have the same direct effect on the money supply. You will also recall that when the central bank buys assets, for example, the accompanying increase in the money supply is generally *larger* than the initial asset purchase because of multiple deposit creation within the private banking system. This *money multiplier* effect, which magnifies the impact of central bank transactions on the money supply, reinforces our main conclusion: *Any central bank purchase of assets automatically results in an increase in the domestic money supply, while any central bank sale of assets automatically causes the money supply to decline.*[5]

Foreign Exchange Intervention and the Money Supply

To see in greater detail how foreign exchange intervention affects the money supply, let's look at an example. Suppose the Bank of Pecunia goes to the foreign exchange market and sells $100 worth of foreign bonds for Pecunian money. The sale reduces official holdings of foreign assets from $1,000 to $900, causing the assets side of the central bank balance sheet to shrink from $2,500 to $2,400.

The payment the Bank of Pecunia receives for these foreign assets automatically reduces its liabilities by $100 as well. If the Bank of Pecunia is paid with domestic currency, the currency goes into its vault and out of circulation. Currency in circulation therefore falls by $100. (A problem at the end of the chapter considers the identical money supply effect of payment by check.) As a result of the foreign asset sale, the central bank's balance sheet changes as follows:

Central Bank Balance Sheet after $100 Foreign Asset Sale (Buyer Pays with Currency)

Assets		Liabilities	
Foreign assets	$900	Deposits held by private banks	$500
Domestic assets	$1,500	Currency in circulation	$1,900

---

[5]For a detailed description of multiple deposit creation and the money multiplier, see Frederic S. Mishkin, *The Economics of Money, Banking, and Financial Markets*, 10th ed., Chapter 14 (Upper Saddle River, NJ: Prentice Hall, 2013).

After the sale, assets still equal liabilities, but both have declined by $100, equal to the amount of currency the Bank of Pecunia has taken out of circulation through its intervention in the foreign exchange market. The change in the central bank's balance sheet implies a decline in the Pecunian money supply.

A $100 *purchase* of foreign assets by the Bank of Pecunia would cause its liabilities to increase by $100. If the central bank paid for its purchase in cash, currency in circulation would rise by $100. If it paid by writing a check on itself, private bank deposits at the Bank of Pecunia would ultimately rise by $100. In either case, there would be a rise in the domestic money supply.

Sterilization

Central banks sometimes carry out equal foreign and domestic asset transactions in opposite directions to nullify the impact of their foreign exchange operations on the domestic money supply. This type of policy is called **sterilized foreign exchange intervention**. We can understand how sterilized foreign exchange intervention works by considering the following example.

Suppose once again that the Bank of Pecunia sells $100 of its foreign assets and receives as payment a $100 check on the private bank Pecuniacorp. This transaction causes the central bank's foreign assets and its liabilities to decline simultaneously by $100, and there is therefore a fall in the domestic money supply. If the central bank wishes to negate the effect of its foreign asset sale on the money supply, it can *buy* $100 of domestic assets, such as government bonds. This second action increases the Bank of Pecunia's domestic assets *and* its liabilities by $100 and thus completely cancels the money supply effect of the $100 sale of foreign assets. If the central bank buys the government bonds with a check, for example, the two transactions (a $100 sale of foreign assets and a $100 purchase of domestic assets) have the following net effect on its balance sheet.

Central Bank Balance Sheet before Sterilized $100 Foreign Asset Sale

Assets		Liabilities	
Foreign assets	$1,000	Deposits held by private banks	$500
Domestic assets	$1,500	Currency in circulation	$2,000

Central Bank Balance Sheet after Sterilized $100 Foreign Asset Sale

Assets		Liabilities	
Foreign assets	$900	Deposits held by private banks	$500
Domestic assets	$1,600	Currency in circulation	$2,000

The $100 decrease in the central bank's foreign assets is matched with a $100 increase in domestic assets, and the liabilities side of the balance sheet does not change. The sterilized foreign exchange sale therefore has no effect on the money supply.

Table 7-1 summarizes and compares the effects of sterilized and nonsterilized foreign exchange interventions.

The Balance of Payments and the Money Supply

In our discussion of balance of payments accounting in Chapter 2, we defined a country's balance of payments (or official settlements balance) as net purchases of foreign assets by the home central bank less net purchases of domestic assets by foreign central

TABLE 7-1	Effects of a $100 Foreign Exchange Intervention: Summary			
Domestic Central Bank's Action	Effect on Domestic Money Supply	Effect on Central Bank's Domestic Assets	Effect on Central Bank's Foreign Assets
Nonsterilized foreign exchange purchase	+$100	0	+$100
Sterilized foreign exchange purchase	0	−$100	+$100
Nonsterilized foreign exchange sale	−$100	0	−$100
Sterilized foreign exchange sale	0	+$100	−$100

banks. Looked at differently, the balance of payments equals the current account plus capital account balances *less* the nonreserve component of the financial account balance, that is, the international payments gap that central banks must finance through their reserve transactions. A home balance of payments deficit, for example, means the country's net foreign reserve liabilities are increasing: Some combination of reserve sales by the home central bank and reserve purchases by foreign central banks is covering a home current plus capital account deficit not fully matched by net private sales of assets to foreigners, or a home current account surplus that falls short of net private purchases of financial claims on foreigners.

What we have learned in this section illustrates the important connection between the balance of payments and the growth of money supplies at home and abroad. *If central banks are not sterilizing and the home country has a balance of payments surplus, for example, any associated increase in the home central bank's foreign assets implies an increased home money supply. Similarly, any associated decrease in a foreign central bank's claims on the home country implies a decreased foreign money supply.*

The extent to which a measured balance of payments disparity will affect home and foreign money supplies is, however, quite uncertain in practice. For one thing, we have to know how the burden of balance of payments adjustment is divided among central banks, that is, how much financing of the payments gap is done through home official intervention and how much through foreign. This division depends on various factors, such as the macroeconomic goals of the central banks and the institutional arrangements governing intervention (discussed later in this chapter). Second, central banks may be sterilizing to counter the monetary effects of reserve changes. Finally, as we noted at the end of Chapter 2, some central bank transactions indirectly help to finance a foreign country's balance of payments deficit, but they do not show up in the latter's published balance of payments figures. Such transactions may nonetheless affect the monetary liabilities of the bank that undertakes them.

How the Central Bank Fixes the Exchange Rate

Having seen how central bank foreign exchange transactions affect the money supply, we can now look at how a central bank fixes the domestic currency's exchange rate through foreign exchange intervention.

To hold the exchange rate constant, a central bank must always be willing to trade currencies at the fixed exchange rate with the private actors in the foreign exchange market. For example, to fix the yen/dollar rate at ¥120 per dollar, the Bank of Japan must be willing to buy yen with its dollar reserves, and in any amount the market desires, at a rate of ¥120 per dollar. The bank must also be willing to buy any amount of dollar assets the market wants to sell for yen at that exchange rate. If the Bank of Japan did not remove such excess supplies or demands for yen by intervening in the market, the exchange rate would have to change to restore equilibrium.

The central bank can succeed in holding the exchange rate fixed only if its financial transactions ensure that asset markets remain in equilibrium when the exchange rate is at its fixed level. The process through which asset market equilibrium is maintained is illustrated by the model of simultaneous foreign exchange and money market equilibrium used in previous chapters.

Foreign Exchange Market Equilibrium under a Fixed Exchange Rate

To begin, we consider how equilibrium in the foreign exchange market can be maintained when the central bank fixes the exchange rate permanently at the level E^0. The foreign exchange market is in equilibrium when the interest parity condition holds, that is, when the domestic interest rate, R, equals the foreign interest rate, R^*, plus $(E^e - E)/E$, the expected rate of depreciation of the domestic currency against foreign currency. However, when the exchange rate is fixed at E^0 and market participants expect it to remain fixed, the expected rate of domestic currency depreciation is *zero*. The interest parity condition therefore implies that E^0 is today's equilibrium exchange rate only if

$$R = R^*.$$

Because no exchange rate change is expected by participants in the foreign exchange market, they are content to hold the available supplies of domestic and foreign currency deposits only if these offer the same interest rate.[6]

To ensure equilibrium in the foreign exchange market when the exchange rate is fixed permanently at E^0, the central bank must therefore hold R equal to R^*. Because the domestic interest rate is determined by the interaction of real money demand and the real money supply, we must look at the money market to complete our analysis of exchange rate fixing.

Money Market Equilibrium under a Fixed Exchange Rate

To hold the domestic interest rate at R^*, the central bank's foreign exchange intervention must adjust the money supply so that R^* equates aggregate real domestic money demand and the real money supply:

$$M^s/P = L(R^*, Y).$$

Given P and Y, the above equilibrium condition tells what the money supply must be if a permanently fixed exchange rate is to be consistent with asset market equilibrium at a foreign interest rate of R^*.

When the central bank intervenes to hold the exchange rate fixed, it must *automatically* adjust the domestic money supply so that money market equilibrium is

---

[6]Even when an exchange rate is currently fixed at some level, market participants may expect the central bank to change it. In such situations, the home interest rate must equal the foreign interest rate plus the expected depreciation rate of the domestic currency (as usual) for the foreign exchange market to be in equilibrium. We examine this type of situation later in this chapter, but for now we assume that no one expects the central bank to alter the exchange rate.

maintained with $R = R^*$. Let's look at an example to see how this process works. Suppose the central bank has been fixing E at the level E^0 and asset markets initially are in equilibrium. Suddenly output rises. A necessary condition for holding the exchange rate permanently fixed at E^0 is that the central bank restore current asset market equilibrium at that rate, *given* that people expect E^0 to prevail in the future. So we frame our question as: What monetary measures keep the current exchange rate constant given unchanged expectations about the future exchange rate?

A rise in output raises the demand for domestic money, and this increase in money demand normally would push the domestic interest rate upward. To prevent the appreciation of the home currency that would occur (given that people expect an exchange rate of E^0 in the future), the central bank must intervene in the foreign exchange market by buying foreign assets. This foreign asset purchase eliminates the excess demand for domestic money because the central bank issues money to pay for the foreign assets it buys. The bank automatically increases the money supply in this way until asset markets again clear with $E = E^0$ and $R = R^*$.

If the central bank does not purchase foreign assets when output increases but instead holds the money stock constant, can it still keep the exchange rate fixed at E^0? The answer is no. If the central bank did not satisfy the excess demand for money caused by a rise in output, the domestic interest rate would begin to rise above the foreign rate, R^*, to balance the home money market. Traders in the foreign exchange market, perceiving that domestic currency deposits were offering a higher rate of return (given expectations), would begin to bid up the price of domestic currency in terms of foreign currency. In the absence of central bank intervention, the exchange rate thus would fall below E^0. To prevent this appreciation, the central bank must sell domestic currency and buy foreign assets, thereby increasing the money supply and preventing any excess money demand from pushing the home interest rate above R^*.

A Diagrammatic Analysis

The preceding mechanism of exchange rate fixing can be pictured using a diagrammatic tool developed earlier. Figure 7-1 shows the simultaneous equilibrium of the foreign exchange and domestic money markets when the exchange rate is fixed at E^0 and is expected to remain fixed at E^0 in the future.

Money market equilibrium is initially at point 1 in the lower part of the figure. The diagram shows that for a given price level, P, and a given national income level, Y^1, the money supply must equal M^1 when the domestic interest rate equals the foreign rate, R^*. The upper part of the figure shows the equilibrium of the foreign exchange market at point 1'. If the expected future exchange rate is E^0, the interest parity condition holds when $R = R^*$ only if today's exchange rate also equals E^0.

To see how the central bank must react to macroeconomic changes to hold the exchange rate permanently at E^0, let's look again at the example of an increase in income. A rise in income (from Y^1 to Y^2) raises the demand for real money holdings at every interest rate, thereby shifting the aggregate money demand function in Figure 7-1 downward. As noted above, a necessary condition for maintaining the fixed rate is to restore *current* asset market equilibrium given that E^0 is still the expected future exchange rate. So we can assume that the downward-sloping curve in the figure's top panel doesn't move.

If the central bank were to take no action, the new money market equilibrium would be at point 3. Because the domestic interest rate is above R^* at point 3, the currency would have to appreciate to bring the foreign exchange market to equilibrium at point 3'.

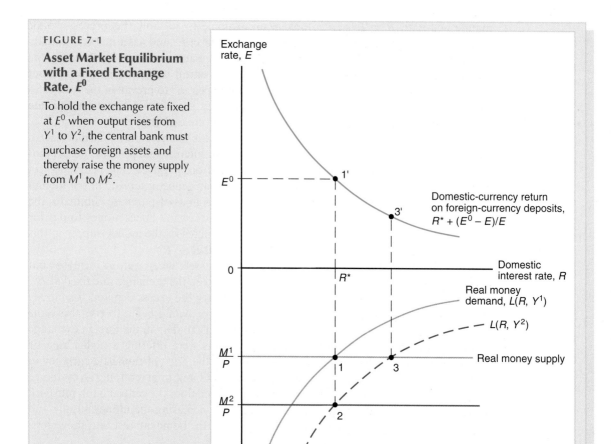

FIGURE 7-1

Asset Market Equilibrium with a Fixed Exchange Rate, E^0

To hold the exchange rate fixed at E^0 when output rises from Y^1 to Y^2, the central bank must purchase foreign assets and thereby raise the money supply from M^1 to M^2.

The central bank cannot allow this appreciation of the domestic currency to occur if it is fixing the exchange rate, so it will buy foreign assets. As we have seen, the increase in the central bank's foreign assets is accompanied by an expansion of the domestic money supply. The central bank will continue to purchase foreign assets until the domestic money supply has expanded to M^2. At the resulting money market equilibrium (point 2 in the figure), the domestic interest rate again equals R^*. Given this domestic interest rate, the foreign exchange market equilibrium remains at point 1′, with the equilibrium exchange rate still equal to E^0.

Stabilization Policies with a Fixed Exchange Rate

Having seen how the central bank uses foreign exchange intervention to fix the exchange rate, we can now analyze the effects of various macroeconomic policies. In this section, we consider three possible policies: monetary policy, fiscal policy, and an abrupt change in the exchange rate's fixed level, E^0.

The stabilization policies we studied in the last chapter have surprisingly different effects when the central bank fixes the exchange rate rather than allowing the foreign exchange market to determine it. By fixing the exchange rate, the central bank gives up its ability to influence the economy through monetary policy. Fiscal policy, however, becomes a more potent tool for affecting output and employment.

As in the last chapter, we use the DD-AA model to describe the economy's short-run equilibrium. You will recall that the DD schedule shows combinations of the exchange rate and output for which the output market is in equilibrium, the AA schedule shows combinations of the exchange rate and output for which the asset markets are in equilibrium, and the short-run equilibrium of the economy as a whole is at the intersection of DD and AA. To apply the model to the case of a permanently fixed exchange rate, we add the assumption that the expected future exchange rate equals the rate at which the central bank is pegging its currency.

Monetary Policy

Figure 7-2 shows the economy's short-run equilibrium as point 1 when the central bank fixes the exchange rate at the level E^0. Output equals Y^1 at point 1, and, as in the last section, the money supply is at the level where a domestic interest rate equal to the foreign rate (R^*) clears the domestic money market. Now suppose that, hoping to increase output, the central bank attempts to increase the money supply through a purchase of domestic assets.

Under a floating exchange rate, the increase in the central bank's domestic assets would push the original asset market equilibrium curve AA^1 rightward to AA^2 and would therefore result in a new equilibrium at point 2 and a currency depreciation. To prevent this depreciation and hold the rate at E^0, the central bank sells foreign assets for domestic money in the foreign exchange market. The money the bank receives goes out of circulation, and the asset market equilibrium curve shifts back toward its initial position as the home money supply falls. Only when the money supply has returned to its original level,

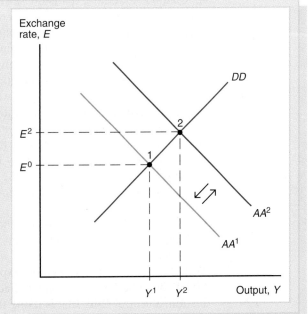

FIGURE 7-2

Monetary Expansion Is Ineffective under a Fixed Exchange Rate

Initial equilibrium is shown at point 1, where the output and asset markets simultaneously clear at a fixed exchange rate of E^0 and an output level of Y^1. Hoping to increase output to Y^2, the central bank decides to increase the money supply by buying domestic assets and shifting AA^1 to AA^2. Because the central bank must maintain E^0, however, it has to sell foreign assets for domestic currency, an action that decreases the money supply immediately and returns AA^2 back to AA^1. The economy's equilibrium therefore remains at point 1, with output unchanged at Y^1

so that the asset market schedule is again AA^1, is the exchange rate no longer under pressure. The attempt to increase the money supply under a fixed exchange rate thus leaves the economy at its initial equilibrium (point 1). *Under a fixed exchange rate, central bank monetary policy tools are powerless to affect the economy's money supply or its output.*

This result is very different from our finding in Chapter 6 that a central bank can use monetary policy to raise the money supply and (apart from liquidity traps) output when the exchange rate floats. So it is instructive to ask why the difference arises. By purchasing domestic assets under a floating rate, the central bank causes an initial excess supply of domestic money that simultaneously pushes the domestic interest rate downward and weakens the currency. Under a fixed exchange rate, however, the central bank will resist any tendency for the currency to depreciate by selling foreign assets for domestic money and thus removing the initial excess supply of money its policy move has caused. Because any increase in the domestic money supply, no matter how small, will cause the domestic currency to depreciate, the central bank must continue selling foreign assets until the money supply has returned to its original level. In the end, the increase in the central bank's domestic assets is exactly offset by an equal *decrease* in the bank's official international reserves. Similarly, an attempt to decrease the money supply through a sale of domestic assets would cause an equal *increase* in foreign reserves that would keep the money supply from changing in the end. Under fixed rates, monetary policy can affect the composition of the central bank's assets but nothing else.

By fixing an exchange rate, then, the central bank loses its ability to use monetary policy for the purpose of macroeconomic stabilization. However, the government's second key stabilization tool, fiscal policy, is more effective under a fixed rate than under a floating rate.

Fiscal Policy

Figure 7-3 illustrates the effects of expansionary fiscal policy, such as a cut in the income tax, when the economy's initial equilibrium is at point 1. As we saw in Chapter 6, fiscal expansion shifts the output market equilibrium schedule to the right. DD^1 therefore shifts to DD^2 in the figure. If the central bank refrained from intervening in the foreign exchange market, output would rise to Y^2 and the exchange rate would fall to E^2 (a currency appreciation) as a result of a rise in the home interest rate (assuming unchanged expectations).

How does central bank intervention hold the exchange rate fixed after the fiscal expansion? The process is the one we illustrated in Figure 7-1. Initially, there is an excess demand for money because the rise in output raises money demand. To prevent the excess money demand from pushing up the home interest rate and appreciating the currency, the central bank must buy foreign assets with money, thereby increasing the money supply. In terms of Figure 7-3, intervention holds the exchange rate at E^0 by shifting AA^1 rightward to AA^2. At the new equilibrium (point 3), output is higher than originally, the exchange rate is unchanged, and official international reserves (and the money supply) are higher.

Unlike monetary policy, fiscal policy can affect output under a fixed exchange rate. Indeed, it is even more effective than under a floating rate! Under a floating rate, fiscal expansion is accompanied by an appreciation of the domestic currency that makes domestic goods and services more expensive in world markets and thus tends to counteract the policy's positive direct effect on aggregate demand. To prevent this appreciation, a central bank that is fixing the exchange rate is forced to expand the money supply through foreign exchange purchases. The additional expansionary effect of

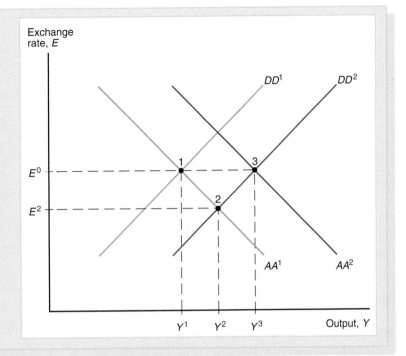

FIGURE 7-3

Fiscal Expansion under a Fixed Exchange Rate

Fiscal expansion (shown by the shift from DD^1 to DD^2) and the intervention that accompanies it (the shift from AA^1 to AA^2) move the economy from point 1 to point 3.

this accompanying increase in the money supply explains why fiscal policy is more potent under a fixed rate than under a floating rate.

Changes in the Exchange Rate

A country that is fixing its exchange rate sometimes decides on a sudden change in the foreign currency value of the domestic currency. This might happen, for example, if the country is quickly losing foreign exchange reserves because of a big current account deficit that far exceeds private financial inflows. A **devaluation** occurs when the central bank raises the domestic currency price of foreign currency, E, and a **revaluation** occurs when the central bank lowers E. All the central bank has to do to devalue or revalue is announce its willingness to trade domestic against foreign currency, in unlimited amounts, at the new exchange rate.[7]

Figure 7-4 shows how a devaluation affects the economy. A rise in the level of the fixed exchange rate, from E^0 to E^1, makes domestic goods and services cheaper relative to foreign goods and services (given that P and P^* are fixed in the short run). Output therefore moves to the higher level Y^2, shown by point 2 on the DD schedule. Point 2, however, does not lie on the initial asset market equilibrium schedule AA^1. At point 2, there is initially an excess demand for money due to the rise in transactions accompanying the output increase. This excess money demand would push the home

---

[7]We usually observe a subtle distinction between the terms *devaluation* and *depreciation* (and between *revaluation* and *appreciation*). Depreciation (appreciation) is a rise in E (a fall in E) when the exchange rate floats, while devaluation (revaluation) is a rise in E (a fall in E) when the exchange rate is fixed. Depreciation (appreciation) thus involves the active voice (as in "the currency appreciated"), while devaluation (revaluation) involves the passive voice (as in "the currency was devalued"). Put another way, devaluation (revaluation) reflects a deliberate government decision, while depreciation (appreciation) is an outcome of government actions and market forces acting together.

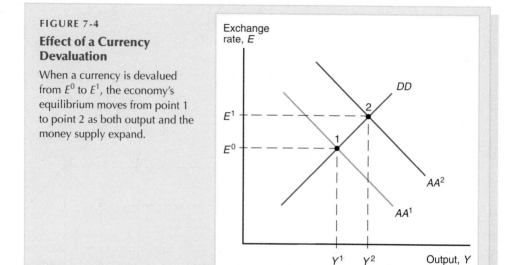

FIGURE 7-4

Effect of a Currency Devaluation

When a currency is devalued from E^0 to E^1, the economy's equilibrium moves from point 1 to point 2 as both output and the money supply expand.

interest rate above the world interest rate if the central bank did not intervene in the foreign exchange market. To maintain the exchange rate at its new fixed level, E^1, the central bank must therefore buy foreign assets and expand the money supply until the asset market curve reaches AA^2 and passes through point 2. Devaluation therefore causes a rise in output, a rise in official reserves, and an expansion of the money supply.[8]

The effects of devaluation illustrate the three main reasons why governments sometimes choose to devalue their currencies. First, devaluation allows the government to fight domestic unemployment despite the lack of effective monetary policy. If government spending and budget deficits are politically unpopular, for example, or if the legislative process is slow, a government may opt for devaluation as the most convenient way of boosting aggregate demand. A second reason for devaluing is the resulting improvement in the current account, a development the government may believe to be desirable. The third motive behind devaluations, one we mentioned at the start of this subsection, is their effect on the central bank's foreign reserves. If the central bank is running low on reserves, a sudden, one-time devaluation (one that nobody expects to be repeated) can be used to draw in more reserves.

Adjustment to Fiscal Policy and Exchange Rate Changes

If fiscal and exchange rate changes occur when there is full employment and the policy changes are maintained indefinitely, they will ultimately cause the domestic price level to move in such a way that full employment is restored. To understand

---

[8]After the home currency is devalued, market participants expect that the new, higher exchange rate, rather than the old rate, will prevail in the future. The change in expectations alone shifts AA^1 the right, but without central bank intervention, this change by itself is insufficient to move AA^1 all the way to AA^2. At point 2, as at point 1, $R = R^*$ if the foreign exchange market clears. Because output is higher at point 2 than at point 1, however, real money demand is also higher at the former point. With P fixed, an expansion of the money supply is therefore necessary to make point 2 a position of money market equilibrium, that is, a point on the new AA schedule. Central bank purchases of foreign assets are therefore a necessary part of the economy's shift to its new fixed exchange rate equilibrium.

this dynamic process, we discuss the economy's adjustment to fiscal expansion and devaluation in turn.

If the economy is initially at full employment, fiscal expansion raises output, and this rise in output above its full-employment level causes the domestic price level, P, to begin rising. As P rises, home output becomes more expensive, so aggregate demand gradually falls, returning output to the initial, full-employment level. Once this point is reached, the upward pressure on the price level comes to an end. There is no real appreciation in the short run, as there is with a floating exchange rate, but regardless of whether the exchange rate is floating or fixed, the real exchange rate appreciates *in the long run* by the same amount.[9] In the present case, real appreciation (a fall in EP^*/P) takes the form of a rise in P rather than a fall in E.

At first glance, the long-run price level increase caused by a fiscal expansion under fixed rates seems inconsistent with Chapter 4's conclusion that for a given output level and interest rate, the price level and the money supply move proportionally in the long run. In fact, there is no inconsistency because fiscal expansion *does* cause a money supply increase by forcing the central bank to intervene in the foreign exchange market. To fix the exchange rate throughout the adjustment process, the central bank ultimately must increase the money supply by intervention purchases in proportion to the long-run increase in P.

The adjustment to a devaluation is similar. In fact, since a devaluation does not change long-run demand or supply conditions in the output market, the increase in the long-run price level caused by a devaluation is proportional to the increase in the exchange rate. A devaluation under a fixed rate has the same long-run effect as a proportional increase in the money supply under a floating rate. Like the latter policy, devaluation is neutral in the long run, in the sense that its only effect on the economy's long-run equilibrium is a proportional rise in all nominal prices and in the domestic money supply.

Balance of Payments Crises and Capital Flight

Until now, we have assumed that participants in the foreign exchange market believe that a fixed exchange rate will be maintained at its current level forever. In many practical situations, however, the central bank may find it undesirable or infeasible to maintain the current fixed exchange rate. The central bank may be running short on foreign reserves, for example, or it may face high domestic unemployment. Because market participants know the central bank may respond to such situations by devaluing the currency, it would be unreasonable for them to expect the current exchange rate to be maintained forever.

The market's belief in an impending change in the exchange rate gives rise to a **balance of payments crisis**, a sharp change in official foreign reserves sparked by a change in expectations about the future exchange rate. In this section, we use our model of asset market equilibrium to examine how balance of payments crises can occur under fixed exchange rates. (In later chapters we will describe a broader range of financial crises.)

Figure 7-5 shows the asset markets in equilibrium at points 1 (the money market) and 1′ (the foreign exchange market) with the exchange rate fixed at E^0 and expected to remain there indefinitely. M^1 is the money supply consistent with this initial equilibrium. Suppose a sudden deterioration in the current account, for example, leads

---

[9]To see this, observe that the long-run equilibrium real exchange rate, EP^*/P, must in either case satisfy the same equation, $Y^f = D(EP^*/P, Y^f - T, I, G)$, where Y^f, as in Chapter 6, is the full-employment output level.

FIGURE 7-5

Capital Flight, the Money Supply, and the Interest Rate

To hold the exchange rate fixed at E^0 after the market decides it will be devalued to E^1, the central bank must use its reserves to finance a private financial outflow that shrinks the money supply and raises the home interest rate.

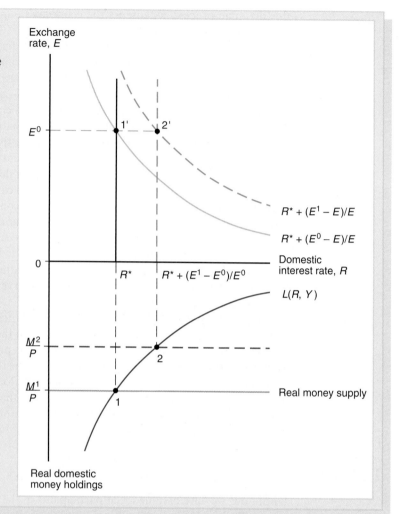

the foreign exchange market to expect the government to devalue in the future and adopt a new fixed exchange rate, E^1, that is higher than the current rate, E^0. The figure's upper part shows this change in expectations as a rightward shift in the curve that measures the expected domestic currency return on foreign currency deposits. Since the current exchange rate still is E^0, equilibrium in the foreign exchange market (point 2′) requires a rise in the domestic interest rate to $R^* + (E^1 - E^0)/E^0$, which now equals the expected domestic currency return on foreign currency assets.

Initially, however, the domestic interest rate remains at R^*, which is below the new expected return on foreign assets. This differential causes an excess demand for foreign currency assets in the foreign exchange market; to continue holding the exchange rate at E^0, the central bank must sell foreign reserves and thus shrink the domestic money supply. The bank's intervention comes to an end once the money supply has fallen to M^2, so that the money market is in equilibrium at the interest rate $R^* + (E^1 - E^0)/E^0$ that clears the foreign exchange market (point 2). *The expectation of a future devaluation causes a balance of payments crisis marked by a sharp fall in reserves and a rise in the home interest rate above the world interest rate. Similarly, an expected revaluation causes an abrupt rise in foreign reserves together with a fall in the home interest rate below the world rate.*

The reserve loss accompanying a devaluation scare is often labeled **capital flight**. Residents flee the domestic currency by selling it to the central bank for foreign exchange; they then invest the foreign currency abroad. At the same time, foreigners convert holdings of home assets into their own currencies and repatriate the proceeds. When fears of devaluation arise because the central bank's reserves are low to begin with, capital flight is of particular concern to the government. By pushing reserves even lower, capital flight may force the central bank to devalue sooner and by a larger amount than planned.[10]

What causes currency crises? Often, a government is following policies that are not consistent with maintaining a fixed exchange rate over the longer term. Once market expectations take those policies into account, the country's interest rates inevitably are forced up. For example, a country's central bank may be buying bonds from the domestic government to allow the government to run continuing fiscal deficits. Since these central bank purchases of domestic assets cause ongoing losses of central bank foreign exchange reserves, reserves will fall toward a point at which the central bank may find itself without the means to support the exchange rate. As the possibility of a collapse rises over time, so will domestic interest rates, until the central bank indeed runs out of foreign reserves and the fixed exchange rate is abandoned. (Appendix 2 to this chapter presents a detailed model of this type, and shows that the collapse of the currency peg can be caused by a sharp *speculative attack* in which currency traders suddenly acquire all of the central bank's remaining foreign reserves.) The only way for the central bank to avoid this fate is to stop bankrolling the government deficit, hopefully forcing the government to live within its means.

In the last example, exhaustion of foreign reserves and an end of the fixed exchange rate are inevitable, given macroeconomic policies. The financial outflows that accompany a currency crisis only hasten an inevitable collapse, one that would have occurred anyway, albeit in slower motion, even if private financial flows could be banned. Not all crises are of this kind, however. An economy can be vulnerable to currency speculation even without being in such bad shape that a collapse of its fixed exchange rate regime is inevitable. Currency crises that occur in such circumstances often are called **self-fulfilling currency crises**, although it is important to keep in mind that the government may ultimately be responsible for such crises by creating or tolerating domestic economic weaknesses that invite speculators to attack the currency.

As an example, consider an economy in which domestic commercial banks' liabilities are mainly short-term deposits, and in which many of the banks' loans to businesses are likely to go unpaid in the event of a recession. If speculators suspect there will be a devaluation, interest rates will climb, raising banks' borrowing costs sharply while at the same time causing a recession and reducing the value of bank assets. To prevent domestic banks from going out of business, the central bank may well lend money to the banks, in the process losing foreign reserves and possibly its ability to go on pegging the exchange rate. In this case, it is the emergence of devaluation expectations among currency traders that pushes the economy into crisis and forces the exchange rate to be changed.

For the rest of this chapter, we continue to assume that no exchange rate changes are expected by the market when exchange rates are fixed. But we draw on the preceding analysis repeatedly in later chapters when we discuss various countries' unhappy experiences with fixed exchange rates.

---

[10]If aggregate demand depends on the real interest rate (as in the *IS-LM* model of intermediate macroeconomics courses), capital flight reduces output by shrinking the money supply and raising the real interest rate. This possibly contractionary effect of capital flight is another reason why policy makers hope to avoid it.

Managed Floating and Sterilized Intervention

Under managed floating, monetary policy is influenced by exchange rate changes without being completely subordinate to the requirements of a fixed rate. Instead, the central bank faces a trade-off between domestic objectives such as employment or the inflation rate and exchange rate stability. Suppose the central bank tries to expand the money supply to fight domestic unemployment, for example, but at the same time carries out foreign asset sales to restrain the resulting depreciation of the home currency. The foreign exchange intervention will tend to *reduce* the money supply, hindering but not necessarily nullifying the central bank's attempt to reduce unemployment.

Discussions of foreign exchange intervention in policy forums and newspapers often appear to ignore the intimate link between intervention and the money supply that we previously explored in detail. In reality, however, these discussions often assume that foreign exchange intervention is being *sterilized*, so that opposite domestic asset transactions prevent it from affecting the money supply. Empirical studies of central bank behavior confirm this assumption and consistently show central banks to have practiced sterilized intervention under flexible and fixed exchange rate regimes alike.

In spite of widespread sterilized intervention, there is considerable disagreement among economists about its effects. In this section, we study the role of sterilized intervention in exchange rate management.[11]

Perfect Asset Substitutability and the Ineffectiveness of Sterilized Intervention

When a central bank carries out a sterilized foreign exchange intervention, its transactions leave the domestic money supply unchanged. A rationale for such a policy is difficult to find using the model of exchange rate determination previously developed, for the model predicts that without an accompanying change in the money supply, the central bank's intervention will not affect the domestic interest rate and therefore will not affect the exchange rate.

Our model also predicts that sterilization will be fruitless under a fixed exchange rate. The example of a fiscal expansion illustrates why a central bank might wish to sterilize under a fixed rate and why our model says that such a policy will fail. Recall that to hold the exchange rate constant when fiscal policy becomes more expansive, the central bank must buy foreign assets and expand the home money supply. The policy raises output but it eventually also causes inflation, which the central bank may try to avoid by sterilizing the increase in the money supply that its fiscal policy has induced. As quickly as the central bank sells domestic assets to reduce the money supply, however, it will have to *buy* more foreign assets to keep the exchange rate fixed. The ineffectiveness of monetary policy under a fixed exchange rate implies that sterilization is a self-defeating policy.

The key feature of our model that leads to these results is the assumption that the foreign exchange market is in equilibrium only when the expected returns on domestic and foreign currency bonds are the same.[12] This assumption is often called

---

[11]In the United States, the Federal Reserve Bank of New York carries out intervention for the Federal Reserve System, and the interventions are routinely sterilized. See Federal Reserve Bank of New York, "Fedpoint: U.S. Foreign Exchange Intervention," http://www.newyorkfed.org/aboutthefed/fedpoint/fed44.html

[12]We are assuming that all interest-bearing (nonmoney) assets denominated in the same currency, whether illiquid time deposits or government bonds, are perfect substitutes in portfolios. The single term "bonds" will generally be used to refer to all these assets.

perfect asset substitutability. Two assets are perfect substitutes when, as our model assumed, investors don't care how their portfolios are divided between them, provided both yield the same expected rate of return. With perfect asset substitutability in the foreign exchange market, the exchange rate is therefore determined so that the interest parity condition holds. When this is the case, there is nothing a central bank can

CASE STUDY   Can Markets Attack a *Strong* Currency? The Case of Switzerland

The Swiss franc has traditionally been a "safe haven" currency: a currency investors buy when they fear instability in the global economy. When a simmering global financial crisis intensified in September 2008 (as we discuss in later chapters), the usual pattern repeated itself. Investors (many of whom were Swiss and owned substantial assets abroad) rushed to put their money into Switzerland. As you can see in Figure 7-6, the Swiss franc price of euros fell sharply (a Swiss franc appreciation), while the reserves of the central bank, the Swiss National Bank (SNB), rose sharply. (Reserves are measured on the figure's right-hand vertical axis.) Reserves rose because the SNB was intervening in the foreign exchange market, buying euros with francs so as to slow the franc's appreciation.

The SNB cut interest rates quickly, both to stimulate economic activity and to discourage appreciation. By November 2008, Swiss short-term interest rates were essentially at zero (where they remained). The Swiss franc's exchange rate briefly stabilized at levels slightly over CHF 1.5 per euro.

But renewed pressure came when the euro zone entered its own financial crisis late in 2009 (as we discuss in Chapter 10). The Swiss franc appreciated dramatically against the euro and reserves ballooned as a result of further foreign exchange purchases. Switzerland began to suffer from deflation and unemployment as import prices fell and as export industries (such as the watch industry) found themselves priced out of world markets. In August 2011, the currency reached CHF 1.12 per euro.

At that point, the SNB took radical action: in September 2011, it pledged to defend a minimal euro price of CHF 1.2 per euro. It would allow the Swiss franc to depreciate up from that floor, but not to appreciate below it. To accomplish this, the SNB had to buy all the euros the market wished to sell it at a rate of CHF 1.2 per euro.

Figure 7-6 shows that Switzerland's international reserves subsequently rose even more rapidly. As money flooded in from speculators betting that the currency floor would not hold, SNB foreign currency reserves reached a level equal to about three-quarters of a year's national output! When a weak currency is under attack, the defending central bank, which is selling reserves, may run out. But is there any limit to its ability to hold down a *strong* currency by *buying* reserves with its own money, which it has the power to print without limit? The main potential brake is that by buying reserves and allowing the money supply to increase, the central bank sparks excessive inflation. But this did not happen. In part because of the neighboring euro zone's dismal economic growth, Switzerland remained in deflation long after it stepped in to limit the Swiss franc's appreciation.

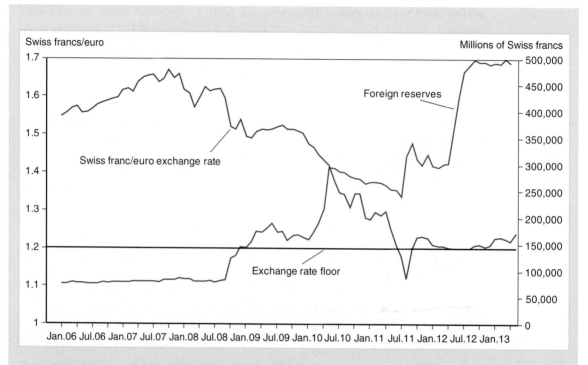

FIGURE 7-6

The Swiss Franc's Exchange Rate against the Euro and Swiss Foreign Exchange Reserves, 2006–2013

The Swiss National Bank intervened heavily to slow the Swiss franc's appreciation against the euro, finally setting a floor under the price of the euro in September 2011.

Source: Swiss National Bank.

do through foreign exchange intervention that it could not do as well through purely domestic open-market operations.

In contrast to perfect asset substitutability, **imperfect asset substitutability** exists when it is possible for assets' expected returns to differ in equilibrium. As we saw in Chapter 3, the main factor that may lead to imperfect asset substitutability in the foreign exchange market is *risk*. If bonds denominated in different currencies have different degrees of risk, investors may be willing to earn lower expected returns on bonds that are less risky. Correspondingly, they will hold a very risky asset only if its expected return is relatively high.

In a world of perfect asset substitutability, participants in the foreign exchange market care only about expected rates of return; since these rates are determined by monetary policy, actions such as sterilized intervention that do not affect the money supply also do not affect the exchange rate. Under imperfect asset substitutability, however, both risk *and* return matter, so central bank actions that alter the riskiness of domestic currency assets can move the exchange rate even when the money supply does not change. To understand how sterilized intervention can alter the riskiness of domestic currency assets, however, we must modify our model of equilibrium in the foreign exchange market.

Foreign Exchange Market Equilibrium under Imperfect Asset Substitutability

When domestic and foreign currency bonds are perfect substitutes, the foreign exchange market is in equilibrium only if the interest parity condition holds:

$$R = R^* + (E^e - E)/E. \qquad (7\text{-}1)$$

When domestic and foreign currency bonds are *imperfect* substitutes, the condition above does not hold in general. Instead, equilibrium in the foreign exchange market requires that the domestic interest rate equal the expected domestic currency return on foreign bonds *plus* a **risk premium**, ρ, that reflects the difference between the riskiness of domestic and foreign bonds:

$$R = R^* + (E^e - E)/E + \rho. \qquad (7\text{-}2)$$

Appendix 1 to this chapter develops a detailed model of foreign exchange market equilibrium with imperfect asset substitutability. The main conclusion of that model is that the risk premium on domestic assets rises when the stock of domestic government bonds available to be held by the public rises and falls when the central bank's domestic assets rise. It is not hard to grasp the economic reasoning behind this result. Private investors become more vulnerable to unexpected changes in the home currency's exchange rate as the stock of domestic government bonds they hold rises. Investors will be unwilling to assume the increased risk of holding more domestic government debt, however, unless they are compensated by a higher expected rate of return on domestic currency assets. An increased stock of domestic government debt will therefore raise the difference between the expected returns on domestic and foreign currency bonds. Similarly, when the central bank buys domestic assets, the market need no longer hold them; private vulnerability to home currency exchange rate risk is thus lower, and the risk premium on home currency assets falls.

This alternative model of foreign market equilibrium implies that the risk premium depends positively on the stock of domestic government debt, denoted by B, less the domestic assets of the central bank, denoted by A:

$$\rho = \rho(B - A). \qquad (7\text{-}3)$$

The risk premium on domestic bonds therefore rises when $B - A$ rises. This relation between the risk premium and the central bank's domestic asset holdings allows the bank to affect the exchange rate through sterilized foreign exchange intervention. It also implies that official operations in domestic and foreign assets may differ in their asset market impacts.[13]

The Effects of Sterilized Intervention with Imperfect Asset Substitutability

Figure 7-7 modifies our earlier picture of asset market equilibrium by adding imperfect asset substitutability to illustrate how sterilized intervention can affect the exchange rate. The lower part of the figure, which shows the money market in equilibrium at point 1, does not change. The upper part of the figure is also much the same

---

[13]The stock of central bank domestic assets is often called central bank *domestic credit*.

FIGURE 7-7

Effect of a Sterilized Central Bank Purchase of Foreign Assets under Imperfect Asset Substitutability

A sterilized purchase of foreign assets leaves the money supply unchanged but raises the risk-adjusted return that domestic currency deposits must offer in equilibrium. As a result, the return curve in the upper panel shifts up and to the right. Other things equal, this depreciates the domestic currency from E^1 to E^2.

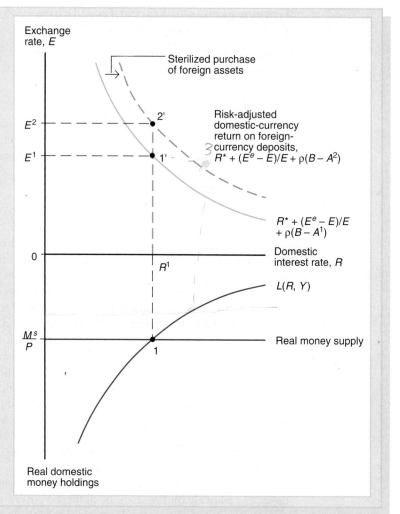

as before, except that the downward-sloping schedule now shows how the *sum* of the expected domestic currency return on foreign assets *and* the risk premium depends on the exchange rate. (The curve continues to slope downward because the risk premium itself is assumed not to depend on the exchange rate.) Equilibrium in the foreign exchange market is at point 1′, which corresponds to a domestic government debt of B and central bank domestic asset holdings of A^1. At that point, the domestic interest rate equals the risk-adjusted domestic currency return on foreign deposits (as in equation (7-2)).

Let's use the diagram to examine the effects of a sterilized purchase of foreign assets by the central bank. By matching its purchase of foreign assets with a sale of domestic assets, the central bank holds the money supply constant at M^s and avoids any change in the lower part of Figure 7-7. As a result of its domestic asset sale, however, the central bank's domestic assets are lower (they fall to A^2) and the stock of domestic assets that the market must hold, $B - A^2$, is therefore higher than the initial stock $B - A^1$. This increase pushes the risk premium ρ upward and shifts to the right the negatively sloped schedule in the upper part of the figure. The foreign exchange market now settles at point 2′ and the domestic currency depreciates to E^2.

With imperfect asset substitutability, even sterilized purchases of foreign exchange cause the home currency to depreciate. Similarly, sterilized sales of foreign exchange cause the home currency to appreciate. A slight modification of our analysis shows that the central bank can also use sterilized intervention to hold the exchange rate fixed as it varies the money supply to achieve domestic objectives such as full employment. In effect, the exchange rate and monetary policy can be managed independently of each other in the short run when sterilized intervention is effective.

Evidence on the Effects of Sterilized Intervention

Little evidence has been found to support the idea that sterilized intervention exerts a major influence over exchange rates independent of the stances of monetary and fiscal policies.[14] As we noted in Chapter 3, however, there is also considerable evidence against the view that bonds denominated in different currencies are perfect substitutes.[15] Some economists conclude from these conflicting results that while risk premiums are important, they do not depend on central bank asset transactions in the simple way our model assumes. Others contend that the tests that have been used to detect the effects of sterilized intervention are flawed. Given the meager evidence that sterilized intervention has a reliable effect on exchange rates, however, a skeptical attitude is probably in order.

Our discussion of sterilized intervention has assumed that it does not change the market's exchange rate expectations. If market participants are unsure about the *future* direction of macroeconomic policies, however, sterilized intervention may give an indication of where the central bank expects (or desires) the exchange rate to move. This **signaling effect of foreign exchange intervention**, in turn, can alter the market's view of future monetary or fiscal policies and cause an immediate exchange rate change even when bonds denominated in different currencies are perfect substitutes.

The signaling effect is most important when the government is unhappy with the exchange rate's level and declares in public that it will alter monetary or fiscal policies to bring about a change. By simultaneously intervening on a sterilized basis, the central bank sometimes lends credibility to this announcement. A sterilized purchase of foreign assets, for example, may convince the market that the central bank intends to bring about a home currency depreciation because the bank will lose money if an appreciation occurs instead. Even central banks must watch their budgets!

However, a government may be tempted to exploit the signaling effect for temporary benefits even when it has no intention of changing monetary or fiscal policy to bring about a different long-run exchange rate. The result of crying, "Wolf!" too often is the same in the foreign exchange market as elsewhere. If governments do not follow up on their exchange market signals with concrete policy moves, the signals soon become ineffective. Thus, intervention signaling cannot be viewed as a policy weapon to be wielded independently of monetary and fiscal policy.[16]

---

[14]For evidence on sterilized intervention, see the Further Readings entry by Sarno and Taylor as well as the December 2000 issue of the *Journal of International Financial Markets, Institutions, and Money.*

[15]See the paper by Froot and Thaler in this chapter's Further Readings.

[16]For discussion of the role played by the signaling effect, see Kathryn M. Dominguez and Jeffrey A. Frankel, *Does Foreign Exchange Intervention Work?* (Washington, D.C.: Institute for International Economics, 1993); and Richard T. Baillie, Owen F. Humpage, and William P. Osterberg, "Intervention from an Information Perspective," *Journal of International Financial Markets, Institutions, and Money* 10 (December 2000), pp. 407–421.

Reserve Currencies in the World Monetary System

Until now, we have studied a single country that fixes its exchange rate in terms of a hypothetical single foreign currency by trading domestic for foreign assets when necessary. In the real world there are many currencies, and it is possible for a country to manage the exchange rates of its domestic currency against some foreign currencies while allowing them to float against others.

This section and the next adopt a global perspective and study the macroeconomic behavior of the world economy under two possible systems for fixing the exchange rates of *all* currencies against each other.

The first such fixed-rate system is very much like the one we have been studying. In it, one currency is singled out as a **reserve currency**, the currency central banks hold in their international reserves, and each nation's central bank fixes its currency's exchange rate against the reserve currency by standing ready to trade domestic money for reserve assets at that rate. Between the end of World War II and 1973, the U.S. dollar was the main reserve currency and almost every country pegged the dollar exchange rate of its money.

The second fixed-rate system (studied in the next section) is a **gold standard**. Under a gold standard, central banks peg the prices of their currencies in terms of gold and hold gold as official international reserves. The heyday of the international gold standard was between 1870 and 1914, although many countries attempted unsuccessfully to restore a permanent gold standard after the end of World War I in 1918.

Both reserve currency standards and the gold standard result in fixed exchange rates between *all* pairs of currencies in the world. But the two systems have very different implications about how countries share the burden of balance of payments financing and about the growth and control of national money supplies.

The Mechanics of a Reserve Currency Standard

The workings of a reserve currency system are illustrated by the system based on the U.S. dollar set up at the end of World War II. Under that system, every central bank fixed the dollar exchange rate of its currency through foreign exchange market trades of domestic currency for dollar assets. The frequent need to intervene meant that each central bank had to have on hand sufficient dollar reserves to meet any excess supply of its currency that might arise. Central banks therefore held a large portion of their international reserves in the form of U.S. Treasury bills and short-term dollar deposits, which pay interest and can be turned into cash at relatively low cost.

Because each currency's dollar price was fixed by its central bank, the exchange rate between any two currencies was automatically fixed as well through arbitrage in the foreign exchange market. How did this process work? Consider the following example based on the French franc and the deutsche mark, which were the currencies of France and Germany prior to the introduction of the euro. Let's suppose the French franc price of dollars was fixed at FFr 5 per dollar while the deutsche mark price of dollars was fixed at DM 4 per dollar. The exchange rate between the franc and the DM had to remain constant at DM 0.80 per franc = (DM 4 per dollar) ÷ (FFr 5 per dollar), even though no central bank was directly trading francs for DM to hold the relative price of those two currencies fixed. At a DM/FFr rate of DM 0.85 per franc, for example, you could have made a sure profit of $6.25 by selling $100 to the former French central bank, the Bank of France, for ($100) × (FFr 5 per dollar) = FFr 500, selling your FFr 500 in the foreign exchange market for (FFr 500) × (DM 0.85 per franc) = DM 425, and then selling the DM to the German Bundesbank (Germany's central bank until

1999) for (DM 425) ÷ (DM 4 per dollar) = $106.25. With everyone trying to exploit this profit opportunity by selling francs for DM in the foreign exchange market, however, the DM would have appreciated against the franc until the DM/FFr rate reached DM 0.80 per franc. Similarly, at a rate of DM 0.75 per franc, pressure in the foreign exchange market would have forced the DM to depreciate against the franc until the rate of DM 0.80 per franc was reached.

Even though each central bank tied its currency's exchange rate only to the dollar, market forces automatically held all other exchange rates—called cross rates—constant at the values implied by the dollar rates. Thus, the post–World War II exchange rate system was one in which exchange rates between any two currencies were fixed.[17]

The Asymmetric Position of the Reserve Center

In a reserve currency system, the country whose currency is held as reserves occupies a special position because it never has to intervene in the foreign exchange market. The reason is that if there are N countries with N currencies in the world, there are only $N-1$ exchange rates against the reserve currency. If the $N-1$ nonreserve currency countries fix their exchange rates against the reserve currency, there is no exchange rate left for the reserve center to fix. Thus, the center country need never intervene and bears none of the burden of financing its balance of payments.

This set of arrangements puts the reserve-issuing country in a privileged position because it can use its monetary policy for macroeconomic stabilization even though it has fixed exchange rates. We saw earlier in this chapter that when a country must intervene to hold an exchange rate constant, any attempt to expand its money supply is bound to be frustrated by losses of international reserves. But because the reserve center is the one country in the system that can enjoy fixed exchange rates without the need to intervene, it is still able to use monetary policy for stabilization purposes.

What would be the effect of a purchase of domestic assets by the central bank of the reserve currency country? The resulting expansion in its money supply would momentarily push its interest rate below those prevailing abroad, and thereby cause an excess demand for foreign currencies in the foreign exchange market. To prevent their currencies from appreciating against the reserve currency, all other central banks in the system would be forced to buy reserve assets with their own currencies, expanding their money supplies and pushing their interest rates down to the level established by the reserve center. Output throughout the world, as well as at home, would expand after a purchase of domestic assets by the reserve country.

Our account of monetary policy under a reserve currency system points to a basic asymmetry. The reserve country has the power to affect its own economy, as well as foreign economies, by using monetary policy. Other central banks are forced to relinquish monetary policy as a stabilization tool and instead must passively "import" the monetary policy of the reserve center because of their commitment to peg their currencies to the reserve currency.

This inherent asymmetry of a reserve system places immense economic power in the hands of the reserve country and is therefore likely to lead eventually to policy disputes within the system. Such problems helped cause the breakdown of the postwar "dollar standard" in 1973, a topic we discuss in Chapter 8.

---

[17]The rules of the postwar system actually allowed currencies' dollar values to move as much as 1 percent above or below the "official" values. This meant cross rates could fluctuate by as much as 4 percent.

The Gold Standard

An international gold standard avoids the asymmetry inherent in a reserve currency standard by avoiding the "Nth currency" problem. Under a gold standard, each country fixes the price of its currency in terms of gold by standing ready to trade domestic currency for gold whenever necessary to defend the official price. Because there are N currencies and N prices of gold in terms of those currencies, no single country occupies a privileged position within the system: Each is responsible for pegging its currency's price in terms of the official international reserve asset, gold.

The Mechanics of a Gold Standard

Because countries tie their currencies to gold under a gold standard, official international reserves take the form of gold. Gold standard rules also require each country to allow unhindered imports and exports of gold across its borders. Under these arrangements, a gold standard, like a reserve currency system, results in fixed exchange rates between all currencies. For example, if the dollar price of gold is pegged at $35 per ounce by the Federal Reserve while the pound price of gold is pegged at £14.58 per ounce by Britain's central bank, the Bank of England, the dollar/pound exchange rate must be constant at ($35 per ounce) ÷ (£14.58 per ounce) = $2.40 per pound. The same arbitrage process that holds cross exchange rates fixed under a reserve currency system keeps exchange rates fixed under a gold standard as well.[18]

Symmetric Monetary Adjustment under a Gold Standard

Because of the inherent symmetry of a gold standard, no country in the system occupies a privileged position by being relieved of the commitment to intervene. By considering the international effects of a purchase of domestic assets by one central bank, we can see in more detail how monetary policy works under a gold standard.

Suppose the Bank of England decides to increase its money supply through a purchase of domestic assets. The initial increase in Britain's money supply will put downward pressure on British interest rates and make foreign currency assets more attractive than British assets. Holders of pound deposits will attempt to sell them for foreign deposits, but no *private* buyers will come forward. Under floating exchange rates, the pound would depreciate against foreign currencies until interest parity had been reestablished. This depreciation cannot occur when all currencies are tied to gold, however. Why not? Because central banks are obliged to trade their currencies for gold at fixed rates, unhappy holders of pounds can sell these to the Bank of England for gold, sell the gold to other central banks for their currencies, and use these currencies to purchase deposits that offer interest rates higher than the interest rate on pounds. Britain therefore experiences a private financial outflow and foreign countries experience an inflow.

This process reestablishes equilibrium in the foreign exchange market. The Bank of England loses foreign reserves since it is forced to buy pounds and sell gold to keep the pound price of gold fixed. Foreign central banks gain reserves as they *buy* gold with their currencies. Countries share equally in the burden of balance of payments adjustment. Because official foreign reserves are declining in Britain and increasing abroad, the British money supply is falling, pushing the British interest rate back up, and foreign money supplies are rising, pushing foreign interest rates down. Once interest rates

---

[18]In practice, the costs of shipping gold and insuring it in transit determined narrow "gold points" within which currency exchange rates could fluctuate.

have again become equal across countries, asset markets are in equilibrium and there is no further tendency for the Bank of England to lose gold or for foreign central banks to gain it. The total world money supply (not the British money supply) ends up being higher by the amount of the Bank of England's domestic asset purchase. Interest rates are lower throughout the world.

Our example illustrates the symmetric nature of international monetary adjustment under a gold standard. Whenever a country is losing reserves and seeing its money supply shrink as a consequence, foreign countries are gaining reserves and seeing their money supplies expand. In contrast, monetary adjustment under a reserve currency standard is highly asymmetric. Countries can gain or lose reserves without inducing any change in the money supply of the reserve currency country, and only the latter country has the ability to influence domestic and world monetary conditions.[19]

Benefits and Drawbacks of the Gold Standard

Advocates of the gold standard argue that it has another desirable property besides symmetry. Because central banks throughout the world are obliged to fix the money price of gold, they cannot allow their money supplies to grow more rapidly than real money demand, since such rapid monetary growth eventually raises the money prices of all goods and services, including gold. A gold standard therefore places automatic limits on the extent to which central banks can cause increases in national price levels through expansionary monetary policies. These limits can make the real values of national monies more stable and predictable, thereby enhancing the transaction economies arising from the use of money (see Chapter 4). No such limits to money creation exist under a reserve currency system; the reserve currency country faces no automatic barrier to unlimited money creation.

Offsetting this potential benefit of a gold standard are some drawbacks:

  1. The gold standard places undesirable constraints on the use of monetary policy to fight unemployment. In a worldwide recession, it might be desirable for all countries to expand their money supplies jointly even if this were to raise the price of gold in terms of national currencies.

  2. Tying currency values to gold ensures a stable overall price level only if the relative price of gold and other goods and services is stable. For example, suppose the dollar price of gold is $35 per ounce while the price of gold in terms of a typical output basket is one-third of a basket per ounce. This implies a price level of $105 per output basket. Now suppose that there is a major gold discovery in South America and the relative price of gold in terms of output falls to one-fourth of a basket per ounce. With the dollar price of gold unchanged at $35 per ounce, the price level would have to rise from $105 to $140 per basket. In fact, studies of the gold standard era do reveal surprisingly large price level fluctuations arising from such changes in gold's relative price.[20]

---

[19]Originally, gold coins were a substantial part of the currency supply in gold standard countries. A country's gold losses to foreigners therefore did not have to take the form of a fall in central bank gold holdings: Private citizens could melt gold coins into ingots and ship them abroad, where they were either reminted as foreign gold coins or sold to the foreign central bank for paper currency. In terms of our earlier analysis of the central bank balance sheet, circulating gold coins are considered to make up a component of the monetary base that is not a central bank liability. Either form of gold export would thus result in a fall in the domestic money supply and an increase in foreign money supplies.

[20]See, for example, Richard N. Cooper, "The Gold Standard: Historical Facts and Future Prospects," *Brookings Papers on Economic Activity* 1 (1982), pp. 1–45.

3. An international payments system based on gold is problematic because central banks cannot increase their holdings of international reserves as their economies grow unless there are continual new gold discoveries. Every central bank would need to hold some gold reserves to fix its currency's gold price and serve as a buffer against unforeseen economic mishaps. Central banks might thereby bring about world unemployment as they attempted to compete for reserves by selling domestic assets and thus shrinking their money supplies.

4. The gold standard could give countries with potentially large gold production, such as Russia and South Africa, considerable ability to influence macroeconomic conditions throughout the world through market sales of gold.

Because of these drawbacks, few economists favor a return to the gold standard today. As early as 1923, the British economist John Maynard Keynes characterized gold as a "barbarous relic" of an earlier international monetary system.[21] While most central banks continue to hold some gold as part of their international reserves, the price of gold now plays no special role in influencing countries' monetary policies.

The Bimetallic Standard

Up until the early 1870s, many countries adhered to a **bimetallic standard** in which the currency was based on both silver and gold. The United States was bimetallic from 1837 until the Civil War, although the major bimetallic power of the day was France, which abandoned bimetallism for gold in 1873.

In a bimetallic system, a country's mint will coin specified amounts of gold *or* silver into the national currency unit (typically for a fee). In the United States before the Civil War, for example, 371.25 grains of silver (a grain being 1/480th of an ounce) or 23.22 grains of gold could be turned into, respectively, a silver or a gold dollar. That mint parity made gold worth $371.25/23.22 = 16$ times as much as silver.

The mint parity could differ from the market relative price of the two metals, however, and when it did, one or the other might go out of circulation. For example, if the price of gold in terms of silver were to rise to 20:1, a depreciation of silver relative to the mint parity of 16:1, no one would want to turn gold into gold dollar coins at the mint. More dollars could be obtained by instead using the gold to buy silver in the market, and then having the silver coined into dollars. As a result, gold would tend to go out of monetary circulation when its relative market price rose above the mint relative price, and silver coin would tend to disappear in the opposite case.

The advantage of bimetallism was that it might reduce the price level instability resulting from use of one of the metals alone. Were gold to become scarce and expensive, cheaper and relatively abundant silver would become the predominant form of money, thereby mitigating the deflation that a pure gold standard would imply. Notwithstanding this advantage, by the late 19th century most of the world had followed Britain, the leading industrial power of the day, onto a pure gold standard.

The Gold Exchange Standard

Halfway between the gold standard and a pure reserve currency standard is the **gold exchange standard**. Under a gold exchange standard, central banks' reserves consist of gold *and* currencies whose prices in terms of gold are fixed, and each central bank

---

[21]See Keynes, "Alternative Aims in Monetary Policy," reprinted in his *Essays in Persuasion* (New York: W. W. Norton & Company, 1963). For a dissenting view on the gold standard, see Robert A. Mundell, "International Monetary Reform: The Optimal Mix in Big Countries," in James Tobin, ed., *Macroeconomics, Prices and Quantities* (Washington, D.C.: Brookings Institution, 1983), pp. 285–293.

fixes its exchange rate to a currency with a fixed gold price. A gold exchange standard can operate like a gold standard in restraining excessive monetary growth throughout the world, but it allows more flexibility in the growth of international reserves, which can consist of assets besides gold. A gold exchange standard is, however, subject to the other limitations of a gold standard listed previously.

The post–World War II reserve currency system centered on the dollar was, in fact, originally set up as a gold exchange standard. While foreign central banks did the job of pegging exchange rates, the U.S. Federal Reserve was responsible for holding the dollar price of gold at $35 an ounce. By the mid-1960s, the system operated in practice more like a pure reserve currency system than a gold standard. For reasons explained in the next chapter, President Richard M. Nixon unilaterally severed the dollar's link to gold in August 1971, shortly before the system of fixed dollar exchange rates was abandoned.

CASE STUDY   The Demand for International Reserves

The chapter explained that a central bank's assets are divided between domestic currency assets, such as domestic government bonds, and foreign currency assets, the bank's international reserves. Historically and up to the present day, international reserves have been prized by central banks because they can be traded to foreigners for goods and services even in circumstances, such as financial crises and wars, when the value of domestic assets may come into doubt. Gold played the role of international reserve asset *par excellence* under the gold standard—and while the U.S. dollar remains the main reserve asset today, economists debate how long that unique American privilege can last. Because central banks and governments may alter their policies to affect national holdings of international reserves, it is important to understand the factors that influence countries' demands for international reserves.

A good starting point for thinking about international reserves is the model in the chapter in which domestic and foreign bonds are perfect substitutes, the exchange rate is fixed, and confidence in the fixed exchange rate is absolute. In that model, our result that monetary policy is ineffective also implies that individual central banks can painlessly acquire all the international reserves they need! They do so simply by an open-market sale of domestic assets, which immediately causes an equal inflow of foreign assets but no change in the home interest rate or in other domestic economic conditions. In real life, matters may not be so easy, because the circumstances in which countries need reserves are precisely those in which the above conditions of perfect confidence in creditworthiness and in the exchange rate peg are likely to be violated. As a result, central banks manage their reserves in a *precautionary* manner, holding a stock that they believe will be sufficient in future times of crisis.[22]

As usual, there are costs as well as benefits of acquiring and holding reserves, and the level of reserves that a central bank wishes to hold will reflect a balance between those costs and benefits. Some monetary authorities (such as that of Hong Kong) value reserves so highly that the entire money supply is backed by foreign

[22]A different problem arises under a system like the gold standard, where the global stock of international reserves may be limited (in contrast to a reserve currency system). The difficulty is that all countries cannot simultaneously increase their reserve holdings, so efforts by many countries to do so at the same time will affect global economic conditions. An end-of-chapter exercise asks you to think about this case.

assets—there are no domestic monetary assets at all. In most cases, however, central banks hold both domestic and foreign assets, with the optimal level of reserves determined by the trade-off between costs and benefits.

Starting in the mid-1960s, economists developed and sought empirical verification of formal theories of the demand for international reserves. In that setting, with international capital markets much more limited than they are today (see Chapter 9), a major threat to reserves was a sudden drop in export earnings, and central banks measured reserve levels in terms of the number of months of import needs those reserves could cover. Accordingly, the variability levels of exports, imports, and international financial flows, all of which could cause reserves to fluctuate too close to zero, were viewed as prime determinants of the demand for international reserves. In this theory, higher variability would raise the demand for reserves. An additional variable raising the average demand for reserves might be the adjustment cost countries would suffer if they suddenly had to raise exports or reduce imports to generate a trade surplus, or raise interest rates to draw in foreign capital. Higher economic openness could make such adjustments easier, thereby reducing the demand for reserves, but might also make an economy more vulnerable to foreign trade shocks, thereby raising desired reserve holdings.[23]

On the other hand, the main cost of holding reserves is their interest cost. A central bank that switches from domestic bonds to foreign reserves loses the interest on the domestic bonds and instead earns the interest on the reserve currency, for example, on dollars. If markets harbor any fears that the domestic currency could be devalued, then domestic bonds will offer a higher interest rate than foreign reserves, implying that it is costly to switch the central bank's portfolio toward reserves. Of course, if the reserve currency does appreciate against domestic currency, the central bank will gain, with a corresponding loss if the reserve currency depreciates.

In addition, reserves may offer lower interest simply because of their higher liquidity. This interest cost of holding relatively liquid reserves is analogous to the interest cost of holding money, which we reviewed in Chapter 4.

It was argued in the 1960s that countries with more flexible exchange rates would find it easier to generate an export surplus if reserves ran low—they could allow their currencies to depreciate, perhaps avoiding the recession that might otherwise be needed to create a trade balance surplus. When industrial countries moved to floating exchange rates in the early 1970s, many economists therefore expected that the demand for international reserves would drop sharply.

Figure 7-8 shows, however, that nothing of the sort happened. For industrial countries, the growth rate of international reserves has not declined since the 1960s. For developing countries, the growth rate of reserves has, if anything, risen on average (though the sharp upsurge in the mid-2000s is to some degree a reflection of huge reserve purchases by China). Accelerating reserve growth has taken place despite the adoption of more flexible exchange rates by many developing countries.

One explanation for this development, which we will discuss further in later chapters, is that the growth of global capital markets has vastly increased the potential variability of financial flows across national borders, especially across the borders

---

[23]An early influential study was by H. Robert Heller, "Optimal International Reserves," *Economic Journal* 76 (June 1966), pp. 296–311.

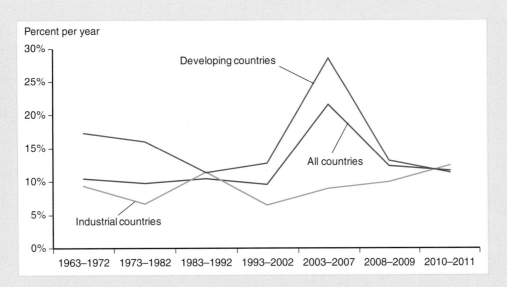

FIGURE 7-8

Growth Rates of International Reserves

Annualized growth rates of international reserves did not decline sharply after the early 1970s. Recently, developing countries have added large sums to their reserve holdings, but their pace of accumulation has slowed starting with the crisis years of 2008–2009. The figure shows averages of annual growth rates.

Source: International Monetary Fund.

of crisis-prone developing countries.[24] The sharp decline in developing-country reserve growth in the 1982–1992 period, shown in the figure, reflects an international debt crisis during the years 1982–1989. In that crisis, foreign lending sources dried up and many developing countries were forced to draw on their reserves. We see another decline in reserve growth during the crisis years of 2008–2009. These episodes illustrate why developing countries have added so eagerly to their reserve holdings. Even a developing country with a floating exchange rate might need to pay off foreign creditors and domestic residents with dollars to avoid a financial crisis and a currency collapse.

Nothing about this explanation contradicts earlier theories. The demand for international reserves still reflects the variability in the balance of payments. The rapid globalization of financial markets in recent years has, however, caused a big increase in potential variability and in the potential risks that variability poses.

Countries can and do choose to hold international reserves in currencies other than the U.S. dollar. They tend to hold only those currencies that are most likely to retain their value over time and to be readily accepted by foreign exporters and creditors. Thanks to the large and generally prosperous geographical region it serves, the euro, introduced in 1999, is the strongest challenger to the dollar's role (although the recent euro area crisis has taken a toll).

[24]Recent works on the modern determinants of the demand for international reserves includes those of Robert Flood and Nancy Marion, "Holding International Reserves in an Era of High Capital Mobility," *Brookings Trade Forum* 2001, pp. 1–47; Joshua Aizenman and Jaewoo Lee, "International Reserves: Precautionary versus Mercantilist Views, Theory and Evidence," *Open Economies Review* 18 (April 2007), pp. 191–214; and Maurice Obstfeld, Jay C. Shambaugh, and Alan M. Taylor, "Financial Stability, the Trilemma, and International Reserves," *American Economic Journal: Macroeconomics* 2 (April 2010), pp. 57–94.

Figure 7-9 shows the importance of four major currencies in countries' international reserve holdings. Since the euro's birth in 1999, its share in global reserves has risen from 18 to 25 percent, while the dollar's share has declined from 71 to 62 percent. Britain's pound sterling was the world's leading reserve currency up until the 1920s. That currency, however, now makes up only about 4 percent of global reserves, while the Japanese yen's share, about three times that of sterling during the mid-1990s, is now slightly lower.

Upon its introduction in 1999, some economists speculated that the euro would overtake the dollar as the main international reserve currency. Despite the apparent trend away from the dollar shown in Figure 7-9, that day seems distant. Yet history certainly shows how leading reserve currencies can be toppled by newcomers.[25]

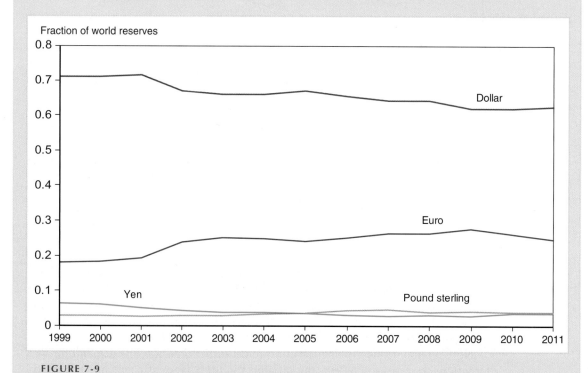

FIGURE 7-9

Currency Composition of Global Reserve Holdings

While the euro's role as a reserve currency has generally increased over time, the dollar remains the overwhelming favorite.

Source: International Monetary Fund, Currency Composition of Foreign Exchange Reserves, at http://www.imf.org/external/np/sta/cofer/eng/index.htm. These data cover only the countries that report reserve composition to the IMF, the major omission being China.

---

[25]A recent assessment of the dollar's reserve status by Eichengreen is listed in Further Readings. Eichengreen presents a comprehensive historical perspective on the dollar's special status in his book *Exorbitant Privilege: The Rise and Fall of the Dollar and the Future of the International Monetary System* (New York: Oxford University Press, 2011). For a formal statistical study, see Menzie Chinn and Jeffrey A. Frankel, "Will the Euro Eventually Surpass the Dollar as Leading International Reserve Currency?" in Richard H. Clarida, ed., *G7 Current Account Imbalances: Sustainability and Adjustment* (Chicago: University of Chicago Press, 2007), pp. 283–322.

SUMMARY

1. There is a direct link between central bank intervention in the foreign exchange market and the domestic money supply. When a country's central bank purchases foreign assets, the country's money supply automatically increases. Similarly, a central bank sale of foreign assets automatically lowers the money supply. The *central bank balance sheet* shows how foreign exchange intervention affects the money supply because the central bank's liabilities, which rise or fall when its assets rise or fall, are the base of the domestic money supply process. The central bank can negate the money supply effect of intervention through *sterilization*. With no sterilization, there is a link between the balance of payments and national money supplies that depends on how central banks share the burden of financing balance of payments gaps.

2. A central bank can fix the exchange rate of its currency against foreign currency if it is willing to trade unlimited amounts of domestic money against foreign assets at that rate. To fix the exchange rate, the central bank must intervene in the foreign exchange market whenever necessary to prevent the emergence of an excess demand or supply of domestic currency assets. In effect, the central bank adjusts its foreign assets—and thus, the domestic money supply—to ensure that asset markets are always in equilibrium under the fixed exchange rate.

3. A commitment to fix an exchange rate forces the central bank to sacrifice its ability to use monetary policy for stabilization. A purchase of domestic assets by the central bank causes an equal fall in its official international reserves, leaving the money supply and output unchanged. Similarly, a sale of domestic assets by the bank causes foreign reserves to rise by the same amount but has no other effects.

4. Fiscal policy, unlike monetary policy, has a more powerful effect on output under fixed exchange rates than under floating rates. Under a fixed exchange rate, fiscal expansion does not, in the short run, cause a real appreciation that "crowds out" aggregate demand. Instead, it forces central bank purchases of foreign assets and an expansion of the money supply. *Devaluation* also raises aggregate demand and the money supply in the short run. (*Revaluation* has opposite effects.) In the long run, fiscal expansion causes a real appreciation, an increase in the money supply, and a rise in the home price level, while devaluation causes the long-run levels of the money supply and prices to rise in proportion to the exchange rate change.

5. *Balance of payments crises* occur when market participants expect the central bank to change the exchange rate from its current level. If the market decides a devaluation is coming, for example, the domestic interest rate rises above the world interest rate and foreign reserves drop sharply as private capital flows abroad. *Self-fulfilling currency crises* can occur when an economy is vulnerable to speculation. In other circumstances an exchange rate collapse may be the inevitable result of inconsistent government policies.

6. A system of *managed floating* allows the central bank to retain some ability to control the domestic money supply, but at the cost of greater exchange rate instability. If domestic and foreign bonds are *imperfect substitutes*, however, the central bank may be able to control both the money supply and the exchange rate through sterilized foreign exchange intervention. Empirical evidence provides little support for the idea that sterilized intervention has a significant direct effect on exchange rates. Even when domestic and foreign bonds are *perfect substitutes*, so that there is no *risk premium*, sterilized intervention may operate indirectly through a *signaling effect* that changes market views of future policies.

7. A world system of fixed exchange rates in which countries peg the prices of their currencies in terms of a *reserve currency* involves a striking asymmetry: The reserve currency country, which does not have to fix any exchange rate, can influence economic activity both at home and abroad through its monetary policy. In contrast, all other countries are unable to influence their output or foreign output through monetary policy. This policy asymmetry reflects the fact that the reserve center bears none of the burden of financing its balance of payments.

8. A *gold standard*, in which all countries fix their currencies' prices in terms of gold, avoids the asymmetry inherent in a reserve currency standard and places constraints on the growth of countries' money supplies. (A related arrangement was the *bimetallic standard* based on both silver and gold.) But the gold standard has serious drawbacks that make it impractical as a way of organizing today's international monetary system. Even the dollar-based *gold exchange standard* set up after World War II ultimately proved unworkable.

KEY TERMS

balance of payments crisis, p. 207
bimetallic standard, p. 220
capital flight, p. 209
central bank balance sheet, p. 195
devaluation, p. 205
gold exchange standard, p. 220
gold standard, p. 216

imperfect asset substitutability, p. 212
managed floating exchange rates, p. 193
perfect asset substitutability, p. 211
reserve currency, p. 216
revaluation, p. 205
risk premium, p. 213

self-fulfilling currency crises, p. 209
signaling effect of foreign exchange intervention, p. 215
sterilized foreign exchange intervention, p. 198

PROBLEMS

MyEconLab

1. Show how an expansion in the central bank's domestic assets ultimately affects its balance sheet under a fixed exchange rate. How are the central bank's transactions in the foreign exchange market reflected in the balance of payments accounts?

2. Do the exercises in the previous problem for an increase in government spending.

3. Describe the effects of an unexpected devaluation on the central bank's balance sheet and on the balance of payments accounts.

4. Explain why a devaluation improves the current account in this chapter's model. (Hint: Consider the *XX* curve developed in the last chapter.)

5. Can you think of reasons why a government might willingly sacrifice some of its ability to use monetary policy so that it can have more stable exchange rates?

6. How does fiscal expansion affect the current account under a fixed exchange rate?

7. Explain why temporary and permanent fiscal expansions do not have different effects under fixed exchange rates, as they do under floating exchange rates.

8. Devaluation is often used by countries to improve their current accounts. Since the current account equals national saving less domestic investment, however (see Chapter 2), this improvement can occur only if investment falls, saving rises, or both. How might devaluation affect national saving and domestic investment?

9. Using the *DD-AA* model, analyze the output and balance of payments effects of an import tariff under fixed exchange rates. What would happen if all countries in the world simultaneously tried to improve employment and the balance of payments by imposing tariffs?

10. When a central bank devalues after a balance of payments crisis, it usually gains foreign reserves. Can this financial inflow be explained using our model? What would happen if the market believed that *another* devaluation would occur in the near future?

11. Suppose that under the postwar "dollar standard" system, foreign central banks had held dollar reserves in the form of green dollar bills hidden in their vaults rather than in the form of U.S. Treasury bills. Would the international monetary adjustment mechanism have been symmetric or asymmetric? (Hint: Think about what happens to the U.S. and Japanese money supplies, for example, when the Bank of Japan sells yen for dollar bills that it then keeps.)

12. "When domestic and foreign bonds are perfect substitutes, a central bank should be indifferent about using domestic or foreign assets to implement monetary policy." Discuss.

13. U.S. foreign exchange intervention is sometimes done by an Exchange Stabilization Fund, or ESF (a branch of the Treasury Department), which manages a portfolio of U.S. government and foreign currency bonds. An ESF intervention to support the yen, for example, would take the form of a portfolio shift out of dollar and into yen assets. Show that ESF interventions are automatically sterilized and thus do not alter money supplies. How do ESF operations affect the foreign exchange risk premium?

14. Use a diagram like Figure 7-7 to explain how a central bank can alter the domestic interest rate, while holding the exchange rate fixed, under imperfect asset substitutability.

15. On page 197 in the text, we analyzed how the sale of $100 worth of its foreign assets affects the central bank's balance sheet. The assumption in that example was that the buyer of the foreign assets paid in the form of domestic currency cash. Suppose instead that the buyer pays with a check drawn on her account at Pecuniacorp, a private domestic bank. Using a balance sheet like the ones presented in the text, show how the transaction affects the central bank's balance sheet and the money supply.

16. We observed in the text that "fixed" exchange-rate systems can result not in absolutely fixed exchange rates but in narrow bands within which the exchange rate can move. For example, the gold points (mentioned in footnote 18) produced such bands under a gold standard. (Typically those bands were on the order of plus or minus 1 percent of the "central" exchange parity.) To what extent would such bands for the exchange rate allow the domestic interest rate to move independently of a foreign rate? Show that the answer depends on the maturity or *term* of the interest rate. To help your intuition, assume plus or minus 1 percent bands for the exchange rate, and consider, alternatively, rates on three-month deposits, on six-month deposits, and on one-year deposits. With such narrow bands, would there be much scope for independence in ten-year loan rates?

17. In a three-country world, a central bank fixes one exchange rate but lets the others float. Can it use monetary policy to affect output? Can it fix both exchange rates?

18. In the Case Study on international reserves (pages 221–224), we asserted that except in the case of a reserve currency system, an attempt by all central banks simultaneously to raise their international reserve holdings through open-market sales of domestic assets could have a contractionary effect on the world economy. Explain by contrasting the cases of a gold standard-type system and a reserve currency system.

19. If a country changes its exchange rate, the value of its foreign reserves, measured in the domestic currency, also changes. This latter change may represent a domestic currency gain or loss for the central bank. What happens when a country devalues its currency against the reserve currency? When it revalues? How might this factor affect the potential cost of holding foreign reserves? Make sure to consider the role of interest parity in formulating your answer.

20. Analyze the result of a permanent devaluation by an economy caught in a liquidity trap of the sort described in Chapter 6.

21. Recall our discussion of the Swiss franc's currency floor in the box on pp. 211–212. Also, recall the last chapter's discussion of the liquidity trap. Because Switzerland has been in a liquidity trap all the time it has defended its currency floor, does our discussion of liquidity trap theory in the last chapter suggest why Swiss inflation has not been raised by the SNB's heavy foreign exchange purchases?

22. Again returning to the case of the Swiss franc currency floor, with Swiss interest rates at zero, what do you think would happen if currency speculators expected the Swiss franc to appreciate by more than the euro rate of interest?

FURTHER READINGS

Graham Bird and Ramkishen Rajan. "Too Much of a Good Thing? The Adequacy of International Reserves in the Aftermath of Crises." *World Economy* 86 (June 2003), pp. 873–891. Accessible review of literature on the demand for international reserves.

William H. Branson. "Causes of Appreciation and Volatility of the Dollar," in *The U.S. Dollar—Recent Developments, Outlook, and Policy Options*. Kansas City: Federal Reserve Bank of Kansas City, 1985, pp. 33–52. Develops and applies a model of exchange rate determination with imperfect asset substitutability.

Barry Eichengreen. "The Dollar Dilemma: The World's Top Currency Faces Competition." *Foreign Affairs* 88 (September/October 2009), pp. 53–68. An assessment of challenges to the dollar's primacy among potential alternative vehicle and reserve currencies.

Milton Friedman. "Bimetallism Revisited." *Journal of Economic Perspectives* 4 (Fall 1990), pp. 85–104. A fascinating reconsideration of economists' assessments of the dual silver-gold standard.

Kenneth A. Froot and Richard H. Thaler. "Anomalies: Foreign Exchange." *Journal of Economic Perspectives* 4 (Summer 1990), pp. 179–192. Clear, nontechnical discussion of the empirical evidence on the interest parity condition.

Karl Habermeier, Annamaria Kokenyne, Romain Veyrune, and Harald Anderson. "Revised System for the Classification of Exchange Rate Arrangements." IMF Working Paper WP/09/211, September 2009. Explains how the International Monetary Fund classifies countries' diverse systems of exchange-rate determination.

Matthew Higgins and Thomas Klitgaard. "Reserve Accumulation: Implications for Global Capital Flows and Financial Markets." *Current Issues in Economics and Finance* 10 (September/October 2004). Analysis of trends in central bank reserve holdings.

Owen F. Humpage. "Institutional Aspects of U.S. Intervention." *Federal Reserve Bank of Cleveland Economic Review* 30 (Quarter 1, 1994), pp. 2–19. How the U.S. Treasury and Federal Reserve coordinate foreign exchange intervention.

Olivier Jeanne. *Currency Crises: A Perspective on Recent Theoretical Developments*. Princeton Special Papers in International Economics 20. International Finance Section, Department of Economics, Princeton University, March 2000. Recent thinking on speculative crises and attacks.

Robert A. Mundell. "Capital Mobility and Stabilization Policy under Fixed and Flexible Exchange Rates." *Canadian Journal of Economics and Political Science* 29 (November 1963), pp. 475–485. Classic account of the effects of monetary and fiscal policies under alternative exchange rate regimes.

Michael Mussa. *The Role of Official Intervention.* Occasional Paper 6. New York: Group of Thirty, 1981. Discusses the theory and practice of central bank foreign exchange intervention under a dirty float.

Christopher J. Neely. "Central Bank Authorities' Beliefs about Foreign Exchange Intervention." Working Paper 2006-045C, Federal Reserve Bank of St. Louis, April 2007. Interesting survey of central bankers' views on the role and limits of intervention.

Maurice Obstfeld. "Models of Currency Crises with Self-Fulfilling Features." *European Economic Review* 40 (April 1996), pp. 1037–1048. More on the nature of balance of payments crises.

Lucio Sarno and Mark P. Taylor. "Official Intervention in the Foreign Exchange Market: Is It Effective and, If So, How Does It Work?" *Journal of Economic Literature* 39 (September 2001), pp. 839–868. An updated survey on foreign exchange intervention.

MyEconLab Can Help You Get a Better Grade

MyEconLab   If your exam were tomorrow, would you be ready? For each chapter, MyEconLab Practice Tests and Study Plans pinpoint sections you have mastered and those you need to study. That way, you are more efficient with your study time, and you are better prepared for your exams.

To see how it works, turn to page 9 and then go to

www.myeconlab.com

Equilibrium in the Foreign Exchange Market with Imperfect Asset Substitutability

This appendix develops a model of the foreign exchange market in which risk factors may make domestic currency and foreign currency assets imperfect substitutes. The model gives rise to a risk premium that can separate the expected rates of return on domestic and foreign assets.

Demand

Because individuals dislike risky situations in which their wealth may vary greatly from day to day, they decide how to allocate wealth among different assets by looking at the riskiness of the resulting portfolio as well as at the expected return the portfolio offers. Someone who puts her wealth entirely into British pounds, for example, may expect a high return, but the wealth can be wiped out if the pound unexpectedly depreciates. A more sensible strategy is to invest in several currencies even if some have lower expected returns than the pound, and thus reduce the impact on wealth of bad luck with any one currency. By spreading risk among several currencies, an individual can reduce the variability of her wealth.

Considerations of risk make it reasonable to assume that an individual's demand for interest-bearing domestic currency assets increases when the interest they offer (R) rises relative to the domestic currency return on foreign currency assets $[R^* + (E^e - E)/E]$. Put another way, an individual will be willing to increase the riskiness of her portfolio by investing more heavily in domestic currency assets only if she is compensated by an increase in the relative expected return on those assets.

We summarize this assumption by writing individual i's demand for domestic currency bonds, B_i^d, as an increasing function of the rate-of-return difference between domestic and foreign bonds,

$$B_i^d = B_i^d[R - R^* - (E^e - E)/E].$$

Of course, B_i^d also depends on other factors specific to individual i, such as her wealth and income. The demand for domestic currency bonds can be negative or positive, and in the former case, individual i is a net borrower in the home currency, that is, a *supplier* of domestic currency bonds.

To find the *aggregate* private demand for domestic currency bonds, we need only add up individual demands B_i^d for all individuals i in the world. This summation gives the aggregate demand for domestic currency bonds, B^d, which is also an increasing function of the expected rate-of-return difference in favor of domestic currency assets. Therefore,

$$\text{Demand} = B^d[R - R^* - (E^e - E)/E]$$
$$= \text{sum for all } i \text{ of } B_i^d[R - R^* - (E^e - E)/E].$$

Since some private individuals may be borrowing, and therefore supplying bonds, B^d should be interpreted as the private sector's *net* demand for domestic currency bonds.

Supply

Since we are interpreting B^d as the private sector's *net* demand for domestic currency bonds, the appropriate supply variable to define market equilibrium is the net supply of domestic currency bonds to the private sector, that is, the supply of bonds that are not the liability of any private individual or firm. Net supply therefore equals the value of domestic currency *government* bonds held by the public, B, less the value of domestic currency assets held by the central bank, A:

$$\text{Supply} = B - A.$$

A must be subtracted from B to find the net supply of bonds because purchases of bonds by the central bank reduce the supply available to private investors. (More generally, we would also subtract from B domestic currency assets held by foreign central banks.)

Equilibrium

The risk premium, ρ, is determined by the interaction of supply and demand. The risk premium is defined as

$$\rho = R - R^* - (E^e - E)/E,$$

that is, as the expected return difference between domestic and foreign bonds. We can therefore write the private sector's net demand for domestic currency bonds as an increasing function of ρ. Figure 7A1-1 shows this relationship by drawing the demand curve for domestic currency bonds with a positive slope.

The bond supply curve is vertical at $B - A^1$ because the net supply of bonds to the market is determined by decisions of the government and central bank and is independent of the risk premium. Equilibrium occurs at point 1 (at a risk premium of ρ^1), where the private sector's net demand for domestic currency bonds equals the net supply.

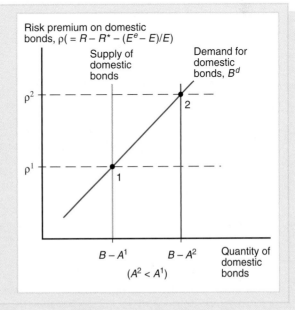

FIGURE 7A1-1

The Domestic Bond Supply and the Foreign Exchange Risk Premium under Imperfect Asset Substitutability

An increase in the supply of domestic currency bonds that the private sector must hold raises the risk premium on domestic currency assets.

Notice that for given values of R, R^*, and E^e, the equilibrium shown in the diagram can also be viewed as determining the exchange rate, since $E = E^e/(1 + R - R^* - \rho)$.

Figure 7A1-1 also shows the effect of a central bank sale of domestic assets that lowers its domestic asset holdings to $A^2 < A^1$. This sale raises the net supply of domestic currency bonds to $B - A^2$ and shifts the supply curve to the right. The new equilibrium occurs at point 2, at a risk premium of $\rho^2 > \rho^1$. Similarly, an increase in the domestic currency government debt, B, would raise the risk premium.

The model therefore establishes that the risk premium is an increasing function of $B - A$, just as we assumed in the discussion of sterilized intervention that led to equation (7-3).

You should recognize that our discussion of risk premium determination is an oversimplification in a number of ways, not least because of the assumption that the home country is small, so that all foreign variables can be taken as given. In general, however, actions taken by foreign governments may also affect the risk premium, which of course can take *negative* as well as positive values. That is, policies or events that make foreign bonds progressively riskier will eventually make investors willing to hold domestic currency bonds at an expected rate of return *below* that on foreign currency bonds.

One way to capture this possibility would be to generalize equation (7-3) in the text and express the risk premium instead as

$$\rho = \rho(B - A, B^* - A^*),$$

where $B^* - A^*$ is the net stock of foreign currency bonds that the public must hold. In this extended formulation, a rise in $B - A$ still raises ρ, but a rise in $B^* - A^*$ causes ρ to fall by making foreign bonds relatively riskier.

The Timing of Balance of Payments Crises

In the text, we modeled a balance of payments crisis as a sudden loss of confidence in the central bank's promise to hold the exchange rate fixed in the future. As previously noted, a currency crisis often is not the result of arbitrary shifts in market sentiment, contrary to what exasperated policy makers embroiled in crises often contend. Instead, an exchange rate collapse can be the inevitable result of government policies inconsistent with maintaining a fixed exchange rate permanently. In such cases, simple economic theory may allow us to predict the date of a crisis through a careful analysis of the government policies and the market's rational response to them.[26]

It is easiest to make the main points using the assumptions and notations of the monetary approach to the balance of payments (as developed in Online Appendix A to this chapter) and the monetary approach to the exchange rate (Chapter 5). To simplify, we will assume that output prices are perfectly flexible and that output is constant at its full-employment level. We will also assume that market participants have perfect foresight concerning the future.

The precise timing of a payments crisis cannot be determined independently of government policies. In particular, we have to describe not only how the government is behaving today, but also how it plans to react to future events in the economy. Two assumptions about official behavior are made: (1) The central bank is allowing the stock of central bank domestic credit, A, to expand steadily, and will do so forever. (2) The central bank is currently fixing the exchange rate at the level E^0, but will allow the exchange rate to float freely forever if its foreign reserves, F^*, ever fall to zero. Furthermore, the authorities will defend E^0 to the bitter end by selling foreign reserves at that price as long as they have any to sell.

The problem with the central bank's policies is that they are inconsistent with maintaining a fixed exchange rate indefinitely. The monetary approach suggests that foreign reserves will fall steadily as domestic assets continually rise. Eventually, therefore, reserves will have to run out and the fixed exchange rate E^0 will have to be abandoned. In fact, speculators will force the issue by mounting a speculative attack and buying all of the central bank's reserves while reserves are still at a positive level.

We can describe the timing of this crisis with the help of a definition and a diagram. The *shadow* floating exchange rate at time t, denoted E_t^S, is the exchange rate that would prevail at time t if the central bank held no foreign reserves, allowed the currency to float, but continued to allow domestic credit to grow over time. We know from the monetary approach that the result would be a situation of *ongoing inflation* in which E_t^S trends upward over time in proportion to the domestic credit growth rate. The upper panel of Figure 7A2-1 shows this upward trend in the shadow floating rate, together with the level E^0 at which the exchange rate is initially pegged. The time T indicated on the horizontal axis is defined as the date on which the shadow exchange rate reaches E^0.

---

[26]Alternative models of balance of payments crises are developed in Paul Krugman, "A Model of Balance-of-Payments Crises," *Journal of Money, Credit and Banking* 11 (August 1979), pp. 311–325; Robert P. Flood and Peter M. Garber, "Collapsing Exchange Rate Regimes: Some Linear Examples," *Journal of International Economics* 17 (August 1984), pp. 1–14; and Maurice Obstfeld, "Rational and Self-Fulfilling Balance-of-Payments Crises," *American Economic Review* 76 (March 1986), pp. 72–81. See also the paper by Obstfeld in Further Readings.

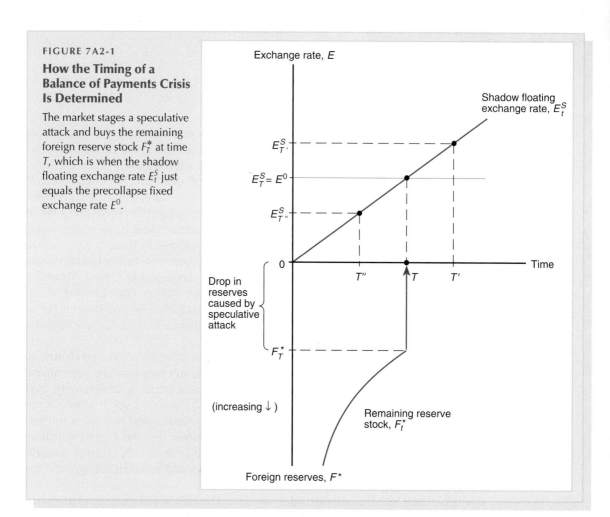

FIGURE 7A2-1

How the Timing of a Balance of Payments Crisis Is Determined

The market stages a speculative attack and buys the remaining foreign reserve stock F_T^* at time T, which is when the shadow floating exchange rate E_t^S just equals the precollapse fixed exchange rate E^0.

The lower panel of the figure shows how reserves behave over time when domestic credit is steadily growing. (An increase in reserves is a move down from the origin along the vertical axis.) We have shown the path of reserves as a kinked curve that falls gradually until time T, at which point reserves drop in a single stroke to zero. This precipitous reserve loss (of size F_T^*) is the speculative attack that forces the end of the fixed exchange rate, and we now argue that such an attack must occur precisely at time T if asset markets are to clear at each moment.

We are assuming that output Y is fixed, so reserves will fall over time at the same rate that domestic credit grows, as long as the domestic interest rate R (and thus the demand for domestic money) doesn't change. What do we know about the behavior of the interest rate? We know that while the exchange rate is convincingly fixed, R will equal the foreign interest rate R^* because no depreciation is expected. Thus, reserves fall gradually over time, as shown in Figure 7A2-1, as long as the exchange rate remains fixed at E^0.

Imagine now that reserves first hit zero at a time such as T', which is *later* than time T. Our shadow exchange rate E^S is defined as the equilibrium floating rate that prevails when foreign reserves are zero, so if reserves first hit zero at time T', the authorities abandon E^0 forever and the exchange rate jumps immediately to the higher level $E_{T'}^S$. There is something wrong with this "equilibrium," however: Each market participant knows that the home currency will depreciate very sharply at time T' and will try to profit by buying foreign reserves from the central bank, at the lower price E^0, just an instant *before* T'. Thus the central bank will lose all of its reserves before T', contrary to our assumption that reserves first hit zero *at* T'. So we have not really been looking at an equilibrium after all.

Do we get to an equilibrium by assuming instead that speculators buy out the official reserve stock at a time like T'' that is *earlier* than time T? Again the answer is no, as you can see by considering the choices facing an individual asset holder. He knows that if central bank reserves reach zero at time T'', the currency will appreciate from E^0 to $E_{T''}^S$ as the central bank leaves the foreign exchange market. It therefore will behoove him not to join any speculative attack that pushes reserves to zero at time T''; in fact, he would prefer to *sell* as much foreign currency as possible to the central bank just before time T'' and then buy it back at the lower market-determined price that would prevail after a crisis. Since every market participant would find it in his or her interest to act in this way, however, a speculative attack simply can't occur before time T. No speculator would want to buy central bank reserves at the price E^0, knowing that an immediate discrete capital loss was at hand.

Only if foreign reserves hit zero precisely at time T are asset markets continually in equilibrium. As noted above, time T is defined by the condition

$$E_T^S = E^0,$$

which states that if reserves suddenly drop to zero at time T, the exchange rate remains initially at its pegged level, and only subsequently floats upward.

The absence of any foreseen initial jump in the exchange rate, either upward or downward, removes the opportunities for arbitrage (described above) that prevent speculative attacks at times like T' or T''. In addition, the money market remains in equilibrium at time T, even though the exchange rate doesn't jump, because two factors offset each other exactly. As reserves drop sharply to zero, the money supply falls. We also know that at the moment the fixed exchange rate is abandoned, people will expect the currency to begin depreciating over time. The domestic interest rate R will therefore move upward to maintain interest parity, reducing real money demand in line with the fall in the real money supply.

We have therefore tied down the exact date on which a balance of payments crisis forces the authorities off the fixed exchange rate. Note once again that in our example, a crisis must occur at *some* point, because profligate monetary policies make one inevitable. The fact that a crisis occurs while the central bank's foreign reserves are still positive might suggest to superficial observers that ill-founded market sentiment is leading to a premature panic. This is not the case here. The speculative attack we have analyzed is the only outcome that does not confront market participants with arbitrage opportunities.[27] However, there are alternative self-fulfilling crisis models in which attacks can occur even when the exchange rate could have been sustained indefinitely in the absence of an attack.

---

[27]Our finding that reserves fall to zero in a single attack comes from our assumptions that the market can foresee the future perfectly and that trading takes place continuously. If we were instead to allow some discrete uncertainty—for example, about the rate of central bank domestic credit growth—the domestic interest rate would rise as a collapse became more probable, causing a series of "speculative" money demand reductions prior to the final depletion of foreign reserves. Each of these preliminary attacks would be similar to the type of crisis described in the chapter.

CHAPTER 8

INTERNATIONAL MONETARY SYSTEMS: AN HISTORICAL OVERVIEW

In the previous two chapters, we saw how a single country can use monetary, fiscal, and exchange rate policies to change the levels of employment and production within its borders. Although this analysis usually assumes that macroeconomic conditions in the rest of the world are not affected by the actions of the country we are studying, that assumption is not, in general, a valid one: Any change in the home country's real exchange rate automatically implies an opposite change in foreign real exchange rates, and any shift in overall domestic spending is likely to change domestic demand for foreign goods. Unless the home country is insignificantly small, developments within its borders affect macroeconomic conditions abroad and therefore complicate the task of foreign policy makers.

The inherent interdependence of open national economies has sometimes made it more difficult for governments to achieve such policy goals as full employment and price level stability. The channels of interdependence depend, in turn, on the monetary, financial, and exchange rate arrangements that countries adopt—a set of institutions called the *international monetary system*. This chapter examines how the international monetary system influenced macroeconomic policy making and performance during four periods: the gold standard era (1870–1914), the interwar period (1918–1939), the post–World War II years during which exchange rates were fixed under the Bretton Woods agreement (1946–1973), and the recent period of widespread reliance on floating exchange rates (1973–present). As we shall see, alternative international monetary arrangements have posed different trade-offs for macroeconomic policy.

In an open economy, macroeconomic policy has two basic goals, internal balance (full employment with price stability) and external balance (avoiding excessive imbalances in international payments). Because a country cannot alter its international payments position without automatically causing an opposite change of equal magnitude in the payments position of the rest of the world, one country's pursuit of its macroeconomic goals inevitably influences how well other countries attain their goals. The goal of external balance therefore offers a clear illustration of how policy actions taken abroad may change an economy's position relative to the position its government prefers.

Throughout the period since 1870, with its various international currency arrangements, how did countries try to attain internal and external balance, and how successful were they? Why did different international monetary systems prevail at different times? Did policy makers worry about the foreign repercussions of their actions, or did each adopt nationalistic measures that were self-defeating for the world economy as a whole? The answers to these questions depend on the international monetary system in effect at the time.

LEARNING GOALS

After reading this chapter, you will be able to:

- Explain how the goals of internal and external balance motivate economic policy makers in open economies.
- Understand the monetary trilemma that policy makers in open economies inevitably face and how alternative international monetary systems address the trilemma in different ways.
- Describe the structure of the international gold standard that linked countries' exchange rates and policies prior to World War I and the role of the Great Depression of the 1930s in ending efforts to restore the pre-1914 world monetary order.
- Discuss how the post–World War II Bretton Woods system of globally fixed exchange rates was designed to combine exchange rate stability with limited autonomy of national macroeconomic policies.
- Explain how the Bretton Woods system collapsed in 1973 and why many economists at the time favored an international financial system such as the current one based on floating dollar exchange rates.
- Summarize how the monetary and fiscal policies of a large country such as the United States are transmitted abroad under floating exchange rates.
- Discuss how the world economy has performed in recent years and what lessons the post-1973 experience teaches about the need for international policy coordination.

Macroeconomic Policy Goals in an Open Economy

In open economies, policy makers are motivated by the goals of internal and external balance. Simply defined, **internal balance** requires the full employment of a country's resources and domestic price level stability. **External balance** is attained when a country's current account is neither so deeply in deficit that the country may be unable to repay its foreign debts in the future nor so strongly in surplus that foreigners are put in that position.

In practice, neither of these definitions captures the full range of potential policy concerns. Along with full employment and stability of the overall price level, for example, policy makers may have a particular domestic distribution of income as an additional internal target. Depending on exchange rate arrangements or other factors, policy makers may worry about swings in balance of payments accounts other than the current account. To make matters even more complicated, the line between external and internal goals can be fuzzy. How should one classify an employment target for export industries, for example, when export growth influences the economy's ability to repay its foreign debts?

The simple definitions of internal and external balance given previously, however, capture the goals that most policy makers share regardless of the particular economic environment. We therefore organize our analysis around these definitions and discuss possible additional aspects of internal and external balance when they are relevant.

Internal Balance: Full Employment and Price Level Stability

When a country's productive resources are fully employed and its price level is stable, the country is in internal balance. The waste and hardship that occur when resources are underemployed is clear. If a country's economy is "overheated" and resources are *over*employed, however, waste of a different (though probably less harmful) kind occurs. For example, workers on overtime might prefer to work less and enjoy leisure, but their contracts require them to put in longer hours during periods of high demand. Machines worked more intensely than usual will tend to suffer more frequent breakdowns and to depreciate more quickly.

Under- and over-employment also lead to general price level movements that reduce the economy's efficiency by making the real value of the monetary unit less certain and thus a less useful guide for economic decisions. Since domestic wages and prices rise when the demands for labor and output exceed full-employment levels and fall in the opposite case, the government must prevent substantial movements in aggregate demand relative to its full-employment level to maintain a stable, predictable price level.

Inflation or deflation can occur even under conditions of full employment, of course, if the expectations of workers and firms about future monetary policy lead to an upward or downward wage-price spiral. Such a spiral can continue, however, only if the central bank fulfills expectations through continuing injections or withdrawals of money (Chapter 4).

One particularly disruptive result of an unstable price level is its effect on the real value of loan contracts. Because loans tend to be denominated in the monetary unit, unexpected price level changes cause income to be redistributed between creditors and debtors. A sudden increase in the U.S. price level, for example, makes those with dollar debts better off, since the money they owe to lenders is now worth less in terms of goods and services. At the same time, the price level increase makes creditors worse off. Because such accidental income redistribution can cause considerable distress to those who are hurt, governments have another reason to maintain price level stability.[1]

Theoretically, a perfectly predictable trend of rising or falling prices would not be too costly, since everyone would be able to calculate easily the real value of money at any point in the future. But in the real world, there appears to be no such thing as a predictable inflation rate. Indeed, experience shows that the unpredictability of the

---

[1] The situation is somewhat different when the government itself is a major debtor in domestic currency. In such cases, a surprise inflation that reduces the real value of government debt may be a convenient way of taxing the public. This method of taxation was quite common in developing countries in the past (see Chapter 11), but elsewhere it has generally been applied with reluctance and in extreme situations (for example, during or just after wars). A policy of trying to surprise the public with inflation undermines the government's credibility and, through the Fisher effect, worsens the terms on which the government can borrow in the future.

general price level is magnified tremendously in periods of rapid price level change. The costs of inflation have been most apparent in the postwar period in countries such as Argentina, Brazil, Serbia, and Zimbabwe, where astronomical price level increases caused the domestic currencies practically to stop functioning as units of account or stores of value.

To avoid price level instability, therefore, the government must prevent large fluctuations in output, which are also undesirable in themselves. In addition, it must avoid inflation and deflation by ensuring that the money supply does not grow too quickly or too slowly.

External Balance: The Optimal Level of the Current Account

The notion of external balance is more difficult to define than internal balance because there are no unambiguous benchmarks like "full employment" or "stable prices" to apply to an economy's external transactions. Whether an economy's trade with the outside world poses macroeconomic problems depends on several factors, including the economy's particular circumstances, conditions in the outside world, and the institutional arrangements governing its economic relations with foreign countries. A country committed to fixing its exchange rate against a foreign currency, for example, may well adopt a different definition of external balance than a country whose currency floats.

International economics textbooks often identify external balance with balance in a country's current account. While this definition is appropriate in some circumstances, it is not appropriate as a general rule. Recall from Chapter 2 that a country with a current account deficit is borrowing resources from the rest of the world that it will have to repay in the future. This situation is not necessarily undesirable, however. For example, the country's opportunities for investing the borrowed resources may be attractive relative to the opportunities available in the rest of the world. In this case, paying back loans from foreigners poses no problem because a profitable investment will generate a return high enough to cover the interest and principal on those loans. Similarly, a current account surplus may pose no problem if domestic savings are being invested more profitably abroad than they would be at home.

More generally, we may think of current account imbalances as providing another example of how countries gain from trade. The trade involved is what we have called *intertemporal trade*, that is, the trade of consumption over time (see Appendix 1 to Chapter 6). Just as countries with differing abilities to produce goods at a single point in time gain from concentrating their production on what they do best and trading, countries can gain from concentrating the world's investment in those economies best able to turn current output into future output. Countries with weak investment opportunities should invest little at home and channel their savings into more productive investment activity abroad. Put another way, countries where investment is relatively unproductive should be net exporters of currently available output (and thus have current account surpluses), while countries where investment is relatively productive should be net importers of current output (and have current account deficits). To pay off their foreign debts when the investments mature, the latter countries export output to the former countries and thereby complete the exchange of present output for future output.

Other considerations may also justify an unbalanced current account. A country where output drops temporarily (for example, because of an unusually bad crop failure) may wish to borrow from foreigners to avoid the sharp temporary fall in its consumption that would otherwise occur. In the absence of this borrowing, the price of present output in terms of future output would be higher in the low-output country than abroad, so the intertemporal trade that eliminates this price difference leads to mutual gains.

Insisting that all countries be in current account equilibrium makes no allowance for these important gains from trade over time. Thus, no realistic policy maker would want to adopt a balanced current account as a policy target appropriate in all circumstances.

At a given point, however, policy makers generally adopt *some* current account target as an objective, and this target defines their external balance goal. While the target level of the current account is generally not zero, governments usually try to avoid extremely large external surpluses or deficits unless they have clear evidence that large imbalances are justified by potential intertemporal trade gains. Governments are cautious because the exact current account balance that maximizes the gains from intertemporal trade is difficult if not impossible to figure out. In addition, this optimal current account balance can change unpredictably over time as conditions in the domestic and global economies change. Current account balances that are very wide of the mark can, however, cause serious problems.

Problems with Excessive Current Account Deficits Why do governments prefer to avoid current account deficits that are too large? As noted, a current account deficit (which means that the economy is borrowing from abroad) may pose no problem if the borrowed funds are channeled into productive domestic investment projects that pay for themselves with the revenue they generate in the future. Sometimes, however, large current account deficits represent temporarily high consumption resulting from misguided government policies or some other malfunction in the economy. At other times, the investment projects that draw on foreign funds may be badly planned and based on overoptimistic expectations about future profitability. In such cases, the government might wish to reduce the current account deficit immediately rather than face problems in repaying debts to foreigners later. In particular, a large current account deficit caused by an expansionary fiscal policy that does not simultaneously make domestic investment opportunities more profitable may signal a need for the government to restore external balance by changing its economic course. Every open economy faces an **intertemporal budget constraint** that limits its spending over time to levels that allow it to pay the interest and principal on its foreign debts. A simple version of that budget constraint was presented in the first appendix to Chapter 6, and a more realistic version is derived in the following box on New Zealand's foreign borrowing and debt.

At times, the external target is imposed from abroad rather than chosen by the domestic government. When countries begin to have trouble meeting their payments on past foreign loans, foreign creditors become reluctant to lend them new funds and may even demand immediate repayment of the earlier loans. Economists refer to such an event as a **sudden stop** in foreign lending. In such cases, the home government may have to take severe action to reduce the country's desired borrowing from foreigners to feasible levels, as well as to repay maturing loans that foreigners are unwilling to renew. A large current account deficit can undermine foreign investors' confidence and contribute to a sudden stop. In the event of a sudden stop, moreover, the larger the initial deficit, the larger and more painful the fall in domestic spending that is needed to make the economy live strictly within its means.

CAN A COUNTRY BORROW FOREVER? THE CASE OF NEW ZEALAND

The small Pacific country of New Zealand (with a population of about 4.5 million) has run current account deficits every year for many years, as far back as the country's official statistics reach. As a result, its net debt to foreign lenders stands at around 70 percent of its national output. Yet lenders continue to extend credit and seem not to worry about repayment (in contrast to many cases that we will study later on). Is it possible for an indebted country to borrow year after year without going broke? Perhaps surprisingly the answer is yes—if it does not borrow too much.

To understand why, we have to think about a country's budget constraint when it can borrow and lend over a long horizon.[2] (Our analysis will also underline why the *IIP* is so important.) Let's continue to let *IIP* stand for a country's net foreign wealth (claims on foreigners less liabilities), and let *GDP* denote its gross domestic product or production within the country's borders. Let *r* stand for the (constant) interest rate the country both earns on wealth held abroad and pays on its liabilities to foreigners.[3] If we assume for simplicity that gross national product Y is the sum of GDP and net foreign investment income, $Y = GDP + rIIP$, then we can express the current account in any year t as

$$CA_t = IIP_{t+1} - IIP_t = Y_t - (C_t + I_t + G_t)$$
$$= rIIP_t + GDP_t - (C_t + I_t + G_t).$$

(Think of IIP_{t+1} as net foreign wealth at the *end* of year t. We saw in Chapter 2's Case Study that the preceding relationship is not quite accurate because of price gains and losses on net foreign liabilities that are not captured in the national income and product accounts. We say more about this at the end.)

Define net exports, the (possibly negative) difference between what a country produces domestically and what it demands, as $NX_t = GDP_t - (C_t + I_t + G_t)$. (Net exports are sometimes referred to as the "balance of trade.") Then we can rewrite the preceding current account equation as

$$IIP_{t+1} = (1 + r)IIP_t + NX_t.$$

Now we have to resort to some simple, but devious, algebra. Imagine that in the last equation we are starting out in some year labeled $t = 0$ and that there is a year T far in the future at which everyone's debts have to be repaid, so that $IIP_T = 0$. We will apply the preceding equation for the *IIP* successively for years 1, 2, 3, and all the way through T. To start off, notice that the preceding equation can be manipulated to become

$$IIP_0 = -\frac{1}{1 + r} NX_0 + \frac{1}{1 + r} IIP_1.$$

But a similar relationship to this last one holds true with IIP_1 on the left hand-side and IIP_2 and NX_1 on the right. If we substitute this in for IIP_1 above, we get

$$IIP_0 = -\frac{1}{1 + r} NX_0 - \frac{1}{(1 + r)^2} NX_1$$
$$+ \frac{1}{(1 + r)^2} IIP_2.$$

Of course, we can continue to make these substitutions until we reach $IIP_T = 0$ (the point at

(Continued)

---

[2]Our discussion is closely related to that in Appendix 1 to Chapter 6, but it is more general because it allows for many time periods (not just two) and for a starting non-zero *IIP*.

[3]A simple interpretation of the model is to imagine that all foreign assets and liabilities are bonds denominated in a single global currency, where *r* is the *nominal* interest rate measured in the global currency. In practice, however, the nominal rates of return on foreign assets and liabilities can differ, and can be somewhat unpredictable, as we discuss further below. In the first appendix to Chapter 6, we interpreted *r* as a global *real* rate of interest, which we could do here too if we measured *GDP*, *Y*, and the *IIP* all in real terms (rather than in terms of the hypothetical global currency).

which all debts have been fully repaid). The resulting equation is the economy's *intertemporal budget constraint*:

$$IIP_0 = -\frac{1}{1+r}NX_0 - \frac{1}{(1+r)^2}NX_1$$
$$-\frac{1}{(1+r)^3}NX_2 - \cdots - \frac{1}{(1+r)^T}NX_{T-1}.$$

If the country has an initially positive *IIP* (foreign assets in excess of liabilities), this intertemporal constraint states that the country can run a stream of net export deficits in the future ($NX < 0$), provided the *present discounted value* of those deficits is not greater than the economy's initial net claims on foreigners. On the other hand, if initially $IIP < 0$, the economy must have future surpluses of net exports sufficient to repay its net debt to foreigners (with interest, which is why future net exports are discounted by r, and discounted more heavily the farther in the future they occur). So an indebted country such as New Zealand definitely cannot have *net export* or *trade balance* deficits forever. At some point the country must produce more goods and services than it absorbs in order to repay what it owes. Otherwise, it is perpetually borrowing more to repay what it owes—a strategy that must eventually collapse when the country runs out of fresh lenders (and probably long before then).[4]

But what about the current account balance, which equals net exports *plus* the negative flow of net interest payments implied by the country's negative *IIP*? Perhaps surprisingly, it turns out that this sum need *never* be positive for the country to remain creditworthy.

To see why, it is helpful to rewrite the preceding intertemporal budget constraint in terms of *ratios* to nominal output (nominal GDP), $iip = IIP/GDP$ and $nx = NX/GDP$. Assume that nominal GDP grows at a constant annual rate g that is below r – meaning that $GDP_t = (1 + g) GDP_{t-1}$.

Then after dividing the intertemporal budget constraint by GDP in year 0, we can see that

$$iip_0 = \frac{IIP_0}{GDP_0} = -\frac{1}{1+r}\frac{NX_0}{GDP_0} - \frac{1}{(1+r)^2}\frac{NX_1}{GDP_1}$$
$$\frac{GDP_1}{GDP_0} - \cdots - \frac{1}{(1+r)^T}\frac{NX_{T-1}}{GDP_{T-1}}\frac{GDP_{T-1}}{GDP_0}$$
$$= -\frac{1}{1+r}nx_0 - \frac{1+g}{(1+r)^2}nx_1 - \frac{(1+g)^2}{(1+r)^3}nx_2$$
$$- \cdots - \frac{(1+g)^{T-2}}{(1+r)^T}nx_{T-1}.$$

Let's now apply this version of the country's budget constraint, which we simplify by assuming that the country's time horizon is very long, making the constraint approximately the same as the infinite-summation expression:

$$iip_0 = -\frac{1}{1+g}\sum_{t=1}^{\infty}\left(\frac{1+g}{1+r}\right)^t nx_{t-1}.$$

To illustrate how a country can easily run a perpetual current account deficit, let us ask what *constant* level of net exports $\overline{nx}$ will allow the country to respect this budget constraint. We find this constant net export level by substituting $\overline{nx}$ into the previous equation and simplifying using the summation formula for a geometric series,[5]

$$iip_0 = -\frac{1}{1+g}\sum_{t=1}^{\infty}\left(\frac{1+g}{1+r}\right)^t \overline{nx} = \frac{-\overline{nx}}{r-g}.$$

This solution implies net exports of $\overline{nx} = -(r - g)iip_0$. For example, if iip_0 is negative – the country is a net debtor – then $\overline{nx}$ will need to be positive and by construction, it is just big enough for the country to repay its debt over time.

What level of the current account balance does this imply, though? The country's current account balance in the initial year $t = 0$ (expressed as a fraction of its GDP) is equal to $ca_0 = r(iip_0) + \overline{nx} = r(iip_0) - (r - g)iip_0 =$

---

[4]Strategies based on always repaying old creditors with money borrowed from new creditors—as opposed to repayment with genuine investment earnings—are known as *Ponzi schemes*. Charles Ponzi (1882–1949) promised gullible Massachusetts investors he could double their money in 90 days, but when he had to pay out to them, he did so with funds supplied by new investors. U.S. authorities arrested Ponzi in 1920 after the fraudulent nature of his business model came to light. More recently, financier Bernard Madoff ran a much bigger Ponzi scheme for many years.

[5]Recall from your high school pre-calculus course that if x is a number less than 1 in absolute value, then $x + x^2 + x^3 + \cdots = \dfrac{x}{1-x}$. In the present example, $x = \dfrac{1+g}{1+r} < 1$.

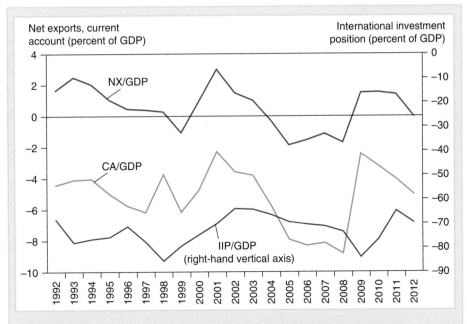

New Zealand's Net Exports, Current Account, and Net International Investment Position, 1992–2012

New Zealand has consistently had a current account deficit for decades, yet its net foreign liabilities have remained near 70 percent of GDP.

Source: Statistics New Zealand.

$g(iip_0)$. For a debtor country such as New Zealand, the initial current account is therefore in deficit. An important further implication of this current account level, however, is that the IIP ratio to GDP will remain constant forever at the level $\overline{iip} = iip_0$, so that the current account will also remain constant at $g(\overline{iip})$: this current account level is just enough to keep the ratio of net foreign assets or debt to nominal GDP constant, given that nominal GDP is growing at the rate g.[6] Thus, if the ratio of net exports to GDP is held constant at the right value, a country with an initial net foreign debt will perpetually run deficits in its current account, while still maintaining a constant ratio of net foreign liabilities to national output.

The accompanying figure shows New Zealand data on net exports and the current account (left-hand vertical axis) and the IIP (right-hand vertical axis), all expressed as percentages of GDP. In recent history, as you can see, New Zealand has had a negative current account balance every year, yet its IIP-to-GDP ratio has remained roughly constant at −70 percent of GDP. How has this been possible? Because the average growth rate of New Zealand's nominal GDP was 5 percent for 1992–2012, our previous formula suggests that at an interest rate of $r = 6$ percent per year, the IIP-to-GDP ratio will remain constant if on average New Zealand has an annual net export surplus equal to

$$\overline{nx} = -(r - g)iip_0 = (.06 - .05) \times (.7)$$
$$= .01 \times .7 = 0.007,$$

or 0.7 percent of GDP. But this is *exactly* the average ratio of New Zealand's net exports to its GDP over the 1992–2012 period shown in the figure![7]

Can we *independently* confirm that the rate of return on New Zealand's IIP was around

(Continued)

---

[6]Thus, if nominal GDP grows by 5 percent per year, the current account will raise net foreign assets or debt by 5 percent as well, leaving the ratio constant. Problem 8 at the end of this chapter asks you to verify this algebraically.
[7]The average current account deficit implied by this calculation is rather large: $g(iip_0) = .05 \times .7 = 3.5$ percent of GDP annually.

6 percent per year over this period? Such estimates are not easy to make because we would need detailed data on the country's foreign liabilities and investments and their rates of return (recall our discussion of the U.S. *IIP* at the end of Chapter 2). We can get a partial answer—partial because it ignores capital gains and losses on foreign assets and liabilities—by looking at New Zealand's balance of international investment income, reckoned as a fraction of the *IIP*. Over 1992–2012, New Zealand paid out on average net interest and dividends equal to 8.3 percent of its net foreign debt. This is higher than the 6 percent rate that stabilizes the *IIP* relative to GDP.

What explains the difference? One possibility is that interest inflows to New Zealand are underestimated in the official data, due to the standard under-reporting problem (Chapter 2). In addition, New Zealand's gross foreign liabilities consist largely of bank debt, denominated in New Zealand (or "kiwi") dollars, while its gross foreign assets include substantial stock shares, plus other assets denominated in foreign currencies. Even though the kiwi has appreciated since 1992 (from about 55 to 80 U.S. cents per kiwi dollar), global stock markets have done very well over that period; for example, the Standard and Poor's 500 index of U.S. stock prices has risen roughly fourfold. Evidently, such gains on foreign assets have helped to reduce the average annual *total* cost of New Zealand's negative *IIP* closer to 6 percent.

Problems with Excessive Current Account Surpluses   An excessive current account surplus poses problems that are different from those posed by deficits. A surplus in the current account implies that a country is accumulating assets located abroad. Why are growing domestic claims to foreign wealth ever a problem? One potential reason stems from the fact that, for a given level of national saving, an increased current account surplus implies lower investment in domestic plant and equipment. (This follows from the national income identity, $S = CA + I$, which says that total domestic saving, S, is divided between foreign asset accumulation, CA, and domestic investment, I.) Several factors might lead policy makers to prefer that domestic saving be devoted to higher levels of domestic investment and lower levels of foreign investment. First, the returns on domestic capital may be easier to tax than those on assets located abroad. Second, an addition to the home capital stock may reduce domestic unemployment and therefore lead to higher national income than an equal addition to foreign assets. Finally, domestic investment by one firm may have beneficial technological spillover effects on other domestic producers that the investing firm does not capture.

If a large home current account surplus reflects excessive external borrowing by foreigners, the home country may in the future find itself unable to collect the money it is owed. Put another way, the home country may lose part of its foreign wealth if foreigners find they have borrowed more than they can repay. In contrast, non-repayment of a loan between domestic residents leads to a redistribution of national wealth within the home country but causes no change in the level of national wealth.[8] Excessive current account surpluses may also be inconvenient for political reasons. Countries with large surpluses can become targets for discriminatory import barriers imposed by trading partners with external deficits. Japan has been in this position in the past, and China's surpluses inspire the most visible protectionist threats today. To avoid such damaging restrictions, surplus countries may try to keep their surpluses from becoming too large.

---

[8]This fact was pointed out by John Maynard Keynes in "Foreign Investment and National Advantage," *The Nation and Athenaeum* 35 (1924), pp. 584–587.

Summary   The goal of external balance is a level of the current account that allows the most important gains from trade over time to be realized without risking the problems discussed previously. Because governments do not know this current account level exactly, they may try to avoid large deficits or surpluses unless there is clear evidence of large gains from intertemporal trade.

There is a fundamental asymmetry, however, between the pressures pushing deficit and surplus countries to adjust their external imbalances downward. While big deficits that continue too long may be forcibly eliminated by a sudden stop in lending, there is unlikely to be a sudden stop in borrowing countries' willingness to absorb funds that are supplied by foreigners! Thus, the adjustment pressures that confront deficit countries are generally much stronger than those facing surplus countries.

Classifying Monetary Systems: The Open-Economy Monetary Trilemma

The world economy has evolved through a variety of international monetary systems since the 19th century. A simple insight from the models we studied in the last part of this text will prove very helpful in understanding the key differences between these systems as well as the economic, political, and social factors that lead countries to adopt one system rather than another. The insight we will rely on is that policy makers in an open economy face an inescapable **monetary trilemma** in choosing the currency arrangements that best enable them to attain their internal and external balance goals.

Chapter 7 showed how a country that fixes its currency's exchange rate while allowing free international capital movements gives up control over domestic monetary policy. This sacrifice illustrates the impossibility of a country's having more than two items from the following list:

1. Exchange rate stability.
2. Monetary policy oriented toward domestic goals.
3. Freedom of international capital movements.

Because this list contains properties of an international monetary system that most economists would regard as desirable in themselves, the need to choose only two is a trilemma for policy regimes. It is a *tri*lemma rather than a *di*lemma because the available options are three: 1 and 2, 1 and 3, or 2 and 3.

As we have seen, countries with fixed exchange rates that allow free cross-border capital mobility sacrifice item 2 above, a domestically oriented monetary policy. On the other hand, if a country with a fixed exchange rate restricts international financial flows so that the interest parity condition, $R = R^*$, does not need to hold true (thereby sacrificing item 3 above), it is still able to change the home interest rate so as to influence the domestic economy (thereby preserving item 2). In this way, for example, the country might be able to reduce domestic overheating (getting closer to internal balance by raising the interest rate) without causing a fall in its exports (preventing a potential departure from external balance due to an appreciation of its currency). Finally, as Chapter 6 showed, a country that has a floating exchange rate (and thus gives up item 1 above) can use monetary policy to steer the economy even though financial flows across its borders are free. But the exchange rate might become quite unpredictable as a result, complicating the economic planning of importers and exporters.

Figure 8-1 shows the preceding three desirable properties of an international monetary regime schematically as the vertices of a triangle. Only two can be reached

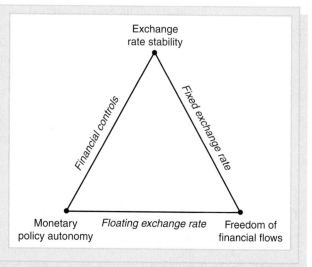

FIGURE 8-1

The Monetary Trilemma for Open Economies

The vertices of the triangle show three features that policy makers in open economies would prefer their monetary system to achieve. Unfortunately, at most two can coexist. Each of the three policy regime labels along the triangle's edges (floating exchange rate, fixed exchange rate, financial controls) is consistent with the two goals that it lies between in the diagram.

simultaneously. Each edge of the triangle represents a policy regime consistent with the two properties shown at the edge's end points.

Of course, the trilemma does not imply that intermediate regimes are impossible, only that they will require the policy maker to trade off between different objectives. For example, more aggressive monetary intervention to manage the exchange rate can reduce exchange rate volatility, but only at the cost of reducing the ability of monetary policy to pursue targets other than the exchange rate. Similarly, a partial opening of the financial account will allow some cross-border borrowing and lending. At the same time, however, fixing the exchange rate in the face of domestic interest rate changes will require larger volumes of intervention, and potentially larger drains on foreign exchange reserves, than would be needed if cross-border financial transactions were entirely prohibited. The central bank's ability to guarantee exchange rate stability (by avoiding devaluations and crises) will therefore decline.

International Macroeconomic Policy under the Gold Standard, 1870–1914

The gold standard period between 1870 and 1914 was based on ideas about international macroeconomic policy very different from those that have formed the basis of international monetary arrangements since World War II. Nevertheless, the period warrants attention because subsequent attempts to reform the international monetary system on the basis of fixed exchange rates can be viewed as attempts to build on the strengths of the gold standard while avoiding its weaknesses. (Some of these strengths and weaknesses were discussed in Chapter 7.) This section looks at how the gold standard functioned in practice before World War I and examines how well it enabled countries to attain goals of internal and external balance.

Origins of the Gold Standard

The gold standard had its origin in the use of gold coins as a medium of exchange, unit of account, and store of value. While gold has played these roles since ancient times, the gold standard as a legal institution dates from 1819, when the British Parliament repealed long-standing restrictions on the export of gold coins and bullion from Britain.

Later in the 19th century, the United States, Germany, Japan, and other countries also adopted the gold standard. At the time, Britain was the world's leading economic power, and other nations hoped to achieve similar economic success by following British precedent. Given Britain's preeminence in international trade and the advanced development of its financial institutions and industry, London naturally became the center of the international monetary system built on the gold standard.

External Balance under the Gold Standard

Under the gold standard, the primary responsibility of a central bank was to fix the exchange rate between its currency and gold. To maintain this official gold price, the central bank needed an adequate stock of gold reserves. Policy makers therefore viewed external balance not in terms of a current account target, but as a situation in which the central bank was neither gaining gold from abroad nor (much more worrisome) losing gold to foreigners at too rapid a rate.

In the modern terminology of Chapter 2, central banks tried to avoid sharp fluctuations in the *balance of payments*, the difference between the current plus capital account balances and the balance of net nonreserve financial flows abroad. Because international reserves took the form of gold during this period, the surplus or deficit in the balance of payments had to be financed by gold shipments between central banks.[9] To avoid large gold movements, central banks adopted policies that pushed the balance of payments toward zero. A country is said to be in **balance of payments equilibrium** when the sum of its current and capital accounts, less the nonreserve component of net financial flows abroad, equals zero, so that the current plus capital account balance is financed entirely by private international lending without official reserve movements.

Many governments took a laissez-faire attitude toward the current account. Britain's current account surplus between 1870 and World War I averaged 5.2 percent of its GNP, a figure that is remarkably high by post-1945 standards. Several borrowing countries, however, did experience difficulty at one time or another in paying their foreign debts. Perhaps because Britain was the world's leading exporter of international economic theory as well as of capital during these years, the economic writing of the gold standard era places little emphasis on problems of current account adjustment.

The Price-Specie-Flow Mechanism

The gold standard contains some powerful automatic mechanisms that contribute to the simultaneous achievement of balance of payments equilibrium by all countries. The most important of these, the **price-specie-flow mechanism,** was recognized by the 18th century (when precious metals were referred to as "specie"). In 1752, David Hume, the Scottish philosopher, described the price-specie-flow mechanism as follows:

> Suppose four-fifths of all the money in Great Britain to be annihilated in one night, and the nation reduced to the same condition, with regard to specie, as in the reigns of the Harrys and the Edwards, what would be the consequence? Must not the

---

[9]In reality, central banks had begun to hold foreign currencies in their reserves even before 1914. (The pound sterling was the leading reserve currency.)

price of all labour and commodities sink in proportion, and everything be sold as cheap as they were in those ages? What nation could then dispute with us in any foreign market, or pretend to navigate or to sell manufactures at the same price, which to us would afford sufficient profit? In how little time, therefore, must this bring back the money which we had lost, and raise us to the level of all the neighbouring nations? Where, after we have arrived, we immediately lose the advantage of the cheapness of labour and commodities; and the farther flowing in of money is stopped by our fulness and repletion.

Again, suppose that all the money in Great Britain were multiplied fivefold in a night, must not the contrary effect follow? Must not all labour and commodities rise to such an exorbitant height, that no neighbouring nations could afford to buy from us; while their commodities, on the other hand, became comparatively so cheap, that, in spite of all the laws which could be formed, they would run in upon us, and our money flow out; till we fall to a level with foreigners, and lose that great superiority of riches which had laid us under such disadvantages?[10]

It is easy to translate Hume's description of the price-specie-flow mechanism into more modern terms. Suppose Britain's current plus capital account surplus is greater than its nonreserve financial account balance. Because foreigners' net imports from Britain are not being financed entirely by British loans, the shortfall must be matched by flows of international reserves—that is, of gold—into Britain. These gold flows automatically reduce foreign money supplies and swell Britain's money supply, pushing foreign prices downward and British prices upward. (Notice that Hume fully understood the lesson of Chapter 4, that price levels and money supplies move proportionally in the long run.)

The simultaneous rise in British prices and fall in foreign prices—a real appreciation of the pound, given the fixed exchange rate—reduces foreign demand for British goods and services and at the same time increases British demand for foreign goods and services. These demand shifts work in the direction of reducing Britain's current account surplus and reducing the foreign current account deficit. Eventually, therefore, reserve movements stop and all countries reach balance of payments equilibrium. The same process also works in reverse, eliminating an initial situation of foreign surplus and British deficit.

The Gold Standard "Rules of the Game": Myth and Reality

In theory, the price-specie-flow mechanism could operate automatically. But the reactions of central banks to gold flows across their borders furnished another potential mechanism to help restore balance of payments equilibrium. Central banks that were persistently losing gold faced the risk of becoming unable to meet their obligations to redeem currency notes. They were therefore motivated to sell domestic assets when gold was being lost, pushing domestic interest rates upward and attracting inflows of funds from abroad. Central banks gaining gold had much weaker incentives to eliminate their own imports of the metal. The main incentive was the greater profitability of interest-bearing domestic assets compared with "barren" gold. A central bank that was accumulating gold might be tempted to purchase domestic assets, thereby lowering home interest rates, increasing financial outflows, and driving gold abroad.

---

[10]Hume, "Of the Balance of Trade," reprinted (in abridged form) in Barry Eichengreen and Marc Flandreau, eds., *The Gold Standard in Theory and History* (London: Routledge, 1997), pp. 33–43.

These domestic credit measures, if undertaken by central banks, reinforced the price-specie-flow mechanism by pushing all countries toward balance of payments equilibrium. After World War I, the practices of selling domestic assets in the face of a deficit and buying domestic assets in the face of a surplus came to be known as the gold standard "rules of the game"—a phrase reportedly coined by Keynes. Because such measures speeded the movement of all countries toward their external balance goals, they increased the efficiency of the automatic adjustment processes inherent in the gold standard.

Later research has shown that the supposed "rules of the game" of the gold standard were frequently violated before 1914. As noted, the incentives to obey the rules applied with greater force to deficit than to surplus countries, so in practice it was the deficit countries that bore the burden of bringing the payments balances of *all* countries into equilibrium. By not always taking action to reduce gold inflows, the surplus countries worsened a problem of international policy coordination inherent in the system: Deficit countries competing for a limited supply of gold reserves might adopt overly contractionary monetary policies that harmed employment while doing little to improve their reserve positions.

In fact, countries often reversed the rules and *sterilized* gold flows, that is, sold domestic assets when foreign reserves were rising and bought domestic assets as foreign reserves fell. Government interference with private gold exports also undermined the system. The picture of smooth and automatic balance of payments adjustment before World War I therefore did not always match reality. Governments sometimes ignored both the "rules of the game" and the effects of their actions on other countries.[11]

Internal Balance under the Gold Standard

By fixing the prices of currencies in terms of gold, the gold standard aimed to limit monetary growth in the world economy and thus to ensure stability in world price levels. While price levels within gold standard countries did not rise as much between 1870 and 1914 as over the period after World War II, national price levels moved unpredictably over shorter horizons as periods of inflation and deflation followed each other. The gold standard's mixed record on price stability reflected a problem discussed in the last chapter: change in the relative prices of gold and other commodities.

In addition, the gold standard does not seem to have done much to ensure full employment. The U.S. unemployment rate, for example, averaged 6.8 percent between 1890 and 1913, whereas it averaged around 5.7 percent between 1948 and 2010.[12]

A fundamental cause of short-term internal instability under the pre-1914 gold standard was the subordination of economic policy to external objectives. Before World War I, governments had not assumed responsibility for maintaining internal balance as fully as they did after World War II. In the United States, the resulting economic distress led to political opposition to the gold standard, as the Case Study that follows explains. In terms of the monetary policy trilemma discussed above, the gold standard allowed high degrees of exchange rate stability and international financial

---

[11]An influential modern study of central bank practices under the gold standard is Arthur I. Bloomfield, *Monetary Policy under the International Gold Standard: 1880–1914* (New York: Federal Reserve Bank of New York, 1959).

[12]Data on price levels are given by Cooper (cited on page 219 in Chapter 7), and data for U.S. unemployment are adapted from the same source. Caution should be used in comparing gold standard and post–World War II unemployment data because the methods used to assemble the earlier data were much cruder. A critical study of pre-1930 U.S. unemployment data is Christina D. Romer, "Spurious Volatility in Historical Unemployment Data," *Journal of Political Economy* 94 (February 1986), pp. 1–37.

capital mobility, but did not allow monetary policy to pursue internal policy goals. These priorities were consistent with the limited political power at the time of those most vulnerable to unemployment.

The importance of internal policy objectives increased after World War II as a result of the worldwide economic instability of the interwar years, 1918–1939. And the unpalatable internal consequences of attempts to restore the gold standard after 1918 helped mold the thinking of the architects of the fixed exchange rate system adopted after 1945. To understand how the post–World War II international monetary system tried to reconcile the goals of internal and external balance, we therefore must examine the economic events of the period between the two world wars.

CASE STUDY

The Political Economy of Exchange Rate Regimes: Conflict over America's Monetary Standard during the 1890s

As we learned in Chapter 7, the United States had a bimetallic monetary standard until the Civil War, with both silver and gold in circulation. Once war broke out, the country moved to a paper currency (called the "greenback") and a floating exchange rate, but in 1879 a pure gold standard (and a fixed exchange rate against other gold-standard currencies such as the British pound sterling) was adopted.

World gold supplies had increased sharply after the 1849 discoveries in California, but the 1879 return of the dollar to gold at the pre–Civil War parity required deflation in the United States. Furthermore, a global shortage of gold generated continuing downward pressure on price levels long after the American restoration of gold. By 1896, the U.S. price level was about 40 percent below its 1869 level. Economic distress was widespread and became especially severe after a banking panic in 1893. Farmers, who saw the prices of agricultural products plummet more quickly even than the general price level, were especially hard hit.

In the 1890s, a broad Populist coalition of U.S. farmers, miners, and others pressed for revival of the bimetallic silver-gold system that had prevailed before the Civil War. They desired a return to the old 16:1 relative mint parity for gold and silver, but by the early 1890s, the market price of gold in terms of silver had risen to around 30. The Populists foresaw that the monetization of silver at 16:1 would lead to an increase in the silver money stock, and possibly a reversal of deflation, as people used gold dollars to buy silver cheaply on the market and then took it to the mint for coining. These developments would have had several advantages from the standpoint of farmers and their allies, such as undoing the adverse terms of trade trends of the previous decades and reducing the real values of farmers' mortgage debts. Western silver mine owners, in particular, were wildly enthusiastic. On the other side, eastern financiers viewed "sound money"—that is, gold and gold alone—as essential for achieving more complete American integration into world markets.

The silver movement reached its high tide in 1896 when the Democratic Party nominated William Jennings Bryan to run for president after a stem-winding convention speech in which he famously proclaimed, "Thou shalt not crucify mankind upon a cross of gold." But by then, new gold discoveries in South Africa, Alaska, and elsewhere were starting to reverse previous deflationary trends across the world, defusing silver as a political issue. Bryan lost the elections of 1896 and 1900 to Republican William McKinley, and in March 1900 Congress passed the Gold Standard Act, which definitively placed the dollar on an exclusive basis of gold.

Modern readers of L. Frank Baum's classic 1900 children's book *The Wonderful Wizard of Oz* usually don't realize that the story of Dorothy, Toto, and their friends is an allegorical rendition of the U.S. political struggle over gold. The yellow brick road represents the false promise of gold, the name "Oz" is a reference to an ounce (oz.) of gold, and Dorothy's silver slippers—changed to ruby slippers in the well-known Hollywood color-film version—offer the true way home to the heavily indebted farming state of Kansas.[13]

Although farming debt is often mentioned as a prime factor in the 1890s silver agitation, Harvard political scientist Jeffry Frieden shows that a more relevant factor was the desire of farming and mining interests to raise the prices of their products relative to nontraded goods.[14] Manufacturers, who competed with imports, had been able to obtain tariff protection as a counterweight to deflation. As a group, they therefore had little interest in changing the currency standard. Because the United States was nearly exclusively an exporter of primary products, import tariffs would have been ineffective in helping farmers and miners. A depreciation of the U.S. dollar, however, promised to raise the dollar prices of primary products relative to the prices of nontradables. Through a careful statistical analysis of congressional voting on bills related to the monetary system, Frieden shows that legislative support for silver was unrelated to debt levels but was indeed highly correlated with state employment in agriculture and mining.

The Interwar Years, 1918–1939

Governments effectively suspended the gold standard during World War I and financed part of their massive military expenditures by printing money. Further, labor forces and productive capacity were reduced sharply through war losses. As a result, price levels were higher everywhere at the war's conclusion in 1918.

Several countries experienced runaway inflation as their governments attempted to aid the reconstruction process through public expenditures. These governments financed their purchases simply by printing the money they needed, as they sometimes had during the war. The result was a sharp rise in money supplies and price levels.

The Fleeting Return to Gold

The United States returned to gold in 1919. In 1922, at a conference in Genoa, Italy, a group of countries including Britain, France, Italy, and Japan agreed on a program calling for a general return to the gold standard and cooperation among central banks

---

[13]An informative and amusing account is Hugh Rockoff, "The 'Wizard of Oz' as a Monetary Allegory," *Journal of Political Economy* 98 (August 1990), pp. 739–760.

[14]See "Monetary Populism in Nineteenth-Century America: An Open Economy Interpretation," *Journal of Economic History* 57 (June 1997), pp. 367–395.

in attaining external and internal objectives. Realizing that gold supplies might be inadequate to meet central banks' demands for international reserves (a problem of the gold standard noted in Chapter 7), the Genoa Conference sanctioned a partial gold *exchange* standard in which smaller countries could hold as reserves the currencies of several large countries whose own international reserves would consist entirely of gold.

In 1925, Britain returned to the gold standard by pegging the pound to gold at the prewar price. Chancellor of the Exchequer Winston Churchill advocated returning to the old parity on the grounds that any deviation from the prewar price would undermine world confidence in the stability of Britain's financial institutions, which had played the leading role in international finance during the gold standard era. Though Britain's price level had been falling since the war, in 1925 it was still higher than in the days of the prewar gold standard. To return the pound price of gold to its prewar level, the Bank of England was therefore forced to follow contractionary monetary policies that contributed to severe unemployment.

British stagnation in the 1920s accelerated London's decline as the world's leading financial center. Britain's economic weakening proved problematic for the stability of the restored gold standard. In line with the recommendations of the Genoa Conference, many countries held international reserves in the form of deposits in London. Britain's gold reserves were limited, however, and the country's persistent stagnation did little to inspire confidence in its ability to meet its foreign obligations. The onset of the Great Depression in 1929 was shortly followed by bank failures throughout the world. Britain left gold in 1931 when foreign holders of sterling (including several central banks) lost confidence in Britain's promise to maintain its currency's value and began converting their sterling to gold.

International Economic Disintegration

As the depression continued, many countries renounced the gold standard and allowed their currencies to float in the foreign exchange market. In the face of growing unemployment, a resolution of the trilemma in favor of fixed exchange rates became difficult to maintain. The United States left gold in 1933 but returned in 1934, having raised the dollar price of gold from $20.67 to $35 per ounce. Countries that clung to the gold standard without devaluing their currencies suffered most during the Great Depression. Indeed, recent research places much of the blame for the depression's worldwide propagation on the gold standard itself (see the Case Study on page 253).

Major economic harm resulted from restrictions on international trade and payments, which proliferated as countries attempted to discourage imports and keep aggregate demand bottled up at home. The Smoot-Hawley tariff imposed by the United States in 1930 was intended to protect American jobs, but it had a damaging effect on employment abroad. The foreign response involved retaliatory trade restrictions and preferential trading agreements among groups of countries. World trade collapsed dramatically. A measure that raises domestic welfare is called a *beggar-thy-neighbor policy* when it benefits the home country at the cost of worsening economic conditions abroad. However, everyone is hurt when countries *simultaneously* adopt beggar-thy-neighbor policies.

Uncertainty about government policies led to sharp reserve movements for countries with pegged exchange rates and sharp exchange rate movements for those with floating rates. Many countries imposed prohibitions on private financial account transactions to limit these effects of foreign exchange market developments. This was another way of addressing the trilemma. Trade barriers and deflation in the industrial economies of America and Europe led to widespread repudiations of private international debts, particularly by Latin American countries, whose export markets were disappearing. Governments in western Europe repudiated their debts to the United States and Britain incurred because of World War I. In short, the world economy disintegrated into increasingly autarkic (that is, self-sufficient) national units in the early 1930s.

In the face of the Great Depression, most countries resolved the choice between external and internal balance by curtailing their trading links with the rest of the world and eliminating, by government decree, the possibility of any significant external imbalance. By reducing the gains from trade, that approach imposed high costs on the world economy and contributed to the slow recovery from depression, which in many countries was still incomplete in 1939. All countries would have been better off in a world with freer international trade, provided international cooperation had helped each country preserve its external balance and financial stability without sacrificing internal policy goals. It was this realization that inspired the blueprint for the postwar international monetary system, the **Bretton Woods agreement**.

CASE STUDY

The International Gold Standard and the Great Depression

One of the most striking features of the decade-long Great Depression that started in 1929 was its global nature. Rather than being confined to the United States and its main trading partners, the downturn spread rapidly and forcefully to Europe, Latin America, and elsewhere. What explains the Great Depression's nearly universal scope? Recent scholarship shows that the international gold standard played a central role in starting, deepening, and spreading the 20th century's greatest economic crisis.[15]

In 1929, most market economies were once again on the gold standard. At the time, however, the United States, attempting to slow its overheated economy through monetary contraction, and France, having just ended an inflationary period and returned to gold, faced large financial inflows. Through the resulting balance of payments surpluses, both countries were absorbing the world's monetary gold at a startling rate. (By 1932, the two countries alone held more than 70 percent of it!) Other countries on the gold standard had no choice but to engage in domestic asset sales and raise interest rates if they wished to conserve their dwindling

---

[15]Important contributions to this research include Ehsan U. Choudhri and Levis A. Kochin, "The Exchange Rate and the International Transmission of Business Cycle Disturbances: Some Evidence from the Great Depression," *Journal of Money, Credit, and Banking* 12 (1980), pp. 565–574; Peter Temin, *Lessons from the Great Depression* (Cambridge, MA: MIT Press, 1989); and Barry Eichengreen, *Golden Fetters: The Gold Standard and the Great Depression, 1919–1939* (New York: Oxford University Press, 1992). A concise and lucid summary is Ben S. Bernanke, "The World on a Cross of Gold: A Review of 'Golden Fetters: The Gold Standard and the Great Depression, 1919–1939,'" *Journal of Monetary Economics* 31 (April 1993), pp. 251–267.

gold stocks. The resulting worldwide monetary contraction, combined with the shock waves from the October 1929 New York stock market crash, sent the world into deep recession.

A cascade of bank failures around the world only accelerated the global economy's downward spiral. The gold standard again was a key culprit. Many countries desired to safeguard their gold reserves in order to be able to remain on the gold standard. This desire often discouraged their central banks from providing troubled private banks with the loans that might have allowed the banks to stay in business. After all, any cash provided to banks by their home central banks would have increased potential private claims to the government's precious gold holdings.[16]

Perhaps the clearest evidence of the gold standard's role is the contrasting behavior of output and the price level in countries that left the gold standard relatively early, such as Britain, and those that chose a different response to the trilemma and instead stubbornly hung on. Countries that abandoned the gold standard freed themselves to adopt more expansionary monetary policies that limited (or prevented) both domestic deflation and output contraction. The countries with the biggest deflations and output contractions over the years 1929–1935 included France, Switzerland, Belgium, the Netherlands, and Poland, all of which stayed on the gold standard until 1936.

The Bretton Woods System and the International Monetary Fund

In July 1944, representatives of 44 countries meeting in Bretton Woods, New Hampshire, drafted and signed the Articles of Agreement of the **International Monetary Fund (IMF)**. Remembering the disastrous economic events of the interwar period, statesmen in the Allied countries hoped to design an international monetary system that would foster full employment and price stability while allowing individual countries to attain external balance without restrictions on international trade.[17]

The system set up by the Bretton Woods agreement called for fixed exchange rates against the U.S. dollar and an unvarying dollar price of gold—$35 an ounce. Member countries held their official international reserves largely in the form of gold or dollar assets and had the right to sell dollars to the Federal Reserve for gold at the official price. The system was thus a gold exchange standard, with the dollar as its principal reserve currency. In the terminology of Chapter 7, the dollar was the "Nth currency"

---

[16]Chang-Tai Hsieh and Christina D. Romer argue that the fear of being forced off gold cannot explain the U.S. Federal Reserve's unwillingness to expand the money supply in the early 1930s. See "Was the Federal Reserve Constrained by the Gold Standard During the Great Depression? Evidence from the 1932 Open Market Purchase Program," *Journal of Economic History* 66 (March 2006), pp. 140–176.

[17]The same conference set up a second institution, the World Bank, whose goals were to help the belligerents rebuild their shattered economies and to help the former colonial territories develop and modernize theirs. In 1947, the General Agreement on Tariffs and Trade (GATT) was inaugurated as a forum for the multilateral reduction of trade barriers. The GATT was meant as a prelude to the creation of an International Trade Organization (ITO), whose goals in the trade area would parallel those of the IMF in the financial area. Unfortunately, the ITO was doomed by the failures of Congress and Britain's Parliament to ratify its charter. In the 1990s, the GATT became the current World Trade Organization (WTO).

in terms of which the $N-1$ exchange rates of the system were defined. The United States itself intervened only rarely in the foreign exchange market. Usually, the $N-1$ foreign central banks intervened when necessary to fix the system's $N-1$ exchange rates, while the United States was responsible in theory for fixing the dollar price of gold.

Goals and Structure of the IMF

The IMF Articles of Agreement, through a mixture of discipline and flexibility, hoped to avoid a repetition of the turbulent interwar experience.

The major discipline on monetary management was the requirement that exchange rates be fixed to the dollar, which, in turn, was tied to gold. If a central bank other than the Federal Reserve pursued excessive monetary expansion, it would lose international reserves and eventually become unable to maintain the fixed dollar exchange rate of its currency. Since high U.S. monetary growth would lead to dollar accumulation by foreign central banks, the Fed itself was constrained in its monetary policies by its obligation to redeem those dollars for gold. The official gold price of $35 an ounce served as a further brake on American monetary policy, since that price would be pushed upward if too many dollars were created.

Fixed exchange rates were viewed as more than a device for imposing monetary discipline on the system, however. Rightly or wrongly, the interwar experience had convinced the IMF's architects that floating exchange rates were a cause of speculative instability and were harmful to international trade.

The interwar experience had shown also that national governments would not be willing to maintain both free trade and fixed exchange rates at the price of long-term domestic unemployment. After the experience of the Great Depression, governments were widely viewed as responsible for maintaining full employment. The IMF agreement therefore tried to incorporate sufficient flexibility to allow countries to attain external balance in an orderly fashion without sacrificing internal objectives or predictable exchange rates.

Two major features of the IMF Articles of Agreement helped promote this flexibility in external adjustment. First, members of the IMF contributed their currencies and gold to form a pool of financial resources that the IMF could lend to countries in need. Second, although exchange rates against the dollar were fixed, these parities could be adjusted with the agreement of the IMF. Such devaluations and revaluations were supposed to be infrequent and carried out only in cases of an economy in *fundamental disequilibrium*. Although the IMF's Articles did not define "fundamental disequilibrium," the term was intended to cover countries that suffered permanent adverse shifts in the demand for their products, so that without devaluation, the countries would face long periods of unemployment and external deficits. The flexibility of an adjustable exchange rate was not available, however, to the "Nth currency" of the Bretton Woods system, the U.S. dollar.

How did the Bretton Woods system resolve the trilemma? In essence, the system was based on the presumption that movements of private financial capital could be restricted, allowing some degree of independence for domestically oriented monetary policies. The new system thus was diametrically opposed to the gold standard's subordination of monetary policy to external considerations such as freedom of financial flows. After the experience of high interwar unemployment, the architects of the Bretton Woods system hoped to ensure that countries would not be forced to adopt contractionary monetary policies for balance of payments reasons in the face of an economic downturn.

Supporting this emphasis on high employment, restrictions on cross-border financial flows would allow "orderly" exchange rate changes in situations of persistent imbalance. In theory, policy makers would be able to change exchange rates in a deliberate fashion, without the pressure of massive speculative attacks. As we shall see, however, while this approach worked well initially, the very success of the Bretton Woods system in rebuilding international trade made it progressively harder for policy makers to avoid speculative attacks as the years passed.

Convertibility and the Expansion of Private Financial Flows

Just as the general acceptability of national currency eliminates the costs of barter within a single economy, the use of national currencies in international trade makes the world economy function more efficiently. To promote efficient multilateral trade, the IMF Articles of Agreement urged members to make their national currencies convertible as soon as possible. A **convertible currency** is one that may be freely exchanged for foreign currencies. The U.S. and Canadian dollars became convertible in 1945. This meant, for example, that a Canadian resident who acquired U.S. dollars could use them to make purchases in the United States, could sell them in the foreign exchange market for Canadian dollars, or could sell them to the Bank of Canada, which then had the right to sell them to the Federal Reserve (at the fixed dollar/gold exchange rate) in return for gold. General *in*convertibility would make international trade extremely difficult. A French citizen might be unwilling to sell goods to a German in return for inconvertible German marks because these marks would then be usable only subject to restrictions imposed by the German government. With no market in inconvertible French francs, the German would be unable to obtain French currency to pay for the French goods. The only way of trading would therefore be through barter, the direct exchange of goods for goods. Most countries in Europe did not restore convertibility until the end of 1958, with Japan following in 1964.

The early convertibility of the U.S. dollar, together with its special position in the Bretton Woods system and the economic and political dominance of the United States, helped to make the dollar the postwar world's key currency. Because dollars were freely convertible, much international trade tended to be invoiced in dollars, and importers and exporters held dollar balances for transactions. In effect, the dollar became an international money—a universal medium of exchange, unit of account, and store of value. Central banks naturally found it advantageous to hold their international reserves in the form of interest-bearing dollar assets.

The restoration of convertibility in Europe in 1958 gradually began to change the nature of policy makers' external constraints. As foreign exchange trading expanded, financial markets in different countries became more tightly integrated—an important step toward the creation of today's worldwide foreign exchange market. With growing opportunities to move funds across borders, national interest rates became more closely linked, and the speed with which policy changes might cause a country to lose or gain international reserves increased. After 1958, and increasingly over the next 15 years, central banks had to be attentive to foreign financial conditions or take the risk that sudden reserve losses might leave them without the resources needed to peg exchange rates. Faced with a sudden rise in foreign interest rates, for example, a central bank would be forced to sell domestic assets and raise the domestic interest rate to hold its international reserves steady.

The restoration of convertibility did not result in immediate and complete international financial integration, as assumed in the model of fixed exchange rates set out in Chapter 7. On the contrary, most countries continued to maintain restrictions on financial account transactions, a practice that the IMF explicitly allowed. But the opportunities for *disguised* capital flows increased dramatically. For example, importers within a country could effectively purchase foreign assets by accelerating payments to foreign suppliers relative to actual shipments of goods; they could effectively borrow from foreign suppliers by delaying payments. These trade practices— known, respectively, as "leads" and "lags"—provided two of the many ways through which official barriers to private capital movements could be evaded. Even though the condition of international interest rate equality assumed in the last chapter did not hold exactly, the links among countries' interest rates tightened as the Bretton Woods system matured. The Bretton Woods resolution of the trilemma was gradually coming undone.

Speculative Capital Flows and Crises

Current account deficits and surpluses took on added significance under the new conditions of increasingly mobile private financial flows. A country with a large and persistent current account deficit might be suspected of being in "fundamental disequilibrium" under the IMF Articles of Agreement, and thus ripe for a currency devaluation. Suspicion of an impending devaluation could, in turn, spark a balance of payments crisis (see Chapter 7).

Anyone holding pound deposits during a devaluation of the pound, for example, would suffer a loss, since the foreign currency value of pound assets would decrease suddenly by the amount of the exchange rate change. If Britain had a current account deficit, therefore, holders of pounds would become nervous and shift their wealth into other currencies. To hold the pound's exchange rate against the dollar pegged, the Bank of England (Britain's central bank) would have to buy pounds and supply the foreign assets that market participants wished to hold. This loss of foreign reserves, if large enough, might force devaluation by leaving the Bank of England without enough reserves to prop up the exchange rate.

Similarly, countries with large current account surpluses might be viewed by the market as candidates for revaluation. In this case, their central banks would find themselves swamped with official reserves, the result of selling the home currency in the foreign exchange market to keep the currency from appreciating. A country in this position would face the problem of having its money supply grow uncontrollably, a development that could push the price level up and upset internal balance. Governments thus became increasingly reluctant to contemplate exchange rate realignments, fearing the resulting speculative attacks.

Balance of payments crises nonetheless became increasingly frequent and violent throughout the 1960s and early 1970s. A record British trade balance deficit in early 1964 led to a period of intermittent speculation against the pound that complicated British policy making until November 1967, when the pound was finally devalued. France devalued its franc and Germany revalued its mark in 1969 after similar speculative attacks, in which France faced speculative financial outflows and Germany faced speculative financial inflows. (The two countries still had their own currencies at that time.) These crises became so massive by the early 1970s that they eventually brought down the Bretton Woods structure of fixed exchange rates. The possibility of a balance of payments crisis therefore lent increased importance to the external goal of a current account target. Even current account imbalances justified by differing international investment opportunities or caused by purely temporary factors might have fueled market suspicions of an impending parity change. In this environment, policy makers had additional incentives to avoid sharp current account changes.

Analyzing Policy Options for Reaching Internal and External Balance

How were individual countries able to reach internal and external balance under the rules of the Bretton Woods system? A simple diagram will help you to visualize the available policy options. (The problem of the United States under the Bretton Woods system was somewhat different, as we describe later.) In line with the approximate conditions later in the Bretton Woods system, we will assume a high degree of financial capital mobility across borders, so that the domestic interest rate cannot be set independently of the exchange rate.

Our diagrammatic framework actually is applicable whether the exchange rate is fixed, as under the Bretton Woods system, or flexible. The diagram shows how a country's position with respect to its internal and external goals depends on the level of its exchange rate, E, and the level of domestic spending; and that position is not necessarily restricted by the exchange rate regime. Throughout, E is the domestic currency price of the foreign currency (the dollar under Bretton Woods). The analysis applies to the short run because the home and foreign price levels (P and P^*, respectively) are assumed to be fixed.

Maintaining Internal Balance

First consider internal balance, which requires that aggregate demand equal the full-employment level of output, Y^f.[18]

Recall that aggregate demand for domestic output is the sum of consumption, C, investment, I, government purchases, G, and the current account, CA. Of this sum, total domestic spending, also called domestic *absorption*, is denoted by $A = C + I + G$. (Of course, some of this overall domestic spending falls on imports, and therefore does not contribute to the aggregate demand for domestic output, whereas foreign demand for our exports adds to that aggregate demand.) In Chapter 6, we expressed the current account surplus as a decreasing function of disposable income and an increasing function of the real exchange rate, EP^*/P. However, because import spending rises as total domestic spending A rises, we can similarly express the current account as a decreasing function of spending and an increasing function of the real exchange rate, $CA(EP^*/P, A)$. Under this new notation, the condition of internal balance (full-employment output equals aggregate demand) is therefore

$$Y^f = C + I + G + CA(EP^*/P, A) = A + CA(EP^*/P, A). \qquad (8\text{-}1)$$

Equation (8-1) suggests the policy tools that affect aggregate demand and, therefore, output, in the short run. The government can directly influence total spending A through fiscal policy, for example. Fiscal expansion (a rise in G or a fall in T) stimulates aggregate demand and causes output to rise, even though a fraction of the additional spending goes toward import purchases. Similarly, a devaluation of the currency (a rise in E) makes domestic goods and services cheaper relative to those sold abroad and thereby increases demand and output. The policy maker can hold output steady at its full employment level, Y^f, through fiscal policy or exchange rate changes.

---

[18]We will assume the domestic price level is stable at full employment, but if P^* is unstable because of foreign inflation, for example, full employment alone will not guarantee price stability under a fixed exchange rate. This complex problem is considered in the following pages, when we examine worldwide inflation under fixed exchange rates.

Notice that monetary policy is not a policy tool under fixed exchange rates. This is because, as shown in Chapter 7, an attempt by the central bank to alter the money supply by buying or selling domestic assets will cause an offsetting change in foreign reserves, leaving the domestic money supply unchanged. If we were interpreting the diagram to apply to a situation of floating exchange rates, however, we would think of monetary policy as potentially bringing about exchange rate changes consistent with a position of internal and external balance.

The II schedule in Figure 8-2 shows combinations of exchange rates and domestic spending that hold output constant at Y^f and thus maintain internal balance. The schedule is downward sloping because currency devaluation (a rise in E) and higher domestic absorption both tend to raise output. To hold output constant, a *revaluation* of the currency (which reduces aggregate demand) must therefore be matched by higher domestic spending (which increases aggregate output demand). Schedule II shows precisely how domestic spending must change as E changes to maintain full employment. To the right of II, spending is higher than needed for full employment, so the economy's productive factors are overemployed. To the left of II, spending is too low, and there is unemployment.

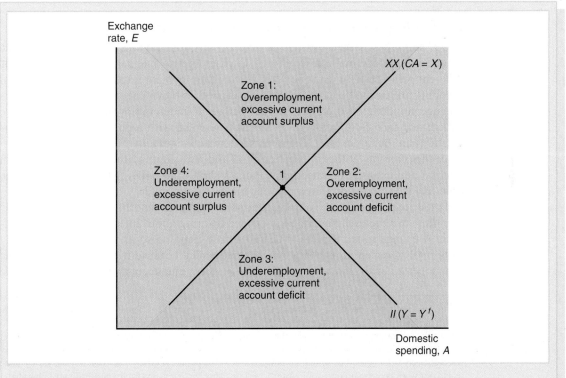

FIGURE 8-2

Internal Balance (II), External Balance (XX), and the "Four Zones of Economic Discomfort"

The diagram shows what different levels of the exchange rate, E, and overall domestic spending, A, imply for employment and the current account. Along II, output is at its full-employment level, Y^f. Along XX, the current account is at its target level, X.

Maintaining External Balance

We have seen how domestic spending and exchange rate changes influence output and thus help the government achieve its internal goal of full employment. How do these variables affect the economy's external balance? To answer this question, assume the government has a target value, X, for the current account surplus. The goal of external balance requires the government to manage domestic spending (perhaps through fiscal policy) and the exchange rate so that the equation

$$CA(EP^*/P, A) = X \qquad\qquad (8\text{-}2)$$

is satisfied.

Given P and P^*, a rise in E makes domestic goods cheaper and improves the current account. A rise in domestic spending, A, however, has the opposite effect on the current account, because it causes imports to rise. To maintain its current account at X as it devalues the currency (that is, as it raises E), the government must enact policies that raise domestic spending. Figure 8-2 therefore shows that the XX schedule, along which external balance holds, is positively sloped. The XX schedule shows the amount of additional spending that will hold the current account surplus at X as the currency is devalued by a given amount.[19] Since a rise in E raises net exports, the current account is in surplus, relative to its target level X, above XX. Similarly, below XX the current account is in deficit relative to its target level.[20]

Expenditure-Changing and Expenditure-Switching Policies

The II and XX schedules divide the diagram into four regions, sometimes called the "four zones of economic discomfort." Each of these zones represents the effects of different policy settings. In zone 1, the level of employment is too high and the current account surplus too great; in zone 2, the level of employment is too high but the current account deficit is too great; in zone 3, there is underemployment and an excessive deficit; and in zone 4, underemployment is coupled with a current account surplus greater than the target level. Together, spending changes and exchange rate policy can place the economy at the intersection of II and XX (point 1), the point at which both internal and external balance hold. Point 1 shows the policy setting that places the economy in the position that the policy maker would prefer.

If the economy is initially away from point 1, appropriate adjustments in domestic spending and the exchange rate are needed to bring about internal and external balance. A change in fiscal policy that influences spending so as to move the economy to point 1 is called an **expenditure-changing policy** because it alters the *level* of the economy's total demand for goods and services. The accompanying exchange rate

---

[19]Can you see how to derive the XX schedule in Figure 8-2 from the different (but related) XX schedule shown in Figure 6-17? (Hint: Use the latter diagram to analyze the effects of fiscal expansion.)

[20]Since the central bank does not affect the economy when it raises its foreign reserves by an open-market sale of domestic assets, no separate reserve constraint is shown in Figure 8-2. In effect, the bank can borrow reserves freely from abroad by selling domestic assets to the public. (During a devaluation scare, this tactic would not work because no one would want to sell the bank foreign assets for domestic money.) Our analysis, however, assumes perfect asset substitutability between domestic and foreign bonds (see Chapter 7). Under imperfect asset substitutability, central bank domestic asset sales to attract foreign reserves would drive up the domestic interest rate relative to the foreign rate. Thus, while imperfect asset substitutability would give the central bank an additional policy tool (monetary policy), it would also make the bank responsible for an additional policy target (the domestic interest rate). If the government is concerned about the domestic interest rate because it affects investment, for example, the additional policy tool would not necessarily increase the set of attractive policy options. Imperfect substitutability was exploited by central banks under Bretton Woods, but it did not get countries out of the policy dilemmas illustrated in the text.

adjustment is called an **expenditure-switching policy** because it changes the *direction* of demand, shifting it between domestic output and imports. In general, both expenditure changing and expenditure switching are needed to reach internal and external balance. Apart from monetary policy, fiscal policy is the main government lever for pushing total domestic expenditure up or down.

Under the Bretton Woods rules, exchange rate changes (expenditure-switching policy) were supposed to be infrequent. This left fiscal policy as the main policy tool for moving the economy toward internal and external balance. But as Figure 8-2 shows, one instrument, fiscal policy, is generally insufficient to attain the two goals of internal and external balance. Only if the economy had been displaced horizontally from point 1 would fiscal policy be able to do the job alone. In addition, fiscal policy is an unwieldy tool, since it often cannot be implemented without legislative approval. Another drawback is that a fiscal expansion, for example, might have to be reversed after some time if it leads to chronic government budget deficits.

As a result of the exchange rate's inflexibility during the Bretton Woods period, policy makers sometimes found themselves in difficult situations. With the spending level and exchange rate indicated by point 2 in Figure 8-3, there is underemployment and an excessive current account deficit. Only the combination of devaluation and spending expansion indicated in the figure moves the economy to internal and external balance (point 1). Expansionary fiscal policy, acting alone, can eliminate the unemployment by moving the economy to point 3, but the cost of reduced unemployment is a larger external deficit. While contractionary fiscal policy alone can bring about external balance (point 4), output falls as a result and the economy moves further from internal balance. It is no wonder that policy dilemmas such as the one at point 2 gave rise to suspicions that the currency was about to be devalued. Devaluation improves the current account and aggregate demand by raising the real exchange rate EP^*/P in one

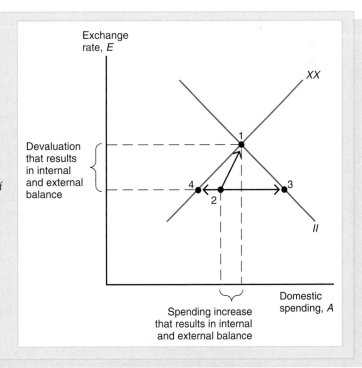

FIGURE 8-3

Policies to Bring about Internal and External Balance

Unless the currency is devalued and the level of domestic spending rises, internal and external balance (point 1) cannot be reached. Acting alone, a change in fiscal policy, for example, enables the economy to attain *either* internal balance (point 3) *or* external balance (point 4), but only at the cost of increasing the economy's distance from the goal that is sacrificed.

stroke; the alternative is a long and politically unpopular period of unemployment to bring about an equal rise in the real exchange rate through a fall in P.[21]

In practice, countries did sometimes use changes in their exchange rates to move closer to internal and external balance, although the changes were typically accompanied by balance of payments crises. Many countries also tightened controls on financial account transactions to sever the links between domestic and foreign interest rates and make monetary policy more effective (in line with the trilemma). In this they were only partly successful, as the events leading to the breakdown of the system were to prove.

The External Balance Problem of the United States under Bretton Woods

The external balance problem of the United States was different from the one faced by the other countries in the Bretton Woods system. As the issuer of the Nth currency, the United States was not responsible for pegging dollar exchange rates. Its main responsibility was to hold the dollar price of gold at $35 an ounce and, in particular, to guarantee that foreign central banks could convert their dollar holdings into gold at that price. For this purpose, it had to hold sufficient gold reserves.

Because the United States was required to trade gold for dollars with foreign central banks, the possibility that other countries might convert their dollar reserves into gold was a potential external constraint on U.S. macroeconomic policy. In practice, however, foreign central banks were willing to hold on to the dollars they accumulated, since these paid interest and were international money *par excellence*. And the logic of the gold exchange standard dictated that foreign central banks should continue to accumulate dollars. Because world gold supplies were not growing quickly enough to keep up with world economic growth, the only way central banks could maintain adequate international reserve levels (barring deflation) was by accumulating dollar assets. Official gold conversions did occur on occasion, and these depleted the American gold stock and caused concern. But as long as most central banks were willing to add dollars to their reserves and forgo the right of redeeming those dollars for American gold, the U.S. external constraint appeared looser than that faced by other countries in the system.

In an influential book that appeared in 1960, economist Robert Triffin of Yale University called attention to a fundamental long-run problem of the Bretton Woods system, the **confidence problem**.[22] Triffin realized that as central banks' international reserve needs grew over time, their holdings of dollars would necessarily grow until they exceeded the U.S. gold stock. Since the United States had promised to redeem these dollars at $35 an ounce, it would no longer have the ability to meet its obligations should all dollar holders simultaneously try to convert their dollars into gold. This would lead to a confidence problem: Central banks, knowing that their dollars were no longer "as good as gold," might become unwilling to accumulate more dollars and might even bring down the system by attempting to cash in the dollars they already held.

One possible solution at the time was an increase in the official price of gold in terms of the dollar and all other currencies. But such an increase would have been inflationary and would have had the politically unattractive consequence of enriching the main gold-supplying countries. Further, an increase in gold's price would

---

[21]As an exercise to test your understanding, show that a fall in P, all else equal, lowers both II and XX, moving point 1 vertically downward.

[22]See Triffin, *Gold and the Dollar Crisis* (New Haven: Yale University Press, 1960).

have caused central banks to expect further decreases in the gold value of their dollar reserve holdings in the future, thereby possibly worsening the confidence problem rather than solving it!

CASE STUDY

The End of Bretton Woods, Worldwide Inflation, and the Transition to Floating Rates

By the late 1960s, the Bretton Woods system of fixed exchange rates was beginning to show strains that would soon lead to its collapse. These strains were closely related to the special position of the United States, where inflation was gathering strength because of higher monetary growth as well as higher government spending on new social programs such as Medicare and on the unpopular Vietnam War.

The acceleration of American inflation in the late 1960s was a worldwide phenomenon. Table 8-1 shows that by the start of the 1970s, inflation had also broken out in European economies.[23] The worldwide nature of the inflation problem was no accident. The theory in Chapter 7 predicts that when the reserve currency country speeds up its monetary growth, as the United States did in the second half of the 1960s, one effect is an automatic increase in monetary growth rates and inflation abroad as foreign central banks purchase the reserve currency to maintain their exchange rates and expand their money supplies in the process. One interpretation of the Bretton Woods system's collapse is that foreign countries were forced to *import* unwelcome U.S. inflation through the mechanism described in Chapter 7. To stabilize their price levels and regain internal balance, they had to abandon fixed exchange rates and allow their currencies to float. The monetary trilemma implies that these countries could not simultaneously peg their exchange rates and control domestic inflation.

TABLE 8-1	Inflation Rates in Industrial Countries, 1966–1972 (percent per year)						
Country	**1966**	**1967**	**1968**	**1969**	**1970**	**1971**	**1972**
Britain	3.6	2.6	4.6	5.2	6.5	9.7	6.9
France	2.8	2.8	4.4	6.5	5.3	5.5	6.2
Germany	3.4	1.4	2.9	1.9	3.4	5.3	5.5
Italy	2.1	2.1	1.2	2.8	5.1	5.2	5.3
United States	2.9	3.1	4.2	5.5	5.7	4.4	3.2

Source: Organization for Economic Cooperation and Development. *Main Economic Indicators: Historical Statistics, 1964–1983.* Paris: OECD, 1984. Figures are percentage increases in each year's average consumer price index over that of the previous year.

---

[23]The U.S. inflation numbers for 1971 and 1972 are artificially low because of President Nixon's resort to government-administered wage and price controls in August 1971. In principle, the U.S. commitment to peg the market price of gold should have limited U.S. inflation, but in practice, the United States was able to weaken that commitment over time, thus allowing the *market* price of gold to rise while still holding to the promise to redeem dollars from central banks at $35 per ounce. By the late 1960s, the United States was therefore the unique country in the system in that it did not face the full monetary trilemma. It enjoyed fixed exchange rates because *other* countries pegged their currencies to the dollar, yet it could still orient monetary policy toward domestic goals. For recent assessments of the worldwide inflation of the 1970s, see Michael Bordo and Athanasios Orphanides, eds., *The Great Inflation* (Chicago: University of Chicago Press, 2013).

Adding to the tensions, the U.S. economy entered a recession in 1970, and as unemployment rose, markets became increasingly convinced that the dollar would have to be devalued against all the major European currencies. To restore full employment and a balanced current account, the United States somehow had to bring about a real depreciation of the dollar. That real depreciation could be brought about in two ways: The first option was a fall in the U.S. price level in response to domestic unemployment, coupled with a rise in foreign price levels in response to continuing purchases of dollars by foreign central banks. The second option was a fall in the dollar's nominal value in terms of foreign currencies. The first route—unemployment in the United States and inflation abroad—seemed a painful one for policy makers to follow. The markets rightly guessed that a change in the dollar's value was inevitable. This realization led to massive sales of dollars in the foreign exchange market.

After several unsuccessful attempts to stabilize the system (including a unilateral U.S. decision in August 1971 to end completely the dollar's link to gold), the main industrialized countries allowed their dollar exchange rates to float in March 1973.[24] Floating was viewed at the time as a temporary response to unmanageable speculative capital movements. But the interim arrangements adopted in March 1973 turned out to be permanent and marked the end of fixed exchange rates and the beginning of a turbulent new period in international monetary relations.

The Mechanics of Imported Inflation

To understand how inflation can be imported from abroad unless exchange rates are adjusted, look again at the graphical picture of internal and external balance shown in Figure 8-2. Suppose the home country is faced with foreign inflation. Above, the foreign price level, P^*, was assumed to be given; now, however, P^* rises as a result of inflation abroad. Figure 8-4 shows the effect on the home economy.

You can see how the two schedules shift by asking what would happen if the nominal exchange rate were to fall in proportion to the rise in P^*. In this case, the real exchange rate EP^*/P would be unaffected (given P), and the economy would remain in internal balance or in external balance if either of these conditions originally held. Figure 8-4 therefore shows that for a given initial exchange rate, a rise in P^* shifts both II^1 and XX^1 downward by the same distance (approximately equal to the proportional increase in P^* times the initial exchange rate). The intersection of the new schedules II^2 and XX^2 (point 2) lies directly below the original intersection at point 1.

If the economy starts out at point 1, a rise in P^* *given* the fixed exchange rate and the domestic price level therefore strands the economy in zone 1 with overemployment and an undesirably high surplus in its current account. The factor that causes this outcome is a real currency depreciation that shifts world demand toward the home country (EP^*/P rises because P^* rises).

If nothing is done by the government, overemployment puts upward pressure on the domestic price level, and this pressure gradually shifts the two schedules back to their original positions. The schedules stop shifting once P has risen in proportion to

---

[24]Many developing countries continued to peg to the dollar, and a number of European countries were continuing to peg their mutual exchange rates as part of an informal arrangement called the "snake." The snake evolved into the European Monetary System (discussed in Chapter 10) and ultimately led to Europe's single currency, the euro.

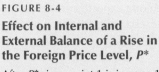

FIGURE 8-4

Effect on Internal and External Balance of a Rise in the Foreign Price Level, P*

After P* rises, point 1 is in zone 1 (overemployment and an excessive surplus). Revaluation (a fall in E) restores balance immediately by moving the policy setting to point 2.

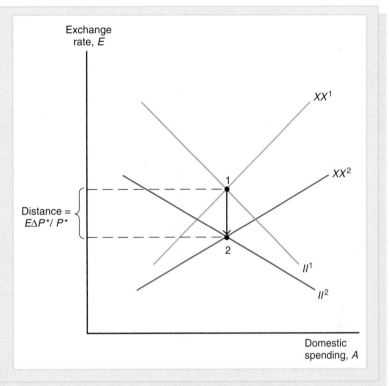

P^*. At this stage, the real exchange rate, employment, and the current account are at their initial levels, so point 1 is once again a position of internal and external balance.

The way to avoid the imported inflation is to revalue the currency (that is, lower E) and move to point 2. A revaluation restores internal and external balance immediately, without domestic inflation, by using the nominal exchange rate to offset the effect of the rise in P^* on the real exchange rate. Only an expenditure-switching policy is needed to respond to a pure increase in foreign prices.

The rise in domestic prices that occurs when no revaluation takes place requires a rise in the domestic money supply, since prices and the money supply move proportionally in the long run. The mechanism that brings this rise about is foreign exchange intervention by the home central bank. As domestic output and prices rise after the rise in P^*, the real money supply shrinks and the demand for real money holdings increases. To prevent the resulting upward pressure on the home interest rate from appreciating the currency, the central bank must purchase international reserves and expand the home money supply. In this way, inflationary policies pursued by the reserve center spill over into foreign countries' money supplies.

Assessment

The collapse of the Bretton Woods system was partly due to the lopsided macroeconomic power of the United States, which allowed it to generate global inflation. But it was also due in large measure to the fact that the key expenditure-switching tool needed for internal and external balance—discrete exchange rate adjustment—inspired speculative attacks that made both internal and external balance progressively more difficult to achieve. The system thus was a victim of the trilemma. As international financial flows became harder to restrain, policy makers faced an increasingly sharp trade-off between exchange rate stability and domestic monetary goals. By the 1970s, however, the electorates of the industrial counties had long expected governments to give priority to the domestic economy. So it was fixed exchange rates that gave way.

The Case for Floating Exchange Rates

As international currency crises of increasing scope and frequency erupted in the late 1960s, most economists began advocating greater flexibility of exchange rates. Many argued that a system of floating exchange rates (one in which central banks do not intervene in the foreign exchange market to fix rates) would not only deliver necessary exchange rate flexibility but would also produce several other benefits for the world economy. Thus, the arrival of floating exchange rates in March 1973 was hailed by many economists as a healthy development in the evolution of the world monetary system, one that would put markets at center stage in determining exchange rates.

The case for floating exchange rates rested on at least four major claims:

1. *Monetary policy autonomy.* If central banks were no longer obliged to intervene in currency markets to fix exchange rates, governments would be able to use monetary policy to reach internal and external balance. Furthermore, no country would be forced to import inflation (or deflation) from abroad.
2. *Symmetry.* Under a system of floating rates, the inherent asymmetries of Bretton Woods would disappear and the United States would no longer be able to set world monetary conditions all by itself. At the same time, the United States would have the same opportunity as other countries to influence its exchange rate against foreign currencies.
3. *Exchange rates as automatic stabilizers.* Even in the absence of an active monetary policy, the swift adjustment of market-determined exchange rates would help countries maintain internal and external balance in the face of changes in aggregate demand. The long and agonizing periods of speculation preceding exchange rate realignments under the Bretton Woods rules would not occur under floating.
4. *Exchange rates and external balance.* Market-determined exchange rates would move automatically so as to prevent the emergence of big current account deficits and surpluses.

Monetary Policy Autonomy

Toward the end of the Bretton Woods fixed-rate system, countries other than the United States had little scope to use monetary policy to attain internal and external balance. Countries could hold their dollar exchange rates fixed only if they kept the domestic interest rate in line with that of the United States. Thus, in the closing years of fixed exchange rates, central banks imposed increasingly stringent restrictions on international payments to keep control over their interest rates and money supplies. However, these restrictions were only partially successful in strengthening monetary policy, and they had the damaging side effect of distorting international trade.

Advocates of floating rates pointed out that removal of the obligation to peg currency values would restore monetary control to central banks. If, for example, the central bank faced unemployment and wished to expand its money supply in response, there would no longer be any legal barrier to the currency depreciation this would cause. Similarly, the central bank of an overheated economy could cool down activity by contracting the money supply without worrying that undesired reserve inflows would undermine its stabilization effort. Enhanced control over monetary policy would allow countries to dismantle their distorting barriers to international payments. In other words, floating rates implied an approach to the monetary trilemma that sacrificed fixed exchange rates in favor of freedom of financial flows and of monetary policy.

Consistent with this view, advocates of floating also argued that floating rates would allow each country to choose its own desired long-run inflation rate rather than having to import passively the inflation rate established abroad. We saw in the last chapter that a country faced with a rise in the foreign price level will be thrown out of balance and ultimately will import the foreign inflation if it holds its exchange rate fixed. By the end of the 1960s, many countries felt that they were importing inflation from the United States. By revaluing its currency—that is, by lowering the domestic currency price of foreign currency—a country can insulate itself completely from an inflationary increase in foreign prices, and so remain in internal and external balance. One of the most telling arguments in favor of floating rates was their ability, in theory, to bring about automatically exchange rate changes that insulate economies from ongoing foreign inflation.

The mechanism behind this insulation is purchasing power parity (see Chapter 5). Recall that when all changes in the world economy are monetary, PPP holds true in the long run: Exchange rates eventually move to offset exactly national differences in inflation. If U.S. monetary growth leads to a long-run doubling of the U.S. price level while Europe's price level remains constant, PPP predicts that the long-run euro price of the dollar will be halved. This nominal exchange rate change leaves the *real* exchange rate between the dollar and the euro unchanged and thus maintains Europe's internal and external balance. In other words, the long-run exchange rate change predicted by PPP is exactly the change that insulates Europe from U.S. inflation.

A money-induced increase in U.S. prices also causes an *immediate* appreciation of foreign currencies against the dollar when the exchange rate floats. In the short run, the size of this appreciation can differ from what PPP predicts, but the foreign exchange speculators who might have mounted an attack on fixed dollar exchange rates speed the adjustment of floating rates. Since they know foreign currencies will appreciate according to PPP in the long run, they act on their expectations and push exchange rates in the direction of their long-run levels.

In contrast, countries operating under the Bretton Woods rules were forced to choose between matching U.S. inflation to hold their dollar exchange rates fixed or deliberately revaluing their currencies in proportion to the rise in U.S. prices. Under floating, however, the foreign exchange market automatically brings about exchange rate changes that shield countries from U.S. inflation. Since this outcome does not require any government policy decisions, the revaluation crises that occurred under fixed exchange rates are avoided.[25]

Symmetry

The second argument put forward by the advocates of floating was that abandonment of the Bretton Woods system would remove the asymmetries that caused so much international disagreement in the 1960s and early 1970s. There were two main asymmetries, both the result of the dollar's central role in the international monetary system. First, because central banks pegged their currencies to the dollar and accumulated dollars as international reserves, the U.S. Federal Reserve played the leading role in determining the world money supply, and central banks abroad had little scope

---

[25]Countries can also avoid importing undesired *deflation* by floating, since the analysis above applies, in reverse, for a fall in the foreign price level.

to determine their own domestic money supplies. Second, any foreign country could devalue its currency against the dollar in conditions of "fundamental disequilibrium," but the system's rules did not give the United States the option to devalue against foreign currencies. Rather, dollar devaluation required a long and economically disruptive period of multilateral negotiation.

A system of floating exchange rates would do away with these asymmetries. Since countries would no longer peg dollar exchange rates, each would be in a position to guide monetary conditions at home. For the same reason, the United States would not face any special obstacle to altering its exchange rate through monetary or fiscal policies. All countries' exchange rates would be determined symmetrically by the foreign exchange market, not by government decisions.[26]

Exchange Rates as Automatic Stabilizers

The third argument in favor of floating rates concerned their ability, theoretically, to promote swift and relatively painless adjustment to certain types of economic changes. One such change, previously discussed, is foreign inflation. Figure 8-5, which uses the DD-AA model presented in Chapter 6, examines another type of change by comparing an economy's response under a fixed and a floating exchange rate to a temporary fall in foreign demand for its exports.

A fall in demand for the home country's exports reduces aggregate demand for every level of the exchange rate, E, and thus shifts the DD schedule leftward from DD^1 to DD^2. (Recall that the DD schedule shows exchange rate and output pairs for which aggregate demand equals aggregate output.) Figure 8-5a shows how this shift affects the economy's equilibrium when the exchange rate floats. Because the demand shift is assumed to be temporary, it does not change the long-run expected exchange rate and so does not move the asset market equilibrium schedule AA^1. (Recall that the AA schedule shows exchange rate and output pairs at which the foreign exchange market and the domestic money market are in equilibrium.) The economy's short-run equilibrium is therefore at point 2; compared with the initial equilibrium at point 1, the currency depreciates (E rises) and output falls. Why does the exchange rate rise from E^1 to E^2? As demand and output fall, reducing the transactions demand for money, the home interest rate must also decline to keep the money market in equilibrium. This fall in the home interest rate causes the domestic currency to depreciate in the foreign exchange market, and the exchange rate therefore rises from E^1 to E^2.

The effect of the same export demand disturbance under a fixed exchange rate is shown in Figure 8-5b. Since the central bank must prevent the currency depreciation that occurs under a floating rate, it buys domestic money with foreign reserves, an action that contracts the money supply and shifts AA^1 left to AA^2. The new short-run equilibrium of the economy under a fixed exchange rate is at point 3, where output equals Y^3.

Figure 8-5 shows that output actually falls more under a fixed rate than under a floating rate, dropping all the way to Y^3 rather than Y^2. In other words, the movement of the floating exchange rate stabilizes the economy by reducing the shock's effect on employment relative to its effect under a fixed rate. Currency depreciation in the floating-rate case makes domestic goods and services cheaper when the demand for them falls, partly offsetting the initial reduction in demand. In addition to reducing

---

[26]The symmetry argument is not an argument against fixed-rate systems in general, but an argument against the specific type of fixed exchange rate system that broke down in the early 1970s. As we saw in Chapter 7, a fixed-rate system based on an international gold standard can be completely symmetric.

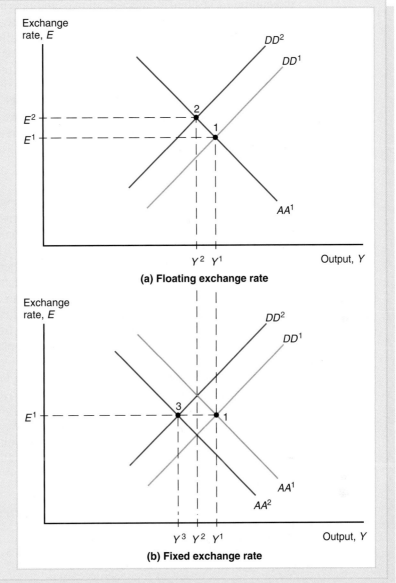

FIGURE 8-5

Effects of a Fall in Export Demand

The response to a fall in export demand (seen in the shift from DD^1 to DD^2) differs under floating and fixed exchange rates. (a) With a floating rate, output falls only to Y^2 as the currency's depreciation (from E^1 to E^2) shifts demand back toward domestic goods. (b) With the exchange rate fixed at E^1, output falls all the way to Y^3 as the central bank reduces the money supply (reflected in the shift from AA^1 to AA^2).

(a) Floating exchange rate

(b) Fixed exchange rate

the departure from internal balance caused by the fall in export demand, the depreciation reduces the increased current account deficit that occurs under fixed rates by making domestic products more competitive in international markets.

We have considered the case of a transitory fall in export demand, but even stronger conclusions can be drawn when there is a *permanent* fall in export demand. In this case, the expected exchange rate E^e also rises and AA shifts upward as a result. A permanent shock causes a greater depreciation than does a temporary shock, and the movement of the exchange rate therefore cushions domestic output more when the shock is permanent.

Under the Bretton Woods system, a fall in export demand such as the one shown in Figure 8-5b would, if permanent, have led to a situation of "fundamental disequilibrium" calling for a devaluation of the currency or a long period of domestic unemployment as wages and prices fell. Uncertainty about the government's intentions would have encouraged speculative capital outflows, further worsening the situation by depleting central bank reserves and contracting the domestic money supply at a time of unemployment. Advocates of floating rates pointed out that the foreign exchange market would automatically bring about the required *real* currency depreciation through a movement in the nominal exchange rate. This exchange rate change would reduce or eliminate the need to push the price level down through unemployment, and because it would occur immediately, there would be no risk of speculative disruption, as there would be under a fixed rate.

Exchange Rates and External Balance

A final benefit claimed for floating exchange rates was that they would prevent the emergence of persistently large current account deficits or surpluses. Because a country with a large current account deficit is borrowing from foreigners and thereby increasing its foreign debt, it will eventually have to generate larger surpluses of exports over imports to pay the interest on that debt. Those larger surpluses, in turn, will require a depreciated currency. Advocates of floating suggested that speculators, anticipating this depreciation, would drive the currency down in advance, making exports more competitive and imports more expensive in the short run. Such stabilizing speculation, it was held, would prevent current account deficits from getting too large in the first place. (The same mechanism, with appreciation replacing depreciation, would limit external surpluses.)

A corollary of this view is that floating exchange rates would not be too volatile, because stabilizing speculators would constantly drive them toward levels consistent with external balance.

How well did these predictions fare after 1973? We shall show that while some predictions were borne out, advocates of floating were on the whole too optimistic that a system of market-determined exchange rates would function free of exchange market turbulence or policy conflicts among countries.

CASE STUDY

The First Years of Floating Rates, 1973–1990

A review of the macroeconomic history of the world economy since 1973 offers key data for judging the successes and shortcomings of the modern international monetary system. We begin with a summary of the first turbulent years of floating exchange rates.

INFLATION AND DISINFLATION, 1973–1982

The opening act of the floating exchange rate era was a quadrupling in the world price of petroleum between late 1973 and early 1974, engineered by the newly assertive Organization of Petroleum Exporting Countries (OPEC), an international cartel that includes most large oil producers. Consumption and investment slowed down everywhere and the world economy was thrown into recession. The current account balances of oil-importing countries worsened.

MyEconLab Real-time data

TABLE 8-2	Macroeconomic Data for Key Industrial Regions, 1963–2012					
Period	**1963–1972**	**1973–1982**	**1983–1992**	**1993–2006**	**2007–2009**	**2010–2012**
	Inflation (percent per year)					
United States	3.3	8.7	4.0	2.7	2.1	2.3
Europe	4.4	10.7	5.1	2.4	2.3	2.5
Japan	5.6	8.6	1.8	0.2	0.0	−0.3
	Unemployment (percent of labor force)					
United States	4.7	7.0	6.8	5.3	6.6	8.9
Europe	1.9	5.5	9.4	9.4	7.8	10.0
Japan	1.2	1.9	2.5	4.0	4.3	4.7
	Per Capita Real GDP Growth (percent per year)					
United States	2.8	0.9	2.4	2.1	−0.9	1.4
Europe	3.9	2.0	3.0	2.1	0.6	0.8
Japan	8.5	2.9	3.4	1.0	−3.8	2.1

Source: International Monetary Fund and Eurostat.

The model we developed in Chapters 3 through 7 predicts that inflation tends to rise in boom periods and fall in recessions. As the world went into deep recession in 1974, however, inflation accelerated in most countries. Table 8-2 shows how inflation in the main industrial regions spurted upward in the decade 1973–1982 even though unemployment was rising.

What happened? An important contributing factor was the oil shock itself: By directly raising the prices of petroleum products and the costs of energy-using industries, the increase in the oil price caused price levels to jump upward. Further, the worldwide inflationary pressures that had built up since the end of the 1960s had become entrenched in the wage-setting process and were continuing to contribute to inflation in spite of the deteriorating employment picture. The same inflationary expectations that were driving new wage contracts were also putting additional upward pressure on commodity prices as speculators built up stocks of commodities whose prices they expected to rise. Over the following years, central bankers proved unwilling to combat these inflationary pressures at the cost of yet-higher unemployment.

To describe the unusual macroeconomic conditions of 1974–1975, economists coined a new word that has since become commonplace: **stagflation**, a combination of stagnating output and high inflation. Stagflation was the result of two factors:

1. Increases in commodity prices that directly raised inflation while at the same time depressing aggregate demand and supply
2. Expectations of future inflation that fed into wages and other prices in spite of recession and rising unemployment

Freed of the need to defend a fixed exchange rate, governments responded with expansionary policies that further fueled inflation. Many countries, moving to a different vertex of the trilemma, had even been able to relax the capital controls they had set up before 1974. This relaxation eased the adjustment problem of the developing countries, which were able to borrow more easily from developed-country financial markets to maintain their own spending and economic growth. In turn, the relative strength of the developing world's demand for industrial-country exports helped mitigate the severity of the 1974–1975 recession. But in the industrial countries, unemployment nonetheless jumped upward and remained stubbornly high, as shown in Table 8-2.

In the mid-1970s, the United States attempted to combat this unemployment through expansionary monetary policy, whereas other countries such as Germany and Japan were more worried about inflation. The result of this policy imbalance—vigorous expansion in the United States that was unmatched by expansion abroad—was a steep depreciation of the dollar after 1976. U.S. inflation reached double-digit levels (as did inflation in a number of other countries, including Canada, France, Italy, and the United Kingdom). The depreciation of the dollar in these years is evident in Figure 8-6, which shows both **nominal and real effective exchange rate indexes** of the dollar. These indexes measure, respectively, the price of a dollar in terms of a basket of foreign currencies and the price of U.S. output in terms of a basket of foreign outputs. Thus, a rise in either index is a (nominal or real) dollar appreciation, while a fall is a depreciation.

To restore faith in the dollar, President Jimmy Carter appointed a new Federal Reserve Board chairman with broad experience in international financial affairs, Paul A. Volcker. The dollar began to strengthen in October 1979, when Volcker announced a tightening of U.S. monetary policy and the adoption by the Fed of more stringent procedures for controlling money supply growth.

The fall of the shah of Iran in 1979 sparked a second round of oil price increases by disrupting oil exports from that country. In 1975 macroeconomic policy makers in the industrial countries had responded to the first oil shock with expansionary monetary and fiscal policies. They responded very differently to this second oil shock.

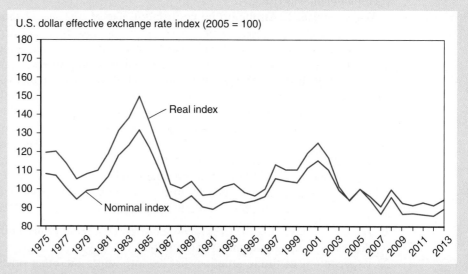

FIGURE 8-6

Nominal and Real Effective Dollar Exchange Rate Indexes, 1975–2013

The indexes are measures of the nominal and real value of the U.S. dollar in terms of a basket of foreign currencies. An increase in the indexes is a dollar appreciation, a decrease a dollar depreciation. For both indexes, the 2005 value is 100.

Source: International Monetary Fund, *International Financial Statistics*.

Over 1979 and 1980, monetary growth was actually *restricted* in most major industrial countries in an attempt to offset the rise in inflation accompanying the oil price increase. This policy approach prevented an upsurge in inflation, but helped cause a worldwide recession.

November 1980 saw the election of President Ronald Reagan, who had campaigned on an anti-inflation platform. In light of the election result and Volcker's monetary slowdown, the dollar's value soared (see Figure 8-6). U.S. interest rates had also risen sharply late in 1979; by 1981, short-term interest rates in the United States were nearly double their 1978 levels.

By pushing up the U.S. interest rate and causing investors to expect a stronger dollar in the future, the U.S. action led to an immediate appreciation of the dollar. This appreciation made U.S. goods more expensive relative to foreign goods, thereby reducing U.S. output.

The dollar's appreciation was not welcomed abroad, however, even though it could, in theory, have lent foreign economies some positive stimulus in a period of slow growth. The reason was that a stronger dollar hindered foreign countries in their own fights against inflation, both by raising the import prices they faced and by encouraging higher wage demands from their workers. A stronger dollar had the opposite effect in the United States, hastening the decline of inflation there. The tight U.S. monetary policy therefore had a beggar-thy-neighbor effect abroad, in that it lowered American inflation in part by exporting inflation to foreign economies.

Foreign central banks responded by intervening in the currency markets to slow the dollar's rise. Through the process of selling dollar reserves and buying their own currencies, some central banks reduced their monetary growth rates for 1980 and 1981, driving interest rates upward. Synchronized monetary contraction in the United States and abroad, following fast on the heels of the second oil shock, threw the world economy into a deep recession, the most severe between the Great Depression of the 1930s and the 2007–2009 crisis a generation later. In 1982 and 1983, unemployment throughout the world rose to levels unprecedented in the post–World War II period. While U.S. unemployment quickly returned to its pre-recession level, unemployment in Japan and especially in Europe remained permanently higher (see Table 8-2). Monetary contraction and the recession it brought quickly led, however, to a dramatic drop in the inflation rates of industrialized countries.

THE STRONG DOLLAR AND THE PLAZA ACCORD

During his election campaign, President Reagan had promised to lower taxes and balance the federal budget. He made good on the first of these promises in 1981. At the same time, the Reagan administration pushed for an acceleration of defense spending. The net result of these and subsequent congressional actions was a ballooning U.S. government budget deficit and a sharp fiscal stimulus to the economy. The U.S. fiscal stance encouraged continuing dollar appreciation (see Figure 8-6). By February 1985, the dollar's cumulative appreciation against the German currency since the end of 1979 was 47.9 percent. The recession reached its low point in the United States in December 1982, and output began to recover both there and abroad as the U.S. fiscal stimulus was transmitted to foreign countries through the dollar's steady appreciation.

While the U.S. fiscal expansion contributed to world recovery, growing federal budget deficits raised serious worries about the future stability of the world economy. Because increasing government deficits were not met with offsetting increases in private saving or decreases in investment, the American current account balance deteriorated sharply. By 1987, the United States had become a net debtor to foreign countries and its current account deficit was at the (then) postwar record level of 3.6 percent of GNP. Some analysts worried that foreign creditors would lose confidence in the future value of the dollar assets they were accumulating and sell them, causing a sudden, precipitous dollar depreciation.

Equally worrisome was the strong dollar's impact on the distribution of income within the United States. The dollar's appreciation had reduced U.S. inflation and allowed consumers to purchase imports more cheaply, but those hurt by the terms of trade change were better organized and more vocal than those who had benefited. Persistently poor economic performance in the 1980s had led to increased pressures on governments to protect industries in import-competing sectors. Protectionist pressures snowballed.

The Reagan administration had, from the start, adopted a policy of "benign neglect" toward the foreign exchange market, refusing to intervene except in unusual circumstances (for example, after a would-be assassin shot President Reagan). By 1985, however, the link between the strong dollar and the gathering protectionist storm became impossible to ignore.

Fearing a disaster for the international trading system, economic officials of the United States, Britain, France, Germany, and Japan announced at New York's Plaza Hotel on September 22, 1985, that they would jointly intervene in the foreign exchange market to bring about dollar depreciation. The dollar dropped sharply the next day and continued to decline through 1986 and early 1987 as the United States maintained a loose monetary policy and pushed dollar interest rates down relative to foreign currency interest rates. (See Figure 8-6.)

Macroeconomic Interdependence under a Floating Rate

Up until now, our modeling of the open economy has focused on the relatively simple case of a small country that cannot affect foreign output, price levels, or interest rates through its own monetary and fiscal policies. That description obviously does not fit the United States, however, with its national output level equal to about a fifth of the world's total product. To discuss macroeconomic interactions between the United States and the rest of the world, we therefore must think about the transmission of policies between countries linked by a floating exchange rate. We will offer a brief and intuitive discussion rather than a formal model, and restrict ourselves to the short run, in which we can assume that nominal output prices are fixed.

Imagine a world economy made up of two large countries, Home and Foreign. Our goal is to evaluate how Home's macroeconomic policies affect Foreign. The main complication is that neither country can be thought of any longer as facing a fixed external interest rate or a fixed level of foreign export demand. To simplify, we consider only the case of *permanent* shifts in monetary and fiscal policy.

Let's look first at a permanent monetary expansion by Home. We know that in the small-country case (Chapter 6), Home's currency would depreciate and its output would rise. The same happens when Home's economy is large, but now, the rest of the world is affected too. Because Home is experiencing real currency depreciation, Foreign must be experiencing real currency *appreciation*, which makes Foreign goods relatively expensive and thus has a depressing effect on Foreign output. The increase in Home output, however, works in the opposite direction, since Home spends some of its extra income on Foreign goods and, on that account, aggregate demand for Foreign output rises. Home's monetary expansion therefore has two opposing effects on Foreign output, with the net result depending on which effect is the stronger. Foreign output may rise or fall.[27]

Next let's think about a permanent expansionary fiscal policy in Home. In the small-country case of Chapter 6, a permanent fiscal expansion caused a real currency appreciation and a current account deterioration that fully nullified any positive effect on aggregate demand. In effect, the expansionary impact of Home's fiscal ease leaked entirely abroad (because the counterpart of Home's lower current account balance must be a higher current account balance abroad). In the large-country case, Foreign output still rises, since Foreign's exports become relatively cheaper when Home's currency appreciates. In addition, now some of Foreign's increased spending increases Home exports, so Home's output actually does increase along with Foreign's.[28]

We summarize our discussion of macroeconomic interdependence between large countries as follows:

1. *Effect of a permanent monetary expansion by Home.* Home output rises, Home's currency depreciates, and Foreign output may rise or fall.
2. *Effect of a permanent fiscal expansion by Home.* Home output rises, Home's currency appreciates, and Foreign output rises.

CASE STUDY   Transformation and Crisis in the World Economy

The fall of the Berlin Wall in 1989 marked the beginning of the end of the Soviet empire. Ultimately, the former Soviet bloc countries would embrace market structures and enter the world economy. At the same time, China was continuing a gradual process of market-oriented reforms begun in 1978, reforms that were starting to lead to rapid economic growth and modernization. These simultaneous changes would greatly increase the size of the global economy and labor force by the turn of the century.

CRISES IN EUROPE AND ASIA, 1990–1999

The reunification of West and East Germany on July 1, 1990, set off inflationary pressures in Germany. At the same time, other European countries were pegging their exchange rates to Germany's former currency, the deutsche mark (DM), within

---

[27]The Foreign money market equilibrium condition is $M^*/P^* = L(R^*, Y^*)$. Because M^* is not changing and P^* is sticky and therefore fixed in the short run, Foreign output can rise only if the Foreign nominal interest rate rises too and can fall only if the Foreign nominal interest rate falls.

[28]By considering the Home money market equilibrium condition (in analogy to the previous footnote), you will see that Home's nominal interest rate must rise. A parallel argument shows that Foreign's interest rate rises at the same time.

the European Union's fixed exchange rate mechanism, the European Monetary System (EMS). Germany's contractionary monetary response to its internal inflation pressures led to slower growth in its EMS partners, many of whom were not afflicted by rising inflation as Germany was. The resulting asymmetric pressures within the EMS led to a massive speculative attack on the EMS fixed parities in 1992.

Japanese inflation rose in 1989, in part the result of a relatively loose monetary policy from 1986 to 1988 designed to avoid further yen appreciation after the sharp post-Plaza Accord rise. Two very visible symptoms of these pressures were skyrocketing prices for Japanese real estate and stocks. The Bank of Japan's strategy of puncturing these asset price bubbles through restrictive monetary policy and high interest rates succeeded well, and Tokyo's Nikkei stock price index lost more than half its value between 1990 and 1992. Unfortunately, the sharp fall in asset prices threw Japan's banking system into crisis and the economy into recession by early 1992.

Recovery never really took hold. By 1998, the Japanese economy seemed to be in free fall, with shrinking GDP, declining prices, and its highest unemployment level in more than four decades. Japan's deflation and stagnation would prove protracted indeed, lasting with little interruption through the following decade and a half.

In 1997–1998, however, the problems of the Japanese economy spilled over to the developing countries in East Asia, with which it trades heavily. As we shall see in Chapter 11, many of these economies had experienced spectacularly rapid rates of GDP growth for many years through 1997. Many of them also held their exchange rates fixed, or in target ranges, against the U.S. dollar. Japan's slowdown in 1997 therefore weakened the East Asian economies.

The eventual result was a cascading series of speculative attacks on East Asian currencies, beginning with Thailand's baht in the spring of 1997 and moving on to Malaysia, Indonesia, and Korea. These economies fell into deep recessions (as we discuss further in Chapter 11), pulled down by Japan but also pulling Japan down in a vicious circle. Russia defaulted on its internal and external debts in 1998, setting off global investor jitters and domestic financial chaos. The fear of a worldwide depression prompted a series of interest rate cuts by the Federal Reserve, as well as an unprecedented coordinated interest rate cut by the 11 European countries preparing to give up their national currencies in 1999 in favor of the euro. These measures helped to avert a global economic meltdown.

THE DOT-COM CRASH AND THE EMERGENCE OF GLOBAL IMBALANCES

The U.S. stock market soared in the late 1990s as money flooded into high-tech, "dot-com" stocks related to new, Internet-based technologies. Investment rose and the U.S. current account deficit swelled. When stock prices began to collapse in 2000, helping to create a recession, the Federal Reserve cut interest rates aggressively. Despite a fall in investment, the U.S. current account deficit was soon on the rise again because of falling saving. One factor reducing U.S. saving was a rapid increase in real estate prices, illustrated in Figure 8-7. Interest rates were low, and as Americans borrowed against their rising home equity values, the net U.S. household saving rate turned negative. As a result, the U.S. current account deficit reached an unprecedented 6 percent of GDP by the middle of the decade (see Figure 2-2), and the dollar began to depreciate (see Figure 8-6). Real estate prices escalated as well in many countries outside the United States, ranging from the United Kingdom to Spain to Estonia, and these countries, like the United States, also tended to run bigger trade deficits.

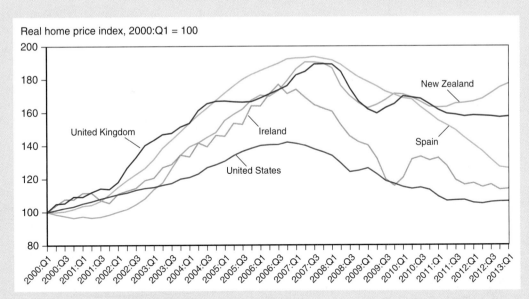

FIGURE 8-7   MyEconLab Real-time data

Real Home Prices in Selected Countries, 2000–2013

Home prices in the United States rose at an accelerating pace through 2006 before collapsing. However, the pace of price increase was even greater in a number of other countries.

Source: Federal Reserve Bank of Dallas, from http://www.dallasfed.org/institute/houseprice/index.cfm. Nominal home price index is divided by a personal consumption price deflator to obtain the real index.

Indeed, during the years after 1999, the pattern of global external imbalances widened sharply. Figure 8-8 gives a picture of this process. It is useful to think of the negative entries in the figure (the deficit entries) as showing net demands for global savings, while the positive entries (the surplus entries) show net supplies of savings (saving in excess of domestic investment needs). In an equilibrium for the global financial markets, the worldwide demand for savings equals the worldwide supply, which is another way of saying that the current account balances of all countries must add up to zero.

On the demand side, the dramatic explosion of the U.S. current account deficit was the dominant development. Because the current account equals saving minus investment, a large U.S. deficit meant that American investment (in effect, a demand for savings) far exceeded the supply of savings generated by American households, firms, and governmental units. Also contributing to the global demand for savings, though on a much smaller scale, was the investment-driven demand coming from the rapidly developing countries of Central and Eastern Europe (see Figure 8-8).

The puzzling feature of the data is that, as the U.S. deficit widened—reflecting an *increase* in American demand for the world's savings—the U.S. real long-term interest rate *fell*, continuing a process that had begun around 2000 when the dot-com crash reduced investment demand and market expectations of future economic growth (see Figure 8-9). Lower real interest rates helped drive American home prices higher, encouraging people to borrow against home equity and spend more out of national income, as noted above. It would seem more natural, instead, for real

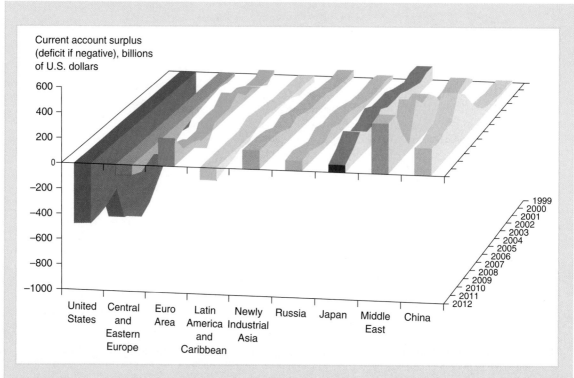

FIGURE 8-8

Global External Imbalances, 1999–2012

During the 2000s, the large increase in the U.S. current account deficit was financed by increases in the surpluses of Asian countries (notably China), Latin America, and oil exporters. After 2007 the imbalances shrank but remained substantial.

Source: International Monetary Fund, *World Economic Outlook* database.

interest rates to have *risen*, encouraging U.S. saving and discouraging U.S. investment. How could the opposite, a fall in real interest rates, have happened? Why, moreover, was this phenomenon also seen in other countries, as shown in Figure 8-9? The answer must lie in a change in saving and investment behavior outside of the United States.

Figure 8-8 shows that over the 2000s, current account surpluses rose in Russia, the Middle East, Asia (notably China, but also Japan and newly industrialized countries such as Singapore and Taiwan), and Latin America. The surplus of Africa (not shown in the figure) also increased. Economists still debate the causes of these surpluses, but a number of likely factors stand out. One of these was the emergence of China as a major player in the world economy, especially after it joined the World Trade Organization in December 2001. Growth in the private Chinese economy starting in the late 1970s led to very rapid economic expansion, but also to economic disruption for much of the country's huge population—for example, a reduction in social benefits such as health care, which state-owned firms had earlier supplied. As a precautionary measure, the Chinese saved more than they had in the past. At the same time, China's torrid economic growth (coupled with rather strong growth in the United States) increased the prices of a range of primary commodities, notably petroleum. The revenues from exporting Brazilian soybeans and iron, Malaysian palm oil, and Russian,

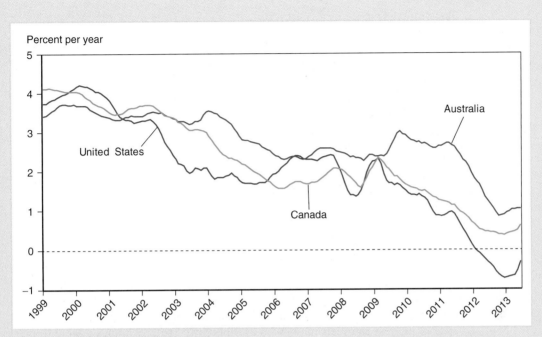

FIGURE 8-9   MyEconLab Real-time data

Long-Term Real Interest Rates for the United States, Australia, and Canada, 1999–2013

Real interest rates fell to low levels in the 2000s. Many countries followed the same trend.

Source: Global Financial Data. Real interest rates are six-month moving averages of monthly interest rate observations on ten-year inflation-indexed government bonds.

Venezuelan, Congolese, and Saudi petroleum all soared. These economic windfalls, running ahead of the recipients' abilities to spend or invest them, also helped to raise worldwide saving.

A second factor was at work in raising current account surpluses outside the United States. The economic and financial crises of the late 1990s had made poorer countries more cautious in their fiscal policies, and also reduced their willingness to invest. Similarly, economic uncertainty in Japan depressed investment demand there. One result of more conservative economic policies in the developing world was the rapid accumulation of U.S. dollar reserves as mentioned previously, an outcome that provided these poorer countries with a welcome cushion against possible future economic misfortunes.

To summarize, the higher supply of savings from countries outside of the United States, coupled with generally lower investment demand, more than offset the effects on the global financial markets of the higher American current account deficit. The result was a fall in global interest rates, which contributed to global house-price appreciation.[29]

---

[29]Problem 13 at the end of this chapter suggests a simple economic framework that will help you think through the effects of shifts in the world's demand and supply curves for savings. The article by Ben Bernanke in Further Readings offers a detailed analysis of the low real interest rates of the mid-2000s.

THE GLOBAL FINANCIAL CRISIS

In August 2007, a serious financial crisis erupted, this time not in the developing world but in the credit markets of the United States and Europe. The crisis spread worldwide, snowballing into a worldwide financial panic and recession in 2008–2009. The roots of the crisis lay in the U.S. home mortgage market. We will study the financial aspects of the crisis and its spread in much greater detail in the next chapter.

One key element leading to the crisis was the period of lower long-term real interest rates, shown in Figure 8-9. Low interest rates contributed to the run-up in home prices in the United States and in many other countries, and in the United States led to much riskier practices among mortgage lenders (for example, lending with minimal or zero down payments, or with temporarily low "teaser" interest rates). To make matters worse, these "subprime" or "nonprime" mortgages were repackaged and sold to other investors worldwide, investors who had little idea in many cases of the risks they were taking on.

Such low real interest rates could not last forever. Eventually, commodity exporters' consumption began to catch up to their income, and world investment demand rose. As you can see in the figure, real interest rates were low from 2003 to the end of 2005, and then rose sharply in the United States. This abrupt rise in interest rates left many who had borrowed to buy homes unable to meet their monthly mortgage payments. In turn, the homeowners' creditors ran into trouble, and the credit crisis of 2007 erupted. At higher interest rate levels, many of the subprime home loans made earlier in the 2000s by aggressive mortgage lenders started to look as if they would never be repaid. The lenders (including banks around the world) then encountered serious difficulties in borrowing themselves.

Despite interest rate cuts by many central banks and other financial interventions aimed at aiding their economies, the world slipped into recession. The recession deepened dramatically as the financial crisis itself intensified in the autumn of 2008 (for details see Chapter 9). Global trade contracted at a rate initially more rapid than during first stage of the Great Depression.[30] Major countries, including the United States and China, rolled out large fiscal stimulus programs while central banks, in many cases, pushed their target nominal interest rates close to zero. (Figure 3-2 shows the interest rates in the United States and Japan.) While these policies prevented the world economy from going into free fall, unemployment rose sharply the world over (see Table 8-2), and output generally contracted in 2009. By 2010, the world economy had stabilized, but growth remained tepid in the industrial world, unemployment was slow to decline, and the recession left many governments with sharply higher fiscal deficits that could not be sustained indefinitely. Global current account imbalances declined but remained significant. In the years following 2009, much of the developing world recovered more robustly from the crisis than did the industrial world, but in the

[30]For a fascinating comparison of 2008 and its aftermath with the Great Depression of the interwar period, see Barry Eichengreen and Kevin Hjortshøj O'Rourke, "What Do the New Data Tell Us?" *Vox: Research-Based Policy Analysis and Commentary from Leading Economists,* March 8, 2010 (at http://www.voxeu.org/article/tale-two-depressions-what-do-new-data-tell-us-february-2010-update#apr609).

United States, Europe, and Japan, recovery from the worst global crisis since the Great Depression remained halting and fragile. Because industrial-country monetary policies remained ultra-loose long after developing countries began to worry again about inflation, developing-country currencies appreciated, causing problems for exporters in those countries. Policymakers in countries such as Brazil accused richer countries of launching "currency wars": easy monetary policies that were forcing poorer countries to choose between less competitive exchange rates and inflation.

In Japan, continuing deflation finally led in 2013, after more than two decades of lethargic economic growth, to an ambitious plan both to revitalize the economy and control a gross government debt that had grown to more than twice the size of GDP. One component of the plan was a Bank of Japan pledge to double the money supply quickly and thereby raise the rate of inflation. The ultimate success of this bold initiative is unknown at the time of writing. In developments that we will take up in Chapter 10, the euro area's recovery stalled and reversed as an existential crisis erupted late in 2009. The euro crisis was driven by the slow growth, unemployment, banking problems, and high public debts bequeathed by the 2007–2009 global crisis, and it also remains unresolved as of this writing.

What Has Been Learned Since 1973?

Earlier in this chapter, we outlined the main elements of the case for floating exchange rates. Having examined the events of the recent floating-rate period, we now briefly compare experience with the predictions made before 1973 by the proponents of floating.

Monetary Policy Autonomy

There is no question that floating gave central banks the ability to control their money supplies and to choose their preferred rates of trend inflation. As a result, floating exchange rates allowed a much larger international divergence in inflation. Did exchange depreciation offset inflation differentials between countries over the floating-rate period? Figure 8-10 compares domestic currency depreciation against the dollar with the difference between domestic and U.S. inflation for the six largest industrial market economies outside the United States. The PPP theory predicts that the points in the figure should lie along the 45-degree line, indicating proportional exchange rate and relative price level changes, but this is not exactly the case. While Figure 8-10 therefore confirms the lesson of Chapter 5 that PPP has not always held closely, even over long periods of time, it does show that on balance, high-inflation countries have tended to have weaker currencies than their low-inflation neighbors. Furthermore, most of the difference in depreciation rates is due to inflation differences, making PPP a major factor behind long-run nominal exchange rate variability.

While the inflation insulation part of the policy autonomy argument is broadly supported as a *long-run* proposition, economic analysis and experience both show that in the short run, the effects of monetary as well as fiscal changes are transmitted across national borders under floating rates. The two-country macroeconomic model

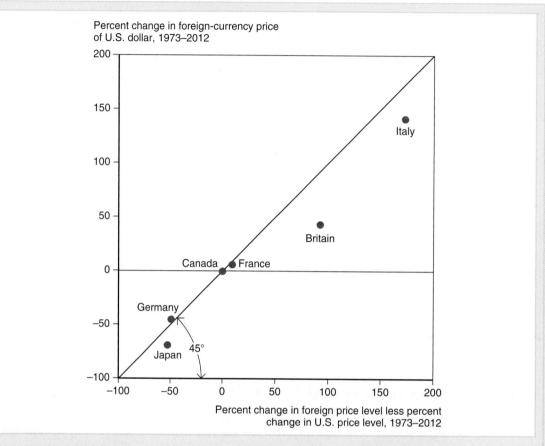

FIGURE 8-10

Exchange Rate Trends and Inflation Differentials, 1973–2012

Over the floating-rate period as a whole, higher inflation has been associated with greater currency depreciation. The exact relationship predicted by relative PPP, however, has not held for most countries. The inflation difference on the horizontal axis is calculated as $(\pi - \pi_{US}) \div (1 + \pi_{US}/100)$ using the exact relative PPP relation given in footnote 1 on page 114.

Source: International Monetary Fund and Global Financial Data.

developed earlier, for example, shows that monetary policy affects output in the short run both at home and abroad as long as it alters the real exchange rate. Skeptics of floating were therefore right in claiming that floating rates would not insulate countries completely from foreign policy shocks.

Symmetry

Because central banks continued to hold dollar reserves and intervene, the international monetary system did not become symmetric after 1973. The euro gained importance as an international reserve currency (and the British pound declined), but the dollar remained the primary component of most central banks' official reserves.

Economist Ronald McKinnon of Stanford University has argued that the current floating-rate system is similar in some ways to the asymmetric reserve currency system underlying the Bretton Woods arrangements.[31] He suggests that changes in the world money supply would have been dampened under a more symmetric monetary adjustment mechanism. In the 2000s, China's policy of limiting its currency's appreciation against the dollar led it to accumulate vast dollar reserves, possibly reinforcing the worldwide economic boom that preceded the 2007–2009 financial crisis. As a result, some economists have characterized the period of the early and mid-2000s as a "revived Bretton Woods system."[32]

The Exchange Rate as an Automatic Stabilizer

The world economy has undergone major structural changes since 1973. Because these shifts changed relative national output prices (Figure 8-6), it is doubtful that any pattern of fixed exchange rates would have been viable without some significant parity changes. The industrial economies certainly wouldn't have weathered the two oil shocks as well as they did while defending fixed exchange rates. In the absence of capital controls, speculative attacks similar to those that brought down the Bretton Woods system would have occurred periodically, as recent experience has shown. Under floating, however, many countries were able to relax the capital controls put in place earlier. The progressive loosening of controls spurred the rapid growth of a global financial industry and allowed countries to realize greater gains from intertemporal trade and from trade in assets.

The effects of the U.S. fiscal expansion after 1981 illustrate the stabilizing properties of a floating exchange rate. As the dollar appreciated, U.S. inflation was slowed, American consumers enjoyed an improvement in their terms of trade, and economic recovery was spread abroad.

The dollar's appreciation after 1981 also illustrates a problem with the view that floating rates can cushion the economy from real disturbances such as shifts in aggregate demand. Even though *overall* output and the price level may be cushioned, some sectors of the economy may be hurt. For example, while the dollar's appreciation helped transmit U.S. fiscal expansion abroad in the 1980s, it worsened the plight of American agriculture, which did not benefit directly from the higher government demand. Real exchange rate changes can do damage by causing excessive adjustment problems in some sectors and by generating calls for increased protection.

Permanent changes in goods market conditions require eventual adjustment in real exchange rates that can be speeded by a floating-rate system. Foreign exchange intervention to peg nominal exchange rates cannot prevent this eventual adjustment because money is neutral in the long run and thus is powerless to alter relative prices permanently. The events of the 1980s show, however, that if it is costly for factors of production to move between sectors of the economy, there is a case for pegging rates in the face of temporary output market shocks. Unfortunately, this lesson leaves policy makers with the difficult task of determining which disturbances are temporary and which are permanent.

External Balance

As Figure 8-8 makes clear, the floating exchange rate system did not prevent large and persistent departures from external balance. True, China's refusal to allow a free

---

[31]Ronald I. McKinnon, *An International Standard for Monetary Stabilization*, Policy Analyses in International Economics 8 (Washington, D.C.: Institute for International Economics, 1984).

[32]See Michael Dooley, David Folkerts-Landau, and Peter Garber, *International Financial Stability: Asia, Interest Rates, and the Dollar*, 2nd edition (New York: Deutsche Bank Securities Inc., 2008).

float of its own currency is part of the story of the large global imbalances of the 2000s. If the Chinese yuan had been free to appreciate in the foreign exchange market, China's surpluses and the corresponding deficits elsewhere in the world might have been smaller.

But even before China's emergence as a world economic power and before the creation of the euro, large current account deficits and surpluses, such as the U.S. deficit of the 1980s and Japan's persistent surpluses, certainly occurred. Financial markets were evidently capable of driving exchange rates far from values consistent with external balance, as suggested by Figure 8-6 for the case of the dollar. Under floating, external imbalances have persisted for years before exchange rates have adjusted. Long swings in real exchange rates that leave countries far from external balance are called *misalignments*, and they frequently inspire political pressures for protection from imports.

The Problem of Policy Coordination

Problems of international policy coordination clearly have not disappeared under floating exchange rates. The problem of resolving global imbalances provides a good example, in the sense that unilateral action by deficit countries to reduce their imbalances would lead to global deflation, while surplus countries have little incentive to avoid that outcome by pumping up their internal demand and appreciating their currencies.

There are other examples that are perhaps even more striking, in the sense that all countries would clearly benefit if they could commit to coordinating their policies rather than going it alone in beggar-thy-neighbor fashion. For example, during the disinflation of the early 1980s, industrial countries as a group could have attained their macroeconomic goals more effectively by negotiating a joint approach to common objectives. The appendix to this chapter presents a formal model, based on that example, to illustrate how all countries can gain through international policy coordination.

Another instance comes from the global fiscal response to the recession that the 2007–2009 crisis caused. We saw earlier in this chapter (and in Chapter 6) that when a country raises government spending, part of the expansionary impact leaks abroad. The country will pay the cost of the policy, however, in the form of a higher government deficit. Since countries do not internalize all the benefits of their own fiscal expansions but pay the cost in full, they will adopt too little of it in a global recession.

If countries could negotiate an agreement *jointly* to expand, however, they might be more effective in fighting the recession (and they might even experience lower fiscal costs). The response to the 2007–2009 crisis was discussed periodically by the Group of Twenty (G20) nations, an informal grouping of leading industrial and developing countries including Argentina, Brazil, China, India, and Russia. In the early stages of the crisis, there was widespread agreement on the fiscal response within the G20. Later on, as countries experienced more divergent rates of recovery, policy coordination became more difficult and G20 meetings yielded fewer concrete results.

Are Fixed Exchange Rates Even an Option for Most Countries?

Is there any practical alternative to floating exchange rates when financial markets are open to international trade? The post-Bretton Woods experience suggests a stark hypothesis: Durable fixed exchange rate arrangements may not even be *possible*. In a financially integrated world in which funds can move instantly between national financial markets, fixed exchange rates cannot be credibly maintained over the long run unless countries are willing to maintain controls over capital movements (as China does), or, at the other extreme, move to a shared single currency with their monetary partners (as in Europe). Short of these measures, the argument goes, attempts to fix exchange rates will necessarily lack credibility and be relatively short-lived. You will recognize that these predictions follow from the trilemma.[33]

This pessimistic view of fixed exchange rates is based on the theory that speculative currency crises can, at least in part, be self-fulfilling events (recall Chapter 7). According to that view, even a country following prudent monetary and fiscal policies is not safe from speculative attacks on its fixed exchange rate. Once the country encounters an economic reversal, as it eventually must, currency speculators will pounce, forcing domestic interest rates sky-high and inflicting enough economic pain that the government will choose to abandon its exchange rate target.

At the turn of the 21st century, speculative attacks on fixed exchange rate arrangements—in Europe, East Asia, and elsewhere—were occurring with seemingly increasing frequency. The number and circumstances of those crises lent increasing plausibility to the argument that it is impossible to peg currency values for long while maintaining open capital markets and national policy sovereignty. Moreover, many countries outside the industrial world have allowed much greater exchange rate flexibility in recent years, and apparently benefited from it, as we shall see in Chapter 11. Some countries appear to be moving toward either greater control over cross-border financial flows or more drastic sacrifices of monetary autonomy (for example, adopting the euro). It seems likely that policy coordination issues will be confronted in the future within a system in which different countries choose different policy regimes, subject to the constraints of the monetary trilemma.

SUMMARY

1. In an open economy, policy makers try to maintain *internal balance* (full employment and a stable price level) and *external balance* (a current account level that is neither so negative that the country may be unable to repay its foreign debts nor so positive that foreigners are put in that position). The definition of external balance depends on a number of factors, including the exchange rate regime and world economic conditions. Because each country's macroeconomic policies have repercussions abroad, a country's ability to reach internal and external balance depends on the policies other countries choose to adopt. A country running large, persistent deficits might appear to be violating its *intertemporal budget constraint*, putting it in danger of facing a *sudden stop* in foreign lending.

2. The limitations of alternative exchange rate regimes can be understood in terms of the open-economy *monetary trilemma*, which states that countries must choose

---

[33]For an early statement of the hypothesis that fixed exchange rates combined with mobile capital can be unstable, see Maurice Obstfeld, "Floating Exchange Rates: Experience and Prospects," *Brookings Papers on Economic Activity* 2 (1985), pp. 369–450. For more recent discussions see Barry Eichengreen, *International Monetary Arrangements for the 21st Century* (Washington, D.C.: Brookings Institution, 1994); Lars E. O. Svensson, "Fixed Exchange Rates as a Means to Price Stability: What Have We Learned?" *European Economic Review* 38 (May 1994), pp. 447–468; Maurice Obstfeld and Kenneth Rogoff, "The Mirage of Fixed Exchange Rates," *Journal of Economic Perspectives* 9 (Fall 1995), pp. 73–96; and the book by Klein and Shambaugh in Further Readings.

two of the following three features of a monetary policy system: exchange rate stability, freedom of cross-border financial flows, and monetary policy autonomy.

3. The gold standard system contained a powerful automatic mechanism for ensuring external balance, the *price-specie-flow mechanism*. The flows of gold accompanying deficits and surpluses caused price changes that reduced current account imbalances and therefore tended to return all countries to external balance. The system's performance in maintaining internal balance was mixed, however. With the eruption of World War I in 1914, the gold standard was suspended.

4. Attempts to return to the prewar gold standard after 1918 were unsuccessful. As the world economy moved into general depression after 1929, the restored gold standard fell apart, and international economic integration weakened. In the turbulent economic conditions of the period, governments made internal balance their main concern and tried to avoid the external balance problem by partially shutting their economies off from the rest of the world. The result was a world economy in which all countries' situations could have been bettered through international cooperation.

5. The architects of the *International Monetary Fund (IMF)* hoped to design a fixed exchange rate system that would encourage growth in international trade while making the demands of external balance sufficiently flexible that they could be met without sacrificing internal balance. To this end, the IMF charter provided financing facilities for deficit countries and allowed exchange rate adjustments under conditions of "fundamental disequilibrium." All countries pegged their currencies to the dollar. The United States pegged to gold and agreed to exchange gold for dollars with foreign central banks at a price of $35 an ounce.

6. After *currency convertibility* was restored in Europe in 1958, countries' financial markets became more closely integrated, monetary policy became less effective (except for the United States), and movements in international reserves became more volatile. These changes revealed a key weakness in the system. To reach internal and external balance at the same time, *expenditure-switching* as well as *expenditure-changing* policies were needed. But the possibility of expenditure-switching policies (exchange rate changes) could give rise to speculative financial flows that would undermine fixed exchange rates. As the main reserve currency country, the United States faced a unique external balance problem: the *confidence problem*, which would arise as foreign official dollar holdings inevitably grew to exceed U.S. gold holdings. A series of international crises led in stages to the abandonment by March 1973 of both the dollar's link to gold and fixed dollar exchange rates for the industrialized countries.

7. Before 1973, the weaknesses of the Bretton Woods system led many economists to advocate floating exchange rates. They made four main arguments in favor of floating. First, they argued that floating rates would give national macroeconomic policy makers greater autonomy in managing their economies. Second, they predicted that floating rates would remove the asymmetries of the Bretton Woods arrangements. Third, they pointed out that floating exchange rates would quickly eliminate the "fundamental disequilibriums" that had led to parity changes and speculative attacks under fixed rates. Fourth, they claimed that these same exchange rate movements would prevent large, persistent departures from external balance.

8. In the early years of floating, floating rates seemed, on the whole, to function well. In particular, it is unlikely that the industrial countries could have maintained fixed exchange rates in the face of the *stagflation* caused by two oil shocks. The

dollar suffered a sharp depreciation after 1976, however, as the United States adopted macroeconomic policies more expansionary than those of other industrial countries.

9. A sharp turn toward slower monetary growth in the United States, coupled with a rising U.S. government budget deficit, contributed to massive dollar appreciation between 1980 and early 1985. Other industrial economies pursued disinflation along with the United States, and the resulting worldwide monetary slowdown, coming soon after the second oil shock, led to a deep global recession. As the recovery from the recession slowed in late 1984 and the U.S. current account began to register record deficits, political pressure for wide-ranging trade restrictions gathered momentum in Washington. At the Plaza Hotel in New York in September 1985, the United States and four other major industrial countries agreed to take concerted action to bring down the dollar.

10. Exchange rate stability was downplayed as a prime policy goal in the 1990s and 2000s. Instead, governments aimed to target low domestic inflation while maintaining economic growth. After 2000, global external imbalances widened dramatically. In the United States and other countries, external deficits were associated with rapidly increasing housing prices. When these collapsed starting in 2006, the global financial system seized up and the world economy went into deep recession.

11. One unambiguous lesson of these experiences seems to be that no exchange rate system functions well when international economic cooperation breaks down. Severe limits on exchange rate flexibility among the major currencies are unlikely to be reinstated in the near future. But increased consultation among international policy makers should improve the performance of the international monetary system.

KEY TERMS

balance of payments
   equilibrium, p. 247
Bretton Woods agreement,
   p. 253
confidence problem, p. 262
convertible currency, p. 256
expenditure-changing policy,
   p. 260

expenditure-switching policy,
   p. 261
external balance, p. 237
internal balance, p. 237
International Monetary Fund
   (IMF), p. 254
intertemporal budget
   constraint, p. 240

monetary trilemma, p. 245
nominal and real effective
   exchange rate indexes, p. 272
price-specie-flow mechanism,
   p. 247
stagflation, p. 271
sudden stop, p. 240

PROBLEMS

MyEconLab

1. If you were in charge of macroeconomic policies in a small open economy, what qualitative effect would each of the following events have on your target for external balance?
   a. Large deposits of uranium are discovered in the interior of your country.
   b. The world price of your main export good, copper, rises permanently.
   c. The world price of copper rises temporarily.
   d. There is a temporary rise in the world price of oil.

2. Under a gold standard of the kind analyzed by Hume, describe how balance of payments equilibrium between two countries, A and B, would be restored after a transfer of income from B to A.

3. Despite the flaws of the pre-1914 gold standard, exchange rate changes were rare for the "core" countries (including the richer European countries and the United States). In contrast, such changes became frequent in the interwar period. Can you think of reasons for this contrast?

4. Under a gold standard, countries may adopt excessively contractionary monetary policies as all countries scramble in vain for a larger share of the limited supply of world gold reserves. Can the same problem arise under a reserve currency standard when bonds denominated in different currencies are all perfect substitutes?

5. A central bank that adopts a fixed exchange rate may sacrifice its autonomy in setting domestic monetary policy. It is sometimes argued that when this is the case, the central bank also gives up the ability to use monetary policy to combat the wage-price spiral. The argument goes like this: "Suppose workers demand higher wages and employers give in, but the employers then raise output prices to cover their higher costs. Now the price level is higher and real balances are momentarily lower, so to prevent an interest rate rise that would appreciate the currency, the central bank must buy foreign exchange currencies and expand the money supply. This action accommodates the initial wage demands with monetary growth, and the economy moves permanently to a higher level of wages and prices. With a fixed exchange rate, there is thus no way of keeping wages and prices down." What is wrong with this argument?

6. Suppose the central bank of a small country with a fixed exchange rate is faced by a rise in the world interest rate, R^*. What is the effect on its foreign reserve holdings? On its money supply? Can it offset either of these effects through domestic open-market operations?

7. How might restrictions on private financial account transactions alter the problem of attaining internal and external balance with a fixed exchange rate? What costs might such restrictions involve?

8. In the box on New Zealand, we derived an equation showing how the *IIP* changes over time: $IIP_{t+1} = (1 + r)IIP_t + NX_t$. Show that if $g = (GDP_{t+1} - GDP_t)/GDP_t$ is the growth rate of nominal output (GDP), and lower-case variables denote ratios to nominal GDP (as in the chapter), we can express this same equation in the form:

$$iip_{t+1} = \frac{(1 + r)iip_t + nx_t}{1 + g}.$$

Use this expression to find the ratio of net exports to GDP that holds the *IIP* to GDP ratio *iip* constant over time.

9. You are an economic adviser to the government of China in 2008. The country has a current account surplus and is facing gathering inflationary pressures.
   a. Show the location of the Chinese economy on a diagram like Figure 8-2.
   b. What would be your advice on how the authorities should move the yuan renminbi's exchange rate?
   What would be your advice about fiscal policy? In that regard, you have three pieces of data: First, the current account surplus is big, in excess of 9 percent of GDP. Second, China currently provides a rather low level of government services to its people. Third, China's government would like to attract workers from the rural countryside into manufacturing employment, so Chinese officials would prefer to soften any negative impact of their policy package on urban employment.

10. Use the *DD-AA* model to examine the effects of a one-time rise in the foreign price level, P^*. If the expected future exchange rate E^e falls immediately in proportion to P^* (in line with PPP), show that the exchange rate will also appreciate immediately in proportion to the rise in P^*. If the economy is initially in internal and external balance, will its position be disturbed by such a rise in P^*?

11. If the foreign *inflation rate* rises permanently, would you expect a floating exchange rate to insulate the domestic economy in the short run? What would happen in the long run? In answering the latter question, pay attention to the long-run relationship between domestic and foreign nominal interest rates.

12. Imagine that domestic and foreign currency bonds are imperfect substitutes and that investors suddenly shift their demand toward foreign currency bonds, raising the risk premium on domestic assets (Chapter 7). Which exchange rate regime minimizes the effect on output—fixed or floating?

13. The Case Study starting on page 275 discussed the big global imbalances of the 2000s and suggested that one can analyze factors determining world real interest rates in terms of the balance between the world demand for savings (in order to finance investment) and the world supply of savings (just as in a closed economy—which the world is). As a first step in formalizing such an analysis, assume there are no international differences in real interest rates due to expected real exchange rate changes. (For example, you might suppose that yours is a long-run analysis in which real exchange rates are expected to remain at their long-run levels.) As a second step, assume that a higher real interest rate reduces desired investment and raises desired saving throughout the world. Can you then devise a simple supply-demand picture of equilibrium in the world capital market in which quantities (saved or invested) are on the horizontal axis and the real interest rate is on the vertical axis? In such a setting, how would an increase in world saving, defined in the usual way as an outward shift in the entire supply-of-savings schedule, affect equilibrium saving, investment, and the real interest rate? Relate your discussion to the last Case Study in the chapter and to the paper by Ben S. Bernanke in Further Readings. [For a classic exposition of a similar model, see Lloyd A. Metzler, "The Process of International Adjustment under Conditions of Full Employment: A Keynesian View," in Richard E. Caves and Harry G. Johnson, eds., *Readings in International Economics* (Homewood, IL: Richard D. Irwin, Inc. for the American Economic Association, 1968), pp. 465–486.]

14. The chapter suggested that because large increases in oil prices transfer income to countries that cannot rapidly increase their consumption or investment and therefore must save their windfalls, world real interest rates fall in the short run. Put together data on the U.S. real interest rate for 1970–1976, a period that includes the first OPEC oil shock. How did the U.S. real interest rate behave? (You may assume that expected inflation rates equal actual inflation rates.)

15. We noted in this chapter that foreign central banks, especially in Asia, accumulated large dollar foreign reserves after 2000. One persistent worry was that those central banks, fearing dollar depreciation, would shift their reserve holdings from dollars to euros. Show that this action would be equivalent to a huge sterilized sale of dollars in the foreign exchange market. What might be the effects? Be sure to spell out your assumption about perfect versus imperfect asset substitutability.

16. Like its neighbor New Zealand, Australia has had a long string of current account deficits and is an international debtor. Go to the Australian Bureau of Statistics website at http://www.abs.gov.au/AUSSTATS and find the data you need to carry out an "external sustainability" analysis of the current account such as the one

for New Zealand in the chapter. You will need data starting in 1992 for nominal GDP, the IIP, the current account, and the balance on goods and services NX (from "time series spreadsheets"). The goal of the exercise is to find the interest rate r on the IIP that stabilizes the ratio IIP/GDP at its most recent value given the historical average of NX and the historical average of nominal GDP growth (all since 1992). Warning: This is a challenging exercise that requires you to navigate the Australian data system and judge the most appropriate data to use in light of what you learned in Chapter 2.

FURTHER READINGS

Liaquat Ahamed. *Lords of Finance: The Bankers Who Broke the World.* New York: Penguin Press, 2009. Lively historical account of international monetary crises between the world wars of the twentieth century.

Ben S. Bernanke. "The Global Saving Glut and the U.S. Current Account Deficit." Sandridge Lecture, March 10, 2005, at www.federalreserve.gov/boarddocs/speeches/2005/200503102/default.htm. The Federal Reserve chairman's diagnosis of the low real interest rates of the mid-2000s.

Olivier J. Blanchard and Gian Maria Milesi-Ferretti. "(Why) Should Current Account Balances Be Reduced?" *IMF Economic Review* 60 (April 2012), pp. 139–150. The authors offer a concise, up-to-date survey of the hazards of very large current account deficits and surpluses.

Richard H. Clarida. *G-3 Exchange Rate Relationships: A Review of the Record and Proposals for Change.* Princeton Essays in International Economics 219. International Economics Section, Department of Economics, Princeton University, September 2000. Critical review of various target zone proposals for limiting exchange rate movements.

W. Max Corden. "The Geometric Representation of Policies to Attain Internal and External Balance." *Review of Economic Studies* 28 (January 1960): 1–22. A classic diagrammatic analysis of expenditure-switching and expenditure-changing macroeconomic policies.

Barry Eichengreen. *Globalizing Capital: A History of the International Monetary System,* 2nd edition. Princeton: Princeton University Press, 2008. Compact, insightful overview of international monetary history from the gold standard to the present day.

Milton Friedman. "The Case for Flexible Exchange Rates," in *Essays in Positive Economics.* Chicago: University of Chicago Press, 1953, pp. 157–203. A classic exposition of the merits of floating exchange rates.

Joseph E. Gagnon. *Flexible Exchange Rates for a Stable World Economy.* Washington, D.C.: Peterson Institute for International Economics, 2011. The author presents an up-to-date case for exchange rate flexibility.

Charles P. Kindleberger. *The World in Depression 1929–1939,* rev. edition. Berkeley and Los Angeles: University of California Press, 1986. A leading international economist examines the causes and effects of the Great Depression.

Michael W. Klein and Jay C. Shambaugh. *Exchange Rate Regimes in the Modern Era.* Cambridge, MA: MIT Press, 2010. Comprehensive analysis of the causes and consequences of alternative exchange rate regimes.

Maurice Obstfeld. "The International Monetary System: Living with Asymmetry," in Robert C. Feenstra and Alan M. Taylor, eds., *Globalization in an Age of Crisis: Multilateral Cooperation in the Twenty-First Century.* Chicago: University of Chicago Press, 2014, pp. 301–336. Overview of the international monetary system in light of the global financial crisis.

Maurice Obstfeld and Alan M. Taylor. *Global Capital Markets: Integration, Crisis, and Growth.* Cambridge, U.K.: Cambridge University Press, 2004. Overview of the linkages between international financial integration and exchange rate regimes.

Robert Solomon. *The International Monetary System, 1945–1981.* New York: Harper & Row, 1982. Excellent chronicle of the Bretton Woods period and the early years of floating. The author was chief of the Federal Reserve's international finance division during the period leading up to the breakdown of fixed exchange rates.

MyEconLab Can Help You Get a Better Grade

MyEconLab   If your exam were tomorrow, would you be ready? For each chapter, MyEconLab Practice Tests and Study Plans pinpoint sections you have mastered and those you need to study. That way, you are more efficient with your study time, and you are better prepared for your exams.

To see how it works, turn to page 9 and then go to

www.myeconlab.com

International Policy Coordination Failures

This appendix illustrates the importance of macroeconomic policy coordination by showing how all countries can suffer as a result of self-centered policy decisions. The phenomenon is another example of the Prisoner's Dilemma of game theory. Governments can achieve macroeconomic outcomes that are better for all if they choose policies cooperatively.

These points are made using an example based on the disinflation of the early 1980s. Recall that contractionary monetary policies in the industrial countries helped throw the world economy into a deep recession in 1981. Countries hoped to reduce inflation by slowing monetary growth, but the situation was complicated by the influence of exchange rates on the price level. A government that adopts a less restrictive monetary policy than its neighbors is likely to face a currency depreciation that partially frustrates its attempts to disinflate.

Many observers feel that in their individual attempts to resist currency depreciation, the industrial countries as a group adopted overly tight monetary policies that deepened the recession. All governments would have been happier if everyone had adopted looser monetary policies, but given the policies that other governments did adopt, it was not in the interest of any individual government to change course.

The argument above can be made more precise with a simple model. There are two countries, Home and Foreign, and each country has two policy options, a very restrictive monetary policy and a somewhat restrictive monetary policy. Figure 8A-1, which is similar to a diagram we used to analyze trade policies, shows the results in Home and Foreign of different policy choices by the two countries. Each row corresponds to a particular monetary policy decision by Home and each column to a decision by Foreign. The boxes contain entries giving changes in Home and Foreign

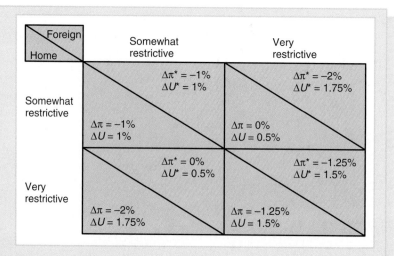

FIGURE 8A-1

Hypothetical Effects of Different Monetary Policy Combinations on Inflation and Unemployment

Monetary policy choices in one country affect the outcomes of monetary policy choices made abroad.

annual inflation rates ($\Delta\pi$ and $\Delta\pi^*$) and unemployment rates (ΔU and ΔU^*). Within each box, lower left entries are Home outcomes and upper right entries are Foreign outcomes.

The hypothetical entries in Figure 8A-1 can be understood in terms of this chapter's two-country model. Under somewhat restrictive policies, for example, inflation rates fall by 1 percent and unemployment rates rise by 1 percent in both countries. If Home suddenly shifts to a very restrictive policy while Foreign stands pat, Home's currency appreciates, its inflation drops further, and its unemployment rises. Home's additional monetary contraction, however, has two effects on Foreign. Foreign's unemployment rate falls, but because Home's currency appreciation is a currency *de*preciation for Foreign, Foreign inflation goes back up to its pre-disinflation level. In Foreign, the deflationary effects of higher unemployment are offset by the inflationary impact of a depreciating currency on import prices and wage demands. Home's sharper monetary crunch therefore has a beggar-thy-neighbor effect on Foreign, which is forced to "import" some inflation from Home.

To translate the outcomes in Figure 8A-1 into policy payoffs, we assume each government wishes to get the biggest reduction in inflation at the lowest cost in terms of unemployment. That is, each government wishes to maximize $-\Delta\pi/\Delta U$, the inflation reduction per point of increased unemployment. The numbers in Figure 8A-1 lead to the payoff matrix shown as Figure 8A-2 .

How do Home and Foreign behave faced with the payoffs in this matrix? Assume each government "goes it alone" and picks the policy that maximizes its own payoff given the other player's policy choice. If Foreign adopts a somewhat restrictive policy, Home does better with a very restrictive policy (payoff $= \frac{8}{7}$) than with a somewhat restrictive one (payoff $= 1$). If Foreign is very restrictive, Home still does better by being very restrictive (payoff $= \frac{5}{6}$) than by being somewhat restrictive (payoff $= 0$). So no matter what Foreign does, Home's government will always choose a very restrictive monetary policy.

Foreign finds itself in a symmetric position. It, too, is better off with a very restrictive policy regardless of what Home does. The result is that both countries will choose very restrictive monetary policies, and each will get a payoff of $\frac{5}{6}$.

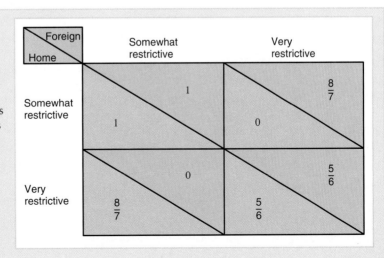

FIGURE 8A-2

Payoff Matrix for Different Monetary Policy Moves

Each entry equals the reduction in inflation per unit rise in the unemployment rate (calculated as $-\Delta\pi/\Delta U$). If each country "goes it alone," they both choose very restrictive policies. Somewhat restrictive policies, if adopted by both countries, lead to an outcome better for both.

Notice, however, that *both* countries are actually better off if they simultaneously adopt the somewhat restrictive policies. The resulting payoff for each is 1, which is greater than $\frac{5}{6}$. Under this last policy configuration, inflation falls less in the two countries, but the rise in unemployment is far less than under very restrictive policies.

Since both countries are better off with somewhat restrictive policies, why aren't these adopted? The answer is at the root of the problem of policy coordination. Our analysis assumed that each country "goes it alone" by maximizing its own payoff. Under this assumption, a situation where both countries were somewhat restrictive would not be stable: Each country would want to reduce its monetary growth further and use its exchange rate to hasten disinflation at its neighbor's expense.

For the superior outcome in the upper left corner of the matrix to occur, Home and Foreign must reach an explicit agreement, that is, they must *coordinate* their policy choices. Both countries must agree to forgo the beggar-thy-neighbor gains offered by very restrictive policies, and each country must abide by this agreement in spite of the incentive to cheat. If Home and Foreign can cooperate, both end up with a preferred mix of inflation and unemployment.

The reality of policy coordination is more complex than in this simple example because the choices and outcomes are more numerous and more uncertain. These added complexities make policy makers less willing to commit themselves to cooperative agreements and less certain that their counterparts abroad will live up to the agreed terms.

CHAPTER 9

FINANCIAL GLOBALIZATION: OPPORTUNITY AND CRISIS

If a financier named Rip van Winkle had gone to sleep in the 1960s and awakened after 50 years, he would have been shocked by changes in both the nature and the scale of international financial activity. In the early 1960s, for example, most banking business was purely domestic, involving the currency and customers of the bank's home country. Five decades later, many banks were deriving a large share of their profits from international activities. To his surprise, Rip would have found that he could locate branches of Citibank in São Paulo, Brazil, and branches of Britain's Barclays Bank in New York. He would also have discovered that it had long since become routine for a branch of an American bank located in London to accept a deposit denominated in Japanese yen from a Swedish corporation, or to lend Swiss francs to a Dutch manufacturer. Finally, he would have noticed much greater participation by nonbank financial institutions in international markets and a huge expansion in the sheer volume of global transactions.

The market in which residents of different countries trade assets is called the **international capital market**. The international capital market is not really a single market; it is instead a group of closely interconnected markets in which asset exchanges with some international dimension take place. International currency trades take place in the foreign exchange market, which is an important part of the international capital market. The main actors in the international capital market are the same as those in the foreign exchange market (Chapter 3): commercial banks, large corporations, nonbank financial institutions, central banks, and other government agencies. And, like the foreign exchange market, the international capital market's activities take place in a network of world financial centers linked by sophisticated communications systems. The assets traded in the international capital market, however, include different countries' stocks and bonds in addition to bank deposits denominated in their currencies.

This chapter discusses four main questions about the international capital market. First, how can this well-oiled global financial network enhance countries' gains from international trade? Second, what has caused the rapid growth in international financial activity since the early 1960s? Third, what dangers are posed by an integrated world capital market straddling national borders? And fourth, how can policy makers minimize problems raised by the global capital market without sharply reducing the benefits it provides?

After reading this chapter, you will be able to:

- Understand the economic function of international portfolio diversification.
- Explain factors leading to the explosive recent growth of international financial markets.
- Analyze problems in the regulation and supervision of international banks and nonbank financial institutions.
- Describe some different methods that have been used to measure the degree of international financial integration.
- Understand the factors leading to the worldwide financial crisis that started in 2007.
- Evaluate the performance of the international capital market in linking the economies of the industrial countries.

The International Capital Market and the Gains from Trade

In earlier chapters, the discussion of gains from international trade concentrated on exchanges involving goods and services. By providing a worldwide payments system that lowers transaction costs, banks active in the international capital market enlarge the trade gains that result from such exchanges. Furthermore, the international capital market brings borrowers and lenders in different countries together in order to finance the global pattern of current account imbalances. But most deals that take place in the international capital market are exchanges of assets between residents of different countries, for example, the exchange of a share of IBM stock for some British government bonds. Although such asset trades are sometimes derided as unproductive "speculation," they do, in fact, lead to gains from trade that can make consumers everywhere better off.

Three Types of Gain from Trade

All transactions between the residents of different countries fall into one of three categories: trades of goods or services for goods or services, trades of goods or services for assets, and trades of assets for assets. At any moment, a country is generally carrying out trades in each of these categories. Figure 9-1 (which assumes that there are two countries, Home and Foreign) illustrates the three types of international transaction, each of which involves a different set of possible gains from trade.

Two of these sources of trade gain may be familiar. The microeconomic theory of international trade shows how countries can gain by concentrating on the production activities in which they are most efficient and by using some of their output to pay for imports of other products from abroad. This type of trade gain involves the exchange of goods or services for other goods or services. The top horizontal arrow in Figure 9-1 shows exchanges of goods and services between Home and Foreign.

FIGURE 9-1

The Three Types of International Transaction

Residents of different countries can trade goods and services for other goods and services, goods and services for assets (that is, for future goods and services), and assets for other assets. All three types of exchange lead to gains from trade.

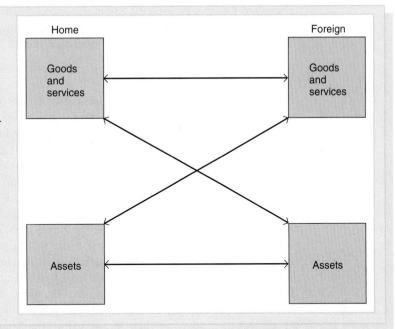

A second set of trade gains results from *intertemporal* trade, which is the exchange of goods and services for claims to future goods and services, that is, for assets (Chapters 6 and 8). When a developing country borrows abroad (that is, sells a bond to foreigners) so that it can import materials for a domestic investment project, it is engaging in intertemporal trade—trade that would not be possible without an international capital market. The diagonal arrows in Figure 9-1 indicate trades of goods and services for assets. If Home has a current account deficit with Foreign, for example, it is a net exporter of assets to Foreign and a net importer of goods and services from Foreign.

The bottom horizontal arrow in Figure 9-1 represents the last category of international transaction, trades of assets for assets, such as the exchange of real estate located in France for U.S. Treasury bonds. In Table 2-2 on page 28, which shows the 2012 U.S. balance of payments accounts, you will see under the financial account both a $97.5 billion purchase of foreign assets by U.S. residents and a $543.9 billion purchase of U.S. assets by foreign residents. (These numbers do not include derivatives; the BEA reports only *net* trade in derivatives.) So while the United States could have financed its current account deficit simply by selling assets to foreigners and not buying any from them, U.S. and foreign residents also engaged in pure asset swapping. Such a large volume of trade in assets between countries occurs in part because international asset trades, like trades involving goods and services, can yield benefits to all the countries involved.

While the preceding distinctions may appear clear-cut in theory, be aware that in the real world, different types of trade may occur together because they are complementary. For example, importers may need to buy foreign goods on the basis of credit from sellers and repay after they have sold the goods to domestic consumers. In this case, the importers' ability to obtain goods today in return for a promise to repay soon after—a form of intertemporal trade—is vital to promoting international exchange of goods and services. As a second example, exporters may need to hedge future foreign exchange receipts in forward exchange markets. In this case, a trade of assets for assets—future foreign currency against future domestic currency—lowers exporters' costs of carrying out goods and services exchanges.

Risk Aversion

When individuals select assets, an important factor in their decisions is the riskiness of each asset's return (Chapter 3). Other things equal, people dislike risk. Economists call this property of people's preferences **risk aversion**. Chapter 7 showed that risk-averse investors in foreign currency assets base their demand for a particular asset on its riskiness (as measured by a risk premium) in addition to its expected return.

An example will make the meaning of risk aversion clearer. Suppose you are offered a gamble in which you win $1,000 half the time but lose $1,000 half the time. Since you are as likely to win as to lose the $1,000, the average payoff on this gamble—its *expected value*—is $\left(\frac{1}{2}\right) \times (\$1,000) + \left(\frac{1}{2}\right) \times (-\$1,000) = 0$. If you are risk averse, you will not take the gamble because, for you, the possibility of losing $1,000 outweighs the possibility that you will win, even though both outcomes are equally likely. Although some people (called risk lovers) enjoy taking risks and would take the gamble, there is much evidence that risk-averse behavior is the norm. For example, risk aversion helps explain the profitability of insurance companies, which sell policies that allow people to protect themselves or their families from the financial risks of theft, illness, and other mishaps.

If people are risk averse, they value a collection (or portfolio) of assets not only on the basis of its expected return but also on the basis of the riskiness of that return. Under risk aversion, for example, people may be willing to hold bonds denominated in several different currencies, even if the interest rates they offer are not linked by the interest parity condition, if the resulting portfolio of assets offers a desirable combination of return and risk. In general, a portfolio whose return fluctuates wildly from year to year is less desirable than one that offers the same average return with only mild year-to-year fluctuations. This observation is basic to understanding why countries exchange assets.

Portfolio Diversification as a Motive for International Asset Trade

International trade in assets can make both parties to the trade better off by allowing them to reduce the riskiness of the return on their wealth. Trade accomplishes this reduction in risk by allowing both parties to diversify their portfolios—to divide their wealth among a wide spectrum of assets and thus reduce the amount of money they have riding on each individual asset. The late economist James Tobin of Yale University, an originator of the theory of portfolio choice with risk aversion, once described the idea of **portfolio diversification** as "Don't put all your eggs in one basket." When an economy is opened to the international capital market, it can reduce the riskiness of its wealth by placing some of its "eggs" in additional foreign "baskets." This reduction in risk is the basic motive for asset trade.

A simple two-country example illustrates how countries are made better off by trade in assets. Imagine there are two countries, Home and Foreign, and residents of each own only one asset, domestic land yielding an annual harvest of kiwi fruit.

The yield of the land is uncertain, however. Half of the time, Home's land yields a harvest of 100 tons of kiwi fruit at the same time as Foreign's land yields a harvest of 50 tons. The other half of the time, the outcomes are reversed: The Foreign harvest is 100 tons, but the Home harvest is only 50. On average, then, each country has a harvest of $\left(\frac{1}{2}\right) \times (100) + \left(\frac{1}{2}\right) \times (50) = 75$ tons of kiwi fruit, but its inhabitants never know whether the next year will bring feast or famine.

Now suppose the two countries can trade shares in the ownership of their respective assets. A Home owner of a 10 percent share in Foreign land, for example, receives 10 percent of the annual Foreign kiwi fruit harvest, and a Foreign owner of a 10 percent share in Home land is similarly entitled to 10 percent of the Home harvest. What happens if international trade in these two assets is allowed? Home residents will buy a 50 percent share of Foreign land, and they will pay for it by giving Foreign residents a 50 percent share in Home land.

To understand why this is the outcome, think about the returns to the Home and Foreign portfolios when both are equally divided between titles to Home and Foreign land. When times are good in Home (and therefore bad in Foreign), each country earns the same return on its portfolio: half of the Home harvest (100 tons of kiwi fruit) plus half of the Foreign harvest (50 tons of kiwi fruit), or 75 tons of fruit. In the opposite case—bad times in Home, good times in Foreign—each country *still* earns 75 tons of fruit. If the countries hold portfolios equally divided between the two assets, therefore, each country earns a *certain* return of 75 tons of fruit—the same as the average or expected harvest each faced before international asset trade was allowed.

Since the two available assets—Home and Foreign land—have the same return on average, any portfolio consisting of those assets yields an expected (or average) return of 75 tons of fruit. People everywhere are risk averse, however, so all prefer to hold the fifty-fifty portfolio described above, which gives a sure return of 75 tons of fruit every year. After trade is opened, therefore, residents of the two counties will swap titles to land until the fifty-fifty outcome is reached. Because this trade eliminates the risk faced by both countries without changing average returns, both countries are clearly better off as a result of asset trade.

The above example is oversimplified because countries can never really eliminate *all* risk through international asset trade. (Unlike the model's world, the real world is a risky place even in the aggregate!) The example does demonstrate that countries can nonetheless *reduce* the riskiness of their wealth by diversifying their asset portfolios internationally. A major function of the international capital market is to make this diversification possible.[1]

The Menu of International Assets: Debt versus Equity

International asset trades can be exchanges of many different types of assets. Among the many assets traded in the international capital market are bonds and deposits denominated in different currencies, shares of stock, and more complicated financial instruments such as stock or currency options. A purchase of foreign real estate and the direct acquisition of a factory in another country are other ways of diversifying abroad.

In thinking about asset trades, it is frequently useful to make a distinction between **debt instruments** and **equity instruments**. Bonds and bank deposits are debt instruments,

---

[1] The Mathematical Postscript to this chapter develops a detailed model of international portfolio diversification. You may have noticed that in our example, countries could reduce risk through transactions other than the asset swap we have described. The high-output country could run a current account surplus and lend to the low-output country, for example, thereby partially evening out the cross-country consumption difference in every state of the world economy. The economic functions of intertemporal trades and of pure asset swaps thus can overlap. To some extent, trade over time can substitute for trade across states of nature, and vice versa, simply because different economic states of the world occur at different points in time. But, in general, the two types of trade are not perfect substitutes for each other.

since they specify that the issuer of the instrument must repay a fixed value (the sum of principal plus interest) regardless of economic circumstances. In contrast, a share of stock is an equity instrument: It is a claim to a firm's profits, rather than to a fixed payment, and its payoff will vary according to circumstances. Similarly, the kiwi fruit shares traded in our example are equity instruments. By choosing how to divide their portfolios between debt and equity instruments, individuals and nations can arrange to stay close to desired consumption and investment levels despite the different eventualities that could occur.

The dividing line between debt and equity is not a neat one in practice. Even if an instrument's money payout is the same in different states of the world, its *real* payout in a particular state will depend on national price levels and exchange rates. In addition, the payments that a given instrument promises to make may not occur in cases of bankruptcy, government seizure of foreign-owned assets, and so on. Assets like low-grade corporate bonds, which superficially appear to be debt, may in reality be like equity in offering payoffs that depend on the doubtful financial fortunes of the issuer. The same has turned out to be true of the debt of many developing countries, as we will see in Chapter 11.

International Banking and the International Capital Market

The Home-Foreign kiwi fruit example above portrayed an imaginary world with only two assets. Since the number of assets available in the real world is enormous, specialized institutions have sprung up to bring together buyers and sellers of assets located in different countries.

The Structure of the International Capital Market

As we noted above, the main actors in the international capital market include commercial banks, corporations, nonbank financial institutions (such as insurance companies, money market funds, hedge funds, and pension funds), central banks, and other government agencies.

1. *Commercial banks.* Commercial banks are at the center of the international capital market, not only because they run the international payments mechanism but also because of the broad range of financial activities they undertake. Bank liabilities consist chiefly of deposits of various maturities, as well as debt and short-term borrowing from other financial institutions, while their assets consist largely of loans (to corporations and governments), deposits at other banks (interbank deposits), and various securities including bonds. Multinational banks are also heavily involved in other types of asset transaction. For example, banks may *underwrite* issues of corporate stocks and bonds by agreeing, for a fee, to find buyers for those securities at a guaranteed price. One of the key facts about international banking is that banks are often free to pursue activities abroad that they would not be allowed to pursue in their home countries. This type of regulatory asymmetry has spurred the growth of international banking over the past 50 years.

2. *Corporations.* Corporations—particularly those with multinational operations such as Coca-Cola, IBM, Toyota, and Nike—routinely finance their investments by drawing on foreign sources of funds. To obtain these funds, corporations may sell shares of stock, which give owners an equity claim to the corporation's

assets, or they may use debt finance. Debt finance often takes the form of borrowing from and through international banks or other institutional lenders; firms also sell short-term commercial paper and corporate debt instruments in the international capital market. Corporations frequently denominate their bonds in the currency of the financial center in which the bonds are being offered for sale. Increasingly, however, corporations have been pursuing novel denomination strategies that make their bonds attractive to a wider spectrum of potential buyers.

  3. *Nonbank financial institutions.* Nonbank institutions such as insurance companies, pension funds, mutual funds, and hedge funds have become important players in the international capital market as they have moved into foreign assets to diversify their portfolios. Of particular importance are *investment banks*, which are not banks at all but specialize in underwriting sales of stocks and bonds by corporations and (in some cases) governments, providing advice on mergers and acquisitions, and facilitating transactions for clients, among other functions. Investment banks may be free-standing but in most cases belong to large financial conglomerates that also include commercial banks. Prominent examples include Goldman Sachs, Deutsche Bank, Citigroup, and Barclays Capital.

  4. *Central banks and other government agencies.* Central banks are routinely involved in the international financial markets through foreign exchange intervention. In addition, other government agencies frequently borrow abroad. Developing-country governments and state-owned enterprises have borrowed substantially from foreign commercial banks, and regularly sell bonds abroad.

On any measure, the scale of transactions in the international capital market has grown much more quickly than world GDP since the early 1970s. One major factor in this development is that, starting with the industrial world, countries have progressively dismantled barriers to private capital flows across their borders.

An important reason for that development is related to exchange rate systems. According to the monetary trilemma of Chapter 8, the widespread adoption of flexible exchange rates since the early 1970s has allowed countries to reconcile open capital markets with domestic monetary autonomy. The individual member countries of the European economic and monetary union (Chapter 10) have followed a different route with respect to their mutual exchange rates. However, the euro floats against foreign currencies and the euro zone as a unit orients its monetary policy toward internal macroeconomic goals while permitting freedom of cross-border payments.

Offshore Banking and Offshore Currency Trading

One of the most pervasive features of today's commercial banking industry is that banking activities have become globalized as banks have branched out from their home countries into foreign financial centers. In 1960, only eight American banks had branches in foreign countries, but now hundreds have such branches. Similarly, the number of foreign bank offices in the United States has risen steadily.

The term **offshore banking** is used to describe the business that banks' foreign offices conduct outside of their home countries. Banks may conduct foreign business through any of three types of institutions:

1. An *agency* office located abroad, which arranges loans and transfers funds but does not accept deposits.
2. A *subsidiary* bank located abroad. A subsidiary of a foreign bank differs from a local bank only in that a foreign bank is the controlling owner. Subsidiaries are

subject to the same regulations as local banks but are not subject to the regulations of the parent bank's country.

3. A foreign *branch*, which is simply an office of the home bank in another country. Branches carry out the same business as local banks and are usually subject to local *and* home banking regulations. Often, however, branches can take advantage of cross-border regulatory differences.

The growth of **offshore currency trading** has gone hand in hand with that of offshore banking. An offshore deposit is simply a bank deposit denominated in a currency other than that of the country in which the bank resides—for example, yen deposits in a London bank or dollar deposits in Zurich. Many of the deposits traded in the foreign exchange market are offshore deposits. Offshore currency deposits are usually referred to as **Eurocurrencies**, which is something of a misnomer since much Eurocurrency trading occurs in such non-European centers as Singapore and Hong Kong. Dollar deposits located outside the United States are called **Eurodollars**. Banks that accept deposits denominated in Eurocurrencies (including Eurodollars) are called **Eurobanks**. The advent of the new European currency, the euro, has made this terminology even more confusing!

One motivation for the rapid growth of offshore banking and currency trading has been the growth of international trade and the increasingly multinational nature of corporate activity. American firms engaged in international trade, for example, require overseas financial services, and American banks have naturally expanded their domestic business with these firms into foreign areas. By offering more rapid clearing of payments and the flexibility and trust established in previous dealings, American banks compete with the foreign banks that could also serve American customers. Eurocurrency trading is another natural outgrowth of expanding world trade in goods and services. British importers of American goods frequently need to hold dollar deposits, for example, and it is natural for banks based in London to woo these importers' business.

World trade growth alone, however, cannot explain the growth of international banking since the 1960s. Another factor is the banks' desire to escape domestic government regulations on financial activity (and sometimes taxes) by shifting some of their operations abroad and into foreign currencies. A further factor is in part political: the desire by some depositors to hold currencies outside the jurisdictions of the countries that issue them. In recent years, the tendency for countries to open their financial markets to foreigners has allowed international banks to compete globally for new business.

The major factor behind the continuing profitability of Eurocurrency trading is regulatory: In formulating bank regulations, governments in the main Eurocurrency centers discriminate between deposits denominated in the home currency and those denominated in others and between transactions with domestic customers and those with foreign customers. Domestic currency deposits generally are more heavily regulated as a way of maintaining control over the domestic money supply, while banks are given more freedom in their dealings in foreign currencies.

Regulatory asymmetries explain why those financial centers whose governments historically imposed the fewest restrictions on foreign currency banking became the main Eurocurrency centers. London is the leader in this respect, but it has been followed by Luxembourg, Bahrain, Hong Kong, and other countries that have competed for international banking business by lowering restrictions and taxes on foreign bank operations within their borders.

The Shadow Banking System

In recent decades, a major regulatory asymmetry has arisen between banks and what is often referred to as the **shadow banking system**. Nowadays, numerous financial institutions provide payment and credit services similar to those that banks provide. U.S. money market mutual funds, for example, provide check-writing services to customers and also are major players in providing credit to firms (through commercial paper markets) and in lending dollars to banks outside the United States. Investment banks also have provided credit to other entities while offering payment services. The shadow banking system even has included investment conduits sponsored by banks but supposedly independent of the banks' own balance sheets. However, shadow banks have usually been minimally regulated compared to banks.

Why has this been the case? Historically, monetary policy makers have viewed banks as the prime focus of concern because of their centrality to the payments system, to the flow of credit to firms and household borrowers, and to the implementation of monetary policy. But the shadow banking system has grown dramatically and taken up many of the same functions as traditional banking. Total shadow banking sector assets are difficult to measure precisely, but in the United States today, they are probably comparable to the assets of the traditional banking sector.

Moreover, shadow banks are closely intertwined with banks as both creditors and borrowers. As a result, the stability of the shadow banking network cannot easily be divorced from that of the banks: If a shadow bank gets into trouble, so may the banks that have loaned it money. This became painfully clear during the 2007–2009 global financial crisis, as we shall see later in this chapter. We now turn to a discussion of banking regulation, but readers should be aware that banks are only one category of player in the international financial markets and that banks' fortunes are likely to depend on those of other players. Most of what we say below regarding "banks" also applies to shadow banks.

Banking and Financial Fragility

Many observers believe that the free-wheeling nature of global banking activity up until now left the world financial system vulnerable to bank failure on a massive scale. The financial crisis of 2007–2009, which we will discuss below, supports that belief. To understand what went wrong with financial globalization, we need first to review the inherent fragility of banking activity, even when undertaken in a hypothetical closed economy, and the safeguards national governments have put in place to prevent bank failures.

The Problem of Bank Failure

A bank fails when it is unable to meet its obligations to its depositors and other creditors. Banks use borrowed funds to make loans and to purchase other assets, but some of a bank's borrowers may find themselves unable to repay their loans, or the bank's assets may decline in value for some other reason. When this happens, the bank might be unable to repay its short-term liabilities, including demand deposits, which are largely repayable immediately, without notice.

A peculiar feature of banking is that a bank's financial health depends on depositors' (and other creditors') confidence in the value of its assets. If depositors, for example, come to believe that many of the bank's assets have declined in value, each has an incentive to withdraw his or her funds and place them in a different bank. A bank faced with a large and sudden loss of deposits—a bank run—is likely to close its doors, even if the asset side of its balance sheet is fundamentally sound. The reason is that many bank assets are illiquid and cannot be sold quickly to meet deposit obligations without substantial loss to the bank. If an atmosphere of financial panic develops, therefore, bank failure may not be limited to banks that have mismanaged their assets. It is in the interest of each depositor to withdraw his or her money from a bank if all other depositors are doing the same, even when the bank's assets, if only they could be held until maturity, would suffice to repay fully the bank's liabilities.

Unfortunately, once a single bank gets into trouble, suspicion may fall on other banks that have lent it money: if they lose enough on the loans, they may be unable to meet their own obligations. When banks are highly interconnected through mutual loans and derivative contracts, bank runs therefore can be highly contagious. Unless policymakers can quickly quarantine the panic, the domino effects of a single bank's troubles can result in a generalized, or *systemic*, banking crisis.

It is easiest to understand a bank's vulnerability by looking at its balance sheet. The stylized balance sheet below shows the relationship between the bank's assets, its liabilities, and their difference, the bank's *capital* (its non-borrowed resources, supplied by the bank's owners, who hold the bank's stock):

Bank Balance Sheet			
Assets		**Liabilities and equity capital**	
Loans	$1,950	Demand deposits	$1,000
Marketable securities	$1,950	Time deposits and long debt	$1,400
Reserves at central bank	$75	Short-term wholesale liabilities	$1,400
Cash on hand	$25	Capital	$200

In this example, the bank's total assets (listed on the Assets side of its balance sheet) are $4,000. They consist of a small amount of cash ($25) and reserves ($75, the latter being deposits at the home central bank), as well as potentially less liquid loans to businesses and households ($1,950) and other securities (such as government or corporate bonds, totaling $1,950). Cash in the bank's vaults obviously can be used any time to meet depositors' withdrawals, as can its central bank deposits, but loans (for example, mortgage loans) cannot be called in at will, and thus are usually highly illiquid. Marketable securities, in contrast, can be sold off, but if market conditions happen to be unfavorable, the bank might have to sell at a loss if forced to do so on short notice. In a financial panic, for example, other banks might simultaneously be trying to unload similar securities, driving down their market prices.

The bank makes its profits by accepting the risk that its assets may fall in value, while at the same time promising depositors and other short-term creditors that they can get their money back whenever they want it. The bank's provision of liquidity to its creditors is reflected on the Liabilities side of its balance sheet. Banks' time deposits and long-term debt ($1,400) are sources of funding that *cannot* flee at the whim of the lenders, and the bank accordingly pays a higher rate of interest on these liabilities than on its two sources of short-term funding, (retail) demand deposits ($1,000) and short-term wholesale liabilities ($1,400). The latter might take various forms, including overnight loans from other banks (including the central bank) or a collateralized *repurchase agreement* (known as "repo"), in which the bank pledges an asset to the lender for cash, promising to buy the asset back later (often the next day) at a slightly higher price. If all wholesale lenders refuse to renew their short-term loans to the bank, however, it will have to scramble for cash by trying to sell off assets, just as in the case of a retail depositor bank run. In general, banks' balance sheets are characterized by *maturity mismatch*—they have more liabilities payable on short notice than they hold of such assets—and this is what makes them vulnerable to runs.

Bank capital (here, $200) is the difference between assets and liabilities, and is the amount the bank could lose on its assets before it becomes *insolvent*, that is, unable to pay off its debts by selling its assets. Bank capital is provided by the investors who buy new issues of the bank's stock shares. Without the buffer of bank capital, the bank would have no margin for error and creditors would never believe in the bank's ability always to repay. In that case, the bank could not conduct its business of exploiting the interest difference or "carry" between its liquid liabilities and less liquid assets. Because a bank depends on the confidence of its creditors, even the suspicion that it could be insolvent may lead creditors to demand instant repayment, forcing it to liquidate assets at a loss and making it insolvent in fact. This scenario is most likely in the case of a systemic financial crisis, in which the prices of marketable assets that the bank normally could sell easily are depressed due to distress selling by numerous financial institutions.[2]

The lower a bank's capital, the higher the chance that it becomes insolvent due to losses in asset values, whether these are due to external events in the economy or due to a run by its creditors. It may therefore surprise you that large globally active banks have tended to operate in the past with fairly slim margins of capital. In our example, which is not unrealistic, the ratio of capital to total bank assets is only $200/$4000 = 5 percent, implying that the bank can tolerate at most a 5 percent loss on assets before it fails. Many large global banks have operated with even lower capital levels! Although banks usually avoid big positions in highly risky assets such as stock shares, and they also avoid unhedged or "open" positions in foreign currencies, numerous banks throughout the world still got into trouble during the global financial crisis of 2007–2009. Because of that experience, international policymakers are attempting to ensure that banks throughout the world maintain higher capital levels, as we explain later in this chapter.

Bank failures obviously inflict serious financial harm on individual depositors who lose their money. But beyond these individual losses, bank failure can harm the economy's macroeconomic stability. One bank's problems may easily spread to sounder banks if they are suspected of having lent to the bank that is in trouble. Such a general loss of confidence in banks undermines the credit and payments system on which the economy runs. A rash of bank failures can bring a drastic reduction in the banking system's ability to finance investment, consumer-durable expenditure, and home purchases, thus reducing aggregate demand and throwing the economy into a slump. There is strong evidence that the string of U.S. bank closings in the early 1930s helped start and worsen the Great Depression, and financial panic certainly worsened the severe worldwide recession that began in 2007.[3]

---

[2]Central banks also have capital positions. Central bank assets normally exceed liabilities and the resulting profits are used to cover the bank's expenses—for example, staff salaries and the operating cost of the central bank's physical plant. Any profits in excess of those expenses are usually turned over to the national treasury. Generally, shares in the central bank's capital are not publicly traded (they are owned by the government), although historically this was not always the case. (To take one notable case, the Bank of England was privately owned from its founding in 1694 until 1946.) If a central bank makes big enough losses—on foreign exchange intervention, for example—this might reduce its capital enough that the central bank is forced to request funding from the government. Central banks prefer not to be in this position because the government might attach conditions that reduce the central bank's independence.

[3]For an evaluation of the 1930s, see Ben S. Bernanke, "Nonmonetary Effects of the Financial Crisis in the Propagation of the Great Depression," Chapter 2 in his *Essays on the Great Depression* (Princeton, NJ: Princeton University Press, 2000). Banking crises may also lead to balance-of-payments crises. The macroeconomic policies needed to counteract the banking system's collapse can make it harder to maintain a fixed exchange rate (as illustrated by the euro area crisis that we discuss later in this book). A classic study is Graciela L. Kaminsky and Carmen M. Reinhart, "The Twin Crises: The Causes of Banking and Balance-of-Payments Problems," *American Economic Review* 89 (June 1999), pp. 473–500.

Government Safeguards against Financial Instability

Because the potential consequences of a banking collapse are so harmful, governments attempt to prevent bank failures through extensive regulation of their domestic banking systems. Well-managed banks themselves take precautions against failure even in the absence of regulation, but the costs of failure extend far beyond the bank's owners. Thus, some banks, taking into account their own self-interest but ignoring the costs of bank failure for society, might be led to shoulder a level of risk greater than what is socially optimal. In addition, even banks with cautious investment strategies may fail if rumors of financial trouble begin circulating. Many of the precautionary bank regulation measures taken by governments today are a direct result of their countries' experiences during the Great Depression.

In most countries, an extensive "safety net" has been set up to reduce the risk of bank failure. The main safeguards are:

1. *Deposit insurance.* One legacy of the Great Depression of the 1930s is deposit insurance. In the United States, the Federal Deposit Insurance Corporation (FDIC) insures bank depositors against losses of up to a current limit of $250,000. Banks are required to make contributions to the FDIC to cover the cost of this insurance. FDIC insurance discourages runs on banks by small depositors who know that their losses will be made good by the government: they no longer have an incentive to withdraw their money just because others are doing so. Since 1989, the FDIC has also provided insurance for deposits with savings and loan (S&L) associations.[4] The absence of government insurance is one reason policymakers sometimes give for the comparatively light regulation of banks' offshore operations as well as of the shadow banking system.

2. *Reserve requirements.* Reserve requirements are one possible tool of monetary policy, influencing the relation between the monetary base and monetary aggregates. At the same time, reserve requirements force the bank to hold a portion of its assets in a liquid form that is easily mobilized to meet sudden deposit outflows. In the United States, banks tend to hold reserves in excess of required reserves, so reserve requirements are not important. In our preceding balance-sheet example, the bank's total liquid reserves (including cash) are $100, only 2.5 percent of its total assets.

3. *Capital requirements and asset restrictions.* U.S. and foreign bank regulators set minimum required levels of bank capital to reduce the system's vulnerability to failure. Other rules prevent banks from holding assets that are "too risky," such as common stocks, whose prices tend to be volatile. Banks must also deal with rules against lending too large a fraction of their assets to a single private customer or to a single foreign government borrower.

4. *Bank examination.* Government supervisors have the right to examine a bank's books to ensure compliance with bank capital standards and other regulations. Banks may be forced to sell assets that the examiner deems too risky or to adjust their balance sheets by writing off loans the examiner thinks will not be repaid. In some countries the central bank is the main bank supervisor, while in others a separate financial supervision authority handles that job.

5. *Lender of last resort facilities.* Banks can borrow from the central bank's discount window or from other facilities the central bank may make available (generally

---

[4]Holders of deposits over $250,000 still have an incentive to run if they suspect trouble, of course, as do uninsured (and uncollateralized) bank creditors other than depositors, including other banks.

after they post assets of comparable or greater value as collateral). While lending to banks is a tool of monetary management, the central bank can also use discounting to prevent or quarantine bank panics. Since a central bank has the ability to create currency, it can lend to banks facing massive deposit outflows as much as they need to satisfy their depositors' claims. When the central bank acts in this way, it is acting as a **lender of last resort (LLR)** to the bank. Indeed, the Federal Reserve was set up in 1913 precisely as a safeguard against financial panic. When depositors know the central bank is standing by as the LLR, they have more confidence in a private bank's ability to withstand a panic and are therefore less likely to run if financial trouble looms. The administration of LLR facilities is complex, however. If banks think the central bank will *always* bail them out, they will take excessive risks. So the central bank must make access to its LLR services conditional on sound management. To decide when banks in trouble have not brought it on themselves through unwise risk taking, the LLR should ideally be closely involved in the bank examination process.

6. *Government-organized restructuring and bailouts.* The central bank's LLR role is intended to tide over banks suffering *temporary* liquidity problems due to jittery creditors. Hopefully the bank will be solvent if the central bank can give it enough time to dispose of assets at favorable prices; and if so, the central bank will not lose money as a result of its intervention. Often, however, creditors are jittery for a good reason and big losses on assets are unavoidable. In this case, the national fiscal authorities, along with taxpayer money, come into the picture. The central bank and fiscal authorities may organize the purchase of a failing bank by healthier institutions, sometimes throwing their own money into the deal as a sweetener. The fiscal authorities may also recapitalize the bank with public monies, in effect making the government a full or part owner of the bank until the bank is back on its feet and the public shares can be sold to private buyers. In these cases, bankruptcy can be avoided thanks to the government's intervention as a crisis manager, but perhaps at public expense. The government may alternatively choose to protect taxpayers by imposing losses—sometimes called *haircuts*—on the claims of unsecured bondholders or uninsured depositors.[5]

How successful have safeguards such as these been? Figure 9-2 shows the frequency of ongoing national banking crises—systemic crises which have affected large portions of countries' banking systems—between 1970 and 2011.[6] Banking crises in the poorer developing and emerging market economies are shown in blue, while crises in industrial economies including the United States are shown in red. Obviously such systemic crises are not rare events! As we will discuss in Chapter 11, through much of recent history poorer countries have regulated their banks much less effectively than richer countries, implying a much greater frequency of financial instability in the developing world. However, that changed in 2007–2009 as many more prosperous economies' banks required extensive government support in order to survive. The 2007–2009 crisis thus revealed serious gaps in the banking safety net, gaps that we will analyze below.

The U.S. commercial bank safety net worked reasonably well until the late 1980s, but as a result of deregulation, the 1990–1991 recession, and a sharp fall in commercial

---

[5]Unsecured bondholders are creditors who have not demanded collateral for their loans. Those who demand collateral receive a lower interest rate because their loans are less risky.

[6]The crisis chronology is taken from Luc Laeven and Fabián Valencia, "Systemic Banking Crises Database," *IMF Economic Review* 61 (June 2013), pp. 225–270.

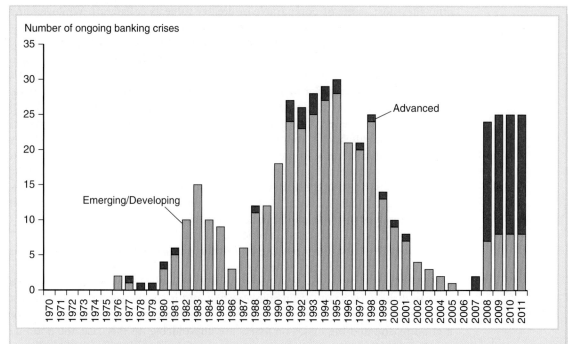

FIGURE 9-2

Frequency of Systemic Banking Crises, 1970–2011

Generalized banking crises have been plentiful around the world since the mid-1970s, but in recent years they have been concentrated in richer countries.

Source: Laeven and Valencia, *op. cit.*

property values, bank closings rose dramatically and the FDIC insurance fund was depleted. Like the United States, other countries that deregulated domestic banking in the 1980s—including Japan, the Scandinavian countries, the United Kingdom, and Switzerland—faced serious problems a decade later. Many overhauled their systems of banking safeguards as a result, but as we shall see, those safeguards were not nearly sufficient to prevent the massive financial crisis of 2007–2009.

Moral Hazard and the Problem of "Too Big to Fail"

The banking safeguards listed above fall into two categories: facilities for emergency financial support to banks or their customers and curbs on unwise risk taking by banks.

It is important to realize that these two types of safeguard are complements, not substitutes. An expectation of LLR support or a government-organized bailout package in case of problems may cause banks to extend excessively risky loans and to provision inadequately for investment losses. Deposit insurance will reassure depositors that they need not monitor the bank management's decisions; and without the threat of a bank run to discipline them, bank managers will pursue riskier strategies on the margin, including maintaining an inadequate capital cushion and holding insufficient cash.

The possibility that you will take less care to prevent an accident if you are insured against it is called **moral hazard**. Domestic bank supervision and balance-sheet restrictions are necessary to limit the moral hazard resulting from deposit insurance and access to the lender of last resort, which otherwise would lead banks to make excessively risky loans and inadequate provision for their possible failure.

The FDIC limit of $250,000 on the size of insured deposits is meant to limit moral hazard by encouraging big depositors, and other bank creditors including interbank lenders, to monitor the actions of bank managers. In principle, those big depositors could take their business elsewhere if their bank appears to be taking unwise risks. The problem is that some banks have become so big in global markets, and so interconnected with other banks and shadow banks that their failure might set off a chain reaction that throws the entire financial system into crisis.

When rumors began circulating in May 1984 that the Continental Illinois National Bank had made a large number of bad loans, the bank began rapidly to lose its large, uninsured deposits. At the time the bank was the seventh biggest in the U.S. and many of its deposits were owned by foreign banks, so its failure could have set off a much bigger global banking crisis. As part of its rescue effort, the FDIC extended its insurance coverage to all of Continental Illinois's deposits, regardless of size. This and later episodes have convinced people that the U.S. government is following a "too-big-to-fail" policy of fully protecting all creditors of the largest banks.

When a financial institution is *systemically important*—that is, "too big to fail" or "too interconnected to fail"—its managers and creditors expect that the government will have no choice but to support it in case it gets into trouble. The resulting moral hazard sets off a vicious circle: Because the institution is perceived to be under the umbrella of government support, it can borrow cheaply and engage in risky strategies that (while times are good) yield high returns. The resulting profits allow the institution to become even bigger and more interconnected, leading to more profits, more growth, and more moral hazard. The entire financial system becomes less stable as a result.

THE SIMPLE ALGEBRA OF MORAL HAZARD

The moral hazard that results from a combination of perceived government guarantees and weak regulation of the guaranteed institution has helped fuel excessively speculative investment in many economies. To see how it works, imagine that there is a potential investment—say, a large real estate development—that will cost $70 million up front. If all goes well, the project will yield a return of $100 million; but there is only a one-third chance of this, and a two-thirds chance that the investment will yield only $25 million. The expected payoff, then, is only $(1/3 \times \$100 \text{ million}) + (2/3 \times \$25 \text{ million}) = \$50$ million, which is far below the $70 million up-front cost. Ordinarily, this investment simply would never be made.

Government bailout guarantees change the result, however. Suppose that a real estate developer is able to *borrow* the entire $70 million, because he can convince lenders that the government will protect them if his project fails and he cannot repay. Then from his point of view, he has a one-third chance of making $30 million (= $100 million − $70 million). Otherwise he simply walks away from the project. It's heads he wins, tails the taxpayers lose.

The preceding example may seem extreme, but this kind of logic has led to financial disasters in many countries. The 2007–2009 financial crisis is the most recent example—and the most costly one to date—but it has many precedents. In the 1980s, the U.S. savings and loan industry was granted what amounted to privilege without responsibility: government guarantees on deposits, without close regulation of risk taking. The eventual bill to U.S. taxpayers was $150 billion. Similar mishandling of the financial sector led to much larger bank losses in the 1990s in industrial countries as diverse as Sweden and Japan.

For this reason, economists are increasingly in favor of curbs on the size of financial firms, despite the possible sacrifice of scale efficiencies. As former Federal Reserve chair Alan Greenspan put it, "If they're too big to fail, they're too big." Many economists also favor forcing large complex banks and shadow banks to draw up "living wills" allowing them to be closed and wound down, in case of insolvency, with minimal disruption and minimal cost to taxpayers. The credible threat of bank closure is necessary for limiting moral hazard—bank managers need to know they can be put out of business if they misbehave—but devising concrete procedures is not easy, especially in an international context.

As we shall see, the problem of moral hazard is central to understanding both the 2007–2009 global financial crisis and the measures being proposed to avoid future crises. Another important element in that crisis and its international transmission, however, was the globalized nature of banking.

The Challenge of Regulating International Banking

In this section, we will learn how the internationalization of banking (and financial institutions more generally) weakens purely national safeguards against banking collapse. At the same time, however, global financial interdependence has made the need for effective safeguards more urgent. The result is a second *trilemma* for international policymakers.[7]

The Financial Trilemma

Offshore banking involves a tremendous volume of interbank deposits—roughly 80 percent of all Eurocurrency deposits, for example, are owned by private banks. A high level of interbank depositing implies that problems affecting a single bank can be highly contagious and spread quickly to banks with which it is thought to do business. Through this domino effect, a localized disturbance can set off a banking panic on a global scale, as in the 2007–2009 crisis that we describe below.

Despite these very high stakes, banking regulations of the type used in the United States and other countries become even less effective in an international environment where banks can shift their business among different regulatory jurisdictions. A good way to see why an international banking system is harder to regulate than a national system is to look at how the effectiveness of the U.S. safeguards that we described earlier (pages 306–307) is reduced as a result of offshore banking activities.

1. Deposit insurance is essentially absent in international banking. National deposit insurance systems may protect domestic and foreign depositors alike, but the amount of insurance available is invariably too small to cover the size of the deposits that are usual in international banking. In particular, interbank deposits and other wholesale funding sources are unprotected.

2. The absence of overseas reserve requirements was historically a major factor in the growth of Eurocurrency trading. While Eurobanks derived a competitive advantage from escaping the required reserve tax, there was a social cost in terms of the reduced stability of the banking system. No country could solve the problem single-handedly by imposing reserve requirements on its own banks' overseas branches. Concerted international action was blocked, however, by the political and technical difficulty of agreeing on an internationally uniform set of regulations and

---

[7]As you will see, the financial trilemma that we introduce in this section is different from the monetary trilemma that we introduced in Chapter 8 and mentioned again earlier in this chapter. However, both trilemmas concern the connections between international financial integration and other potential policy goals.

by the reluctance of some countries to drive banking business away by tightening regulations. Nowadays, reserve requirements are less important in many countries. In part this is because governments simply realized the requirements' futility in a world of globalized banking.

3. and 4. Bank examination to enforce capital requirements and asset restrictions becomes more difficult in an international setting. National bank regulators usually monitor the balance sheets of domestic banks and their foreign branches on a consolidated basis. But they are less strict in keeping track of banks' foreign subsidiaries and affiliates, which are in theory more tenuously tied to the parent bank but whose financial fortunes may well affect the parent's solvency. Banks have often been able to take advantage of this laxity by shifting risky business that home regulators might question to regulatory jurisdictions where fewer questions are asked. This process is known as **regulatory arbitrage**. Further, it is often unclear which group of regulators would ideally be responsible for monitoring a given bank's assets. Suppose the London subsidiary of an Italian bank deals primarily in Eurodollars. Should the subsidiary's assets be the concern of British, Italian, or American regulators?

5. There is uncertainty over which central bank, if any, is responsible for providing LLR assistance in international banking. The problem is similar to the one that arises in allocating responsibility for bank supervision. Let's return to the example of the London subsidiary of an Italian bank. Should the Fed bear responsibility for saving the subsidiary from a sudden drain of dollar deposits? Should the Bank of England step in? Or should the European Central Bank bear the ultimate responsibility? When central banks provide LLR assistance, they increase their domestic money supplies and may compromise domestic macroeconomic objectives. In an international setting, a central bank may also be providing resources to a bank located abroad whose behavior it is not equipped to monitor. Central banks are therefore reluctant to extend the coverage of their LLR responsibilities.

6. When a bank has assets and liabilities in many countries, several governments may have to share operational and financial responsibility for a rescue or reorganization. The resulting uncertainties can slow down or even impede the operation. Big, complex, highly interconnected global banks know how hard it would be for governments to shut them down and reorganize them rather than simply bailing them out, and this can encourage excessive risk taking.

The preceding difficulties in regulating international financial institutions show that a **financial trilemma** constrains what policymakers in an open economy can achieve. At most two goals from the following list of three are simultaneously feasible:

1. Financial stability.
2. National control over financial safeguard policy.
3. Freedom of international capital movements.

For example, a country that closes itself financially from the outside world can regulate its banks strictly without worrying about regulatory arbitrage across borders, thereby promoting domestic financial stability regardless of what foreign regulators do. On the other hand, if countries were to delegate the design and implementation of financial safeguards to a global regulatory body immune to national political pressures, they could enjoy greater financial stability and financial openness at the same time.[8]

---

[8]For a recent examination of international banking in the context of the financial trilemma, see Dirk Schoenmaker, *Governance of International Banking: The Financial Trilemma* (Oxford: Oxford University Press, 2013).

The utopian goal of an omniscient global financial authority is remote, of course. In its absence, however, national regulators for four decades have been trying to reconcile growing financial integration with financial stability through a process of ever-increasing international cooperation. It is no accident that this process began precisely when the new system of floating exchange rates allowed countries to move to a new edge of the *monetary* trilemma (Chapter 8) by liberalizing international capital movements.

International Regulatory Cooperation through 2007

In the early 1970s, the new regime of floating exchange rates presented a new source of disturbance: a large, unexpected exchange rate change that might wipe out the capital of an exposed bank.

In response to this threat, central bank heads from 11 industrialized countries in 1974 set up a group called the **Basel Committee**, whose job is to achieve "a better coordination of the surveillance exercised by national authorities over the international banking system...." (The group got its name from Basel, Switzerland, the home of the central bankers' meeting place, the Bank for International Settlements, or BIS.) The Basel Committee remains the major forum for cooperation among bank regulators from different countries.

In 1975, the Basel Committee reached an agreement, called the Concordat, which allocates responsibility for supervising multinational banking establishments between parent and host countries. In addition, the Concordat calls for the sharing of information about banks by parent and host regulators and for "the granting of permission for inspections by or on behalf of parent authorities on the territory of the host authority."[9] In 1988, the Basel Committee suggested a minimally prudent level of bank capital (generally speaking, 8 percent of assets) and a system for measuring capital. These guidelines, widely adopted throughout the world, have become known as Basel I. The committee revised the Basel I framework in 2004, issuing a new set of rules for bank capital known as Basel II.

A major change in international financial relations has been the rapidly growing importance of new **emerging markets** as sources and destinations for private capital flows. Emerging markets are the capital markets of industrializing countries that have liberalized their financial systems to allow at least some private asset trade with foreigners. Countries such as Brazil, Mexico, Indonesia, and Thailand were all major recipients of private capital inflows from the industrial world after 1990.

Emerging market financial institutions have, however, proven to be weak in the past. This vulnerability contributed to the emerging markets' severe financial crisis of 1997–1999 (Chapter 11). Among other problems, developing countries tended to lack experience in bank regulation, had looser prudential and accounting standards than developed countries, and had been prone to moral hazard by offering domestic banks implicit guarantees that they will be bailed out if they get into trouble.

Thus, the need to extend internationally accepted "best practice" regulatory standards to emerging market countries became a priority for the Basel Committee. In September 1997, the Committee issued its *Core Principles for Effective Banking Supervision*, worked out in cooperation with representatives from many developing countries (and revised in 2006). That document set out 25 principles deemed to describe the minimum necessary requirements for effective bank supervision, covering

---

[9]The Concordat was summarized in these terms by W. P. Cooke of the Bank of England, then chairman of the Basel Committee, in "Developments in Co-operation among Banking Supervisory Authorities," *Bank of England Quarterly Bulletin* 21 (June 1981), pp. 238–244.

licensing of banks, supervision methods, reporting requirements for banks, and cross-border banking. The Basel Committee and the IMF were monitoring the international implementation of the revised *Core Principles* and Basel II when the global financial crisis erupted in August 2007. The crisis revealed weaknesses in Basel II that led the Basel Committee to agree on a new framework, Basel III, which we will describe further below. The international activities of nonbank financial institutions are another potential trouble spot. The failure of a major actor in the shadow banking system, like the failure of a bank, could seriously disrupt national payments and credit networks. Increasing **securitization** (in which bank assets are repackaged in readily marketable forms and sold off) and trade in options and other derivative securities have made it harder for regulators to get an accurate picture of global financial flows by examining bank balance sheets alone. Indeed, as we shall see, securitization and derivatives were at the heart of the 2007–2009 crisis, which is the subject of the following Case Study.

CASE STUDY The Global Financial Crisis of 2007–2009

The global financial and economic meltdown of 2007–2009 was the worst since the Great Depression. Banks throughout the world failed or required extensive government support to survive; the global financial system froze; and the entire world economy was thrown into recession. Unlike some recessions, this one originated in a shock to financial markets, and the shock was transmitted from country to country by financial markets, at lightning speed.

The crisis had a seemingly unlikely source: the United States mortgage market.[10] Over the course of the mid-2000s, with U.S. interest rates very low and U.S. home prices bubbling upward (recall Chapter 8), mortgage lenders had extended loans to borrowers with shaky credit. In many cases, the borrowers planned to hold the homes only for brief periods, selling them later for a profit. Many people borrowed at low, temporary "teaser" rates of interest, when in fact they lacked the financial means to meet mortgage payments if interest rates were to rise. And then U.S. interest rates started moving up as the Federal Reserve gradually tightened monetary policy to ward off inflation. U.S. housing prices started to decline in 2006.

The total amount of shaky, "subprime" U.S. mortgage loans was not very big compared to total U.S. financial wealth. However, the subprime loans were securitized quickly and sold off by the original lenders, often bundled with other assets. This factor made it very hard to know exactly which investors were exposed to the risk that subprime mortgage loans would not be repaid. In addition, banks throughout the world, but especially in the United States and Europe, were avid buyers of securitized subprime-related assets, in some cases setting up—outside of the reach of regulators—opaque, off-balance-sheet vehicles for that purpose. A major motivation was regulatory arbitrage. Banks were eager to exploit loopholes in prudential rules, including the Basel II guidelines, in order to minimize the amount of capital

---

[10]For useful accounts of the crisis, see Markus Brunnermeier, "Deciphering the Liquidity and Credit Crunch of 2007–2008," *Journal of Economic Perspectives* 23 (Winter 2009), pp. 77–100; Gary B. Gorton, *Slapped in the Face by the Invisible Hand: The Panic of 2007* (New York: Oxford University Press, 2010); Chapter 9 in Frederic S. Mishkin, *The Economics of Money, Banking, and Financial Markets*, 10th edition (Upper Saddle River, NJ: Prentice Hall, 2013); and the book by Blinder in Further Readings.

they were required to hold against assets and thereby maximize the amount they could borrow to buy securitized credit products. Funding for these banks' securitized asset purchases came from U.S. lenders, including money market mutual funds.[11] Much of the European banks' demand was for U.S. products, but as we noted in Chapter 8, the housing boom of the 2000s was a global phenomenon (recall Figure 8-7), and European banks were also heavily exposed to downturns in highly-priced housing markets outside of the U.S. House prices in those markets would soon follow U.S. prices downward. (In the next chapter, we will see how the problems of Europe's banks led to a crisis in the euro zone.)

As subprime borrowers increasingly missed their payments during 2007, lenders became more aware of the risks they faced, and pulled back from markets. No one could tell who was exposed to subprime risk, or how vulnerable he or she was. Borrowing costs rose, and many participants in financial markets had no choice but to sell assets to get cash. A number of the derivative assets being offered for sale were so poorly understood by the markets that potential buyers could not value them.

During the week of August 9, 2007, central banks provided markets with the most extensive liquidity support since the September 11, 2001, terrorist attacks. On August 9, a major French bank, BNP Paribas, disclosed that three of its investment funds faced potential trouble due to subprime-related investments. Credit markets went into panic, with interbank interest rates rising above central bank target rates around the world. Banks feared that other banks would go under and be unable to repay, and fearing an inability to obtain interbank funding themselves, they all hoarded cash. The European Central Bank stepped in as lender of last resort to the European interbank market, and the Fed followed suit in the United States, announc-

ing that it would accept mortgage-backed securities as collateral for loans to banks. Stock markets fell everywhere. The U.S. economy slipped into recession late in 2007, pushed by the disappearance of credit and a collapsing housing market.

More trouble lay ahead. In March 2008, institutional lenders refused to roll over their short-term credits to the fifth largest investment bank, Bear Stearns, which had extensive subprime-related investments. Even though Bear Stearns was not a bank, it effectively suffered a run by its lenders. In a hastily organized rescue, the Fed bought $30 billion of Bear's "toxic" assets in order to persuade the bank J.P. Morgan Chase to buy Bear at a fire-sale price.

---

[11]For documentation of the two-way financial flows between Europe and the U.S. prior to the crisis, see Ben S. Bernanke, Carol Bertaut, Laurie Pounder DeMarco, and Steven Kamin, "International Capital Flows and the Returns to Safe Assets in the United States, 2003–2007," *Financial Stability Review*, Banque de France 15 (2011), pp. 13–26. Viral V. Acharya and Philipp Schnabl illustrate regulatory arbitrage in "Do Global Banks Spread Global Imbalances? Asset-Backed Commercial Paper during the Financial Crisis of 2007–09," *IMF Economic Review* 58 (August 2010), pp. 37–73. Many securitized U.S. mortgage-backed securities (MBS) were bundled by their issuers so that they would pay off fully except in circumstances where nonpayment of mortgage obligations was extremely widespread—essentially, a severe housing market collapse affecting most regions of the United States. Because rating agencies deemed such an event highly improbable, they gave the MBS their highest ratings. Under the Basel capital guidelines, however, banks were required to hold relatively less capital against such seemingly bullet-proof assets. So European banks piled into MBS and related securities both because of their (slightly) higher returns and because they could thereby borrow and lend on slimmer capital bases.

The Fed was criticized for not wiping out Bear's shareholders (to deter moral hazard) and for putting taxpayer money at risk.

But even after this bailout, financial stability did not return. Foreclosures on delinquent U.S. mortgages were mounting, home prices were still heading downward, and yet banks and shadow banks retained on their books toxic assets that were difficult to value or sell. Against this background the U.S. government took control of the two giant privately owned but government-sponsored mortgage intermediaries, Fannie Mae and Freddie Mac.

The investment bank Lehman Brothers filed for bankruptcy on September 15, 2008, after frantic but unsuccessful efforts by the U.S. Treasury and the Fed to find a buyer. There is still controversy about the legal standing of the U.S. authorities to have prevented the collapse; surely they were still smarting from the criticism over Bear, and hoping that the Lehman fallout could be contained. Instead, the situation quickly spun out of control. A day after Lehman's filing, the giant insurance firm American International Group (AIG, with over $1 trillion in assets) suffered a run. Apparently without the approval of senior management, traders for the firm had issued more than $400 billion in derivatives called *credit default swaps* (CDS), which are insurance policies against nonrepayment of loans (including loans made to Lehman, as well as mortgage-backed securities). With the world financial system in a state of meltdown, those CDS looked increasingly likely to be triggered, yet AIG lacked the funds to cover them. The Fed stepped in immediately with an $85 billion loan, and ultimately the U.S. government loaned AIG billions more.

In the same month, money American market mutual funds (some with claims on Lehman) suffered a run and had their liabilities guaranteed by the U.S. Treasury; Washington Mutual Bank (the sixth largest in the United States) failed; ailing Wachovia (the fourth largest bank) and investment bank Merrill Lynch were bought by Wells Fargo Bank and Bank of America, respectively; the last two independent U.S. investment banks, Goldman Sachs and Morgan Stanley, became bank-holding companies subject to Fed supervision but with access to the Fed's lending facilities; interbank lending spreads over Treasury bill rates reached historic levels; and world stock markets swooned. The U.S. Congress, after much debate, passed a bill allocating $700 billion to buy troubled assets from banks, in hopes that this would allow them to resume normal lending—but the funds were not, in the end, used for that purpose. The post-Lehman turmoil spread to Europe, where a number of financial institutions failed and EU governments issued blanket deposit guarantees to head off bank runs. In addition, a number of countries guaranteed interbank loans. But by this time, the economic downturn had gone global, with devastating effects on output and employment throughout the world.

Limited space prevents a detailed review of the many financial, fiscal, and unconventional monetary policies that central banks and governments undertook to end the global economy's seeming free fall in late 2008 and the first part of 2009.[12] (The box on the next page explores one aspect of the policy response that is especially relevant to international monetary economics.) With housing markets depressed in the industrial countries, however, recovery of financial and household-sector balance sheets was slow, as was the recovery in aggregate demand.

---

[12]A readable account of Fed policies during the crisis is David Wessel, *In Fed We Trust: Ben Bernanke's War on the Great Panic* (New York: Crown Business, 2009). A more comprehensive review of government policy responses is the book by Blinder in Further Readings.

FOREIGN EXCHANGE INSTABILITY AND CENTRAL BANK SWAP LINES

Traditionally, the lender of last resort provides liquidity in its own currency, which it can print freely. The crisis of 2007–2009 made clear, however, that in the modern world of globalized finance, banks may need liquidity in currencies other than that of their home central bank. One area in which central banks innovated during the crisis was in making such support readily available to foreign central banks. In effect, the Federal Reserve, which pioneered this approach, became a *global* LLR for U.S. dollars.

Why was this necessary? The need was a spill-over effect of the disruption in U.S. credit markets, particularly interbank markets. As we pointed out above, in the years leading up to the crisis, European banks had invested heavily in U.S. mortgage-backed securities and other similar securitized assets. The European banks did not, however, wish to bear the currency risk of holding these dollar-denominated claims. Lacking an ability to obtain dollars through retail deposits, they borrowed short-term dollars in wholesale markets (from U.S. banks and money market funds) to finance their purchases of U.S. asset-backed securities.

Then the crisis hit and interbank credit markets stopped functioning. European banks did not want to sell their now-toxic U.S. assets at a loss (even if they had been able to), so they needed to borrow dollars to repay their short-term loans and maintain their hedged positions in dollars. Even though the banks' dollar liabilities were on paper balanced with dollar assets, the liquidity mismatch between the assets and liabilities created a currency mismatch once the assets could no longer be sold quickly at face value. Where could these banks get dollars loans quickly now that private dollar credit markets were frozen?

Some, but not all, were able to borrow from the Fed through U.S. affiliates. Other European banks lacked collateral acceptable to the Fed. To make matters worse, the Fed was closed during European morning trading.

The ECB could print euros and lend them to banks, but it could not print U.S. dollars. European banks thus tried to swap the borrowed euros into dollars (selling them in the spot market for dollars and buying them back with forward dollars in the forward market). Under *covered* interest parity (Chapter 3), this complicated operation has the same cost as a straight loan of dollars. But covered interest parity was breaking down because banks did not want to lend dollars to each other. Swaps of euros into dollars thus yielded too few spot dollars and too few forward euros. In particular, this dollar shortage led to a tendency for the dollar to strengthen sharply in the spot market.

The Fed's swap lines, initially extended to the ECB and the Swiss National Bank (SNB) in December 2007, were intended to remedy the shortage and prevent disorderly conditions in foreign exchange markets. The lines allowed the ECB and SNB to borrow dollars directly from the Fed and lend them to domestic banks in need.

But the dollar shortage became much more severe after the Lehman collapse in September 2008. The Fed extended the swaps to a wider set of central banks, including four in emerging countries (Brazil, Mexico, Korea, and Singapore), and made the swap lines unlimited for several industrial-country central banks (including the ECB and SNB), thus fully outsourcing its LLR function. Ultimately the Fed lent hundreds of billions of dollars in this way.*

---

*For further discussion, see Maurice Obstfeld, Jay C. Shambaugh, and Alan M. Taylor, "Financial Instability, Reserves, and Central Bank Swap Lines in the Panic of 2008," *American Economic Review* 99 (May 2009), pp. 480–486; Patrick McGuire and Götz von Peter, "The US Dollar Shortage in Global Banking and the International Policy Response," BIS Working Papers No. 291, October 2009; and Linda S. Goldberg, Craig Kennedy, and Jason Miu, "Central Bank Dollar Swap Lines and Overseas Dollar Funding Costs," *Economic Policy Review*, Federal Reserve Bank of New York (May 2011), pp. 3–20.

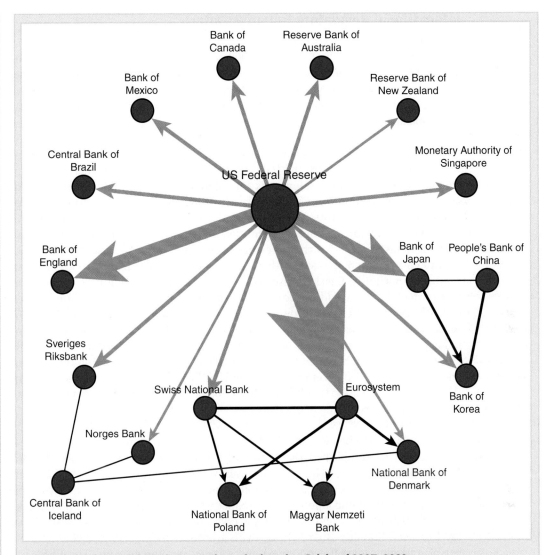

Network of Central Bank Swap Lines during the Crisis of 2007–2009

Light arrows show loans of dollars, dark arrows loans of other currencies. An arrow's direction shows the direction of lending, when known. Arrow thickness is proportional to the size of the swap line or, when the line was unlimited, to the amount lent.

Source: Patrick McGuire and Götz von Peter, "The US Dollar Shortage in Global Banking and the International Policy Response," BIS Working Papers No. 291, October 2009, from http://www.bis.org/publ/work291.pdf © Bank for International Settlements ("BIS")

Central banks other than the Fed likewise extended swap lines in their currencies, though typically these were more limited in scope than the Fed's. The figure above illustrates the remarkable network of swap lines that emerged.

The Fed wound down its swap lines in February 2010 but reactivated some when the European debt crisis erupted shortly afterward and interbank markets again became jittery (Chapter 10). Recent experience clearly shows the need for global lenders of last resort in different currencies, but it is doubtful that national central banks will or can play this role on a permanent basis. One possibility is to assign that function to the IMF, which saw its lending resources triple as world governments responded to the crisis.

International Regulatory Initiatives after the Global Financial Crisis

The severity and breadth of the 2007–2009 crisis have led to initiatives to reform both national financial systems and the international system. We now describe some of these measures, which have sought to fill gaps in existing regulatory frameworks while also paying more attention to the macroeconomic causes and consequences of banking problems.

Basel III   The financial crisis made obvious the inadequacies of the Basel II regulatory framework, so in 2010, the Basel Committee proposed a tougher set of capital standards and regulatory safeguards for international banks, Basel III. Regarding capital, the new Basel framework makes it harder for banks to get around capital requirements (for example, it takes a broader view of the risks banks are running, including through off-balance sheet entities, and also requires banks to guard against more pessimistic scenarios than previously). But like Basel II, Basel III still attaches risk weights to different assets, with assets deemed less risky leading to lower required capital. Importantly, Basel III also proposes to phase in a Liquidity Coverage Ratio, under which banks would be required to hold enough cash or highly liquid bonds to cover thirty days of cash outflow in specified crisis conditions. A Net Stable Funding Ratio seeks to limit banks' reliance on short-term wholesale funding (in contrast to retail deposits). As of the end of March 2013, only 11 countries (not including the U.S. and the EU) had fully implemented Basel III; but many more were in the process of adopting its rules. In December 2011, the U.S. Federal Reserve announced its intention to apply the Basel III rules not only to banks, but also to other financial institutions with assets exceeding $50 billion.[13]

The Financial Stability Board   In 1999, policymakers from a handful of industrialized countries established the Financial Stability Forum, housed (like the Basel Committee) in the BIS. The goal, however, was to promote international coordination over a broader set of financial stability issues (including, but going beyond, bank regulation), and among a potentially broader group of macroeconomic policymakers. In April 2009, at the height of the global crisis, the Financial Stability Forum became the Financial Stability Board (FSB), with a broader membership (including a number of emerging market economies) and a larger permanent staff. The FSB's job is to monitor the global financial system and make recommendations for global policy coordination and reform, sometimes in cooperation with other international agencies such as the IMF.

National Reforms   Individual countries have not limited themselves to implementing the Basel III recommendations. In a number of cases, including the euro zone, the United Kingdom, and the United States, countries have embarked on far-reaching reforms of their domestic financial systems. In 2010, the U.S. Congress passed the Dodd-Frank act, which, among other things, empowers the government to regulate nonbank financial institutions deemed "systemically important" (such as Lehman or AIG) and also allows the government to take over those firms in much the same way that the FDIC takes over and resolves failing banks.[14]

---

[13]You can explore the Basel III framework (and its implementation) on your own at http://www.bis.org/bcbs/basel3.htm?ql=1, on the BIS website.
[14]See Mishkin, *op. cit.*

The Macroprudential Perspective   An important lesson of the global financial crisis is that it is not enough for financial regulators to ensure that each individual financial institution is sound. This in itself will not ensure that the financial system *as a whole* is sound, and in fact, measures that would make an individual institution more resilient, given that the broader financial system is healthy, could put the broader system into jeopardy if implemented simultaneously by all institutions. The **macroprudential perspective** on financial regulation seeks to avoid such fallacies of composition at the aggregate level.[15]

As an example, consider the Basel capital standards, which apply different risk weights to different assets to determine the amount of capital banks need to hold. If there are two assets, A and B, with similar returns, but asset B has the lower Basel risk weight, all banks will wish to hold asset B rather than asset A. But in this case, the system *as a whole* will be more vulnerable to a fall in asset B's price than if banks were more diversified between the two assets. This is exactly what happened in 2007 when U.S. and European banks were all so heavily invested in securities tied to the U.S. housing market, and therefore all vulnerable to the U.S. housing downturn. A major concern about the new Basel rules is that they do not do enough to correct this system-level problem.

However, in other respects the Basel III proposals recognize the macroprudential problem. For example, the Basel Committee has proposed that banks increase their capital ratios during lending booms in order to make the system more resilient during downturns, at which time capital requirements would be loosened. Why is this plan for "countercyclical capital buffers" helpful? If instead all banks simultaneously sell assets to increase their capital buffers in a financial crisis—which is what a *micro* prudential approach might suggest that they do—the result would be an asset "fire sale" that depresses securities prices and therefore endangers the solvency of the system as a whole.

In the United States, the Dodd-Frank act set up a Financial Stability Oversight Council (FSOC), which includes the Fed chair and the Treasury Secretary, to monitor macroeconomic aspects of financial stability, including risks from the shadow banking system. The FSOC has the power to designate individual financial institutions as systemically important and subject them to enhanced supervision. It can also recommend breaking up institutions that are so big or interconnected as to pose a threat to the economy. However, the biggest financial institutions are, if anything, even bigger after the financial crisis, and many observers remain concerned that the U.S. and other countries have done too little to solve the "too big to fail" problem and reduce moral hazard in financial markets. After seeing the effects of the Lehman failure, policymakers still may remain too fearful of contagion to allow a major international bank to fail.

National Sovereignty and the Limits of Globalization   National financial regulators often face fierce lobbying from their home financial institutions, which argue that stricter rules would put them at a disadvantage relative to foreign rivals (while also being ineffective due to the foreign competition). The Basel multilateral process, like multilateral trade liberalization under the GATT and the WTO, plays an essential rule in allowing governments to overcome domestic political pressures against adequate oversight and control of the financial sector. The process partially addresses the financial trilemma by facilitating some limited delegation of national sovereignty over financial policy. The constraints of the trilemma are still important, however.

---

[15]The monograph by Brunnermeier et al. in Further Readings provides an excellent overview.

For example, a country wishing to control a domestic housing boom may forbid its banks from lending too much to prospective home buyers, but may be unable to prevent foreign banks from lending. In this case, there is a tradeoff between financial stability and financial integration; and countries may be tempted to react through capital controls or other measures that segregate domestic financial markets. Unless governments can successfully contain the risks posed by financial markets, it seems unlikely that financial globalization can continue to proceed as it has over recent decades.

How Well Have International Financial Markets Allocated Capital and Risk?

The present structure of the international capital market involves risks of financial instability that can be reduced only through the close cooperation of bank and financial supervisors in many countries. But the same profit motive that leads multinational financial institutions to innovate their way around national regulations can also provide important gains for consumers. As we have seen, the international capital market allows residents of different countries to diversify their portfolios by trading risky assets. Further, by ensuring a rapid international flow of information about investment opportunities around the world, the market can help allocate the world's savings to their most productive uses. How well has the international capital market performed in these respects?

The Extent of International Portfolio Diversification

Since accurate data on the overall portfolio positions of a country's residents are sometimes impossible to assemble, it can be difficult to gauge the extent of international portfolio diversification by direct observation. Nonetheless, some U.S. data can be used to get a rough idea of changes in international diversification in recent years.

In 1970, the foreign assets held by U.S. residents were equal in value to 6.2 percent of the U.S. capital stock (including residential housing). Foreign claims on the United States amounted to 4.0 percent of its capital stock. By 2008, U.S.-owned assets abroad equaled 46.6 percent of U.S. capital, while foreign assets in the United States had risen to about 54.7 percent of U.S. capital.

The recent percentages are much larger than those in 1970 but still seem too small. With full international portfolio diversification, we would expect them to reflect the size of the U.S. economy relative to that of the rest of the world. Thus, in a fully diversified world economy, something like 80 percent of the U.S. capital stock would be owned by foreigners, while U.S. residents' claims on foreigners would equal around 80 percent of the value of the U.S. capital stock. Moreover, the numbers in the previous paragraph describe total foreign assets—stocks, foreign direct investment, and bonds alike—not just stocks and FDI, which alone represent claims on capital. (For the U.S., fewer than half of its foreign assets are stocks and FDI, while less than a third of its foreign liabilities are stocks and FDI.) What makes the apparently incomplete extent of international equity portfolio diversification even more puzzling is the presumption most economists would make that the potential gains from diversification are large. An influential study by the French financial economist Bruno Solnik, for example, estimated that a U.S. investor holding only American stocks could more than halve the riskiness of her portfolio by further diversification into stocks from

European countries.[16] Thus, the observed *home bias* in equity holdings is hard to understand.

The data do show, however, that international asset trade has increased substantially as a result of the growth of the international capital market. Further, international asset holdings are large in absolute terms. At the end of 2012, for example, U.S. claims on foreigners were equal to about 138 percent of the U.S. GNP in that year, while foreign claims on the United States were about 163 percent of U.S. GNP. (Recall Figure 2-3, page 34.) Stock exchanges around the world have established closer communication links, and companies are showing an increasing readiness to sell shares on foreign exchanges. The seemingly incomplete extent of international equity diversification attained so far, however, is not necessarily a strong indictment of the world capital market. The market has certainly contributed to a stunning rise in asset trade in recent decades. Further, the U.S. experience is not necessarily typical. Table 9-1 illustrates the trend over two decades for a sample of industrial countries, showing the countries' gross foreign assets and liabilities as percentages of their GDPs. The United Kingdom, already the world's financial center in the early 1980s, was deeply

TABLE 9-1	Gross Foreign Assets and Liabilities of Selected Industrial Countries, 1983–2011 (percent of GDP)			
		1983	**1993**	**2011**
Australia				
	Assets	12	34	83
	Liabilities	43	87	140
France				
	Assets	63	80	256
	Liabilities	46	89	289
Germany				
	Assets	38	64	230
	Liabilities	31	54	205
Italy				
	Assets	22	43	106
	Liabilities	26	55	131
Netherlands				
	Assets	93	148	450
	Liabilities	72	133	421
United Kingdom				
	Assets	150	202	694
	Liabilities	134	198	711
United States				
	Assets	31	40	146
	Liabilities	26	46	173

Source: Philip R. Lane and Gian Maria Milesi-Ferretti, "The External Wealth of Nations, Mark II: Revised and Extended Estimates of Foreign Assets and Liabilities, 1970–2004," *Journal of International Economics* 73 (November 2007), pp. 223–250. The table's 2011 figures come from the updated data reported on Philip Lane's home page, http://www.philiplane.org/EWN.html.

[16]See Solnik, "Why Not Diversify Internationally Rather Than Domestically?" *Financial Analysts Journal* (July–August 1974), pp. 48–54.

engaged in international financial markets then and is even more so now. A small country such as the Netherlands tends to have a high level of foreign assets and liabilities, while all countries in the euro zone (including the Netherlands) have increased their gross foreign investment positions since 1993 as a result of European capital market unification. The same trend is evident, albeit more mildly, for Australia and the United States. Even some emerging markets have begun to engage in significant asset swapping.

The welfare significance of these numbers is far from clear. To the extent that they represent greater diversification of economic risks, as in our analysis at the start of this chapter, they point to a more stable world economy. But most of these external asset and liabilities are debt instruments, including bank debts, in some cases driven by regulatory arbitrage. It is likely that they include systemically risky borrowing, as when a bank in the U.K. borrows short-term funds to invest in less liquid securities abroad. Thus, even though these data show that the volume of international asset transactions has increased enormously over the past decades, they also remind us that there is no foolproof measure of the socially optimal extent of foreign investment.

The Extent of Intertemporal Trade

An alternative way of evaluating the performance of the world capital market was suggested by economists Martin Feldstein and Charles Horioka. Feldstein and Horioka pointed out that a smoothly working international capital market allows countries' domestic investment rates to diverge widely from their saving rates. In such an idealized world, saving seeks out its most productive uses worldwide, regardless of their location; at the same time, domestic investment is not limited by national saving because a global pool of funds is available to finance it.

For many countries, however, differences between national saving and domestic investment rates (that is, current account balances) have not been large since World War II: Countries with high saving rates over long periods also have usually had high investment rates, as Figure 9-3 illustrates. Feldstein and Horioka concluded from this evidence that cross-border capital mobility is low, in the sense that most of any sustained increase in national saving will lead to increased capital accumulation at home. The world capital market, according to this view, does not do a good job of helping countries reap the long-run gains of intertemporal trade.[17]

The main problem with the Feldstein-Horioka argument is that it is impossible to gauge whether the extent of intertemporal trade is deficient without knowing if there are unexploited trade gains, and knowing this requires more knowledge about actual economies than we generally have. For example, a country's saving and investment may usually move together simply because the factors that generate a high saving rate (such as rapid economic growth) also generate a high investment rate. In such cases, the country's gain from intertemporal trade may simply be small. An alternative explanation of high saving-investment correlations is that governments have tried to manage macroeconomic policy to avoid large current account imbalances. In any case, events appear to be overtaking this particular debate. For industrialized countries, the empirical regularity noted by Feldstein and Horioka seems to have weakened recently in the face of the high external imbalances of the United States, Japan, Switzerland, and some of the euro zone countries.

---

[17]See Martin Feldstein and Charles Horioka, "Domestic Savings and International Capital Flows," *Economic Journal* 90 (June 1980), pp. 314–329.

FIGURE 9-3

Saving and Investment Rates for 24 Countries, 1990–2011 Averages

OECD countries' saving and investment ratios to output tend to be positively related. The straight regression line in the graph represents a statistician's best guess of the level of the investment ratio, conditional on the saving ratio, in this country sample.

Source: World Bank, *World Development Indicators.*

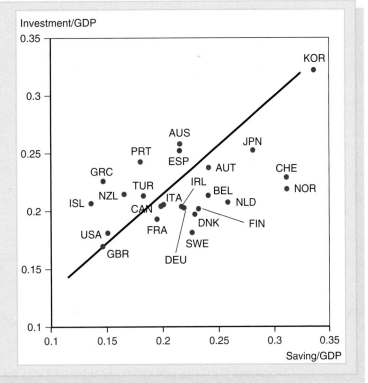

Onshore-Offshore Interest Differentials

A quite different barometer of the international capital market's performance is the relationship between onshore and offshore interest rates on similar assets denominated in the same currency. If the world capital market is doing its job of communicating information about global investment opportunities, these interest rates should move closely together and not differ too greatly. Large interest rate differences would be strong evidence of unrealized gains from trade.

Figure 9-4 shows data since the end of 1990 on the interest rate difference between two comparable bank liabilities, three-month dollar deposits in London and three-month certificates of deposit issued in the United States. These data are imperfect because the interest rates compared are not measured at precisely the same moment. Nonetheless, they provide no indication of any large unexploited gains in normal times. The pattern of onshore-offshore interest differences is similar for other industrial countries.

The London-U.S. differential does begin to creep up with the outbreak of global financial turbulence in August 2007, and it reaches a peak in October 2008, the month after the Lehman Brothers collapse. Evidently, investors perceived that the dollar deposits of U.S. banks would be backstopped by the U.S. Treasury and Federal Reserve, but that dollar deposits in London might not receive the same protection.

The Efficiency of the Foreign Exchange Market

The foreign exchange market is a central component of the international capital market, and the exchange rates it sets help determine the profitability of international transactions of all types. Exchange rates therefore communicate important economic

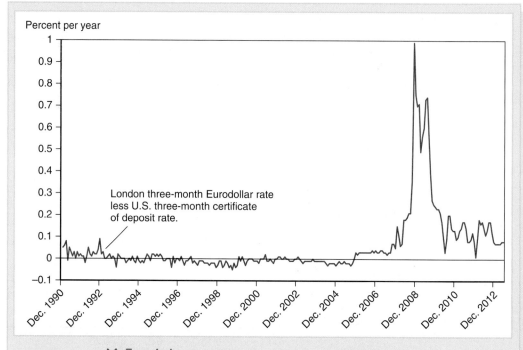

FIGURE 9-4   MyEconLab Real-time data

Comparing Onshore and Offshore Interest Rates for the Dollar

The difference between the London and U.S. interest rates on dollar deposits is usually very close to zero, but it spiked up sharply in the fall of 2008 as the investment bank Lehman Brothers collapsed.

Source: Board of Governors of the Federal Reserve System, monthly data.

signals to households and firms engaged in international trade and investment. If these signals do not reflect all available information about market opportunities, a misallocation of resources will result. Studies of the foreign exchange market's use of available information are therefore potentially important in judging whether the international capital market is sending the right signals to markets. We examine three types of tests: tests based on interest parity, tests based on modeling risk premiums, and tests for excessive exchange rate volatility.

Studies Based on Interest Parity   The interest parity condition that was the basis of the discussion of exchange rate determination in Chapter 3 has also been used to study whether market exchange rates incorporate all available information. Recall that interest parity holds when the interest difference between deposits denominated in two different currencies is the market's forecast of the percentage by which the exchange rate between those currencies will change. More formally, if R_t is the date t interest rate on home currency deposits, R_t^* is the interest rate on foreign currency deposits, E_t is the exchange rate (defined as the home currency price of foreign currency), and E_{t+1}^e is the exchange rate that market participants expect when the deposits paying interest R_t and R_t^* mature, the interest parity condition is

$$R_t - R_t^* = (E_{t+1}^e - E_t)/E_t. \tag{9-1}$$

Equation (9-1) implies a simple way to test whether the foreign exchange market is doing a good job of using current information to forecast exchange rates. Since the interest difference, $R_t - R_t^*$, is the market's forecast, a comparison of this *predicted* exchange rate change with the *actual* exchange rate change that subsequently occurs indicates the market's skill in forecasting.[18]

Statistical studies of the relationship between interest rate differences and later depreciation rates show that the interest difference has been a very bad predictor, in the sense that it has failed to catch any of the large swings in exchange rates. We noted this failure in Chapter 3's discussion of the carry trade. Even worse, as we noted there, the interest difference has, on average, failed to predict correctly the *direction* in which the spot exchange rate would change. If the interest rate difference were a poor but unbiased predictor, we could argue that the market is setting the exchange rate according to interest parity and doing the best job possible in a rapidly changing world where prediction is inherently difficult. The finding of bias, however, seems at odds with that interpretation of the data.

The interest parity condition also furnishes a test of a second implication of the hypothesis that the market uses all available information in setting exchange rates. Suppose that E_{t+1} is the actual future exchange rate people are trying to guess; then the forecast error they make in predicting future depreciation, u_{t+1}, can be expressed as actual minus expected depreciation:

$$u_{t+1} = (E_{t+1} - E_t)/E_t - (E_{t+1}^e - E_t)/E_t. \tag{9-2}$$

If the market is making use of all available information, its forecast error, u_{t+1}, should be statistically unrelated to data known to the market on date t, when expectations were formed. In other words, there should be no opportunity for the market to exploit known data to reduce its later forecast errors.

Under interest parity, this hypothesis can be tested by writing u_{t+1} as actual currency depreciation less the international interest difference:

$$u_{t+1} = (E_{t+1} - E_t)/E_t - (R_t - R_t^*). \tag{9-3}$$

Statistical methods can be used to examine whether u_{t+1} is predictable, on average, on the basis of past information. A number of researchers have found that forecast errors, when defined as above, *can* be predicted. For example, past forecast errors, which are widely known, are useful in predicting future errors.[19]

The Role of Risk Premiums   One explanation of the research results described above is that the foreign exchange market simply ignores easily available information in setting exchange rates. Such a finding would throw doubt on the international capital

---

[18]Most studies of exchange market efficiency study how the forward exchange rate premium does as a predictor of subsequent spot exchange rate changes. That procedure is equivalent to the one we are following if the covered interest parity condition holds, so that the interest difference $R_t - R_t^*$ equals the forward premium (see the appendix to Chapter 3). As noted in Chapter 3, there is strong evidence that covered interest parity holds when the interest rates being compared apply to deposits in the same financial center—for example, London Eurocurrency rates.

[19]For further discussion, see Robert E. Cumby and Maurice Obstfeld, "International Interest Rate and Price Level Linkages Under Flexible Exchange Rates: A Review of Recent Evidence," in John F. O. Bilson and Richard C. Marston, eds., *Exchange Rate Theory and Practice* (Chicago: University of Chicago Press, 1984), pp. 121–151; and Lars Peter Hansen and Robert J. Hodrick, "Forward Exchange Rates as Optimal Predictors of Future Spot Rates: An Econometric Analysis," *Journal of Political Economy* 88 (October 1980), pp. 829–853.

market's ability to communicate appropriate price signals. Before jumping to this conclusion, however, recall that when people are risk averse, the interest parity condition may *not* be a complete account of how exchange rates are determined. If, instead, bonds denominated in different currencies are *imperfect* substitutes for investors, the international interest rate difference equals expected currency depreciation *plus* a risk premium, ρ_t:

$$R_t - R_t^* = (E_{t+1}^e - E_t)/E_t + \rho_t \qquad (9\text{-}4)$$

(see Chapter 7). In this case, the interest difference is not necessarily the market's forecast of future depreciation. Thus, under imperfect asset substitutability, the empirical results just discussed cannot be used to draw inferences about the foreign exchange market's efficiency in processing information.

Because people's expectations are inherently unobservable, there is no simple way to decide between equation (9-4) and the interest parity condition, which is the special case that occurs when ρ_t is always zero. Several econometric studies have attempted to explain departures from interest parity on the basis of particular theories of the risk premium, but none has been entirely successful.[20]

The mixed empirical record leaves the following two possibilities: Either risk premiums are important in exchange rate determination, or the foreign exchange market has been ignoring the opportunity to profit from easily available information. The second alternative seems unlikely in light of foreign exchange traders' powerful incentives to make profits. The first alternative, however, awaits solid statistical confirmation. It is certainly not supported by the evidence reviewed in Chapter 7, which suggests that sterilized foreign exchange intervention has not been an effective tool for exchange rate management. More sophisticated theories show, however, that sterilized intervention may be powerless even under imperfect asset substitutability. Thus, a finding that sterilized intervention is ineffective does not necessarily imply that risk premiums are absent. Another possibility, raised in Chapter 3's Case Study on the carry trade, is one of expected large but infrequent reversals in currency trends that standard statistical techniques are ill-equipped to detect.

Tests for Excessive Volatility   One of the most worrisome findings is that statistical forecasting models of exchange rates based on standard "fundamental" variables like money supplies, government deficits, and output perform badly—even when *actual* (rather than predicted) values of future fundamentals are used to form exchange rate forecasts! Indeed, in a famous study, Richard A. Meese of Barclays Global Investors and Kenneth Rogoff of Harvard University showed that a naive, "random walk" model, which simply takes today's exchange rate as the best guess of tomorrow's, performs better. Some have viewed this finding as evidence that exchange rates have a life of their own, unrelated to the macroeconomic determinants we have emphasized in our models. More recent research has confirmed, however, that while the random walk outperforms more sophisticated models for forecasts up to a year away, the

---

[20]For useful surveys, see Charles Engel, "The Forward Discount Anomaly and the Risk Premium: A Survey of Recent Evidence," *Journal of Empirical Finance* 3 (1996), pp. 123–192; Karen Lewis, "Puzzles in International Finance," in Gene M. Grossman and Kenneth Rogoff, eds., *Handbook of International Economics*, Vol. 3 (Amsterdam: North-Holland, 1996); and Hanno Lustig and Adrien Verdelhan, "Exchange Rates in a Stochastic Discount Factor Framework," in Jessica James, Ian W. Marsh, and Lucio Sarno, eds., *Handbook of Exchange Rates* (Hoboken, NJ: John Wiley & Sons, 2012), pp. 391–420.

models seem to do better at horizons longer than a year and have explanatory power for long-run exchange rate movements.[21]

An additional line of research on the foreign exchange market examines whether exchange rates have been excessively volatile, perhaps because the foreign exchange market "overreacts" to events. A finding of excessive volatility would prove that the foreign exchange market is sending confusing signals to traders and investors who base their decisions on exchange rates. But how volatile must an exchange rate be before its volatility becomes excessive? As we saw in Chapter 3, exchange rates *should* be volatile, because to send the correct price signals, they must move swiftly in response to economic news. Exchange rates are generally less volatile than stock prices. It is still possible, though, that exchange rates are substantially more volatile than the underlying factors that move them—such as money supplies, national outputs, and fiscal variables. Attempts to compare exchange rates' volatility with those of their underlying determinants have, however, produced inconclusive results. A basic problem underlying tests for excessive volatility is the impossibility of quantifying exactly all the variables that convey relevant news about the economic future. For example, how does one attach a number to a political assassination attempt, a major bank failure, or a terrorist attack?

The Bottom Line   The ambiguous evidence on the foreign exchange market's performance warrants an open-minded view. A judgment that the market is doing its job well would support a laissez-faire attitude by governments and a continuation of the present trend toward increased cross-border financial integration in the industrial world. A judgment of market failure, on the other hand, might imply a need for increased foreign exchange intervention by central banks and a reversal of the global trend toward external financial liberalization. The stakes are high, and more research and experience are needed before a firm conclusion can be reached.

SUMMARY

1. When people are *risk averse*, countries can gain through the exchange of risky assets. The gains from trade take the form of a reduction in the riskiness of each country's consumption. International *portfolio diversification* can be carried out through the exchange of *debt instruments* or *equity instruments*.

2. The *international capital market* is the market in which residents of different countries trade assets. One of its important components is the foreign exchange market. Banks are at the center of the international capital market, and many operate offshore, that is, outside the countries where their head offices are based.

3. Regulatory and political factors have encouraged *offshore banking*. The same factors have encouraged *offshore currency trading*, that is, trade in bank deposits

---

[21]The original Meese-Rogoff study is "Empirical Exchange Rate Models of the Seventies: Do They Fit Out of Sample?" *Journal of International Economics* 14 (February 1983), pp. 3–24. On longer-run forecasts, see Menzie D. Chinn and Richard A. Meese, "Banking on Currency Forecasts: How Predictable Is Change in Money?" *Journal of International Economics* 38 (February 1995), pp. 161–178; and Nelson C. Mark, "Exchange Rates and Fundamentals: Evidence on Long-Horizon Predictability," *American Economic Review* 85 (March 1995), pp. 201–218. A recent survey is Pasquale Della Corte and Ilias Tsiakas, "Statistical and Economic Methods for Evaluating Exchange Rate Predictability," in Jessica James, Ian W. Marsh, and Lucio Sarno, eds., *Handbook of Exchange Rates* (Hoboken, NJ: John Wiley & Sons, 2012), pp. 221–263.

denominated in currencies of countries other than the one in which the bank is located. Such *Eurocurrency* trading received a major stimulus from the absence of reserve requirements on deposits in *Eurobanks*.

4. Creation of a Eurocurrency deposit does not occur because that currency leaves its country of origin; rather, all that is required is that a Eurobank accept a deposit liability denominated in the currency. Eurocurrencies therefore pose no threat to central banks' control over their domestic monetary bases, and fears that *Eurodollars*, for example, will some day come "flooding into" the United States are misplaced.

5. Offshore banking is largely unprotected by the safeguards that national governments have imposed to prevent domestic bank failures. In addition, the opportunity that banks have to shift operations offshore, thereby profiting from *regulatory arbitrage*, has undermined the effectiveness of national bank supervision. These problems create a *financial trilemma* that international policymakers have tried to mitigate through increasingly ambitious cross-border collaboration. Since 1974, the *Basel Committee* of industrial-country bank supervisors has worked to enhance global regulatory cooperation, including international standards for *bank capital*. A third generation of proposed prudential regulations (Basel III) was released in 2010 and is in process of implementation by national regulators. There is still uncertainty, however, about a central bank's obligations as an international *lender of last resort*. That uncertainty may reflect an attempt by international authorities to reduce *moral hazard*. The trend toward securitization has increased the need for international cooperation in monitoring and regulating nonbank financial institutions. So has the rise of *emerging markets* and of large *shadow banking systems*. Gaps in the global financial safety net became evident during the global financial crisis of 2007–2009. A key lesson of the crisis is that governments should adopt a *macroprudential perspective* in evaluating financial risks, rather than worrying only about the soundness of individual institutions.

6. The losses caused by financial crises must be evaluated against the gains that international capital markets potentially offer. The international capital market has contributed to an increase in international portfolio diversification since 1970, but the extent of diversification still appears incomplete compared with what economic theory would predict. Similarly, some observers have claimed that the extent of intertemporal trade, as measured by countries' current account balances, has been too small. Such claims are hard to evaluate without more detailed information about the functioning of the world economy than is yet available. Less ambiguous evidence comes from international interest rate comparisons, and this evidence points to a well-functioning market (apart from rare periods of international financial crisis). Rates of return on similar deposits issued in the major financial centers are normally quite close.

7. The foreign exchange market's record in communicating appropriate price signals to international traders and investors is mixed. Tests based on the interest parity condition of Chapter 3 seem to suggest that the market ignores readily available information in setting exchange rates; but because the interest parity theory ignores risk aversion and the resulting risk premiums, the theory may be an oversimplification of reality. Attempts to model risk factors empirically have not, however, been very successful. Tests of excessive exchange rate volatility also yield a mixed verdict on the foreign exchange market's performance. Together with the recent history of financial crises, this is not good news for those who favor a pure laissez-faire approach to financial globalization.

KEY TERMS

bank capital, p. 305
Basel Committee, p. 312
debt instrument, p. 299
emerging markets, p. 312
equity instrument, p. 299
Eurobank, p. 302
Eurocurrencies, p. 302
Eurodollar, p. 302

financial trilemma, p. 311
international capital market, p. 295
lender of last resort (LLR), p. 307
macroprudential perspective, p. 319
moral hazard, p. 308

offshore banking, p. 301
offshore currency trading, p. 302
portfolio diversification, p. 298
regulatory arbitrage, p. 311
risk aversion, p. 298
securitization, p. 313
shadow banking system, p. 303

PROBLEMS

MyEconLab

1. Which portfolio is better diversified, one that contains stock in a dental supply company and a candy company or one that contains stock in a dental supply company and a dairy product company?

2. Imagine a world of two countries in which the only causes of fluctuations in stock prices are unexpected shifts in monetary policies. Under which exchange rate regime would the gains from international asset trade be greater, fixed or floating?

3. The text points out that covered interest parity holds quite closely for deposits of differing currency denominations issued in a single financial center. Why might covered interest parity fail to hold when deposits issued in *different* financial centers are compared?

4. When a U.S. bank accepts a deposit from one of its foreign branches, that deposit is subject to the Fed's reserve requirements. Similarly, Fed reserve requirements are imposed on any loan from a U.S. bank's foreign branch to a U.S. resident, or on any asset purchase by the branch bank from its U.S. parent. What do you think is the rationale for these regulations?

5. The Swiss economist Alexander Swoboda has argued that the Eurodollar market's early growth was fueled by the desire of banks outside the United States to appropriate some of the revenue the United States was collecting as issuer of the principal reserve currency. (This argument is made in *The Euro-Dollar Market: An Interpretation*, Princeton Essays in International Finance 64, International Finance Section, Department of Economics, Princeton University, February 1968.) Do you agree with Swoboda's interpretation?

6. After the developing-country debt crisis began in 1982 (see Chapter 11), U.S. bank regulators imposed tighter supervisory restrictions on the lending policies of American banks and their subsidiaries. Over the 1980s, the share of U.S. banks in London banking activity declined. Can you suggest a connection between these two developments?

7. Why might growing securitization make it harder for bank supervisors to keep track of risks to the financial system?

8. Return to the example in the text of the two countries that produce random amounts of kiwi fruit and can trade claims on that fruit. Suppose the two countries also produce raspberries that spoil if shipped between countries and therefore are nontradable. How do you think this would affect the ratio of international asset trade to GNP for Home and Foreign?

9. Sometimes it is claimed that the international equality of *real* interest rates is the most accurate barometer of international financial integration. Do you agree? Why or why not?

10. If you look at data on the website of the Bureau of Economic Analysis, you will see that between the end of 2003 and the end of 2007, the net foreign debt of the United States rose by far less than the sum of its current account deficits over those years. At the same time, the dollar depreciated. Do you see any connection? (Hint: The United States borrows mostly in dollars but has substantial foreign currency assets.)

11. In interpreting ratios such as those in Table 9-1, one must be cautious about drawing the conclusion that diversification is rising as rapidly as the reported numbers rise. Suppose a Brazilian buys a U.S. international equity fund, which places its client's money in Brazil's stock market. What happens to Brazilian and U.S. gross foreign assets and liabilities? What happens to Brazilian and U.S. international diversification?

12. Banks are not happy when regulators force them to raise the ratio of capital to total assets: they argue that this reduces their potential profits. When a bank *borrows* more in order to purchase more risky assets, however, the interest rate it must pay on the borrowing should be high enough to compensate the lenders for the risk that the bank cannot repay in full—and the higher interest rate reduces bank profits. In light of this observation, is it obvious to you that it is more profitable for the bank to finance its asset purchase by borrowing, rather than by issuing additional shares of stock (and thereby increasing rather than reducing its ratio of capital to total assets)?

13. How would your answer to the last question change if the bank's creditors expect the government sometimes to step in with a bailout that prevents losses on the bank's debt liabilities?

14. If you return to Figure 9-4, you will notice that London Eurodollar interest rates tend to exceed U.S. certificate of deposit rates after the global financial crisis, but not before. Why do you think this is the case? (Be sure to return to this question after you read the next chapter!)

FURTHER READINGS

Viral V. Acharya, Nirupama Kulkarni, and Matthew Richardson. "Capital, Contingent Capital, and Liquidity Requirements," in Viral V. Acharya, Thomas F. Cooley, Matthew P. Richardson, and Ingo Walter, eds., *Regulating Wall Street: The Dodd-Frank Act and the Architecture of Global Finance.* Hoboken, NJ: John Wiley & Sons, 2011, pp. 143–180. Clear discussion of the goals and limitations of the Dodd-Frank act and Basel III.

Anat Admati and Martin Hellwig. *The Bankers' New Clothes: What's Wrong with Banking and What to Do about It.* Princeton, NJ: Princeton University Press, 2013. A lucid account of banks' incentives to propagate financial fragility by financing their asset holdings with debt rather than capital.

Alan S. Blinder. *After the Music Stopped: The Financial Crisis, the Response, and the Work Ahead.* New York: Penguin Press, 2013. An influential economist's account of the origins and repercussions of the global financial crisis of 2007–2009.

Markus K. Brunnermeier, Andrew Crockett, Charles A. E. Goodhart, Avinash Persaud, and Hyun Song Shin. *The Fundamental Principles of Financial Regulation.* Geneva and London: International Center for Monetary and Banking Studies and Centre for Economic Policy Research, 2009. Comprehensive review of regulatory approaches to financial crisis prevention, with emphasis on the macroprudential perspective.

Stijn Claessens, Richard J. Herring, and Dirk Schoenmaker. *A Safer World Financial System: Improving the Resolution of Systemic Institutions.* Geneva and London: International Center for Monetary and Banking Studies and Centre for Economic Policy Research, 2010. Discusses the reorganization of insolvent institutions in a global setting.

Nicolas Coeurdacier and Hélène Rey. "Home Bias in Open Economy Financial Macroeconomics." *Journal of Economic Literature* 51 (March 2012), pp. 63–115. Advanced theoretical and empirical overview of home bias in international asset portfolios.

Barry Eichengreen. "International Financial Regulation after the Crisis." *Daedalus* (Fall 2010), pp. 107–114. Description and critique of the current institutional framework for global cooperation in regulating international finance.

Stanley Fischer. "On the Need for an International Lender of Last Resort." *Journal of Economic Perspectives* 13 (Fall 1999): 85–104. Focuses on the IMF's ability to function as an international LLR.

Charles A. E. Goodhart. "Myths about the Lender of Last Resort." *International Finance* 2 (November 1999), pp. 339–360. Clear discussion of the theory and practice of the LLR function.

Charles P. Kindleberger and Robert Aliber. *Manias, Panics, and Crashes: A History of Financial Crises*, 5th edition. Hoboken, NJ: John Wiley & Sons, 2005. An historical review of international financial crises from the 17th century to the present day.

Richard M. Levich. "Is the Foreign Exchange Market Efficient?" *Oxford Review of Economic Policy* 5 (1989), pp. 40–60. Valuable survey of research on the efficiency of the foreign exchange market.

Haim Levy and Marshall Sarnat. "International Portfolio Diversification," in Richard J. Herring, ed. *Managing Foreign Exchange Risk*. Cambridge, U.K.: Cambridge University Press, 1983, pp. 115–142. A nice exposition of the logic of international asset diversification.

Nelson C. Mark. *International Macroeconomics and Finance*. Oxford: Blackwell Publishers, 2001. Chapter 6 discusses the efficiency of the foreign exchange market.

Maurice Obstfeld. "The Global Capital Market: Benefactor or Menace?" *Journal of Economic Perspectives* 12 (Fall 1998), pp. 9–30. Overview of the functions, operations, and implications for national sovereignty of the international capital market.

Maurice Obstfeld and Kenneth Rogoff. "Global Imbalances and the Financial Crisis: Products of Common Causes," in Reuven Glick and Mark Spiegel, eds. *Asia and the Global Financial Crisis*. San Francisco, CA: Federal Reserve Bank of San Francisco, 2010. An analysis of the links between global financial flows and the financial crisis of 2007–2009.

Carmen M. Reinhart and Kenneth S. Rogoff. *This Time Is Different: Eight Centuries of Financial Folly*. Princeton, NJ: Princeton University Press, 2009. Data-based historical overview of the precedents and effects of financial crises around the world.

Garry J. Schinasi. *Safeguarding Financial Stability: Theory and Practice*. Washington, D.C.: International Monetary Fund, 2006. Thorough overview of financial stability threats in a context of globalized financial markets.

MyEconLab Can Help You Get a Better Grade

MyEconLab   If your exam were tomorrow, would you be ready? For each chapter, MyEconLab Practice Tests and Study Plans pinpoint sections you have mastered and those you need to study. That way, you are more efficient with your study time, and you are better prepared for your exams.

To see how it works, turn to page 9 and then go to

www.myeconlab.com

CHAPTER 10

OPTIMUM CURRENCY AREAS AND THE EURO

On January 1, 1999, 11 member countries of the European Union (EU) adopted a common currency, the euro. They have since been joined by seven more EU members. Europe's bold experiment in economic and monetary union (EMU), which many had viewed as a visionary fantasy only a few years earlier, created a currency area with more than 335 million consumers—roughly 7 percent more populous than the United States. If the countries of Eastern Europe all eventually enter the euro zone, it will comprise more than 25 countries and stretch from the Arctic Ocean in the north to the Mediterranean Sea in the south, and from the Atlantic Ocean in the west to the Black Sea in the east. Figure 10-1 shows the extent of the euro zone as of 2014.

The birth of the euro resulted in fixed exchange rates between all EMU member countries. In deciding to form a monetary union, however, EMU countries sacrificed even more sovereignty over their monetary policies than a fixed exchange rate regime normally requires. They agreed to give up national currencies entirely and to hand over control of their monetary policies to a shared European Central Bank (ECB). The euro project thus represents an extreme solution to the monetary policy trilemma of Chapter 8: absolute exchange rate stability, absolute openness to financial trade, but no monetary autonomy whatsoever.

The European experience raises a host of important questions. How and why did Europe set up its single currency? What benefits has the euro delivered for the economies of its members, and why have they found themselves in a protracted crisis? How does the euro affect countries outside of EMU, notably the United States? And what lessons does the European experience carry for other potential currency blocs, such as the Mercosur trading group in South America?

This chapter focuses on Europe's experience of monetary unification to illustrate the economic benefits and costs of fixed exchange rate agreements and more comprehensive currency unification schemes. As we see in Europe's experience, the effects of joining a fixed exchange rate agreement are complex and depend crucially on microeconomic *and* macroeconomic factors. Our discussion

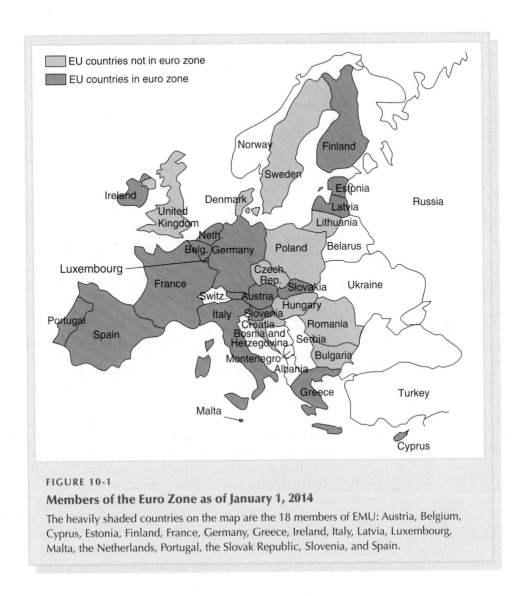

FIGURE 10-1

Members of the Euro Zone as of January 1, 2014

The heavily shaded countries on the map are the 18 members of EMU: Austria, Belgium, Cyprus, Estonia, Finland, France, Germany, Greece, Ireland, Italy, Latvia, Luxembourg, Malta, the Netherlands, Portugal, the Slovak Republic, Slovenia, and Spain.

of Europe will throw light not only on the forces promoting greater unification of national economies but also on the forces that make a country think twice before giving up completely its control over monetary policy.

LEARNING GOALS

After reading this chapter, you will be able to:

- Discuss why Europeans have long sought to stabilize their mutual exchange rates while floating against the U.S. dollar.
- Describe how the European Union, through the Maastricht Treaty of 1991, placed itself on the road to having a single currency, the euro, issued and managed by a European Central Bank (ECB).

- Detail the structure of the ECB, the European System of Central Banks, and the European Union's arrangements for coordinating member states' economic policies.
- Articulate the main lessons of the theory of optimum currency areas.
- Recount how the 18 countries using the euro have fared so far in their currency union, and the steps they are taking in response to their prolonged economic crisis.

How the European Single Currency Evolved

Until its demise in 1973, the Bretton Woods system fixed every member country's exchange rate against the U.S. dollar and as a result also fixed the exchange rate between every pair of nondollar currencies. EU countries allowed their currencies to float against the dollar after 1973, but have tried progressively to narrow the extent to which they let their currencies fluctuate against each other. These efforts culminated in the birth of the euro on January 1, 1999.

What Has Driven European Monetary Cooperation?

What prompted the EU countries to seek closer coordination of monetary policies and greater mutual exchange rate stability? Two main motives inspired these moves and have remained major reasons for the adoption of the euro:

1. *To enhance Europe's role in the world monetary system.* The events leading up to the collapse of the Bretton Woods system were accompanied by declining European confidence in the readiness of the United States to place its international monetary responsibilities ahead of its national interests (Chapter 8). By speaking with a single voice on monetary issues, EU countries hoped to defend more effectively their own economic interests in the face of an increasingly self-absorbed United States.
2. *To turn the European Union into a truly unified market.* Even though the 1957 Treaty of Rome founding the EU had established a customs union, significant official barriers to the movements of goods and factors within Europe remained. A consistent goal of EU members has been to eliminate all such barriers and transform the EU into a huge unified market on the model of the United States.

TABLE 10-1	A Brief Glossary of Euronyms
ECB	European Central Bank
EFSF	European Financial Stability Facility
EMS	European Monetary System
EMU	Economic and Monetary Union
ERM	Exchange Rate Mechanism
ESCB	European System of Central Banks
ESM	European Stability Mechanism
EU	European Union
OMT	Outright Monetary Transactions
SGP	Stability and Growth Pact
SRM	Single Resolution Mechanism
SSM	Single Supervisory Mechanism

European officials believed, however, that exchange rate uncertainty, like official trade barriers, was a major factor reducing trade within Europe. They also feared that exchange rate swings causing large changes in intra-European relative prices would strengthen political forces hostile to free trade within Europe.[1]

The key to understanding how Europe has come so far in both market and monetary unification lies in the continent's war-torn history. After the end of World War II in 1945, many European leaders agreed that economic cooperation and integration among the former belligerents would be the best guarantee against a repetition of the 20th century's two devastating wars. The result was a gradual ceding of national economic policy powers to centralized European Union governing bodies, such as the European Commission in Brussels, Belgium (the EU's executive body), and the European Central Bank in Frankfurt, Germany.

The European Monetary System, 1979–1998

The first significant institutional step on the road to European monetary unification was the **European Monetary System (EMS)**. The eight original participants in the EMS's exchange rate mechanism—France, Germany, Italy, Belgium, Denmark, Ireland, Luxembourg, and the Netherlands—began operating a formal network of mutually pegged exchange rates in March 1979. A complex set of EMS intervention arrangements worked to restrict the exchange rates of participating currencies within specified fluctuation margins.[2]

The prospects for a successful fixed-rate area in Europe seemed bleak in early 1979, when recent yearly inflation rates ranged from Germany's 2.7 percent to Italy's 12.1 percent. Through a mixture of policy cooperation and realignment, however, the EMS fixed exchange rate club survived and even grew, adding Spain to its ranks in 1989, Britain in 1990, and Portugal early in 1992. Only in September 1992 did this growth suffer a sudden setback when Britain and Italy left the EMS exchange rate mechanism at the start of a protracted European currency crisis that forced the remaining members to retreat to very wide exchange rate margins.

The EMS's operation was aided by several safety valves that initially helped reduce the frequency of such crises. Most exchange rates "fixed" by the EMS until August 1993 actually could fluctuate up or down by as much as 2.25 percent relative to an assigned par value. A few members were able to negotiate bands of ±6 percent, making a greater sacrifice of exchange rate stability but gaining more room to choose their own monetary policies. In August 1993, EMS countries decided to widen nearly all of the bands to ±15 percent under the pressure of speculative attacks.

As another crucial safety valve, the EMS developed generous provisions for the extension of credit from strong- to weak-currency members. If the French franc (France's former currency) depreciated too far against the deutsche mark (or DM,

---

[1] A very important administrative reason Europeans have sought to avoid big movements in European cross-exchange rates is related to the Common Agricultural Policy (CAP), the EU's system of agricultural price supports. Prior to the euro, agricultural prices were quoted in terms of the European Currency Unit (ECU), a basket of EU currencies. Exchange rate realignments within Europe would abruptly alter the real domestic value of the supported prices, provoking protests from farmers in the revaluing countries. While the annoyance of administering the CAP under exchange rate realignments was undoubtedly crucial in starting Europeans on the road to currency unification, the two motives cited in the text are more important in explaining how Europe ultimately came to embrace a common currency.

[2] As a technical matter, all EU members were members of the EMS, but only those EMS members who enforced the fluctuation margins belonged to the EMS *exchange rate mechanism (ERM)*.

Germany's former currency), Germany's central bank, the Bundesbank, was expected to lend the Bank of France DM to sell for francs in the foreign exchange market.

Finally, during the system's initial years of operation several members (notably France and Italy) reduced the possibility of speculative attack by maintaining capital controls that directly limited domestic residents' sales of home for foreign currencies.

The EMS went through periodic currency realignments. In all, 11 realignments occurred between the start of the EMS in March 1979 and January 1987. Capital controls played the important role of shielding members' reserves from speculators during these adjustments. Starting in 1987, however, a phased removal of capital controls by EMS countries increased the possibility of speculative attacks and thus reduced governments' willingness openly to consider devaluing or revaluing. The removal of controls greatly reduced member countries' monetary independence (a consequence of the monetary policy trilemma), but freedom of payments and capital movements within the EU had always been a key element of EU countries' plan to turn Europe into a unified single market.

For a period of five and a half years after January 1987, no adverse economic event was able to shake the EMS's commitment to its fixed exchange rates. This state of affairs came to an end in 1992, however, as economic shocks caused by the reunification of East and West Germany in 1990 led to asymmetrical macroeconomic pressures in Germany and in its major EMS partners.

The result of reunification was a boom in Germany and higher inflation, which Germany's very inflation-averse central bank, the Bundesbank, resisted through sharply higher interest rates. (Germany's very high inflation after both world wars left permanent scars.) Other EMS countries such as France, Italy, and the United Kingdom, however, were not simultaneously booming. By matching the high German interest rates to hold their currencies fixed against Germany's, they were unwillingly pushing their own economies into deep recession. The policy conflict between Germany and its partners led to a series of fierce speculative attacks on the EMS exchange parities starting in September 1992. By August 1993, as previously noted, the EMS was forced to retreat to very wide (± 15 percent) bands, which it kept in force until the introduction of the euro in 1999.

German Monetary Dominance and the Credibility Theory of the EMS

Earlier, we identified two main reasons why the European Union sought to fix internal exchange rates: a desire to defend Europe's economic interests more effectively on the world stage and the ambition to achieve greater internal economic unity.

Europe's experience of high inflation in the 1970s suggests an additional purpose that the EMS grew to fulfill. By fixing their exchange rates against the DM, the other EMS countries in effect imported the German Bundesbank's credibility as an inflation fighter and thus discouraged the development of inflationary pressures at home—pressures they might otherwise have been tempted to accommodate through monetary expansion. This view, the **credibility theory of the EMS**, holds that the political costs of violating an international exchange rate agreement may be useful. They can restrain governments from depreciating their currencies to gain the short-term advantage of an economic boom at the long-term cost of higher inflation.

Policy makers in inflation-prone EMS countries, such as Italy, clearly gained credibility by placing monetary policy decisions in the hands of the inflation-fearing German central bank. Devaluation was still possible, but only subject to EMS restrictions. Because politicians also feared that they would look incompetent to voters

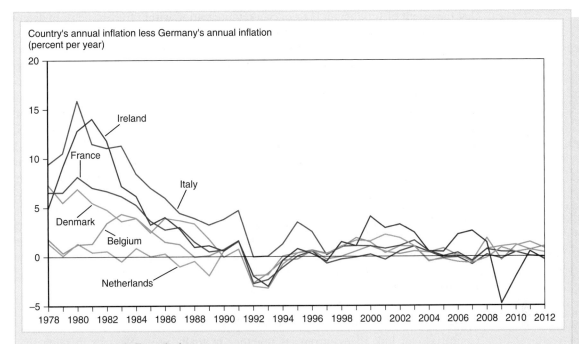

Country's annual inflation less Germany's annual inflation
(percent per year)

FIGURE 10-2 MyEconLab Real-time data

Inflation Convergence for Six Original EMS Members, 1978–2012

Shown are the differences between domestic inflation and German inflation for six of the original EMS members: Belgium, Denmark, France, Ireland, Italy, and the Netherlands.

Source: CPI inflation rates from International Monetary Fund, *International Financial Statistics*.

if they devalued, a government's decision to peg to the DM reduced both its willingness and its ability to create domestic inflation.[3]

Added support for the credibility theory comes from the behavior of inflation rates relative to Germany's, shown in Figure 10-2 for six of the other original EMS members.[4] As the figure shows, annual inflation rates gradually converged toward the low German levels.[5]

Market Integration Initiatives

The EU countries have tried to achieve greater internal economic unity not only by fixing mutual exchange rates, but also through direct measures to encourage the free flow of goods, services, and factors of production. Later in this chapter you will learn

---

[3]The general theory that an inflation-prone country gains from vesting its monetary policy decisions with a "conservative" central bank is developed in an influential paper by Kenneth Rogoff. See "The Optimal Degree of Commitment to an Intermediate Monetary Target," *Quarterly Journal of Economics* 100 (November 1985), pp. 1169–1189. For application to the EMS, see Francesco Giavazzi and Marco Pagano, "The Advantage of Tying One's Hands: EMS Discipline and Central Bank Credibility," *European Economic Review* 32 (June 1988), pp. 1055–1082.

[4]Figure 10-2 does not include the tiny country of Luxembourg because before 1999, that country had a currency union with Belgium and an inflation rate very close to Belgium's.

[5]Those skeptical of the credibility theory of EMS inflation convergence point out that the United States, Britain, and Japan also reduced inflation to low levels over the 1980s, but did so without fixing their exchange rates. Many other countries have done the same since.

that the extent of product and factor market integration within Europe helps to determine how fixed exchange rates affect Europe's macroeconomic stability. Europe's efforts to raise *microeconomic* efficiency through direct market liberalization have also increased its preference for mutually fixed exchange rates on *macroeconomic* grounds.

The process of market unification that began when the original EU members formed their customs union in 1957 was still incomplete 30 years later. In a number of industries, such as automobiles and telecommunications, trade within Europe was discouraged by government-imposed standards and registration requirements. Often government licensing or purchasing practices gave domestic producers virtual monopoly positions in their home markets. In the Single European Act of 1986 (which amended the founding Treaty of Rome), EU members took the crucial political steps to remove remaining internal barriers to trade, capital movements, and labor migration. Most important, they dropped the Treaty of Rome's requirement of unanimous consent for measures related to market completion, so that one or two self-interested EU members could not block trade liberalization measures as in the past. Further moves toward market integration have followed. Financial capital, for example, now can move quite freely, not only within the European Union, but also between the European Union and outside jurisdictions.

European Economic and Monetary Union

Countries can link their currencies together in many ways. We can imagine that the different modes of linkage form a spectrum, with the arrangements at one end requiring little sacrifice of monetary policy independence and those at the other end requiring independence to be given up entirely.

The early EMS, characterized by frequent currency realignments and widespread government control over capital movements, left some scope for national monetary policies. In 1989, a committee headed by Jacques Delors, president of the European Commission, recommended a three-stage transition to a goal at the extreme end of the policy spectrum just described. That goal was an **economic and monetary union (EMU)**, a European Union in which national currencies would be replaced by a single EU currency managed by a sole central bank operating on behalf of all EU members.

On December 10, 1991, the leaders of the EU countries met at the ancient Dutch city of Maastricht and agreed to propose for national ratification far-reaching amendments to the Treaty of Rome. These amendments were meant to place the EU squarely on the road to EMU. Included in the 250-page **Maastricht Treaty** was a provision calling for the introduction of a single European currency and a European Central Bank no later than January 1, 1999. By 1993, all 12 countries then belonging to the EU had ratified the Maastricht Treaty. The 16 countries that joined the EU afterward accepted the Treaty's provisions upon joining (see Figure 10-1).[6]

Why did the EU countries move away from the EMS and toward the much more ambitious goal of a single shared currency? There were four reasons:

1. They believed a single EU currency would produce a greater degree of European market integration than fixed exchange rates by removing the threat of EMS currency realignments and eliminating the costs to traders of converting one EMS

---

[6]Denmark and the United Kingdom, however, ratified the Maastricht Treaty subject to special exceptions that allow them to "opt out" of the treaty's monetary provisions and retain their national currencies. Sweden has no formal opt out, but it has exploited other technicalities in the Maastricht Treaty to avoid joining the euro zone so far.

currency into another. The single currency was viewed as a necessary complement to plans for melding EU markets into a single, continent-wide market.

2. Some EU leaders thought that Germany's management of EMS monetary policy had placed a one-sided emphasis on German macroeconomic goals at the expense of its EMS partners' interests. The European Central Bank that would replace the German Bundesbank under EMU would have to be more considerate of other countries' problems, and it would automatically give those countries the same opportunity as Germany to participate in system-wide monetary policy decisions.

3. Given the move to complete freedom of capital movements within the EU, there seemed to be little to gain, and much to lose, from keeping national currencies with fixed (but adjustable) parities rather than irrevocably locking parities through a single currency. Any system of fixed exchange rates among distinct national currencies would be subject to ferocious speculative attacks, as in 1992–1993. If Europeans wished to combine permanently fixed exchange rates with freedom of capital movements, a single currency was the best way to accomplish this.

4. As previously noted, all of the EU countries' leaders hoped the Maastricht Treaty's provisions would guarantee the political stability of Europe. Beyond its purely economic functions, the single EU currency was intended as a potent symbol of Europe's desire to place cooperation ahead of the national rivalries that often had led to war in the past. Under this scenario, the new currency would align the economic interests of individual European nations to create an overwhelming political constituency for peace on the continent.

The Maastricht Treaty's critics denied that EMU would have these positive effects and opposed the treaty's provisions for vesting stronger governmental powers with the European Union. To these critics, EMU was symptomatic of a tendency for the European Union's central institutions to ignore local needs, meddle in local affairs, and downgrade prized symbols of national identity (including, of course, national currencies). Germany's citizens in particular, traumatized by memories of severe postwar inflations, feared that the new European Central Bank would not fight inflation as fiercely as their Bundesbank did.

The Euro and Economic Policy in the Euro Zone

How were the initial members of EMU chosen, how are new members admitted, and what is the structure of the complex of financial and political institutions that govern economic policy in the euro zone? This section provides an overview.

The Maastricht Convergence Criteria and the Stability and Growth Pact

The Maastricht Treaty requires EU countries to satisfy several macroeconomic convergence criteria prior to admission to EMU. Among these criteria are:

1. The country's inflation rate in the year before admission must be no more than 1.5 percent above the average rate of the three EU member states with the lowest inflation.

2. The country must have maintained a stable exchange rate within the ERM without devaluing on its own initiative.

3. The country must have a public-sector deficit no higher than 3 percent of its GDP (except in exceptional and temporary circumstances).

4. The country must have a public debt that is below or approaching a reference level of 60 percent of its GDP.

The treaty provides for the ongoing monitoring of criteria 3 and 4 mentioned previously by the European Commission even after admission to EMU, and for the levying of penalties on countries that violate these fiscal rules and do not correct situations of "excessive" deficits and debt. The surveillance and sanctions over high deficits and debts place national governments under constraints in the exercise of their national fiscal powers. For example, a highly indebted EMU country facing a national recession might be unable to use expansionary fiscal policy for fear of breaching the Maastricht limits—a possibly costly loss of policy autonomy, given the absence of a national monetary policy!

In addition, a supplementary **Stability and Growth Pact (SGP)** negotiated by European leaders in 1997 tightened the fiscal straitjacket further. The SGP set out "the medium-term budgetary objective of positions close to balance or in surplus." It also set a timetable for the imposition of financial penalties on countries that fail to correct situations of "excessive" deficits and debt promptly enough. What explains the macroeconomic convergence criteria, the fear of high public debts, and the SGP? Before they would sign the Maastricht Treaty, low-inflation countries such as Germany wanted assurance that their EMU partners had learned to prefer an environment of low inflation and fiscal restraint. They feared that otherwise, the euro might be a weak currency, falling prey to the types of policies that have fueled French, Greek, Italian, Portuguese, Spanish, and United Kingdom inflation at various points since the early 1970s. A highly indebted government that continues to borrow may find that the market demand for its bonds disappears—a nightmare scenario that finally came to pass for several European countries in the euro crisis starting in 2009. Another fear about EMU was that the new European Central Bank would face pressures to purchase government debt directly in such situations, thereby fueling money supply growth and inflation. Voters in traditionally low-inflation countries worried that prudent governments within EMU would be forced to pick up the tab for profligate governments that borrowed more than they could afford to repay. This was especially true in Germany, where taxpayers in the country's western part were bearing the cost of absorbing the formerly Communist east. Consistent with this fear, the Maastricht Treaty also contained a "no bailout clause" prohibiting EU member countries from taking on other members' debts.

As EMU came closer in 1997, German public opinion therefore remained opposed to the euro. The German government demanded the SGP as a way of convincing domestic voters that the new European Central Bank would indeed produce low inflation and avoid bailouts. Ironically, because Germany (along with France) is one of the countries that was subsequently in violation of the Maastricht fiscal rules, the SGP was not enforced in practice during the euro's first decade—even though later experience showed the concerns that motivated it to be valid, as we shall see.

By May 1998, it was clear that 11 EU countries had satisfied the convergence criteria on the basis of 1997 data and would be founding members of EMU: Austria, Belgium, Finland, France, Germany, Ireland, Italy, Luxembourg, the Netherlands, Portugal, and Spain. Greece failed to qualify on any of the criteria in 1998, although it ultimately appeared to pass all of its tests and entered EMU on January 1, 2001. Since then, Slovenia (on January 1, 2007), Cyprus and Malta (both on January 1, 2008), the Slovak Republic (January 1, 2009), Estonia (January 1, 2011), and Latvia (January 1, 2014) also have joined the euro zone.

The European Central Bank and the Eurosystem

The *Eurosystem* conducts monetary policy for the euro zone and consists of the *European Central Bank* (ECB) in Frankfurt plus the 18 national central banks of the euro area, which now play roles analogous to those of the regional Federal Reserve banks in the United States. Decisions of the Eurosystem are made by votes of the governing council of the ECB, consisting of the six-member ECB executive board (including the president of the ECB) and the heads of the national central banks of the euro area. The European System of Central Banks (ESCB) consists of the ECB plus all 28 EU central banks, including those of countries that do not use the euro. Like members of the Eurosystem, non-euro area central banks are committed to pursue domestic price stability as well as various forms of cooperation with the Eurosystem.

The authors of the Maastricht Treaty hoped to create an independent central bank free of the political influences that might lead to inflation.[7] The treaty gives the ECB an overriding mandate to pursue price stability and includes many provisions intended to insulate monetary policy decisions from political influence. In addition, unlike any other central bank in the world, the ECB operates above and beyond the reach of any single national government. In the United States, for example, Congress could easily pass laws reducing the independence of the Federal Reserve. In contrast, while the ECB is required to brief the European Parliament regularly on its activities, the European Parliament has no power to alter the statute of the ECB and ESCB. That would require an amendment to the Maastricht Treaty approved by legislatures or voters in every member country of the EU. However, critics of the treaty argue that it goes too far in shielding the ECB from normal democratic processes.

The Revised Exchange Rate Mechanism

For EU countries that are not yet members of EMU, a revised exchange rate mechanism—referred to as ERM 2—defines broad exchange rate zones against the euro (± 15 percent) and specifies reciprocal intervention arrangements to support these target zones. ERM 2 was viewed as necessary to discourage competitive devaluations against the euro by EU members outside the euro zone and to give would-be EMU entrants a way of satisfying the Maastricht Treaty's exchange rate stability convergence criterion. Under ERM 2 rules, either the ECB or the national central bank of an EU member with its own currency can suspend euro intervention operations if they result in money supply changes that threaten to destabilize the domestic price level. In practice ERM 2 is asymmetric, with peripheral countries pegging to the euro and adjusting passively to ECB decisions on interest rates.

The Theory of Optimum Currency Areas

There is little doubt that the European monetary integration process has helped advance the *political* goals of its founders by giving the European Union a stronger position in international affairs. The survival and future development of the European monetary experiment depend more heavily, however, on its ability to help countries reach their *economic* goals. Here the picture is less clear because a country's decision to fix its exchange rate can in principle lead to economic sacrifices as well as benefits.

We saw in Chapter 8 that by changing its exchange rate, a country may succeed in cushioning the disruptive impact of various economic shocks. On the other hand, exchange rate flexibility can have potentially harmful effects, such as making relative

---

[7]Several studies show that central bank independence appears to be associated with lower inflation. A recent assessment is offered by Christopher Crowe and Ellen E. Meade, "Central Bank Independence and Transparency: Evolution and Effectiveness," *European Journal of Political Economy* 24 (December 2008), pp. 763–777.

prices less predictable or undermining the government's resolve to keep inflation in check. To weigh the economic costs against the advantages of joining a group of countries with mutually fixed exchange rates, we need a framework for thinking systematically about the stabilization powers a country sacrifices and the gains in efficiency and credibility it may reap.

In this section, we show that a country's costs and benefits from joining a fixed exchange rate area such as the euro zone depend on how integrated its economy is with those of its potential partners. The analysis leading to this conclusion, which is known as the theory of **optimum currency areas**, predicts that fixed exchange rates are most appropriate for areas closely integrated through international trade and factor movements.[8]

Economic Integration and the Benefits of a Fixed Exchange Rate Area: The *GG* Schedule

Consider how an individual country, for example, Norway, might approach the decision of whether to join an area of fixed exchange rates, for example, the euro zone. Our goal is to develop a simple diagram that clarifies Norway's choice.

We begin by deriving the first of two elements in the diagram, a schedule called *GG* that shows how the potential gain to Norway from joining the euro zone depends on Norway's trading links with that region. Let us assume that Norway is considering pegging its currency, the krone, to the euro.

A major economic benefit of fixed exchange rates is that they simplify economic calculations and, compared to floating rates, provide a more predictable basis for decisions that involve international transactions. Imagine the time and resources American consumers and businesses would waste every day if each of the 50 United States had its own currency that fluctuated in value against the currencies of all the other states! Norway faces a similar disadvantage in its trade with the euro zone when it allows its krone to float against the euro. The **monetary efficiency gain** from joining the fixed exchange rate system equals the joiner's savings from avoiding the uncertainty, confusion, and calculation and transaction costs that arise when exchange rates float.[9]

In practice, it may be hard to attach a precise number to the total monetary efficiency gain Norway would enjoy as a result of pegging to the euro. We can be sure, however, that this gain will be higher if Norway trades a lot with euro zone countries. For example, if Norway's trade with the euro zone amounts to 50 percent of its GNP while its trade with the United States amounts to only 5 percent of GNP, then, other things equal, a fixed krone/euro exchange rate clearly yields a greater monetary efficiency gain to Norwegian traders than a fixed krone/dollar rate. Similarly, the efficiency gain from a fixed krone/euro rate is greater when trade between Norway and the euro zone is extensive than when it is small.

---

[8]The original reference is Robert A. Mundell's classic article "The Theory of Optimum Currency Areas," *American Economic Review* 51 (September 1961), pp. 717–725. Subsequent contributions are summarized in the book by Tower and Willett listed in Further Readings. Mundell was trying to make the point that the optimum currency area need not coincide with national boundaries. As we shall see, however, recent experience in the euro area suggests that if the currency area does reach beyond national borders, some key governmental functions may need to be delegated to supra-national authorities acting on behalf of the currency union as a whole.

[9]To illustrate just one component of the monetary efficiency gain, potential savings of commissions paid to brokers and banks on foreign exchange transactions, Charles R. Bean of the Bank of England estimated that in 1992, a "round-trip" through all the European Union currencies would result in the loss of fully *half* the original sum. See his paper "Economic and Monetary Union in Europe," *Journal of Economic Perspectives* 6 (Fall 1992), pp. 31–52.

The monetary efficiency gain from pegging the krone to the euro will also be higher if factors of production can migrate freely between Norway and the euro area. Norwegians who invest in euro zone countries benefit when the returns on their investments are more predictable. Similarly, Norwegians who work in euro zone countries may benefit if a fixed exchange rate makes their wages more stable relative to Norway's cost of living.

Our conclusion is that *a high degree of economic integration between a country and a fixed exchange rate area magnifies the monetary efficiency gain the country reaps when it fixes its exchange rate against the area's currencies.* The more extensive are cross-border trade and factor movements, the greater is the gain from a fixed cross-border exchange rate.

The upward-sloping *GG* curve in Figure 10-3 shows the relation between a country's degree of economic integration with a fixed exchange rate area and the monetary efficiency gain to the country from joining the area. The figure's horizontal axis measures the extent to which Norway (the joining country in our example) is economically integrated into euro zone product and factor markets. The vertical axis measures the monetary efficiency gain to Norway from pegging to the euro. *GG*'s positive slope reflects the conclusion that the monetary efficiency gain a country gets by joining a fixed exchange rate area rises as its economic integration with the area increases.

In our example, we have implicitly assumed that the larger exchange rate area, the euro zone, has a stable and predictable price level. If it does not, the greater variability in Norway's price level that would follow a decision to join the exchange rate area would likely offset any monetary efficiency gain a fixed exchange rate might provide. A different problem arises if Norway's commitment to fix the krone's exchange rate is not fully believed by economic actors. In this situation, some exchange rate uncertainty would remain and Norway would therefore enjoy a smaller monetary efficiency gain. If the euro zone's price level is stable and Norway's exchange rate commitment is firm, however, the main conclusion follows: When Norway pegs to the euro, it gains from the stability of its currency against the euro, and this efficiency gain is greater the more closely tied are Norway's markets with euro zone markets.

FIGURE 10-3

The *GG* Schedule

The upward-sloping *GG* schedule shows that a country's monetary efficiency gain from joining a fixed exchange rate area rises as the country's economic integration with the area rises.

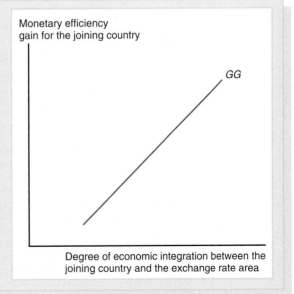

Monetary efficiency gain for the joining country

GG

Degree of economic integration between the joining country and the exchange rate area

Earlier in this chapter, we learned that a country may wish to peg its exchange rate to an area of price stability to import the anti-inflationary resolve of the area's monetary authorities. When the economy of the pegging country is well integrated with that of the low-inflation area, however, low domestic inflation is easier to achieve. The reason is that close economic integration leads to international price convergence and therefore lessens the scope for independent variation in the pegging country's price level. This argument provides another reason why high economic integration with a fixed exchange rate area enhances a country's gain from membership.

Economic Integration and the Costs of a Fixed Exchange Rate Area: The *LL* Schedule

Membership in an exchange rate area may involve costs as well as benefits, even when the area has low inflation. These costs arise because a country that joins an exchange rate area gives up its ability to use the exchange rate and monetary policy for the purpose of stabilizing output and employment. This **economic stability loss** from joining, like the country's monetary efficiency gain, is related to the country's economic integration with its exchange rate partners. We can derive a second schedule, the *LL* schedule, that shows the relationship graphically.

In Chapter 8's discussion of the relative merits of fixed and floating exchange rates, we concluded that when the economy is disturbed by a change in the output market (that is, by a shift in the *DD* schedule), a floating exchange rate has an advantage over a fixed rate: It automatically cushions the economy's output and employment by allowing an immediate change in the relative price of domestic and foreign goods. Furthermore, you will recall from Chapter 7 that when the exchange rate is fixed, purposeful stabilization is more difficult to achieve because monetary policy has no power at all to affect domestic output. Given these two conclusions, we would expect changes in the *DD* schedule to have more severe effects on an economy in which the monetary authority is required to fix the exchange rate against a group of foreign currencies. The *extra* instability caused by the fixed exchange rate is the economic stability loss.[10]

To derive the *LL* schedule, we must understand how the extent of Norway's economic integration with the euro zone will affect the size of this loss in economic stability. Imagine that Norway is pegging to the euro and that there is a fall in the aggregate demand for Norway's output—a leftward shift of Norway's *DD* schedule. If the *DD* schedules of the other euro zone countries happen simultaneously to shift to the left, the euro will simply depreciate against outside currencies, providing the automatic stabilization we studied in the last chapter. Norway has a serious problem only when it *alone* faces a fall in demand—for example, if the world demand for oil, one of Norway's main exports, drops.

[10]You might think that when Norway unilaterally fixes its exchange rate against the euro but leaves the krone free to float against noneuro currencies, it is able to keep at least some monetary independence. Perhaps surprisingly, this intuition is *wrong*. The reason is that any independent money supply change in Norway would put pressure on krone interest rates and thus on the krone/euro exchange rate. So by pegging the krone even to a single foreign currency, Norway completely surrenders its domestic monetary control. This result has, however, a positive side for Norway. After Norway unilaterally pegs the krone to the euro, domestic money market disturbances (shifts in the *AA* schedule) will no longer affect domestic output, despite the continuing float against noneuro currencies. Why? Because Norway's interest rate must equal the euro interest rate, any pure shifts in *AA* will result in immediate reserve inflows or outflows that leave Norway's interest rate unchanged. Thus, a krone/euro peg alone is enough to provide automatic stability in the face of any monetary shocks that shift the *AA* schedule. This is why the discussion in the text can focus on shifts in the *DD* schedule.

How will Norway adjust to this shock? Since nothing has happened to budge the euro, to which Norway is pegged, its krone will remain stable against *all* foreign currencies. Thus, full employment will be restored only after a period of costly slump during which the prices of Norwegian goods and the wages of Norwegian workers fall.

How does the severity of this slump depend on the level of economic integration between the Norwegian economy and those of the EMU countries? The answer is that greater integration implies a shallower slump, and therefore a less costly adjustment to the adverse shift in *DD*. There are two reasons for this reduction in the cost of adjustment: First, if Norway has close trading links with the euro zone, a small reduction in its prices will lead to an increase in euro zone demand for Norwegian goods that is large relative to Norway's output. Thus, full employment can be restored fairly quickly. Second, if Norway's labor and capital markets are closely meshed with those of its euro zone neighbors, unemployed workers can easily move abroad to find work, and domestic capital can be shifted to more profitable uses in other countries. The ability of factors to migrate abroad thus reduces the severity of unemployment in Norway and the fall in the rate of return available to investors.[11]

Notice that our conclusions also apply to a situation in which Norway experiences an *increase* in demand for its output (a rightward shift of *DD*). If Norway is tightly integrated with euro zone economies, a small increase in Norway's price level, combined with some movement of foreign capital and labor into Norway, quickly eliminates the excess demand for Norwegian products.[12]

Closer trade links between Norway and countries *outside* the euro zone will also aid the country's adjustment to Norwegian *DD* shifts that are not simultaneously experienced by the euro zone. However, greater trade integration with countries outside the euro zone is a double-edged sword, with negative as well as positive implications for macroeconomic stability. The reason is that when Norway pegs the krone to the euro, euro zone disturbances that change the euro's exchange rate will have more powerful effects on Norway's economy when its trading links with noneuro countries are more extensive. The effects would be analogous to an increase in the size of movements in Norway's *DD* curve and would raise Norway's economic stability loss from pegging to the euro. In any case, these arguments do not change our earlier conclusion that Norway's stability loss from fixing the krone/euro exchange rate falls as the extent of its economic integration with the euro zone rises.

An additional consideration that we have not yet discussed strengthens the argument that the economic stability loss to Norway from pegging to the euro is lower

---

[11]Installed plant and equipment typically are costly to transport abroad or to adapt to new uses. Owners of such relatively immobile Norwegian capital therefore will always earn low returns on it after an adverse shift in the demand for Norwegian products. If Norway's capital market is integrated with those of its EMU neighbors, however, Norwegians will invest some of their wealth in other countries, while at the same time part of Norway's capital stock will be owned by foreigners. As a result of this process of international wealth *diversification* (see Chapter 9), unexpected changes in the return to Norway's capital will automatically be shared among investors throughout the fixed exchange rate area. Thus, even owners of capital that cannot be moved can avoid more of the economic stability loss due to fixed exchange rates when Norway's economy is open to capital flows.

When international labor mobility is low or nonexistent, higher international capital mobility may *not* reduce the economic stability loss from fixed exchange rates, as we discuss in evaluating the European experience in the Case Study on pages 349–352.

[12]The preceding reasoning applies to other economic disturbances that fall unequally on Norway's output market and those of its exchange rate partners. A problem at the end of this chapter asks you to think through the effects of an increase in demand for EMU exports that leaves Norway's export demand schedule unchanged.

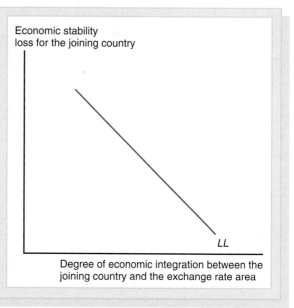

FIGURE 10-4

The *LL* Schedule

The downward-sloping *LL* schedule shows that a country's economic stability loss from joining a fixed exchange rate area falls as the country's economic integration with the area rises.

Economic stability loss for the joining country

LL

Degree of economic integration between the joining country and the exchange rate area

when Norway and the euro zone engage in a large volume of trade. Since imports from the euro zone make up a large fraction of Norwegian workers' consumption in this case, changes in the krone/euro exchange rate may quickly affect nominal Norwegian wages, reducing any impact on employment. A depreciation of the krone against the euro, for example, causes a sharp fall in Norwegians' living standards when imports from the euro zone are substantial; workers are thus likely to demand higher nominal wages from their employers to compensate for the loss. In this situation the additional macroeconomic stability Norway gets from a floating exchange rate is small, so the country has little to lose by fixing the krone/euro exchange rate.

We conclude that *a high degree of economic integration between a country and the fixed exchange rate area that it joins reduces the resulting economic stability loss due to output market disturbances.*

The *LL* schedule shown in Figure 10-4 summarizes this conclusion. The figure's horizontal axis measures the joining country's economic integration with the fixed exchange rate area, the vertical axis the country's economic stability loss. As we have seen, *LL* has a negative slope because the economic stability loss from pegging to the area's currencies falls as the degree of economic interdependence rises.

The Decision to Join a Currency Area: Putting the *GG* and *LL* Schedules Together

Figure 10-5 combines the *GG* and *LL* schedules to show how Norway should decide whether to fix the krone's exchange rate against the euro. The figure implies that Norway should do so if the degree of economic integration between Norwegian markets and those of the euro zone is at least equal to θ_1, the integration level determined by the intersection of *GG* and *LL* at point 1.

Let's see why Norway should peg to the euro if its degree of economic integration with euro zone markets is at least θ_1. Figure 10-5 shows that for levels of economic integration below θ_1, the *GG* schedule lies below the *LL* schedule. Thus, the loss Norway would suffer from greater output and employment instability after joining exceeds the monetary efficiency gain, and the country would do better to stay out.

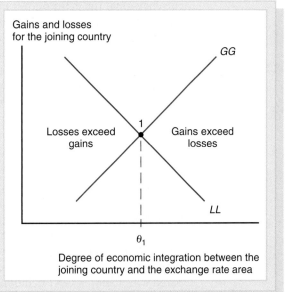

FIGURE 10-5

Deciding When to Peg the Exchange Rate

The intersection of *GG* and *LL* at point 1 determines a critical level of economic integration, θ_1, between a fixed exchange rate area and a country considering whether to join. At any level of integration above θ_1, the decision to join yields positive net economic benefits to the joining country.

Gains and losses for the joining country

Losses exceed gains

Gains exceed losses

Degree of economic integration between the joining country and the exchange rate area

When the degree of integration is θ_1 or higher, however, the monetary efficiency gain measured by *GG* is greater than the stability sacrifice measured by *LL*, and pegging the krone's exchange rate against the euro results in a net gain for Norway. Thus the intersection of *GG* and *LL* determines the minimum integration level (here, θ_1) at which Norway will desire to peg its currency to the euro.

The *GG-LL* framework has important implications about how changes in a country's economic environment affect its willingness to peg its currency to an outside currency area. Consider, for example, an increase in the size and frequency of sudden shifts in the demand for the country's exports. As shown in Figure 10-6, such a change pushes LL^1 upward to LL^2. At any level of economic integration with the

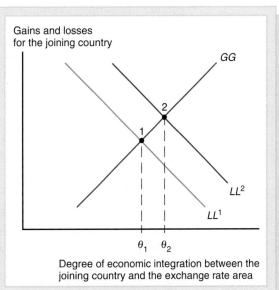

FIGURE 10-6

An Increase in Output Market Variability

A rise in the size and frequency of country-specific disturbances to the joining country's product markets shifts the *LL* schedule upward from LL^1 to LL^2 because for a given level of economic integration with the fixed exchange rate area, the country's economic stability loss from pegging its exchange rate rises. The shift in *LL* raises the critical level of economic integration at which the exchange rate area is joined to θ_2.

Gains and losses for the joining country

Degree of economic integration between the joining country and the exchange rate area currency area, the extra output and unemployment instability the country suffers by fixing its exchange rate is now greater. As a result, the level of economic integration at which it becomes worthwhile to join the currency area rises to θ_2 (determined by the intersection of GG and LL^2 at point 2). Other things equal, increased variability in their product markets makes countries less willing to enter fixed exchange rate areas— a prediction that helps explain why the oil price shocks after 1973 made countries unwilling to revive the Bretton Woods system of fixed exchange rates (Chapter 8).

What Is an Optimum Currency Area?

The *GG-LL* model we have developed suggests a theory of the optimum currency area. *Optimum currency areas* are groups of regions with economies closely linked by trade in goods and services and by factor mobility. This result follows from our finding that a fixed exchange rate area will best serve the economic interests of each of its members if the degree of output and factor trade among the included economies is high.

This perspective helps us understand, for example, why it may make sense for the United States, Japan, and Europe to allow their mutual exchange rates to float. Even though these regions trade with each other, the extent of that trade is modest compared with regional GNPs, and interregional labor mobility is low.

Other Important Considerations

While the *GG-LL* model is useful for organizing our thinking about optimum currency areas, it is not the whole story. At least three other elements affect our evaluation of the euro currency area's past and prospective performances.

Similarity of Economic Structure   The *GG-LL* model tells us that extensive trade with the rest of the currency area makes it easier for a member to adjust to product market disturbances that affect it and its currency partners differently. But it does not tell us what factors will reduce the frequency and size of member-specific product market shocks.

A key element in minimizing such disturbances is similarity in economic structure, especially in the types of products produced. Euro zone countries, for example, are not entirely dissimilar in manufacturing structure, as evidenced by the very high volume of *intra-industry trade*—trade in similar products—within Europe. There are also important differences, however. The countries of northern Europe are better endowed with capital and skilled labor than the countries in Europe's south, and EU products that make intensive use of low-skill labor thus are likely to come from Portugal, Spain, Greece, or southern Italy. The different export patterns of northern and southern European countries create more opportunities for asymmetric shocks.

We can view greater structural dissimilarity between a country and its potential currency union partners as shifting the LL schedule upward, raising the degree of economic integration required before membership in the currency union becomes a good idea.

Fiscal Federalism   Another consideration in evaluating a currency area is its ability to transfer economic resources from members with healthy economies to those suffering economic setbacks. In the United States, for example, states faring poorly relative to the rest of the nation automatically receive support from Washington in the form of welfare benefits and other federal transfer payments that ultimately come out of the taxes other states pay. In addition, the federal tax revenues sent back to Washington automatically decline when the local economy suffers. Such **fiscal federalism** can help offset the economic stability loss due to fixed exchange rates, as it does in the United States. More fiscal federalism shifts the *LL* curve downward.[13]

Banking Union   Suppose that countries in an area of mutually fixed exchange rates maintain national control over banking regulation, supervision, and resolution but at the same time allow freedom of financial transactions across borders, including for banks (and other financial institutions). As we saw in Chapter 9, the *financial tri-lemma* implies that their financial systems will be less stable than with centralized, supra-national control over financial regulatory policy.

The problem is even worse than usual in an area of fixed exchange rates, however. If member countries print money in large quantities while acting as lenders of last resort, for example, they may run out of international reserves and find themselves in a currency crisis (Chapter 7). Each central bank will therefore be reluctant to act as LLR for its domestic banks, and public perceptions of this reluctance could, in itself, encourage bank runs and thereby raise the risk of financial instability and currency crises. In terms of our *GG-LL* framework, less area-wide unification of banking policy raises the *LL* schedule. As we shall see, this problem has been central to the recent crisis in the euro area, although the preceding example based on the central bank's LLR function works in the EMU context in a more complex fashion.

As the financial trilemma suggests, one way to maintain fixed exchange rates, while retaining national control over financial policy, is to prohibit cross-border capital movements. This is not an option within a currency union such as EMU, with a single shared central bank, because the central bank's interest rate policy could not be transmitted to all the member states if they prevented cross-border borrowing and lending.

CASE STUDY

Is Europe an Optimum Currency Area?

The critical question for judging the economic success of EMU is whether Europe itself makes up an optimum currency area. A nation's gains and losses from pegging its currency to an exchange rate area are hard to measure numerically, but by combining our theory with information on actual economic performance, we can evaluate the claim that Europe, most of which is likely to adopt or peg to the euro, is an optimum currency area.

THE EXTENT OF INTRA-EUROPEAN TRADE

Our earlier discussion suggested that a country is more likely to benefit from joining a currency area if the area's economy is closely integrated with the country's. The overall degree of economic integration can be judged by looking at the integration of product markets, that is, the extent of trade between the

---

[13]The classic statement of the role of fiscal federalism in the theory of optimum currency areas is by Peter B. Kenen, "The Theory of Optimum Currency Areas: An Eclectic View," in Robert Mundell and Alexander Swoboda, eds., *Monetary Problems of the International Economy* (Chicago: University of Chicago Press, 1969), pp. 41–60. Perhaps surprisingly, the Kenen argument is valid even when people have access to very efficient private markets for sharing risks. See Emmanuel Farhi and Iván Werning, "Fiscal Unions," Working Paper 18280, National Bureau of Economic Research, August 2012.

joining country and the currency area, and at the integration of factor markets, that is, the ease with which labor and capital can migrate between the joining country and the currency area.

In January 1999, at the time of the euro's launch, most EU members exported from 10 to 20 percent of their output to other EU members. That number is far larger than the extent of EU-U.S. trade. While the average volume of intra-EU trade has increased somewhat since the late 1990s, however, it remains below the level of trade between regions of the United States. If we take trade relative to GNP as a measure of goods-market integration, the *GG-LL* model of the last section suggests that a joint float of Europe's currencies against those of the rest of the world is a better strategy for EU members than a fixed dollar/euro exchange rate would be. The extent of intra-European trade, however, is not large enough to convey an overwhelming reason for believing that the European Union itself is an optimum currency area.

When the euro was created, supporters entertained high hopes that it would promote trade substantially within the currency union. These hopes were bolstered by an influential econometric study by Andrew K. Rose, of the University of California—Berkeley, who suggested that on average, members of currency unions trade three times more with each other than with nonmember countries—even after one controls for other determinants of trade flows. A more recent study of EU trade data by Richard Baldwin, of Geneva's Graduate Institute of International and Development Studies, has greatly scaled back the estimates as they apply to the euro zone's experience so far.[14] Baldwin estimated that the euro increased the mutual trade levels of its users only by about 9 percent, with most of the effect taking place in the euro's first year, 1999. But he also concluded that Britain, Denmark, and Sweden, which did not adopt the euro, saw their trade with euro zone countries increase by about 7 percent at the same time. These EU countries therefore would gain little more if they adopted the euro.

EU measures aimed at promoting market integration following the Single European Act of 1986 probably have helped to bolster intra-EU trade. For some goods (such as consumer electronics), there has been considerable price convergence across EU countries, but for others, among them cars, similar items still can sell for widely differing prices in different European locations. One hypothesis about the persistence of price differentials that is favored by euro enthusiasts is that multiple currencies made big price discrepancies possible, but these were bound to disappear under the single currency. Has the euro itself contributed to market integration? In a careful study of European price behavior since 1990, economists Charles Engel of the University of Wisconsin and John Rogers of the Federal Reserve find that intra-European price

---

[14]See Baldwin, *In or Out: Does It Matter? An Evidence-Based Analysis of the Euro's Trade Effects* (London: Centre for Economic Policy Research, 2006). Rose reports his initial analysis and results in "One Money, One Market: The Effects of Common Currencies on Trade," *Economic Policy* 30 (April 2000), pp. 8–45. He based his methods on the "gravity model" of international trade. Rose scaled down his estimate in Andrew K. Rose and Eric van Wincoop, "National Money as a Barrier to International Trade: The Real Case for Currency Union," *American Economic Review* 91 (May 2001), pp. 386–390. Using a more sophisticated model of international trade patterns, Rose and van Wincoop calculated the trade-creating effect of a currency union to be roughly a 50 percent increase in trade. Even this estimate appears much larger than the increase that followed the euro's introduction.

discrepancies indeed decreased over the 1990s. They find no evidence, however, of further price convergence after the euro's introduction in 1999.[15]

On balance, considering both the price and the quantity evidence to date, it seems unlikely that the combination of Single European Act reforms and the single currency has yet turned the euro zone into an optimum currency area.

HOW MOBILE IS EUROPE'S LABOR FORCE?

The main barriers to labor mobility within Europe are no longer due to border controls. Differences in language and culture discourage labor movements between European countries to a greater extent than is true, for example, between regions of the United States. In a 1990 econometric study comparing unemployment patterns in U.S. regions with those in EU countries, Barry Eichengreen of the University of California–Berkeley found that differences in regional unemployment rates are smaller and less persistent in the United States than are the differences between national unemployment rates in the European Union.[16] Figure 10-7 shows the evolution of selected EU unemployment rates since the early 1990s; the evident divergence after the late 2000s is the result of the recent crisis and will be discussed in the next section.

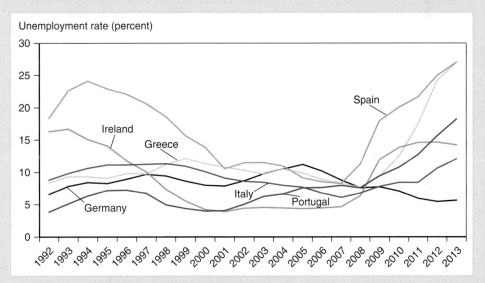

FIGURE 10-7   MyEconLab   Real-time data

Unemployment Rates in Selected EU Countries

Widely divergent unemployment rates moved closer together after the euro's launch in 1999 but since the late 2000s have moved sharply apart.

Source: International Monetary Fund, *World Economic Outlook* database, April 2013. Numbers for 2013 are IMF forecasts.

[15]See their paper "European Product Market Integration after the Euro," *Economic Policy* 39 (July 2004), pp. 347–381. For confirmation, see Jesús Crespo Cuaresma, Balázs Égert, and Maria Antoinette Silgoner, "Price Level Convergence in Europe: Did the Introduction of the Euro Matter?" *Monetary Policy and the Economy*, Oesterreichische Nationalbank (Q1 2007), pp. 100–113.

[16]See Eichengreen, "One Money for Europe? Lessons of the U.S. Currency Union," *Economic Policy* 10 (April 1990), pp. 118–166. Further study of the U.S. labor market has shown that regional unemployment is eliminated almost entirely by worker migration rather than by changes in regional real wages. See Olivier Jean Blanchard and Lawrence F. Katz, "Regional Evolutions," *Brookings Papers on Economic Activity* 1 (1992), pp. 1–75.

TABLE 10-2	People Changing Region of Residence in the 1990s (percent of total population)			
Britain		**Germany**	**Italy**	**United States**
1.7		1.1	0.5	3.1

Sources: Peter Huber, "Inter-regional Mobility in Europe: A Note on the Cross-Country Evidence," *Applied Economics Letters* 11 (August 2004), pp. 619–624; and "Geographical Mobility, 2003–2004," U.S. Department of Commerce, March 2004. Table data are for Britain in 1996, Germany in 1990, Italy in 1999, and the United States in 1999.

Even *within* European countries, labor mobility appears limited, partly because of government regulations. For example, the requirement in some countries that workers establish residence before receiving unemployment benefits makes it harder for unemployed workers to seek jobs in regions that are far from their current homes. Table 10-2 presents evidence on the frequency of regional labor movement in three of the largest EU countries, as compared with that in the United States. Although these data must be interpreted with caution because the definition of "region" differs from country to country, they do suggest that in a typical year, Americans are significantly more footloose than Europeans.[17]

There is some evidence that labor mobility has increased in response to the extreme unemployment rates visible in Figure 10-7. But to some degree this is a mixed blessing. The workers that tend to be most mobile are younger and more productive, while those that remain are closer to retirement. This migration pattern can deprive governments of the tax base they need to fund pension and health benefits, thereby worsening fiscal deficits in countries already hit hard by deep recession.

OTHER CONSIDERATIONS

Previously, we identified three additional considerations (alongside economic integration) that are relevant to the costs and benefits of forming a currency area: similarity of structure, fiscal federalism, and the unification of policy toward bank and financial market stability. On all three counts, the EU comes up short, reinforcing the hypothesis that the EU is not an optimum currency area.

As we have noted, EU members have very different export mixes and therefore different vulnerabilities to identical economic disturbances. For example, Portugal competes with China in export markets, whereas China is a big destination market for German machine tools. Thus, higher Chinese growth has very different effects on the Portuguese and German economies.

Regarding fiscal federalism, it is quite limited in the EU, which has no substantial centralized fiscal capacity. Country-specific shocks therefore are not offset by any inflows of budgetary resources from currency-union partners. Finally, regarding financial stability policy, the Maastricht Treaty left virtually all powers at the national level, giving the Eurosystem no explicit authority to oversee financial markets. The story of the euro crisis, to which we turn next, is intimately related to these last two shortcomings in the architecture underlying the single currency.

---

[17]For a more detailed discussion of the evidence, see Maurice Obstfeld and Giovanni Peri, "Regional Non-Adjustment and Fiscal Policy," *Economic Policy* 26 (April 1998), pp. 205–259.

The Euro Crisis and the Future of EMU

Like the rest of the world, the euro area was battered by the global financial crisis of 2007–2009 (described in Chapters 8 and 9). It was only toward the end of the acute phase of the global financial crisis, however—late in 2009—that the euro zone entered a new crisis so severe as to threaten its continuing existence. In this section we help you to understand the nature of the euro crisis, the ways in which it has been managed so far, and the implications for the future of EMU.

Origins of the Crisis

The spark that ignited the crisis came from an unlikely source: Greece, which accounted for only 3 percent of the euro area's output. However, the spark landed on a broad and deep pile of very dry tinder, assembled during the period of low interest rates, real estate speculation, and heightened financial-market growth that preceded the global financial crisis.

The Tinder   The global assets of internationally-active banks grew rapidly in the years leading up to the 2007–2009 crisis, but especially so for European banks, and especially banks in the euro zone. The asset sides of their balance sheets grew through purchases of U.S. credit-backed products, but also through lending to other euro zone countries, including purchases of government debt and lending to finance consumption spending, housing investment, and mortgage lending. This lending helped to fuel, and in turn was fueled by, massive housing booms, especially in Ireland and Spain (recall Figure 8-7). An important factor promoting these developments, as you learned in Chapter 8, was an environment of very low global interest rates, which induced banks to take greater risks in search of profits.

As a result of this credit expansion, bank assets grew to very large levels compared to the GDPs of the banks' home countries. Table 10-3 illustrates the positions of some large euro area banks at the end of 2011; balance sheets were even larger relative to output in 2007. In a number of countries individual banks had become "too big to

TABLE 10-3	Assets of Some Individual Banks as a Ratio to National Output, End-2011	
Bank	**Home country**	**Bank assets**
Erste Group Bank	Austria	0.68
Dexia	Belgium	1.10
BNP Paribas	France	0.97
Deutsche Bank	Germany	0.82
Bank of Ireland	Ireland	0.95
UniCredit	Italy	0.59
ING Group	Netherlands	2.12
Banco Commercial Português	Portugal	0.57
Banco Santander	Spain	1.19

Source: GDP data from International Monetary Fund, *World Economic Outlook* database. Data on bank assets from Viral V. Acharya and Sascha Steffen, "The 'Greatest' Carry Trade Ever? Understanding Eurozone Bank Risks," Discussion Paper 9432, Centre for Economic Policy Research, April 2013.

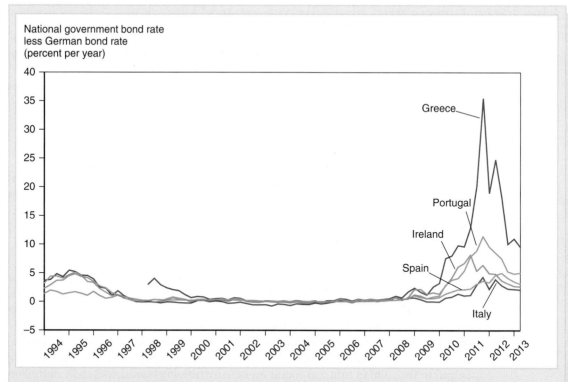

National government bond rate
less German bond rate
(percent per year)

FIGURE 10-8

Nominal Government Borrowing Spreads over Germany

Euro countries' long-term government bond yields converged to Germany's level as they prepared to join the euro. The yields began to diverge again with the global financial crisis of 2007–2009, and moved sharply apart after the euro crisis broke out late in 2009.

Source: European Central Bank. Ten-year government bond interest rates.

save" based on the resources the home government could raise from the home economy alone; and the government's predicament would of course be much worse in a systemic crisis, with several banks in trouble at the same time. For example, if a failed bank's assets are equal to GDP and the government must inject capital equal to 5 percent of assets to restore the bank to solvency, then the government would have to issue debt or raise taxes by 5 percent of GDP—a very big fraction—to keep the bank in operation. And what if several large banks all fail at the same time?

With exchange-rate risk now eliminated between euro area countries, government bond yields moved closer to equality. In addition, markets seemed convinced that no European government would ever **default** on its debts—after all, no advanced country anywhere had done so since the late 1940s. As a result, spreads between the governments judged most creditworthy by ratings agencies such as Moody's (for example, Germany) and the least creditworthy (for example, Greece) became very small—often on the order of 25 basis points or below (see Figure 10-8). This development encouraged more spending and borrowing in countries including Greece, Portugal, and Spain. (A default occurs when a debtor does not make the debt payments it has promised to creditors. The event is called a *sovereign default* when the debtor is a country's government.)

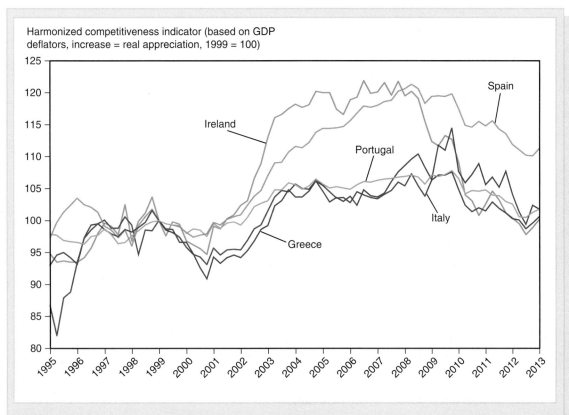

FIGURE 10-9

Real Appreciation in Peripheral Euro Zone Countries

After entry into the euro, real appreciation set in for peripheral euro zone countries, most noticeably the two with massive housing booms, Ireland and Spain.

Source: Eurostat. Harmonized multilateral competitiveness index based on GDP deflators. An increase in the index is a real appreciation (loss in competitiveness).

But with higher spending also came higher inflation relative to the German level. As a result, countries on the euro zone periphery—Ireland, Portugal, Spain, Italy, and Greece—all saw their currencies appreciate in real terms, not only relative to Germany, but relative to all of their trading partners, both within and outside of EMU. Figure 10-9, which reports European Commission indexes of real appreciation with respect to GDP deflators, shows how all of these countries lost competitiveness after the early 2000s, most notably the two countries with the most extreme housing booms, Ireland and Spain. With higher inflation than Germany's, but essentially equal bond rates, these countries had lower *real* interest rates during the mid-2000s, a factor that spurred spending and inflation even further (see Figure 10-10 for real interest rates).[18]

---

[18]This type of monetary instability was predicted by Sir Alan Walters, an economic adviser to Prime Minister Margaret Thatcher of Britain and a prominent opponent of fixed exchange rates within Europe. See his polemical book *Sterling in Danger: Economic Consequences of Fixed Exchange Rates* (London: Fontana, 1990).

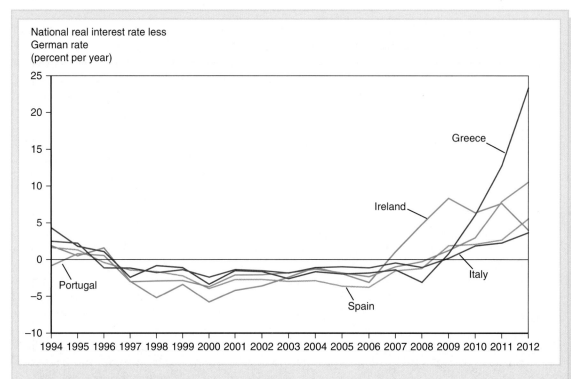

National real interest rate less
German rate
(percent per year)

FIGURE 10-10

Divergent Real Interest Rates in the Euro Zone

As the 1999 launch date for the euro approached, nominal long-term bond rates in prospective member countries converged, leading to lower real interest rates in those countries with relatively high inflation. The graph
shows each country's long-term real interest rate minus Germany's long-term real interest rate. Real interest rates
are average nominal rates on ten-year government bonds minus the same year's inflation rate.

Source: Datastream.

As a result, while Germany had growing current account surpluses, the peripheral
countries had growing deficits, in some cases very large ones, as Table 10-4 shows.
So external debts built up, raising the question of how these countries would ever
generate the net export surpluses necessary to repay foreign creditors. The dilemma

TABLE 10-4	**Current Account Balances of Euro Zone Countries, 2005–2009 (percent of GDP)**					
	Greece	**Ireland**	**Italy**	**Portugal**	**Spain**	**Germany**
2005	−7.5	−3.5	−1.7	−9.4	−7.4	5.1
2006	−11.2	−4.1	−2.6	−9.9	−9.0	6.5
2007	−14.4	−5.3	−2.4	−9.4	−10.0	7.6
2008	−14.6	−5.3	−3.4	−12.0	−9.8	6.7
2009	−11.2	−2.9	−3.1	−10.3	−5.4	5.0

Source: International Monetary Fund.

became more acute once growth slowed as a result of the 2007–2009 global crisis. Because currency devaluation by individual euro area countries was not an option to spur net exports, it became increasingly likely that the adjustment to a more competitive real exchange rate would require a period of low inflation or even deflation, in all likelihood accompanied by significant unemployment due to the rigidity of labor and product markets. Among other negative effects, protracted recession would weaken banks.

In these circumstances, countries with conventional fixed exchange rates might well have fallen victim to speculative currency attacks, forcing the government to devalue. In EMU, however, countries do not have their own currencies, so conventional attacks are not possible. Nonetheless, a different sort of speculation set in, working through bank runs and government debt markets. The effects were devastating.

The Spark The 2007–2009 crisis certainly caused headaches in the euro zone. Some banks were in trouble due to their exposure to U.S. real estate markets. Also troublesome were exposures to European housing markets, which began to fall following the U.S. example (and with Ireland leading the way; see Figure 8-7). But markets had few fears about the creditworthiness of euro zone governments until Greece's intractable fiscal problems became apparent late in 2008. This was

the spark that ignited the tinder of overextended banks and uncompetitive, indebted economies.

The crisis began when a new Greek government was elected in October 2009. Very quickly the new government announced some bad news: The Greek fiscal deficit stood at 12.7 percent of GDP, more than double the numbers announced by the previous government. Apparently the previous government had been misreporting its economic statistics for years, and the public debt actually amounted to more than 100 percent of GDP.

Holders of Greek bonds, including many banks within the euro zone, began to worry about the Greek government's ability to close its yawning deficit and repay its debts. In December 2009, the major rating agencies all downgraded Greek government debt. (As Figure 10-8 shows, the Greek government's borrowing spread over German bonds rose to levels previously seen in late 2008 and early 2009, when global financial markets had been in turmoil over the fallout from the subprime crisis). The Greek government announced harsh budget cuts and raised some taxes in the first months of 2010, but was soon faced with street protests and strikes. Further downgrades followed and Greek borrowing costs soared, making it even harder for the country to repay creditors. Investors began to worry that other deficit countries might face problems similar to those of Greece. The figure shows that borrowing costs for Portugal and Ireland, and even for two larger countries, Spain and Italy, came under pressure. World stock markets plunged as the prospect of a much wider financial crisis in Europe grew.

How did the EU deal with the Greek crisis? A bailout of Greece by richer EU countries would have quelled the market turmoil, but that was exactly the outcome that countries like Germany had wished to avoid when they negotiated the Maastricht Treaty and the SGP. In mid-March 2010, euro zone finance ministers declared their intention to help Greece but provided no details of what they planned to do. With the EU unable to take concrete action, the crisis snowballed, and the value of the euro fell in the foreign exchange markets.

Finally, in mid-April 2010, euro zone countries, working with the IMF, agreed on a €110 billion loan package for Greece. But by this time, the panic over government debt had spread, and the Portuguese, Spanish, and Italian governments (following what Ireland had already undertaken late in 2008) were proposing their own deficit-reduction measures in an effort to keep borrowing spreads from rising to Greek levels. Fearing a continental meltdown, the euro zone's leaders embedded the Greek support within a broader European Financial Stability Facility (EFSF), with funding of €750 billion provided by its own borrowing from markets, the European Commission, and the IMF. (The EFSF was explicitly temporary, but was replaced by a permanent European Stability Mechanism, or ESM, in October 2012.) The ECB then reversed a policy it had earlier announced and began to purchase the bonds of troubled euro zone debtor countries, sparking accusations that it was violating the spirit of the Maastricht Treaty by rewarding fiscal excesses. In fact, the ECB's motivation was to avoid a banking panic by supporting the prices of assets widely held by European banks.

Greek borrowing costs remained high, and soon Ireland's market borrowing rates rose sharply as it became clear that the government's cost of supporting shaky Irish banks would amount to a large fraction of GDP. Late in 2010, Ireland negotiated a €67.5 billion EFSF loan package with the *troika* consisting of the European Commission, ECB, and IMF. Portugal negotiated a €78 billion *troika* loan in May 2011.[19] Both loans, like the Greek loan, came with conditions requiring the recipients to slash government budgets and institute structural economic reforms (such as labor-market deregulation). The *troika* was in charge of monitoring compliance.

Self-Fulfilling Government Default and the "Doom Loop"

Why did market panic develop and spread so quickly? The contentious debate surrounding the initial Greek package made it clear that the northern European countries such as Germany, Finland, and the Netherlands had only a very limited willingness to underwrite the borrowing of countries like Greece facing unfavorable market conditions, either directly or indirectly through support for ECB bond purchases. Some politicians from northern Europe had spoken openly about default by Greece, or even about the possibility that it would exit the euro. Thus, sovereign default on Greek debt, even though EU officials initially denied it as a possibility, appeared eminently possible, as did default by other countries (such as Portugal) with rapidly growing government debts.

The fear of default was a particular problem of the euro area: The government of the United States can always print dollars to pay off its debts, and so is very unlikely to default, but countries using the euro cannot, since the decision to print euros rests with the ECB, not national governments. (This is why Greece, Portugal, and Ireland were in the anomalous position of borrowing euros—their own currency—from the IMF.) The possibility of default gives rise to a self-fulfilling dynamic that is analogous to a bank run (as discussed in Chapter 9) or a self-fulfilling currency crisis (as discussed in Chapter 7): If markets expect a default, they will charge the borrowing government very high interest rates, and if it is unable to raise taxes or cut spending sufficiently,

---

[19]The term "*troika*" came into widespread use during the euro crisis. The word is Russian and refers to a three-horse harness setup for pulling a sleigh.

it will be forced to miss debt repayments and therefore it will default. This is exactly what happened in the euro area.[20]

Because bank balance sheets had become so big, the weakened state of the euro countries' banks strongly reinforced the likelihood of government default. Countries needing to support their banking systems with infusions of public money had to borrow the money, leading to big increases in public debt levels and heightened market fears of default. Figure 10-11 shows the evolution of public debts (as a ratio to GDP) in the euro area. While Greece had by far the largest debt (reaching a staggering 170 percent of GDP by 2011), you can see that other countries' debts were increasing rapidly, fueled in part, in most cases, by the need to bail out banks. Ireland provides the most dramatic example, with debt rising from only 25 percent of GDP in 2007 to more than 90 percent in 2010, driven not only by recession but by a bailout of the banks that had driven the Irish property boom.[21]

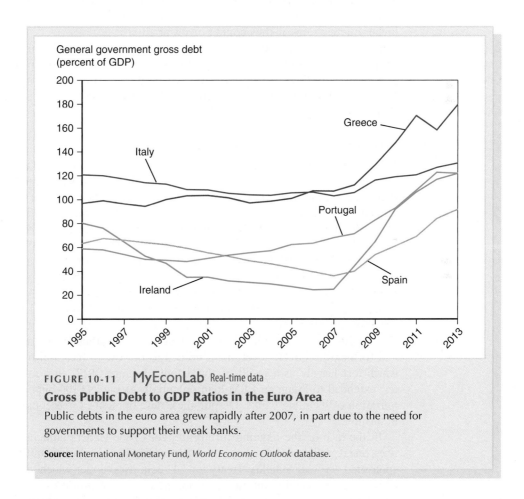

FIGURE 10-11   MyEconLab   Real-time data

Gross Public Debt to GDP Ratios in the Euro Area

Public debts in the euro area grew rapidly after 2007, in part due to the need for governments to support their weak banks.

Source: International Monetary Fund, *World Economic Outlook* database.

[20]For a model of this process, see Guillermo A. Calvo, "Servicing the Public Debt: The Role of Expectations," *American Economic Review* 78 (September 1988): 647–661. The model is applied to the euro crisis in the paper by De Grauwe in Further Readings.
[21]Vivid accounts of the Greek and Irish crises are included in Michael Lewis, *Boomerang: Travels in the New Third World* (New York: W.W. Norton & Company, 2011).

To make matters worse, the perilous state of each government's credit, in turn, weakened the solvency of domestic banks. For one thing, banks were heavily invested in their governments' bonds, so when those bonds' prices fell, bank assets and bank capital were reduced. In addition, banks' lenders (including depositors) understood that if the government itself could not obtain cash, it might be unable to make good on promises to support banks, for example, through injections of public capital or deposit insurance.

The two-way feedback from bank distress to government borrowing problems has been labeled a **doom loop** by economists. As a result of the doom loop, private money fled from banks in countries where the government was having trouble borrowing. These countries experienced a *sudden stop* in private lending, and to keep their banks from collapsing, the ECB had to engage in lender of last resort operations on a massive scale. In effect, the euro zone's financial market became segmented along national lines, with the creditworthiness of banks in the weaker countries judged by the creditworthiness of their governments. Firms and households in those countries faced higher interest rates, if they could borrow at all.

Because of fiscal cutbacks and the credit squeeze, output plummeted and unemployment soared. Many observers questioned whether the austerity programs included in governments' financial support packages, and being practiced more generally in the EU, were actually helping in reducing public debts, especially when implemented by several neighboring countries simultaneously.

A Broader Crisis and Policy Responses

Even after its initial rescue package, Greece proved unable to put its public debt onto a sustainable path. European leaders began openly to discuss the need for mechanisms that would allow insolvent countries to restructure their debt in the future. With officially sanctioned default now on the table, Italy's bond spreads rose sharply in the second half of 2011. Italy was much bigger than Greece, Ireland, or Portugal and its fiscal problems were too big to be addressed without a much bigger budgetary commitment from its euro zone partners. Borrowing costs for Spain, another large country, had also been edging up in view of its very big banking sector, which had been seriously weakened by the country's housing collapse.

In March 2012, Greece finally did restructure its government debt, imposing big losses on private bond holders. However, the country's overall debt fell only slightly (Figure 10-11). By then, much of the debt was held officially (notably by the ECB), and further, the Greek government needed to borrow to recapitalize domestic banks, which lost heavily as a result of the default. In June 2012, euro area finance ministers extended to Spain an ESM loan potentially as big as €100 billion to cover recapitalization of its ailing banks. Despite these developments, Greece and Spain remained in turmoil.

In the face of the ongoing turbulence, euro zone leaders launched two key initiatives, one regarding fiscal policy and one regarding banking policy unification. Germany sponsored a Fiscal Stability Treaty for EU countries, under which signatories commit themselves to amend domestic legislation in a way that produces government budgets that are more nearly in balance. The treaty, an updated and more stringent version of the SGP, was motivated by similar concerns and reflected the official German position that the main cause of the crisis was the fiscal misbehavior of national governments. It came into force for the 16 countries that had signed it at the start of 2013.

Critics of the Fiscal Stability Treaty pointed out that countries such as Ireland and Spain had favorable fiscal indicators, with falling levels of debt relative to GDP, prior to the crisis (Figure 10-11). While the German diagnosis described Greece, other countries' debts exploded because their banking systems melted down, and the German strategy did nothing to improve bank supervision, or to break the doom loop between banks and sovereign governments. As in our discussion of optimum currency areas, a closer *banking union* would be needed in order to stabilize the euro zone.

This second direction also was pursued by EU leaders, who met in June 2012 and directed the European Commission to prepare a blueprint for a Single Supervisory Mechanism (SSM) with powers to police banks throughout the euro zone. The leaders also recommended that once the SSM was in place, the ESM should have the power to recapitalize banks *directly*, that is, with any resulting borrowing showing up as a liability of the ESM, that is, as a joint liability of the euro zone and not of any member government, regardless of where the recapitalized banks reside. This important recommendation was intended to reduce the force of the doom loop at the national level, but it made some governments uneasy at the prospect of being forced to bail out banks in other countries.

In response to the summit directive, the Commission in September 2012 recommended a three-pronged approach to banking union, meant to centralize financial supervision, deposit insurance, and the resolution of insolvent banks within the euro area. These measures, as just noted, were meant to deactivate the doom loop at the national level and enhance the quality and credibility of financial oversight for the currency union. Specifically, the Commission recommended the creation of an SSM, of a euro-area wide deposit insurance scheme, and of a Single Resolution Mechanism (SRM), to be operated (like the SSM) at the level of the euro area. In December 2012, the EU leaders endorsed the SSM, housing it in the ECB (although retaining a significant degree of home-country autonomy in the regulation of smaller banks). As of this writing, the SRM remains a work in progress while the idea of centralized euro area deposit insurance is strongly opposed by a group of countries led by Germany. Thus, the doom loop remains substantially in place, and it is hard to see how the ECB will be able to enforce its supervisory edicts if it does not actually have the clout and financial resources to close down and reorganize failing banks in the face of potential opposition from national politicians.

Many observers have recommended that the euro area enhance fiscal federalism through a larger centralized budget, managed by a fiscal authority with the capability to tax, spend, and issue joint eurobonds. This approach is strongly opposed by Germany and other countries and is unlikely to become reality anytime soon.[22]

ECB Outright Monetary Transactions

Despite the preceding reform efforts, markets for peripheral euro zone sovereign debts remained volatile through the summer of 2012, with investors speculating that Greece might even leave EMU. Such an outcome—known colloquially as a "Grexit"—would have destabilized other countries' borrowing rates even more by setting the precedent that a government might abandon the euro and introduce a national currency in its place. On July 26, 2012, ECB President Mario Draghi made the dramatic statement: "Within our mandate, the ECB is ready to do whatever it takes to preserve the euro. And believe me, it will be enough." Six weeks later he unveiled a program called

---

[22]For a survey of eurobond proposals see Stijn Claessens, Ashoka Mody, and Shahin Vallée, "Paths to Eurobonds," Working Paper WP/12/172, International Monetary Fund, July 2012.

Outright Monetary Transactions (OMT) under which the ECB would do exactly that—purchase sovereign bonds, potentially without limit, to prevent their interest rates from rising too far. To qualify for OMT, countries would first have to agree to an ESM stabilization plan.

As of this writing OMT have not been used, but nonetheless, bond yields in the peripheral countries have receded sharply, as Figure 10-11 shows, simply because of the *expectation* of what the ECB could do with its unlimited monetary firepower. However, it is unclear how long this relative calm can last. To start, no one knows what will happen if OMT actually have to be used (and the very idea has been challenged in Germany's constitutional court). In addition, the breathing space given by OMT may have blunted national governments' determination to carry out structural reforms, as well as EU leaders' determination to deliver on necessary institutional innovations. This is just another form of moral hazard, one that encourages governments to postpone tough decisions.

The Future of EMU

Europe's single currency experiment is the boldest attempt ever to reap the efficiency gains from using a single currency over a large and diverse group of sovereign states. If EMU succeeds, it will promote European political as well as economic integration, fostering peace and prosperity in a region that could someday include all of Eastern Europe and even Turkey. If the euro project fails, however, its driving force, the goal of European political unification, will be set back.

EMU must overcome some difficult challenges, however, if it is to survive its current crisis and prosper:

1. Europe is not an optimum currency area. Therefore, asymmetric economic developments within different countries of the euro zone—developments that might well call for different national interest rates under a regime of individual national currencies—will remain hard to handle through monetary policy. The single currency project has taken economic union to a level far beyond what the EU has so far been able (or willing) to do in the area of political union. Nonetheless, in response to the euro crisis, the EU is increasing the centralized control over economic policy beyond the initial ECB blueprint through the Fiscal Stability Treaty, enhanced powers for the Commission, and the euro zone banking union. Many Europeans hoped that economic union would lead to closer political union, but it is possible that continuing quarrels over economic policies will sabotage that aim. Enhanced governmental powers at the center of EMU require enhanced democratic accountability as well, but little has been done to fulfill this need. There is a danger that voters throughout Europe will come to view the euro's superstructure as being under the control of a distant and politically unaccountable group of technocrats who are unresponsive to people's needs.

2. In most EU countries, labor markets remain highly unionized and subject to employment taxes and regulations that impede labor mobility between industries and regions. The result has been persistently high levels of unemployment. Unless labor markets become much more flexible, as in the United States' currency union, individual euro zone countries will have a difficult time adjusting toward full employment and competitive real exchange rates. Other structural problems abound.

It remains to be seen if the euro zone will develop more elaborate institutions for carrying out fiscal transfers from country to country. At the least, some sort of centralized fiscal backstop for the planned banking union is essential to ensure its effectiveness. The euro crisis showed the need for enough of a centralized European fiscal capacity to deal rapidly with inherently contagious member-country financial instability. It also showed the strength of opposition in some countries to such an institutional change. But as we have seen, the economic and political fissures that the crisis revealed have been present from the euro project's start.

Thus, the euro faces significant challenges in the years ahead. The experience of the United States shows that a large monetary union comprising diverse economic regions can work quite well. For the euro zone to achieve comparable economic success, however, it will have to make progress in creating more flexible labor and product markets, in reforming its fiscal and financial regulatory systems, and in deepening its political union. European unification itself will be imperiled unless the euro project and its defining institution, the ECB, succeed in delivering prosperity as well as price stability.

SUMMARY

1. European Union countries have had two main reasons for favoring mutually fixed exchange rates: They believe monetary cooperation will give them a heavier weight in international economic negotiations, and they view fixed exchange rates as a complement to EU initiatives aimed at building a common European market.

2. The *European Monetary System* of fixed intra-EU exchange rates was inaugurated in March 1979 and originally included Belgium, Denmark, France, Germany, Ireland, Italy, Luxembourg, and the Netherlands. Austria, Britain, Portugal, and Spain joined much later. Capital controls and frequent realignments were essential ingredients in maintaining the system until the mid-1980s, but since then, controls have been abolished as part of the European Union's wider program of market unification.

3. In practice, all EMS currencies were pegged to Germany's former currency, the deutsche mark (DM). As a result, Germany was able to set monetary policy for the EMS, just as the United States did in the Bretton Woods system. The *credibility theory of the EMS* holds that participating governments profited from the German Bundesbank's reputation as an inflation fighter. In fact, inflation rates in EMS countries ultimately tended to converge around Germany's generally low inflation rate.

4. On January 1, 1999, 11 EU countries initiated an *economic and monetary union (EMU)* by adopting a common currency, the euro, issued by a European Central Bank (ECB) headquartered in Frankfurt, Germany. (The initial 11 members were joined by several other countries later on.) The Eurosystem consists of euro members' national central banks and the ECB, whose governing council runs monetary policy in EMU. The transition process from the EMS's fixed exchange rate system to EMU was spelled out in the *Maastricht Treaty* signed by European leaders in December 1991.

5. The Maastricht Treaty specified a set of macroeconomic convergence criteria that EU countries would need to satisfy in order to qualify for admission to EMU. A major purpose of the convergence criteria was to reassure voters in low-inflation countries such as Germany that the new, jointly managed European currency would be as resistant to inflation as the DM had been. A *Stability and Growth Pact (SGP)*, devised by EU leaders in 1997 at Germany's insistence, was intended to limit government deficits and debt at the national level.

6. The theory of *optimum currency areas* implies that countries will wish to join fixed exchange rate areas closely linked to their own economies through trade and factor mobility. A country's decision to join an exchange rate area is determined by the difference between the *monetary efficiency gain* from joining and the *economic stability loss* from joining. The *GG-LL* diagram relates both of these factors to the degree of economic integration between the joining country and the larger, fixed exchange rate zone. Only when economic integration passes a critical level is it beneficial to join.

7. The European Union does not appear to satisfy all of the criteria for an optimum currency area. Although many barriers to market integration within the European Union have been removed since the 1980s and the euro appears to have promoted intra-EU trade, the level of trade still is not very extensive. In addition, labor mobility between and even within EU countries appears more limited than that within other large currency areas such as the United States. Finally, the level of *fiscal federalism* in the European Union is too small to cushion member countries from adverse economic events, and policies for banking sector stability are not adequately centralized.

8. The euro crisis was sparked by Greek fiscal problems revealed at the end of 2009, but the crisis spread so widely because euro area banks were overextended and some countries had suffered big real appreciations that they could not unwind through devaluation. The prospect that some governments might *default* on their debts hurt banks, and conversely, bank weakness forced governments into expensive bailouts, in a self-reinforcing *doom loop*. The results were soaring government borrowing rates and capital flight from fiscally stressed countries. The ECB offered massive lender of last resort support to peripheral banks as money fled; at the same time, their governments required loans from other EU members and the IMF, loans that came on condition of fiscal austerity and structural reforms. Austerity combined with tight credit in so many neighboring countries gave rise to deep recessions.

9. Responses to the crisis include revamped fiscal restrictions on euro area governments as well as incomplete progress toward a euro zone banking union. The most effective initiative in pushing government borrowing rates down, however, has been the ECB's promise of Outright Monetary Transactions. But as of this writing, the OMT weapon remains untested.

KEY TERMS

credibility theory of the EMS, p. 336

default, p. 354

doom loop, p. 360

economic and monetary union (EMU), p. 338

economic stability loss, p. 344

European Monetary System (EMS), p. 335

fiscal federalism, p. 348

Maastricht Treaty, p. 338

monetary efficiency gain, p. 342

optimum currency areas, p. 342

Stability and Growth Pact (SGP), p. 340

PROBLEMS

MyEconLab

1. Why might EMS provisions for the extension of central bank credits from strong-to-weak-currency members have increased the stability of EMS exchange rates?

2. In the EMS before September 1992, the Italian lira/DM exchange rate could fluctuate by up to 2.25 percent up *or* down. Assume that the lira/DM central parity

and band were set in this way and could not be changed. What would have been the maximum possible difference between the interest rates on *one-year* lira and DM deposits? What would have been the maximum possible difference between the interest rates on *six-month* lira and DM deposits? On *three-month* deposits? Do the answers surprise you? Give an intuitive explanation.

3. Continue with the last question. Imagine that in Italy, the interest rate on five-year government bonds was 11 percent per annum and that in Germany, the rate on five-year government bonds was 8 percent per annum. What would have been the implications for the credibility of the current lira/DM exchange parity?

4. Do your answers to the last two questions require an assumption that interest rates and expected exchange rate changes are linked by interest parity? Why or why not?

5. Suppose that soon after Norway pegs to the euro, EMU benefits from a favorable shift in the world demand for non-Norwegian EMU exports. What happens to the exchange rate of the Norwegian krone against noneuro currencies? How is Norway affected? How does the size of this effect depend on the volume of trade between Norway and the euro zone economies?

6. Use the *GG-LL* diagram to show how an increase in the size and frequency of unexpected shifts in a country's money demand function affects the level of economic integration with a currency area at which the country will wish to join.

7. During the speculative pressure on the EMS exchange rate mechanism (ERM) shortly before Britain allowed the pound to float in September 1992, the *Economist*, a London weekly news magazine, opined as follows:

> The [British] government's critics want lower interest rates, and think this would be possible if Britain devalued sterling, leaving the ERM if necessary. They are wrong. Quitting the ERM would soon lead to higher, not lower, interest rates, as British economic management lost the degree of credibility already won through ERM membership. Two years ago British government bonds yielded three percentage points more than German ones. Today the gap is half a point, reflecting investors' belief that British inflation is on its way down—permanently. (See "Crisis? What Crisis?" *Economist*, August 29, 1992, p. 51.)

   a. Why might the British government's critics have thought it possible to lower interest rates after taking sterling out of the ERM? (Britain was in a deep recession at the time the article appeared.)

   b. Why did the *Economist* think the opposite would occur soon after Britain exited the ERM?

   c. In what way might ERM membership have gained credibility for British policy makers? (Britain entered the ERM in October 1990.)

   d. Why would a high level of British nominal interest rates relative to German rates have suggested an expectation of high future British inflation? Can you think of other explanations?

   e. Suggest two reasons why British interest rates might have been somewhat higher than German rates at the time of writing, despite the alleged "belief that British inflation is on its way down—permanently."

8. Imagine that the EMS had become a monetary union with a single currency but that it had created no European Central Bank to manage this currency. Imagine instead that the task had been left to the various national central banks, each of which was allowed to issue as much of the European currency as it liked and to conduct open-market operations. What problems can you see arising from such a scheme?

9. Why would the failure to create a unified EU labor market be particularly harmful to the prospects for a smoothly functioning EMU, if at the same time capital is completely free to move among EU countries?

10. Britain belongs to the EU, but it has not yet adopted the euro, and fierce debate rages over the issue.

   a. Find macro data on the British economy's performance since 1998 (inflation, unemployment, real GDP growth) and compare these with euro zone data.

   b. What were nominal interest rates in Britain and the euro zone after 1998? How would Britain have fared if the ECB had been setting Britain's nominal interest rate at the euro zone level and the pound sterling's euro exchange rate had been fixed?

11. Movements in the euro's external exchange rate can be seen as goods-market shocks that have asymmetric effects on different euro zone members. When the euro appreciated against China's currency in 2007, which country suffered the greater fall in aggregate demand, Finland, which does not compete directly with China in its export markets, or Spain, which does? What would have happened had Spain retained its old currency, the peseta?

12. In the United States' currency union, we seem never to worry if a state has a big current account deficit. Have you ever seen such data in the newspaper? Can you even find the data in any U.S. government statistical sources? For example, one would guess that the state of Louisiana ran large current account deficits after it was devastated by Hurricane Katrina in 2005. But Louisiana's possible current account deficit was not deemed worthy of coverage by the financial press. We do know, however, that in 2008, Greece had a current account deficit of 14.6 percent of GDP, Portugal had a deficit of 12 percent of GDP, and Spain had a deficit of 9.8 percent of GDP (Table 10-4). Should the governments of these countries worry about such large deficits? (Hint: Relate your answer to the debate over the need for the SGP.)

13. Go to the IMF website at www.imf.org and find the *World Economic Outlook* database; then download data on the current account balance (as a percent of GDP) for Greece, Spain, Portugal, Italy, and Ireland. What happens to the current accounts of these countries after 2009 during the euro crisis? Can you explain what you see?

14. Suppose it is possible for a country to leave the euro zone and begin printing its own currency. Suppose also that there is some point at which the ECB (perhaps it is worried about financial losses) will stop lending to the country's banks. What would happen if creditors suddenly begin to flee from the country's banks?

15. In the spring of 2013 Cyprus followed Greece, Ireland, and Portugal in agreeing to an emergency loan from the *troika* of the EU, ECB, and IMF. The cause was big losses in the Cypriot banking system. After imposing losses on some Cypriot bank deposits, the government, with EU approval, imposed capital controls to prevent residents from taking money abroad. Why do you think this step (which violated the EU's single-market philosophy) was taken?

FURTHER READINGS

Alberto Alesina and Francesco Giavazzi, eds. *Europe and the Euro.* Chicago: University of Chicago Press, 2010. Essays on the euro's first decade.

Carlo Bastasin. *Saving Europe: How National Politics Nearly Destroyed the Euro.* Washington, D.C.: Brookings Institution, 2012. Detailed historical account of the political backdrop to the euro crisis and the policy response through 2011.

Lars Calmfors and others. *EMU: A Swedish Perspective.* Berlin: Springer, 1997. This book, which argued against Swedish membership in EMU, is based on a report commissioned by the government of Sweden prior to the launch of the euro.

W. Max Corden. *Monetary Integration.* Princeton Essays in International Finance 32. International Finance Section, Department of Economics, Princeton University, April 1972. Classic analysis of monetary unification.

Paul De Grauwe. "The Governance of a Fragile Eurozone." *Australian Economic Review* 45 (September 2012), pp. 255–268. Interprets the crisis in the euro zone in terms of self-fulfilling speculation in sovereign debt markets.

Barry Eichengreen and Peter Temin. "Fetters of Gold and Paper." *Oxford Review of Economic Policy* 26 (Autumn 2010), pp. 370–384. Explores similarities between the implications of fixed exchange rates in the euro zone, and of the gold standard during the Great Depression.

Martin Feldstein. "The Political Economy of the European Economic and Monetary Union: Political Sources of an Economic Liability." *Journal of Economic Perspectives* 11 (Fall 1997), pp. 23–42. A leading American economist makes the case against EMU.

Harold James. *Making the European Monetary Union.* Cambridge, MA: Harvard University Press, 2012. Detailed historical account of the pre-history of EMU, including negotiations over the design of the ECB.

Peter B. Kenen and Ellen E. Meade. *Regional Monetary Integration.* Cambridge, U.K.: Cambridge University Press, 2008. A comprehensive overview of the euro zone's experience and of the prospects for other large currency areas in East Asia and Latin America.

Philip R. Lane. "The European Sovereign Debt Crisis." *Journal of Economic Perspectives* 26 (Summer 2012), pp. 49–68. Concise overview of the euro area's debt crisis.

Silvia Merler and Jean Pisani-Ferry. "Sudden Stops in the Euro Area." Bruegel Policy Contribution 2012/06, March 2012. An analysis of destabilizing private financial flows within EMU.

Jean Pisani-Ferry, André Sapir, Nicolas Véron, and Guntram B. Wolff. "What Kind of European Banking Union?" Bruegel Policy Contribution 2012/12, June 2012. Compact review of issues in setting up a banking union within the EU.

Jay C. Shambaugh. "The Euro's Three Crises." *Brooking Papers on Economic Activity* 1 (2012), pp. 157–211. A broad look at the euro zone problems leading to the crisis.

Edward Tower and Thomas D. Willett. *The Theory of Optimal Currency Areas and Exchange Rate Flexibility.* Princeton Special Papers in International Economics 11. International Finance Section, Department of Economics, Princeton University, May 1976. Surveys the theory of optimum currency areas.

CHAPTER 11

DEVELOPING COUNTRIES: GROWTH, CRISIS, AND REFORM

Until now, we have studied macroeconomic interactions between industrialized market economies like those of the United States and Western Europe. Richly endowed with capital and skilled labor, these politically stable countries generate high levels of income for their residents. And their markets, compared to those of some poorer countries, have long been relatively free of direct government control.

Several times since the 1980s, however, the macroeconomic problems of the world's developing countries have been at the forefront of concerns about the stability of the entire international economy. Over the decades following World War II, trade between developing and industrial nations has expanded, as have developing-country financial transactions with richer lands. In turn, the more extensive links between the two groups of economies have made each group more dependent than before on the economic health of the other. Events in developing countries therefore have a significant impact on welfare and policies in more advanced economies. Since the 1960s, some countries that once were poor have increased their living standards dramatically, while others have fallen even further behind the industrial world. By understanding these contrasting development experiences, we can derive important policy lessons that can spur economic growth in all countries.

This chapter studies the macroeconomic problems of developing countries and the repercussions of those problems on the developed world. Although the insights from international macroeconomics that we gained in previous chapters also apply to developing countries, the distinctive problems those countries have faced in their quest to catch up to the rich economies warrant separate discussion. In addition, the lower income levels of developing areas make macroeconomic slumps there even more painful than in developed economies, with consequences that can threaten political and social cohesion.

After reading this chapter, you will be able to:

- Describe the persistently unequal world distribution of income and the evidence on its causes.
- Summarize the major economic features of developing countries.
- Explain the position of developing countries in the world capital market and the problem of default by developing borrowers.
- Recount the recent history of developing-country financial crises.
- Discuss proposed measures to enhance poorer countries' gains from participation in the world capital market.

Income, Wealth, and Growth in the World Economy

Poverty is the basic problem that developing countries face, and escaping from poverty is their overriding economic and political challenge. Compared with industrialized economies, most developing countries are poor in the factors of production essential to modern industry: capital and skilled labor. The relative scarcity of these factors contributes to low levels of per capita income and often prevents developing countries from realizing the economies of scale from which many richer nations benefit. But factor scarcity is largely a symptom of deeper problems. Political instability, insecure property rights, and misguided economic policies frequently have discouraged investment in capital and skills, while also reducing economic efficiency in other ways.

The Gap between Rich and Poor

The world's economies can be divided into four main categories according to their annual per capita income levels: low-income economies (including Afghanistan, Bangladesh, Nepal, Cambodia, and Haiti, along with parts of sub-Saharan Africa); lower middle-income economies (including China, India, Pakistan, the Philippines, Indonesia, several Middle Eastern countries, many Latin American and Caribbean countries, many former Soviet countries, and most of the remaining African countries); upper middle-income economies (including the remaining Latin American countries, a handful of African countries, a number of Caribbean countries, Turkey, Malaysia, Poland, Latvia, Lithuania, and Russia); and high-income economies (including the rich industrial market economies; the remaining Caribbean countries; a handful of exceptionally fortunate former developing countries such as Israel, Korea, and Singapore; oil-rich Kuwait and Saudi Arabia; and some successfully transitioned Eastern European countries such as the Czech and Slovak Republics, Hungary, and Estonia). The first two categories consist mainly of countries at a backward stage of development relative to industrial economies, while the last two comprise most of the emerging market economies (as well as the industrial economies, of course). Table 11-1 shows 2011 average per capita annual income levels for these country groups, together with another indicator of economic well-being, average life expectancy at birth.

Table 11-1 illustrates the sharp disparities in international income levels in the second decade of the 21st century. Average national income per capita in the richest economies is 69 times that of the average in the poorest developing countries! Even the upper middle-income countries enjoy only about one-sixth of the per capita income

TABLE 11-1	**Indicators of Economic Welfare in Four Groups of Countries, 2011**	
Income Group	**GDP Per Capita (2011 U.S. dollars)**	**Life Expectancy (years)***
Low-income	635	57
Lower middle-income	2,298	66
Upper middle-income	7,239	72
High-income	43,718	80

*Simple average of male and female life expectancies.
Source: World Bank.

of the industrial group. The life expectancy figures generally reflect international differences in income levels. Average life spans fall as relative poverty increases.[1]

Has the World Income Gap Narrowed Over Time?

Explaining the income differences among countries is one of the oldest goals of economics. It is no accident that Adam Smith's classic 1776 book was entitled the *Wealth of Nations.* Since at least a century before Smith's time, economists have sought not only to explain why countries' incomes differ at a given point in time, but also to solve the more challenging puzzle of why some countries become rich while others stagnate. Debate over the best policies for promoting economic growth has been fierce, as we shall see in this chapter.

Both the depth of the economic growth puzzle and the payoff to finding growth-friendly policies are illustrated in Table 11-2, which shows per capita output *growth rates* for several country groups between 1960 and 2010. (These real output data have been corrected to account for departures from purchasing power parity.) Over that period, the United States grew at roughly the 2 to 2.5 percent annual per capita rate that many economists would argue is the long-run maximum for a mature economy. The industrial countries that were most prosperous in 1960 generally grew at mutually comparable rates. As a result, their income gaps compared to the United States changed relatively little. The poorest industrialized countries as of 1960, however, often grew much more quickly than the United States on average, and as a result, their per capita incomes tended to catch up to that of the United States. For example, Ireland, which had been 48 percent poorer than the United States in 1960, was less than 1 percent poorer in 2010—thereby having virtually erased the earlier income gap.

Ireland's catching-up process illustrates the tendency for differences among *industrial* countries' living standards to narrow over the postwar era. The theory behind this observed **convergence** in per capita incomes is deceptively simple. If trade is free, if capital can move to countries offering the highest returns, and if knowledge itself moves across political borders so that countries always have access to cutting-edge production technologies, then there is no reason for international income gaps to persist for long. Some gaps do persist in reality because of policy differences across

---

[1]Chapter 5 showed that an international comparison of *dollar* incomes portrays relative welfare levels inaccurately because countries' price levels measured in a common currency (here, U.S. dollars) generally differ. The World Bank supplies national income numbers that have been adjusted to take account of deviations from purchasing power parity (PPP). Those numbers greatly reduce, but do not eliminate, the disparities in Table 11-1. Table 11-2 reports some PPP-adjusted incomes.

TABLE 11-2	Output Per Capita in Selected Countries, 1960–2010 (in 2005 U.S. dollars)		
	Output Per Capita		
Country	**1960**	**2010**	**1960–2010 Annual Average Growth Rate (percent per year)**
Industrialized in 1960			
Canada	12,946	35,810	2.1
France	9,396	29,145	2.3
Ireland	7,807	41,558	3.4
Italy	7,924	27,227	2.5
Japan	4,404	31,815	4.0
Spain	6,008	25,797	3.0
Sweden	11,710	33,627	2.1
United Kingdom	11,884	32,034	2.0
United States	15,136	41,858	2.1
Africa			
Kenya	978	1,287	0.5
Nigeria	1,442	1,923	0.6
Senegal	1,567	1,480	−0.1
Zimbabwe	3,847	3,959	0.1
Latin America			
Argentina	6,585	12,862	1.3
Brazil	2,354	8,750	2.7
Chile	3,915	12,871	2.4
Colombia	2,814	7,430	2.0
Mexico	5,033	12,189	1.8
Paraguay	1,990	4,666	1.7
Peru	3,939	7,466	1.3
Venezuela	7,307	9,762	0.6
Asia			
China	405	8,727	6.3
Hong Kong	4,518	44,070	4.7
India	734	3,413	3.1
Malaysia	1,624	11,863	4.1
Singapore	3,170	42,360	5.3
South Korea	1,610	28,702	5.9
Taiwan	2,061	32,865	5.7
Thailand	772	8,467	4.9

Note: Data are taken from the Penn World Table, Version 8.0, and use PPP exchange rates to compare national incomes. For a description, see the Penn World Table website at http://www.rug.nl/research/ggdc/data/penn-world-table.

industrial countries; however, the preceding forces of convergence seem to be strong enough to keep industrial-country incomes roughly in the same ballpark. Remember, too, that differences in output *per capita* may overstate differences in output *per employed worker* because most industrial countries have higher unemployment rates and lower labor-force participation rates than the United States.

Despite the appeal of a simple convergence theory, no clear tendency for per capita incomes to converge characterizes the world as a whole, as the rest of Table 11-2 shows. There we see vast discrepancies in long-term growth rates among different regional country groupings, but no general tendency for poorer countries to grow faster. Several countries in sub-Saharan Africa, although at the bottom of the world income scale, have grown (for most of the postwar years) at rates far below those of the main industrial countries.[2] Growth has also been relatively slow in Latin America, where only a few countries (notably Brazil and Chile) have surpassed the average growth rate of the United States, despite lower income levels.

In contrast, East Asian countries *have* tended to grow at rates far above those of the industrialized world, as the convergence theory would predict. South Korea, with an income level close to Senegal's in 1960, has grown nearly 6 percent per year (in per capita terms) since then and in 1997 was classified as a high-income developing country by the World Bank. Singapore's 5.3 percent annual average growth rate likewise propelled it to high-income status. Some of the Eastern European countries that lived under Soviet rule until 1989 have also graduated rapidly to the upper income brackets.

A country that can muster even a 3 percent annual growth rate will see its real per capita income double every generation. But at the growth rates seen in East Asian countries such as Hong Kong, Singapore, South Korea, and Taiwan, per capita real income increases *fivefold* every generation!

What explains the sharply divergent long-run growth patterns in Table 11-2? The answer lies in the economic and political features of developing countries and the ways these have changed over time in response to both world events and internal pressures. The structural features of developing countries have also helped to determine their success in pursuing key macroeconomic goals other than rapid growth, such as low inflation, low unemployment, and financial-sector stability.

Structural Features of Developing Countries

Developing countries differ widely among themselves these days, and no single list of "typical" features would accurately describe all developing countries. In the early 1960s, these countries were much more similar to each other in their approaches to trade policy, macroeconomic policy, and other government interventions in the economy. Then things began to change. East Asian countries abandoned import-substituting industrialization, embracing an export-oriented development strategy instead. This strategy proved very successful. Later on, countries in Latin America also reduced trade barriers while simultaneously attempting to rein in government's role in the economy, reduce chronically high inflation, and, in many cases, open capital accounts to private transactions. These efforts initially met with mixed success but increasingly are bearing fruit.

While many developing countries therefore have reformed their economies to come closer to the structures of the successful industrial economies, the process remains incomplete and many developing countries tend to be characterized by at least some of the following features:

1. There is a history of extensive direct government control of the economy, including restrictions on international trade, government ownership or control of large industrial firms, direct government control of internal financial transactions,

---

[2]On the other hand, other countries in sub-Saharan Africa have now reached upper middle-income status. Botswana in southern Africa did so early. The country enjoyed an average per capita growth rate well above 5 percent per year during the three decades after 1960.

and a high level of government consumption as a share of GNP. Developing countries differ widely among themselves in the extent to which the role of government in the economy has been reduced in these various areas over the past decades.

2. There is a history of high inflation. In many countries, the government was unable to pay for its heavy expenditures and the losses of state-owned enterprises through taxes alone. Tax evasion was rampant, and much economic activity was driven underground, so it proved easiest simply to print money. **Seigniorage** is the name economists give to the real resources a government earns when it prints money that it spends on goods and services. When their governments were expanding money supplies continually to extract high levels of seigniorage, developing countries experienced inflation and even hyperinflation. (See, for example, the discussion of inflation and money supply growth in Latin America in Chapter 4, page 95.)

3. Where domestic financial markets have been liberalized, weak credit institutions often abound. Banks frequently lend funds they have borrowed to finance poor or very risky projects. Loans may be made on the basis of personal connections rather than prospective returns, and government safeguards against financial fragility, such as bank supervision (Chapter 9), tend to be ineffective due to incompetence, inexperience, and outright fraud. While public trade in stock shares has developed in many emerging markets, it is usually harder in developing countries for shareholders to find out how a firm's money is being spent or to control firm managers. The legal framework for resolving asset ownership in cases of bankruptcy typically is also weak. Notwithstanding the recent instability in advanced-country financial markets, it is still true that by comparison, developing countries' financial markets remain less effective in directing savings toward their most efficient investment uses. As a result, developing countries remain even more prone to crisis.

4. Where exchange rates are not pegged outright (as in China), they tend to be managed more heavily by developing-country governments. Government measures to limit exchange rate flexibility reflect both a desire to keep inflation under control and the fear that floating exchange rates would be subject to huge volatility in the relatively thin markets for developing-country currencies. There is a history of allocating foreign exchange through government decree rather than through the market, a practice (called *exchange control*) that some developing countries still maintain. Most developing countries have, in particular, tried to control capital movements by limiting foreign exchange transactions connected with trade in assets. More recently, however, many emerging markets have opened their capital accounts.

5. Natural resources or agricultural commodities make up an important share of exports for many developing countries—for example, Russian petroleum, Malaysian timber, South African gold, and Colombian coffee.

6. Attempts to circumvent government controls, taxes, and regulations have helped to make corrupt practices such as bribery and extortion a way of life in many if not most developing countries. Even though the development of underground economic activity has in some instances aided economic efficiency by restoring a degree of market-based resource allocation, on balance it is clear from the data that corruption and poverty go hand in hand.

For a large sample of developing and industrial countries, Figure 11-1 shows the strong positive relationship between annual real per capita output and an inverse index of corruption—ranging from 1 (most corrupt) to 10 (cleanest)—published by

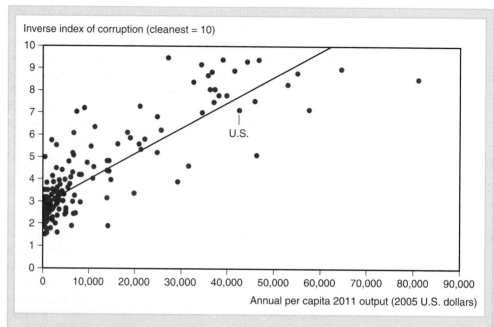

FIGURE 11-1

Corruption and Per Capita Output

Corruption tends to rise as real per capita output falls.

Note: The figure plots 2011 values of an (inverse) index of corruption and 2011 values of PPP-adjusted real per capita output, measured in 2005 U.S. dollars (the amount a dollar could buy in the United States in 2005). The straight line represents a statistician's best guess of a country's corruption level based on its real per capita output.

Source: Transparency International, Corruption Perception Index; World Bank, World Development Indicators.

the organization Transparency International.[3] Several factors underlie this strong positive relationship. Government regulations that promote corruption also harm economic prosperity. Statistical studies have found that corruption itself tends to have net negative effects on economic efficiency and growth.[4] Finally, poorer countries

---

[3]According to Transparency International's 2011 rankings, the cleanest country in the world was New Zealand (scoring a high 9.5), and the most corrupt was Afghanistan (scoring a dismal 1.5). The score for the United States was 7.1. For detailed data and a general overview of the economics of corruption, see Vito Tanzi, "Corruption around the World," *International Monetary Fund Staff Papers* 45 (December 1998), pp. 559–594.

[4]There is, of course, abundant anecdotal evidence on the economic inefficiencies associated with corruption. Consider the following description from 1999 of doing business in Brazil, which had a 2011 Transparency International ranking of 3.8:

> Corruption goes well beyond shaking down street sellers. Almost every conceivable economic activity is subject to some form of official extortion.
>
> Big Brazilian companies generally agree to pay bribes, but multinationals usually refuse and prefer to pay fines. The money—paid at municipal, state and federal levels—is shared out between bureaucrats and their political godfathers. They make sure that it is impossible to comply fully with all of Brazil's tangle of laws, regulations, decrees and directives.
>
> The bribes and fines make up part of the "Brazil Cost," shorthand for the multitude of expenses that inflate the cost of conducting business in Brazil.

See "Death, Decay in São Paulo May Stir Reformist Zeal," *Financial Times*, March 20/21, 1999, p. 4.

lack the resources to police corruption effectively, and poverty itself breeds a greater willingness to go around the rules.

Many of the broad features that still characterize developing countries today took shape in the 1930s and can be traced to the Great Depression (Chapter 8). Most developing countries experimented with direct controls over trade and payments to conserve foreign exchange reserves and safeguard domestic employment. Faced with a massive breakdown of the world market system, industrial and developing countries alike allowed their governments to assume increasingly direct roles in employment and production. Often, governments reorganized labor markets, established stricter control over financial markets, controlled prices, and nationalized key industries. The trend toward government control of the economy proved much more persistent in developing countries, however, where political institutions allowed those with vested financial interests in the status quo to perpetuate it.

Cut off from traditional suppliers of manufactures during World War II, developing countries encouraged new manufacturing industries of their own. Political pressure to protect these industries was one factor behind the popularity of import-substituting industrialization in the first postwar decades. In addition, colonial areas that gained independence after the war believed they could attain the income levels of their former rulers only through rapid, government-directed industrialization and urbanization. Finally, developing-country leaders feared that their efforts to escape poverty would be doomed if they continued to specialize in primary-commodity exports such as coffee, copper, and wheat. In the 1950s, some influential economists argued that developing countries would suffer continually declining terms of trade unless they used commercial policy to move resources out of primary exports and into import substitutes. These forecasts turned out to be wrong, but they did influence developing countries' policies in the first postwar decades.

Developing-Country Borrowing and Debt

One further feature of developing countries is crucial to understanding their macroeconomic problems: Many have relied heavily on financial inflows from abroad to finance domestic investment. Before World War I and in the period up to the Great Depression, developing countries (including the United States for much of the 19th century) received large financial inflows from richer lands. Britain was the biggest international lender, but France, Germany, and other European powers contributed as well to finance industrial development in some then-developing countries (such as Argentina, Australia, Canada, and the United States) and natural resource extraction or plantation agriculture in others (such as Brazil, Peru, Kenya, and Indonesia).

In the decades after World War II, many developing economies again tapped the savings of richer countries and built up a substantial debt to the rest of the world (around $7 trillion in gross terms at the end of 2013). Developing-country debt was at the center of several international lending crises that preoccupied economic policy makers throughout the world starting in the early 1980s.

The Economics of Financial Inflows to Developing Countries

As stated above, many developing countries have received extensive financial inflows from abroad and now carry substantial debts to foreigners. Table 11-3 shows the pattern of borrowing since 1973 by non–oil developing countries (see the second column of data). As you can see, developing countries were consistent borrowers until the very end of the last century (leaving aside the major oil exporters, who run big surpluses

TABLE 11-3	Cumulative Current Account Balances of Major Oil Exporters, Other Developing Countries, and Advanced Countries, 1973–2012 (billions of dollars)		
	Major Oil Exporters	Other Developing Countries	Advanced Countries
1973–1981	252.9	−246.1	−183.8
1982–1989	−64.6	−143.3	−426.6
1990–1998	−58.2	−522.7	−105.9
1999–2012	3,445.9	1,766.1	−5,576.6

Source: International Monetary Fund, *International Financial Statistics.* Global current accounts generally do not sum to zero because of errors, omissions, and the exclusion of some countries in some periods.

when the world oil price is high). What factors have caused financial inflows to the developing world, and why did the pattern apparently change around the start of the twenty-first century?

Recall the identity (analyzed in Chapter 2) that links national saving, S, domestic investment, I, and the current account balance, $CA : S − I = CA$. If national saving falls short of domestic investment, the difference equals the current account deficit. Because of poverty and poor financial institutions, national saving often is low in developing countries. Because these same countries are relatively poor in capital, however, the opportunities for profitably introducing or expanding plant and equipment can be abundant. Such opportunities justify a high level of investment. By running a deficit in its current account, a country can obtain resources from abroad to invest even if its domestic saving level is low. However, a deficit in the current account implies that the country is borrowing abroad. In return for being able to import more foreign goods today than its current exports can pay for, the country must promise to repay in the future either the interest and principal on loans or the dividends on shares in firms sold to foreigners.

Thus, much developing-country borrowing could potentially be explained by the incentives for *intertemporal trade* examined in Chapter 8. Low-income countries generate too little saving of their own to take advantage of all their profitable investment opportunities, so they must borrow abroad. In capital-rich countries, on the other hand, many productive investment opportunities have been exploited already but saving levels are relatively high. Savers in developed countries can earn higher rates of return, however, by lending to finance investments in the developing world.

Notice that when developing countries borrow to undertake productive investments that they would not otherwise be able to carry out, both they and the lenders reap gains from trade. Borrowers gain because they can build up their capital stocks despite limited national savings. Lenders simultaneously gain because they earn higher returns on their savings than they could earn at home.

While the reasoning above provides a rationale for developing countries' external deficits and debt, it does not imply that all loans from developed to developing countries are justified. Loans that finance unprofitable investments—for example, huge shopping malls that are never occupied—or imports of consumption goods may result in debts that borrowers cannot repay. In addition, faulty government policies that artificially depress national saving rates may lead to excessive foreign borrowing. The 1982–1989 fall in developing-country borrowing evident in Table 11-3 is associated with difficulties that some poorer countries had in keeping up their payments to creditors.

A surprising development starting around 2000 was that developing countries (including many that were not oil exporters) ran surpluses, a counterpart of wealthier countries' deficits (mainly that of the United States). Contrary to what simple economic theory would predict, capital was flowing *uphill*, from poorer to richer countries. We mentioned this pattern of global imbalances in Chapter 8 (pages 277–279), and probe further into the phenomenon later in this chapter. One reason for these surpluses was developing countries' strong desire to accumulate international reserves, as we discuss in the box on page 387.

The Problem of Default

Potential gains from international borrowing and lending will not be realized unless lenders are confident they will be repaid. As we noted in Chapter 10, a loan is said to be in *default* when the borrower, without the agreement of the lender, fails to repay on schedule according to the loan contract. Both social and political instability in developing countries, as well as the frequent weaknesses in their public finances and financial institutions, make it much more risky to lend to developing than to industrial countries. And indeed, the history of financial flows to developing countries is strewn with the wreckage of financial crises and defaulted loan contracts:

1. In the early 19th century, a number of American states defaulted on the European loans they had taken out to finance the building of infrastructure such as canals.
2. Throughout the 19th century, Latin American countries ran into repayment problems. This was particularly true of Argentina, which sparked a global financial crisis in 1890 (the Baring Crisis) when it proved unable to meet its obligations.
3. In 1917, the new communist government of Russia repudiated the foreign debts that had been incurred by previous rulers. The communists closed the Soviet economy to the rest of the world and embarked on a program of centrally planned economic development that was often ruthlessly enforced.
4. During the Great Depression of the 1930s, world economic activity collapsed and developing countries found themselves shut out of industrial-country export markets by a wall of protection (recall Chapter 8). Nearly every developing country defaulted on its external debts as a result, and private financial flows to developing countries dried up for four decades. Several European countries defaulted on their World War I debts to allied governments, mainly the United States.
5. Many developing countries have defaulted (or restructured their foreign debts) in recent decades. For example, in 2005, after lengthy negotiations, most of Argentina's private creditors agreed to settle for only about a third of the contractual values of their claims on the country.

Sharp contractions in a country's output and employment invariably occur after a *sudden stop* in which the country suddenly loses access to all foreign sources of funds (recall Chapter 8). At a very basic level, the necessity for such contractions can be seen from the current account identity, $S - I = CA$. Imagine that a country is running a current account deficit that is 5 percent of its initial GNP, when suddenly foreign lenders become fearful of default and cut off all new loans. Since this action forces the current account balance to be at least zero ($CA \geq 0$), the identity $S - I = CA$ tells us that through some combination of a fall in investment or a rise in saving, $S - I$ must immediately rise by at least 5 percent. The required sharp fall in aggregate demand necessarily depresses the country's output dramatically. Even if the country were not on the verge of default initially—imagine that foreign lenders were originally seized by a sudden irrational panic—the harsh contraction in output that the country would suffer would make default a real possibility.

Indeed, matters are likely to be even worse for the country than the preceding example suggests. Foreign lenders will not only withhold new loans if they fear default, they will naturally also try to get as much money out of the country as possible by demanding the *full* repayment on any loans for which principal can be demanded on short notice (for example, liquid short-term bank deposits). When the developing country repays the principal on debt, it is increasing its *net* foreign wealth. To generate the corresponding positive current account item (see Chapter 2), the country must somehow raise its net exports. Thus, in a sudden stop crisis, the country will not only have to run a current account of zero, it will also actually be called upon to run a *surplus* ($CA > 0$). The bigger the country's *short-term* foreign debt—debt whose principal can be demanded by creditors—the larger the rise in saving or compression of investment that will be needed to avoid a default. You already may have noticed that developing-country sudden stops and default crises can be driven by a self-fulfilling mechanism analogous to the ones behind self-fulfilling balance of payments crises (Chapter 7), bank runs (Chapter 9), and the sovereign debt problems in the euro area (Chapter 10). Indeed, the underlying logic is the same. Furthermore, default crises in developing countries are likely to be accompanied by balance of payments crises (when the exchange rate is pegged) *and* bank runs. A balance of payments crisis results because the country's official foreign exchange reserves may be the only ready means it has to pay off foreign short-term debts. Through running down its official reserves, the government can cushion aggregate demand by reducing the size of the current account surplus needed to meet creditors' demands for repayment.[5] But the loss of its reserves leaves the government unable to peg the exchange rate any longer. At the same time, the banks get into trouble as domestic and foreign depositors, fearing currency depreciation and the consequences of default, withdraw funds and purchase foreign reserves in the hope of repaying foreign-currency debts or sending wealth safely abroad. Since the banks are often weak to begin with, the large-scale withdrawals quickly push them to the brink of failure. Finally, a negative impact on the public finances may complete the doom loop. If the government needs to issue more debt as a result of bailing out the banks, then its own credit standing is weakened, which causes higher borrowing costs and a greater chance of a sovereign default.

Because each of these crisis "triplets" reinforces the others, a developing country's financial crisis is likely to be severe, to have widespread negative effects on the economy, and to snowball very quickly. The immediate origin of such a pervasive economic collapse can be in the financial account (as in a sudden stop), in the foreign exchange market, or in the banking system, depending on the situation of the particular country.

When a government defaults on its obligations, the event is called a *sovereign* default. A conceptually different situation occurs when a large number of *private* domestic borrowers cannot pay their debts to foreigners. In practice in developing countries, however, the two types of default go together. The government might bail out the private sector by taking on its foreign debts, thereby hoping to avoid widespread economic collapse. In addition, a government in trouble may provoke private defaults

---

[5]Make certain you understand why this is so. If necessary, review the open-economy accounting concepts from Chapter 2. For a statistical analysis of the characteristics of default, banking, and currency crises, see Pierre-Olivier Gourinchas and Maurice Obstfeld, "Stories of the Twentieth Century for the Twenty-First," *American Economic Journal: Macroeconomics* 4 (January 2012): 226–265.

by limiting domestic residents' access to its dwindling foreign exchange reserves. That action makes it much harder to pay foreign currency debts. In either case, the government becomes closely involved in the subsequent negotiations with foreign creditors.

Default crises were rare in the first three decades after World War II: Debt issue by developing countries was limited, and the lenders typically were governments or official international agencies such as the International Monetary Fund (IMF) and World Bank. As the free flow of private global capital expanded after the early 1970s, however, major default crises occurred repeatedly (as we shall see), leading many to question the stability of the world capital market.[6]

Alternative Forms of Financial Inflow

When a developing country has a current account deficit, it is selling assets to foreigners to finance the difference between its spending and its income. Although we have lumped these asset sales together under the catchall term *borrowing*, the financial inflows that finance developing countries' deficits (and, indeed, any country's deficit) can take several forms. Different types of financial inflows have predominated in different historical periods. Because different obligations to foreign lenders result, an understanding of the macroeconomic scene in developing countries requires a careful analysis of the five major channels through which these countries have financed their external deficits.

  1. *Bond finance.* Developing countries have sometimes sold bonds to private foreign citizens to finance their deficits. Bond finance was dominant in the period up to 1914 and in the interwar years (1918–1939). It regained popularity after 1990 as many developing countries tried to liberalize and modernize their financial markets.

  2. *Bank finance.* Between the early 1970s and late 1980s, developing countries borrowed extensively from commercial banks in the advanced economies. In 1970, roughly a quarter of developing-country external finance was provided by banks. In 1981, banks provided an amount of finance roughly equal to the non–oil developing countries' aggregate current account deficit for that year. Banks still lend directly to developing countries, but in the 1990s the importance of bank lending shrank.

  3. *Official lending.* Developing countries sometimes borrow from official foreign agencies such as the World Bank or the Inter-American Development Bank. Such loans can be made on a "concessional" basis, that is, at interest rates below market levels, or on a market basis, which allows the lender to earn the market rate of return. Over the post-World War II period, official lending flows to developing nations have shrunk relative to total flows but remain dominant for some countries, for example, many of those in sub-Saharan Africa.

---

[6]On the history of default through the mid-1980s, see Peter H. Lindert and Peter J. Morton, "How Sovereign Debt Has Worked," in Jeffrey D. Sachs, ed., *Developing Country Debt and Economic Performance*, Vol. 1 (Chicago: University of Chicago Press, 1989). A good overview of private capital inflows to developing countries over the same period is given by Eliana A. Cardoso and Rudiger Dornbusch, "Foreign Private Capital Inflows," in Hollis Chenery and T. N. Srinivasan, eds., *Handbook of Development Economics*, Vol. 2 (Amsterdam: Elsevier Science Publishers, 1989). A more recent overview of default crises is in Atish Ghosh et al., *IMF-Supported Programs in Capital Account Crises*, Occasional Paper 210 (Washington, D.C.: International Monetary Fund, 2002). For a comprehensive historical survey, see Carmen Reinhart and Kenneth Rogoff, *This Time Is Different: Eight Centuries of Financial Folly* (Princeton, NJ: Princeton University Press, 2009). Reinhart and Rogoff document that for developing countries, default crises can occur at comparatively low levels of external debt relative to output.

4. *Foreign direct investment.* In foreign direct investment, a firm largely owned by foreign residents acquires or expands a subsidiary firm or factory located in the host developing country. A loan from IBM to its assembly plant in Mexico, for example, would be a direct investment by the United States in Mexico. The transaction would enter Mexico's balance of payments accounts as a financial asset sale (and the U.S. balance of payments accounts as an equal financial asset acquisition). Since World War II, foreign direct investment has been a consistently important source of developing-country capital.

5. *Portfolio investment in ownership of firms.* Since the early 1990s, investors in developed countries have shown an increased appetite for purchasing shares of stock in developing countries' firms. The trend has been reinforced by many developing countries' efforts at **privatization**—that is, selling to private owners large state-owned enterprises in key areas such as electricity, telecommunications, and petroleum. In the United States, numerous investment companies offer mutual funds specializing in emerging market shares.

The five types of finance just described can be classified into two categories: *debt* finance and *equity* finance (Chapter 9). Bond, bank, and official finance are all forms of debt finance. In this case, the debtor must repay the face value of the loan, plus interest, regardless of its own economic circumstances. Direct investment and portfolio purchases of stock shares are, on the other hand, forms of equity finance. Foreign owners of a direct investment, for example, have a claim to a share of the investment's net return, not a claim to a fixed stream of money payments. Adverse economic events in the host country thus result in an automatic fall in the earnings of direct investments and in the dividends paid to foreigners.

The distinction between debt and equity finance is useful in analyzing how developing-country payments to foreigners adjust to unforeseen events such as recessions or terms of trade changes. When a country's liabilities are in the form of debt, its scheduled payments to creditors do not fall even if its real income falls. It may then become very painful for the country to continue honoring its foreign obligations—painful enough to cause the country to default. Life often is easier, however, with equity finance. In the case of equity, a fall in domestic income automatically reduces the earnings of foreign shareholders without violating any loan agreement. By acquiring equity, foreigners have effectively agreed to share in both the bad and the good times of the economy. Equity rather than debt financing of its investments therefore leaves a developing country much less vulnerable to the risk of a foreign lending crisis.

The Problem of "Original Sin"

When developing countries incur debts to foreigners, those debts are often denominated in terms of a major foreign currency—the U.S. dollar, the euro, or the yen. This practice is not always a matter of choice. In general, lenders from richer countries, fearing the extreme devaluation and inflation that have occurred so often in the past, insist that poorer countries promise to repay them in the lenders' own currencies. If sovereign debts were denominated in domestic rather than foreign currencies—in other words, if the loan contract was a promise to repay foreign lenders with domestic currency—then developing-country governments could simply print their own currencies to repay their creditors. Governments would never need to default, although by creating inflation they would be reducing the *real* value of their obligations.

In contrast to developing countries, richer countries almost always borrow in terms of their own currencies. Thus, the United States borrows dollars from foreigners, Britain borrows pounds sterling, Japan borrows yen, and Switzerland borrows Swiss francs.

For these richer countries, the ability to denominate their foreign debts in their own currencies, while holding foreign assets denominated in foreign currencies, is a considerable advantage—even apart from the leeway it gives to repay in a currency that the home government can print. For example, suppose a fall in world demand for U.S. products leads to a dollar depreciation. We saw in Chapter 8 how such a depreciation can cushion output and employment in the United States. The U.S. portfolio of foreign assets and liabilities, in fact, yields a further cushioning advantage: Because U.S. assets are mostly denominated in foreign currencies, the dollar value of those assets *rises* when the dollar depreciates against foreign currencies. At the same time, because U.S. foreign liabilities are predominantly (about 95 percent) in dollars, their dollar value rises very little. So a fall in world demand for U.S. goods leads to a substantial wealth transfer from foreigners to the United States—a kind of international insurance payment.

For poor countries that must borrow in a major foreign currency, a fall in export demand has the opposite effect. Because poorer countries tend to be net debtors in the major foreign currencies, a depreciation of domestic currency causes a transfer of wealth to foreigners by *raising* the domestic currency value of the net foreign debt. This amounts to negative insurance!

A country that can borrow abroad in its own currency can reduce the real resources it owes to foreigners, without triggering a default, simply by depreciating its currency. A developing country forced to borrow in foreign currency lacks this option, and can reduce what it owes to foreigners only through some form of outright default.[7]

Economists Barry Eichengreen of the University of California–Berkeley and Ricardo Hausmann of Harvard University coined the phrase **original sin** to describe developing countries' inability to borrow in their own currencies.[8] In these economists' view, that inability of poor countries is a structural problem caused primarily by features of the global capital market—such as the limited additional diversification potential that a small country's currency provides to creditors from rich countries, who already hold all the major currencies in their portfolios. Other economists believe that the "sin" of developing countries is not particularly "original" but instead derives from their own histories of ill-advised economic policies. The debate is far from settled, but whatever the truth, it is clear that because of original sin, debt finance in international markets is more problematic for developing than for developed economies.

A related but distinct phenomenon is the large scale of private, *internal* borrowing in dollars or other major foreign currencies in many developing countries. As a result, foreign currency debtors may find themselves in considerable difficulty when the domestic currency depreciates.[9]

---

[7]As we saw in Chapter 10, Greece's government defaulted on its debt in 2012, the first default by a high-income country since the 1940s. Some other euro zone countries could default in the future. Euro zone countries face a unique constraint compared to other high-income countries, however. Because monetary policy is controlled by the ECB, a single euro zone government cannot choose to devalue its debts legally through depreciation of the domestic currency.

[8]See their paper "Exchange Rates and Financial Fragility" in *New Challenges for Monetary Policy* (Kansas City, MO: Federal Reserve Bank of Kansas City, 1999), pp. 329–368.

[9]For insight into the reasons for foreign-currency liability denomination, see the item by Rajan and Tokatlidis in Further Readings. When the currency of denomination is the U.S. dollar, the phenomenon is called **dollarization**. Increasingly, some of the more prosperous emerging market economies' governments have been able to issue domestic-currency bonds in home bond markets, with some demand coming from foreign investors (notably mutual funds). This development has helped to mitigate the original sin problem somewhat.

The Debt Crisis of the 1980s

In 1981–1983, the world economy suffered a steep recession. Just as the Great Depression made it hard for developing countries to make payments on their foreign loans—quickly causing an almost universal default—the great recession of the early 1980s also sparked a crisis over developing-country debt.

Chapter 8 described how the U.S. Federal Reserve in 1979 adopted a tough anti-inflation policy that raised dollar interest rates and helped push the world economy into recession by 1981. The fall in industrial countries' aggregate demand had a direct negative impact on the developing countries, of course, but three other mechanisms were also important. Because the developing world had extensive adjustable-rate dollar-denominated debts (original sin in action), there was an immediate and spectacular rise in the interest burden that debtor countries had to carry. The problem was magnified by the dollar's sharp appreciation in the foreign exchange market, which raised the real value of the dollar debt burden substantially. Finally, primary commodity prices collapsed, depressing the terms of trade of many poor economies.

The crisis began in August 1982 when Mexico announced that its central bank had run out of foreign reserves and that it could no longer meet payments on its foreign debt. Seeing potential similarities between Mexico and other large Latin American debtors such as Argentina, Brazil, and Chile, banks in the industrial countries—the largest private lenders to Latin America at the time—scrambled to reduce their risks by cutting off new credits and demanding repayment on earlier loans.

The results were a widespread inability of developing countries to meet prior debt obligations and a rapid move to the edge of a generalized default. Latin America was perhaps hardest hit, but also hit were Soviet bloc countries like Poland that had borrowed from European banks. African countries, most of whose debts were to official agencies such as the IMF and World Bank, also fell behind on their debts. Most countries in East Asia were able to maintain economic growth and avoid rescheduling their debt (that is, stretching out repayments by promising to pay additional interest in the future). Nonetheless, by the end of 1986 more than 40 countries had encountered severe external financing problems. Growth had slowed sharply (or gone into reverse) in much of the developing world, and developing-country borrowing fell dramatically. Initially, industrial countries, with heavy involvement by the International Monetary Fund, attempted to persuade the large banks to continue lending, arguing that a coordinated lending response was the best assurance that earlier debts would be repaid. Policy makers in the industrialized countries feared that banking giants like Citicorp and Bank of America, which had significant loans in Latin America, would fail in the event of a generalized default, dragging down the world financial system with them.[10] (As you can see, there was more than one near miss on the road to the 2007–2009 financial meltdown!) But the crisis didn't end until 1989 when the United States, fearing political instability to its south, insisted that American banks give some form of debt relief to indebted developing countries. In 1990, banks agreed to reduce Mexico's debt by 12 percent, and within a year, debt-reduction agreements had also been negotiated by the Philippines, Costa Rica, Venezuela, Uruguay, and Niger. When Argentina and Brazil reached preliminary agreements with their creditors in 1992, it looked as if the debt crisis of the 1980s had finally been resolved, but only after years of economic stagnation.

---

[10]By 1981, the developing country loans of the eight largest U.S. banks amounted to 264 percent of their capital, so loan losses of 50 percent would have made them insolvent. See table 5.1a in Federal Deposit Insurance Corporation, *History of the 80s: Lessons for the Future. Volume I: An Examination of the Banking Crises of the 1980s and Early 1990s* (Washington: FDIC, 1997).

Reforms, Capital Inflows, and the Return of Crisis

The early 1990s saw a renewal of private capital flows into developing countries, including some of the highly indebted Latin American countries at the center of the previous decade's debt crisis. As Table 11-3 shows, the foreign borrowing of non–oil-developing countries as a group expanded sharply.

Low interest rates in the United States in the early 1990s certainly provided an initial impetus to these renewed capital flows. Perhaps more important, however, were serious efforts in the recipient economies to stabilize inflation, a move requiring governments to limit their roles in the economy and raise tax revenues. At the same time, governments sought to lower trade barriers, to deregulate labor and product markets, and to improve the efficiency of financial markets. Widespread privatization served both the microeconomic goal of fostering efficiency and competition, and the macroeconomic goal of eliminating the government's need to cover the losses of sheltered and mismanaged state-owned firms.

What finally pushed countries to undertake serious reform despite the vested political interests favoring the status quo? One factor was the 1980s debt crisis itself, which resulted in what many commentators have called a "lost decade" of Latin American growth. Many of the relatively young policy makers who came to power in Latin America as the debt crisis ended were well-trained economists who believed that misguided economic policies and institutions had brought on the crisis and worsened its effects. Another factor was the example of East Asia, which had survived the 1980s debt crisis largely unscathed. Despite having been poorer than Latin America as recently as 1960, East Asia now was richer.

Recent economic reforms have taken different shapes in different Latin American countries, and some have made significant progress. Here we contrast the macroeconomic aspects of the approaches taken in four large countries that have made wide-ranging (though not equally successful) reform attempts.

Argentina Argentina suffered under military rule between 1976 and 1983, but the economy remained a shambles even after the return of democracy. Following years marked by banking crises, fiscal instability, and even hyperinflation, Argentina finally turned to radical institutional reform in the early 1990s. Import tariffs were slashed, government expenditures were cut, major state companies including the national airline were privatized, and tax reforms led to increased government revenues.

The most daring component of Argentina's program, however, was the new Convertibility Law of April 1991 making Argentina's currency fully convertible into U.S. dollars at a *fixed* rate of exactly one peso per dollar. The Convertibility Law also required that the monetary base be backed entirely by gold or foreign currency, so in one stroke it sharply curtailed the central bank's ability to finance government deficits through continuing money creation. Argentina's Convertibility Law represented an extreme version of the exchange rate–based approach to reducing inflation that had been tried many times in the past, but had typically ended in a currency crisis. The 1991 monetary law requiring 100 percent foreign exchange backing for the monetary base made Argentina an example of a **currency board**, in which the monetary base is backed entirely by foreign currency and the central bank therefore holds no domestic assets at all. This time, the approach worked for nearly a decade. Backed as it was by genuine economic and financial reforms, Argentina's plan had a dramatic effect on inflation, which remained low after dropping from 800 percent in 1990 to well under 5 percent by 1995. However, continuing inflation in the first years of the convertibility plan, despite a fixed exchange rate, implied a steep real appreciation of the peso, about

30 percent from 1990 to 1995. The real appreciation led to unemployment and a growing current account deficit.

In the mid-1990s the peso's real appreciation process ended, but unemployment remained high because of rigidities in labor markets. Although by 1997 the economy was growing rapidly, growth subsequently turned negative and the government deficit once again swelled out of control. As the world economy slipped into recession in 2001, Argentina's foreign credit dried up. The country defaulted on its foreign debts in December 2001 and abandoned the peso/dollar peg in January 2002. The peso depreciated sharply and inflation soared once again. Argentine output fell by nearly 11 percent in 2002, although growth returned in 2003 as inflation fell. As of this writing, Argentina is trying to negotiate a settlement with holdout foreign creditors that will allow it to re-enter international capital markets as a borrower.

Brazil   Like Argentina, Brazil suffered runaway inflation in the 1980s as well as multiple failed attempts at stabilization accompanied by currency reforms. The country took longer to get inflation under control, however, and approached its disinflation less systematically than the Argentines did.[11]

In 1994, the Brazilian government introduced a new currency, the real (pronounced ray-AL), pegged to the dollar. At the cost of widespread bank failures, Brazil defended the new exchange rate with high interest rates in 1995, then shifted to a fixed, upwardly crawling peg in the face of substantial real appreciation. Inflation dropped from an annual rate of 2,669 percent (in 1994) to under 10 percent in 1997.

Economic growth remained unimpressive, however. Although Brazil's government undertook a reduction in import barriers, privatization, and fiscal retrenchment, the country's overall progress on economic reform was much slower than in the case of Argentina, and the government's fiscal deficit remained worryingly high. A good part of the problem was the very high interest rate the government had to pay on its debt, a rate that reflected skepticism in markets that the limited upward crawl of the real against the dollar could be maintained.

Finally, in January 1999, Brazil devalued the real by 8 percent and then allowed it to float. Very quickly, the real lost 40 percent of its value against the dollar. Recession followed as the government struggled to prevent the real from going into a free fall. But the recession proved short-lived, inflation did not take off, and (because Brazil's financial institutions had avoided heavy borrowing in dollars), financial-sector collapse was avoided. Brazil elected a populist president, Ignacio Lula da Silva, in October 2002, but the market-friendly policies he ultimately (and rather unexpectedly) adopted have preserved Brazil's access to international credit markets. Economic growth has been healthy and Brazil has become a power in the emerging world. A key factor in Brazil's success has been its strong commodity exports, notably to China.

Chile   Having learned the lessons of deep unemployment and financial collapse at the start of the 1980s, Chile implemented more consistent reforms later in the decade. Very importantly, the country instituted a tough regulatory environment for domestic financial institutions and removed an explicit bailout guarantee that had helped to worsen Chile's earlier debt crisis. A crawling peg type of exchange rate regime was used to bring inflation down gradually, but the system was operated flexibly to avoid extreme real appreciation. The Chilean central bank became independent of the fiscal

---

[11]For an account, see Rudiger Dornbusch, "Brazil's Incomplete Stabilization and Reform," *Brookings Papers on Economic Activity* 1 (1997), pp. 367–404.

authorities in 1990 (the same year a democratic government replaced the military regime of General Pinochet). That action further solidified the commitment not to finance government deficits by ordering the central bank to print money.[12]

Another new policy required all capital inflows (other than equity purchases) to be accompanied by a one-year, non-interest-bearing deposit equal to as much as 30 percent of the transaction. Because the duration of the deposit requirement was limited, the penalty fell disproportionately on short-term inflows, those most prone to be withdrawn by foreign investors in a crisis. One motivation for the implied capital inflow tax was to limit real currency appreciation; the other was to reduce the risk that a sudden withdrawal of foreign short-term funds would provoke a financial crisis. There is considerable controversy among economists as to whether the Chilean capital inflow barriers succeeded in their aims, although it is doubtful that they did much harm.[13]

Chile's policies have paid off handsomely. Between 1991 and 1997, the country enjoyed GDP growth rates averaging better than 8 percent per year. At the same time, inflation dropped from 26 percent per year in 1990 to only 6 percent by 1997. Chile has been rated not only as being the least corrupt country in Latin America, but also as being less corrupt than several European Union members and the United States.

Mexico   Mexico introduced a broad stabilization and reform program in 1987, combining an aggressive reduction in public-sector deficits and debt with exchange rate targeting and wage-price guidelines negotiated with representatives of industry and labor unions.[14] That same year, the country made a significant commitment to free trade by joining the GATT. (Mexico subsequently joined the Organization for Economic Cooperation and Development and, in 1994, joined the North American Free Trade Agreement.)

Mexico fixed its peso's exchange rate against the U.S. dollar at the end of 1987, moved to a crawling peg at the start of 1989, and moved to a crawling band at the end of 1991. The government kept a level ceiling on the peso's possible appreciation but announced each year after 1991 a gradually rising limit on the currency's allowable extent of depreciation. Thus, the range of possible exchange rate fluctuation was permitted to increase over time.

Despite this potential flexibility, the Mexican authorities held the exchange rate near its appreciation ceiling. The peso therefore appreciated sharply in real terms, and a large current account deficit emerged. During 1994, the country's foreign exchange reserves fell to very low levels. Civil strife, a looming presidential transition, and devaluation fears contributed to this fall. Another important factor behind the

---

[12]For an overview of aspects of the Chilean approach to economic reform, see Barry P. Bosworth, Rudiger Dornbusch, and Raúl Labán, eds., *The Chilean Economy: Policy Lessons and Challenges* (Washington, D.C.: Brookings Institution, 1994). A classic account of Chilean financial problems at the start of the 1980s is Carlos F. Díaz-Alejandro, "Goodbye Financial Repression, Hello Financial Crash," *Journal of Development Economics* 19 (September/October 1985), pp. 1–24. This paper is highly recommended, as the problems discussed by Díaz-Alejandro have proven relevant far beyond the specific context of Chile.

[13]For a discussion, see Chapter 5 of the book by Kenen listed in this chapter's Further Readings. Also see Kevin Cowan and José De Gregorio, "International Borrowing, Capital Controls, and the Exchange Rate: Lessons from Chile," in Sebastian Edwards, ed., *Capital Controls and Capital Flows in Emerging Economies* (Chicago: University of Chicago Press, 2007), pp. 241–296.

[14]The ideas underlying the Mexican approach are explained by one of its architects, Pedro Aspe Armella, an economist trained at the Massachusetts Institute of Technology who was Mexico's finance minister for the period 1988–1994. See his book *Economic Transformation the Mexican Way* (Cambridge, MA: MIT Press, 1993). See also Nora Lustig, *Mexico: The Remaking of an Economy* (Washington, D.C.: Brookings Institution, 1992).

foreign reserve leakage, however, was a continuing extension of government credits to banks experiencing loan losses. Mexico had rapidly privatized its banks without adequate regulatory safeguards, and it had also opened its capital account, thus giving the banks free access to foreign funds. Because banks were confident they would be bailed out by the government if they met trouble, moral hazard was rampant. Hoping to spur growth and reduce a current account deficit that by then was nearly 8 percent of GNP, the new Mexican government that took over in December 1994 devalued the peso 15 percent beyond the depreciation limit promised a year before. The devalued currency peg was immediately attacked by speculators, and the government retreated to a float. Foreign investors panicked, pushing the peso down precipitously, and soon Mexico found itself unable to borrow except at penalty interest rates. As in 1982, default loomed again. The country avoided disaster only with the help of a $50 billion emergency loan orchestrated by the U.S. Treasury and the IMF.

Inflation, which had dropped from 159 percent in 1987 to only 7 percent in 1994, soared as the peso depreciated. Mexico's national output shrank by more than 6 percent in 1995. Unemployment more than doubled amid sharp fiscal cutbacks, sky-high interest rates, and a generalized banking crisis. But the contraction lasted only a year. By 1996, inflation was falling and the economy was recovering as the peso continued to float. Mexico regained access to private capital markets and repaid the U.S. Treasury ahead of schedule. A major achievement of Mexico has been expanding its democratic institutions and moving away from the virtual one-party rule that had characterized much of the country's 20th-century history.

East Asia: Success and Crisis

At the start of 1997, the countries of East Asia were the envy of the developing world. Their rapid growth rates were bringing them far up the development scale, putting several in striking distance of advanced-country status (which several have now reached). Then they were overwhelmed by a disastrous financial crisis. The speed with which East Asia's economic success turned into economic chaos came as a rude shock to most observers. East Asia's setback sparked a broader crisis that engulfed developing countries as distant as Russia and Brazil. In this section, we review the East Asian experience. The lessons, as we will see, reinforce those from Latin America.

The East Asian Economic Miracle

As we saw in Table 11-2, South Korea was a desperately poor nation in the 1960s, with little industry and apparently few economic prospects. In 1963, however, the country launched a series of sweeping economic reforms, shifting from an inward-looking, import-substitution development strategy to one that emphasized exports. And the country began a remarkable economic ascent. Over the next 50 years, South Korea increased its real per capita GDP by a factor of about 16—more than the increase that the United States has achieved over the past century.

Even more remarkable was that South Korea was not alone. Its economic rise was paralleled by that of a number of other East Asian economies. In the first wave were Hong Kong, Taiwan, and Singapore, all of which began growing rapidly in the 1960s. In the course of the 1970s and 1980s, the club of rapidly growing Asian economies expanded to include Malaysia, Thailand, Indonesia, and—awesomely—China, the world's most populous nation. For the first time since the rise of Japan as an industrial power in the late nineteenth century, a substantial part of the world appeared to be making the transition from third world to first.

There remains considerable dispute about the reasons for this economic "miracle." In the early 1990s, it was fashionable among some commentators to ascribe Asia's growth to a common Asian system of industrial policy and business-government cooperation. However, even a cursory look at the economies involved makes the claim of a common system dubious. The high-growth economies did include regimes such as South Korea's, where the government took an active role in the allocation of capital among industries; but it also included regimes such as those of Hong Kong and Taiwan, where this type of industrial policy was largely absent. Some economies, such as those of Taiwan and Singapore, relied heavily on the establishment of local subsidiaries of multinational firms. Others, such as South Korea and Hong Kong, relied mainly on domestic entrepreneurs.

WHY HAVE DEVELOPING COUNTRIES ACCUMULATED SUCH HIGH LEVELS OF INTERNATIONAL RESERVES?

Developing countries facing financial crises typically find that their international reserves have reached very low levels. A country that is fixing its exchange rate may have little choice but to let its currency depreciate once its reserves have run out. A country without liquid foreign exchange reserves may have no means to repay lenders who have previously extended short-term foreign currency loans. Like a run on a bank, market fears about potential default or depreciation can be self-fulfilling. If market confidence fails, reserves will quickly disappear and no new borrowing from foreigners will be possible. The resulting liquidity crunch may make it impossible for a country to meet its remaining foreign obligations.

This type of "bank run" mechanism has been at the heart of many developing-country crises, including the Asian economic crisis of 1997–1998, which we discuss below. Following the Asian crisis, which affected a large number of countries throughout the world, several economists suggested that developing countries take matters into their own hands. Because foreign credit tends to dry up precisely when it is most needed, countries could best protect themselves by accumulating large war chests of ready cash—dollars, euros, and other widely acceptable foreign currencies.

When countries had little involvement with world capital markets (as during the 1950s and early 1960s), reserve adequacy was judged largely by reference to the likelihood that export earnings might temporarily fall short of import needs. But in today's world of globalized finance, the volume of reserves needed to deter an attack might be orders of magnitude greater. As economist Martin Feldstein of Harvard put it, "The most direct way for a country to achieve liquidity is to accumulate substantial amounts of liquid foreign reserves.... [A] government should not judge the adequacy of its reserves in relation to the value of imports. A common reserve goal of, say, six months of imports ignores the fact that currency crises are about capital flows, not trade financing. What matters is the value of reserves relative to the potential selling of assets by speculators even if the country's fundamental economic conditions do not warrant a currency deterioration."*

We touched on the growth of international reserves in Chapter 7. As we observed in that chapter, while reserves have grown for all countries, since the debt crisis of the 1980s they have grown especially quickly for developing countries. For developing countries as a group, however, the pace of reserve accumulation has accelerated most dramatically since the financial crises of the late 1990s. The accompanying figure shows international reserve holdings as a fraction of national output for the group of all developing countries, as well as for Brazil, Russia, India, and China. (These four countries are often referred to as the "BRICs" in view

*See Feldstein, "A Self-Help Guide for Emerging Markets," *Foreign Affairs* 78 (March/April 1999), pp. 93–109. For a recent analytical treatment, see Olivier Jeanne, "International Reserves in Emerging Market Countries: Too Much of a Good Thing?" *Brookings Papers on Economic Activity* 1 (2007), pp. 1–79.

(*Continued*)

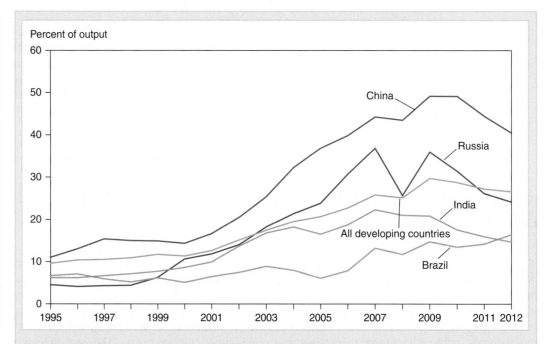

Percent of output

International Reserves Held by Developing Countries

Since the 1990s, developing countries have sharply increased their holdings of foreign currency reserves, mostly U.S dollars.

Source: World Bank, World Development Indicators.

of their recent strong growth performances.) In all the cases shown, reserves better than doubled (as a share of national product) between 1999 and 2009, before falling in three of the four countries. China's reserve ratio rose by a factor of 3.3 over that period and Russia's increased by a factor of 5.7.[†]

For a number of developing countries, the levels of reserves are so high as to exceed their total short-term foreign currency debts to foreigners. These large reserve holdings therefore provide a high degree of protection against a sudden stop of capital inflows. Indeed, they helped the developing countries weather the industrial-country credit crunch of 2007–2009 (recall Chapter 9). As you can see in the figure, developing countries generally spent some reserves to shield themselves during the 2007–2009 crisis.

The self-insurance motive for holding reserves is not the entire story, however. In some cases, reserve growth has been an undesired byproduct of

intervention policies to keep the currency from appreciating. China provides a case in point. China's development strategy has relied on increasing export levels of labor-intensive goods to fuel a rapid rise in living standards. In effect, appreciation of the Chinese renminbi makes Chinese labor more expensive relative to foreign labor, so China has tightly limited the currency's appreciation over time by buying up dollars. Despite capital controls limiting inflows of foreign funds, speculative money entered the country in anticipation of future appreciation, and reserves swelled enormously. The government has gradually loosened its capital outflow controls, hoping that reserves will fall as Chinese investors go abroad, but the tactic has had only limited success so far. At the end of 2012, China's reserves still stood at more than 40 percent of national output. We discuss China's policies in greater detail in a Case Study later in this chapter.

[†]Developing countries hold roughly a 60 percent share of their reserves in the form of U.S. dollars. They hold the balance mostly in euros, but also in a few alternative major currencies such as the Japanese yen, British pound, and Swiss franc.

TABLE 11-4	East Asian Current Accounts (annual averages, percent of GDP)		
	1990–1997	1998–2000	2001–2013
China	1.5	2.1	4.7
Hong Kong	0.5	3.9	8.0
Indonesia	−2.5	4.4	1.2
Malaysia	−5.8	12.7	11.7
South Korea	−1.3	6.7	2.4
Taiwan	3.9	2.2	8.4
Thailand	−6.2	10.2	2.5

Source: International Monetary Fund, World Economic Outlook Database, April 2013.

What the high-growth economies did have in common were high rates of saving and investment; rapidly improving educational levels among the work force; relatively moderate inflation rates; and if not free trade, at least a high degree of openness to and integration with world markets.

Perhaps surprisingly, before 1990 most rapidly growing Asian economies financed the bulk of their high investment rates out of domestic savings. In the 1990s, however, the growing popularity of emerging markets among investors in the advanced world led to substantial lending to developing Asia; as Table 11-4 shows, several of the Asian countries began running, as a counterpart to these loans, large current account deficits as a share of GDP. A few economists worried that these deficits might pose the risk of a crisis similar to the one that had hit Mexico in late 1994, but most observers regarded large capital flows to such rapidly growing and macroeconomically stable economies as justified by the expected profitability of investment opportunities.

Asian Weaknesses

As it turned out, in 1997 Asian economies did indeed experience a severe financial crisis. And with the benefit of hindsight, several weaknesses in their economic structures—some shared by Latin American countries that had gone through crises—became apparent. Three issues in particular stood out:

1. *Productivity.* Although the rapid growth of East Asian economies was not in any sense an illusion, even before the crisis a number of studies had suggested that some limits to expansion were appearing. The most surprising result of several studies was that the bulk of Asian output growth could be explained simply by the rapid growth of production *inputs*—capital and labor—and that there had been relatively little increase in productivity, that is, in output per unit of input. Thus in South Korea, for example, the convergence toward advanced-country output per capita appeared to be mainly due to a rapid shift of workers from agriculture to industry, a rise in educational levels, and a massive increase in the capital-labor ratio within the nonagricultural sector. Evidence for a narrowing of the technological gap with the West was unexpectedly hard to find. The implication of these studies was that continuing high rates of capital accumulation would eventually produce diminishing returns, and, possibly, that the large financial inflows taking place were not justified by future profitability after all.

WHAT DID EAST ASIA DO RIGHT?

The growth of East Asian economies between the 1960s and the 1990s demonstrated that it is possible for a country to move rapidly up the development ladder. But what are the ingredients for such success?

One way to answer this question may be to look at the distinctive attributes of what the World Bank, in its 1993 study entitled *The East Asian Miracle*, dubs the HPAEs, the high-performing Asian economies.

One important ingredient was a high saving rate: In 1990, HPAEs saved 34 percent of GDP, compared with only half that in Latin America, slightly more in South Asia.

Another important ingredient was a strong emphasis on education. Even in 1965, when the HPAEs were still quite poor, they had high enrollment rates in basic education:

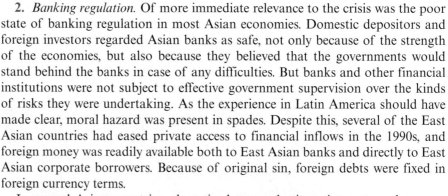

Essentially all children received basic schooling in Hong Kong, Singapore, and South Korea, and even desperately poor Indonesia had a 70 percent enrollment rate. By 1987, rates of enrollment in secondary school in East Asia were well above those in Latin American nations such as Brazil.

Finally, two other characteristics of the HPAEs, as noted earlier, were a relatively stable macroeconomic environment, free from high inflation or major economic slumps, and a high share of trade in GDP. These features made the East Asian economies look quite different from crisis-prone countries in Latin America. These contrasts played an important role in the "conversion" of many leaders in Latin America and elsewhere to the idea of economic reform, in terms of both a commitment to price stability and the opening of markets to the world.

2. *Banking regulation.* Of more immediate relevance to the crisis was the poor state of banking regulation in most Asian economies. Domestic depositors and foreign investors regarded Asian banks as safe, not only because of the strength of the economies, but also because they believed that the governments would stand behind the banks in case of any difficulties. But banks and other financial institutions were not subject to effective government supervision over the kinds of risks they were undertaking. As the experience in Latin America should have made clear, moral hazard was present in spades. Despite this, several of the East Asian countries had eased private access to financial inflows in the 1990s, and foreign money was readily available both to East Asian banks and directly to East Asian corporate borrowers. Because of original sin, foreign debts were fixed in foreign currency terms.

In several Asian countries, close ties between business interests and government officials appear to have helped foster considerable moral hazard in lending. In Thailand, so-called finance companies, often run by relatives of government officials, lent money to highly speculative real estate ventures; in Indonesia, lenders were far too eager to finance ventures by members of the president's family. These factors help to explain how, despite high saving rates, several East Asian countries were led to invest so much that their current accounts were in deficit prior to the crisis.

Some analysts have suggested that excessive lending, driven by moral hazard, helped create an unsustainable boom in Asian economies—especially in real estate—that temporarily concealed the poor quality of many of the investments; and that the inevitable end of this boom caused a downward spiral of declining prices and failing banks. However, while moral hazard was certainly a factor in the run-up to the crisis, its importance remains a subject of considerable dispute.

3. *Legal framework.* One important weakness of Asian economies became apparent only after they'd stumbled: the lack of a good legal framework for dealing with companies in trouble. In the United States, there is a well-established procedure for bankruptcy—that is, for dealing with a company that cannot pay its debts. In such a procedure, the courts take possession of the firm on behalf of its creditors, and then seek to find a way to satisfy their claims as adequately as possible. Often this means keeping the company in existence and converting the debts it cannot pay into ownership shares. In Asian economies, however, bankruptcy law was weak, in part because the astonishing growth of the economies had made corporate failures a rare event. When times did turn bad, a destructive impasse developed. Troubled companies would simply stop paying their debts. They then could not operate effectively because nobody would lend to them until the outstanding debts were repaid. Yet the creditors lacked any way to seize the limping enterprises from their original owners.

Of course, every economy has weaknesses, but the performance of the East Asian economies had been so spectacular that few paid much attention to theirs. Even those who were aware that the "miracle" economies had problems could hardly have anticipated the catastrophe that overtook them in 1997.

The Asian Financial Crisis

The Asian financial crisis is generally considered to have started on July 2, 1997, with the devaluation of the Thai baht. Thailand had been running a huge current account deficit and showing signs of financial strain for more than a year. During 1996, it became apparent that far too many office towers had been built; first the nation's real estate market, then its stock market, went into decline. In the first half of 1997, speculation about a possible devaluation of the baht led to an accelerating loss of foreign exchange reserves, and on July 2 the country attempted a controlled 15 percent devaluation. As in the case of Mexico in 1994, however, the attempted moderate devaluation spun out of control, sparking massive speculation and a far deeper plunge.

Thailand itself is a small economy. However, the sharp drop in the Thai currency was followed by speculation against the currencies first of its immediate neighbor, Malaysia; then of Indonesia; and eventually of the much larger and more developed economy of South Korea. All of these economies seemed to speculators to share with Thailand the weaknesses previously listed; all were feeling the effects in 1997 of renewed economic slowdown in their largest industrial neighbor, Japan. In each case, governments were faced with awkward dilemmas, stemming partly from the dependence of their economies on trade and partly from the fact that domestic banks and companies had large debts denominated in dollars. If the countries had simply allowed their currencies to drop, rising import prices would have threatened to produce dangerous inflation, and the sudden increase in the domestic currency value of debts might have pushed many potentially viable banks and companies into bankruptcy. On the other hand, defending the currencies would have required at least temporary high interest rates to persuade investors to keep their money in the country, and these high interest rates would themselves have produced an economic slump and caused banks to fail.

All of the afflicted countries except Malaysia thus turned to the IMF for assistance and received loans in return for implementation of economic plans that were supposed to contain the damage: higher interest rates to limit the exchange rate depreciation, efforts to avoid large budget deficits, and "structural" reforms that were supposed to deal with the weaknesses that had brought on the crisis in the first place. Despite the IMF's aid, however, the result of the currency crisis was a sharp economic downturn. All of the troubled countries went from growth rates in excess of 6 percent in 1996 to a severe contraction in 1998.

Worst of all was the case of Indonesia, where economic crisis and political instability reinforced each other in a deadly spiral, all made much worse by the collapse of domestic residents' confidence in the nation's banks. By the summer of 1998, the Indonesian rupiah had lost 85 percent of its original value, and few if any major companies were solvent. The Indonesian population was faced with mass unemployment and, in some cases, the inability to afford even basic foodstuffs. Ethnic violence broke out.

As a consequence of the collapse in confidence, the troubled Asian economies were also forced into a dramatic reversal of their current account positions. As Table 11-4 shows, most moved abruptly from sometimes large deficits to huge surpluses. Most of this reversal came not through increased exports but through a huge drop in imports, as the economies contracted.

Currencies eventually stabilized throughout crisis-stricken Asia and interest rates decreased, but the direct spillover from the region's slump caused slowdowns or recessions in several neighboring countries, including Hong Kong, Singapore, and New Zealand. Japan and even parts of Europe and Latin America felt the effects. Most governments continued to take the IMF-prescribed medicine, but in September 1998 Malaysia—which had never accepted an IMF program—broke ranks and imposed extensive controls on capital outflows, hoping that the controls would allow the country to ease monetary and fiscal policies without sending its currency into a tailspin. China and Taiwan, which maintained capital controls and had current account surpluses over the pre-crisis period, were largely unscathed in the crisis.

Fortunately, the downturn in East Asia was "V-shaped": After the sharp output contraction in 1998, growth returned in 1999 as depreciated currencies spurred higher exports. However, not all of the region's economies fared equally well, and controversy remains over the effectiveness of Malaysia's experiment with capital controls. The economies that instead relied on IMF help were generally unhappy with its management of the crisis, which they viewed as clumsy and intrusive. These resentments have proved to be long lived: While governments can turn to the IMF for conditional funding in case of a sudden stop, the Asian crisis countries vowed never to do so again. This determination has been an important motive for "self-insurance" with large stockpiles of international reserves.

Lessons of Developing-Country Crises

The emerging market crisis that started with Thailand's 1997 devaluation produced what might be called an orgy of finger-pointing. Some Westerners blamed the crisis on the policies of the Asians themselves, especially the "crony capitalism" under which businesspeople and politicians had excessively cozy relationships. Some Asian leaders, in turn, blamed the crisis on the machinations of Western financiers; even

Hong Kong, normally a bastion of free market sentiment, began intervening to block what it described as a conspiracy by speculators to drive down its stock market and undermine its currency. And almost everyone criticized the IMF, although some were saying that it was wrong to tell countries to try to limit the depreciation of their currencies, others that it was wrong to allow the currencies to depreciate at all.

Nonetheless, some very clear lessons emerge from a careful study of the Asian crisis and earlier developing-country crises in Latin America and elsewhere.

1. *Choosing the right exchange rate regime.* It is perilous for a developing country to fix its exchange rate unless it has the means and commitment to do so, come what may. East Asian countries found that confidence in official exchange rate targets encouraged borrowing in foreign currencies. When devaluation occurred nonetheless, much of the financial sector and many corporations became insolvent as a result of extensive foreign currency-denominated debts. The developing countries that have successfully stabilized inflation have adopted more flexible exchange rate systems or moved to greater flexibility quickly after an initial period of pegging aimed at reducing inflation expectations. Even in Argentina, where the public's fear of returning to the hyperinflationary past instilled a widely shared determination to prevent inflation, a fixed exchange rate proved untenable over the long term. Mexico's experience since 1995 shows that larger developing countries can manage quite well with a floating exchange rate, and it is hard to believe that, if Mexico had been fixing, it would have survived the Asian crisis repercussions of 1998 without developing a currency crisis of its own.

2. *The central importance of banking.* A large part of what made the Asian crisis so devastating was that it was not purely a currency crisis, but rather a currency crisis inextricably mixed with banking and financial crises. In the most immediate sense, governments were faced with the conflict between restricting the money supply to support the currency and the need to print large quantities of money to deal with bank runs. More broadly, the collapse of many banks disrupted the economy by cutting off channels of credit, which made it difficult for even profitable companies to stay in business. This should not have come as a surprise in Asia. Similar effects of banking fragility played roles in the crises of Argentina, Chile, and Uruguay in the 1980s; of Mexico in 1994–1995; and even in those of industrial countries like Sweden during the 1992 attacks on the EMS (Chapter 10). Unfortunately, Asia's spectacular economic performance prior to its crisis blinded people to its financial vulnerabilities. In the future, wise governments everywhere will devote a great deal of attention to shoring up their banking systems to minimize moral hazard, in the hope of becoming less vulnerable to financial catastrophes.

3. *The proper sequence of reform measures.* Economic reformers in developing countries have learned the hard way that the order in which liberalization measures are taken really does matter. That truth also follows from basic economic theory: The principle of the *second best* tells us that when an economy suffers from multiple distortions, the removal of only a few may make matters worse, not better. Developing countries generally suffer from many, many distortions, so this point is especially important for them. Consider the sequencing of financial account liberalization and financial sector reform, for example. It is clearly a mistake to open up the financial account before sound safeguards and supervision are in place for domestic financial institutions. Otherwise, the ability to borrow abroad will simply encourage reckless lending by domestic banks. When the economy slows down, foreign capital will flee, leaving domestic banks insolvent. Thus, developing

countries should delay opening the financial account until the domestic financial system is strong enough to withstand the sometimes violent ebb and flow of world capital. Economists also argue that trade liberalization should precede financial account liberalization. Financial account liberalization may cause real exchange rate volatility and impede the movement of factors of production from nontraded into traded goods industries.

4. *The importance of contagion.* A final lesson of developing-country experience is the vulnerability of even seemingly healthy economies to crises of confidence generated by events elsewhere in the world—a domino effect that has come to be known as **contagion**. Contagion was at work when the crisis in Thailand, a small economy in Southeast Asia, provoked another crisis in South Korea, a much larger economy some 2,000 miles away. An even more spectacular example emerged in August 1998, when a plunge in the Russian ruble sparked massive speculation against Brazil's real. The problem of contagion, and the concern that even the most careful economic management may not offer full immunity, has become central to the discussion of possible reforms of the international financial system, to which we now turn.

Reforming the World's Financial "Architecture"

Economic difficulties lead, inevitably, to proposals for economic reforms. The Asian economic crisis and its repercussions suggested to many people that the international financial and monetary system, or at least the part of it that applies to developing countries, was in need of change. Proposals for such an overhaul have come to be grouped under the impressive if vague title of plans for a new financial "architecture."

Why did the Asian crisis convince nearly everyone of a need for rethinking international monetary relations, when earlier crises of the 1990s did not? One reason was that the Asian countries' problems seemed to stem primarily from their connections with the world capital market. The crisis clearly demonstrated that a country can be vulnerable to a currency crisis even if its own position looks healthy by normal measures. None of the troubled Asian economies had serious budget deficits, excessive rates of monetary expansion, worrisome levels of inflation, or any of the other indicators that have traditionally signaled vulnerability to speculative attack. If there were severe weaknesses in the economies—a proposition that is the subject of dispute, since some economists argue that the economies would have been quite healthy had it not been for the speculative attacks—they involved issues such as the strength of the banking system that might have remained dormant in the absence of sharp currency depreciations.

The second reason for rethinking international finance was the apparent strength of contagion throughout the international capital markets. The speed and force with which market disturbances could be spread between distant economies suggested that preventive measures taken by individual economies might not suffice. Just as a concern about economic interdependence had inspired the Bretton Woods blueprint for the world economy in 1944, world policy makers again put the reform of the international system on their agendas after the Asian crisis.

Developing countries generally recovered quickly from the financial crisis of 2007–2009—this time, unlike after 1982, the rich countries were the ones that suffered protracted recessions (Chapter 8). But it was unclear whether developing-country resilience was due to reforms adopted after the Asian crisis, higher holdings of international reserves, strong commodity prices, greater flexibility of exchange rates, or the historically low interest rates enforced by industrial-country central banks. In view of the breathtaking contagion again displayed as the 2007–2009 crisis spread across the globe, sentiment that international finance needs an overhaul has remained strong. Here we look at some of the main issues involved.

Capital Mobility and the Trilemma of the Exchange Rate Regime

One effect of the Asian crisis was to dispel any illusions we may have had about the availability of easy answers to the problems of international macroeconomics and finance. The crisis and its spread made it all too clear that some well-known policy trade-offs for open economies remain as stark as ever—and perhaps have become even more difficult to manage.

Chapter 8 spelled out the basic *monetary trilemma* for open economies. Of the three goals that most countries share—independence in monetary policy, stability in the exchange rate, and the free movement of capital—only two can be reached simultaneously. Exchange rate stability is more important for the typical developing country than for the typical developed country. Developing countries have less ability to influence their terms of trade than developed countries, and exchange rate stability can be more important for keeping inflation in check and avoiding financial stress in developing countries. In particular, the widespread developing-country practice of borrowing in dollars or other major currencies (both externally and internally) means that currency depreciations can sharply increase the real burden of debts.

The conundrum facing would-be reformers of the world's financial architecture can then be summarized as follows: Because of the threat of the kind of currency crises that hit Mexico in 1994–1995 and Asia in 1997, it seems hard if not impossible to achieve all three objectives at the same time. That is, to achieve one of them, a country must give up one of the other two objectives. Until the late 1970s, most developing countries maintained exchange controls and limited private capital movements in particular, as we have seen. (Some major developing countries, notably China and India, still retain such controls.) While there was considerable evasion of the controls, they did slow up the movement of capital. As a result, countries could peg their exchange rates for extended periods—producing exchange rate stability—yet devalue their currencies on occasion, which offered considerable monetary autonomy. The main problem with controls was that they imposed onerous restrictions on international transactions, thus reducing efficiency and contributing to corruption.

In the last two decades of the 20th century, capital became substantially more mobile, largely because controls were lifted, but also because of improved communications technology. This new capital mobility made adjustable peg regimes extremely vulnerable to speculation, since capital would flee a currency on the slightest hint that it might be devalued. (The same phenomenon occurred among developed countries in the 1960s and early 1970s, as we saw in Chapter 8.) The result has been to drive developing countries toward one or the other sides of the triangle in Figure 8-1: either rigidly fixed exchange rates and a renunciation of monetary autonomy, like dollarization or the currency board system described above, or flexibly managed (and even floating) exchange rates. But despite the lesson of experience that intermediate positions are dangerous, developing countries have been uncomfortable with both extremes. While a major economy like the United States can accept a widely fluctuating exchange rate, a smaller, developing economy often finds the costs of such volatility hard to sustain, in part because it is more open and in part because it suffers from original sin. As a result, even countries claiming to "float" their currencies may display a "fear of floating" and instead limit currency fluctuations over long periods.[15] Meanwhile, a rigid system like a currency board can deprive a country of flexibility, especially when it is dealing with financial crises in which the central bank must act as the lender of last resort.

Several respected economists, including Columbia University's Jagdish Bhagwati and Joseph Stiglitz and the Institute for Advanced Study's Dani Rodrik, have argued that developing countries should keep or reinstate restrictions on capital mobility to be able to exercise monetary autonomy while enjoying stable exchange rates.[16] In the face of the Asian crisis, China and India, for example, put plans to liberalize their capital accounts on hold; some countries that had liberalized capital movements considered the possibility of reimposing restrictions (as Malaysia actually did). Most policy makers, both in the developing world and in the industrial countries, continue to regard capital controls as either difficult to enforce for long or disruptive of normal business relationships (as well as a potent source of corruption). These reservations apply most strongly to controls on capital *outflows*, because restrictions are particularly hard to maintain effectively when wealth owners are fleeing abroad to avoid potentially big losses.

Nonetheless, in recent years a number of emerging market countries, ranging from Brazil to Israel, have become more open to imposing limited controls on financial *inflows*, and even the IMF has become more open to their use. One reason for this change is a *macroprudential* motive: limits on financial inflows could limit excessive bank lending during booms, and thereby temper the resulting contraction in case of a sudden stop or financial-flow reversal later. Equally (if not more) important as a motivation has been the desire to limit real currency appreciation, and the resulting harm to exports, without resorting to inflationary monetary policies.[17]

While there is a renewed openness to capital inflow controls, most discussion of financial architecture has focused instead on meliorative measures—ways to make the remaining choices less painful even when capital controls are not used.

"Prophylactic" Measures

Since the risk of financial crisis is what makes the decisions surrounding the choice of exchange rate regime so difficult, some recent proposals focus on ways to reduce that risk. Typical proposals include calls for the following:

More "transparency." At least part of what went wrong in Asia was that foreign banks and other investors lent money to Asian enterprises without any clear idea of what the risks were, and then pulled their money out equally blindly when it became clear that those risks were larger than they had imagined. There have therefore been many proposals for greater "transparency"—that is, better provision of financial information—in the same way that corporations in the United States are required to provide accurate public reports of their financial positions. The hope is that increased transparency will reduce both the tendency of too much money rushing into

---

[15]See Guillermo A. Calvo and Carmen M. Reinhart, "Fear of Floating," *Quarterly Journal of Economics* 117 (May 2002), pp. 379–408.

[16]See Jagdish N. Bhagwati, "The Capital Myth," *Foreign Affairs* 77 (May–June, 1998), pp. 7–12; Dani Rodrik, "Who Needs Capital-Account Convertibility?" in Stanley Fischer et al., *Should the IMF Pursue Capital-Account Convertibility?* Princeton Essays in International Finance 207 (May 1998); and Joseph E. Stiglitz, *Globalization and Its Discontents* (New York: W. W. Norton & Company, 2003).

[17]As an indication of the IMF's current approach, see, for example, Jonathan D. Ostry, Atish R. Ghosh, Marcos Chamon, and Mahvash S. Qureshi, "Capital Controls: When and Why?" *IMF Economic Review* 59 (2011), pp. 562–580.

a country when things are going well, and the rush for the exits when the truth turns out to be less favorable than the image.

Stronger banking systems. As we have seen, one factor that made the Asian crisis so severe was the way that the currency crisis interacted with bank runs. It is at least possible that these interactions would have been milder if the banks themselves had been stronger. So there have also been many proposals for strengthening banks, through both closer regulation of the risks they take and increased capital requirements, which ensure that substantial amounts of the owners' own money is at risk. Of course, the 2007–2009 crisis demonstrated that industrial-country financial markets were actually less robust than they had seemed. The need for greater transparency and stricter regulation of financial institutions is universal.

Enhanced credit lines. Some reformers also want to establish special credit lines that nations could draw on in the event of a currency crisis, in effect adding to their foreign exchange reserves. The idea would be that the mere existence of these credit lines would usually make them unnecessary: As long as speculators knew that countries had enough credit to meet even a large outflow of funds, they would not hope or fear that their own actions would produce a sudden devaluation. Such credit lines could be provided by private banks, or by public bodies such as the IMF. This reform area, too, can be seen as applicable to richer countries after the events of 2007–2009 (see the box on central bank currency swaps in Chapter 9, pages 316–317).

Increased equity capital inflows relative to debt inflows. If developing countries financed a greater proportion of their private foreign capital inflows through equity portfolio investment or direct foreign investment rather than through debt issuance, the probability of default would be much lower. The countries' payments to foreigners would then be more closely linked to their economic fortunes, and would fall automatically when times were hard. In fact, there has been a trend toward greater emerging-market reliance on foreign equity rather than debt finance, and this development probably enhanced emerging markets' resilience in the face of the 2007–2009 global financial crisis.[18]

The international community recognizes that developing countries play increasingly important roles, as lenders as well as borrowers, in world financial markets. Ongoing discussions, in Basel and elsewhere, of global cooperation in bank regulation increasingly include the main emerging market countries as key participants.

Coping with Crisis

Even with the proposed prophylactic measures, crises would still surely happen. Thus there have also been proposals to modify the way the world responds to such crises.

Many of these proposals relate to the role and policies of the IMF. Here opinion is bitterly divided. Some conservative critics believe that the IMF should simply be abolished, arguing that its very existence encourages irresponsible lending by making borrowers and lenders believe that they will always be saved from the consequences of their actions—a version of the moral hazard argument previously described. Other critics argue that the IMF is necessary, but that it has misconstrued its role—by, for example, trying to insist on structural reform when it should instead restrict itself to

---

[18]This trend is documented by Eswar S. Prasad, "Role Reversal in Global Finance," in *Achieving Maximum Long-Run Growth: A Symposium Sponsored by the Federal Reserve Bank of Kansas City* (Kansas City, MO: Federal Reserve Bank of Kansas City, 2012), pp. 339–390. See also the paper by Forbes listed in Further Readings.

narrow financial issues. A number of Asian countries bitterly resented having to follow IMF advice during their crisis in the late 1990s; for them, as we have seen, one motive for reserve accumulation has been to avoid having to borrow IMF dollars—and accept IMF conditions. Finally, defenders of the IMF—and also some of its critics—argue that the agency has simply been underfunded for its task, that in a world of high capital mobility, it needs to have the ability to provide much larger loans much more quickly than it presently can. IMF resources rose sharply as a result of the 2007–2009 crisis, and moves are afoot to raise the IMF's perceived legitimacy in the developing world by giving poorer countries a greater voting share in the IMF's management. Measures like these should improve the functioning of the international system.

Another set of proposals is based on the idea that sometimes a country simply cannot pay its debts, and that international contracts should therefore be structured so as to speed—and reduce the costs of—renegotiation between creditors and debtors. As we noted in our discussion of the debt crisis of the 1980s, limited debt write-offs did bring that crisis to an end. Even in the euro zone, sovereign bond issues starting in January 2013 contained clauses making it easier for governments to renegotiate their debts with private creditors. Critics argue that such provisions would be either ineffective or counterproductive because they would encourage countries to borrow too much, in the knowledge that they could more easily renegotiate their debts—moral hazard once again.

CASE STUDY   China's Pegged Currency

Over the first decade of the 2000s, China developed a substantial overall current account surplus and a large bilateral trade surplus with the United States. In 2006, the current account surplus reached $239 billion, or 9.1 percent of China's output, and the bilateral surplus with the United States, at $233 billion, was of similar size. A good part of China's exports to the United States consists of reassembled components imported from elsewhere in Asia, a factor that reduces other Asian countries' exports to the United States and increases China's. Nonetheless, trade frictions between the United States and China have escalated, with American critics focusing on China's intervention in currency markets to prevent an abrupt appreciation of its currency, the yuan renminbi, against the U.S. dollar.

Figure 11-2 shows how China fixed the exchange rate at 8.28 yuan per dollar between the Asian crisis period and 2005. Facing the threat of trade sanctions by the U.S. Congress, China carried out a 2.1 percent revaluation of its currency in July 2005, created a narrow currency band for the exchange rate, and allowed the currency to appreciate at a steady, slow rate. By January 2008, the cumulative appreciation from the initial 8.28 yuan-per-dollar rate was about 13 percent—well below the 20 percent or more undervaluation alleged by trade hawks in Congress. Early in the summer of 2008, in the midst of the financial crisis, China pegged its exchange rate once again, this time at roughly 6.83 yuan to the dollar. In response to renewed foreign pressure, China in June 2010 announced it was adopting a "managed float" exchange rate regime, and under this arrangement, the yuan had appreciated to about 6.12 per dollar by the fall of 2013—a further appreciation of about 10 percent.

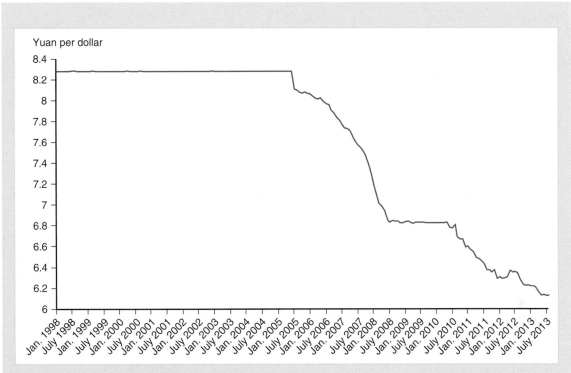

FIGURE 11-2   MyEconLab Real-time data

Yuan/Dollar Exchange Rate, 1998–2013

China's yuan was fixed in value against the U.S. dollar for several years before July 2005. After a 2.1 percent initial revaluation, the currency has appreciated gradually against the dollar.

China's government has moved so slowly because of fears that it would lose export competitiveness and redistribute income domesically by allowing a large exchange rate change. Many economists outside of China believe, however, that a further appreciation of the yuan would be in China's best interest. For one thing, the large reserve increases associated with China's currency peg have caused inflationary pressures in the Chinese economy. Foreign exchange reserves have grown quickly not only because of China's current account surplus, but also because of speculative inflows of money betting on a substantial currency revaluation. To avoid attracting further financial inflows through its porous capital controls, China has hesitated to raise interest rates and choke off inflation. In the past, however, high inflation in China has been associated with significant social unrest.

What policy mix makes sense for China? Figure 11-3 shows the position of China's economy, using the diagram developed earlier in this book as Figure 8-2. In the early 2010s, China was at a point such as 1 in Figure 11-3, with an external surplus and growing inflation pressures—but with a strong reluctance to raise unemployment and thereby slow the movement of labor from the relatively backward countryside into industry. The policy package that moves the economy to both internal and external balance at Figure 11-3's point 2 is a rise in absorption, coupled with currency appreciation. The appreciation works to switch expenditure toward imports and lower inflationary pressures; the absorption increase works

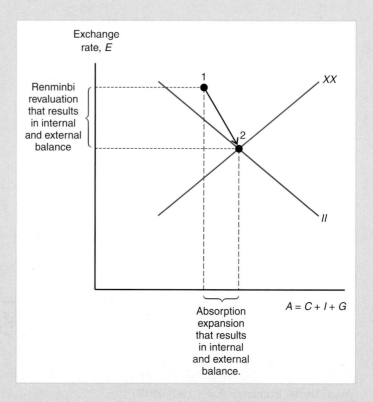

FIGURE 11-3

Rebalancing China's Economy

China faces a current account surplus and inflationary pressures. It can fix both without raising unemployment by expanding absorption and revaluing its currency.

directly to lower the export surplus, at the same time preventing the emergence of unemployment that a stand-alone currency appreciation would bring.

Economists argue further that China should focus on raising both private and government consumption.[19] China's savers put aside more than 45 percent of GNP every year, a staggering number. Saving is so high in part because of a widespread lack of basic services that the government earlier supplied, such as health care. The resulting uncertainty leads people to save in a precautionary manner against the possibility of future misfortunes. By providing a better social safety net, the government would raise private and government consumption at the same time. In addition, there is a strong need for expanded government spending on items such as environmental cleanup, investment in cleaner energy sources, and so on.[20]

While China's leaders have publicly agreed with the needs to raise consumption and appreciate the currency, they have moved very cautiously so far, accelerating their reforms only when external political pressures (such as the threat of trade sanctions) become severe. Whether this pace of change will satisfy external critics, as well as the demands of the majority of Chinese people for higher security and living standards, remains to be seen.

---

[19]For a clear discussion, see Nicholas R. Lardy, "China: Toward a Consumption-Driven Growth Path," *Policy Briefs in International Economics* (Washington, D.C.: Institute for International Economics, October 2006).

[20]Firms also contribute to the very high rate of saving. China's firms pay out relatively little to investors in dividends, retaining their earnings instead and thereby raising corporate saving.

Understanding Global Capital Flows and the Global Distribution of Income: Is Geography Destiny?

As we pointed out at the start of this chapter, today's world is characterized by a vast international dispersion in levels of income and well-being. In contradiction of a simple theory of convergence, however, there is no systematic tendency for poorer countries' income levels to converge, even slowly, to those of richer countries.[21] In conventional macroeconomic models of economic growth, countries' per capita real incomes depend on their stocks of physical and human capital, whose marginal products are highest where stocks are low relative to the stock of unskilled labor. Because high marginal products of investment present strong incentives for capital accumulation, including capital inflows from abroad, the standard models predict that poorer countries will tend to grow more quickly than rich ones. Ultimately, if they have access to the same technologies used in richer countries, poor countries will themselves become rich.

In practice, however, this happy story is the exception rather than the rule. Furthermore, relatively little capital flows to developing countries, despite the prediction of the simple convergence theory that the marginal product of capital, and therefore the returns to foreign investment, should be high there. The scale of capital flows to the developing world is dwarfed by the gross flows between advanced countries. And since the late 1990s (see Table 11-3), net flows to developing countries have reversed as the United States has sucked in most of the world's available current account surpluses.

In fact, the risks of investing in several of the developing countries limit their attractiveness for investors, both foreign and domestic alike; and those risks are closely related to the countries' poor economic growth performances. When governments are unwilling or unable to protect property rights, investors will be unwilling to invest in either physical or human capital, so growth will be nonexistent or low. (The box on the next page probes more deeply into the behavior of capital flows from rich to poor countries.)

What explains the fact that some countries have grown very rich while some attract little or no foreign investment and remain in extreme poverty? Two main schools of thought on the question focus, alternatively, on countries' *geographical features* and on their *institutions of government*.

A leading proponent of the geography theory is UCLA geographer Jared Diamond, whose fascinating and influential book *Guns, Germs, and Steel: The Fates of Human Societies* (New York: W. W. Norton & Company, 1997) won a Pulitzer Prize in 1998. In one version of the geography view, aspects of a country's physical environment such as climate, soil type, diseases, and geographical accessibility determine its long-run economic performance. Thus, for example, unfriendly weather, an absence of easily domesticated large animal species, and the presence of yellow fever and malaria doomed tropical zones to lag behind the more temperate regions of Europe, which could support agricultural innovations such as crop rotation. For these reasons, Diamond argues, it was the Europeans who conquered the inhabitants of the New World and not vice versa.

---

[21]While this statement is true when the unit of study is the country, it is less accurate when the unit of study is the individual. A preponderance of the world's poor in 1960 lived in China and India, two countries that have experienced relatively rapid growth in recent years. A main cause of their growth, however, has been market-friendly economic reforms. For further discussion, see Stanley Fischer, "Globalization and Its Challenges," *American Economic Review* 93 (May 2003), pp. 1–30.

CAPITAL PARADOXES

Although many developing countries have borrowed from developed lenders over the years since World War II, the global pattern of financial flows from rich to poor countries has diverged increasingly from what basic economic theory would seem to predict: a strong flow of lending from high-income countries, rich in capital, to low-income countries, where capital is scarce and where investment opportunities therefore are presumably abundant.

The accompanying figure illustrates the global pattern of current account balances since 1970. Borrowing by non-oil producing developing countries was quite limited, with the partial exception of the decade of the 1990s, when a number of developing borrowers (among them Mexico, Thailand, and the Czech Republic) eventually came to grief. At the same time, current account surpluses by the group of rich countries were small or non-existent. Then, in the 2000s, non-oil developing countries (along with the oil exporters) developed sizable surpluses,

while the rich countries borrowed extensively from the poor.

In general, non-oil producing developing countries have not run the big current account deficits predicted by simple development theories. In the early twenty-first century global current account imbalances expanded sharply, but rich countries ran the deficits.

Just before the developing-country borrowing boomlet of the 1990s got under way, economist Robert E. Lucas, Jr., of the University of Chicago, observed that the big income disparities between rich and poor countries, if caused by differences in capital endowments, should imply large opportunities for foreign capital to move profitably into the developing world. Why, then, was investment not far below saving in rich countries, and far higher than saving in poor countries? Lucas suggested that the answer was related to the scarcity in poor countries of *human* capital—in the form of a highly educated work force and managerial know-how. Other scholars put more weight on the

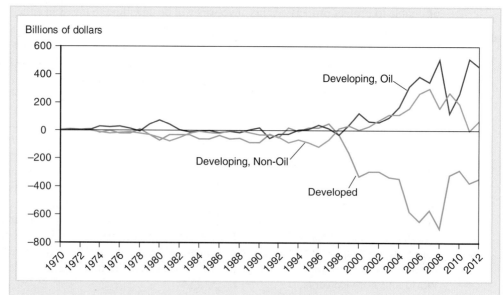

Current Account Balances of Major Country Groups, 1970–2012

Source: International Monetary Fund, *International Financial Statistics.* Note that regional imbalances generally do not sum to zero due to errors and omissions.

greater fragility of property rights and government stability in poorer countries, a position that was partially borne out by the crises of the 1990s.*

Interestingly, the limited postwar flow of capital from rich to poor countries was predicted in the early 1950s by the Columbia University economist Ragnar Nurkse. The nineteenth-century saw a boom in European overseas investment, during which Britain, the leading global lender, invested roughly 4 percent of its income abroad annually for the five decades preceding World War I. Nurkse argued that the conditions of this lending were very special and unlikely to be replicated after World War II. Most of the investment, he noted, flowed to a very few countries of "recent settlement," funding infrastructure (such as railways) needed by the waves of European migrants that accompanied the flow of capital. These migrants transplanted European know-how, as well as governance institutions that made the successful use of investment resources more likely. Not surprisingly, most of the recipient countries—notably Australia, New Zealand, Canada, and the United States—are rich, while most of the poorer "extractive" economies that received a much smaller share of foreign investment before 1914 remain poor today.[†]

Developments in the twenty-first century made the international pattern of capital flows look even more paradoxical than before. Not only was capital failing to flow from rich to poor countries in appreciable amounts; it was actually flowing *uphill*, from poor to rich, and on a huge scale. Behind this pattern lay a number of specific developments: Asset booms in rich countries spurred consumption and housing investment, for example, causing big current account deficits, while rapid growth in rich countries and especially China boosted commodity prices, allowing many relatively poor exporters of raw materials to run surpluses. As economists looked more carefully at this surprising configuration, however, they discovered new paradoxes even more puzzling than the one Lucas had raised in 1990.

First, experience since 1970 has revealed that on average, foreign capital does not appear to drive economic growth. Instead, the countries that have grown fastest are those that have relied most on domestic savings and run the smallest current account deficits (and often-times, surpluses). For example, the successful economies of East Asia, notably China, generally have had high saving levels. A second, related, paradox, highlighted by Pierre-Olivier Gourinchas of the University of California–Berkeley and Olivier Jeanne of Johns Hopkins University, is called the "allocation puzzle": Countries with lower growth in the productivity of labor and capital actually attract relatively more foreign financial inflows than countries with high productivity growth.

Researchers are still seeking to resolve these new puzzles. Many poor countries have weak financial systems that cannot handle big foreign lending inflows without a high risk of crisis. Thus, countries that generate large volumes of savings themselves may have a growth advantage. Gourinchas and Jeanne suggest their allocation puzzle is related to accumulation of international reserves by some fast-growing economies (such as China's). These economies often do receive substantial inflows of foreign direct investment, but their saving is so high that they still run overall surpluses in their current accounts.[‡]

---

*These theories are not mutually exclusive; as mentioned above, investment in human capital is discouraged by poor protection of property rights. On the puzzle of low capital flows to poor countries, see Robert E. Lucas, Jr., "Why Doesn't Capital Flow from Rich to Poor Countries?" *American Economic Review* 80 (May 1990), pp. 92–96. A study that ties limited capital flows to poor institutional quality is Laura Alfaro, Sebnem Kalemli-Ozcan, and Vadym Volosovych, "Why Doesn't Capital Flow from Rich to Poor Countries? An Empirical Investigation," *Review of Economics and Statistics* 90 (May 2008), pp. 347–368. Carmen Reinhart and Kenneth Rogoff ascribe the Lucas puzzle to the likelihood of developing-country default. See "Serial Default and the 'Paradox' of Rich-to-Poor Capital Flows," *American Economic Review* 94 (May 2004), pp. 53–58.

[†]See Nurkse, "International Investment To-Day in the Light of Nineteenth-Century Experience," *Economic Journal* 64 (December 1954), pp. 744–758.

[‡]See Eswar Prasad, Raghuram Rajan, and Arvind Subramanian, "The Paradox of Capital," *Finance & Development* 44 (March 2007); and Gourinchas and Jeanne, "Capital Flows to Developing Countries: The Allocation Puzzle," *Review of Economic Studies* 80 (October 2013), pp. 1484–1515.

Another factor stressed in some geographical theories is access to international trade. Countries that are landlocked and mountainous trade less with the outside world—and therefore fare worse—than those countries blessed with good ocean harbors, navigable internal waterways, and easily traveled roadways.

In contrast, those favoring the institutions of government as the decisive factor for economic prosperity focus on the success of government in protecting private property rights, thereby encouraging private enterprise, investment, innovation, and ultimately economic growth. According to this view, a country that cannot protect its citizens from arbitrary property confiscation—for example, through extortion by private gangsters or crooked public officials—will be a country in which people do not find it worthwhile to exert effort in the pursuit of wealth.[22] This mechanism is one factor underlying the positive association between lower corruption and higher per capita income shown in Figure 11-1: A low corruption level promotes productive economic activity by ensuring investors that the fruits of their labors will not be arbitrarily seized. As we noted in discussing this evidence, however, the positive slope in the figure is not decisive evidence that national institutions determine national income. It could be, for example, that the slope shown is primarily caused by richer countries' desire to stem corruption and the greater resources they can devote to that task. Even if this is the case, it might still be true that geography determines income levels, and thereby ultimately determines institutions as well. However, if more favorable geography leads to higher income and, through higher income, to a better institutional environment (characterized, among other things, by lower corruption), then the geography school of thought would appear to have it right. For policy makers, the possibility of enhancing economic growth through the reform of institutions would appear bleaker.[23]

How can we hope to distinguish among the various statistical possibilities? One strategy is to find some measurable factor that influences the institutions governing private property but is otherwise unrelated to current per capita income levels. Statisticians call such a variable an *instrumental variable* (or more simply, an *instrument*) for institutions. Because the instrument is not affected by current income, its measured statistical relationship with current income reflects a causal effect of institutions on income rather than the reverse. Unfortunately, because of the complex interrelationships among economic variables, valid instrumental variables are, as a general rule, notoriously hard to find.

Economists Daron Acemoglu and Simon Johnson of the Massachusetts Institute of Technology and James Robinson of Harvard University suggest an imaginative

---

[22]See, for example, Douglass C. North, *Institutions, Institutional Change, and Economic Performance* (Cambridge: Cambridge University Press, 1990).

[23]In countries that formerly were European colonies, current institutions often were implanted by foreign rulers. Geography itself played a role in the types of institutions that colonizers set up. Thus, in the West Indies and the American South, climates and soil were conducive to plantation agriculture based on slave labor and an increasing-returns technology that ensured large farming units and an unequal income distribution. The resulting institutions—even if set up by colonists whose mother countries had limited enlightened rule—were fundamentally hostile to egalitarian political ideals and property protection. Inequality of wealth and power perpetuated itself in many cases, thus hampering long-term growth. For a classic discussion, see Stanley L. Engerman and Kenneth D. Sokoloff, "Factor Endowments, Institutions, and Differential Paths of Growth among New World Economies: A View from Economic Historians of the United States," in Stephen Haber, ed., *How Latin America Fell Behind* (Stanford, CA: Stanford University Press, 1997). The institutions hypothesis allows geography to affect income, but requires that geography affect income only (or mainly) by influencing institutions.

approach to this dilemma. They propose historical mortality rates of early European settlers in former colonies as an instrument for institutional quality.[24] Their case that settler mortality provides a useful instrument rests on two arguments.

First, they argue that the level of settler mortality determined the later institutions governing property rights. (This is another case of geography influencing income *through* its effect on institutions.) In areas with high mortality rates (such as the former Belgian Congo in Africa), Europeans could not settle successfully. Many of these areas were relatively densely populated before Europeans arrived, and the European colonizers' goal was to plunder wealth as effectively as possible, oppressing the native people in the process. The institutions Europeans set up were thus directed to the goal of resource extraction rather than to the protection of property rights, and those exploitative institutions were taken over by new, indigenous ruling elites when the former colonies gained independence. In contrast, Europeans themselves settled in sparsely populated low-mortality regions such as North America and Australia and demanded institutions that would protect political and economic rights, safeguarding private property against arbitrary seizures. (Recall the dispute over taxation without representation that sparked the American Revolution!) Those countries received the biggest inflows of foreign capital in the nineteenth century, and they prospered and are rich today.

A valid instrument must satisfy a second requirement besides having an influence on institutions. It must otherwise not affect today's per capita incomes. Acemoglu, Johnson, and Robinson argue that this requirement is satisfied also. As they put it,

> The great majority of European deaths in the colonies were caused by malaria and yellow fever. Although these diseases were fatal to Europeans who had no immunity, they had limited effect on indigenous adults who had developed various types of immunities. These diseases are therefore unlikely to be the reason why many countries in Africa and Asia are very poor today.... This notion is supported by the [lower] mortality rates of local people in these areas.[25]

Acemoglu, Johnson, and Robinson show that the effect of early European settler mortality rates on current per capita income, operating through the influence of mortality on later institutions, is large. They further argue that once the latter effect is taken into account, geographical variables such as distance from the equator and malarial infection rates have no independent influence on current income levels. Provided that one accepts the premises of the statistical analysis, the institutions theory would seem to emerge victorious over the geography theory. But the debate has not ended there.

Some critics have suggested that Acemoglu, Johnson, and Robinson's measures of institutional quality are inadequate; others argue that their mortality data are faulty or even that historical mortality rates could be related directly to productivity today. In one recent paper, a group of economists argues that the main influence on institutions is human capital, that is, the accumulated skills and education of the population. Even an authoritarian dictatorship may establish democracy and property rights as its citizens become more educated. These writers point out that South Korea did just this, and suggest that perhaps European settlers' human capital, not their transplantation

---

[24]The data cover soldiers, sailors, and bishops and are drawn from the seventeenth through the nineteenth centuries. See Daron Acemoglu, Simon Johnson, and James Robinson, "The Colonial Origins of Comparative Development: An Empirical Investigation," *American Economic Review* 91 (December 2001), pp. 1369–1401.
[25]Acemoglu, Johnson, and Robinson, *ibid.*, p. 1371.

of institutions, is what spurred subsequent growth.[26] As we pointed out earlier, one cause of East Asia's high subsequent growth was a high level of investment in education, often decreed by nondemocratic governments.

A number of Asian former colonies arguably offer counterexamples to the theory of Acemoglu, Johnson, and Robinson. India, Indonesia, and Malaysia, for example, all were European colonies with overwhelmingly indigenous populations, yet their economic growth rates generally have exceeded those of the advanced economies.

SUMMARY

1. There are vast differences in per capita income and in well-being among countries at different stages of economic development. Furthermore, developing countries have not shown a uniform tendency of *convergence* to the income levels of industrial countries. However, some developing countries, notably several in East Asia, have seen dramatic increases in living standards since the 1960s. Explaining why some countries remain poor and which policies can promote economic growth remains one of the most important challenges in economics.

2. Developing countries form a heterogeneous group, especially since many have embarked on wide-ranging economic reform in recent years. Many have at least some of the following features: heavy government involvement in the economy, including a large share of public spending in GNP; a track record of high inflation, usually reflecting government attempts to extract *seigniorage* from the economy in the face of ineffective tax collection; weak credit institutions and undeveloped capital markets; pegged exchange rates and exchange or capital controls, including crawling peg exchange rate regimes aimed at either controlling inflation or preventing real appreciation; a heavy reliance on primary commodity exports. Corruption seems to increase as a country's relative poverty rises. Many of the preceding developing-country features date from the Great Depression of the 1930s, when industrialized countries turned inward and world markets collapsed.

3. Because many developing economies offer potentially rich opportunities for investment, it is natural for them to have current account deficits and to borrow from richer countries. In principle, developing-country borrowing can cause gains from trade that make both borrowers and lenders better off. In practice, however, borrowing by developing countries has sometimes led to default crises that generally cause currency and banking crises. Like currency and banking crises, default crises can contain a self-fulfilling element even though their occurrence depends on fundamental weaknesses in the borrowing country. Often default crises begin with a sudden stop of financial inflows.

4. In the 1970s, as the Bretton Woods system collapsed, countries in Latin America entered an era of distinctly inferior macroeconomic performance with respect to

---

[26]See Edward L. Glaeser, Rafael La Porta, Florencio Lopez-de-Silanes, and Andrei Shleifer, "Do Institutions Cause Growth?" *Journal of Economic Growth* 9 (September 2004), pp. 271–303. In support of institutional over geographical explanations, see Dani Rodrik, Arvind Subramanian, and Francesco Trebbi, "Institutions Rule: The Primacy of Institutions over Geography and Integration in Economic Development," *Journal of Economic Growth* 9 (June 2004), pp. 131–165. For a contrary view, see Jeffrey D. Sachs, "Institutions Don't Rule: Direct Effects of Geography on Per Capita Income," Working Paper 9490, National Bureau of Economic Research, February 2003. The role of international trade in growth is another focus of current research. Rodrik and his co-authors argue that openness to international trade is not a prime direct determinant of per capita income, but rather that openness leads to better institutions, and, through that indirect channel, to higher income.

growth and inflation. Uncontrolled external borrowing led, in the 1980s, to a generalized developing-country debt crisis, its greatest impact being in Latin America and Africa. Starting with Chile in the mid-1980s, some large Latin American countries started to undertake more thorough economic reform, including not just disinflation but also control of the government budget, vigorous *privatization*, deregulation, and trade policy reform. Argentina adopted a *currency board* in 1991. Not all the Latin American reformers succeeded equally in strengthening their banks, and failures were evident in a number of countries. For example, Argentina's currency board collapsed after ten years.

5. Despite their astoundingly good records of high output growth and low inflation and budget deficits, several key developing countries in East Asia were hit by severe panics and devastating currency depreciation in 1997. In retrospect, the affected countries had several vulnerabilities, most of them related to widespread moral hazard in domestic banking and finance and linked to the *original sin* of foreign currency denominated debts. The effects of the crisis spilled over to countries as distant as Russia and Brazil, illustrating the element of *contagion* in modern-day international financial crises. This factor, plus the fact that the East Asian countries had few apparent problems before their crises struck, has given rise to demands for rethinking the international financial "architecture." These demands were reinforced by the global nature of the 2007–2009 financial crisis.

6. Proposals to reform the international architecture can be grouped as preventive measures or as ex post (that is, after the fact) measures, with the latter applied once safeguards have failed to stop a crisis. Among preventive measures are greater transparency concerning countries' policies and financial positions; enhanced regulation of domestic banking; and more extensive credit lines, either from private sources or from the IMF. Ex post measures that have been suggested include more extensive and flexible lending by the IMF. Some observers suggest more extensive use of capital controls, both to prevent and manage crises, but in general not too many countries have taken this route. In the years to come, developing countries will no doubt experiment with capital controls, *dollarization*, floating exchange rates, and other regimes. The architecture that will ultimately emerge is not at all clear.

7. Recent research on the ultimate determinants of economic growth in developing countries has focused on geographical issues such as the disease environment, institutional features such as government protection of property rights, and human capital endowments. The flow of capital from rich to poor countries also depends on these factors. While economists agree that all of these determinants are important, it is less clear where policy should focus first in its attempts to lift poor countries out of their poverty. For example, institutional reform might be an appropriate first step if human capital accumulation depends on the protection of property rights and personal security. On the other hand, it makes little sense to create an institutional framework for government if there is insufficient human capital to run government effectively. In that case, education should come first. Because the statistical obstacles to reaching unambiguous answers are formidable, a balanced effort on all fronts is warranted.

KEY TERMS

contagion, p. 394
convergence, p. 370
currency board, p. 383

dollarization, p. 407
original sin, p. 381

privatization, p. 380
seigniorage, p. 373

PROBLEMS

1. Can a government always collect more seigniorage simply by letting the money supply grow faster? Explain your answer.

2. Assume that a country's inflation rate was 100 percent per year in both 1990 and 2000 but that inflation was falling in the first year and rising in the second. Other things equal, in which year was seigniorage revenue greater? (Assume that asset holders correctly anticipated the path of inflation.)

3. In the early 1980s, Brazil's government, through an average inflation rate of 147 percent per year, got only 1.0 percent of output as seigniorage, while Sierra Leone's government got 2.4 percent through an inflation rate less than a third as high as Brazil's. Can you think of differences in financial structure that might partially explain this contrast? (Hint: In Sierra Leone, the ratio of currency to nominal output averaged 7.7 percent; in Brazil, it averaged only 1.4 percent.)

4. Suppose an economy open to international capital movements has a crawling peg exchange rate under which its currency is pegged at each moment but is continuously devalued at a rate of 10 percent per year. How would the domestic nominal interest rate be related to the foreign nominal interest rate? What if the crawling peg is not fully credible?

5. The external debt buildup of some developing countries (such as Argentina) in the 1970s was due, in part, to (legal or illegal) capital flight in the face of expected currency devaluation. (Governments and central banks borrowed foreign currencies to prop up their exchange rates, and these funds found their way into private hands and into bank accounts in New York and elsewhere.) Since capital flight leaves a government with a large debt but creates an offsetting foreign asset for citizens who take money abroad, the consolidated net debt of the country as a whole does not change. Does this mean that countries whose external government debt is largely the result of capital flight face no debt problem?

6. Much developing-country borrowing during the 1970s was carried out by state-owned companies. In some of these countries, there have been moves to privatize the economy by selling state companies to private owners. Would the countries have borrowed more or less if their economies had been privatized earlier?

7. How might a developing country's decision to reduce trade restrictions such as import tariffs affect its ability to borrow in the world capital market?

8. Given output, a country can improve its current account by cutting either investment or consumption (private or government). After the debt crisis of the 1980s began, many developing countries achieved improvements in their current accounts by cutting investment. Was this a sensible strategy?

9. Why would Argentina have to give the United States seigniorage if it gave up its peso and completely dollarized its economy? How would you measure the size of Argentina's sacrifice of seigniorage? (To complete this exercise, think through the actual steps Argentina would have to take to dollarize its economy. You may assume that the Argentine central bank's assets consist of 100 percent of interest-bearing U.S. Treasury bonds.)

10. Early studies of the economic convergence hypothesis, which looked at data for a group of currently industrialized countries, found that those that were relatively poor a century ago subsequently grew more quickly. Is it valid to infer from this finding that the convergence hypothesis is true?

11. Some critics of the adoption of fixed exchange rates by emerging market economies argue that these exchange rates create a kind of moral hazard. Do you agree?

(Hint: Might borrowers behave differently if they knew exchange rates were changeable from day to day?)

12. In some emerging market economies, not only are debt obligations to foreigners denominated in dollars, but so are many of the economies' internal debts, that is, debts of one domestic resident to another. In the chapter, we called this phenomenon liability dollarization. How might liability dollarization worsen the financial market disruption caused by a sharp depreciation of the domestic currency against the dollar?

13. Suppose the production function for aggregate output in the United States is the same as in India, $Y = AK^{\alpha}L^{1-\alpha}$, where A is a total productivity factor, K is the capital stock, and L is the supply of labor. From Table 11-2, calculate the ratio of per capita incomes Y/L in India and the United States in 2010. Use this information to figure out the ratio of capital's marginal product in India and the U.S. (The marginal product of capital is given by $\alpha AK^{\alpha-1}L^{1-\alpha}$.) Relate the answer to the Lucas puzzle of capital flows from rich to poor. How much would A have to differ between India and the U.S. to make the marginal product of capital the same in the two countries?

FURTHER READINGS

Jahangir Aziz, Steven V. Dunaway, and Eswar Prasad, eds. *China and India: Learning from Each Other*. Washington, D.C.: International Monetary Fund, 2006. Essays on Chinese and Indian strategies for promoting economic stability and growth.

Guillermo A. Calvo and Frederic S. Mishkin. "The Mirage of Exchange Rate Regimes for Emerging Market Countries." *Journal of Economic Perspectives* 17 (Winter 2003), pp. 99–118. Argues that institutions are more important than exchange rate regimes for understanding developing-country macroeconomic performance.

Barry Eichengreen and Ricardo Hausmann, eds. *Other People's Money: Debt Denomination and Financial Instability in Emerging Market Economies*. Chicago: University of Chicago Press, 2005. Essays on original sin.

Albert Fishlow. "Lessons from the Past: Capital Markets During the 19th Century and the Interwar Period." *International Organization* 39 (Summer 1985), pp. 383–439. Historical review of the international borrowing experience, including comparisons with the post-1982 debt crisis.

Kristin Forbes. "The 'Big C': Identifying and Mitigating Contagion." In *The Changing Policy Landscape: A Symposium Sponsored by the Federal Reserve Bank of Kansas City*. Kansas City, MO: Federal Reserve Bank of Kansas City, 2013, pp. 23–87. A comprehensive survey of contagious shock transmission through international markets.

Morris Goldstein. *Managed Floating Plus*. Washington, D.C.: Institute for International Economics, 2002. A proposal for managing exchange rate flexibility by emerging market economies.

Morris Goldstein and Nicholas R. Lardy. *The Future of China's Exchange Rate Policy*. Washington, D.C.: Peterson Institute for International Economics, 2009. Compact but thorough analysis of China's macroeconomic challenges.

Peter B. Kenen. *The International Financial Architecture: What's New? What's Missing?* Washington, D.C.: Institute for International Economics, 2001. Reviews emerging market crises and the consequent proposals to reform the global financial system.

M. Ayhan Kose and Eswar S. Prasad. *Emerging Markets: Resilience and Growth amid Global Turmoil*. Washington, D.C.: Brookings Institution, 2010. A wide-ranging study of the relative resilience of emerging economies in the face of the 2007–2009 global financial crisis.

David S. Landes. *The Wealth and Poverty of Nations*. New York: W. W. Norton & Company, 1999. Broad-ranging overview of the global development experience.

Ronald I. McKinnon. *The Order of Economic Liberalization: Financial Control in the Transition to a Market Economy*, 2nd edition. Baltimore: Johns Hopkins University Press, 1993. Essays on the proper sequencing of economic reforms.

Edward Miguel. *Africa's Turn?* Cambridge, MA: MIT Press, 2009. A presentation of perspectives on Africa's economic performance and prospects.

Peter J. Montiel. *Macroeconomics in Emerging Markets.* Cambridge: Cambridge University Press, 2003. Comprehensive analytical overview of macroeconomic policy issues for developing economies.

Raghuram G. Rajan and Ioannis Tokatlidis. "Dollar Shortages and Crises." *International Journal of Central Banking* 1 (September 2005), pp. 177–220. Excellent overview of the institutional weaknesses in developing economies that give rise to liability dollarization.

Dani Rodrik. *One Economics, Many Recipes: Globalization, Institutions, and Economic Growth.* Princeton: Princeton University Press, 2007. Essays on the interplay of institutions and globalization in the process of economic growth.

Nouriel Roubini and Brad Setser. *Bailouts or Bail-ins? Responding to Financial Crises in Emerging Economies.* Washington, D.C.: Institute for International Economics, 2004. Analysis and proposals on the international financial "architecture."

Joseph E. Stiglitz and others. *The Stiglitz Report: Reforming the International Monetary and Financial Systems in the Wake of the Global Crisis.* New York: The New Press, 2010. Report of a United Nations commission of financial experts, with a focus on implications for developing economies.

MyEconLab Can Help You Get a Better Grade

MyEconLab   If your exam were tomorrow, would you be ready? For each chapter, MyEconLab Practice Tests and Study Plans pinpoint sections you have mastered and those you need to study. That way, you are more efficient with your study time, and you are better prepared for your exams.

To see how it works, turn to page 9 and then go to www.myeconlab.com

Risk Aversion and International Portfolio Diversification

This postscript develops a model of international portfolio diversification by risk-averse investors. The model shows that investors generally care about the risk as well as the return of their portfolios. In particular, people may hold assets whose expected returns are lower than those of other assets if this strategy reduces the overall riskiness of their wealth.

A representative investor can divide her real wealth, W, between a Home asset and a Foreign asset. Two possible states of nature can occur in the future, and it is impossible to predict in advance which one it will be. In state 1, which occurs with probability q, a unit of wealth invested in the Home asset pays out H_1 units of output and a unit of wealth invested in the Foreign asset pays out F_1 units of output. In state 2, which occurs with probability $1 - q$, the payoffs to unit investments in the Home and Foreign assets are H_2 and F_2, respectively.

Let α be the share of wealth invested in the Home asset and $1 - \alpha$ the share invested in the Foreign asset. Then if state 1 occurs, the investor will be able to consume the weighted average of her two assets' values,

$$C_1 = [\alpha H_1 + (1 - \alpha)F_1] \times W. \tag{9P-1}$$

Similarly, consumption in state 2 is

$$C_2 = [\alpha H_2 + (1 - \alpha)F_2] \times W. \tag{9P-2}$$

In either state, the investor derives utility $U(C)$ from a consumption level of C. Since the investor does not know beforehand which state will occur, she makes the portfolio decision to maximize the average or *expected* utility from future consumption,

$$qU(C_1) + (1 - q)U(C_2).$$

An Analytical Derivation of the Optimal Portfolio

After the state 1 and state 2 consumption levels given by (9P-1) and (9P-2) are substituted into the expected utility function above, the investor's decision problem can be expressed as follows: Choose the portfolio share α to maximize expected utility,

$$qU\{[\alpha H_1 + (1 - \alpha)F_1] \times W\} + (1 - q)U\{[\alpha H_2 + (1 - \alpha)F_2] \times W\}.$$

This problem is solved (as usual) by differentiating the expected utility above with respect to α and setting the resulting derivative equal to 0.

Let $U'(C)$ be the derivative of the utility function $U(C)$ with respect to C; that is, $U'(C)$ is the *marginal utility* of consumption. Then α maximizes expected utility if

$$\frac{H_1 - F_1}{H_2 - F_2} = -\frac{(1 - q)U'\{[\alpha H_2 + (1 - \alpha)F_2] \times W\}}{qU'\{[\alpha H_1 + (1 - \alpha)F_1] \times W\}}. \tag{9P-3}$$

This equation can be solved for α, the optimal portfolio share.

For a risk-averse investor, the marginal utility of consumption, $U'(C)$, falls as consumption rises. Declining marginal utility explains why someone who is risk averse will not take a gamble with an expected payoff of zero: The extra consumption made possible by a win yields less utility than the utility sacrificed if the gamble is lost. If the marginal utility of consumption does not change as consumption changes, we say the investor is *risk neutral* rather than risk averse. A risk-neutral investor is willing to take gambles with a zero expected payoff.

If the investor is risk neutral, however, so that $U'(C)$ is constant for all C, equation (9P-3) becomes

$$qH_1 + (1 - q)H_2 = qF_1 + (1 - q)F_2,$$

which states that *the expected rates of return on Home and Foreign assets are equal.* This result is the basis for the assertion in Chapter 3 that all assets must yield the same expected return in equilibrium when considerations of risk (and liquidity) are ignored. Thus, the interest parity condition of Chapter 3 is valid under risk-neutral behavior, but not, in general, under risk aversion.

For the analysis above to make sense, neither of the assets can yield a higher return than the other in *both* states of nature. If one asset did dominate the other in this way, the left-hand side of equation (9P-3) would be positive while its right-hand side would be negative (because the marginal utility of consumption is usually assumed to be positive). Thus, (9P-3) would have no solution. Intuitively, no one would want to hold a particular asset if another asset that *always* did better were available. Indeed, if anyone did wish to do so, other investors would be able to make riskless arbitrage profits by issuing the low-return asset and using the proceeds to purchase the high-return asset.

To be definite, we therefore assume that $H_1 > F_1$ and $H_2 < F_2$, so that the Home asset does better in state 1 but does worse in state 2. This assumption is now used to develop a diagrammatic analysis that helps illustrate additional implications of the model.

A Diagrammatic Derivation of the Optimal Portfolio

Figure 9P-1 shows indifference curves for the expected utility function described by $qU(C_1) + (1 - q)U(C_2)$. The points in the diagram should be thought of as contingency plans showing the level of consumption that will occur in each state of nature. The preferences represented apply to these contingent consumption plans rather than to consumption of different goods in a single state of nature. As with standard indifference curves, however, each curve in the figure represents a set of contingency plans for consumption with which the investor is equally satisfied.

To compensate the investor for a reduction of consumption in state 1 (C_1), consumption in state 2 (C_2) must rise. The indifference curves therefore slope downward. Each curve becomes flatter, however, as C_1 falls and C_2 rises. This property of the curves reflects the property of $U(C)$ that the marginal utility of consumption declines when C rises. As C_1 falls, the investor can be kept on her original indifference curve only by successively greater increments in C_2: Additions to C_2 are becoming less beneficial at the same time as subtractions from C_1 are becoming more painful.

Equations (9P-1) and (9P-2) imply that by choosing the portfolio division given by α, the investor also chooses her consumption levels in the two states of nature. Thus, the problem of choosing an optimal portfolio is equivalent to the problem of optimally choosing the contingent consumption levels C_1 and C_2. Accordingly, the indifference

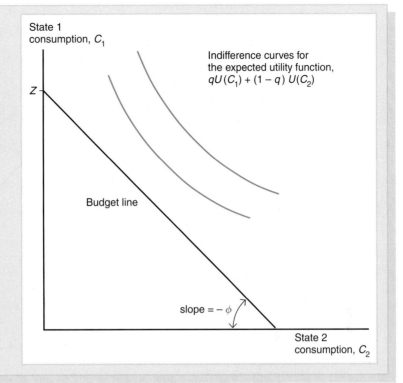

Indifference Curves for Uncertain Consumption Levels

The indifference curves are sets of state-contingent consumption plans with which the individual is equally happy. The budget line describes the trade-off between state 1 and state 2 consumption that results from portfolio shifts between Home and Foreign assets.

curves in Figure 9P-1 can be used to determine the optimal portfolio for the investor. All that is needed to complete the analysis is a budget line showing the trade-off between state 1 consumption and state 2 consumption that the market makes available.

This trade-off is given by equations (9P-1) and (9P-2). If equation (9P-2) is solved for α, the result is

$$\alpha = \frac{F_2 W - C_2}{F_2 W - H_2 W}.$$

After substitution of this expression for α in (9P-1), the latter equation becomes

$$C_1 + \phi C_2 = Z, \tag{9P-4}$$

where $\phi = (H_1 - F_1)/(F_2 - H_2)$ and $Z = W \times (H_1 F_2 - H_2 F_1)/(F_2 - H_2)$. Notice that because $H_1 > F_1$ and $H_2 < F_2$, both ϕ and Z are positive. Thus, equation (9P-4) looks like the budget line that appears in the usual analysis of consumer choice, with ϕ playing the role of a relative price and Z the role of income measured in terms of state 1 consumption. This budget line is graphed in Figure 9P-1 as a straight line with slope $-\phi$ intersecting the vertical axis at Z.

To interpret ϕ as the market trade-off between state 2 and state 1 consumption (that is, as the price of state 2 consumption in terms of state 1 consumption), suppose the investor shifts one unit of her wealth from the Home to the Foreign asset. Since the Home asset has the higher payoff in state 1, her net loss of state 1 consumption is H_1 *less* the Foreign asset's state 1 payoff, F_1. Similarly, her net gain in state 2 consumption is $F_2 - H_2$. To obtain additional state 2 consumption of $F_2 - H_2$, the investor therefore must sacrifice $H_1 - F_1$ in state 1. The price of a single unit of C_2 in terms

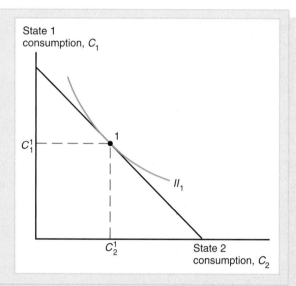

FIGURE 9P-2

Maximizing Expected Utility

To maximize expected utility, the investor makes the state-contingent consumption choices shown at point 1, where the budget line is tangent to the highest attainable indifference curve, II_1. The optimal portfolio share, α, can be calculated as $(F_2 W - C_2^1) \div (F_2 W - H_2 W)$.

of C_1 is therefore $H_1 - F_1$ divided by $F_2 - H_2$, which equals ϕ, the absolute value of the slope of budget line (9P-4).

Figure 9P-2 shows how the choices of C_1 and C_2—and, by implication, the choice of the portfolio share α—are determined. As usual, the investor picks the consumption levels given by point 1, where the budget line just touches the highest attainable indifference curve, II_1. Given the optimal choices of C_1 and C_2, α can be calculated using equation (9P-1) or (9P-2). As we move downward and to the right along the budget constraint, the Home asset's portfolio share, α, falls. (Why?)

For some values of C_1 and C_2, α may be negative or greater than 1. These possibilities raise no conceptual problems. A negative α, for example, means that the investor has "gone short" in the Home asset, that is, issued some positive quantity of state-contingent claims that promise to pay their holders H_1 units of output in state 1 and H_2 units in state 2. The proceeds of this borrowing are used to increase the Foreign asset's portfolio share, $1 - \alpha$, above 1.

Figure 9P-3 shows the points on the investor's budget constraint at which $\alpha = 1$ (so that $C_1 = H_1 W$, $C_2 = H_2 W$) and $\alpha = 0$ (so that $C_1 = F_1 W$, $C_2 = F_2 W$). Starting from $\alpha = 1$, the investor can move upward and to the left along the constraint by going short in the Foreign asset (thereby making α greater than 1 and $1 - \alpha$ negative). She can move downward and to the right from $\alpha = 0$ by going short in the Home asset.

The Effects of Changing Rates of Return

The diagram we have developed can be used to illustrate the effect of changes in rates of return under risk aversion. Suppose, for example, the Home asset's state 1 payoff rises while all other payoffs and the investor's wealth, W, stay the same. The rise in H_1 raises ϕ, the relative price of state 2 consumption, and therefore steepens the budget line shown in Figure 9P-3.

We need more information, however, to describe completely how the position of the budget line in Figure 9P-3 changes when H_1 rises. The following reasoning fills the gap. Consider the portfolio allocation $\alpha = 0$ in Figure 9P-3, under which all wealth is

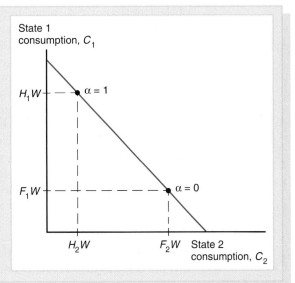

FIGURE 9P-3

Nondiversified Portfolios

When $\alpha = 1$, the investor holds all her wealth in the Home asset. When $\alpha = 0$, she holds all her wealth in the Foreign asset. Moves along the budget constraint upward and to the left from $\alpha = 1$ correspond to short sales of the Foreign asset, which raise α above 1. Moves downward and to the right from $\alpha = 0$ correspond to short sales of the Home asset, which push α below 0.

invested in the Foreign asset. The contingent consumption levels that result from this investment strategy, $C_1 = F_1 W$, $C_2 = F_2 W$, do not change as a result of a rise in H_1, because the portfolio we are considering does not involve the Home asset. Since the consumption pair associated with $\alpha = 0$ does not change when H_1 rises, we see that $C_1 = F_1 W$, $C_2 = F_2 W$ is a point on the new budget constraint: After a rise in H_1, it is still feasible for the investor to put all of her wealth into the Foreign asset. It follows that the effect of a rise in H_1 is to make the budget constraint in Figure 9P-3 pivot clockwise around the point $\alpha = 0$.

The effect on the investor of a rise in H_1 is shown in Figure 9P-4, which assumes that initially, $\alpha > 0$ (that is, the investor initially owns a positive amount

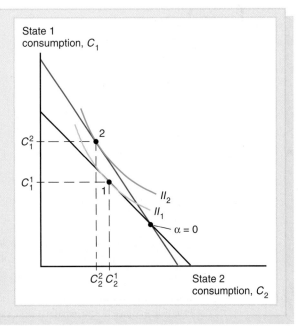

FIGURE 9P-4

Effects of a Rise in H_1 on Consumption

A rise in H_1 causes the budget line to pivot clockwise around $\alpha = 0$, and the investor's optimum shifts to point 2. State 1 consumption always rises; in the case shown, state 2 consumption falls.

of the Home asset).[1] As usual, both a "substitution" and an "income" effect influence the shift of the investor's contingent consumption plan from point 1 to point 2. The substitution effect is a tendency to demand more C_1, whose relative price has fallen, and less C_2, whose relative price has risen. The income effect of the rise in H_1, however, pushes the entire budget line outward and tends to raise consumption in *both* states (as long as $\alpha > 0$ initially). Because the investor will be richer in state 1, she can afford to shift some of her wealth toward the Foreign asset (which has the higher payoff in state 2) and thereby even out her consumption in the two states of nature. Risk aversion explains the investor's desire to avoid large consumption fluctuations across states. As Figure 9P-4 suggests, C_1 definitely rises while C_2 may rise or fall. (In the case illustrated, the substitution effect is stronger than the income effect, and C_2 falls.)

Corresponding to this ambiguity is an ambiguity concerning the effect of the rise in H_1 on the portfolio share, α. Figure 9P-5 illustrates the two possibilities. The key to understanding this figure is to observe that if the investor does *not* change α in response to the rise in H_1, her consumption choices are given by point 1′, which lies on the new budget constraint vertically above the initial consumption point 1. Why is this the case? Equation (9P-2) implies that $C_2^1 = [\alpha H_2 + (1 - \alpha)F_2] \times W$ doesn't

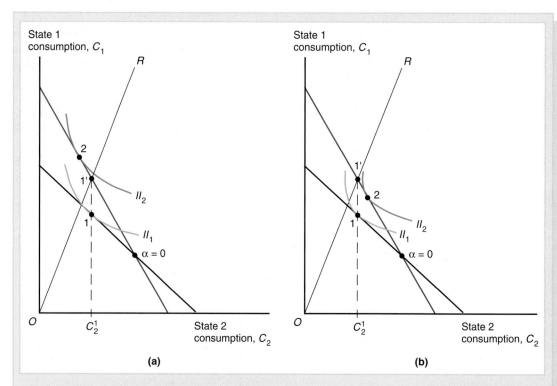

(a)   **(b)**

FIGURE 9P-5

Effects of a Rise in H_1 on Portfolio Shares

Panel (a): If the investor is not too risk averse, she shifts her portfolio toward the Home asset, picking a C_1/C_2 ratio greater than the one indicated by the slope of OR. Panel (b): A very risk-averse investor might increase state 2 consumption by shifting her portfolio toward the Foreign asset.

---

[1]The case in which $\alpha < 0$ initially is left as an exercise.

change if α doesn't change; the new, higher value of state 1 consumption corresponding to the original portfolio choice is then given by the point on the new budget constraint directly above C_2^1. In both panels of Figure 9P-5, the slope of the ray OR connecting the origin and point $1'$ shows the ratio C_1/C_2 implied by the initial portfolio composition after the rise in H_1.

It is now clear, however, that to shift to a lower value of C_2, the investor must raise α above its initial value, that is, shift the portfolio toward the Home asset. To raise C_2, she must lower α, that is, shift toward the Foreign asset. Figure 9P-5a shows again the case in which the substitution effect outweighs the income effect. In that case, C_2 falls as the investor shifts her portfolio toward the Home asset, whose expected rate of return has risen relative to that on the Foreign asset. This case corresponds to those we studied in the text, in which the portfolio share of an asset rises as its relative expected rate of return rises.

Figure 9P-5b shows the opposite case, in which C_2 rises and α falls, implying a portfolio shift toward the Foreign asset. You can see that the factor giving rise to this possibility is the sharper curvature of the indifference curves II in Figure 9P-5b. This curvature is precisely what economists mean by the term *risk aversion*. An investor who becomes more risk averse regards consumptions in different states of nature as poorer substitutes, and thus requires a larger increase in state 1 consumption to compensate her for a fall in state 2 consumption (and vice versa). Note that the paradoxical case shown in Figure 9P-5b, in which a rise in an asset's expected rate of return can cause investors to demand *less* of it, is unlikely in the real world. For example, an increase in the interest rate a currency offers, other things equal, raises the expected rate of return on deposits of that currency in all states of nature, not just in one. The portfolio substitution effect in favor of the currency therefore is much stronger.

The results we have found are quite different from those that would occur if the investor were risk neutral. A risk-neutral investor would shift all of her wealth into the asset with the higher expected return, paying no attention to the riskiness of this move.[2] The greater the degree of risk aversion, however, the greater the concern with the riskiness of the overall portfolio of assets.

---

[2]In fact, a risk-neutral investor would always like to take the maximum possible short position in the low-return asset and, correspondingly, the maximum possible long position in the high-return asset. It is this behavior that gives rise to the interest parity condition.

CREDITS

Key

	$200–690
	$700–1480
	$1500–3490
	$3530–5800
	$6090–11,760
	$12,210–30,390
	$31,800–183,150
	No data available

GREENLAND

CANADA

UNITED STATES

MEXICO

THE BAHAMAS

CUBA
DOM. REP.
JAMAICA HAITI
BELIZE
HONDURAS
GUATEMALA
EL SALVADOR NICARAGUA
PANAMA
COSTA RICA

VENEZUELA GUYANA
SURINAME
FRENCH GUIANA
COLOMBIA

ECUADOR

PERU

BRAZIL

BOLIVIA

PARAGUAY

CHILE

ARGENTINA

URUGUAY

FALKLAND ISLANDS

SOUTH GEORGIA ISLAN

Canary I

SENE
GAMBI
GUINEA B

SI

Source: World Bank, *World Development Indicators,* 2013. Data are measured in 2011 United States dollars.